Frank and LaVonne Amaral

What a Wonderful Life

PART V, continued
Part VI
Appendix A–E

(Volume three)

By LaVonne Amaral

Contact:

Frank and LaVonne Amaral: What a Wonderful Life
P.O. Box 67
Nevada City, California, 95959

Editor: Mark Bancroft

First edition editor: Michael Sion

Contributing editor: Wylene Dunbar

50 years at 211 Reward St., Nevada City

IN LATE FALL 1999, after Frank was home from the hospital, he was lying out on the patio, looking up at the stars, and said, "August 8th of 2000, we'll have been here 50 years, so let's have a party."

I told him we can't have a big party with the tennis court in the condition it is in; we would have to do something about getting it re-cemented. He said, "No way, it's OK the way it is now." I told him that the Music in the Mountains people told me it was too dangerous to have a large group on; someone could get hurt and then we would be in trouble. This was right after his 81st birthday, during the time he was recording the tapes of his life history. Then, in September, we went to the Clarke Ranch for the Kruger–Evenson family reunion, so we sort of put the party on the back burner.

In November 1999, he brought up the party again, so without doing any hard thinking on the subject, I asked Frank to call and have someone come out to give us a bid on the tennis court. In the meantime, Frank must have changed his mind about getting the tennis court done because he then called Bernie Franza to come over and see what it would cost to re-do the court. This would include rebarring and cross-rebarring the whole court, putting in 6 inches of gravel over the whole court, and then pouring 6 to 10 inches of cement over the whole area. This needed to be done in three stages and it had to slope to drain at the north corner. Also, large rocks would have to be brought in to replace the wooden wall that was there.

After some negotiations, the price was settled at around $19,000, about the price we had paid for the house in 1950. The job was started on the first week of January 2000. Everything had to be brought into the site from the back of Frank's office, so I had to remove all the shrubs in that area and store them, so the trucks could come in with gravel and cement.

The tractor making its way through the lawn to the tennis court

Laying the gravel and getting ready to pour cement

Pouring cement

After the job was finished, all the damage done to the back lawn had to be taken care of. This was a big job and it took me, along with Richard, our gardener, into March to get it all done. The first thing we did was re-plant all the shrubs. Then we removed all the spilled cement and rock that was all over the old lawn. The rains came and held up the job for a few days before we could start to remove all the pine and cedar tree roots that were in the ground.

After a few days of Richard working on the ground, I started to rake the ground to start to seed. This was on Monday, which was the gardener's day off. I didn't get very far into the job when I discovered the roots were still there. So I started from one end of the yard and dug down a foot and turned the soil over in every inch of the area. I removed about three small truckloads of roots from the area. I then spent two days leveling it out the best we could. I ended up with a very nice lawn. I used pure Manhattan rye seed. I believe this was the first time the ground had ever been turned, for there was never a lawn in that area until the 1960s that I know of. And I don't know when the tennis court was first put in, but it could have been during Jacob's time.

In April, I had a tree crew come in to take out a tree that was hanging directly over our house.

The tree over the house is to the right. The stump rotted away and was taken out in 2010.

Frank watching the leaning tree being removed

4

Removing the tree in front of the art room

Mark watching the job being done

This is what was left of the tree that was leaning over the house

50 years at 211 Reward St. invitation.
The picture is of the yard near the BBQ house.
The scarf was made by my dad.

The backyard ready for the party

By May 2000, the lawn was looking good, so we started to get the rest of the yard ready for that "50 Years in One Place" party for Frank in August. We ended up having around 180 people; it was a beautiful evening and everyone had a really good time. We had only local people who were from all walks of life, people we had known for years, friends as well as business people.

We bought 10 streetlights that had four light bulbs on each post. They were painted white and placed all along the tennis court. It was very effective. We later gave eight of them to Music in the Mountains. In 1994, we had purchased a foldaway dance floor for M.I.M. and we used that at the party.

The front yard ready for the party

On Aug. 5, 2000, we celebrated our 50 years at 211 Reward St. in Nevada City. The party included an evening of entertainment, dinner, and dance, with everyone wearing dressy attire and having a great time. My cost for the party was a fair share. So I now know what it costs M.I.M. to give a party here in the yard, and I know what to expect on how much is spent and how much they want to make at a party.

Frank welcoming the guests to the party

The yard was in great shape for flowers, and the new tennis court really turned out great—no more cracks in the cement to stub your toes on. We live in a very secluded place, even though we are in the city limits. All the cars were parked either on Reward Street, at the clinic, or at St. Canice Hall. The guests were given a ride in a golf cart up the driveway to our house, where I greeted them at the entrance to the yard.

The men were given women's nametags and the women got men's nametags. Each person then had to go find their own name, and after that, they had to go find what table they were assigned to sit at—no couples sat at the same table. This was a great mixer and made everyone say hello to everybody else. We had excellent hors d'oeuvres, plenty of good hard liquor, wine, and soft drinks with dinner that was served up on the tennis court. In addition to the music and entertainment, there were two couples in costumes doing Vienna waltz dances. There was open dancing later in the evening.

Viennese dancers

It was Frank's wish to have this party to celebrate the 50 years we have lived here at 211 Reward St. Everyone had a good time, and I was later told it was one of the better parties and would be one that many people will remember.

Me and Frank celebrating
50 years at 211 Reward St.

Julia taking the lead in a fun night of dancing after the waltz performance

Trip to Italy and France

BY SEPT. 22, 2000, the entire family had left for a trip to Italy and France. Frank had not been feeling well for some time and was having a great deal of trouble sleeping. He was taking heavy dosages of sleeping pills that kept him from feeling well. So we decided to make a trip with the kids while he could still do it. We all agreed on going to Italy and staying in a villa, and we thought Mark's parents might like to join us, which they did. Everyone left about a week ahead of us.

So this is a family trip to the Tuscany area of Italy. Julia set it up and paid for the villa for all of us. We would be venturing out to see different places from the villa, and at the end of 10 days, we would all go in different directions. In the meantime, Julia and Mark had already been there for two weeks with other friends.

When the family travels together, we try not to have all six of us on the same plane, and it's even better that each couple travels on separate planes. On this trip, everyone left at different times. We were the last ones to arrive at the villa that day, with Curt and Kay arriving a day or so ahead of us.

Frank and I rented a car from home, left at 7 a.m., and drove to the airport in San Francisco, where we dropped off the car before checking in at Air France to fly business class. A few hours later, we were on our way to Paris. From there we went to Rome, and after getting our luggage and finding the driver and car that were there to meet us, it was 27 hours later. I gave the driver the road directions that we had so he could drive us to the villa, called Le Corti-Montoro. The owners were Mr. and Mrs. Vici, and the villa was near the town of Casti Florer.

I think Kay and Curt had come over a week earlier to see Paris and Rome. Laurence and his family also came a few days earlier, and I think they saw Paris first. It was planned for all of us to be at the villa on the day Frank and I arrived.

Looking down on the villa

The villa was way out in the country and took two hours to get to from Rome. As we drove up to the parking area, Laurence greeted us by looking out his upstairs bedroom window.

It was such a good greeting that I got a picture of it. Julia was out at the gate going to the house, for she had heard us driving into the property on the gravel road leading up to the villa.

Laurence greeting us at the villa

There were three rental cars in the parking lot, so we knew everyone had arrived ahead of us. Gloria, Laurence, and Spence had a car, and Kay and Curt had their rental, as did Mark and Julia. We went everywhere with them. Having different cars made it possible for us to go in different ways if we wanted. The roads were so dusty that every morning the three cars received a wash job before going anywhere.

Kay and Mark enjoying the villa patio

After our hugs and greetings with everyone, we took our luggage up to our second-story bedroom. We looked out our bedroom window and saw Kay and Mark down on the patio enjoying the sun and visiting, so I took a picture of them enjoying the relaxation.

I think Julia had arranged for the people to take care of preparing and cooking our main meals on the days we were going to be at the villa, and we would take care of the other meals on our own. It turned out to be a nice arrangement. We spent the rest of the day and evening enjoying the villa and exploring the grounds. Curt made a trip to the local store for coffee, fruits, juices, and bread, along with eggs and bacon — everything needed for a good breakfast.

Dinner was brought in around 7 p.m., so we set up the big table in the dining room for a pasta dinner, big salad, and all the trimmings and a cake to top it off. There was little work on our part other than doing the dishes. With everyone helping, the job was done in short order. Afterward, we spent the evening visiting, playing games, watching TV, and then finally went to bed.

After breakfast on Sept. 24, I think around 10 a.m., the three cars, with us, our daypacks, and gear took off for the day, along with our drivers who had talked to the villa's owners to find out where to go. They decided that our first stop of the day would be Vertine. To get there we went over a winding road that took us through the red wine country that has quite a view in every direction. We finally got to Vertine, which is near Gaiole in Chianti. Vertine is a walled-in city with narrow streets that sits on a hill with quite a view.

Cleaning the cars before heading out for the day

Julia and Kay at the entrance to Vertine

Streets of Vertine (Laurence, Gloria, Kay, and Julia)

After visiting Vertine, we drove on a one-way winding road with wonderful views to Badia, another village with wall-to-wall houses built right up to the street. If you are in luck, you may be able to see the Romanesque church called San Lorenzo, but it was closed when we were there. The wine, honey, and oil from this area are considered among the best in the country. Our next stop was Volpaia, which was a military lookout back in the 16th century. Its towers and castles have a history all their own.

Julia, Kay, and Frank at Volpaia

We took off from Volpaia for Radda, which is located in Chianti. We arrived in time to have lunch out under shady trees at LeVigne Restaurant that has a great view of the valley below. It's a very popular place. There were many tables that could seat 10 people and all of them were full. We ate a variety of foods and none of us had a bad dish. Being so far out in the country with nothing around it except for the wonderful food, you wondered where all the people came from. We were in no hurry to leave this area, and we did do a lot of visiting.

Lunchtime at LeVigne Restaurant:
Spence, Julia,
Gloria, Frank, and Laurence

Mark checking out the road signs

We wandered along on out-of-the-way roads, and somehow we came to a villa called Panzano in Chianti that was crowded with people, so we stopped to see what was going on. Before we knew it, we were in a crowd of people who all had wine glasses in their hands. The object was to go from booth to booth and sample the different wines. Their job was to keep your wine glass half-full as you went around sampling the wines, and if you didn't like what you were tasting, you could pour it out in a barrel nearby and get something else to taste. My guess is that they hoped you would end up buying a case of wine.

The event had already been going on for several hours, so it had become a rather happy place. Before too long we said, "Let's get out of here." And we did. We headed back to our villa on a scenic and winding road stopping at little out-of-the-way shops along the way. That night, we all drove to a casual dining place near Castellina. We then returned to the villa for an evening of cards and games and then went to bed.

The next morning, Sept. 25, after breakfast was over and the dishes were washed, as well as whoever needed to have some laundry done and hung out to dry, we took off to go to Monteriggioni, which is between Castellina and Siena. It is considered among the better-preserved medieval villages in Italy. It was built around 1203 and became a walled city in 1260, with the walls built in the shape of an oval. This was done to protect them from Florence, and, if I remember right, the streets also followed the contour of the walls, and this included the 14 towers.

Julia getting a picture of Monteriggioni

The place sits on a hill and overlooks a vast amount of countryside that includes many vineyards. Today it is a rather expensive city to visit, but we did enjoy a shop and spent some money. Curt and Kay joined us about the same time that Laurence's family was leaving. After that, we headed for Siena where we all arrived in time to have lunch together sitting on the ground in the square, along with many other people. No cars were allowed in this area. This is a large area, and from there you can venture in several directions to see interesting places, churches, shops, and restaurants.

Siena sits on the ridges of three hills, and during 1260 it was a flourishing city; its wealth made this one of Europe's wealthiest places. Then the Black Plague came in 1348 and killed three-fourths of the population. It took a long time for the city to recover. Around 1530, they had a spiritual upheaval that set them back. Then about 1559, they had a military war, and after that, the town suffered centuries of neglect. It's only lately that they have turned the tables with agriculture, banking, and tourism. I would say that tourism is the major thing going on today.

There was a great deal to see in this area, so we all ventured out in different directions, having decided upon a place to meet when we were done. Spence and Laurence went to the top of the striking bell tower of the Sienese Cathedral, which was built of black-and-white tile. When we met up with them later, they said, "What a view!" So Julia and I took off and did the same thing and found you could look down and see the plaza. The people below looked like walking ants. We looked out over the countryside and took pictures from high up in the tower.

We went inside the Duomo, which has many statues worth taking the time to see. We took in several churches, and, along the way, we stopped at stores that sold lots of postcards. As we got ready to leave, I got a picture of everyone discussing their purchases as we gathered to walk back down to the cathedral. Then it was back to our cars to drive back to the villa. By the time we got back, the wet clothes that were hung out were now dry, so Gloria did some ironing and later we went out to dinner.

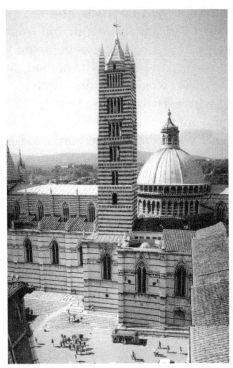
Bell tower of the Sienese Cathedral

Julia getting pictures from the bell tower

Sept. 26. Once again, Curt went to town before breakfast to bring back a lot of goodies, and someone else was washing their clothes today. After breakfast, finishing the dishes, and putting the wash out to dry, no one was in a hurry, so by the time we took off to Assisi, it was closer to noon. For lunch, we had sandwiches at Assisi. I don't have any pictures of Laurence and his family this day, so they must have taken off to see something else for the day. I know Laurence was interested in getting some wine to send home, for he likes collecting different kinds of wine for his cellar.

Cathedral at Assisi

After parking the cars, we walked down to the Basilica of St. Clare, and from there we walked downhill to the Basilica of St. Francis that was built around the 13th century. It was built just for the burial of the saint, and it is really two churches. After we entered the beautiful carved doors, we were met with many paintings on the walls. Seeing them took some time. We finally made our way down to the Lower Church where the presbytery is.

The family getting its plans together

Julia and I got even farther down to where the burial was along with other things. We saw many paintings everywhere we went. In time, Kay and Curt left us to go see something else, so it ended up just being the four of us: Frank, Julia, Mark, and me.

After spending so much time looking at the good art, we decided to head back up the hill, enjoying the shops as we went. As we walked up the hill, Frank spent most of his time just sitting on one doorstep going up to the next, waiting for the rest of us to finish looking into the shops.

Frank waiting for us to catch up

Julia, Mark, and Frank undecided at the market

We finally got back to the car and headed for Castiglione del Lago, where we more or less went through what turned out to be a meat market on both sides of the street. As we walked from one meat shop to another, not really buying very much, we went to a store across the narrow street. This turned out to be kind of fun on our part, for the owners of the other stores were watching us.

One lady, clutching a big fork in one hand and holding her other hand on her hip, watched us leave her shop and go across the narrow street to another meat store. Mark found what he wanted, and we ended up buying several things to take with us to the villa. The fork lady wasn't very happy with us; she said, "What am I doing wrong?" We said, "Nothing," and ended up laughing. It was interesting to see their display of meats, so I took several pictures of this area.

The fork lady asking herself,
"What have I done wrong?"

The medieval streets of Cortona

We left there and headed for Cortona, with its medieval streets, churches, and art galleries, along with a nice view of Lake Trasimeno and some flatlands that have olive trees and vineyards. Cortona is considered one of Italy's oldest towns, with the first set of the town's walls built around the fourth century B.C. You can still see traces of them to this day.

The first thing we noticed was how steep the streets were; it was either walk uphill or downhill. One of the first places we stopped at was an art gallery that drew my attention. Julia and Mark were also interested in the gallery, for they are always on the lookout for a good piece of art. Not seeing anything that satisfied our taste, we continued walking up the street and came to the Piazza della Repubblica, which took us to the 30-some-odd steps leading up to the church of San Francesco.

Frank and Julia at the top of the steps

After climbing the hill to the steps leading to the first church that was built outside of Assisi, Julia and I took pictures of each other climbing the famous 30-some-odd steps. Her pictures were taken from the top looking down on us and the town, and my pictures are of her and Frank at the top, with the church in the background. The steps were inviting to walk up, sit down on, and relax and take in the view of the town below from this high vantage point. After doing this, we went inside to see the church. It was the third-oldest altar, and that took my interest, but there wasn't much else to see.

Mark, Frank, and Julia in front of the church with the famous 30-some-odd steps

If you like a picturesque town to spend a night in, this would be a great choice, for the view of the area is extraordinarily nice. I'm sure the sunset would be great, and there are plenty of good hotels and dining places to choose from. I would say this would be a fun town for an overnight stay.

Toward evening, we headed for Montoro and our villa. On the way, we passed through the flat, freshly plowed, brown farming countryside. We saw a wonderful sunset that turned the freshly plowed ground and all the buildings a light-golden brown. There were very few trees or shrubs to cast shadows. We stopped to take pictures of it. Mine were taken from inside the car; Julia's were taken out in the open. They both turned out good.

A golden sunset out in the country on our way back to the villa

We arrived back at the villa, and I don't know if we stayed there for dinner or went out. But I know that by now a good deal of spare time was being filled by washing and drying clothes and getting things ironed. The others had already been traveling for more than a week or so and would be traveling for another 10 days after leaving the villa. But I knew it would be my turn to wash clothes before we left for Paris in a few days.

The villa had four full bedrooms and three full bathrooms upstairs. Laurence and his family were in one side of the upstairs. We used a spare bedroom next to the stairs between them and us to store our extra luggage. On the other side, the house had two full bedrooms with baths, so Mark and Julia had one, and Frank and I were in the other. I know we sometimes shared our shower because it was off by itself. Downstairs, there was a full kitchen with a large kitchen table and benches to have breakfast, and many windows for light. Near the kitchen was a door leading to the patio area where we took our clothes out to dry. Nearby, a walkway led outside to a two-bedroom cottage that had a living room and kitchen. This is where Kay and Curt stayed.

The main floor of the villa had a full-sized dining room that could seat 12 or more people, and off to the side there was a good-sized entrance hall that also led to the upstairs. This is the area where we all did our ironing and where we nearly always talked about where we were going for the day. The hall was big enough to have a three-by-nine-foot table in the room for road maps, travel books, magazines, and the fruit and candy we had put out, along with keys, purses, and bottled water. On the wall were hooks for backpacks and coats, and there were chairs. Off the living room was a TV and game room, and on the other side of the living room was the service room, which had a washer and dryer; but most of the time we hung the clothes out to dry. There was also a large swimming pool and recreation area a little ways from the house, so no one sleeping inside would be disturbed. The layout was ideal for all of us; we all had plenty of room.

The villa was about five miles from the nearest town. On the other side of the villa, about 20 feet away, was the caretaker's home. He and his family lived there full time. The owners lived in town but came out every day, for the business office was in the basement of the villa. They said the villa was continuously rented year round. The place was also a working farm and had a big vineyard. They made their own wine to sell and were harvesting grapes when we were there.

The next morning, Sept. 27, after Curt had gone into town and bought a bunch of doughnuts, goody buns, and rolls, along with the usual fresh fruits and juices, we ate a hearty breakfast. Someone always wanted bacon and eggs, along with the pastries. After doing the dishes, we packed overnight suitcases, for all the Amarals were headed for Lucca, Pisa, Carrara, Levanto, and La Spezia. We were staying overnight in Levanto. Curt and Kay were staying at the villa but would be taking in some of the places we had seen when they weren't with us.

So after getting the dirt off the cars and the windows washed from all the dust, we were on our way to Lucca, and because we were in separate cars, our destination was Levanto. Laurence and his family had already visited some of the places we were going to see along the way, so they were taking in other sites.

Lucca is a walled-in city and has many Romanesque churches, towers, monuments, and museums. The city center is closed to car traffic. The most interesting places to see are Duomo, San Michele in Foro, San Martino, and San Frediano. Museo Anfiteatro and the city's magnificent walls are also interesting to see. Lucca was a Roman colony and became Tuscany's first Christian town. Its medieval wealth was based on banking and the silk industry, and it still makes and sells underwear. It is also rich in agriculture. Lucca remained an independent republic for 500 years, which ended about 1799 when Napoleon came into the picture and changed a few things. In 1847, it came into the Kingdom of Italy. We learned that one of the reasons the walls are in such good shape today is because very few wars were fought there.

Mark studying the unusual architecture of Duomo di San Martino

We took in Duomo di San Martino, which took over 400 years to complete. By the time it was done, things sort of blended together with the skills of the different builders. There was a lot to see on the outside and inside of this building and how it all came together in the end, but you could clearly see that changes had to be made to make it possible.

We went in and walked all through the inside of the building. We saw the marble tomb of Ilaria del Carretto and looked at the incredible details done to the carving of the body and the folds of the garment. From there, we walked over to the Fonta Listrale where we saw more delicate carvings done in marble, along with many other pieces. There were lots of mosaic works on the walls. Everywhere we looked, we could see great works of art; you couldn't begin to take it all in.

Finally, we walked the grounds. One of the fascinating things we saw was the church bell tower, which sat atop a tall structure and was at least eight stories high. Starting at the second floor, there was a window, and going up each floor, two more windows were added, and on the top floor, there were eight windows side-by-side each other. At the top, we went out to look over the countryside. The bell tower gave you quite a view. We later saw other towers with the same pattern of windows going up, with one window at the bottom level and more windows the higher up you went.

Bell tower at
Duomo di San Martino

Our final jaunt took us to see the city wall that stands about four feet high in some places and much higher in others. A wide swath of lawn makes the place look nice and peaceful, but at one time, anyone coming up the river to do battle could be seen. Today, the lawns, along with the trees that have since been planted, make the town attractive and offer a very nice park, but I do not think they use it for that. We noticed that everyone inside the town walls has beautiful gardens.

Julia with the crowds at the leaning tower

We left Lucca and drove to Pisa to see the leaning tower that Frank and I had seen in 1968. It was a disappointment for us this time because back then we were able to go to the top. The top was now closed, and we weren't able to get close to the tower because of the crowds of people. However, if you had never seen the Tower of Pisa before you would not know the difference.

We drove up to a parking place, got out of the car, and walked to see the leaning tower. I don't think the kids had seen it before. On our first visit, we noticed many places in disrepair due to damage from WWII. Now those old buildings had been restored or replaced and are being used as a nice storage area.

Construction of the leaning tower started in 1173, and right away, it started leaning to the right due to the soil that was beneath the sea at one time. It is now being protected with cables. It leans more than 16 feet off center. Next to it is the Duomo, or cathedral, that was started in 1063 and has bronze doors that were cast in 1180. The doors caught my eye again, just as they had before. This church was among the first to be decorated with black and white stripes. After going through the church, we left going out the doors that led to the baptistery across the street, which was started around 1152 and has many good paintings worth seeing. I don't know if the black stripes are painted or if they are made of black rock of some kind.

Mark, Frank, and Julia at the Tower of Pisa

We stayed overnight in the picturesque town of Levanto

After seeing everything, we headed back toward the car. On the way, I think we bought hot dogs for lunch, and then we headed for Levanto and Monterosso, a busy coastal port, busy even back in the 18th century. To get there, we drove through the towns of Massa and Carrara, where they make the marble we saw on our way. We arrived around 5 p.m. and the town was very active. This was Sept. 27, a religious holiday, and although our rooms were paid for, it was sort of like taking potluck.

I don't know how Laurence and his family had fared, for they were not in the Hotel 5 Terre building that we were in; all I remember is we were very crowded in our room. We had no more than gotten in our room when we hurried out to the center of town, for there was so much activity going on. And we ran into the kids. The owner of our hotel told us we had better get our dinner reservations in somewhere, or we may not get to eat early. So Mark, Julia, and Laurence went looking for a place to eat. There were plenty of places, but they were filling up fast. They finally found one they thought we would all like.

There were hundreds of people in the center of town. In this area, there was something that looked like an altar that had been set up. From there the people formed a line with the priest and altar boys carrying the statue of a saint; I don't remember her name. The people started saying the Rosary while walking along the waterfront from one end of town to the other. It was at least a mile. Somehow we lost Julia, but Mark finally found her in the line saying the Rosary. She caught on faster than I did as to what was going on.

The ceremony lasted until after dark, with people going up and back along the waterfront, which was also the main street in town. When it was finished, the people went down to the water, lit candles in a wax holder, and floated them out in the bay. It was quite a sight to see with all that light reflecting off the water. After this was done, we went and had dinner. We then wandered the streets together, for there was still a lot of activity going on.

At the end of the 18th century, there were 80,000 people living in Livorno (Leghorn). During 1943–44, the port took a lot of hammering from air raids when it was under German occupation. It is not an outstanding town today, but it is busy.

Sept. 28. The next morning the family had breakfast together. We had to be out of the hotel by 10 a.m. with the cars, so Mark and Laurence took the cars and parked them down at the pier where all the cars had to park for the day. There was plenty of room and our car stayed there for the day. We would be driving back to the villa later on after a full day of sightseeing. Laurence and his family stayed in town for a while and then left for Lucca on their way back to the villa for the night.

The four of us took water, toilet paper, Kleenex, and some food in backpacks as we headed out for our walking trip from Monterosso to Vernazza, which took us 1 hour and 45 minutes. From there we planned to take the train to Corniglia, but we ended up taking it to Manarola and then walked to Riomaggiore.

The walking trail from Monterosso to Vernazza was quite rough, but we saw many interesting things along the way. We climbed a high mountain, and in doing so, we went up and down ravines. In several places, we saw big orange nets tied to trees. We were told they were used to catch olives when it's time to harvest them. We learned that October is the season, so they were getting ready for that. We walked under many olive trees. Many places on the trail were very narrow and steep, so Mark found a stick for Frank to use as a cane. This wasn't an easy trip for Frank, and fortunately, as we got closer to Vernazza, we began walking downhill and the trail became wider and easier.

Frank walking down
the trail to Vernazza

Going toward the water in Vernazza

The view of the city nestled against the rocky hill, and the clear blue water of the ocean with different colored boats tied up at the shore, was a wonderful sight. We took quite a few pictures of this area.

After reaching the town of Vernazza, one of the first things we did was find a restroom and a good place to eat. The restaurant we found had a good view of the water and surrounding area. The place was crowded with people, and everyone was enjoying the wonderful weather.

The streets of Vernazza

After lunch, we walked the streets in town and then headed for the train station to go to Manarola. Once we were at the station it was "Hurry up and wait."

Cooling our heels at the train station

We originally planned to take the train to Corniglia and then walk the rest of the way to Riomaggiore. But after cooling our heels for three hours, we were starting to feel the morning walk, so we changed our tickets to take us to Manarola instead. And we really had to cool our heels waiting for the train that took forever to arrive; it was off schedule by two hours. This meant we would now be getting home later than Mark had planned, and we were now left with very little time to spend at Riomaggiore. Finally, the train arrived. We were now traveling along the mountain cliffs looking down at the ocean below us, as we went through tunnels, across winding hills, and past small towns. The trains and tracks were very modern.

The last three towns we passed were built along the mountainside and extended down to the ocean. The houses stood wall to wall, and they were painted in light colors. All you could see were rows and rows of solid light-colored houses climbing the mountain. The forever-hanging clothes out the windows had become part of the decor. We saw ramps down at the water's edge to lie on and get a suntan, for there were no sandy beaches that I could see, mostly solid rocks right down to the sea.

Well, we finally made it to Riomaggiore, and the first thing Mark had us do was buy our 4 p.m. boat tickets back to Levanto, where our car was. So we walked to the part of town near

where the water is deep and where the big boats that can hold 50 people come into dock. After finding this and taking care of the tickets, we spent some time walking the town and saw a beach where small boats come in. After a while, we walked back up to the main boat area together. It was sort of relaxing and Frank was with us. Then all of a sudden, here comes our boat. Where is Frank? He didn't tell us he was leaving, nor did he know why we were up where we were waiting on some big boulders in the hot sun.

Me, Mark, and Frank walking down to where the boats come in

The three of us took off with our backpacks and ran back to the central area where there was a lot of activity. We had to find Frank. I headed for all the different men's bathrooms thinking he might be there. The three of us were calling his name. When we finally found him, it was already too late to catch the boat. He was down near the shallow bay ramp, leaning against the wall, waiting there for the boat; he thought the big boat would come in there.

We missed the boat to go back to our car, so we would now have to wait another hour for the boat to return to take us back to Levanto. This meant it would be up to Mark to make the long drive back to the villa, driving at night through a strange country. I know he wasn't thrilled about it.

Frank thought he was doing great, but he hadn't understood what we said and had gotten his signals mixed up. A little later, he lost his cool. When we finally found him, we were all hollering to him to hurry to us. He just stood there. And, of course, the three of us were really giving him hell and telling him what he did wrong. He cannot apologize when he makes a mistake; it just cannot be his fault, nor can he be quiet about it. He hurt Mark and Julia's feelings very much, and I knew then we all had to settle down. So I told Julia and Mark to go take a walk and explore the town. I assured them Frank and I would get back to the boat ramp in time. Mark was afraid I would not be able to find it, but I told him to go and enjoy the town.

I noticed a bench sitting along the retaining wall leading to town where all this happened, so I pulled Frank down on it with me and we rested awhile, for it had been a hot day and we were all upset with him. After we sat down, I explained to him what he had done. I finally said, "Let's go walk back up to where we have to catch the boat. Maybe we can both just cool off."

It was then that he told me he didn't know we had to be up there and that he didn't hear us say a word about it, nor did he let us know he didn't hear us. And I know this is right, for he never asks people to repeat anything if he doesn't know or hear what they said. So I could see why he got so mad at us; he thought he was doing the right thing. At the same time, I am aware he wasn't getting enough sleep and was taking too many sleeping pills. The results of this were with him most of the time. Added to all that there was his trouble with not hearing very well, and his stool problem that can put him on the irritable side at times.

Frank did take time to rest and cool down. He took his shoes and socks off and put his feet in the deep Mediterranean Sea. He sat there on a rock next to the water in deep meditation. I really felt sorry for him, but he now owed Mark and Julia an apology for what he had said, and I hoped they would forgive him. I got a picture of him in deep thought over it. About 10 minutes before boat time, Mark and Julia came back. Frank didn't say a thing to them about what had happened. He honestly thought he had done right and had no way to retract what he had said. I really think he gets mad at himself, and he knew he had gotten me mad. It took me awhile to settle down.

Frank meditating on his mistake

Finally, the boat came back. We made sure Frank was on board before it pulled away and headed back to Levanto. Neither of us had really gotten to see the town, except from the boat as we went by on our way back to the car. Frank owed Julia and Mark one for that. On the way, we got a great view of the city of Riomaggiore as we drifted slowly away from the town. And I was able to get a good picture of the surrounding area and the people on the big flat rock

platform by the water's edge getting a suntan and swimming in the ocean. As we were looking high up on the hill, we saw the town of Montenero, which we had walked by earlier. And as we passed Manarola, we could see the city up on the hill and the train tracks and train along the rim of the mountain. We went by Corniglia, the city down by the side of the mountain with railroad tracks above and below the town.

Julia looking at the view from the boat pulling away from Riomaggiore

The sun was getting low as we went by Vernazza, but we could still get a picture of where we had eaten lunch out on the deck. Because of the shadows, the town had sharper colors on the wall-to-wall houses that climb the mountainside from the rock cliffs just above the ocean. We continued seeing train tracks and homes as we continued by boat to Monterosso and Levanto. Seeing the area this way, the area we had been to earlier in the day by walking and by train, was a wonderful way to end such a nice trip, even with Frank's faux pas.

The vast view from the boat heading back to Levanto

We headed for the car as soon as we docked and took off on the two-hour or longer drive back to our villa, stopping only for gas. We finally got back to our villa much later that night. Everyone else was back by the time we got there, so we took a quick shower, changed our clothes, and we all went out to dinner, except Kay and Curt. They ate dinner in their cottage due to Kay's accident.

While we were gone for the day, Kay and Curt had taken a trip to another area. While walking down some steps, she fell on cement and did a great deal of damage to the side of her face, arm, and hip, and also a good job on her left knee and leg that required a doctor. The lady at the villa called her family doctor. He took care of Kay and gave her pain pills, along with anything else she had to take. Thank the good Lord she did not break any bones.

She needed many ice packs and had to stay in bed for a couple of days for the swelling to go down, so they could leave for the States in a few days when we'd all be leaving the villa. By the time we saw her, she was already black and blue. She ended up going through a few weeks of pain and having black and blue spots on her body after she got home, but she was a good sport through it all.

Julia doing some shopping in Greve

Sept. 29. Friday morning was another washday, and this time we all joined in so the washing would go faster. The clotheslines were really full. After what had happened yesterday, nobody was in a hurry to go far from the villa, at least until we were well organized and knew what we'd be getting ourselves into. We all spent some time with Kay so that Curt could have some free time. We sat out on the patio in the sun with Kay joining us. Around noon, Julia and I had everything done except the ironing, and the suitcases were pretty well organized. So we took off for the town of Greve, where Julia did some shopping for silk sheets. I think she found some and had them shipped home. While driving to the town, I took pictures of the surrounding area that I could put together when I placed them in the travel album after the trip.

We then went to the town of Montefioralle to see a quaint little villa and make arrangements to have a nice dinner party there for our last night together. This was quite a nice place to walk around, seeing all the red and pink brick houses, walls, archways, and patios. It seemed like every house was joined to the next; then you come to an alley that gives you a wonderful view of the surrounding area. We then went back to Greve, where we ran into Laurence and Gloria. They joined us for lunch, and then the four of us walked the town and had a very nice time together.

Then it was back to the villa, where everyone spent the rest of the day out on the patio playing card games with Kay. She was a good sport even though she was all black and blue, but she didn't hurt as much. We took more pictures of all of us together and of the area and swimming pool. After one person finished their ironing, the next person went in to use the iron until all the ironing was done. The clothes were in and off the line as Mark brought out his last load. Laurence put some of his luggage in his car so he would be ready to leave in the morning. Kay, Spence, and Frank spent their time out on the sundeck playing Mexican Train; everyone was out there at one time or another playing the game with her. Curt took care of their packing.

Playing cards with Kay on the patio

Walkway to the pool

We had a wonderful time at dinner, and nobody was in a hurry to leave the quaint little place at Montefioralle. The dinner was served family style. It was obviously a popular place, for it was packed with people.

We all enjoyed this wonderful trip to Montoro and the Chianti area. Frank and I had this part of our trip paid for by Julia, Mark, Laurence, and Gloria, and we thanked them for giving us such a nice gift.

Saturday morning, Sept. 30, we were up and had our last breakfast, with Curt going into town to get fresh fruits and fresh bakery goods so we wouldn't have to cook. I took a

picture of him sitting at the kitchen table with the rest of the family. By 9 a.m., Curt and Kay, with her black-and-blue face, had left to drive back to Rome to catch their plane home. The rest of us finished breakfast, with Laurence, Gloria, and Spence getting that last cup of coffee at the table. Then all the luggage was taken out and loaded up. Last minute pictures of the place were taken, and we said a goodbye to the owner of the villa who had really gone out of her way to help us in everyway she could.

Curt, Laurence, Mark, Kay, Gloria,
and Spence at our last breakfast together in Italy

We took a picture of Laurence, Gloria, and Spence as they drove off on their way to Florence and then to Vienna. They would be gone for 10 more days. We then said goodbye to Mark and Julia as they headed for Naples. As I said earlier, they had already been at the villa two weeks before we arrived with other friends who had joined them at that time.

Laurence, Gloria, and Spence
getting ready to drive to Florence

Frank feeling lonely after everyone had left

Frank and I were now left all by ourselves with no car in this great big villa out in the country. I took a picture of him climbing the steps with no one around; he looked rather lonely. About 10 a.m., the owner came over to us and said the same taxi driver that brought us out would arrive in 10 minutes, and he did. Of course, she knew who he was, for he had done this service for her many times.

He drove us to the airport in Florence, and we then headed for Paris for 10 days. Thus, we come to the end of a wonderful week with the family in Italy.

Paris

ON SEPT. 30, AFTER everyone went in different directions, Frank and I ended up in Paris. Julia had booked us at the Ritz for 10 days, knowing that was something we would never do for ourselves. The place was a great location for seeing that part of Paris, but the Ritz was really wasted on both Frank and me. We never did use the dining room. We ate our breakfast at one of the street cafés where we could watch what was going on, or we simply ate fruit and sweet rolls in our room.

Frank has a hard time spending that kind of money on pleasure; he just cannot relax and enjoy spending his hard-earned money. Frank's comment was saying "no" to the price, and then admitting he could well afford it, but his "mind" could not. I liked his comment for it really said it all.

We checked in at the hotel and had a nice big room with all the luxuries, along with a big bowl of fruit. When that was gone, we bought more fruit, for that was part of our breakfast each day. There was also a big box of mixed candies. After hanging up our clothes, we settled in and put everything else where it would be for the week, including our jar of peanut butter and a box of crackers. Frank and I were not inclined to open the refrigerator to get anything out of it, so I set our food on top of it because we did not have a coffee table.

We headed out to see the sights. A movie was being made in front of the Ritz, so traffic was tied up to some degree. They were filming right up until the day before we left. This made it hard to get a good picture of the front of the hotel. And it rained off and on the week we were there.

When checking in at the Ritz Hotel, they told us not to forget to get the five-day pass to go to the museums. The pass would keep us from having to stand in long lines, and it was good for 65 museums. So we decided to get it on Monday; in the meantime, we walked the area. It was a rather clear day. The Ritz is at 15 Place Vendome, and it was close to everything we wanted to see, including Tuileries Gardens, which was just a half-block away. We walked through that place, then started walking down Rue de Rivoli and saw a big Ferris wheel, so we stopped and checked it out. We found out it was given to Paris on Jan. 1, 2000, and was scheduled to be removed in 2001. It was in a good spot, standing on the corner of Roosevelt and François, but we did not ride on it.

Frank splurging at the Ritz, thanks to Julia and Mark

We continued walking to the Arc de Triomphe and went up to see the view from the top. It's quite a view looking down at the Notre Dame Cathedral and all the surroundings, and it helped us get oriented to the area. We stayed at the top just long enough to see the city lights come on, including the lights from the Ferris wheel and the Eiffel Tower. It really made a wonderful sight. The Arc was built in 1805 to celebrate Napoleon's military victories. You can't go to Paris and not take it in. I was happy to get some nice pictures of the area.

The two of us having a good time exploring Paris

It was getting dark, so we headed back towards the hotel, taking our time and enjoying the people and all the activities going on as we went. We got back around 10:30. Julia called us from Naples and said it had rained all day, so it must have started raining right after we left Italy.

Sunday, Oct. 1. We got up in time to go to High Mass at Notre Dame. We took a taxi so we would get there in time; we didn't know the way and did not want to be late. It was showing signs of rain, so we took our backpacks and raincoats with us, along with a bottle of water, for we planned to walk and sightsee the rest of the day.

The church was beautiful with all its colorful stained-glass windows, and the singing was nice to hear. Even though this is a very big place, it was still crowded inside. After Mass, we walked around the grounds and saw Sainte–Chapelle. We took the footbridge over to Ile St. Louis where we walked around and found a nice place to have lunch. We then walked down to the water's edge of Quai Saint-Bernard and found a nice warm spot to sit down and watch the birds in the water.

After watching the birds, we walked over to the Opera Bastille and found our way back to Notre Dame, ending up in front of a set of doors made of iron that Frank especially liked. He also liked the big fancy downspout next to the doors. This was the Hotel de Lauzun, which I'm sure was a great hotel in its day. From there, we went over to Cluny La Sorbonne. The museum was open, so we went in and enjoyed spending time there. It was very good. We saw a lot of work from the Middle Ages, and several rooms were well worth taking the time to see.

Frank was fascinated by
these doors and downspout

We ended up going through the Orsay Museum that covers 19th century art. This turned out to be a big place, so we more or less glanced it over as we walked, knowing we would be back the next day. We crossed over the Seine River on our way back to our hotel and saw people selling flowers along the bank of the river. We walked through Tuileries Gardens and then went to our room, changed clothes, and were soon back on the street to find a place to have dinner.

After walking to the Arc de Triomphe, we wandered back toward the hotel. On the way, we made reservations to go to Giverny by bus on Oct. 4. We finally got back to our room and played a game of Mexican Train on our bed. As I said earlier, there was no coffee table in our room. In such a big, fancy hotel, this was not satisfactory.

We started the next day, Monday, Oct. 2, with fruit in our room, followed by breakfast around the corner from the hotel. Frank wasn't too happy paying $4 for a cup of coffee, but they did serve a nice breakfast. We went back to our room, packed our bag for the day, and went down to buy tickets at the hotel desk to see the flamenco opera at 7:30 p.m. Next, we walked to the office by the Louvre to stand in line to get our five-day museum pass. We then stood in line to enter the Louvre Pyramid (Pyramide du Louvre). After that, you are on your own. We walked down into a huge underground complex divided into many large rooms with the pyramid dome providing a lot of light in this area.

We saw so much art that it kept us busy looking for the rest of the day. There were more than 30,000 pieces of art to look at. Frank finally found the Mona Lisa; it was a stopper for him. Another must-see piece is The Wedding at Cana. We did not take a tour, for we found you could hear enough from other tours to fill in the gaps if you needed more information. We spent the whole day there walking from one room to another, and we had lunch along the way.

Wedding at Cana

Frank and his Mona Lisa

Before the day was over, Frank made the rounds three times to see the Mona Lisa. She was his delight. I took a picture of him looking at her and got many other pictures of paintings. Around 5 p.m., we headed back to the hotel, going over by a market on the way to get more fruit and some sweets for our breakfast in the morning. We dressed for dinner and went to the opera near the hotel. It was raining when we went back to the hotel. It's sad to say, but I don't remember much about the opera, so it must not have been very impressive or outstanding.

Inside the Musee d'Orsay

We got up Tuesday, Oct. 3, ready to go to Musee d'Orsay to see the Impressionist painters. By this time, we were having fruit and rolls in our room for breakfast, and Frank was drinking hot water; he said he could wait to get home for his coffee. We left the hotel with our rain gear on, for it was still raining. We now knew our way around Paris so we walked to the museum. Musee d'Orsay has a lot of French art that is on the Impressionist side, and the artists include Manet, Monet, Renoir, Degas, van Gogh, Gauguin, and Cezanne.

The museum building was made from an old train station around 1970. It is two stories high and has excellent lighting. They did a good job turning it into a place to show art. Once again, we enjoyed all the art, and time does go by fast when you have so much wonderful art to see. We ended up having our lunch in their nice restaurant. The food was very good, and above all, it was hot.

"Cain flying before Jehovah's Curse" by Fernand Cormon

One of the paintings that Frank liked was "The Harvest Done," perhaps because it was the wife in the painting who collected the money. There were others paintings we especially liked, including, "Cain flying before Jehovah's Curse," "Romans of the Fall," and the one of "Van Gogh" that was done in reds and browns.

We finally decided we had seen enough. We left the museum around 4 p.m. and headed back to the hotel, once again taking in the fruit stand and bakery on the way to stock up for breakfast the following morning. By now it was really raining, so I had my one-piece rain jacket over my hat and coat to help keep me dry as we walked to the hotel. As Frank was getting the key to our room, it became obvious that the bellboy was not going to let me in the hotel lobby. Frank saw what was happening and came over to help me out of my rain gear. The bellboy then cooperated. I guess I was not dressed to his taste to enter the Ritz; we had a good laugh over that.

We went up to our room and rested up; then we spent the rest of the day walking through the hotel's many hallways looking at all the small shops and the displays of jewelry, furs, crystals, and other items. I really enjoyed looking at all of the things. Dinnertime found us out on the street looking for a good restaurant, and I think we spent this night having dinner at a real authentic spaghetti house. The food was very good, but the place was very crowded with people, which meant you couldn't linger over your dinner very long. The waiter made sure of that. It was still raining outside, and we didn't feel like walking the streets in the rain, so we took a cab back to the hotel.

Back in our hotel room, we got our Hand and Foot card decks out, which included five decks in all, and decided to go down to the lobby to one of the tables to play cards. We found a table by the check-in counter that was out of the way and in a nice, quiet spot. We ended up having the clerks and bellboys enjoying watching us play as they waited around. They had never seen the game before. We did this a few more evenings while we were there.

On Oct. 4, Tuesday, we took a tour bus at 10 a.m. for a trip to Giverny for the day to see where Van Gogh had spent the last few months of his life. This is also the place where Monet lived from 1883 to 1926. Our trip out on the bus was interesting to us, for we had not seen Paris before, nor had we seen the surrounding area. On the way out, we went by the Eiffel Tower before heading out into the countryside.

When we arrived at the Normandy home and garden of Claude Monet, our driver parked the bus out in the parking lot and told us we could come back to the bus at any time. He would be staying in the bus, so we left our rain gear and a few other items behind, knowing we could go back and get them if we needed to. The first thing we did was walk the garden and then the lily ponds. There were a few ponds and the lilies were in bloom. The flowers looked very nice and there were so many to see. No wonder Monet's paintings showed so many lilies.

Lily pond at Claude Monet's home   Frank exploring the beautiful gardens

Monet also had a nice rose garden and many other kinds of flowerbeds, along with several weeping willow trees. After spending time at the gardens and ponds, we took in the tour of his two-and-one-half-story house. There was one window high up, and from there I took a picture of the grounds and road below, which ran right along the sidewalk up against the wall of the house. I also took a picture of the ice cream vendor cart.

We ate lunch at the Jardins de Giverny restaurant, which was also near the parking lot. It was separated by the narrow main road from the house and garden. After lunch, we took in the museum that at one time was Monet's art studio; it was in among the flowerbeds. There were many prints and postcards of the area for sale, along with other things you could buy. I ended buying a couple of things.

After doing some shopping, we walked over to the restaurant area and bought two homemade ice cream cones from the vendor on the street. They tasted very good. Frank, while waiting for the bus to arrive, was feeding the birds with what was left of the cones. There were many different kinds of birds just waiting for a tasty handout.

On our way back to Paris, just outside of Giverny, we came to a palace. Our driver stopped and told us the reason it was still standing was that the Germans used it as their headquarters during WWII. Our driver said the Germans destroyed anything of value unless they were using it. As we continued driving, he told us interesting stories about things that had happened during that time.

This palace outside of Giverny was occupied by the Germans in WWII

We got back to Paris around 5 p.m. and had the bus driver drop us off near the Arc. We walked back to our hotel from there, stopping for dinner on the way. Back at the Ritz, it was time to relax and play a game of cards, and then we got ready to take off in the morning for Versailles (vehr-sigh).

On Oct. 5, we ate a breakfast of fruits, sweet buns, and hot water. By 10 a.m., we were ready to board a minivan, which held six people. As we started leaving the city, we were waylaid by President Clinton's entourage, headed by Secretary of State Madeleine Albright, which had taken up the road outside of Paris on our way to Versailles. This was during the time she had gone to Paris handling the conflict between Israel and Palestine. They were all out in this area. We had to stop until a road was cleared that would allow us to take a side road out of the congested area they had caused.

Then we were on our way to Versailles to see the Sun King, Louis XIV's dream palace and grounds. As we entered the gate, we saw a hand-laid stone walkway in the courtyard that covered a huge area surrounded by the palace buildings. The six of us had special B passes, so we were able to move right along once we got inside the palace. I don't remember which rooms we saw first, so I will tell you what I remember from the pictures I took.

We saw the War Room with lots of guns, knives, swords, and other things hanging on dark mahogany-paneled walls. The crystal chandeliers were one of the things Frank loved and took a special interest in. Another was the Hall of Mirrors that was 250 feet long and had 17 arched mirrors on one side of the hall. On the opposite wall were 17 matching windows you could look out and see the fabulous cookie-cutter gardens and shrub areas. They were breathtaking and extensive; you could look at them a long time and not get tired of what you were seeing. There were 24 gilded crystal candelabras in the hall that held at least 24 tapered white candles each. Additional candelabras lined the walls. Can you image all 1,000 or more candles lit up with all the crystal sparkling and reflecting in the mirrors, along with all the formal gowns and wigs?

There also were 23 busts and statues, along with some good paintings. A pipe organ was on the second floor looking down on the main floor. And we learned that the throne could be moved into this room, which is where the WWI Treaty was signed.

Frank checking out the candelabras

Room where the WWI Treaty was signed

We saw the throne room, which was called the Apollo Room, and there was the Peace Room. At the end of the Peace Room, we entered the Queen's Room. Her quarters were very well decorated and, of course, in good taste. It was restored to what it was when she lived there in 1789. From there we saw the Queen's Antechamber, where the royal family entertained dinner guests and family.

We had our lunch in an outside cafeteria before going on to see more. After lunch, we went into the gardens. We were taken over to a place where a bridge went over a good-sized lake that was built in the shape of a cross. After that, we were taken by van to Trianon to see Marie Antoinette's small, private house. It was a half-story palace with another house built beside it, making it spread out along a lakeside. She raised pigs, goats, chickens, and many other kinds of animals at this place. She also had a garden and fruit trees. This was quite a change from the big fancy palace. Marie Antoinette entertained her friends, put on shows, and had fun here. Afterward, we headed back to the city for the evening.

Frank saying goodbye to Marie Antoinette's small house

We had found a nice little cafeteria close to the hotel, and we ate most of our dinners at that place. They would serve us hot water and the food was good. After a meal, and if the weather was good, we would go for a walk and buy our fruit for breakfast. We always had peanut butter and crackers on hand if we needed more to eat. If it were raining, we would play Hand and Foot in the lobby in the evenings. The table we sat at was a good place to observe people coming and going. I will say that some of the men's tuxes were quite elaborate and went well with their overweight egos.

Oct. 6, Thursday, we got ready to meet our private driver, Raphael, outside at the limo at 10 a.m. He spoke good English and worked for the hotel. This was going to be a long day, taking us to see many interesting places. The first place we went to was Vaux le Vicomte (voh-

luh-vee-komt), which was about 20 miles away. We got to see some of what 17th century life was like at this place. Our guide took a great deal of pride in telling us the history of how the palace building got started and the wars that went on; he had Frank asking questions throughout the day. Our guide showed us the fine horse carriages and old stables, the drawbridge, the ponds, and the lakes with their spraying fountains. Like Versailles, which set the standard for palaces to come, the gardens were set in a cookie-cutter oblong pattern.

Frank and me overlooking Chateau de Vaux le Vicomte

My only problem was I did not take enough notes.

After entering the main room and looking down the grand hall and ballroom, we saw enough chandeliers to hold 1,300 candles. Frank liked this room and spent some time looking at all the different things. I took a picture of him and the guide talking, and I marveled at how

one's voice sounded in the room. Napoleon welcomed the Pope in this room, and General Patton, on his way to Berlin, set up his headquarters in this ballroom.

We saw the music room and the pipe organ and then went to the dining room, with its elaborate carved wood and china setting. We also saw the billiard room and even got to go into the Chinese Room, which was closed to the rest of the tours.

Raphael and Frank in the grand hall

Trinity Chapel ceiling

Major art works are held in this art gallery that was built around 1528. The gallery is in a wing of the building that provides passage from Trinity Chapel. The room itself is 60 meters long and 6 meters wide. The chapel is done in beautiful wood with light blue paint, and the décor dates from Henry IV–Louis XIII.

We saw several small bedrooms that were very well done and on the cozy side. One room we saw is what I will call the bathroom. It had chairs with seats that went up. Under the chairs was a big copper pot with a lid on it that would obviously be used as a potty or toilet.

There was also a copper bathtub covered with a wood cover that you could use as a place to rest when not in use to take a bath. The items were done in wood and were real nice pieces of furniture. All the rooms had nice flocked wallpaper and drapes that went from ceiling to floor, and each room had many painting on the walls.

The bathroom

Our guide took us up a bunch of narrow, steep, winding wrought-iron steps to the attic, where we got a view of the entire surrounding area. You could look down and see all the buildings from there. It was a very good place from which to supervise the grounds. You could keep an eye on your workers and watch how the work was being done. There were many buildings, and they all looked like homes, but some were for the horses and other animals, and there was a shed for buggies; however, you could not tell this from the outside.

From the attic, we went downstairs to the first floor to see the kitchen. This was one big room, with one entire wall made of copper. Copper pots and lids hung in rows on the wall, and there was a huge fireplace where the cooking was done. There was also a big table used for preparing meals. Cupboards ran above and below one wall that had a working space to wash dishes in copper dishpans. The windows were high up so they sat above ground level, but the kitchen itself was below ground taking up the entire first floor.

Frank checking out the large kitchen

The wine and vegetable cellar was beneath the first floor, and no doubt that is where clothing and linens were washed and where winter wood was stored.

Frank outside the entrance to the palace

Before we left, Raphael told us to look at the different styles of rocks and bricks used during the construction of each building. One of the last things done was the entrance to the palace. It had curved stairways on each side that allowed horses and their carriages to go straight up to the main level to let people out. From there the people would walk up the steps to the grand doors. This whole section was completed in the 19th century.

Each building has its own name. One was called the "Building of the Keep," but I have since forgotten if it means for animals or for the working people. There was a good story to go with it, and I took a picture of Frank standing at the entrance. From there we wandered through the gardens.

Two pictures together showing the lecturing Frank was getting on the building

Frank inspecting the Eiffel Tower

During our tour, Raphael took us to the restaurant for tourists. He knew what to order, which was nice, and the food was very good. After we had finished taking in the gardens, we headed back to Paris. We had Raphael stop at the Eiffel Tower so we could take a picture of it, and we asked to get out so we could see it. He let us, even though he wasn't supposed to. We got out and took a good close look at it. We walked all around it and looked high up to take it all in. It is a massive piece of construction. After staying for a half-hour, Raphael took us back to the hotel. It had indeed been a long day. He told us that Le Grand Café was a very nice place to have dinner, and it was.

Friday, Oct. 7. We were with Raphael, our Ritz chauffeur guide, for the day and went to Fontainebleau. I can't remember exactly what we saw, but I know we had a nice time. I do remember Raphael telling us that the employees of the Ritz had a staff of people working in a full kitchen that served them three choices of food at each meal. The employees had their own dining room, and if you worked six hours, you got one meal, and after eight hours, you got three meals and a place to stay overnight. He said there were 500 employees. All employees received very good wages and no tips, for tips were included in the billings. He also said that 44% of their earnings go to the government. I thought that was very interesting.

We spent Saturday, Oct. 8, window-shopping, and I bought myself a big light-blue print silk scarf. I don't remember buying anything else. We walked a great deal and Frank got a haircut along the way. I remember seeing all the high heels in the stores and thought to myself, "Great, I'm so glad I didn't throw mine away." Everyone back home was wearing big thick heels at this time. Paris fashion was now back to the thin high heels, so after just a matter of time, we would be, too. (Note: In 2006, as I am going through this, the heels being worn today are very high and have straps to hold them on. I wasn't far off, for what goes around comes around; it's just a matter of time.) We then walked to the Arc and over to the Eiffel Tower and took in the Ferris wheel again, taking our time walking the streets. I don't remember what else we did this day, but we did go to the nice eating place called Le Grand Café, and, yes, it was good.

Going to see the Eiffel Tower again

We went to the opera this night, which was within walking distance from the hotel. After the opera, we had a late dinner snack at an expensive neighbor hotel that was the only place open for a meal at that hour. Thinking we would split an order, we ordered one meal and found it was meat only. The size was no larger than four inches square, and this was all that was on the plate. So Frank and I got two bites each and left hungry, deciding that was enough fine dining in Paris for us. From then on, we would stick to the street cafes where you got something for your money. We ended up finding a nice café near the hotel to have lunch at. If we were nearby in the afternoon, we would go there. They would serve me hot water with no questions asked.

Sunday morning, Oct. 9, after having fruit and a pastry in our room, we walked to the Notre Dame Cathedral for High Mass services. This time I found it more interesting, for we got right up close to the front altar and could hear everything that was said. We could follow it using a paper that had the service in both English and French. As before, the music was nice to hear.

We left the church around noon and took in the museum near the church. It was a nice day, so we continued our walk and crossed over the Seine River and saw lots of people down on it. There was a houseboat being used as a cafeteria, so we took time out, had our lunch there, and enjoyed watching the people.

Afterwards, we walked over to Cluny Museum, taking our time going through it. From there we headed over to the Orsay Museum and ended up spending the rest of the day at the Louvre, seeing all the art we really liked. We took our time looking at everything, including the Mona Lisa again. And, of course, I took photos of all the pieces we wanted to remember.

We then walked over and went through Tuileries Gardens and enjoyed seeing everything. This is a very large, beautiful garden, and I took pictures of Frank saying goodbye, with all the statues and big buildings in the background. After seeing this part of Paris, we crossed over the Rue de Rivoli and walked up a side street that took us to the place we had found to buy our fruit and sweet rolls for breakfast. We stocked up for one last breakfast and then returned to our room and rested awhile.

Having rested up, we continued our sightseeing for the day by going over to the Arc de Triomphe and taking in everything along the way. We ended up eating dinner at the American Dream, on Ave Daunou, which served spare ribs and was close to the Ritz. The movie people moved out this day, so I got a picture of the Ritz entrance, only now it was busy with limos, taxis, and car traffic. I never did get a good picture of the place. Getting back to the hotel, we walked all throughout the lobby and enjoyed taking in all the showcases and boutique rooms once again. Finally, it was time to go back to our room for the night and do some packing. Frank is not one to pack, so I do it for the two of us. This holds true for all our trips. I really don't mind doing it, and he never complains about how things are packed. In the meantime, as I pack, he confirms our plane reservations and checks to make sure we have paid all our bills.

Frank saying goodbye to Tuileries Gardens

On Monday, Oct. 9, the sun was out. It was a nice day to finish packing and have our fruit and sweet rolls. We took one more walk around the garden before our Ritz hotel driver and escort took us to the airport at 11 a.m. to fly Air France non-stop to San Francisco. Julia had arranged a wheelchair and an assistant for Frank to accompany us to the lounge, boarding gate, and baggage claim area. She did this when she had set up the program, and it turned out to be very handy, for Frank was having a hard time getting around. Having the assistant made it much easier for me to handle all of our luggage.

The Lufthansa airliner that Julia and Mark arrived in

We flew out of Paris at 1:15 p.m. and had a nice flight back to the States. Flying business class, we had good flight attendants and good food along the way. We even got some sleep. We came into the airport at San Francisco on time at 3:35 p.m., taxiing right up to an Atlantic Airlines plane that was getting loaded up for takeoff. I was able to get a picture of it, and I got a picture of the plane Julia and Mark had come in on an hour ahead of us, a Lufthansa airliner. Heavy cargo was still being unloaded off that plane as we taxied to a stop.

It was planned by Julia that the four of us would come home at the same time, with Julia and Mark arriving in San Francisco an hour ahead of us. Her plan gave Mark time to go to a car rental agency to get a large van for the four of us and our luggage to go home in. We had just landed as Julia was getting their luggage ready to go through Customs. The timing was perfect; she was there to help us get our luggage and go through Customs as well. By this time, Mark was there ready for us to put things in the van. We were very happy to see that we did not have to wait or go looking for them, nor did they have to wait or go looking for us. And we got to come home together, which was nice.

On our way home, we stopped at the Chevy's Fresh Mex restaurant in Auburn for a baby-back rib dinner. I have a feeling Mark had that in mind long before he got off his plane in San Francisco. After eating, we finished our drive home. The weather was nice. The rest of the family arrived home a day later. When Laurence and his family got home, they had lost some of their luggage, but it ended up arriving at their home a few days later.

It is always nice to take the family on a trip. We get to be together. We have a good time, along with some bad times, and all I hope is that all is forgiven in the end. We won't be making many more of these trips unless Frank's mental health improves, for he now has a hard time remembering.

It is always great to plan and look forward to a trip, but it is even better getting home from one.

Fire in the kitchen

ON DEC. 26, 2000, I had the house all decorated for the Christmas holidays—candles and everything, with some candles burning on the kitchen drain board. We had Betty and Brayton Hahn over this night and went into the living room to play bridge together. I forgot the candles were burning in the kitchen. I smelled something and thought I was burning my dinner, so I went to check on it. When I got in the kitchen, I saw that a candle fire had started. I put it out quickly and went back to playing bridge while the dinner continued to cook.

The fire itself was not too bad, but the damage the soot did to the whole house was another thing. It took a whole month just to get the house painted and all the rugs cleaned, and so on.

Betty and Brayton were over for bridge and dinner, and we enjoyed eating a nice holiday dinner with them, not knowing that soot was everywhere. We didn't see the soot at that time, which was a good thing, for it did not deter us from enjoying the dinner and the rest of the evening. However, after they left, Frank and I went into the kitchen to do the dishes and clean up; to do this we had to turn the lights up to see better. It was then that we found that every place we touched was black with soot; even the floor and the rugs had soot on them. In the end, all the walls, floors, dishes, drapes, and rugs had to be cleaned throughout the whole house because soot had gotten into all the air ducts. And all the cupboards in the kitchen had to be professionally cleaned. They do not look as nice as they did before, but, for now, I will have to live with it. But who knows? Maybe I'll live long enough to have them redone.

Frank, Betty and Brayton Hahn enjoying a holiday dinner at our place

Frank's sister passes away

ON JAN. 18, 2001, Frank's sister, Marie Souza, passed away. She was 88 and died while living at the Townsend House in Chico, CA, where she had been living for more than a year.

Anna Marie was her only child. She is married to Ron Dillard and they have two children. One child is Amber, who married Brian Weathers, and they have three children (Colton and the twin girls Makenzie and Makaela). Their other child is Jordan, who will be out of high school in the spring as I write this. It was at the gravesite that Anna gave Frank his dad's cross and plaque that Marie had from the time Frank's mother died. This brought tears to Frank's eyes, for he had wanted that cross for a long time. The cross now hangs by his parent's wedding picture in the den.

Laurence falls off a ladder

ON JAN. 27, 2001, Laurence fell off a two-foot ladder while hanging some drapes for Gloria in their bedroom. I am pretty sure he hit the back of his head on a brick wall as he went down. The back of his head was cut open and he suffered a concussion; he passed out, stopped breathing, turned blue, and his eyes were wide open. He bled and I think he threw up. To his good luck, Gloria came to see why he was on the floor, and when she saw what he looked like, she thought he was dead. She called 911. The operator told her to pull his chest up to see if she could get him to breathe again; she did so and it worked. I think I have all that right.

She called their friends the Petersons, who lived nearby, to come help her. She then called Brad, Penny, and us and told everyone to meet them at the hospital in 20 minutes, which we all did. Laurence was then taken from the hospital by helicopter down to Auburn Faith Hospital. All of this happened when there was about three feet of snow outside their home.

After about four hours, we began to have some faith that he was going to make it. He was in the hospital overnight. If Gloria had not been there when she was, he would not be here today. I thank you, Gloria, with all my heart. And Laurence, the good Lord has given you a grace period that is a gift to take advantage of.

If this accident had happened while he was handing those 60,000 lights on the trees and shrubs at Christmastime, we would not have been so taken aback.

Julia and Mark were off skiing at Utah, or somewhere in that area, so they were not there. We did not tell them what had happened until they got home.

Going away party for the Kellermanns and other parties at 211 Reward St.

ON MARCH 18, 2001, we hosted a going away party for Dr. Scott and Carol Kellermann at our home. This was with the help of Brayton and Betty Hahn. It was a potluck, and all their friends brought food. It turned out to be a very nice day, so we were able to enjoy the outside. The Kellermanns had given me a list of all their friends whom they wanted to say goodbye to before they left for Africa for a year or so. It was a successful party; everyone had a good time.

In the process of giving the party, I discovered that the electrical plugs in the basement were not able to handle all the hot plates that were needed to keep the food warm. It was then that Laurence told me I was always blowing fuses in that room and that I needed to have a change made. So, a few days later, I called Frank Lasner, told him what was happening, and asked if he could come and see what needed to be done. He looked at it and said it was impossible for me not to have a setup in place already that would take care of the problem, for I was always looking ahead in all the years he had worked for me. And sure enough, I had a 220-volt setup in the furnace room. He strung the necessary wires and put outlets in a couple of places so I would have enough outlets for hot plates and other small appliances in the basement room. At this time, I also had him put in one more light post along the driveway. Now, everything inside and outside the house was ready for a party at any time. I have done this mostly so that Music in the Mountains can have the use of the yard for fundraisers.

Later the following year, in spring 2002, Julia and Mark traveled to Uganda and visited the Kellermanns. At that time, they were the only people from this area who had gone over to visit them since they had moved there to work with the pigmy people. Mark and Julia stayed with the Kellermanns for five days. The Kellermanns were very happy to see them. Later, other people went over to see them. I'll tell more about this later in the story.

Through the years, there have been many big parties in the yard for the kids as they were growing up, as well as after-golf barbecue parties and lots of bridge parties up through and into the 1970s. We had many indoor dinner parties: the party for Laurence and Gloria the night before their wedding, the shower party for Kellie, our godchild, and Julia and Mark's engagement party. And, of course, the Amaral family reunions, but never the Kruger–Evenson reunions—too many people, so we held those at the ranch. And there was Frank's 70th birthday party in 1988. I'm just highlighting a few of the parties we've had over the later years.

There is not much more in the way of any major projects that have to be done to change this place. There will always be small, fun things to do at 211 Reward St., which lends itself well to parties, both large and small.

Sharon Truman passes away

ON MARCH 22, 2001, my niece, Sharon (Anderson) Davis Truman, died of cancer at her home. She was 57 and left behind her husband Harold, a daughter, and three granddaughters. Sharon was the twin to Sandra and the daughter to my sister Helena Kruger-Anderson-Holton.

Sharon was a very sick lady during her last few months, but she continued taking her walks and worked as long as she could. There was a large family attendance at her funeral. She loved to come to the ranch, and she came to all the reunions. She is now at peace.

Allen Harsin funeral in Fresno

ON APRIL 13, 2001, Allen Harsin died, leaving his wife Ella (Gutherige) Nelson-Evenson-Asbury-Harsin, my sister-in-law by marriage to my brother Jim Evenson, who died in 1961.

Attending the funeral were all four boys and a girl by Nelson; Ray, by my brother Jim Evenson; Jeffrey Asbury; Ray's two half-sisters, Kitty and Corinda; half-brother James by Jim Evenson; and Allen's daughter. There were also all the spouses and grandchildren and sisters, and brothers-in-law on both sides of the family. We all ended up at Ella's house for a visit and some food.

Me, LaVena, and Nick at Ella's

Me and Nick talking at Ella's house

My brother Nick was also there. We had one of the nicest visits I have ever had with him. We were never very close, so that made it nice for me, and, no doubt, for him as well. He told me he would be up for my birthday or some time in May. I called him on his birthday, April 21; he was 75. We had a picture taken of my sister LaVena, Nick, and I together after the funeral.

My brother Nick passes away May 19, 2001

Nick at the Clarke Ranch, July '79

ON MAY 19, 2001, my brother, Nick Kruger, passed away. Two weeks earlier, as I've mentioned, I saw Nick at Allen's memorial service and later at Ella's house. Nick and I had a great talk about our life in Minnesota, up to when we lived in Durham and why we moved from there, right up to the present day. After we finished talking about our younger years, I told him I wondered if I should tell about our life in Durham in my book. He said we were the only ones left who remembered it, other than LaVena, and she could not talk anymore because of her stroke. So he said just leave it alone, so I said I would do just that.

That was one of the best conversations I had ever had with Nick, and it left me with a good feeling for him. He shared what he knew about what went on in Durham; I thought I was the only one left that knew. He also shared some of the experiences he had while living there. It was then that he really came into close ties with God. As the years went by, we all got used to his, "Praise the Lord," and, "Alleluia."

He later called me on May 13 to wish me a happy Mother's Day and a belated happy birthday. He said he was coming up to see us in two weeks; well, in two weeks he was gone. He had gone to work on Saturday on some church function, and when he was through working for the day, he told someone he would like a glass of cold water. The person went to get the water and then heard a loud bump. When they returned to him with the water, Nick had already dropped dead. This was Saturday, May 19, 2001.

Nick went so peacefully. Having had such a nice visit with him, I feel at peace with him, whereas our brother Jack, who died in 1999, really had a struggle at the end. It took about three months until Jack died. He wasted away to skin and bones before he left us. His passing left a great void inside me. I still cannot go up to the ranch without thinking of Jack, for we did so many things together, all of which were on the happy side of life.

20th anniversary Music in the Mountains dinner

Frank outside the new
Amaral Family Festival Center

ON WEDNESDAY, JUNE 13, 2001, we celebrated the 20th anniversary of Music in the Mountains at the Nevada County Fairgrounds with a gala dinner. This was the grand opening night of The Amaral Family Festival Center.

The event started with wine and hors d'oeuvres served from 5:45 to 6:15 p.m., followed by dinner at 6:15 in the Pine Building. The dinner was black tie optional. Everyone was dressed in the best they had; it was a beautiful and successful evening. They could have had a lot more people at the dinner, but the hall was filled to capacity and couldn't hold more people. So it was first call, and so on. The hall held about 250 people, and the ladies were presented with a conductor pin designed by Marian Gallaher.

The evening was followed by a performance in the new Amaral Family Festival Center. I was told that about 600 people attended. The hall will hold 700 people when full.

This hall is a great addition for the community, and I'm sure everyone will enjoy it very much for the next 10 years or so. But I feel that someday the fairgrounds people may decide not to renew the contract. They, themselves, may figure they can operate the hall on their own and not need Music in the Mountains, so it would pay for M.I.M. to keep their eyes open and keep their feelers moving.

Music in the Mountains anniversary party at 211 Reward St.

ON JUNE 15, 2001, Music in the Mountains put on "Elegance Under the Stars — A Night in Old Vienna." The performance was held at the Amaral Gardens at 211 Reward St. Two hundred and six guests attended, and it was a very successful night. The event featured Claus and Donna de Rond and Stan and Popi Dunn, as dancers; Stephanie Johnson, soprano and Linus Eukel, tenor (a husband and wife team); Robin Mayforth and Rae Ann Goldberg, violin; Janet Sims, viola; Cheryl Fippen, cello; Tim Spears, bass; Jane Lenior, flute; Neil Tatman, oboe; Tom Rose, clarinet; John Fuller, harp; and Paul Perry, the pianist-conductor. And there was a wonderful crew of workers for the evening cleanup. The event started at 8 p.m. and was over too soon, at 10 p.m.

Musician's rehearsal

The evening could not have been better, and as the owner of the place, I believe it was one of those magical nights. The evening was warm, the air was calm, and the sky was so clear you could see the stars. Everyone was dressed for the occasion, and the seating arrangement of the tables and chairs was done just right. Above all, the music was heard by all, regardless of where you were sitting, and it sounded just as if you were inside a hall. It was even heard down on Woodpecker Lane, two blocks away.

The cleanup crew worked until 11 p.m., and the next morning they came by to clean up the rest. I was told that this event could have been sold three times over and that it was sold out on the second day the tickets went out. (I knew they would sell at $100 a ticket the following year if I had my say.) Too much work goes into something like this not to make some money on it. It would be cheaper for me to just give them some money and spend less on the yard, and not have the party.

It takes three months in the spring from April through June to get the yard in shape. The work includes getting the deadheading done on all the camellias, rhodes, and azaleas. Also, the spring and summer flowers for the season have to be put in. This goes on every year. The amount of time it takes depends on how good the gardener is and how much work is needed to get everything done. This year I did double duty, but I have to admit it helped keep me in shape.

September 2001 — trouble with the new gardener

IN SEPTEMBER 2001, WITHIN two weeks after my new gardener was at our house, he took a blank check out of Frank's desk drawer and wrote it out by hand for $402. He had the check made out to the neighbor and had her sign her name. She, in turn, gave the gardener the money. Well, the police finally got involved, and in the process, we discovered that he was making methamphetamine in the gardener's cottage. The end result was that he left without saying a word, nor did he take his clothes or personal things, which I had to dispose of. He just took his "drug stuff" and we didn't hear from him again.

He also left me with a clogged drain in the bathtub and bathroom sink, and I had to replace the linoleum in a section by the kitchen sink and clean the carpets to try to get rid of the odor. I now had to find someone else to help me with the yard work. My friends would say, "What's new?" for I do seem to go through gardeners quite often; but then, I'll hire one who stays for several years.

I have been told that I should have a chapter on just the gardeners, which I think I will go ahead and add by the time this book is finished (included as Appendix C). With the drug-making gardener, I even managed to hit the local paper this time, instead of Frank, which upset my son very much. He said we all hit the paper enough without my having to be in it too, and, of course, he had a point there.

Terrorism attack on Sept. 11

AT 8:46 A.M. EST, ON Sept. 11, 2001, five hijackers flew American Airlines Flight 11 into the North Tower of the World Trade Center. There were 76 passengers and 11 crewmembers on board, and the plane was full of fuel. Approximately 18 minutes later, at 9:03 a.m., United Airlines Flight 175, with 51 passengers and 9 crewmembers, was flown into the South Tower of the World Trade Center. Flight 11 impacted the North Tower between the 93rd and 99th floors. Flight 175 crashed between the 77th and 85th floors. Each plane was carrying around 10,000 gallons of jet fuel. Fire started right away and became so hot that it melted the steel inside the buildings, resulting in structural failure. The buildings collapsed of their own weight, killing many more innocent people and 479 rescue workers.

Hundreds of people had gone to work in the buildings, and when they felt something, they went to the windows to look out. They saw smoke and debris everywhere, so some started to leave and make their way down to the exits. Fortunately, many were able to get out alive. It is estimated that around 17,000 people were inside the World Trade Center complex when the attacks occurred. However, many did not make it out, including the estimated 1,434 people who died in the North Tower and the estimated 599 people who died in the South Tower. Nor was it true for the passengers and crewmembers. In all, around 2,800 people perished in the World Trade Center collapse.

Just about a half-hour after Flight 175 hit the South Tower, at 9:37 a.m., terrorists crashed American Airlines Flight 77 into the pentagon, killing 125 people on the ground, 53 passengers, and 6 crewmembers. Then at 10:03 a.m., the fourth jet, United Airlines Flight 93, went into the ground in Pennsylvania, saving the White House or some other government building that was the target. There were 7 crewmembers and 33 passengers on board, not counting the 4 hijackers. The people in the plane chose to keep the hijackers from killing any more innocent people, knowing that their lives would not be saved. They took it upon themselves to fight the hijackers and force the plane down into open space.

There is no doubt that there was quite a struggle inside the plane as passengers and crew attempted to take it away from the hijackers before it went down. We do know that some of the people on board the plane had contacted their families by cell phone, so passengers had learned about the Twin Towers. At that time, they said goodbye to their families, knowing they would be killed when they crashed.

This tragedy started on Tuesday morning. Of course, it was on TV. We could see the fire and devastation. We watched as people were trying to get out of the way and saw people being killed from the fire. It was shown all over the world and continued through Sunday. The world was in mourning along with us. The fallout from these terrorist attacks will go on for some time, maybe many years, before we see the end result—"If ever."

People from all over the world went to churches and meeting places to pray for us here in America. One of the things that should come out of this is that we are all Americans. And we should start to think that way, instead of black, white, yellow, or any other color or religion, and including being Democrats or Republicans.

I am writing this 10 days after 911 happened, and things have really only begun to unfold, so I will leave it at this for now.

It's now a couple of weeks later, and on Oct. 7, 2001, the United States and the United Kingdom did a night air raid bombing attack on Afghanistan's airports. After that was complete, they went in during the daytime. Now the airfields have been destroyed. President Bush still carries the strong support of the American people and support from most of the world, for this is a world war on terrorists. It is now part of history, so more can be read about it in the libraries in America. This will go on and will change all our lives for some time, perhaps many years, and in some ways forever.

Nevada County prayer breakfast

NEVADA COUNTY HELD A prayer breakfast on Nov. 9, 2001. Among the many speakers, Julia gave the invocation. She did such an outstanding job that I thought I would like to have her prayer in my book. There were about 200 people at the breakfast, which was held at the Alta Sierra Country Club. Other people asked her for a copy, so she made a few and gave one to me. Here it is:

Good Morning Jesus!

We praise You and thank You for the many blessings we have received.
We especially thank You for the blessings of living in the United States
and especially in Nevada County, California.
Yet we enthusiastically ask You to bless us even more and to enlarge our
territory for You. We ask that You help us dispel fear by making us
ambassadors of trust in You individually in our separate circles of
influence and collectively as a community. We know we cannot succeed
alone so we ask you, Lord, to guide us and help us always stay
connected to (abide in) You.
Jesus, keep us from evil that we do not cause pain in others.
As we pray for ourselves this morning Lord, we also make these prayers
for others.

First, that You would inspire our local leaders as well as our President and

all world leaders with wisdom and courage, that they will work to create a peaceful world.

Second, that You heal the wounds of all people who are or have been

victims of evil.

And third, that You touch those of your children who plan and do evil that

they will have a change of heart.

Thank you Jesus for hearing our prayers and answering them according to

Your will.

[This was, and is, Julia's Prayer as she said it.]

An article by Gloria

OUR DAUGHTER-IN-LAW, Gloria, wrote the following article for the Hospice of the Foothills newsletter of November 2001. She was president of the organization's board of directors. Here is her article:

To head this letter with the usual greetings of Merry Christmas and Happy New Year, seems a little out of place considering the recent events that have affected all of us in one way or another. But the wish that all of you will have a holiday season that will bring you warmth and joy is still very real. Now, more than ever, we should treasure all that is good in our lives: family, friends, good health, and beauty of every kind. And while we are enjoying the colors and music and festivities we associate with the season, we here at Hospice will be ever mindful too of our patients, and the Hospice team that cares for them.

In this season of giving, we are also grateful for the financial support of the Friends of Hospice as well as the contributions of the community at large.

Personally, I wish to express my gratitude to the other members of the Hospice Board and to Dennis Fournier, who have been generous with their time and support. To them and to all the Hospice family, I wish for a year that will bring peace to all.

Happy Holidays

Gloria Amaral

President, Board of Directors

I include Julia and Gloria's writings to let the girls know that I like what they do and to keep on doing whatever is right by them. They have my support and best wishes at all times. And may "God Bless" you both in all your endeavors.

Olympia Plaza

Frank's story

FRANK REMEMBERS THAT OLYMPIA Plaza is the rest of the land the kids own together near what is the Exxon gas station off Brunswick Road. Apparently, they were working on getting that land into commercial operation of some kind that will work out well for them.

Frank hopes that it does work out. He had actually made a deal for a gas station from one of those low-priced gas outfits. He can't think of its name now, but he believes it was Regal. Regal had a whole bunch of stations all over northern California and elsewhere, during 1980 to 1985. Frank did make that deal for the gas station with Regal. Following that, Exxon purchased all of the Regal gas stations. That is how it became an Exxon gas station on Brunswick Road.

On Nov. 30, 2001, all four of the kids came over to our house for a business talk with Frank regarding the Olympia Plaza project. They talked about how the project would be paid for. Later, we had dinner. We had a very productive evening, and Frank would be the banker.

The annexation that the kids applied for to build a shopping center in what is called the Glenbrook Basin area was approved. The land was in Nevada County. They wanted it in Grass Valley so they could gain access to Grass Valley's sewer services. This was for 13 acres. The next hurdle they had to get over was with the Grass Valley Planning Department. After that, it should be rather easy to finish the project. Once they get approval, they can begin construction, sometime in the summer 2002, on the future Olympia Plaza Shopping Center.

The newspaper reported that Julia Amaral said the first phase would cost about $4 million and would include a 35,880-square-foot, two-story retail and office building. Ten apartments could be built over the retail space. Briar Patch Co-op Community Market was hoping to be the tenant for 10,000 square feet.

As of this writing, Olympia Plaza Shopping Center is an ongoing project that is in three phases; it is expected to remain ongoing for the next 20 years.

Julia, you did a good job with all your homework and all the trust that you had in the good Lord to help you, for I knew you prayed a lot over this. We also have to give Andy Casano a big "Thank you."

War still not over in Afghanistan

IN DECEMBER 2001, I had the feeling that the Afghanistan War was going to take years, seeing how it was set off by the World Trade Center being destroyed on Sept. 11. As the years have gone by since then, the Afghanis have had an election. We hope their new government and country improves, so our troops can leave their country to them and have them protect themselves.

Family tree decorating

ON DEC. 5, 2001, we had Julia, Mark, Laurence, and Gloria, Gloria's mother Winnie, and Spence come over around 3 p.m. to decorate the Christmas tree. After we were done, we had our Christmas dinner. Brad and Penny were unable to attend this year.

This has been a tradition for us for the past few years, ever since the time we had the tree fall over and break half the ornaments that were on it. Many of the ornaments were really nice, and we had had them since 1945. We had to redo the hardwood floor due to the water spill, and, afterwards, the kids said they would put up the tree and decorate it. And they have; it works out for all of us. This way each family is free to do what they want later in the month.

To get our tree, we go five miles upcountry on Highway 20 to a place that cuts trees every year for people to buy. They will get you just the size you want, and you can go up after Thanksgiving to get the tree that had been set aside for you.

Frank and I had set the tree up in the living room before the kids got there. We were then ready for them to take over. Laurence and Gloria put up the lights on the tree, and then Julia and I do the top part of the tree. When that is done, everyone pitches in to finish up the project. Of course, we have a very good gallery (group of spectators) by the fellows, and their comments are always needed.

This year, when the tree was finished, we had a real nice sit-down dinner in the dining room that was all set up for the occasion. Each family brings a dish, so that cuts down on the cooking chore. I am not one for potluck, but for this occasion, it comes in handy. We don't exchange gifts, but we do enjoy the time visiting, which is really a nice time for me, and I hope the rest of the family enjoys it as well.

Mark's parents came up on Tuesday before the Christmas holidays. His mother, Kay, was cooking dinner that night over at the kids' place and invited us up to join them. Then on Christmas Eve, his two sisters and their families came up, so we were invited over again for their "White Christmas dinner," and to open gifts. Frank and I no longer exchange gifts, but we had a good time watching Santa play his part with Chelsea, their only granddaughter.

On Christmas Day, we went to church. Later on, Mark and Julia had us over to their place again for a crab dinner that night. It was a nice easy meal. They were all tired by this time, especially Mark and Julia. After dinner, we had all been invited to Laurence and Gloria's to see their outside lights and have dessert. The plan was to be there around 7 p.m., after they had finished their dinner. When we got to their place, they had not started to eat their dinner, for they had outside guests who had dropped in to see them and wish them season's greetings.

So dinner was held up until the guests finally left. Laurence and Gloria finally sat down to a full-course dinner with their houseguests who had already been there for three days. So we walked into a house that had two tired people who had cooked a not-so-easy dinner and served food late. Frank and I sort of helped out by serving the soup dishes and dinner plates and washing some dishes. Later, once they had eaten, dessert was served.

Frank and I had pulled up chairs and sat by each end of the dinner table, holding our dessert plates in our laps as we visited with everyone. After a while, I dozed off with my dish of ice cream held neatly in my hand on my lap. Frank saw this and came over and said to me, "Don't you think we should be going home?" By this time, it must have been close to 9 p.m. I agreed, so we left. I later told Frank I should have stayed to help Gloria finish doing the dishes, for they were both so tired; you could see it in their faces and by the way, they were doing things. Julia, Mark, and his family decided to skip dessert, and, instead, they went driving around to see the lights. I am sure this was a blessing for Gloria and Laurence.

This was one of the nicest Christmas seasons I've had in a long time, with no work on my part. I thank you Julia, Mark, Laurence, and Gloria for giving us such a nice time.

December 7, 2001 — Pearl Harbor 60 years ago

DEC. 7, 2001, WAS the 60th anniversary of the Japanese attack on Pearl Harbor, which brought our nation into World War II.

What was I doing at that time in my life in 1941? I was living in Oakland, California, with a family. My job was to babysit two little boys and help with housecleaning in return for a place to live while attending the California College of Arts and Crafts. It was a Sunday when the attack happened, around noon our time as I remember. The family I lived with had all gone to church; I went to another one near where they lived. Later, I was left to babysit the boys while their mother and father went to be with her parents. I don't remember their names, but he was a lawyer. I think he worked in San Francisco. After they got back from church, she was very afraid, so they went to stay overnight with her parents, leaving me home with the two boys. I never understood why they were not concerned about them, but they must have had a lot of confidence in me.

I was going steady with Ed Hull at the time. I had yet to meet Frank. Frank was living at home with his mother and brother in Stockton, working as a clerk for the state of California, doing clerical work in what he says was a "dumb job." (I have told this story earlier.)

December 2001 — Deer Creek Park

Frank's story

FRANK REMEMBERS THAT IN December 2001 Laurence was winding up his project at Deer Creek Park that he had been working on during the year. Lowell Robinson was logging and hauling out the trees that had been cut so that if approval could ever be obtained, the next phase of the development project could get started. But no doubt, it would take a few years before the "powers that be" would even come close to agreeing on anything.

Laurence, I pray that the good Lord will help you and see you through it.

December 2001 — Olympia Plaza

Frank's story

FRANK REMEMBERS THAT JULIA, in December 2001, was neck-deep in paperwork trying to get her project at Olympia Plaza ready to build in summer 2002. This had been one long drawn-out project, but it finally looked like it might come to fruition. I knew all four of them would be relieved once it got started. This had been going on for several years, and all the trouble with the planning department and the public input can sort of get a person down.

With all your prayers Julia, I'm sure it has helped you through the struggle you have gone through. It makes you wonder why you try to do anything worthwhile. But keep on praying; it will work out in the end.

The Amaral–Robinson North Star project

Frank's story

FRANK RECALLS THAT THE North Star project, in December 2001, had been an on-and-off project for many years, and it seemed that it would never go anywhere. A meeting was scheduled at the city's L.O.V.E. building (Local Organized Volunteer Effort) on Dec. 12 that year. We hoped the property would be annexed by the city. Then maybe they could start doing something the following year. If nothing else, they could just try to sell it.

God Bless all of you for the trouble you have with people who have no idea what it's like having to deal with those who have nothing else to do but make trouble and to see how much damage they can do to others, not realizing what may be in store down the road.

The meeting had a good turnout with about 100 people showing up. And, yes, there were people who had their say, but they were not as mean as they could have been. I liked the way the evening was handled. Julia had finally learned how to handle the people and the public. She knew what to say to them, and this is when Laurence learned how to do the same.

We were very proud of what our children were doing in business and how they had grown into wonderful adults.

Mark and Julia go to Ethiopia

ON JAN. 7, 2002, Mark and Julia left on a trip to Ethiopia. They would also visit the Kellermanns in Uganda the last week of their trip and then return home in February.

Stanford called us on Jan. 24 to let us know that the kids had finished their trip to Ethiopia and were doing fine when they left for Uganda. We hoped the rest of the trip would also be fine for them. As it turned out, Julia fell and broke her right little finger and was not able to get it set until after she got home a few weeks later. It's a good thing she is left-handed. It came out all right in the end.

My blood pressure

ON JAN. 13, 2002, my blood pressure was 101 over 60 when lying down; when sitting up, it was 90 over 60. No wonder I was dizzy and short of energy when first getting out of bed. I was told that salt and water were now my best friends. I had been staying away from salt for years because of Frank's high blood pressure, so now they were telling me different. I was also told that my condition was caused from a pinched nerve in my neck, so I had Doctor Greenlee take a complete set of X-rays of my back and neck. He didn't find any pinched nerves, so we would go forward from there.

Dr. Mallery took a set of MRIs on my neck and head and found nothing that would cause the pain. I guess I will live and maybe find out later in life what is going on.

Morgan House to be repaired?

ON JAN. 22, 2002, there was front-page news. A particular person who wanted the Morgan House restored and opened to the general public decided to trespass and see if the North Star property was really under the supervision of on-site caretakers, which it was, and the house was boarded up and fenced.

When he was on the property, he said he couldn't find anyone. Just maybe the people were out shopping? And what were you doing on the property without letting the owner or Andy Casano, who is the planner, know that you were going onto the property and taking pictures? I'd say, just maybe, you did some damage to the chicken wire just to stir up more problems.

No wonder the "NO on 2020" signs sprouted up. I wonder if it is people like you, those that don't respect private property, who have caused the trouble to start with.

I remember back in the late 1970s when Frank and I went around the whole property putting up "No Trespassing" signs, using a ladder and tacking them to the trees so they would be up high, only to find them all torn down a few days later. I now wonder if you were one of the culprits. Perhaps so you could walk the property anytime you wanted to. We also boarded up the windows on the house and put a fence around it, but in a short time, they were gone.

There has always been trouble with dope and drug trespassers on that property, which made it unsafe to go out there at night. The people had respect neither for the property, nor for the owners. At first, we would go out on the property at night to check on it, but years later, it was not safe to go out there at night, unless you had a gun or had the police do the job for you.

If people like the fellow who came onto the property like it so much, why don't they just buy it? Then they would find out that it is no "bed of roses." It's also too bad that our local paper didn't bother to get both sides of the story before going to print. Doing so would have given readers honest and objective reporting on the Morgan House.

Barry Bonifas takes over M.I.M.

ON JAN. 28, 2002, Barry Bonifas became Music in the Mountain's new executive director. He had been the interim executive director of the Santa Cruz Symphony, and he has served at many other such places. Our hope was that he could fill the bill and help M.I.M. grow in the years to come.

It snowed his first day on the job; we hoped the office workers greeted him more warmly than the weather. Not having a place to stay while looking for a house, he stayed in our gardener's house, which is now called a guesthouse, until he could find a house to move into. He stayed with us about six weeks and left the place clean.

Evelyn Schroeder passes away

ON FEB. 7, 2002, Evie Schroeder passed away. She was my stepsister. When my brother Jim was born, she nursed him, along with her son Henry, who was 10 days older than Jim was. My mother did not have any milk to nurse Jim; at that time, she was living in Akeley. Evie later moved to Park Rapids, Minnesota. She was 94 when she died and was a good Christian person all her life.

When my immediate family left Minnesota in 1935, Evie was the last family member we saw. So, when Frank and I went back 50 years later in 1985, she was the first person I saw. She was my stepfather Julius' oldest child, followed by Joe (who died Jan. 21, 1953, in Eureka, California), Art, and Aggie. Then in 1934, my half-brother Jim was born. He died in the 1960s.

Evie left behind a son and daughter-in-law, several grandchildren, her sister Aggie and brother Art, and lots of nieces and nephews.

Laurence and Gloria's trip to Las Vegas

ON FEB. 17, 2002, Laurence and Gloria took a trip to Las Vegas and Southern California for a couple of weeks with their friends, the Petersons, just before Frank and I left for Carefree, Arizona.

On their way to Las Vegas, Laurence and Gloria saw the fresh snow on the mountains that we'd see a day later on our trip to Carefree. The two of them make many little trips with their friends and enjoy visiting many places.

Frank and I drive to Carefree, Arizona

ON FEB. 18, 2002, Frank and I left home around 10:30 a.m. and drove to Lake Tahoe. We then headed south to highways 267, 50, and 395. We spent the night in a hotel just off Highway 10. It was a beautiful drive heading over the freshly frozen snow-capped mountains. Except for the road, everything was covered with pure white snow. We were still driving through the mountains when the sun started to set. By this time, it had already turned into a rather long drive. Frank drove the whole way, and as the sun set I began looking for a place to stop for the night. But Frank was determined to make it to Highway 10 before calling it quits for the day, so we kept driving into the night.

By about 9 p.m. Frank was just too tired to drive, so when I saw a big sign that said "Truck Stop," I ordered him to turn off to the right. And with luck he did. We had made it all the way to San Bernardino.

One thing I've come to learn in all our travels is that when you see a "Truck Stop" sign, there are two things you can safely bet on: a place to eat that has good food, and a clean, cheap hotel. On this night, it was a Motel 6, and we were in luck at that late hour. We got a clean room but with not a lot of extras. There was a phone, but you could not place a long-distance call from it. Our room was warm and had a good-sized bed, a clean bathroom, plenty of towels, and a TV, so I could not complain about Motel 6. I have to say this was the first time, in I don't know how many years, that we had stayed at a budget-priced hotel. However, I know I will never be afraid to stay at a Motel 6 again.

Because it was so late and Frank was so tired, he had sort of lost his thinking power. He tried using the new cell phone Laurence had given us to use in the car, in case we got into trouble, but he forgot how it worked, and I hadn't yet learned how to use it. Neither of the kids had wanted us to drive to Carefree at our age. Frank was 83, and I was 79 experiencing light dizziness first thing in the mornings, but by this time, I was much better. This trip was a worry for them; that's the reason for the cell phone.

But we couldn't get the phone to work, nor could we call out from the phone in our room, not even using a credit card. Frank finally had the hotel operator call Julia to tell her to call us in our room, which she did. Julia told us that maybe the cell phone didn't have a signal and couldn't be used at our location, and that turned out to be the case.

After a good night's sleep and a good breakfast, we left San Bernardino and took Highway 10 east to Blythe, California, where we stopped to gas up and have a picnic lunch in the car. I then drove the rest of the way to Carefree. There was a lot of traffic, but Frank directed me through all the road signs, and by 4 p.m., we were safe in our room. We had forgotten that there is an hour time difference, so it was now 5 p.m. instead of 4. And we still needed to unpack, change clothes, get something to eat, and find our way to Pinnacle Presbyterian Church for the 8 p.m. Haydn Seek performance.

The only reason we went to Carefree was to see Paul Perry, who was serving as the director at the annual Desert Foothills Musicfest for the next several days. Well, forget about dinner. However, we managed to get to the church in time to see Paul before the performance. He told us where to sit, and as usual, we walked to the front seats. As we were reading the program, some people from home came up to say hello to us. I'm sorry I can't remember their names.

A little later, the Hahns came down from the balcony to say hello and to let us know they were glad we got there safely. Both couples had gone several years ago to see Paul at this event, and both couples traveled and stayed in their RVs. There were also a couple of women that went every year who also greeted us.

When the string ensemble came on stage and saw us in the audience, their mouths flew open; I wonder what the people in the audience behind us thought. Most of the musicians in the string ensemble also perform for Music in the Mountains and know us very well. They later told us that for a moment they thought they were in Nevada City when they saw us sitting in the front seats. This was a very good performance, and after it was all over, we still had to find a place to eat, for Frank does not do well on an empty stomach.

It was now late in the night, and Carefree is a lot like Nevada City; it closes up shop early. So we went back to our hotel where we talked to the people at the Carefree Inn & Conference Center to see if they could help with food of some kind. They called a local place called Harold's and told them to keep the kitchen open until we got there and to please take care of us, which they did. But as soon as we got our super-big hamburger, the bar took over. What a noisy place! It was obvious that this is a well-liked place by the local people, and the dining and dancing area could easily hold 200 people.

The next day, after eating a late breakfast, we decided to find out how to get to the rest of the places we would be going to for the concerts over the next several days. We got all kinds of help at the hotel desk, including detailed directions to The Desert Mountain Cochise Geronimo Clubhouse, where we had been invited for the Maestro's Party that night. On Thursday night, The Tastes of the Foothills and Concert would be at Our Lady of Joy Catholic Church. On Friday, there would be dinner at the church for all the musicians, the donors, and their families, including the people from Nevada City. We were entertained Friday night by two young boys with the piano and the bass viola. On Saturday night, we were at Desert Hills Presbyterian Church for a nighttime concert followed by dessert. Then Sunday afternoon was the Grand Finale at Desert Hills Presbyterian Church. We hoped we could find these places when we needed to.

One place we were having trouble finding was The Desert Mountain Clubhouse, so we finally ended up at the Our Lady of Joy Church, where we asked a lady how to get to the place. She said it was a hard place to find and difficult to get through the guard gate. She told us she could get us in, so she rode with us and got us up to the gate. She told the guards we were due there later that night and asked if we could drive up to the clubhouse so we'd know the way. The gate guard found our name on that night's guest list and let us drive in through the course to the clubhouse and back out again. This place has six golf courses, all designed by Jack Nicklaus.

We took the kind woman back to Our Lady of Joy and then drove to the Pinnacle Presbyterian Church. Across the street from the church was a shopping center, so we took a look at it, had lunch, and bought Frank three shirts. Then it was back to the hotel to get ready to go back to the Desert Mountain Clubhouse for the formal-dress Maestro's Party. We wanted to arrive early enough to be able to enjoy the view of the course from inside the dining room.

Some people overheard us talking about the course, and without us knowing it, they made a note to tell Paul that they would get us a game of golf with them on Saturday morning. We were the only outside people besides Paul and the musicians being invited to the Maestro's Party; the rest were large local donors and patrons for Musicfest. We couldn't understand why we were invited to this occasion.

We were given a place at the head table with Nan and Ralph (Sam) Mullen and John and Mary Gosule. Paul sat next to us, and I asked him why we were invited when no one else from home was. He said he intended it that way. It became obvious that Paul was using us, and he told me so at the time, saying he intended to use us the whole time we were there to help get those people off the dime and moving in the right direction.

The reason, of course, was we were the main donor for Music in the Mountains, and Musicfest was trying to get started in the same direction. They were not sure it would work, and Paul wanted to help them along, so he used us to let them know that if they got going, the money would come in, but first they had to commit themselves to doing it.

Before the evening was over, 10 people came up with the money needed to do the job, and the credit was given to us just for being there to let the donors know it could be done. For the rest of the time we were in Carefree, we got a lot of attention from the local people. Our time was certainly filled up.

Paul Perry, me, John Gosule, Frank, and Lew Lehr at the Maestro's reception

The next day, Frank had the hotel staff call to make a game of golf at one of the local courses, Rancho Mirage. We played with a pro and his wife from Boise, and everyone had a nice time. And what a view of the area from all the different tees! After we finished and were getting ready to leave, we could not get the car started; it would turn over but would not start. So after a half-hour, Frank had the cart attendant call AAA. It took awhile for them to show up, and in the meanwhile, we had to get back to the hotel to get ready to go to the concert at Our Lady of Joy Catholic Church. The cart attendant said he would stay with the car and take care of it when AAA showed up, so we gave him the car key. In the meantime, the hotel had sent a car to pick us up and take us back to the hotel.

We had dinner at the hotel and were ready to have the hotel get a driver to take us to the church. We were surprised when they said, "Here is your key to your car. It is ready to be picked up." They said they'd take us to the car. We were told the cart attendant had delivered the key and said AAA had asked him to start the car. Well, it started right up with no trouble, so there was nothing they could do. They figured it might have been a vapor lock. So that took care of that, but it did get the Hahns and Paul nervous about us driving around at night, especially when we did not show up for the Tastes of the Foothills at 6 o'clock. They were really glad when we got there in time for the concert.

We took it easy on Friday and had lunch with the Tatman family. Both Neil and Mutsuko played in the program; they also play in Music in the Mountains at home, staying at our daughter Julia's place when they come to Nevada City. Then it was off to Our Lady of Joy for an early Tastes of the Foothills buffet put on by a chef from Utah who came in just for the occasion. The food was very light and tasty, put on for all the musicians and donors. All the people from Nevada City were also there.

Two young brothers, who play the piano and the cello, entertained us during dinner. They did a very good job. This same chef was hired to put on the late Sunday afternoon buffet that we would also be attending. It was at this time we were told that we had a game of golf at the Cochise Geronimo Club House. Paul introduced us to Mary and Chuck Goldthwaite, who live at Desert Mountain, and they told us we had a game of golf with them at nine in the morning. About this time, Nan Mullen came up and said, "I'll pick you up at 8:30 to take you to the club house," which she did. She said we'd all have lunch together after we got through playing golf, and Paul would join us, along with a few other local friends.

Saturday. We were off for our golf game at 8:30 a.m., with Nan right on time. She also lives in this great golf complex area. The only way you get to play a game is with someone who lives in Desert Mountain. Mary took me into their locker room area, and what a layout; this was no Alta Sierra Country Club. Then, as we went to play our game of golf, I noticed I didn't have my purse. I decided it had to be in Nan's car, for Mary said she knew I didn't have it when we went into the locker room. I am not one to be careless with my purse. Casual? Yes, I always have been. So I left it at that, for there was nothing I could do about it at the time. We went on to play a course that was really tough, but we did have a good time. Mary and Chuck were very good sports to play with these old duffers.

After the game, we went inside to have lunch. Paul had also joined us with Nan and Ralph, and Nan came walking in swinging her purse along with mine. That brought a good feeling inside of me, for I do carry a great deal of money when we travel anywhere. After a very pleasant day of golf and lunch, we all adjourned, knowing we'd see everyone at the concert that evening at Pinnacle Presbyterian Church. This had been a long day, ending a nice time with everyone we had met.

On Sunday, we went to Mass at Our Lady of Joy Catholic Church. It is a very big church with excellent acoustics, which is something all the churches in this area have. That is why many of the concerts we went to were held in churches. Our Lady of Joy could easily hold 1,000 people and Sunday was no exception. Fortunately, we were in luck, for we got there early enough to sit rather close to the front. There was an 8 a.m. Mass and another Mass at 11. We were told that all the services were filled that way every Sunday, and not just at Lady of Joy, but at all the other churches in the area as well.

After church, we went back to the hotel and did some packing, for we planned to be on our way home by 9:30 Monday morning, which we were. Later, we attended the afternoon concert at Desert Hills Presbyterian Church. We had planned a month earlier to take Paul out to dinner with Betty and Brayton after this concert; however, the local people insisted that Paul attend the buffet. He told them he couldn't and explained why. They insisted we also attend, so we did. We could tell that Paul really had to attend the buffet.

So we followed Paul from the concert to the home where the buffet was being held. When we arrived, there were Rolls Royce and Bentley cars in the driveway, along with lots of Mercedes, and so on. We got to see what a home built in the desert looks like inside, which I found interesting.

Paul left the party with us. I told him he would have to set up something for these people when they came to visit us in June, for we now owed them something in return for all their warm hospitality. He said he had thought of that already. He then led us back to the main road out of Desert Mountain so we could find our way back to the hotel. The Hahns decided not to go with us. They were having crab and champagne dinner for two and would then spend time relaxing in their RV. We never did get together with the Hahns for bridge and dinner in their home on wheels.

This had been a fast week for us in Carefree, with the Desert Mountain people showing us a good time, but we never did get to see the surrounding area. Frank was having trouble driving at night and having difficulty getting on the right roads, so one of the things they said was, "Next year you fly. We will get you a car to drive while you're here."

Monday morning we were on the road by 9:30 just as we had planned. Frank was driving while I read the map to get us back to Highway 10. As we drove we kept having the right side of the hood pop up about six inches, and it would really bounce around when a truck passed us. I tried to get him to stop to fix it, but he said it wouldn't stay down. I could see where I would have to have a new hood put on after we got home, for this one would surely wind up getting bent out of shape.

After driving several hours, he finally pulled off the road and tried to get the hood down, but to no avail. At this time, I didn't know he was also having trouble with the right headlight staying in place, a problem caused by the wind coming in from the open hood.

We stopped at Blythe and had lunch. Frank was looking for a Big Mac but we couldn't find a McDonalds, so we ate at another burger place instead. From there I took over the driving heading north on Highway 95. This was a new route for us. We enjoyed the scenery. There weren't many cars, so I was able to drive at a rather good clip. Then we entered an area of rolling hills. I began to realize that the trucks and cars coming toward us from the opposite direction could not see to pass each other on this narrow road without some risk. If I didn't pay close attention to this, I knew we could get into trouble. So I dropped down to 60 mph and felt safe at that speed. Frank, in the meantime, had taken a nap, which he does when I'm driving. He has always said he has no trouble with me driving. In all our life together, I have never heard him complain about my driving, not even at the fast pace that I usually go.

About this time, I had to put on the brakes. Frank woke up to see a car coming straight at us that was passing about 20 cars and trucks on those rolling hills. There was no place to pull off. I could not believe what I saw; not one truck or car slowed down for him to move back into the southbound lane. By this time, I had nearly come to a full stop, which allowed the driver to get in front of the last truck he had to get around. If I had been going at any decent speed at all, we would have been goners right then. But luck was with us; there were no cars behind us to rear end us. I know that if I hadn't been able to stop, there would have been one hell of a pileup on that road for some time.

We recovered nicely from that and talked about it for a few minutes. Frank then went back to sleep as I continued driving to Highway 40 to Barstow. We gassed up there and Frank took over to drive us into Bakersfield. On the way, he was talking about driving all the way home. I was holding my thought on that one, for I figured it would be midnight before we got home, and he was not good at driving at night. Then again, I should have remembered that the good Lord would look after us as He always does.

We were no more than an hour from Bakersfield when Frank said we were out of gas, and we had just filled up! So when we came to a gas station, he went to fill it up again; no gas would go in. We continued driving, and he noticed that the speedometer wasn't working, nor the clock, lights, or brake lights. When we got to Bakersfield, we went to the nearest service station we could find off Highway 99. We asked them where the closest Mercedes service shop was located. They said six miles south on one of the side streets.

We had a hard time finding the place. When we finally got there, it was just after 5 p.m. They were getting ready to close shop, but the mechanic put his lunch pail down. They took one look at the car and guessed what was the matter. We had lost the right headlight that had shorted the whole thing out. All that was needed were some fuses, and a new headlight unit needed to be installed. They could tell it wouldn't take long to fix, and they knew we could not go anywhere by that time because it was now dark outside. They also knew that to get it fixed tomorrow would no doubt take all day, for their schedule was filled. So they worked on the car, and within a half-hour, everything was fine. Frank told them he had bought our little Mercedes from them years ago. They also showed Frank how to close the hood of the car by using both hands and closing it from the center of the hood. It closed fine and this upset him.

Then we got ready to leave, but Frank could not find his way back to the freeway. By this time, we knew we were not driving home that night. At one time, we had been coming to this area for many years and knew the area well. But after all the trouble he had with the car, Frank had used up all his energy. It was time for him to get something to eat, for lately he had not been doing well on an empty stomach.

When we got ready to leave to get back to the highway heading north, he had forgotten how to get around Bakersfield. He just couldn't figure how to get back to highways 99 and 58, which is where we needed to get to in order to find a hotel for the night. After about an hour and a half, trying to find our way around, driving over medians, and so on, I began to see that I was going to have to do something and do it fast. I told him where to go. I saw a sign that said Lamont south. I now knew where we were. Frank wasn't able to figure it out.

I ordered Frank to get on the ramp going south. At this time, he could not understand what I was trying to do, but he listened to what I said. We were lucky; all this time there were no cars around us. His driving wasn't good, and he even wanted to cross over a side barrier to get to the opposite freeway. Somehow his thinking powers had almost completely shut down.

As soon as we got on Highway 99 south to Lamont, in an ordering voice I said, "Now go over the overpass and take the turnoff ramp onto Highway 99 north." He did, but he didn't understand why. From there I said, "Do you know where you are now?" But he didn't know. Soon he saw the turnoff for Highway 58, and that was where I said, "Now get off to the right," which he did. Only instead of getting over to take the north turnoff exit that led to the hotels, he exited right going south on one of the side streets. This told me he still didn't know where he was at.

After driving south for about a mile, with no cars around us, I got him to turn around and make a U-turn on the four-lane road going north. He was finally able to get to the place where the hotels were, but he still didn't know where he was.

At no time was this easy on Frank; he kept saying, "I don't know where I am or what I'm doing." I was working very hard to keep my mind working at full speed, while at the same time keeping him calm and alert to his many mistakes. I also did my best to make him aware of all the traffic around us, for I never knew what he would do next. This sure wasn't easy for me, for I kept thinking he had completely forgotten his way around Bakersfield. He didn't even know the roads going to Julia's oil property, which had been ours for many years. It was better for me to direct him than for me to drive and try to find my way alone.

While we were doing this, one of the things that came out of it was that he said, "I can't drive at night in strange places again or take any more long trips." This was a very easy decision for him to make. No one had to tell him; he came to this on his own. What was going on inside his head must have been devastating to him, for, no doubt, he was also remembering what went on in Carefree that one night.

We finally got to the hotel and got a room that was nice and quiet. We had a nice dinner right at the hotel. This hotel was new since the last time we had been in the area, which was at least five years before.

The next morning we got up and I asked Frank if he wanted to check on any of the properties. He said no. Then he drove to Stockton and was fine; I drove home from there. So as I said earlier, the good Lord was looking after us that night. And, of course, this was to make a big change in our life, but then again Frank was going on 84 and I was going on 80, and so far we had done fine and would continue to do so.

It was interesting that at our local April Spring Fest, Paul came up and told us that a man in Carefree came up with $100,000 for Musicfest. He said we were the ones who had made it possible. He thanked us for going to Carefree so that those people could meet us and know that there were people who did do things like that. It also encouraged others to do the same.

This, he said, would also make it possible for him to see an end to going to Carefree in a few years, knowing he was leaving that area in good hands as he backed out, for he intended to retire in a few years, or so he said. Anyway, something good did come out of our trip to Carefree, and we had a nice time together.

Gloria's mother falls

IN MARCH 2002, GLORIA'S mother fell and crushed part of her left arm. This made Gloria and Laurence and the kids have second thoughts, for Winnie was 88 and might not be able to take care of herself anymore. Her fall laid her up for a month or so, and her children had to think about what to do for her and the apartment she had; she might have to go to some other care facility.

Winnie was still rather sharp at thinking and good-witted. She would be around for a few more years, anyway. And she did sort of remind Frank and me of ourselves.

Israel and Palestine's War

IN APRIL 2002, ISRAEL and the Palestinians were in a big war with each other. America was having to step in and tell them to settle their differences, and soon, or this could lead to a worldwide war. America tried to broker a deal so that they would each have a state of their own. We were hoping it would work after 50 years of fighting each other.

But it didn't turn out; they just continued to fight and kill each other.

Julia and I prepare to go to Holland

IN APRIL 2002, JULIA and I went to Holland to see the big tulip show. It was a mother-daughter thing, which I was looking forward to—if only I could get over the flu and the plugged-up right ear I had before we left. This would be the first time I had ever left Frank to go on a fun trip, so I felt rather guilty about leaving him home; however, several people had already set up dinner dates with him, so he would be kept busy at night, anyway.

I got the gardeners lined up to get things done, for as soon as I got home, 20 flats of spring flowers would arrive on May 1 to be put in the ground for the June 14 Music in the Mountains concert being held in the yard. Paul had a lot of things lined up for that evening; I was looking forward to seeing what he had in mind. I believe they had hopes for 220 people attending, and they upped the price to $100 a head

As I have said earlier, I spend a great deal of time, money, and effort on this place so that they can make some money using it. One of the improvements this year was the brick walkway up to the barbecue house and around that area where they intended to have the bar set up.

Along with all of the dizziness I was having, I accidentally ran into our tall oriental vase of around 100 years old that we have had over 50 years. The top six inches of the vase broke off, so what was of real value was now kaput. Yes, I did get better, but I lost some hearing in my right ear. I took the vase to a lady in Sacramento that does high-end repair work on porcelain. She said she would put the pieces back and then call us to come and look at it, and from there we could decide how much more repair work we wanted done.

She called us after two weeks and we went down to see what she had done. She did a good job of putting the parts back, but there were a few pieces missing, so we told her to do more repair work, but to hold off on the extra-refined work at this time.

Unless you look very closely at the vase now, you won't notice the damage. So this is where we were at with the vase. The repair lady would have it until we picked it up after Christmas. It was interesting to learn that when you break something, it has a memory, and when you put the parts back in place, it adjusts itself to it.

Trip to Holland with Julia

ON APRIL 18, 2002, Julia picked me up at the house at 10 a.m. in a rental car. I had taken a good half-teaspoon of salt, thinking it might help with my blood pressure, which was low. By the time we got to the airport in San Francisco, I was fine. I called home to let Frank know that I was feeling better, but he wasn't there, so I left a nice message for him. That message was still on the answering machine when I got home 10 days later. He said when he wanted to hear my voice he would just play the tape. (This reminds me that maybe we should make a tape of each other's voices for the future.)

Julia in front of the Beach Hotel

We had a good flight over the Atlantic and arrived at the Golden Tulip Beach Hotel in Noordwijk, where we would be staying the next two nights. We had time to take a walk along the beach before the cocktail hour and dinner. This hotel faces the beach, with the main highway running between it and the beach. The road was closed off for the parade being held the following day.

Me relaxing in one of the shade chairs outside the Beach Hotel

We were up early the next day to see the flower parade, which is sort of like our Rose Parade, only everything is in tulips and hyacinths. We could see the parade from our room, but we decided to go walking down the main road so we could get close to the floats, take some good pictures, and really enjoy everything that was going on. There were big floats, and they decorate cars of all makes. This would be a tulip trip, and the floats set the tone for the next eight days. After seeing the parade, our tour took us out into the fields, where tulips could be seen for miles in every direction. We got to walk among the tulips and took lots of wonderful pictures.

Julia getting pictures of the parade

Exploring the colorful tulip fields

On April 21–22, we stayed at Palace Het Loo in Apeldoorn. This place is on the outskirts of town and is one of the most popular places in Holland. We arrived early enough to take a long walk to town for dinner; we walked back just before dark. While in town, we saw the place that holds the Dutch monarchs' collection of furniture, paintings, and tapestries. We also saw the gardens, which are sometimes referred to as a "little Versailles." This is the king's garden, and there is the queen's garden that has a wonderful colonnade with fountains. We ate lunch and drove to De Hoge Veluwe National Park, where we visited the Kroller Muller Museum. The museum houses works of Impressionists and several paintings of Van Gogh. There were banks of daffodils and tulips along the main walkway. Then it was back to the hotel in Apeldoorn for dinner and sleep.

The gardens at Palace Het Loo

Tuesday, April 23, we left for Amsterdam, stopping on our way to visit the private garden of Mrs. Hobijn, in Breukelen. On our way, our driver, who was supposed to know the area, and our guide, who did not know how to get us to this place, drove us for miles on narrow inter-country roads; I wondered if they knew where they were going. When we finally got there, we were all very relieved, happy, and glad that there was hot tea and food waiting for us. The house dates from 1700 and consists of a linked coach house and stable buildings with an inner courtyard that contains a formal box garden with a central pool.

This is a very expensive place to keep up. The country has a crew of men who do nothing but go around and trim the box hedges that residents have grown and are keeping up. The residents are charged for this. Mrs. Hobijn and her family were trying to keep the estate in one piece and trying to maintain it in the same condition as when her parents and the relatives before them lived there.

Then WWII came along. This place is very close to Germany and the Germans used this place as they saw fit. The family, of course, was forced to leave. The box hedges were badly damaged, along with many other things. A lot of valuable things were pillaged from the house. It is a place the country wants to keep, so the family was opening it to the public in order to bring in money to help cover the expense. I enjoyed seeing this place and could understand what a big job she had on her hands; it was several acres and had farming to go with it. We continued our trip to Amsterdam and learned the history on close to five centuries of urban gardens, from Baroque to contemporary design.

Our next stop was at an 18th century merchant home, which is now a museum where Huis Van Loon lives. From what I could see, this place was really in the Dark Ages. It was difficult to imagine anyone wanting to live in a place so old and rundown that offered next to nothing in the way of comfortable living. The yard was nothing special, just ordinary. However, what was really worth seeing was the house and the way she and her family lived. We had a light buffet lunch in the yard, and from there we drove to our hotel and checked in early and had dinner together with the group. We stayed at Hotel Sofitel in Amsterdam, the hotel we would stay at through Saturday, April 27.

Julia and me at Museum Van Loon

Me checking out the red-light district

Julia and I decided to check out the "red-light district" that was only a few blocks away from the hotel. One other lady went with us, and she and Julia decided to go into a "weed store" and check out some shirts to buy for the husbands, but they were not allowed to go past the counter without a pass. All they wanted to do was buy a shirt to take home that had the "weed picture" stamped on the front of the shirt, but they couldn't find what they wanted.

In the meantime, I was watching the lady behind the counter as she started to take out a sheet of white thin paper and put some grass on it. She then rolled it to look like a cigarette, lit it, and started to smoke it. After a few minutes, Julia and our friend started coughing. In the meantime, I had stepped outside the open door so I wouldn't smell the sweet odor. After a few minutes, the girls decided to leave laughing, thinking they just might get a little high if they stayed any longer. Anyway, we had a good laugh and on we went through the red-light district.

To my surprise, the red-light district had changed a lot since Frank and I walked those streets many, many years before. It was now very open; the so-called ladies were right out in front of their individual spaces that were no longer dark but clean-looking. The girls lacked any shyness. (But then again, look at what now goes on at the public beaches.) Their profession is now legal and protected by the government. After our sojourn into the red-light district, we stopped by a large building that at one time was a church but is now used to show famous pictures that had been taken in the years 2001–02. It is also used for concerts and other events. Then we were on our way back to the hotel to change for dinner. We passed by a very active carnival center along the way.

Wednesday, April 24, our group drove to Keukenhof to see the Keukenhof Exhibition. This is on a 70-acre estate where 6 million bulbs are planted annually by local growers. There were blooming tulips, daffodils, and hyacinths everywhere, all put to every kind of use. Just seeing this place made the trip worthwhile. If only we could go back again the next day, for it was so big and had so much to see. However, we were only given three to four hours to see the place, so Julia and I had to take it all in as fast as we could. Our cameras never stopped taking pictures. We also got a Keukenhof book on the flowers, for our cameras just would not do it justice.

Me enjoying the beautiful flowers that were everywhere

Julia at the Keukenhof Exhibition

We returned to Amsterdam around 4 p.m. It was early enough, so Julia and I got dropped off near an art museum that we had tickets for. This kept us busy for more than four hours, and it was still light out when we left the museum. As we walked back to our hotel, we walked along two streets that had many places to eat at. It was now getting dark, and we had to eat somewhere, but we weren't sure what we wanted to gamble on. We finally came across a place that had spareribs and corn on the cob, so we had our dinner there. We were served enough food to feed four people. The meal was good. We took the leftovers back to the hotel, but we never had a chance to eat them. We walked close together and were very careful with our purses on our way back to the hotel. We got back around 11 p.m. with no problems.

For this trip, Julia had upgraded every room we had in each hotel from standard to deluxe accommodations; even so, the rooms were never very big.

We woke up very early on Thursday to see the Aalsmeer Flower Auction, the world's largest flower auction. We tried to get there early enough to see it in its full glory, but the auction was over by the time we got there. However, we did get to see how things were put together into carts and how they were packaged for distribution to all parts of the world. The flowers are shipped out of this huge building by 10 every morning, making their way by plane, boat, ship, or bus to wherever they are going.

A very small section of the Aalsmeer Flower Auction

This was one huge building that covered several acres, all under one roof. A walkway ran high above the main floor so visitors could walk along and see the main floor and all the action taking place below. I found this place very interesting, and I realized how much Frank would have loved to have been there with us. I could just imagine him down on the auction floor doing some bidding.

It was at this place that you could buy your tulip or other bulbs to take home or order and have them delivered later, but we did not do that; we waited until we got home and then placed our orders. We tried taking picture of the inside of this place, but it was just too much for a small camera to do it justice.

Our next stop this day was at the Historical Garden Aalsmeer, which has a display of the history of horticulture in the Aalsmeer area. We took a little boat ride down the canals to see different shrubs, trees, and herbaceous plants. There were garden buildings, frames, plants, pots, baskets, barrels, and tools, and even boats used to transport flowers to market. We were shown entire fields that people owned but could not live on. They were only allowed to have a little shed for day use; they couldn't stay overnight. Along this part of our trip, we were shown how lilacs are grown and how to cut them back, and we learned how the Dutch are trying to keep some of the old shrubs, bulbs, roses, and other things from the past, so they will not lose the history of their flowers.

Julia at the canal

We then went to a quaint Dutch village to visit the Hortus Bulborum in Limmen, where rare species of flowering bulbs can be seen. They can be traced back to the 17th and 18th centuries, and there are more than 100 varieties of tulips. Some of the tulips are no more than six inches high. These fields are best described as a patchwork of color. This is a place with a great deal of history on tulips; I found it very interesting and so did Julia.

After visiting the village, we went back to our hotel for the evening. Before we left home, Mark had found a real nice restaurant he thought we should try out if we had the time. So Julia made a reservation in the morning for us, and we were told it is a real dressy place. We decided to walk to the place, which was a rather long distance from our hotel, but we had been told that ladies' purses were being stolen. So after hearing about the purse-snatchers, we decided not to carry too much money with us, especially since we were all dressed up. We figured if we both took €100 Euros (equal to about $180 U.S.D.) we would have enough for a real nice dinner and a taxi ride home. So off we went on a very enjoyable walk, feeling safe enough not to worry about anything.

Neither Julia nor I took a purse with us, and we left all our credit cards behind; but, at the last moment, Julia decided to take at least one identification card with her just in case we needed it. I think it was her driver's license. When we got to this real nice place, we were seated at a very nice table with a white tablecloth and all the trimmings; we were given a nice view out the window. We got a lot of attention from different waiters, and we got our water right away without asking for it. They also brought us some nice, small, warm buns that were really tasty. I should add that we had been charged $10 for water everywhere we went.

We got the menu and started to look through it, and as we did Julia about choked after she saw the prices of each entrée, which included the salad, main dish, desserts, and wine. No doubt, there was something fancy in each item. She began adding up the cost, including the $10 for water, the tax, and the service fee; she could see we didn't have enough money to cover the meals.

Julia hadn't said anything to me yet. In the meantime, I had gone to the back page of the menu that had the whole dinner for $8, knowing I could eat from that selection. I told her what I would have; she then told me what the problem was. This became a joke with us, for we could have had anything we wanted on the menu if we had taken our credit cards with us, but now we were in the position of having to count pennies, which was really something for us to have to do.

Anyway, she did find something but ended up settling for much less and gave up the glass of wine and dessert. In the end, we had a very good dinner. Mine had large portions of everything, so I split half of everything I had. It was way too much for me and Julia's portions were small. And those real good buns kept right on coming, along with the water, and, yes, we got it hot. My dessert was enough for both of us and tasted very good. When our bill came, we had enough to cover it. The water was actually free and tips were included with the meal. We also had enough money leftover to take a taxi back to the hotel if we wanted to.

Julia then told the headwaiter about our problem; he said it wasn't a problem at all. They would have driven us to the hotel, so we could have gotten our credit card to cover the expenses. He told us that all the gratuities were included in the price of each item—not like it is in the States. He said they have the same problem when they come to our country, only in reverse, for they forget that they have to add it onto the bill. By this time, it was around 11 p.m., and we had a long walk back to the hotel, taking streets where there wasn't much traffic. The headwaiter told us to stick to the lighted streets, even if it was longer; however, he felt we would be safe, and, yes, we made it back to the hotel with no problem.

Friday, April 26. We were up early again, had breakfast, and then went to see the Floriade Flower Festival. This is the world's largest horticultural exhibition and only takes place once every 10 years. This year's theme was, "Feel the Art of Nature." The exhibition was held on a 65-acre site. There were more than 300 exhibits from 29 countries around the world. The 2002 exhibit showed every aspect of Dutch horticulture. This event was the reason Julia had me take this trip to Holland. So there we were, and the weather was cold and rainy, just as it had been almost the whole time we were there. Julia and I were in our red North Pole jackets, and I mean *red*. We wore them most of the time. The people in the group said they got to looking for the two red coats, and when they saw them, they knew the group was nearby. At times, it was hard for everyone in the group to keep up together.

Floriade Flower Festival 2002, with me in my red North Pole jacket over to the left

Julia and me in our
North Pole jackets

The Floriade Flower Festival covers all phases of flowers from producer to consumer. A wide range of horticulture is covered as well, including bulbs, plants, trees, bushes, shrubs, vegetables, and fruits. Besides the Dutch exhibits, there were many exhibitors from all over the world. There were display gardens from the Philippines, India, Brazil, Kenya, Colombia, Russia, Germany, and Hungary. We were given only two hours to see the whole exhibit and didn't have enough time to really enjoy looking at all the things that were there. We eventually ended up in the Floriade Green Trade Centre, which was nice, and it was all under a roof.

The group all wanted to stay longer, so it was voted on, and we stayed for three hours instead of two. However, this did not really give us much time to go back and see what we had already rushed past earlier, and by now it was really raining outside. So Julia and I, after trying to see some of the outdoor exhibits, ended up in a section that was showing ways to grow vegetables and shrubs, including roses. The demonstrations were all on tracks that kept on rotating throughout the day. We got a bite to eat and then rushed back to the group.

My picture of Julia taking pictures of the lovely flowers

On our way back to the hotel, I got to thinking that after seeing Keukenhof, this was sort of a disappointment after all the hype and publicity. We should have seen this exhibition first. I would say no to going back to see the Floriade exhibition; however, to see Keukenhof again? Yes, absolutely.

Julia had arranged for us to go to dinner at an Indonesian restaurant this night and then to a concert. A couple of sisters from the Midwest decided to join us. It was raining again, so we decided to take the city streetcar near the hotel, rather than walk to the theater to pick up our tickets. From there we walked to the restaurant for dinner. We had a very good dinner with lots of choices to indulge in; then after dinner we walked to the theater in the rain. After the performance was over, the four of us hurried downstairs to get our coats. We literally ran to the streetcar so we could get on and beat the traffic. We didn't want to wind up standing in the rain at 11 p.m. waiting for the next car to show up. And we weren't the only ones doing this, for it was really raining. The sisters had to get into high gear to keep up with us. They said if LaVonne could do it, so could they. We had a nice time together with them.

Saturday, April 27, Laurence's 56th birthday. Today was set up to be a leisure day in Amsterdam.

A group of us decided to join our tour guide, Emmy, in visiting a restored canal house and garden. The place had been redone by a couple of young fellows who had really taken pride in their work. It was a narrow three-story building, and each room was the width of the building. On the main floor was a narrow hallway that led to the main living area, and at the end it went upstairs. On the main floor, facing the street, was the living room with a piano that extended to a dining room and on to the kitchen and outdoor area. It had been arranged very well to make the most of the narrow space.

Off the kitchen was a door that led out to a small, narrow garden that was the same width as the house. I would say at the most 25 feet wide. At the end there was a small building, no doubt a tool shed at one time that had been made into a guest bedroom and bath. In the main house and on the second floor facing the street, there was a big room used as an office or family room, and there was a guest bath under the stairwell. The next room was a bedroom and bath, and I believe this led to a porch off the bedroom. I never did get up to see the third floor, but Julia did. I forgot what she said was up there. Not many got to see that area, but knowing Julia, I knew she would get in to see it.

Me outside the restored canal house

We had tea and dessert in the kitchen. As we did, the mother of one of the fellows was making tulip bouquets of flowers for each of us to take home to the States with us. She was showing us how you make them with the bulbs still attached to the stems of the tulips. These tulips were on short stems. They were small but lovely bouquets and would last for days, but what they did not know was we couldn't take them into California. Therefore, that night for dinner, we gave ours to Emmy to take home.

Julia on the streets of Amsterdam

After leaving this adventure of visiting the home, Julia and I walked the streets to the hotel. Along the way we bought chocolates to bring home as gifts. That was all I bought while we were there; I didn't buy anything for myself. That night, all of us got together in the hotel and had our last meal together. It was a good time.

April 28. We left for home after having breakfast. At the airport, I bought some cheese to bring home to Frank. Our trip home was nice, and when we got to San Francisco, we rented a car and drove home.

Thank you, Julia, for a wonderful time together. May you always have good memories of this trip, for I know I will—even if I did wake you up in the mornings by touching you so we could start our day together.

After I got home, I found the phone message that I had left for Frank from the airport when we left on our trip. As I've said, it was still on the answering machine. Frank said he left it on there to hear my voice anytime he wanted to. Many of our friends said they doubted that I would be able to go again and leave him behind. It's sort of nice to know that you are missed.

Frank later told me that if anything had happened to me on the trip, he would have never removed my voice from the machine. He said that what I had said on the message made him feel good inside. But I don't remember what I said!

The highlight of our trip,
Julia and me at Keukenhof

My 80th birthday

Pictures of my life

ON MAY 11, 2002, Julia and Mark gave me my 80th birthday party that lasted until the morning of the 12th, which is my birthdate. It was a very nice birthday with all my close friends. Julia had also taken pictures out of the family album that covered the years of 1932 to 2002. She had them enlarged and put on six large sheets of butcher paper. She had them hanging on the wall outside of their house so we could all see and enjoy the ups and downs of my life. We did this while eating all kinds of goodies and having drinks. She had also done this for Frank's 80th birthday party four years earlier, only she had used pictures from Frank's side of the family, on up to the present day.

Julia had the meal catered. We went into the house for dinner to enjoy a multi-course meal, and a group of people came in and did some singing. She did a very good job of it, as she does with everything she sets her mind to. Everyone had such a good time that they didn't want to go home. There were 24 of us altogether. And, of course, we took pictures. Later, after the party, I had the butcher paper with the pictures on it rolled up and put in one of Frank's office map drawers for safekeeping.

Me standing in front of an
unfinished watercolor of myself that I did in 1971

Karen Wood, John and Madelyn DiMugno, Bev Erickson, Frank, Joe and Netta Kandell

We got up early to go to 9:30 Mass on Sunday, which was also Mother's Day. As we walked into church, Father McKnight said to me very quietly, "Happy birthday," and I wondered how he knew. Sharon Seck heard him say it, so she said, "Why don't we sing Happy Birthday to her?"

Father McKnight had a sad lecture to give us, pertaining to what the church was going through with what a few priests had been doing to make a lot of trouble for the church—trouble that sure didn't help the good priests, and he was feeling sad about it. After the church service was over, he said he wished all the mothers a happy Mother's Day.

He then said something to the effect that his mother had always told him never to ask a woman her age. He then did something that, in all the 52 years that I have gone to that church, I had never heard any priest do before. He told the congregation that it was my birthday and that I was 80 years old. Well, all the people clapped, so I stood and thanked them, only to sit down after he said, "Let's sing Happy Birthday to her," so again I got up and thanked them. But more than anything else, he ended the service on a positive note for himself and the people after his sad lecture by reinforcing everything that was still good in our parish.

I had people come up to me and say that in no way would they want their age mentioned. I told them that all anyone had to do was put together my kids' ages and when they started school at St. Mary's, and they would know how old I was, so it was OK by me, or something to that effect. Before the next Mass was over, and even before it started, my age was mentioned at the SPD store, so some people found out that way as well. When we got home and I read the bulletin, I saw where Julia had requested a Mass to be said for me; there were nine requests in all. I now understood why and how Father knew it was my birthday and how old I was.

Julia had told me earlier that she would be at Mass with us, rather than attend her church in Grass Valley. So she was with us, but she did not know that Father was going to wish me a happy birthday. I was glad that Julia was with us to hear Father say it. Anyway, I felt honored. A few months later, someone got recognition for their 61st wedding anniversary, so maybe we would be hearing more about these occasions from now on.

Father saw us on the 12th hole at Alta Sierra Country Club a few weeks later, and he said to me, "LaVonne, I am sorry I mentioned your age; now the whole world knows it." I told him it was OK and that it didn't bother me. I have never been afraid to tell my age. Thus ends my 80th birthday on a happy note.

Flowers Frank gave me for my birthday

Music in the Mountains Gala, 2002

Getting ready for the Music in the Mountains Gala at 211 Reward St.

ON JUNE 14, 2002, Music in the Mountains had its first performance of the season. It was held here in the yard at 211 Reward St., starting at 6:30 p.m. with wonderful hot finger foods served along with wine, and so on. It was somewhat like a walking dinner before the

Tables set up along the driveway

concert, which started at eight. It was a very successful evening and everyone had a good time, and I was glad when it was over. I had spent months trying to get the yard in shape, along with getting a new brick walkway done. Doing all this with a dizzy head, along with my trip to Holland with Julia and my 80th birthday really kept me busy. The week before the M.I.M. event, we had a huge storm that really did a job on the yard. I had to call in for help to get things back in shape for the gala. Fortunately, with all the help from M.I.M., I got the yard in great shape and everyone had a good time.

There was a good turnout when you consider that "the price had been upped by me," with Music in the Mountains accepting $100 per person for the first time. The event started early in the evening with the serving of the hot finger foods that could work as a dinner of sorts. People were given time to walk the yard, socialize, and enjoy themselves. I refused to have any more doings in my yard for anything less than that price, for the cost to me was far greater than what they had been making. I knew I could comfortably accommodate 220 guests, along with the added 50 people it took to work the event. It was up to the committee to sell the tickets and to get people to come.

Laurence and Gloria, Beth Morehead,
and the couple we met on our golfing trip to Japan in 1985

From the comments I received from the people who attended and from outsiders who did not attend, it was a very successful evening. I was asked for the use of the yard for the next year's event, and at my recommended admission price.

I do not ask for any money; I donate the use of my yard as a way for M.I.M. to make money. It's nice that people enjoy taking in the yard. One of the things that helped me at the last moment, or I should say the last few days before the event, was all the help I received from my family and members of M.I.M. They all helped me get the yard ready after that bad storm we'd had. They were so good to offer their time and to show up prepared to work. I had gotten so far behind in deadheading my rhodes and azaleas that I really needed help. The helpers got right in and did the work, so I thank all of them for their help.

Frank, Gloria, and Laurence enjoying the party

Brickwork

AND NOW ON TO the next project, which is to finish the brick wall around the pump house lawn and have it done in July with David's help. He ended up finishing the rest of that area and went on to remove more roots under another walkway. He also put an electrical line under the walkway in the area of the fishpond so there would be an electrical outlet there. This outlet was something I have wanted done for a long time, for M.I.M. has needed light in that area many times.

July 2002 — Frank has a fall

IN JULY 2002, FRANK got up to go to the bathroom in the middle of the night, but he forgot to open his eyes. When he got up off the toilet, he accidentally walked into the bathtub. I heard the noise. I was going to tell him to open his eyes, and then I thought to myself to be quiet—I say it too often; leave him alone. When I heard the loud noise, I thought he was just getting toilet paper out of the cabinet under the sink, so I went back to sleep. The next morning when I went to the bathroom to take a shower, I saw all this brownish-looking stuff in the far side of the bathtub. I wondered if he had taken a shower.

I waited for him to wake up before I took my shower. When we talked about it, he told me he'd had trouble. He didn't know what had happened last night, only that he'd had a bad time getting out of the tub and didn't know where he was. I noticed blood on his left arm pajama top, so I thought he might have hurt his arm. I started looking very closely for where so much blood could have come from. I then looked at his face and saw his left eye. It was black and blue, as big as an egg, and had been bleeding from a cut on his eyebrow. I think it could have been cut from the faucet. It had bled a lot during the rest of the night. He neither felt it nor knew he was hurt. I put ice packs on it and had him go see Dr. Johnston that morning, in case he had hurt something. Luckily, he was all right and just needed time to heal. It took about 10 days for the black eye to heal, and he ended up taking a lot of ribbing over it.

Scott and Carol Kellermann

ON AUG. 7, 2002, Scott and Carol Kellermann came to visit and showed us their slides of the area where they were doing missionary work in Uganda. They also wanted to see our slides from the time we were in Uganda in 1968. They really enjoyed seeing our slides of Africa in comparison to what it is like today. They had come home for a month to renew their visa and to visit family and friends. They were showing their slides to several churches to raise money to continue their missionary work and build a clinic of sorts. They were also working to fund a school for Carol to teach the kids where she and Scott were operating. Indeed, they were able to raise money for these projects during their visit back to the States.

Scott and Carol home for a short visit

They called to say goodbye on Aug. 30. They were leaving the next morning, Sept. 1, and said they planned to be gone for another year. I remember telling them they would pass Mark and Julia in flight, for they would be in Singapore at the same time. Carol said it would take them three days to get there. I hoped Carol and Scott would be able to find the kids who were on their way home from Kimbe, New Guinea. If they had seen each other, it would've been a thrill for all four of them.

Frank and a ladder

ON AUG. 15, 2002, Frank climbed a ladder to pick peaches off the peach tree. He had two big peaches in each hand, and he forgot he had to have a hand on the ladder. As a result, he ended up falling off the last two steps and broke the bone on his left hand along the little finger. I put it on ice right away, but by the time the doctor saw it and had taken an X-ray, his hand was too swollen. Frank was sent to see Dr. Butler to have a half-cast put on it. Four days later Frank had to go to the hospital to get it set.

At the hospital, Frank had quite a few visits from people who were in the hospital and from doctors, among them Dr. Kellermann. Laurence was at the hospital with me while this was going on, and I am very glad he was there. Frank got to enjoy nice visits before going in to get his hand set around 4:30 p.m. They put four pins in his hand. It took about three hours before I was called to come get him and take him home.

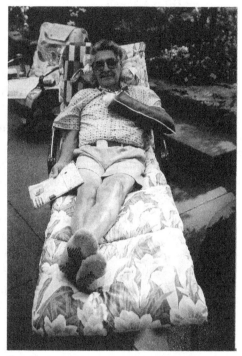

Frank's hand in a cast, picture taken Aug. 17

Laurence and Gloria, along with their friends Dale and Bob Peterson, helped bring Frank home. I couldn't handle him at that time because he was still under too much sedation. I am grateful for their help. We got him home and into the house and fed him a big bowl of turkey and rice soup. His last meal had been at 6 p.m. the night before. It was now past 8 p.m. Needless to say, he was pretty hungry by the time he got home. He ate and went right to bed.

Now it was a matter of waiting for three weeks to go by before Frank went back in to see Dr. Butler to find out what would happen next. The hand, of course, kept getting in his way. He did a lot of walking to town and back, but he wasn't able to drive just yet because he was on medication; after a few days he wouldn't need it. He had taken a few ribbings from church friends and anyone that saw him.

A couple of weeks later, Laurence went with Frank to see the doctor. The word was eight weeks in the cast. Frank took it rather well. The period needed to be extended because his hand was healing rather slowly.

The cast finally came off on Oct. 16. They also pulled the pins out. Three pins were one inch long and another was two inches long. The doctor pulled the pins out with what looked like a pair of pliers; he did it with one full pull each time. It wasn't too bad. We were actually surprised at how easily they came out. Frank kept his hand out of water for four days until the openings from the pins had healed. He would have physical therapy for the next few weeks and maybe longer. He was not supposed to lift anything for another two to three months, for his hand hadn't healed very well yet. His little finger was very stiff.

A year later, after all of this, the middle joint of his little finger was still on the stiff side. No doubt, it would remain that way. It wasn't easy playing golf with a stiff finger, but he still continued to play.

The North Star in escrow

Frank's story

FRANK REMEMBERS THAT IN 2002 buyers made an offer for the asking price set by the Amarals and the Robinson Lumber Co. for the North Star property. The buyers put down a deposit to hold the property for three months to see if they still wanted it. They had until Sept. 24 to come up with the money, which they did, but not in cash as they were supposed to. Now it was left to see what the lawyers would come up with and to see if everything was OK. If so, it meant the North Star had been sold and the buyers' problems were to begin, and now the Amarals and the Robinson Timber people could relax. All the negativity from the local community about developing the property, along with all the vilifying of the owners, who were being called the "Gang of Four," was now over.

Now, the issue about access to the Morgan House no longer needed to keep us awake at night over something that was not our fault. The fault really should have been credited to the Footes people who had owned it and then given it to a Christian school who'd really done damage to the house. The school went into bankruptcy and that is how we came to own it. After that, the Footes people wanted the Morgan House restored by us; I said they should have done it themselves. So another chapter in our lives had come to an end.

For years, the Amarals and the Robinsons had wanted to put an 18-hole golf course on the property and have nice homes built on it. We older folks had planned to build our last homes there and retire on the property, but no such luck! We knew that for the past 10 or more years, with all the negativity started by people who didn't know what they were saying, the project wasn't going to happen. We wished the new buyers luck and success. At least they weren't local people; therefore, they might get better treatment.

Fall 2002 — dryness, then rain

IN 2002, WE'D HAD a very warm summer, and the warm weather had continued into fall. There still had been no rain. Pinecones had dropped off the trees all summer long and were still falling; they are not due to fall until around December, so it remained to be seen what winter would be like.

We got into November, and it rained so hard that in a few days it made up for lost time. Along with the rain, all the dead needles came down off the pine trees. They covered the acre-and-a-half of land we are on with about an inch of brown needles. It took a couple of days just to get a few lawns and the driveway clean between storms.

Trip on the Mississippi Queen

IN 2002, FRANK WANTED to take a trip to Costa Rica, but it was too far for Gloria to go and leave her mother, who wasn't doing well. So we settled on the Mississippi River trip, scheduling it as close to our Nov. 26 wedding anniversary as we could get, yet still be home for our 60th anniversary party that the kids were planning to give us.

We would also be home for Thanksgiving on Nov. 28, and that would give Laurence and Gloria time to finish decorating and putting lights up on their outside trees in time for Thanksgiving evening and the Christmas season. Their Christmas lights display has turned into an annual tradition in the community. I've talked about this earlier. Gloria and Laurence really didn't want to go traveling at this time of the year; they said it would be too cold, and neither one likes cold weather. They said it several times, right up until a few days before leaving on our trip together. We had already put out the money, and we really wanted to go for our anniversary, so we left it that way, and both Frank and I prayed for good weather so they would not be too cold.

On Nov. 13, the six of us — Frank and I, Laurence and Gloria, Julia and Mark — had an early flight scheduled out of Sacramento, so we left the day before, rented two cars, and dropped Laurence and Gloria off at the Sacramento airport. All six of us stayed at the hotel near the airport. We had an early dinner and went to bed. Julia and Mark would be at the airport to check in their luggage at 4 a.m. and fly out at 6 a.m. The long wait was all due to the 911 terrorist attacks. They were going to Memphis, Tennessee, for a few days before getting on the boat on Saturday, Nov. 16. Laurence, Gloria, Frank, and I checked in our luggage at 5 a.m. and flew out at 7 a.m.

We had a nice flight, and along the way, Frank got to talking with one of the flight attendants. He told her about our 60th anniversary, telling her what we were going to do and about the party we were having after we got home. Later, she and the captain came up to us and gave us a big bottle of champagne to celebrate with the kids on the boat.

After we arrived at St. Louis, Laurence rented a large van for the four of us and all our luggage. It was high enough off the ground to really see things as we drove. We stayed at the Adams Mark Hotel, the same one Frank and I stayed at when we were there in 1994. At that time, we had a room on the 17th or 18th floor that faced towards the Gateway Arch. This time, we were on the 17th floor and faced the street side, but we could still see the Arch. We went into St. Louis just so Frank could go to the top of the great Arch one more time in his life.

There were also things that Laurence and Gloria wanted to see, and they weren't too interested in going to the Arch. Knowing this, I said we could see it in a hurry and then go on to do what they wanted to do. So after we got checked in, they came to our room to see if we were ready, which we weren't, so they went back to their room that was right next to ours; but, I thought they had gone on to the Arch.

Frank and I took off to meet them at the Arch, but after we got to the top, they weren't there. Now I was worried. I told Frank we would stay put until they showed up.

After a while, I saw them cross the street as we looked down from the top of the Arch. I took a picture of Gloria and Laurence crossing the highway and hoped it would turn out. (It

did, but not so you could tell who it was.) They let me know that they would not leave like that without telling us, and I was glad to hear them say that. What they had done was have a light lunch, and that is why we missed them. Of course, if I had knocked on their door in the first place, I could have saved all the commotion. After going to the top of the Arch, we took in the museum that is there. It was well worth seeing. By this time, Laurence and Gloria had decided to continue to see the rest of the Arch. Then we went out to dinner, which was so-so.

Frank having a good time looking out of the Arch

A wonderful birds-eye view of St. Louis as seen from the Arch

The next morning after breakfast, we checked out and then drove around until we found the place that had the "Drew Ice Cream" that Laurence had read about in one of the travel books. The place didn't open until 10 a.m., so we drove around the area to kill time. We went back and got our choice of ice cream at that early, cold hour. There were many people there just to get the ice cream, and I could understand why; it makes a good cold breakfast, and the taste is excellent. Then we started our leisurely drive to Memphis for the night. We joined up with Julia and Mark at a hotel across the street from them; they were staying at the Peabody Hotel.

All six of us did some sightseeing by foot and then had a sparerib dinner that our friend, Brayton Hahn, had told us not to miss. Julia and Mark, having been there a couple of days earlier, had already found the place. After that, we all went for a walk around town, and in the process, the four of them were able to get into a late show to see Jerry Seinfeld at $67 each. These were the last seats available and were in the orchestra section with the W.C. (wheelchair people).

As I said, the house was sold out, but they had two chairs in that section, and the kids talked the ushers into putting two more in with them. They had some time to kill, so they decided to walk us back to the hotel. As we left the building, two men came up to us and said, "Lucky you! We took time out to decide if we wanted to be in that section, and while we talked it over, you came and bought the last tickets." In walking back to the hotel, we all got some ice cream, and then the kids went back to the Orpheum Theater to see the show. Frank and I went into the hotel and went to bed. The next day they said they had the best seats in the house.

The duck show at the Peabody Hotel as seen from the balcony

Our hotel was not too great, but Julia and Mark, as I said, were staying at the Peabody Hotel across the street. So the next day the four of us went over to Julia and Mark's hotel at the time the ducks were scheduled to make their appearance from the elevator to the center fountain, where they would spend the day swimming in the water until 4 p.m. A large crowd of people shows up just to see this quaint, little show. I was able to get up into the balcony and get a real good spot. The kids joined us, so when the ducks came walking to the fountain, Julia took the picture. She is so much steadier with a camera than I am. While waiting for this to happen, I was able to buy Frank a nice sweater in a shop near where we were standing.

Julia and Mark had things they were going to do until it was time to go to the boat. So the four of us checked out of our hotel and drove around to see the town. We then took our luggage down to the port. We still had a lot of time on our hands, so we drove around the Mud Island area to see the homes. We then went out into the country. After a while, Laurence sort of got lost, so when we saw the airport sign, we all ended up going with him to turn in the van at the airport. After that was done, we took the taxi back to board the Mississippi Queen. Julia and Mark were already there waiting for us, so they got a picture of us walking down the ramp. I also took some photos.

The Mississippi Queen was nice and we enjoyed looking at each other's rooms. Frank had made the room arrangements for all of us. Julia and Mark's room was on the fourth floor at the front of the ship, room No. 402. Their room was on the quiet side and off by itself; it was above the lounge and the chart room. It was situated close to where breakfast and lunch were served and where daytime entertainment took place. They loved it and were able to do some reading.

Laurence and Gloria's room was at the other end of the ship on the second floor. I think it was No. 275. It was near the paddlewheel, and above them were the late dance and music shows, as well as the music from the calliope. A lot of activity went on in the evening and they

Checking out our rooms

joined in with it, especially since there was too much noise to sleep. Both rooms were larger than any of the other rooms, giving them a little space to breathe. Frank and I had a nice room in the middle of the boat on the third floor, No. 326. We were near the stairs in a quiet room that was a little smaller than the kids' rooms. All three rooms had their own balcony. Everyone was as happy with their quarters as you can be on any boat.

We had a late dinner hour, and our table was in the center of the dining room. We had great waiters but the room was on the noisy side. Having three people in our group not being able to hear very well, we asked to be moved to a quiet table and asked to have the same people waiting on us, which they did for the rest of the trip.

Our first day, heading out of Memphis, was spent relaxing and enjoying the boat and the scenery. The next day we went to Vicksburg, where the kids took a walking tour of the town, and I took care of Frank. About 2 p.m., someone on the boat brought a beautiful bouquet of flowers to our room. It sure cheered up the room; the card said, "Happy 60th Anniversary." The flowers were from Julia and Mark, and at that time it was really a welcomed gift. (That bouquet lasted the whole trip. On the last morning, I left it with the purser on her desk.)

Frank and our cheerful bouquet of flowers

Later, Julia and Mark came back, and then Julia and I went for a fast walk of the town just so I could get off the boat and get some exercise. Mark said he would look after Frank.

We were scheduled to leave around 5 p.m. Then it was all aboard and down the river until we reached the next stop, which was Natchez, Tennessee, on Nov. 19. Around 9 a.m., most people had left the boat and either walked or took the bus into town. I waited for Frank and thought he was all right to walk to the town. We got about two blocks. He then stopped and said he wasn't going any farther. So that left me sort of stranded. He could see the boat from where we were and could get back to it OK, so with the map that the purser had given us, I told him I would walk the tour on my own. Now I have to admit, this is something I don't, as a rule, do on my own in a strange town. But I decided it was time to break loose from the mold and start doing things on my own, in case I would have to do so in the near future.

I had done very well on my own and was on my way towards the Catholic Church. About this time, here comes Mark and Julia in a horse and carriage with a driver and another couple with them. Mark had the driver stop and pick me up. From there, we continued to see the town, some of which I had already seen earlier in the day; however, I did not know all the history on the historical homes. That sure made the ride interesting. Later, we had lunch and then went to see the church. Mark then headed back to the boat, telling us to be sure we were on the boat before 4:30 p.m.

Julia and I continued on to see the important sights, including Magnolia Hall, which was the last great mansion built in Natchez prior to the War Between the States. We then took a taxi to Longwood to see what is called the grandest octagonal house in the United States. Construction on the house was started in 1860–61, and then the war broke out putting a stop to it. The family went broke during the war, as did many plantations, and this is one place they did not plan to restore. It was interesting to hear how they would build a house so that air would circulate from the center of the first floor up to the ceiling, cooling rooms on each floor as the air rose up and out the top dome. Hallways and stairs in the middle of the house were used the same way. We discovered that many such homes are being restored and brought back to their original condition.

Julia's picture of me in front of the octagonal house in Natchez, TN

Time ran out, but fortunately, for us, the taxi man got us back to the boat just in time. One man had to run to get on the gangplank as it was being lifted up from shore; he had been to the gambling boathouse next to us and lost track of time. We were then on to our next stop, St. Francisville, Louisiana.

Later that evening we had our dinner in a quieter place on the boat and enjoyed the champagne that was given to us by the flight attendants. The waiters even sang "Happy Anniversary" to us. Unfortunately, Frank got to feeling sick before he could enjoy it. This lasted for the next two days, and after some laxatives, along with All-Bran, prunes, and water, we finally got rid of his problem. And the three sleeping pills he had taken made him feel like a zombie, so no more pills. After that, he enjoyed the rest of the trip, although he was still not feeling too well, and his ankles were swelling.

Anniversary dinner at the quiet dinner spot on the boat

During the night, the Delta Queen riverboat had pulled up and was tied to us, and in the morning, we were able to go across to see it. Passengers of the Delta Queen had to come onto the Mississippi Queen to get on shore.

It was now Nov. 20, and we had arrived at St. Francisville, Louisiana. Out of the six of us, Julia and I were the only ones to sign up to take a bus to see the Greenwood Plantation. The place was built in 1830 and later caught fire. Richard Barnes spent 16 years restoring the house. When we were there, he and his family were living on the third floor. The public wasn't allowed to see that part of the house. However, he was very generous in telling you the story, and you were welcomed to walk and sit anywhere you wished on the first two floors. As he said, "It's a home to live in." He restored it as close as possible to its original state, and this included no bathrooms on the first two floors. He added them on the third floor where the family lived. Tours of the house were used to pay the bills and help keep it going. It was still a plantation, but not as large as it was in the 1830s.

Top: Our boat was used as a bridge for people on the Delta Queen
Bottom: Me in front of the Greenwood Plantation

We also saw the Louisiana State Penitentiary at Angola, which is something everyone should see if they are in the area. You will get to learn how the "prisoners for life" live on this 18,000-acre site. And you learn how well it sustains itself; there is no wasted space, and it's a productive farm, including raising cattle and other livestock.

Going into the Louisiana State Penitentiary

It was then time to head back to our boat to see the Delta Queen pull away from us. They played the calliope for a long time after leaving, and we left once they were out of the area. This was around 4:30 or 5 p.m. While the Delta Queen was tied up to our boat, Frank and I went over to see it and enjoyed reminiscing about old times when we were on it in 1994. Frank even remembered our room number, No. 210. He also remembered that the lifeboat was right outside our room.

Laurence, Julia, and Gloria
enjoying the nice weather

We were on our way downriver once again, and sometime during the night, we tied up at Baton Rouge on Nov. 21. Frank, who was still not up to par, remained behind, while the rest of us took off by foot with a guide to see the Governor's Mansion that was designed and built for Huey P. Long in 1930. It was built to look like the White House, along with the 30-foot-high white columns. Long had a great deal to say and do while he was governor of the state, including having a bridge built over the river. He had it constructed too low for big ships to go under; the object, I guess, was to put more people to work unloading and reloading smaller ships. In the end, I think the state was the loser.

Time was beginning to run out on us at this point. A liftoff and a shipboard renewal of vows was taking place together at 4:30 p.m., and some of us were in it, including Frank and me. We still wanted to see the capitol and it was a long walk to get there. If we were to see it, we'd have to get walking in high gear. This would leave a few people out who had trouble walking fast, including Gloria and Laurence, so that group took a leisurely walk back to the boat.

The rest of us really walked fast. We got to see the capitol and went clear to the top of the building. We saw where Huey Long was shot and where some of the bullet marks were still in the wall. After leaving the building, a few of us really took off for the boat; we had about a mile to walk, and I think Julia, Mark, a couple of other people, and myself made it back in 15 minutes. Luckily, the rest of the group had enough time to get back. It was a good thing I hurried because I ended up having only three minutes to change and look halfway decent for the vows. Frank had changed and was waiting for me. The boat was now leaving the shore as we headed on to our next stop.

Frank and me cutting the cake

There were 17 couples that had been married from 1 year up to 50 years. Frank and I were the only ones who had reached 60 married years together. We had our pictures taken under white bells, and then we all marched up and had the vows read. I said a quiet prayer for God to forgive all our sins that covered all our married years. The captain was very good at what he had to say. Because we were the last to go through the line, Frank and I were the first couple to cut the cake. As we were doing this, the photographer asked, "Where is your wedding ring?" I said I never travel with my rings. And, of course, he didn't know the kinds of rings I have. During this time, the kids were busy taking pictures.

We had a very nice evening and enjoyed the evening's show; it was then time for our dinner. We had a good time, and extra attention was given to our table by our two headwaiters. Somewhere about this time, we tied up near the U.S.S. Kidd (DD-661) from World War II, which had been historically restored. I didn't get to see it, but Frank, Gloria, and Laurence did.

Nov. 22 saw us docked at the west bank of the Mississippi River across from the Oak Alley Plantation. This plantation was built in 1837–39 and has 28 windows and 28 Doric columns. It is one of the antebellum mansions. It has 28 live oak trees that were planted about 300 years ago that formed an arch canopy from the entrance on River Road to the mansion. All the slave houses were being restored and used for shops, and so on.

Oak Alley Plantation

From there all six of us took the Cajun Swamp Tour. We missed seeing any live animals but did see a few birds. We got to learn a little about the area and how they were trying to keep the swampland intact. We also learned why the trees have so much moss on them and that it doesn't kill the trees. We visited a farm-like area that had a crocodile and saw different kinds of birds that they raised. From there we headed back to the Mississippi Queen, leaving the banks of the Mississippi River and enjoying our trip downstream, seeing all the long barges full of things going and coming to market. Later on this day, we would be enjoying the last night's show and dinner.

We sure didn't see much animal life in the swamp

We continued down to New Orleans with our luggage out in front of our door by 2 a.m. We had all had a good time on the trip, but we knew it was time to move on. The weather could not have been better.

On the morning of Nov. 23, we arrived at New Orleans. We saw that the Mississippi Queen had tied up alongside the company warehouse. The American Queen was tied up just ahead of us and was undergoing repair work. They have a very big warehouse here, and all the boat companies have cars and buses ready to take you wherever you want to go.

By 7 a.m. we were ready to enjoy a hearty good breakfast and say goodbye to all the nice people we had met on the boat. Frank and I took the nice bouquet that I talked about earlier to the purser; she had been a lot of help to us during the trip when we needed help. She said she would really enjoy the bouquet, at least for several more days. After we left her, other people who were still waiting their turn to check out said she was very happy to have the flowers to look at.

Me saying goodbye to the Mississippi Queen

We were off the boat before Mark and Julia, who were near the exit, so we took some pictures of them as they left their room and the area where they had stayed. We had a big van waiting for us to load our luggage into. We loaded up and then drove to our hotel near the Ritz.

Some rooms at the hotel were ready for us, but Mark and Julia's room wasn't ready, so the hotel management stored their luggage. We then rented a tour bus to take us around the city and show us the sights. The city had really changed since the last time we were there around 1986, when we were drilling for oil.

French Quarter, New Orleans

We wanted to see all the changes and could tell that the town had really changed and grown. That night we had dinner with Julia and Mark, and then we took a walk down near the French Quarter. It too had really changed. Laurence and Gloria had arranged to go somewhere else earlier for dinner. By the time we got back to the hotel, we were tired, so we went to bed early. Laurence and Gloria would be leaving us in the morning to catch an early plane home; Mark and Julia were leaving on a later flight.

During the night, Frank was having a hard time breathing, and during the past several days his legs really began to swell. So around two in the morning, he put on his bathrobe and went down to the lobby and out the front door for some fresh air. The night watchman on duty for the three big hotels stayed and talked with Frank. When he left the room, I thought, "What kind of identification does he have on him to show who he is if something should happen to him?" Then I remembered he could not get back into the hotel without his room card, so I knew he was covered on that ground.

An hour later he came back, only to go back downstairs again around 4 a.m. When he came back this time, we stayed up, got everything ready to leave at 7 a.m., and got ready to go down to the lobby to have breakfast. Around this time, Laurence and Gloria came down the elevator, and the night watchman told them all about Frank's episode. Frank said that at 2 a.m. the city was full of people having a good time, and at 4 a.m. the streets were empty, except for the people who were going to work. He couldn't believe the change in the streets in just two hours.

We got home safely on Monday and Frank went to see his doctor. Frank had so much water in his system that it interfered with his lungs and breathing, so the doctor gave him some water tablets, which caused him to lose 10 pounds in 24 hours. After two weeks, more tests were done, and so far everything looked fine. During this time, Laurence was calling or stopping by to make sure Frank saw the doctor, and when he didn't, Julia would make sure her father made it to his appointments.

One of the things Frank and I began noticing was that all four of the children were really paying more attention to us and to how we were doing, which we love, for it means they care. May God bless the four of you and walk with you always.

Our 60th anniversary party, given by the kids

ON TUESDAY, NOV. 26, 2002, Frank and I got up early and went to 8 a.m. Mass. This was our anniversary — the day we got married 60 years ago. Julia joined us; she had already been to 6 o'clock mass in Grass Valley and had Mass said for us at her church. We didn't know that Father was going to announce during Mass that it was our 60th anniversary, so we got a wonderful blessing from everyone for our 60 years together.

Frank and me wearing our corsages at our 60th anniversary party

Our anniversary party, given to us by Julia and Laurence, along with the help of their spouses, took place later that evening. It had been planned before we left for our trip on the Mississippi Queen. The four of them really do things up right, and I thank the Lord for giving them to us.

Julia and Gloria used our wedding picture for the front of the invitation; they got many good comments on that. The party was black-tie optional and no gifts. It started at 6 p.m. and consisted of dinner and dancing at the historic Holbrooke Hotel in Grass Valley, California.

The girls decorated the tables up in two shades of lavender and had bouquets of the long-stemmed little white orchids as the centerpiece for each table. I did not want a wedding cake per se, so they had several other kinds of cakes available that gave everyone a good choice.

The dinner was a nine-course meal with music being played by Wally Brooks for dancing between courses. The girls had a gardenia corsage for us to wear, just like our wedding corsage of 60 years ago. Upon arriving, guests got their pictures taken by Ron Sanchez. With everyone so well dressed in tuxedos and long dresses, it was a perfect occasion to have pictures taken. I later gave each person their picture as a gift.

A variety of cakes were available for all to enjoy

On planning the party, the girls had asked for a list of names of people I wanted to have, and they gave me no limit. I remembered thinking back to our 25th anniversary party that Julia and Laurence gave us. There were so many people from out of town, along with all the relatives, that we did not have a chance to visit with all the people that were there. And the next day everybody was gone, so I said no to having that many guests this time around. I mainly just wanted locals who were always doing things for us. So I limited the invite list to 58 guests, and we were able to visit with everybody that came.

Julia had asked me to come up with the seating arrangements for the tables, so I did. I had one member of the family at the head of each table, and then taking their personality, I placed the guests—quiet and talkative at each table, equal men and women, and no couples together. I had a good number of comments on the seating arrangements at the tables, and I was told how everyone had such a good time mixing.

Frank having a good time telling stories

Both Julia and Laurence gave delivered remarks about us at the party. I did not hear everything Laurence said, but I got the tail end of it. It was something like, "Mother was the glue that held us together." He got many laughs on that. And Julia told a little story about how Dad always had us tightening our belts when they were little, and he still does, but here we were having a party this night, or something to that effect. She got a lot of laughs on that one too. Frank also had a few stories to tell as well.

It was a lovely, crisp evening, so the furs came out of the closet and felt very nice to wear. The hotel management did a nice job, and I'm sure they got referrals from our event. This was their first big party since the new owners had recently taken over.

No gifts were requested, but a few presents showed up anyway. We received a $100 gift in our name to Music in the Mountains, a lovely azalea plant, and a white marble carving of the Last Supper from Jim and Hank Maxwell that we really treasure. It sits on top of the Mathushek piano in the living room. I thank the kids for all their efforts and of thinking of us enough to give such a lovely party. It took no effort on our part whatsoever. I still have my corsages from 1942 and 1967, and now I will add this one to them.

Everyone having a good time at the Holbrooke

For several months leading up to the party, I had not been feeling very well. My blood pressure was very low and I was somewhat dizzy off and on. So when the kids said they were going to do the party, I wasn't sure that it was a good idea. I felt that the Mississippi River trip would be enough and that was our gift to them. However, the kids said they wanted to give this to us and that the 60th is a milestone. They assured me it would not be that hard to arrange and that they were going to have it catered, so it would take little effort on their part.

It was a very relaxed evening for everyone.

The family together celebrating at the Holbrooke
Brad, Penny, Laurence, Gloria, me, Frank, Julia, Mark, and Spence

Christmas tree time

ON DEC. 10, 2002, the kids came over in the afternoon for our annual tradition of putting up the Christmas tree. Laurence put up the lights, while the rest of us gave him a bad time. Mark fixed the lights on the angel that had been around and seen many Christmas seasons; she even survived 1993 — the year the tree crash-landed in the living room, with half of the old ornaments going with it. After the lights were all done, Julia climbed the ladder to put the ornaments on the top part of the tree, while Gloria handed them to her, with the critique given by all three men.

By this time, it was after 6 p.m. and dinner was ready, so we enjoyed a leisurely leg-of-lamb dinner and had a good time together. Spence, Brad, and Penny were not able to come for dinner. While Frank and I did the dishes, the rest of the family finished putting the rest of the ornaments on the tree. It was now 10 p.m. and time to call it quits. We always have a good time, for this is our Christmas as a family. And now the kids were free to go and visit the rest of the families on Christmas Day.

85-mile-per-hour windstorm, tree goes down

ON MONDAY, DEC. 16, 2002, we had a very heavy windstorm that "they said" was 85 miles an hour. At 3:15 a.m. I heard what sounded like a tree that had fallen, and the power went out. I got up to look out all the windows to see if I could see where it went down, but I couldn't see anything, except for a large one-inch power line lying across the kitchen porch. I went and woke up Frank; he looked around and tried to call for help, but the phone line was dead. So we used the cell phone and called Laurence, which was a mistake, for he couldn't do anything at that hour. He was also out of power and had snow on the ground. So we put another blanket on our bed and went back to sleep.

Frank got up at 8 a.m. to build a fire in the fireplace; he said to me, "You had better get up." He saw men in our yard looking at the power damage and all the trouble we had.

As it turned out, our neighbor had called the power company and reported the damage at 4 a.m. After I got up, I saw that the tree had fallen across the pump house lawn. It took out the PG&E power pole line that held the telephone and electrical wires; it broke our water lines

Before: New brick walkway and hourglass fixture

and ripped out underground electrical wires to the pump house and outside lights. It broke sprinkling water lines, knocked down fencing, and broke the new, large hourglass fixture that I had bought that summer. When the roots of the tree let go, it fell in the direction of the barbecue house, hitting the side of the building and going into the neighbor's yard, hitting one of their cars and ripping out and breaking a light post. A large hole was left where the tree had stood. It had also ripped up my new brick walkway.

After: The tree that fell on Dec. 16, 2002

Storm takes its toll on yard

The Union photo/John Hart

Sunday's storm uprooted this tree in the yard of Frank Amaral Sr. on Reward Street in Nevada City, taking out a water line and damaging a small building.

The tree had lots of big roots, but it didn't have a long taproot, which surprised Robinson's men who came to take it out and cut the tree into logs. Over the years, the tree roots had grown around and into the sprinkling system, water lines, and the electrical wires that went to the pump house and all the outside lights. The men we had on site were able to restore the water line enough so we could have some water in the house. This was not the only damage; the tree also took out the power box to Frank's office. When the line went down, it pulled all the power-box lines to the outside lights.

The fallen tree also made the local newspaper

Our neighbor lost trees and suffered some damage to the back porch of their small rental house. One of the trees crossed over to a corner of the house next to it. After three days, we got electricity restored to the house and telephone service was back on the fourth day. The office got fixed a week later, the day before Christmas.

We spent the first two nights after the storm at Julia and Mark's place. On Wednesday morning, I got a dilly of a dizzy spell that lasted for two days. The night before, I had told Frank and Mark what I would have to do the next day, and the first thing was to get an electrician on the job. God bless Mark. He got his friend David Schwarz to come over to show him what had to be done; David got things working for me. He had to order a new meter box with all new parts, so it took several days. The job was finished the day before Christmas, and Frank now had heat and lights in his office again. In the meantime, I found out that Laurence was also getting someone lined up to do the repair work. I thank him for working on it; Mark's guy was just a little faster getting on the job.

On Saturday, Julia and Mark brought over a big pot of pumpkin soup and all the goodies to go with it, and we had dinner at our place. I was still not up to par. Then on Christmas Eve, we went to the early Mass, as did the Hahns. They brought over a crab dinner with all the trimmings, which we really enjoyed, along with a game of bridge that lasted until about midnight. It's nice having friends like that. Then on Christmas Day, Gloria and Laurence had us over for dinner with the Petersons to see their outside lights that Frank and I had not yet seen that year. So with all this mess, and with my ups and downs, and with a bout of the flu, Laurence made sure I got medicine to take care of myself. Overall, we fared very well with the help and support of good family and friends.

It was now Dec. 28 and snowing. The pump house still did not have any pressure, nor were the outside lights and the barbecue house lights working. I had contacted B&P Landscaping to come do the repair work to the sprinkling system and to have them work on the lawn, replace the lamppost, and fill the hole with sod. They also needed to replace the new brick walkway, which I had put in between January through March of this year, and which was now gone and had to be redone. While they worked on those things, I'd also have them put in one more sprinkling station, which should have been done earlier. And I was able to get someone to fix the grape fence that was knocked down.

I called Julio Salcido to see if he was available to put the upper part of the barbecue house back into place. Fortunately, the three-foot-high brick wall of the building was not damaged, and neither were the stained-glass windows. However, the hexagon roof would have to be raised to fix the wood sidings of the building. Julio said he could do it, but he was busy for a few weeks. This is the same building I had done several years ago with Tom Barney.

Now it was just a matter of time for the snow to melt and to get people over to do the work on clear, sunny days. So this was some Christmas, but at least no one had been hurt by the tree falling. Many other people in our area had far worse things happen to them; some lost parts of their homes and some were out of power for a week, including Laurence. Frank took care of the insurance claim and the landscape contractor. He is very good at doing things like that, but doing labor work, forget it.

So I thank the Lord that we were not hurt and asked Him to give us patience to see the job done.

Making up losses in oil and gas investments

Frank's story

FRANK REMEMBERS THAT BY December 2002 the Aspen Exploration Corp. had drilled 15 wells. We had taken enough out of the Aspen at a lower tax bracket to more than cover all of our losses we had had on all our other adventures into oil and gas.

This same year, on the Denverton Gas field, we were in a much lower tax bracket, so now we were far ahead. This one was an ongoing project.

Repairing damage from the 85-mile-an-hour windstorm

IT LOOKED IN JANUARY that 2003 would start off as a busy year, for my work had already been cut out for me to do, mostly supervising the repairs after the 85-mile-an-hour windstorm in December. I did get the work done on the lawn area; B&P Landscape did the job. Now we needed to have the sun shine long enough to get the new grass seed to grow. B&P had to do most everything over twice. Somehow their workers didn't want to take any orders from me, so in the end they got things fouled up in the plumbing and the electrical wiring. I had a map that had everything lined out in the yard, so I knew where everything was. The brick walkway was done twice and it still wasn't done like I'd had it done before.

Julio said it was a poor job, so I told him to call Peter at B&P and tell him that. I told Peter that in the summertime, I would re-lay it. He said he wanted to see it when I did. I told him that I had already planned to call him after I got the job done. But it would be awhile, for Music in the Mountains would be holding its annual fundraiser in our yard on June 1, and re-laying the brick would have to wait until that was over.

Julio had just a few touchup jobs left to do on the barbecue house and then he would be done. The damaged part of the fence was fixed, and now I wanted to repair the rest of the fence so it would look sharp again; after 50 years it was in need of a facelift. I got all of this done the first week in April, and it looks like it should last for the rest of my time at this place. A young man by the name of John Lawrence finished the job. He also said he was available to help me with yard work if I needed him.

I had David work on repairing all the old brick walkways that were damaged from the tree and the places where the workers set up their equipment to cut the tree into logs. This took a few days. I was then back in business again and going ahead with the May project.

The hyacinths were in bloom, and when that happens it always snows, but so far we hadn't had any. Then we had hail and snow April 11–13, followed by a few real cold showers the next few days. The tulips that were up took a real beating; some were still hanging in there.

I planted 500 tulips that year; the trip to Holland with Julia had really inspired me.

Frank really enjoyed his gardens

Julia in escrow on the Anaheim property

Frank's story

FRANK RECALLS THAT IN March 2002, the last phase of The Orange County Sportsman Club in Anaheim (the restaurant later was known as the Hungry Tiger, and after that it became a Mexican food restaurant) had finally come to an end. The property had been in our family since 1980.

The land and its location were worth more in some other business than a restaurant, but the new owners were the same people who had been operating it as a restaurant for several years. Julia hoped the sale would be completed by the end of 2003 and hoped to make a trade with the money. (Indeed, the sale and trade were completed in 2004.)

North Star in escrow from 2002

Frank's story

FRANK REMEMBERS THAT THE North Star property was finally sold in 2003, after going into escrow in 2002. Julia and Laurence were looking for a trade on this property, which had been in our family, with the Robinson Enterprise, since 1978. They had cut timber off the property at least three times and also sold gravel and rented the buildings. There had been a lot of headaches over this property, so Julia and Laurence were glad to move on to something else.

They sold it, but it was worth more than what they got for it. Frank and I had sold out of it to the kids in the late 1980s.

2003 — As we grow older

IN 2003, FRANK HAD his blood test taken. His cholesterol was on the high side, and he needed to take it down before going to his appointment with the doctor in May. Also, Frank's left little finger was still on the stiff side from when he broke it the previous June. This interfered with him playing golf, so he threatened to quit the game. I told him he needed the exercise and said it would be nice if he would join the men's group so he would have some people to play with when I wasn't able to join him.

I had been having trouble with my ring finger. It didn't want to bend, which had kept me from playing golf. I just hoped the fever I was having would go away soon so it wouldn't be so painful. Months later, the pain did go away, but it remained stiff enough that I couldn't use that finger other than to wear my wedding ring. So the finger was still good for something, and as time went on, it continued to get better.

Frank and I enjoyed each other's company, even if we weren't spending a lot of time together. I had my projects and a big beautiful yard to give me space to wander around in, and he played the market every morning. We had our exercise classes three times a week and this helped keep the pains down. Frank also took his walk every day; sometimes I joined him. He tried to do at least a mile each day. Neither one of us needed a lot of outside company, so we enjoyed our quiet time together.

Traveling to Carefree to see Musicfest

ON FEB. 23, 2003, Frank and I flew to Carefree for the Musicfest. Flying there would be a lot easier than driving, which we had done the time before. It rained the whole time we were there, so we did not do much other than go to the music concerts and receptions. They were excellent as they always are and the people were nice. We stayed at the Carefree Hotel. The management had someone pick us up at the airport, and when we got to the hotel, we rented a car. The roads were so bad in places from the rain that they were closed off and on during the week.

A week later, we were driven back to the airport; this made our trip much easier. Even so, traveling had become hard for Frank, so we would not be going again unless his state of health improved.

We bomb Iraq

ON MARCH 19, 2003, our military took action to get rid of Iraqi dictator Saddam Hussein and his army and his alleged weapons of mass destruction. Our military continued the invasion until April 9. By then we had gotten rid of all his main forces; they had either left the country, got caught in the crossfire, or vanished somewhere, no doubt into another country. This operation continued for a few more days; then it was a matter of cleaning up. The Iraqi people started to realize he was gone. They were now free on Easter Sunday to celebrate in the streets of Baghdad, or any other city or town.

As we know, our soldiers would be there for an extended period of time, but the major mess, I hoped, was done. But it didn't turn out that way.

In 2005, the Iraqis had their election. Let's hope it works out for that side of the world. This is world history, so I will leave the rest for you to read up on at your local library as the years go by.

Music in the Mountains, 2003

PAUL PERRY AND HIS crew were at our house in April 2003 to set the date for the June party that they planned to have in the yard as the annual Music in the Mountains fundraiser. They later decided to hold it on June 1, from 4 p.m. to 6 p.m. About 100 invitations would go out to the people who had donated $1,000 or more to M.I.M., to show M.I.M.'s appreciation for what they had given. Drinks and light hors d'oeuvres would be served around the barbecue area, and there would be live music piped throughout the yard. Dessert would be served up on the tennis court, where everyone would all gather to hear Paul give a thank you talk.

The tulips had been doing exceptionally well, especially considering we'd had snow as late as May 11. I have a picture somewhere of snowdrifts that were 35 inches high. On May 20, I had the group of people over who'd helped me with the deadheading of shrubs the previous year. I invited them for a light lunch and wanted to give them a chance to see how their work had turned out, for some really didn't know how to trim azaleas. We had a nice time. The yard was now full of pollen from the pine trees, so I hoped a light shower would come our way to wash it away before the party on June 1.

Saturday, May 31. A storm came up during the very early morning hours while it was still dark outside. By sunrise, pine needles were just everywhere, and this, of course, was after we'd had a nice clean yard all ready for M.I.M. to use. As I got out of bed, I experienced a bad case of vertigo that started at 7 a.m. It stayed with me all day toward six that night; I was able to get out of bed and do nothing more than hold my own. In the meantime, Julia had come over and fixed me something to eat. About 10 a.m., Gloria and Laurence had gotten back from their Los Angeles vacation and dropped in to see us.

When Gloria and Laurence saw me in bed, they said, "Don't worry about the yard. We will go home, change clothes, and come back to wash down all the pollen and help David and John clean up the yard." When they said that, I just let go and relaxed. I knew they would do it just as I would. Julia and Frank also got into the act, and by 4 p.m., the place was in top shape for the party. An hour later, about 5 p.m., Laurence and Gloria came back and made a barbecue dinner outside for the six of us. By 6 p.m., I was able to get up and do little more than hold my own to enjoy their company.

I thank them for all they did; it's wonderful when family helps you out like that. I hope someday I will be able to pay them back in kind.

Sunday, June 1, the Music in the Mountains people showed up at our place by 9 a.m. to start setting up tables for the afternoon party. I still had vertigo but was able to get out of bed and hold my own.

I was not able to go to church, which was another change in our life. The bishop had changed our priests and said we had to consolidate our 9:30 a.m. and 11 a.m. Masses at St. Canice Hall on Reward Street. This change wasn't going over very well with any of us. Sometime in the middle of the week, we were told that both Masses would be at 9:30 a.m. and held at St. Canice Church in Nevada City. We waited to see how it would all turn out. And it did. Everyone was happy the next Sunday. It turned out that 11 o'clock Mass would be combined with 9:30 a.m. Mass, and it would always be held at the church and not at the hall. The noon Sunday Mass would be said in North San Juan one week and in Downieville the next.

By 3:30 p.m., I was dressed and still holding my own, standing straight and not lying down as I had been on Saturday. The yard and lawns looked their best. All the azaleas and rhodes were in full bloom, and the backyard by the tennis court was at its best for this time of year. Tables were set up with colorful tablecloths that blended in with the flowers both in the front yard and on the tennis court. There were plenty of goodies and desserts to eat, and drinks of your choice. Paul gave a thank you talk to all who were there and said how he appreciated their help supporting M.I.M. Berry Bonifas and Hazel Shewell thanked all the working crew who helped make everything doable, and, of course, there were thanks said to Frank and me for the use of the yard.

With the help of family and friends, the yard was ready for the M.I.M. party

It was a beautiful, warm day and everyone seemed to enjoy being there; if they didn't, it was their fault. The yard and spring flowers were an array of color wherever you turned. All the work that was put into it, in addition to repairing the damage from the tree that fell in December, had all come together very nicely in the end. The brick walkway still had to be redone, and as long as I had my dizziness problem, it would have to wait. There was a change in that part of the yard, but in a way, maybe it's for the better. And the new fence was a blessing to me; I had never thought I would get it repaired in my lifetime.

The yard in full bloom for the M.I.M. party (azaleas and some camellias)

John, our gardener, came over on Monday and told me how surprised he was to see the place looking so good. He appreciated all the work the family had done and said he really liked how everyone pulled together to make the job easier. He even commented on Frank having gotten into the act.

I later received a very nice thank you note from a couple that lived in the Los Angeles area who were at the M.I.M. party. They referred to the yard and said it was in the class, only smaller, of Butchart Gardens in Victoria, B.C. This sort of made me feel like all my effort was worth it.

By Thursday, I was still having vertigo trouble. David hadn't been to work since noon on Monday, so I was out deadheading by myself. Frank, believe it or not, was out washing the cars. We concluded that I had to let David go, which I decided to do the next day if he showed up for work.

It wasn't until June 9 that David showed up to work. I told him he was through working for me. He asked for one more chance, but I said no, that he had been given that already. But I was sorry I didn't get his phone number, for he was good with bricks. John Lawrence asked for the job, so we'd have to see how he worked out. He wasn't a gardener, but he wanted to learn to be one, to add to the other things he did to make a living, and he was a willing worker. We would have to see how well he learned and how fast and good he was at taking orders and remembering what I wanted done.

Frank and the market in 2003

Frank's story

FRANK REMEMBERS THAT IN 2003, ever since the Iraq war had started, the stock market and other commerce had really slowed down. So on April 23, I called Howard Epstein, the broker with whom Frank had been doing business with for many years. I asked him to give me a quote on General Electric, a stock Frank had liked through the years. Howard could only go back on the computer to 1981. He said that in 1981 GE had split and adjusted to a low of $2 a share. In 2000, GE stock was at $58, and on April 23, 2003, it was at $30 a share. So this gives you an idea of the changes that Frank had dealt with, but it doesn't go back to 1960. Maybe somewhere in Frank's files or records we can find some comparison prices from earlier years.

The news media was blaming the slump on President Bush and the war. But when it is all said and done, I have a feeling that the slump will be caused by the scandals at the large companies that gave large bonuses to their heads and were not keeping good records. These companies had decided to take a run while they still could, and it caught up with them and the world in the end. And, of course, the war in Iraq had a negative effect on the market. Until Saddam Hussein is caught, it will be a troubling spot for Bush. Blame can also be shared by the people reporting the news, some of whom are excessively liberal.

(In time, we did catch Saddam. He had been hiding in an underground bunker and was not very clean when we caught him. I hoped that now the Iraqi people would wake up to a chance for a better life, like the one they had back before he and his two sons, who were now dead, came into power.)

I have vertigo

FOR A MONTH, FROM May 30 to June 30, 2003, I suffered from vertigo. This was a long time to be dizzy. Because of this, Julia made a decision that we had to make a change in doctors, especially if she was going to be looking after Frank and me in the future.

My move was to Dr. Christine Newsom, and Frank went to Dr. John Lace. Frank went to see him for swelling in one ankle and for having a hard time breathing, along with not sleeping. We found out he had fluid in his lungs and an infection in his sinuses. Dr. Lace put Frank on Lasix and gave him some nose drops. The doctor told Frank he would not give him any stronger sleeping pills; if he did, he would be on some kind of dope and its effectiveness would wear off after a few months, and then where would he be?

After a few days and losing 10 pounds of water weight, Frank decided he didn't need to take the pills any longer. But a few days later, he was right back to where he was before, so he now knew he had to stay on the medicine. As for the sleeping pills, Dr. Lace suggested Frank stop taking the catnaps throughout the day, so he could sleep at night. Frank had been on sleeping pills for more than three years and did nothing but complain about not sleeping; however, he would sleep all day. It was like he was drugged. He was not as alert, not remembering things very well, and bitching about everything, even to the kids.

One day I said to him, "Too bad Ollie Hause is not alive." Frank asked why. I told him he quit cigarettes for Ollie and has always bragged about how he had no trouble quitting. "So why can't you do the same with the sleeping pills?" I asked him. So Frank tried it for the first night and slept some.

He had no hangover the next day, and while at exercise class with Roxanna, he told her about not sleeping. She proceeded to tell him about her round of troubles many years before, and how when you still can't sleep, you take more. After a while, you are on them day and night. You end up taking them and finally you have to make a choice to get off them or be a real druggie. Roxanna also told him how hard it was to get off them, but once you did you wouldn't go back.

After Frank was off the pills for a few days, I threw all the pills in the garbage, and we would go from there. And so we did. He soon became his old self and was much nicer to be around. Even the kids noticed it.

I hoped he would be able to stay off the sleeping pills. It's true that he does have a hard time sleeping; no doubt, he is playing the market or doing business all night long in his mind.

When it came to me, Dr. Newsom had me get a blood test; it was found that I had *H. pylori* and amylase. Dr. Newsom did a CAT scan and audiometric exam for the ear, nose, and throat. The doctor also did a VNG, called videonystagmography, for the inner ear. It was found I had trouble on the left side. Next was a mammogram and a MRA/MRI for the head, brain, and neck. Next on the list was the urologist.

As of this writing, I have not found out what the results were. I did want to know why I was getting vertigo. The tests showed I was in great shape from my neck down!

During this time, the temperature had been in the 90s for many days. It was the hottest summer I can remember in Nevada City. Usually at this time of year, it is hot three days in a row and then the temperature will drop three days in a row. Sometimes the hot streak will last for nine days, but not this year. Everything in the yard really needed watering every day.

June 2003 — Laurence and Deer Creek Park

Frank's story

FRANK REMEMBERS THAT IN June 2003 he began work on another parcel in the Deer Creek Park subdivision, and the "powers that be" had already tried to put the damper on the project. I believe the environmental restriction book on the project was around 150 pages alone.

There was a public meeting, and the whole town showed up trying to shut him down on the project, but at this point it was wait and see. Frank has more patience with the "do-gooders" than I have; I call them, "Those 'do-good-doers' who can produce nothing, but are great for stirring up trouble."

Many positive and negative stories have been in the newspaper about the project, and Frank got his picture in the paper on the good ones. This turned into an ongoing project with many more acres to develop.

July 2003 — Julia back on the Olympia Park project

Frank's story

FRANK RECALLS THAT IN June 2003 a local prospective tenant was back in the picture for moving into Olympia Plaza, but not much was settled and it was still up in the air. After all the trouble we'd gotten from the "do-good-doers," Julia was thinking about selling the project to someone else and letting them have the headache.

Labor Day Weekend 2003

AUGUST 2003 WAS A real hot month, so on Labor Day weekend we went up to the Clarke Ranch for a break from all that was going on at home—the doctor visits, keeping up with the heat, business matters, and the air conditioning that wasn't always working. I was originally planning to go to my sister's 80th birthday in Manteca, CA, which was put on by Barbara at her place. But Julia said it was too hot in the Central Valley and it was a four-day holiday. There would be lots of traffic and it would not be too good for Frank and me to drive down there. So we ended up going to the ranch with Julia and Mark. They flew us there in their plane; we were there in one hour. Driving to the ranch takes at least four hours and even longer in holiday traffic.

On Monday, we got a call at the ranch from Laurence telling us there had been a severe lightning storm in Nevada City and damage had been done at our home. He did not know it until John, our gardener, came to work and saw the mess from the tree branches that were everywhere, and he had left the yard in tip-top shape on Friday.

John didn't know what to do, nor did he know how to get in touch with us. So he went up to Laurence's place and told him what the yard looked like. Laurence, Gloria, and Brad came to see it and took pictures for the insurance people. A neighbor told them he'd been sitting out on his porch Sunday morning about 8:30 waiting for his wife to get his breakfast. He said he saw the lightning hit the top part of our tree by the carport. He then saw the top 30 feet of a 200-foot pine tree explode all over the place. It made a lot of noise and a big mess; debris was everywhere.

The storm took out our electricity in all the buildings. Laurence took care to get the power back on to the pump house. He and Brad helped John clean up the yard as best they could without taking away too much damage for the insurance people to see firsthand.

Laurence called Alvin Cyrus, a tree man who had done our trees before, to come over to see the tree. They also took pictures of the yard before cleaning it up. It turns out that during the storm, electricity came down the TV cable wire all the way from the pole near Brock Road, and then on down the wire to the gardener's house. From there, the wire ran above the lawn area to the tree. It was hooked through the eye of an iron spike nailed into the big 200-foot pine tree. The electrical jolt entered at the spike and traveled down the center of the tree, all the way down and through the six-foot base and into the ground. At the spike, the electrical charge also took off on the wire going to our house, where the TV cable entered the house. It pushed the cable box through the wall into the living room, burning the outside of the house where the cable was attached.

It burned the air-conditioning wires and heater, blew out the TVs in the living room and in the kitchen, and fried the VCR and radio. It took out the vacuum system, got Frank's fax machine that was in his office away from the house, and took out the sprinkling system panel that was on the outside office wall. It also took out the pump and disrupted the water system, took out the telephone system, and stripped the antenna wires and other electrical wires that were inside the roof of the house.

When we got home Monday evening, we were told by our insurance people that we could not stay in the house until the tree was taken down or until it was proved safe for us to stay at home. The concern was that another storm could come along and split the tree, which could fall on the house and hurt us. Up to now, the damage had been caused by an act of God, but the next time we would not be covered by insurance, unless we took the tree down. So we spent the night at Julia and Mark's place, and the next day we had some tree men come and check the tree. It was deemed safe for the time being, so we were able to stay at our home.

Removing the tree hit by lightning.
Cyrus is hanging onto the cable line.

On Tuesday, John continued spending the whole day moving big branches into piles, while we spent the time trying to get a hold of the telephone company to repair the phone line. It took four days to get the phone working. Frank got some tree men to come out and give us a bid to take the tree down in eight large sections, or logs, so that Robinson's crew could take out the logs. As I've said, the tree was 200 feet high and 6 feet at its trunk. We finally got Cyrus to do the job, and a week later he had an 85-ton crane, the biggest he could get, come in and do the job. Of course, this meant there was another big mess to clean up.

They ended up cutting eight 16-foot logs; Robinson Timber removed them for us. This was the second tree within nine months that had come down at our place. I sure hoped the good Lord would say that was enough for the Amarals for a while. It was a good thing we weren't home when the electrical storm hit, for Frank had been using the electric blanket and we don't know what could have happened. All the neighbors said the noise was really something. Even people who were in a church a half-mile away said they heard it. Their pastor said it was "God's will."

In the meantime, we were still trying to get the TV people to come out to get things going again. And we needed to replace the fax machine. It took three weeks to replace the furnace and air conditioner, the same for the TVs. We had the burned spot on the house painted. We had to have all the electrical wires in the house checked. It took an entire day to get the tree down, and, of course, we took pictures of it. We needed this tree to fall down like a hole in the wall, for it was a sound tree for its height. What a mess it made! It took a long time to get the lawns back in shape. We had the same problems after losing the other tree at Christmas time.

The tree was first stripped of branches and then removed in 16 large sections

Frank was beginning to think that the good Lord was trying to tell us something; I told him He was testing our patience. But getting a new furnace and heater did make me happy. And I now had a six-foot tree stump standing one-foot high in my yard that was a good topic of conversation. You could see right where the electricity went

through to the ground. We counted 92 rings on the stump and hoped this would be the last tree to fall while living in this place.

Frank was a lumberman who knew his trees. This one could've easily lived another 30 years.

Frank and his tree that grew from 30 rings to 93 rings in the time we lived here

In the meantime, both Frank and I were seeing our doctors and continuing with the tests that had been going on all summer. For me, they had finally come to a conclusion about what I have and will continue to have; it's something that makes it so I have to watch what I do. Frank had two leaking valves from his heart and had a dead kidney that was full of stones. They decided to leave it alone. The kidney was no doubt damaged from the radiation he'd had 20 years ago for his prostate cancer, which had also disrupted his bowel line.

Frank decided he didn't care for Dr. Lace and went back to Dr. Johnston. He told the doctor about the sleeping pills he was taking for several years, and the doctor said they were doing him more harm than good. Frank told the doctor that I took the $3-a-pill bottle and threw it in the garbage; I think there were at least 50 pills left in the bottle. He said, "Good!" for they only deaden the brain and help you lose memory. I told the doctor if he prescribed any more sleeping pills for Frank, I would do the same thing again.

He told Frank, "Anything you take to help you relax the muscles is fine, but don't overdo them, either." He suggested Frank take ibuprofen, or something along that line, and he said that taking a nap during the day was OK. Frank still complained about not sleeping and did take catnaps during the day instead of a nap, but at least he was a nicer person to be around. He didn't complain nearly as much and he acted alive. He stood tall and was willing to do things again.

By this time, Frank had gotten very hard of hearing. I know life must have been rather rough for him at times, for he had a lot to talk about and loved being around people. But not knowing what they were saying, it kind of got boring for him and he soon lost interest. He could hear the voice but not the words, so he tuned it all out.

He liked his TV programs, but he had trouble handling the satellite dish and would rather go back to the cable service we'd had before the lightning took it out. However, the cable people had not been able to figure out how to put the line back and have it approved by management. Mark told me not to cave in over the satellite dish. He said to make Frank use his brain; we didn't want that to go dormant. Frank liked watching the ticker tape every morning during the time he played the stock market, and he remained active and doing well in the market.

We have since heard from the doctor; Frank's MRI turned out fine. There were no signs of strokes or anything like that. He had nothing wrong with him for a man his age, so we could forget about there being any trouble with the brain. He just needed to stay off sleeping pills. His blood test showed he was low in both vitamin B12 and thyroid hormone, so he now had supplements for that, along with his high blood pressure pills and Lasix to take care of the fluid in his body. His PSA was 1.7 and his one kidney was doing fine. As of this point, with God's help, Frank was doing fine health-wise.

Things weren't fine with everything else going on around the house, with the tree damage and the yard, and the pump not putting out enough water for the yard or house. These sort of things really got to Frank. He would rather move somewhere else, but I told him, "You think you will get rid of all the things like that by moving?" And so went our daily life. Yes, he loved the yard; he just didn't want to have anything to do with it. Of course, the yard was food for me and my soul.

After all the things that had been going on during this period, I tried to figure out how to keep the stress from getting to me. The kids came to the conclusion that I had vertigo or dizzy spells right after all these things started happening. I started remembering what either Dr. Black or Dr. Frey had told me way back in the 1940s, that I was a lucky person who had a "built-in pop-off valve" to relieve pressure instead of going off my rocker. I am a person in high gear all the time and move very fast; when things have to be done, I do them, or I get them done by someone else.

So this time, with this storm, I began thinking along the lines of not letting things get to me—if it doesn't get done today, we'll let tomorrow take care of it. I'd have to say that so far I was riding the storm fairly well. I wasn't always sure-footed, but that's OK, at least I wasn't unsteady all the time. The doctor told me not to stay in bed when dizzy. He said I needed to get up and see it through, even if all I could do was sit down.

After all the excitement going around this place, I had my appointment with Dr. Blaha. I kept wondering why I had to go see him. But Dr. McKennan, from Sacramento, and Dr. Newsom, who was my local doctor, wanted to have Dr. Blaha's thoughts and opinions to see if what they had come up with was the same as his opinion. I will also say it was to help give peace of mind to Julia, who had taken over supervising her mother's health care in my old age. It had been close to 15 years since the last time I'd seen Dr. Blaha as a doctor. We were friends and had seen each other on occasion, so we chitchatted before getting down to business.

I told Dr. Blaha about all the tests I had undergone and gave him a copy of the results. I shared with him what I knew about my problem, and I let him know that nothing had changed since the last time he had seen me. I still had the same troubles, except the dizziness and vertigo had changed in the way it affected me. He tested me by having me close my eyes and having me stand with one foot in front of another for five seconds with my eyes closed. His comment was, "Nothing is wrong with you." He said he hoped when he got to 81 that he would be in as good of shape as I was.

After talking for a while, I told him about the "pop-off valve" story. He said I was right, that it is something that just happens to me and I was lucky. He admitted he had never heard the expression before, but it made sense. I told him I knew I was wasting his time and my money with this visit, but it was for Julia and Dr. McKennan's peace of mind. He said he would talk to Dr. McKennan, who was a friend of his. So I came to the conclusion that all the trouble was at the base of the brainstem going to the inner ear and the neck. It was more or less an arthritic problem.

He said I had never been a pill popper and that I was one to know my body. He also mentioned how all the work I did in the yard was keeping me looking so young. I admitted to him that when I did have vertigo, it was hard to see a doctor (it had taken two months to see him), and by the time you got your appointment, it was over and had passed. He told me, "You call, and we'll see you."

Hospice of the Foothills

ALONG WITH ALL THE commotion of the past few weeks, we had some good things happen too.

Hospice of the Foothills had a dinner party to honor and give awards to three hard-working people. One was a doctor for all the things that she did in so many fields. The other two awards went to Laurence and Gloria in recognition for all the hard work they had done through the years, going back to about 1985 when they decorated St. Canice Hall for the first Silver Ball dinner dance. While they were decorating the hall, Laurence fell from a ladder while hanging something to the ceiling. And from then on, the two of them had given their free labor to any function Hospice put on, including "The Starry Starry Night" dinner dance, the Hospice breakfast at St. Canice, and many other events during the years. This was quite an honor for them and we were very glad to see them get it. A few weeks later, they received an award in Sacramento for some of the same things down there.

As I'm sitting here working on this story, Frank asked me to go to the Miners Foundry Cultural Center to attend a reading of the Dylan Thomas play *Under Milk Wood*. Donna Brown, a friend of ours, was one of the readers. I said I would go with him and asked if he really wanted to go, knowing he couldn't hear what they said. His comment was, "No, I'd rather be dead," and I told him I knew he felt that way. I told him I felt the same way when I had my dizzy spells. So off we went. And we both enjoyed it, even if we both dozed off a few times and neither one of us heard nor understood everything that was being said the whole time.

Afterward I found out we weren't the only ones who did not understand them; but we all enjoyed the acting, and their facial expressions were great.

Mount St. Mary's and a Spanish teacher

JULIA WAS ON THE board at St. Mary's, along with Terry McAteer, who was also the Nevada County Superintendent of Schools. In 2003 they wanted to hire a Spanish teacher who could teach each class enough Spanish to help the students when they went to the public high school. The only problem was the school was short of money to pay the teacher. Julia asked me if I would go in with her, and together we volunteered to put up the money for three years of salary. Then, by that time, the school would be able to continue without our aid. So we agreed to pay the teacher's salary to help the students learn Spanish.

For the past few years, the school had been under bad management, so some of the students weren't coming back. However, by putting in this curriculum, it would entice students to return. I have always said I would support the school, and Julia knew it.

They found and hired a lady who spoke four languages; she was very happy to get the job. McAteer said that if we couldn't pay her salary, he would hire her for the public school. They could tell she was that good. But as long as St. Mary's could pay her salary, he would not suggest any school change. Julia and I planned to make our donation so it could be used with income tax reports. The donation would be from me and not from Frank, for he thought the students should learn English and forget any other language. He remembered his mother who could not speak English very well during her life, something that made it hard not only for herself but for her children as well.

A party for Gloria and Laurence

IN OCTOBER OF 2003, Frank and I gave Gloria and Laurence a surprise party at the Holbrooke Hotel. We had invited several of their friends and told them it was to be a surprise. Everyone kept it quiet. I had set up a private room in the hotel so we could be by ourselves for the evening. When Gloria and Laurence arrived, I think they were surprised, as well as a little confused, for everyone that was there acted as if they were meeting someone else, until we got into the room that was set up for us.

I had ordered flowers for the tables that were set up in a square so that no one would be sitting with their backs to anyone and could see everyone. I was not able to get Stephanie and

her family to be with us, but Brad and his wife and Spence with a friend were there, along with Julia and Mark, and several close couples of theirs. There were some that could not make it. I tried to arrange it so that no couples sat together, so they could visit with other people. I felt that everyone had a good time. I wanted to give Laurence and Gloria a nice party for their anniversary. And, yes, I think they were surprised. I hope they had a good time.

Gloria, Brad, me, Lisa, and Laurence arriving for the party

I had ordered a few different kinds of yummy cakes so there would be several choices, and it was served with the ice cream of their choice, along with their choice of wine. If I recall right, the cakes that were left over were used for guests in the regular dinning room.

People coming into the private dining room

Getting ready for dinner

Putting up the Christmas tree, December 2003

ON DEC. 9, 2003, all four kids came over to our house to make sure the Christmas tree would not fall over; then Laurence and Gloria put the lights on the tree. After the lights were done, the rest of us decorated the nine-foot-tall tree in the living room, with me climbing the ladder and Julia hanging onto it, while at the same time handing me ornaments to put on the top branches. Supervision was given by the crew below. After that, the rest took over. When we were all done, we admired our creative job.

By the time we finished, it was evening and time for dinner. This year we had a crab feed, while Gloria had salad and French bread with garlic. I had forgotten she didn't like crab, so she didn't fare as well as the rest of us. The next time I served crab dinner, I'd make sure there was some kind of fish for her.

A few days later, we had some friends over in the afternoon to enjoy the tree and play bridge. While this was going on, I had a strange thing happen to me on my right side. I guess it pertained to the heart. It lasted about 10 minutes, and then I was fine and went on to have a very nice evening. Two days later, I went to Yuba Docs, a local clinic, to see what had caused it. The doctor ended up sending me to the emergency room at the hospital, where I stayed overnight. It was some type of checkup, I guess. They put me on a treadmill the following day, where I stayed for 9 minutes and 15 seconds. Dr. Mallery said I was very healthy for my age.

He was not sure what caused all my trouble, so they set me up for more tests in four weeks. In the meantime, they gave me a "nitro patch" to wear every day. It gave me a real headache, along with other side effects. A few days later, I had some more pains in the middle of my chest, so I went back to Yuba Docs. The doctor said, "It's not the heart but your esophagus that is giving you that heartbeat-like feeling." So more pills, and, as I've said, I'm not a pill popper. This time I took them for the chest pain.

I went home and forgot about the problems with my heart. It was good for another 10 years, or so they said.

My heart and chest problems

AROUND JAN. 8, 2004, a few days before my doctor's appointment, at 2:15 a.m. something was really going wrong in my chest. Frank was sound asleep for a change, and I hated to do it, but I reached over and put his left hand over my chest so he could feel it beating, knowing this would wake him up. And it did.

He called 911 and then went down and opened the driveway gate. I unlocked the front door, turned on the lights, and went back to bed to wait. When the ambulance arrived, the technicians checked my pulse and the pain I was having. My pulse was 140. They said I had done the right thing by calling them. In the emergency room, it got up to 160. This was around 4 a.m., and by this time, my whole family was in the emergency room with me.

The doctors finally told them to go home so that the staff could get my blood pressure down and treat the pain I was having, which was now worse. It was about 6 a.m. before they got me stabilized and out of danger. It wasn't until 9 a.m. that they got me upstairs and into a room. The male nurses said I was "one tough nut to crack."

I was in the hospital for two more nights and was given a bunch of tests, along with another treadmill test (this time I went 12 minutes, 10 seconds) and all the rest that goes with it. They also did an angiogram to check my heart and found it was in very good shape. Other than a little plaque in a couple of veins, my heart, along with everything else, was in very good shape for my age. I was told I would be around for another 10 years.

They did say I should have my esophagus and stomach checked, and that was the next step, for the doctors thought I might have *H. pylori* or an ulcer that could be causing the heavy chest pain that went clear to my back. But the bottom line, as far as I could tell, was I had atrial fibrillation and a big "A" for anxiety, but otherwise I am a very healthy person. But it seems like I'm on the dizzy side most of the time. I have no signs of *H. pylori*, so I am fine that way.

While all of this was going on, Julia, with Mark, was finally doing what she moved up to Nevada City to do—take care of her parents, with Laurence and Gloria's help. In addition to everything that was going on, Frank wasn't in the best of shape, but at least he was holding his own, even if he had left the basement door open when he left the house, thinking he had locked the door. We had a good laugh over that.

In the meantime, I was working on getting this book done.

2004—End of Sportsman at Anaheim

IN 2004, JULIA AND Mark bought a new home site up past where they were currently living near the airport. They planned to have the fire department burn down the old buildings there. They cut some trees, opening the view looking toward Lake Tahoe, and started working on plans to build their next dream home in another year or so.

As of Jan. 7, 2004, Julia had sold what had previously been the Sportsman's Club in Anaheim. She had been renting the building to the owners of a Mexican food restaurant for many years. The sale turned out well for her, and Frank said the investment turned out very profitable. This was one more project we had turned over to her. Julia was now looking into a place to roll over her gain, rather than have Uncle Sam take it.

Three days later, she succeeded in her exchange into a business building at 3101 N.E. Orchard Ave., McMinnville, Oregon. The place was operated by Gruma Corp. In putting the project together, Julia got her dad involved in a 30% share. Now Frank was back into owning something that gave him a tax base and something to think about. She would operate the property. This gave Frank something else to put his mind on, besides his puts and calls, picking up pinecones, buying groceries, and cooking dinners—tasks he'd taken on since his wife was still busy working on her book.

January 2004 — End of the North Star

Frank's story

FRANK REMEMBERS THAT IN January 2004, after Julia and Laurence completed the sale of the North Star, they made an exchange into some property in the Gold Flat area called "138 New Mohawk." I believe Laurence operates it, and at the moment, he had his hands full.

Laurence was also working on another project in the Deer Creek Park subdivision, so he was kept busy. He managed to get his name and picture in the paper, along with all the comments from the "do-gooders" aimed to hold things up, costing him more money. But in the end it would all come through, for what is right usually does.

Julia was still struggling with the Lake Olympia property, but now that all her headaches were over from the previous years' projects, she would no doubt look into it again.

The gate and railing project

A fancy new gate after 53 years

LAURENCE AND GLORIA DECIDED we needed hand railings to go down our basement steps—after 53 years—so in 2004 they had them put in. Julia also decided we needed a better security gate at our driveway entrance and was having that done. I thought about having the name "Amaral Gardens" put on the gate, which I did.

We were all getting older. It seemed hard to believe that Julia would be 60 and Laurence 58 in spring 2004, and that they had grown up in this yard. With the good Lord's help, we would continue doing what we had to do to keep our spirits up. And I finally had Victor, a very good gardener, who needed very little advice from me. The kids were very happy that I employed him. I thank you, Lord, for looking after me on that score in my twilight years.

Dr. Blaha

IN 2004, I WENT back to visit Dr. Blaha. True to his word, after I'd suffered a spell of vertigo, I called for an appointment—I was scheduled to see him within an hour. This time, my dizziness felt like being off balance, and when I looked down, I would experience vertigo.

Julia went with me, for when I am like that I do not drive. She asked the doctor all kinds of questions and wanted answers, along with why I was not able to have a stint put in. Dr. Blaha told her that that was out of his expertise, and it could turn out to be that my veins might be too small; but he really didn't know.

Dr. Blaha gave me some exercises to do to break the stiffness in my neck and told me to get therapy from Jim Saccomanno. I mentioned to Dr. Blaha that some of the pills my other doctors had given me were coming up into my nose at night, and in the morning, I was throwing them up. He said my body was rejecting them and to stop taking them, and later the other doctors told me the same thing. He said that anyone as old as I was and in such good shape knew a little of what their body would and wouldn't take. He said he knew I preferred taking vitamins and minerals to drugs of any kind. He wished me good luck and believed he had done all he could do.

Later, the doctors decided to take an MRI and MRA. They found that everything was rather well for a person of my age, and the blood was flowing rather well to my brain. I was told my best bet was Jim Saccomanno; they turned out to be right.

I still have some dizziness when lying down and getting up, but other than that, I'm fine. I am able to spend a full day deadheading shrubs and flowers without falling over, as long as I don't look down or too far up with my head.

Mark's 51st, Julia's 60th birthday

MARK PASSED THE HALFWAY point to 100 when he reached his 51st birthday on April 10, 2004. Julia celebrated her 60th birthday and Laurence his 58th within 16 days, with Frank and I still around to see this happen.

Julia celebrating 60

Mark gave Julia a big 60th birthday party with all her friends from all walks of life at the Holbrooke Hotel. The theme of the party was, "A Woman of Style." The invitation read: Please Dress "In Style"—Hats Encouraged—"Fabulous" Fifties—"Hippie" Sixties—"Swinging" Seventies—"Elegant" Eighties—"Dress Down" Nineties—"Do Your Own Thing" Millennium. And there was her mother, not too steady but still able to wear her pink graduation gown from her high school years before ("WWII" Thirties), with Frank in a "Sports Jacket" of the Forties. And there was Julia wearing the same "Black Gown with Black Umbrella" from the turn of the century that she wore at her 40th birthday, with Mark in an "up to date" black tuxedo.

115

Fun was had by all, by both the men, as well as the women, who were surprised at my being able to wear my high school prom gown 61 years later. The only change had to do with my boobs; they were much smaller now. After the war, a gown made like that went out of fashion, and gowns have never been made like that again.

That spring Laurence and Gloria took a trip to celebrate his 58th and her 68th birthdays, on the respective dates of April 27 and May 3. I can't remember what they did but hope they had a good time.

This family has so many birthdays in the spring that sometimes the parties run together. On May 12, my 82nd birthday was celebrated at Julia's with all the family being there, along with a family pow-wow. I also hit the garden page of *The Union* with a story about my yard. It was headlined, "Grand dame of the garden." For once, something nice was said about the Amarals in the paper.

Mark, Cindy Pickett, Julia, Joe and Pat Pittelkow

Me, Frank, Julia, and Laurence at the Holbrooke, with me
in my high school graduation dress and Julia is in her 40th birthday dress

Then on June 19, we all celebrated Frank's 86th birthday. We were all getting older, but I don't know how much wiser, I'm not sure.

I wrote something to both of the kids on their birthdays, which I'll include here.

116

JULIA THE 60 GAL
HAPPY BIRTHDAY

By LaVonne

Julia had a hard time deciding,
To check into this world.
But when she did, she wasted no time.

She was a tiny little thing,
With a mind of her own.
She struggled for a while to live,
But removing her tonsils took care of that.

At three she took her sand pail and went for a walk,
Through town and up to the sawmill to see her dad.
The men shut the mill down to get her dad's attention and it did.

She went through grammar school in a breeze.
With high school no trouble, and plenty of boys to spare.
With a new Pontiac for graduation,
With the car door open, she backed into a pine tree.

Off to Holy Names, four years for learning.
With a boys' school just down the road,
No time for boredom, for plenty of them around.

Out of college and now to fly the coop.
Sales clerk for a time, but not for long.
Then off to fly with World, for a while.

She changed her career to real estate.
Won her first million-plaque award.
And traveled without fear, on the lean, all over the world,
With a bag of clothes, a tent, peanut butter and bread.

Along the line, she gained a plane.
Bought a house or two or maybe three or more.
Traveling became a lodge, steak, and wine.
With real estate being still her game.

She became 40, with we, no hopes of a man in sight.
Her folks gave her a party, thinking that was it.
She dressed all in black, with an umbrella and a feather stole,
And danced the night with a shining Mister Tin Man tall.

There were lots of changes, along with ups and downs.
Going and taking trips, along with her parents to China.

Still flying, making a living, along with taking on the family projects.
Mark came along, and her acoustic neuroma surgery.

Mark learned to fly her plane, then came wedding bells.
While traveling now first class, champagne and all.
In time, she came back to be near the coop,
To take care of her parents in their feeble years.

May the 60s bring you and Mark much pleasure,
With a new house now in line.
Happy Birthday Julia, and many more to come.

Thank you Julia, for your love and care.
May the Lord walk with you both always.

Your mother, who loves you very much from the heart.

HAPPY BIRTHDAY LAURENCE

By LaVonne

58 happy years.
Not too bad at taking your time,
With ten days at the most.
A big, cuddly baby that is for sure.

You outgrew the size of your sister in a very short time.
Carried you both everywhere I went.
Never much trouble, content as could be.
Entertained yourself in the yard by the hours.

Entered grammar school, that was a struggle.
Reading was hard but math was a cinch.
Struggled to breathe and swallow, until tonsils came out.
Well-liked fella, by everyone in class.
Grew taller than most at St. Mary's including the high school.

Was expected much because of your size.
Ended up being Mother's right-hand man.
Grew up around women and Sisters, no Dad around.

Off to Bellarmine to be around men.
Only to have Dad come home to stay.
Had a little trouble with a few cans of beer.
Paid the price, home in the early senior year.
Off to USF College before it was time.
Had a lot of fun, learned bridge and cards.
Spent some time at Sierra College.
Worked at the sawmill for Dad for a while.
Picked up a girlfriend or two.
Back to USF to finish on time.

Out of school with a government job in line.
Flew the coop away from Mom.
Off to Alaska for a few years of knowledge.
Along with a fling with a broad or two.
Hard of hearing that we did not know, found out later.

Dad was told by friends to bring you home,
Government jobs would spoil him good.
So home to the coop and work in real estate for Dad.
With Deer Creek Park his training ground.

He did a good job, no doubt about that.
Had decided that life alone was not too good.
So after a few dates here and there,
He found what he liked, Gloria, family and all.
Married and brought them home to Deer Creek Park.

May ending your fifties and going into your sixties,
Bring you both much happiness.

Thank you Laurence, for all your love and caring.
May the Lord walk with you always.

Your Mother, who loves you very much and from the heart.

Working in the yard, spring 2004

IN SPRING 2004, I was deadheading all the spring shrubs getting things ready for Music in the Mountains. They would be in our yard again on June 6 to start the opening of the summer concerts. There was also Frank's 86th birthday on June 19 to celebrate. What made it especially nice was that we were still able to enjoy what was going on around us. The new gate finally got finished, and we were enjoying it more than we thought we would. It added the finishing touch to the yard, which had recovered nicely from the tree damage.

Music in the Mountains starting off the 2004 concert season at 211 Reward St.

Bev Erickson came over and made a videotape of the yard, a nice memento to take with us in case we have to leave this place before our time.

Family life in general, 2004

IN JULY 2004, THE war in Iraq was still going on. I continued having dizzy spells, along with vertigo. The doctors had done a good job of scaring me off from having a chiropractic treatment, so I didn't go see Dr. Greenlee. But after he checked my MRI and MRA, he called me to come down to see him. It turned out I was out in three places in my neck. After a treatment, the vertigo went away, but it comes back when I need an adjustment.

Most of the time when I was off balance, I believe it was caused by the Coreg pill that I take for my heart. Otherwise, I was doing fine, except for the pain I had been having behind my upper right ear that had been there for so many years. Nothing had ever been found to take care of it. I had come to accept it and had given up telling the doctors about it. I simply used ice packs when it got too bad.

Frank was coming along fine—now that he had gotten rid of the side effects from those worthless sleeping pills. At least he stayed in bed, even though he didn't sleep very well. But that was OK, neither did I, and I guess in our old age that just comes with the territory. Frank was even feeling good enough to get out and play in a golf tournament at Alta Sierra Country Club with Brad and Laurence. They had a really good time together.

Brad, Frank, and Laurence enjoying a game of golf

Julia and Mark's Africa trip and new home

IN JULY 2004, JULIA and Mark made a six-week trip to Africa. While they were there, they were in a small airplane crash that totaled the plane at Kayo near Buhoma in Bwindi. Fortunately, no one was hurt. The crash made the local paper, the *New Vision,* Aug. 19, 2004. The story in the paper said the tourists went on to track the endangered mountain gorillas. An African pilot was flying the plane; let's hope he didn't lose his job.

At the time, they were on their way to see the Kellermanns. While visiting with them, Julia became a godmother to a Catholic African baby girl whose father was the cook for the Kellermanns. Julia intended to set the man up in the chicken business. He planned to call it the Julianna Farm, named after the little girl's name, Julianna. He had already bought enough ground to build a home on it and enough room to raise 100 chickens. So let's hope that helped him get started toward a future.

When Julia and Mark got back, they started building their new home. It would take the builders a year to finish it. In the meantime, they stayed in the little gardener's cottage at our place.

Laurence and Gloria fixing up the stump dump

GLORIA AND LAURENCE ADDED a new addition to their yard and put in a great big new rock wall down where the stump dump is. They included a nice-sized wine cellar and put in a storage place in this area for his yard equipment. It is inserted into the bank wall on the lower level of their lot. On top of the two built-in buildings, they put a nice patio with walkways going all through the area and incorporated it into the rest of the landscape on the hillside. It looks over toward Highway 20 and Harmony Ridge.

Laurence and Gloria hosted Brad and Lisa's wedding in this area of the yard on Sept. 25, 2004. They really outdid themselves, especially with the yard and all its lights. It made it a very nice evening for the kids' wedding. Dancing took place after dinner. Frank was given the garter; I was given the bridal bouquet. Instead of throwing it over their shoulder, they gave it to the oldest married couple dancing. We got it by having been married 62 years.

Frank, me, Lisa, Brad, Gloria, Laurence, Gloria's mother Celeste, and Spence

We loved it, and it was nice to receive the recognition. I dried the bouquet, put it in a box, and gave it to Lisa to keep.

Frank and our health

ON OCT. 27, 2004, I had all the kids over for Gloria and Laurence's anniversary dinner. I had fixed a lot of spareribs and put a real good spicy sauce on them, or so I thought. But what I actually ended up doing was filling up Frank with too much sodium, and later during the night, he couldn't breathe. I took him to the hospital around 2:30 in the morning.

By 4 a.m., the doctors told me to go home and get some sleep. They said Frank would be all right, but he would be in the hospital for at least two days. So I drove home and went back to bed.

I didn't call the kids right away. Instead, I waited until around eight in the morning to tell them what had happened. The end result was that Frank was full of fluid. After it had been removed, he got better and could breathe. Since then we've had to watch his sodium intake and he seems to be fine. Along with the pills to remove the fluid, he had to keep his weight down.

If he gained four pounds, he was required to take two extra pills. He ended up doing fine under that regimen as long as he followed orders. I also raised his side of the bed, which helped him sleep.

Other than this, Frank and I were in good health for our age. I still had the dizzy spells, but they were on the mild side. You might call it floating, and they usually occurred when I got up from lying down. With the help of a good chiropractor, it was something I could live with.

Frank still had his prostate problems that he handled very well. And he now had a new pair of hearing aids so he could hear me a little better. He even laughed occasionally at what the deacon said in church on Sunday, rather than falling asleep during the service. As long as he kept his ears clean of wax and the hearing aids clean, I knew he could hear what was going on.

I was hoping he would be much happier being able to hear again. His only problem now was he was still learning how to put them in his ears.

November 24, election time

THE ELECTION SEASON IN November 2004 was rather ugly, with all the news media being so one sided. I sure hoped that President Bush would come out ahead, if for no other reason than to help keep our moral at a higher level, and to help the Iraqi people establish their freedom.

In fact, he did win reelection, and I thank the Lord for that. You must never cave in when it comes to a war. If you do, you have another Vietnam, and later another war to finish what did not get finished in the first go-around. And by that time the enemy has come to see you as a weak.

We had definitely become to be seen as that to the enemy aggressor under President Clinton's term. To live the way we live in the United States will always be the envy of other countries. To do the right thing, you may have to be the aggressor, and in a bully's world, you become a person to be respected, regardless of being liked. All we have to do is think about what Jesus went through.

Thanksgiving 2004

JULIA AND MARK CELEBRATED Thanksgiving 2004 a few days early for the Amarals, for they wanted to go to Hawaii with Mark's family, who were spending a week there during the holiday to be together as a family. While at their place, we took a drive over to see Mark and Julia's new house and went all through it. We really liked the view, but I thought it was going to be on the windy side when the wind came up. They really had a nice site and a good layout plan for the house. I believe all the Strates left for Hawaii the next day.

Gloria and Laurence had us over to their place on Thanksgiving Day. We had a very nice dinner with some of their friends, and we got to see some of the Christmas lights.

Christmas tree decorating, 2004

ON DEC. 5, 2004, our kids came over around two in the afternoon to help put up the Christmas tree. Laurence and Mark put up all the lights, and Gloria made sure all the strings and bulbs were working right. After the lights were all on, we started the ornaments.

Frank got into the season spirit by hanging the ornaments he liked where he liked them. Not one of us was going to tell him differently. We were having a good time together, with Julia decorating the top two feet of the nine-foot-tall tree. I let her go up the ladder to reach the top of the tree. With my not-too-stable head, it was better for me to hand her the ornaments to decorate the top of the tree. Around 4 p.m., Brad and his new wife, Lisa, came to help finish the job, and along the way, Spence arrived to finish up the hors d'oeuvres.

Once the top of the tree was done, I left and went into the kitchen to work on my dinner. We always have our Christmas dinner right after the tree is decorated. As I've said before, this frees everyone up to be with other sides of the families on Christmas Day. After what had happened several years back with our tree falling over, it's a real gift just getting help putting the tree up.

I had the dining room table set up in Christmas colors and served a nice dinner. We had mashed potatoes, and somehow I managed to get a serving fork stuck in the eggbeaters. I was lucky the job was finished, and so too was the eggbeater. Then I forgot to get the gravy started, so I ended up using more butter. Otherwise, the evening was a great success. After dinner, we went back to the living room to enjoy the tree. It was rather off balance with ornaments more on one side of the tree, but we all liked it anyway, and no one was ready to leave to go home.

After everyone had gone home, Frank and I did the dishes, cleaned up the dining room, and then went off to bed. We were both rather tired by this time.

Another dizzy spell

I WAS STILL HAVING trouble with being off balance. The problem had now been with me for about a year leading from one thing into another. A few days before decorating the Christmas tree, I had gone to see Dr. Newsom for some help with hemorrhoid trouble; otherwise, all was fine, except for feeling off balance. Whenever I lay down and got up, it would occur for a short time, and it happened if I looked up too high. Dr. Newsom was unable to find out why I had this trouble, so she told me to go see if I could get some help from a physical therapist. After she had finished the examination, she said, "I want you to have the flu shot," which she gave to me. This year, due to the vaccination shortage, the flu shot was only being given to at-risk people, mostly those in their seventies and older.

A few minutes, after getting the shot, I left the doctor's office feeling fine. I was walking down the sidewalk when I suddenly passed out cold and landed on the lawn next to the sidewalk. I wasn't out long and wondered what had happened to me. I thought, "Could it have been the flu shot that had done it?" There were two gardeners working in the area. They came right over and told me not to move while they went to get help. I was able to tell them who my doctor was and said I had just had a flu shot, thinking that might be what caused it.

They got the doctor right away. Within minutes, several people, along with Dr. Newsom and dear Maggie, were there to put me in a wheelchair. They did this after checking me over to make sure I hadn't broken any bones or suffered a head injury. They took me back to her office to be rechecked to see if they could find what went wrong.

They gave me all kinds of tests and an EKG. All was fine, and I even had the same blood count I'd had 10 minutes earlier. The doctor told me to get a tilt table test at the hospital to rule out anything, only to find out I had to wait until Feb. 1 for an appointment. After an hour, they called Julia to come get me. I went home and was fine by nighttime, other than that off-balance or light-headedness thing, which I had sort of felt I might have to live with the rest of my life, along with the pain I've had for years behind my upper right ear.

I kept thinking, "What if I had gotten in the car and was driving home?" I definitely would have had an accident. And that thought really got me to thinking.

On Dec. 8, about four in the morning, I got up to go to the bathroom and was fine, other than being a little off-balance. I went back to bed to lie down; then I felt the whole world go around for about 10 minutes. I remember thinking that the vertigo might be back again, but then maybe it was my heart acting up. I remained still for a while and told myself to go to sleep, and if I had vertigo I would go see Dr. Greenlee in the morning.

When I woke up and rolled over at 7 a.m. to shut off the alarm, I no longer had any dizziness or feeling of being off-balance. I got out of bed fine, and the pain I'd had behind my right ear for so many years was gone. Since then I have been back to having no problems with my head, other than the arthritis in my neck. Maybe passing out on the lawn started something new happening inside my system, or maybe my prayers were answered.

I visited the physical therapist five days later and told her I was fine. She gave me some exercises to do and said the balance in my inner ear may have gone back to normal. She said something like, "We have crystals in the inner ear and sometimes they get off balance." That could be what had happened to me years ago and they finally moved back into place.

So I continued moving forward in life, hoping to end this year with my head in working order after all these years. And during the process of everything going on during the past two weeks, I lost 210 pages of Frank's story I'd been working on recently. This was material in an earlier draft of this book that I decided to organize as "Book Three" on the computer. Fortunately, I was lucky enough to have had most of it in print. I could just type it back into the computer. I was hoping to have the first draft of his whole story done by Christmas 2004, but no such luck.

At this time, I was aiming to finish the book before the end of July 2005, six years after having started writing it in 1999.

Winnie Sanchez passes away

ON DEC. 12, 2004, Gloria's mother, Winnie, who had been in failing health for several years and was living at a nice rest home, peacefully passed away just short of 90 years old.

Two days earlier, Winnie was drinking milk with a straw with the help of a nurse holding the glass, and Laurence was there and asked her how her milk was. Her reply was, "Dried up, how is yours?" That was the last bit of humor she said.

When I saw her the next two days, she was no longer responding and was very quiet and still. Gloria had taken very good care of her mother all through the years, along with Laurence's help. I'm sure it was a relief that she had passed on, even though they would both miss her.

Gloria gave her mother a 90th birthday party on her birth date as a farewell, rather than having memorial services for her. All relatives and close friends were invited. It was held at the Chinese restaurant where Winnie had celebrated her 89th birthday party a year earlier.

We had a very nice time, and some people talked about things they had done with Winnie. My talk was about how she wanted to go back to the Catholic Church and wanted to know how to do it. I think I told her to call the church and ask to speak to a priest and see if he would come to her apartment, which he did. After talking with her and hearing her confession, she was reinstated. Julia took Communion to her many times and I did it when Julia was not available.

My sister LaVena

IN 2004, MY SISTER LaVena was in the same condition with her health, just thinner. She still couldn't talk and one wondered how much she retained in her mind, but she did move about and still lived with her daughter Barbara.

Barbara's daughter and granddaughter were hit side-on in an auto accident the night before Christmas. They had to have many adjustments done on their necks, but otherwise they came out all right. So that household had its hands full most of the time.

Around this time, Elmer, the husband to my sister Helena's daughter Patty, went into the hospital in Chico to treat a heart problem, only to find out he had one artery almost fully blocked at 95% and two others were at 85% in his neck. After five days, he was doing fine and went home. He would have the remaining arteries cleared in three weeks after the holidays were over. Patty's remark was that Elmer was feeling his oats for the first time in a long time. He later did have the rest of the surgery and was doing fine. The rest of my relatives were also doing fine.

Christmas season 2004

IN THE HOLIDAY SEASON of 2004, I was running out of time sending letters to all the relatives, which is one of the things I like to do. This year, it ended up being the same letter for everyone. I prefer to write each person a note, but I was trying to get this book in order and was sort of having fun seeing what I could do with it. But between my stiff fingers hitting the wrong keys, the spelling, and not knowing much about a computer, I got myself into a lot of trouble. I had to call on someone to help me out of my mistakes, which was not always convenient.

Now that Jonix, the local computer man, had moved to Oregon, I was calling upon my family to help. Julia ended up helping me whenever she had the time, and when Mark would drop by, he would say, "Need any help?" He said they would help me get the job done, so I didn't feel quite so bad when I had to call upon them.

All four of the kids were into helping with different charities and raising money for them. Laurence asked us if we would do for Hospice what we had done for M.I.M., and we said yes. He would have to give $15,000 and the Amaral Family Trust would give $85,000.

I don't know all the different charitable organizations the four of them were involved with. I know that Julia and Mark were involved with Music in the Mountains, Foothill Theatre, CABPRO, Adopted Children, and church groups. They also helped on acoustic neuroma fundraising for research work. They were involved with a lot of other things, but I don't know what they were. Laurence and Gloria were keeping very busy with Hospice in the Foothills, the Silver Ball fundraiser, Starry Starry Night, Rotary, and many other organizations that we are not involved in. Both men really worked hard when it came to putting up props, and so on, to help raise money. I had also told Hospice they could use the yard for fundraising or for a "Thank you" party for a select group if they wanted to. I told CABPRO they could do the same.

We hadn't done any traveling this year, thinking it safer for us to stay at home. Frank continued to play the puts and calls, take his daily walks, and, between reading and catnapping, had a relaxed day. He didn't complain as much about not sleeping at night; he would just get up and spend some time reading and then go back to bed.

Christmas Day was spent at Julia and Mark's place with all his family there for a couple of days. We had their white Christmas dinner on Christmas Eve, and later they opened their gifts. At the time, Curt, Mark's dad, was having trouble with the food he was eating. He felt something was wrong and he was going to see a doctor after they got home. The next day we were over again after Mark's sisters and family had left to go home. Laurence and Gloria came over for a few hours in the afternoon, and that evening we had a crab feed with Curt and Kay.

Gloria and Laurence spent Christmas Eve at their home with their family and friends. Their home and yard are always busy this time of year, with the yard so beautifully decorated with so many lights. As I've said earlier, people come from all over to see the lights. They also get to visit with "Eddie the Elf," who is there to talk to the kids. If timed right, Santa is there to meet with the young kids and pass out candy canes.

Dec. 26, 2004 — A 9.0 earthquake in the Indian Ocean

ON DEC. 26, 2004, a tsunami with waves up to 100 feet tall hit 11 countries along the Indian Ocean, with Sri Lanka and Indonesia being hit the worst. The tsunami killed more than 230,000 people; their bodies were washed back onto the beaches in piles. Debris from destroyed buildings, electrical wires and poles, waterlines, communication wires, toilets, bathtubs, stoves, beds — everything that one would have in a home, schools, churches, hotels, or offices — all of it was piled up, along with the bodies. Bodies were even found up in the trees.

The people who survived were devastated and needed water and food. Everything was contaminated with the ocean's salt water, spilled oil, and sewage. One wonders if God was trying to tell us something, for I understand these areas are heavily populated with Muslims, along with some Christians and tourists from all over the world. This was a paradise country to go to for a vacation.

Help was sent from all over the Christian world as soon as planes were available to fly relief aid over to them. And this would be going on for some time. They were still finding bodies a month later. Where were the people who survived going to live? What were they going to do with all the children with no relatives? One thing they were trying to do was get the children into some kind of makeshift school to get them under a roof and among friends who could help take care of them.

It is going to take a long time for this part of the world to get back to normal again, and I doubt it will in my lifetime. I wondered about Bali and all the beautiful parts of that country we'd seen a few years before, for the devastation was along the coastline. But in the end, they were all right.

January 2005 — Mark's parents, Kay and Curt

JAN. 6, 2005, WAS Mark's mother Kay's birthday, and on this day she was informed that her husband had pancreatic cancer two inches in diameter, plus two spots on his liver. The doctor gave him six months to live. A day later, they found out he had even less time, and Kay brought Hospice into the picture. A day or so after that, on a Friday afternoon, Mark flew to the Los Angeles area to see if he could help in any way, such as helping to get all the paperwork in order and to meet with any lawyers if needed. Curt's condition was a shock to all of them and us.

Julia stayed with us that night. Mark called Julia the next morning and told her to fly down that day, for it looked like Curt might not make it through the next few days. So she did, and by Sunday, the rest of their family had gone down to be with them. Julia stayed as long as her help was needed. Then on Monday, Curt took a turn for the better and could keep some food down, so Julia and Mark came home that night. By this time, the original shock had worn off, and they had accepted what was facing them in the next few weeks or months ahead.

Just over a month ago, Curt, at age 70, had had all his family in Hawaii for a week to celebrate Thanksgiving. Three or so weeks later, they all went to Mark and Julia's for Christmas for a few days. Everyone had a good time, even if Curt looked like he was losing weight. The doctor had just given him a clean bill of health, or so he thought. Without knowing what was going on, they all had a good time making all the different kinds of white foods for their traditional Christmas Eve white dinner, something that even Frank and I had gotten to like.

While making the rice in a double boiler, it exploded and went all over the stove area in the kitchen, including the cabinets, floor, and ceiling, but luck was with them. No one was standing near the stove. It took about three hours with all of them working together to clean up the mess, and Curt was right in there doing his job, cleaning the ceiling by standing up on a ladder. By the time we got there, everything was well in order, even if they were all tired and worn out.

We all went to see how Julia and Mark's new house was progressing. We decided it would not be done in time for Christmas the following year, at least not with a tree up and decorated. Later that night was the opening of gifts and watching Chelsea, the only grandchild, open hers. There would be good memories for everyone. Sometime on Christmas Day, the two daughters and husbands and Chelsea left to go home. But the Amaral side of the family, with Laurence and Gloria, stopped by for the afternoon. We all took another trip to the new house, for Laurence and Gloria hadn't seen it in its latest stage. That evening, Frank and I stayed on for the crab feed we have on Christmas Day with Julia, Mark, and his parents almost every year. Curt ate other food this year, knowing the crab food would not stay down. Early the next morning, Curt and Kay left for their home in the Dana Point area, having good weather, which we'd had all throughout the holiday.

It was a few days after his parents got home in Dana Point that they got the bad news about the cancer.

Repair work in the house

NOW THAT I HAD lost the pain in my head, I decided to do some house repair. I had the floor in Julia's bathroom replaced and put in 1-foot-square tiles that blended in with the tile on the walls, sink, and shower. And I had a sealer put on the old tile to prevent the grout from mildewing. I also replaced the showerhead so it would put out more water. The job turned out nice. I hired the son of Sam Ramie, who had done the first tile work, to do the job. The tile was just as it was the day he put it in back in the late 1960s. I still had some things to do in our bathroom, but that would have to wait until I was sure what to do with the mildew behind the tile in my bathroom.

I had Julio retouch some of the windows and scars that had been done by housekeepers over the years. I then ordered new sheer curtains to replace all the old ones that could no longer be dry-cleaned. I had automatic outside shade screens put up on the windows in the kitchen area of the house to cut out the summer sun, and I replaced 15 windowpanes that had picked up moisture between the panes due to age. I also replaced two sets of windows in Frank's office and repaired leaks in the roof of the garage. My next project was replacing the old carpet in Julia and Laurence's bedrooms, the closets, and the hallways.

The cleaning people had accidentally ruined a few pieces of furniture, and the china cabinet would have to be stripped and redone. The cleaning girls had done something to the varnish. I had several people look at it and say it couldn't be polished out. So that would cost their boss some money; she had agreed to take care of it. She also said she couldn't afford the girls working at my house, and I agreed with her, for I couldn't afford them either. So I have since replaced them. The rest of the repairs I would have to have done on my own, for I didn't want a sloppy repair job done.

Music in the Mountains had already asked for the yard for the first week of June for their annual fundraiser, so I had my work cut out for me. Now I hoped my head continued to be in good operation. I had some bad spots in the lawn, so I took care of them, hoping the new seed would come up and the lawn would look nice for the party.

2005 — elections here and in Iraq

THE 2004 PRESIDENTIAL ELECTION came out with President George Bush winning his second term, and the Democrats were having a hard time accepting it. Back when they were in power, we were in their shoes, and I don't remember feeling too bad about it, other than when Clinton was president and I didn't like how he lowered the morals of our country. So the country is a little divided right now, largely because the Democrats lost. Rather than looking at what we could do to make things work right and what was best for our country, the question became, "What is best for the party?" That should have been a concern for everybody.

The Iraqi people held their election on Jan. 30, 2005. This was another historic event to have taken place during my lifetime. Now let's hope their budding democracy will work so that people can have their freedom and be able to think and choose whom they want in power without being killed.

The tilt table test

ON FEB. 1, 2005, I finally got my appointment to take the tilt table test at the hospital. Dr. Mallery was there to watch what was going on, along with Tom, who was in charge of the neurocardiac department. He was kind enough to try to explain everything to me and said, "We are going to make you pass out." I had lain for 20 minutes strapped down to a table that was then tilted up with me on it. The straps were needed to keep me from falling if I happened to pass out. There were monitors of some kind taped to my body so they could record my heartbeat and my pulse, I think.

After the 20 minutes were up, Dr. Mallery tilted me into a standing position. He had me open my mouth, and then he sprayed a strong dosage of what I think was nitroglycerin into my mouth. I soon had trouble swallowing and talking. Then came the blurry eyes, and somewhere along the way, I momentarily passed out. It must have been at that time that they put the table back to a lying position, for when I came to I was lying down. He said it took me eight minutes to pass out and they had expected it to happen sooner. My blood pressure went to 50. It took me at least 10 minutes to get my bearings back so I could dress and have Frank bring me home.

It wasn't until a couple of hours of being at home that I felt all right again.

The test lasted about an hour and a half, and after an hour, Frank came looking for me. He was in the room as I came out of the short relapse. The result was that I had had this problem all my life, and it had been the main source of all my problems all those years. My reaction was, "Why had it taken about 70 years for them to find it out?" With all the tests I had been through, why hadn't anyone done a tilt table test on me before?

They told me I would continue to have the dizziness for the rest of my life, and now that they knew what I had, they could work on finding the right medicine. One thing was for sure, I wouldn't die from it, and it would likely happen more often in my later years. It was around this time that Dr. Mallery said, "I changed my mind, I've upped the 10 years to 15 more years that you will live," and I said, "Who wants to live to be over 100?"

What I have is called "neurocardiac syncope." And what could I do for it? Drink lots of water, avoid standing for a long time, and sit or lie down when dizzy. Walking is fine, and I need to control stress. (That last one is my biggest problem.) I was told to consider medication and to not golf in hot weather, but wait for evening. Shots of any kind can trigger it, which is what happened at Dr. Newsom's office after she had given me the flu shot. I needed to avoid taking water pills. When my legs swell, it means they are filling up with fluid, which means the blood is not getting to the brain, thus vertigo is part of it. Also, my heart was fine. It's what is happening around it that makes it contract and expand. I learned that this problem does not show up on an MRA or MRI test, and I have had many of those throughout the years for this very problem.

Now I knew what has been wrong with my head all these years, and knowing this would make a big difference in how I handled it from now on. I asked about driving. They said, "No problem, for you know when it comes on," and that part was true. I never drive if I don't feel good, and when sitting down I never have any problems with it.

As I've said, Frank was with me the last half-hour of the test, so he got to hear everything the doctors said. Now, how was Frank? He was doing fine since he got off all the sleeping pills, and as he said, he slept the same without them as he did with them. And now that he was off them, he was a different person and much happier during the day. He took his walk almost every day if the weather permitted, even if I didn't go with him. He saw Dr. Callahan and was told he was doing well enough that he could wait three months before seeing him again, unless a problem came up. And his blood pressure was fine.

And we now hoped that Curt was doing well enough to try chemotherapy, for he had gained six pounds in the past week and was able to keep food down.

Julia and Mark's house in escrow

FOR THE PAST SEVERAL years, Mark and Julia have been living in their home next to the airport on Loma Rica Drive, in the Wawona Madrona subdivision. They are now building their dream house at the end of the subdivision. Their new home site has a spectacular view of the mountains. The view is breathtaking!

We had known all along that there was a chance Mark and Julia would have to move out of the house they were selling before their new place was completed. And that's what ended up happening—they had to move out nine months before their new house was ready to move into. It was now time for Mark and Julia to figure out where to move all the things they would need for the next nine months.

They came up with a plan, which they ended up going with. They would set up camp in the gardener's cottage at our place. All their clothes would go into our spare bedroom and be hung on racks. Our basement, which would be used for storage, had already started filling up with boxes. And Julia planned to move some of her office equipment into Frank's office. Mark's office equipment would go into a room at one of Terra Alta's buildings, which I think is called Mohawk. The rest of their household would go into storage. It must be interesting for them, going from a 6,000-square-foot home to about a 600-square-foot cottage.

Julia and Mark have named their new home *Nyumbani*, which I think means *My Home* or *At Home*. It is a Swahili name.

March, April 2005 — things happening in our life

IN SPRING 2005, FRANK and I were holding our own very well for our age. He had a PSA test result of 79.01 in March, which wasn't too good, but we'd wait for another test in a month before we were sure if anything had gone wrong. I was in the best of health in many years, although I had trouble with my hemorrhoids, but I hoped that could be taken care of soon. The kids were doing fine—keeping busy with social life and taking care of their businesses. Mark's father was not doing well from his pancreatic cancer, and after three months of troubles, it looked like we might be losing him in a few days. He decided in his mind he would be gone the week after Easter, but a week later, he was still with us, so God still wanted him around.

Frank, Spence, and I spent our last Easter Sunday at Mark and Julia's old home by the airport, which was now in escrow. Laurence and Gloria were with friends in Washington for the holidays. Through the years, we have had many holidays together, so we sort of missed them not being with us this time. But we still colored Easter eggs and had our Easter egg hunt.

Frank continued to walk about a mile each day, and I joined him at times. He had no trouble walking downtown, but he had trouble walking back, for it is all uphill. He got out of breath and had to stop, whereas I could move right along. But we'd stop to give him some rest. It was about two miles and was a hike I liked to make. So when he decided to go to town, I liked to go with him and take the cell phone, just in case we needed it. He enjoyed living so close to everything and walked to the store to get the groceries. He still played the market and enjoyed doing the puts and calls.

Late in March one evening, I received a phone call from my nephew, Raymond Evenson, who lives in Campbell, California. He said he had just received a call from a person by the name of Agnes Evenson. She wondered if he might be related to her. I think he said she had found his name in the telephone book. They got to talking. She said her father was Art and that he lived at Laurel, Montana, but he had died a few years back. She also said her aunt Aggie, who lived in Red Bluff, California, had also died in the past couple of years.

She told him her mother was Jane Hurley. Raymond finally told her he did not know if they were related, but he said he would call me to find out and would let her know right away. So he called me and told me about the conversation they had. As soon as he said Jane Hurley, I said, "Yes, you are related." I told him he had seen her father at the family reunion in Minnesota and had talked to him, and that he was the brother to Evie, whom he had spent a lot of time getting the Evenson history from. Also, she was the first of six children. I told him I was in the process of getting the family tree done, and as soon as I did, I would send it to him. I found it strange that this would happen after all these years.

I had a picture of Jane and me taken in Minnesota back around 1933, so I decided to make a copy of it for him to give to her. (see photo, 1-44.)

Things happening in 2005

AS I WAS WRITING this in spring 2005, the final major thing happening in the world around us at the time was the death of Pope John Paul II at the Vatican in Rome. Closer to home, Mark's father, Curtis, passed away on April 8. Julia had her 61st birthday on April 10, which was sort of bad timing, but, of course, she couldn't really help it. Laurence turned 59 on April 27, and on May 3, Gloria turned 69. I turned 83 on May 12, and Frank's 87th birthday was around the corner on June 19. And we now had a new Pope called Pope Benedict the XVI.

On the beautiful spring day I wrote this section of the book, if you had come into the yard of our house at 211 Reward St., you would have seen the red leaf maple trees, the white and pink dogwood trees, and the camellias in full bloom. The rhododendrons, ex-berry trees, and azaleas were just starting to go into full color. The tulips, daffodils, grape hyacinth, and all the other spring bulbs were still showing good color. The lilies of the valley that have been in the same spot for more than 70 years, before we moved here, were just beginning to show color, along with all the other spring flowers, and then there were those ever-so-green lawns that I am known for having.

The rhododendrons and azaleas in May 2005

On June 5, Music in the Mountains was here again for its annual fundraiser. The yard was in really good shape. I noticed that people enjoyed the yard more each year. Now that they knew the area, they started roaming around the yard more, looking at different things. And the lawns always capture the men's attention. The tennis court ended up being the place where all the goodies were served, with all the colorful tablecloths on small tables with chairs set around the area. The banquet tables were full of lots of goodies that Desmond Galagher always saw to. And again, they used the cottage to heat different finger foods.

The oldest and largest rhododendron at our place

Victor worked hard to get the yard in shape. He and his family had planned to take a vacation that week, so he wasn't there the day of the party, but the weather held out for us, which meant no major cleanup was needed this year. And I was in very good health to carry on what needed to be done.

On June 19, Frank, very much alive and in good spirits, celebrated his 87th birthday. He was in fair health. A few months later, Dr. Harris gave us our warning that Frank had six months to a year or two at the most to live. His PSA had climbed to 217. It was at this time that Frank decided to give Foothill Theatre a generous gift while he could enjoy the fun of giving. They turned it into a matching gift and received the money in a very short time.

Later, Frank gave a very large and generous donation on a matching fund to the Sierra Memorial Hospital Foundation for the new Diagnostic Imaging Center. The plan was to give 20% of the total gift at the time, 60% in 2006, and the remaining 20% in 2007, unless more matching money came in sooner, which it did. However, when we got the news about Frank's PSA, he decided to finish the donation in its entirety in 2006.

About this time, in June, Julia and Mark moved into the cottage at 211 Reward St. It took awhile for them to adjust living in such a small space. But after a short time, they decided it was great, since there was no work to keeping the place up. The cottage has a washer and dryer, along with a refrigerator and an electric stove; but, as they said, it was on the cheap side, and they were right.

A quiet Thanksgiving and anniversary, Christmas 2005

IN NOVEMBER 2005, WE spent a quiet Thanksgiving and wedding anniversary with our family. After that we went into getting ready to put the tree up the first week in December, with the family there to help. Brad and Lisa could not make it, but Spence arrived in time for dinner. I had lots of different kinds of finger foods to eat while putting up the tree.

Frank and me with our Christmas tree

That year we had a soup dinner, with Gloria and Julia making different kinds of soups. We enjoyed eating it in the living room, wherever we could find space between the tree trimmings and so on; and, of course, we also had dessert. As the girls said, there were not too many dishes to do afterwards, which was nice. We finished decorating the tree and enjoyed our evening together.

I had 10 people in for a sit-down dinner during the holiday season. They were also here to enjoy the family's handiwork with the Christmas tree. And that year, it was one of the straightest trees I'd ever had. So I had Julia take a picture of Frank and me standing beside it. I thought I might use it as a Christmas card the following year.

This year, Julia said she and Mark had never spent Christmas with her side of the family in all the years they had been married, so she made a point to see to it that the whole family was together this year. This was very nice. Julia and Mark left a few days before Christmas to go up to his sister's place in Washington to be with all his family for a few days. They stayed there until the day before Christmas and then flew home to be with us on Christmas Eve at Gloria and Laurence's place. This was Kay and her family's first Christmas without Curt.

On Christmas Eve, we all had a very good time visiting and enjoyed a wonderful dinner. The whole family was there. After dinner, their family opened gifts and we stayed until around 11 p.m. When we left, they were still going strong on opening gifts and guessing what was inside the wrapping.

Julia and Mark went to church with us the next morning. Crabs were not available, so we had a small turkey dinner.

Another tree went down

The tree that fell by Frank's office

ON JAN. 1, 2006, having had a very wet rainy season, a wind came up and blew over the cedar tree by Frank's office. It fell in the direction of our neighbor's house, the Painters', but in so doing, it got caught up in another tree of ours and one of theirs. This kept it from falling into their house and damaging their home. The result was we had to have all three trees removed, the stumps ground up, and a property-line fence replaced. Along with that went the big camellia and rhodies that were along the property line. The flower area between the house and office had really taken the brunt of it. When the cedar tree went over, it raised all the shrubs high up off the ground, along with all the tree roots. Some were eight feet off the ground, and the rock wall was badly damaged.

This raised a lot of commotion in the area, for again more trees from our place had fallen. I was hoping this would be the end of all these falling trees. Not being one to spend much time waiting before getting things done, Mark and Julia, who were living in the cottage, heard the tree fall and called the fire department. They came out and told Julia and Mark what had to be done. Frank and I had gone to a New Year's Day party at Bev and Bill Riddle's place; we found out about the tree after we got home at 4 p.m. We drove up to our place and saw all the lights on in the yard and a lot of people standing around in the rain.

We had to remove all the files and everything else that could be damaged by water from Frank's office and put them into the house. We put the things in Julia's bedroom off the kitchen, in case the tree fell into the office before being taken down. The Painters had to leave their home for the same reason until the trees were fully down. We also had to pull the power switch to the office, in case of a fire. And this whole time it was raining cats and dogs; it continued this way for several days. As soon as the trees were removed, we put all the things back into the office so that Julia and Frank would be back in business. This took a few days.

In the meantime, Victor dug up all the damaged shrubs with the chipping machine. He stored all the other ones that had been uprooted from the tree roots coming out of the ground. He placed them among the other shrub areas.

The cleanup took a few weeks, but eventually Dave Merrill was able to come in and repair and replace the old wall using the volcanic cinder blocks that I had around the yard. He did this sometime in late February. Victor and I had all the shrubs replaced, and by March, that end of the yard looked like nothing had really happened, but that area of the yard did have a different look to it.

Cottage Life

FRANK AND I TRIED to stay out of Julia and Mark's hair while they were living in the cottage. We wanted them to have their small, temporary home to themselves, and not resent us. One good thing that came out of it though is that anything that needed repair work done to it inside the cottage got done while they were staying in it. They put in a new garbage disposal (there had not been one there) and replaced the handle to the toilet. They had trouble with water backing up due to too small of a pipe that had been put in sometime around 1924. So when the new garbage disposal went in, I had a bigger water line put in from the outside to take care of the problem.

Julia brought in a three-by-five-foot cupboard to store food and dishes. That was an asset to the cottage. They also left their old microwave oven. The kitchen area was now in good shape. In the living room, they left one of their sofas, along with a couple of lamps, small coffee tables, and rocking chairs. They also hooked up the TV.

When they moved into the cottage, they took all of my stuff they didn't want to the thrift store and brought in some of their things. They also replaced the bed with their king-size one. When they moved out and took their good bed with them, we put in a new queen-size bed.

The place was now in good shape, other than needing a paint job. And during this time, I had new covered gutters put on so I wouldn't have to clean them out anymore.

Julia and Mark had us over to the cottage for dinner a couple of times. It was very enjoyable, even if Mark had to cook dinner in such tight quarters. During the summer months, they sometimes had their dinners out on the little rock table in the flower garden by the cottage. This is the table that has the year "1937" inscribed on the pedestal. It was nice seeing that area being used. They would also eat out on the porch, where they had their small, white patio table set. Mark barbecued most of their evening meals outside when they were home. Frank and I had them in a few times for dinner as well. The two of them were busy doing something all the time and they liked to eat later than we did.

Later in the evenings, Julia would work in the office, while Mark watched TV. I spent my time working on this book, and Frank would read. We would then play Hand and Foot before going to bed. During the time Julia and Mark were staying in the cottage, they took a month off to do some traveling. We also had dinners with Laurence and Gloria, both here and at their home and out to dinner.

During this time, as I was taking something down to the cottage for Julia and Mark, I tripped and fell on the cement walkway that had a big crack in it. The crack was about an inch high. I went scooting on my stomach for about 10 feet, hurting my left hand and thumb. Fortunately, I didn't break any bones. So I told myself that was the next project to get going on.

I had Dave replace the rock wall, which would replace the wall to the old walkway. We were having so much rain at the time that it was hard for him to get much of anything done, so it took a few months before it was all finished. I had Creative Curbs do the cement work.

In order to do the job, Dave needed more cinder block, the type made from volcano cinders found in the Skillman Flat area off Highway 20. At the time, there was too much snow to get up in that area, and you can't buy that kind of rock just anywhere. However, work on the project was able to continue. I knew that under our house there were all the old cinder blocks dating back to the early 1920s, so I had Victor and Dave get them out from under the house. Some of it was the old porch and steps that I had painted red to match the brick and walkway back in the 1960s. Dave chiseled off the paint, and the cinder rock was used as the foundation for the walkway wall. By doing this, I was able to maintain the old flavor of this place dating to its beginnings in the 1920s.

When this area was done, I would finish the old walkway going to the cottage from the garage area. The old cement walkways would all need to be replaced. Once completed, they should hold up for another 80 or so years. During this time, I had the work shed, or garage, re-roofed with corrugated green iron sheets. After 80-some-odd years, it was really leaking in the shed. Now I would have to have the side painted green to look fresh to match the roof.

We had two more dinner parties and took care of our old friends that I felt I should entertain while Frank and I could still enjoy having people over. I believe it rained during most of these months, with maybe a few snowflakes along the way. So this was a good time to do some entertaining. We didn't have our children over for these dinner parties, nor do I think they expected to be invited; I really wanted to have friends over whom I hadn't had invited over in a long time.

Julia and Mark move into their new home

JULIA AND MARK'S NEW home was finished in mid-February 2006. They moved out of our small three-room cottage and into their new 5,000-square-foot home. Their place has a wonderful view of the Crystal Range in Desolation Wilderness about 40 miles to the east. These mountains are part of the Sierra Nevada Mountain Range. And at night, you can see the lights of Roseville off to the south. They have done a great job on their home.

I understood that M.I.M. would have a party in Julia and Mark's yard in 2006 and not at 211 Reward St. I welcomed this, for it would give me some real time to get the yard back in shape, along with getting the roofs taken care of.

Before their new house was finished, Julia and Mark had a lot of landscaping done so they would not have all the dirt to deal with later. However, they would still have more work to do, for it's a 10-acre piece of property. Both of our children got the gardening bug from me, and we each have different kinds of landscaping at our homes.

Frank's charity gifts

Frank and me receiving the M.I.M. award
presented to us with a few tears by Paul Perry

FRANK GAVE FOOTHILL THEATRE another donation as a matching gift in 2006. The theatre people hoped to put it into a big fundraising project of $300,000, which would help get the organization into a better future position. And we still owed M.I.M. another installment in May to finish this year's gift.

We received the 2005 Maestros Award in 2006. It was a very nice honor, and we later received an award for being a member between 20–25 years. This was part of M.I.M.'s 25-year celebration.

This year I decided to have a marketing study done by Karen Wood to see what could be done about getting a performing arts center started in the community. She started the study in January; it took until June for it to be completed. It took Frank awhile to come on board with me. We met with Karen every Tuesday for two months, and going into the second month, he said, "When do we have our next meeting?" I noticed that was the first time he used the words "we" and "our." It was interesting to see how the meetings would turn out and to see if the community thought it was worthwhile.

Foothill Theatre receives $50,000 gift

Cash from Amarals helps company to meet $300,000 fundraising goal

BY PAM JUNG
Staff writer

The Foothill Theatre Company in Nevada City received quite a gift in celebrating its 30th anniversary — $50,000 from Frank and Lavonne Amaral, getting the theater company well on its way to meeting its fundraising goal this year.

"We set a goal to raise $300,000 this year and Frank and Lavonne's very generous gift brings us to 40 percent of that goal," said board of directors' president Cheri Flanigan. "We thank them for their won-

derful support of the arts in our community."

Foothill Theatre Company, founded in 1977, has grown through the years in prestige and scope. Today, its $1 million budget helps produce a season of diverse plays, provides student matinees to thousands of students who come from neighboring counties, and continues to produce the Lake Tahoe Shakespeare Festival (at Sand Harbor) and the Sierra Shakespeare Festival (at Grass Valley).

A new venture is Studio

See FOOTHILL A12

Submitted photo

Lavonne and Frank Amaral, left, have presented a $50,000 gift to Foothill Theatre Company's Board President Cheri Flanigan.

Union Newspaper article

Karen interviewed around 70 individual people. This gave us some idea as to where we would spend our money on charity work. For a long time I had thought it would be nice to have a performing arts center that had a music school for children in the area to get a better feeling for music and encourage some to go on to higher learning in music. I also thought it'd be nice to have a real good-sized concert hall that had wonderful acoustics in each room. I asked Karen to have the project completed before the M.I.M. Summer Fest, so people who knew about it could have a chance to talk it over if they wanted to, and she did.

139

This community started during the Gold Rush era, and along with the gold came Lola Montez and her pet bear. She built her home, which is still standing, in Grass Valley. As mentioned earlier in this book, I was told she had danced on the piano that we have in our living room today. It's a Mathushek, number 12456, and was built around 1848. It has a good sounding board. At that time, pianos were painted black ebony. It was still that color but in very bad shape when I bought it for our home sometime around 1953. I had it refinished as it is today. During their heyday, these pianos were very popular, and there were several of them at the historic National Hotel in Nevada City at the time I bought mine. One drawback with these pianos is they don't keep their tune for very long.

Along with the gold mining came families. Some of them built rather nice homes, and the folks became rather well-known people in the community at that time. Many of these homes have been restored.

Nevada City never went through the Great Depression of the 30s. Then in the late 1940s, the federal government decided to shut down gold mining because of the war effort, so the mines were closed. Afterward, this area went into the lumber era, and then in the late 1980s the environmentalists did their job of shutting down the mills. During this time, about 1981, Paul Perry started a music group that later became Music in the Mountains. His group joined other music groups and arts that were already going strong in the area. And as of this writing in 2006, our town is sort of in limbo wondering what to do. We have a large population of rather middle-aged retired people who have some money and enjoy the arts we have here, and they want to be active doing something with their talent and time. Maybe we can make it an active music and arts community for another 100 years so we won't have to go Sacramento or San Francisco for that quality of entertainment.

As of this writing, Karen had appointed a committee to start working on getting different people organized. It was now just a matter of time before things would start moving in the right direction. I'm sure that our children will be on a committee in some capacity, for neither Frank nor I will be. We had already done the major thing, which was laying the groundwork. It is now a matter of getting people who know how to organize this type of project involved, something that will no doubt take awhile to do.

When that happens, I feel I will have left my mark in life with the help of Frank, my children, and God's ever-guiding hand.

Spring of 2006

SPRING 2006 WAS ONE of the most beautiful springs I have ever had in my yard. It started out with a lot of rain. The first crop of camellias started to bloom, holding their flowers going into the next group of shrubs. The azaleas and rhodies were all loaded with many flowers and very few green leaves were showing. Walking through the shrubs, you felt like you were engulfed in many different-colored flowers, and you could really feel their presence. This was true throughout the back and side yard, and we are talking about 50 shrubs or more. And soon all of these would have to be deadheaded.

Carol Hamilton enjoying the garden at a party we had in 2006

Along with this were all the teardrops, daffodils, tulips, irises, and grape hyacinths of which I have many. Then came the tree peonies, the lilies of the valley, and the lilac shrubs. From there, the yard went into the summer flowers. I hoped that the following year they would do it again. I was happy that Frank and I both got to see this wonderful display at least once in our lives.

My yard is always great, but never had it been like that. And as we went into the summer, the roses also outdid themselves. As always, the lawns were looking great.

In June, I had Creative Curbs remove and replace a section of cement in the back patio that was raised from tree damage. However, after it was done, I wasn't too crazy about how the color came out. Now that the cement was down and it was into July, Tom Barney would start doing some repair work on the house. It was necessary to have the work done, but it wouldn't make Frank very happy. I had the roof checked and a paint job done on the house, the cottage, and tool shed (or garage, as I call it). And all the roofs were sprayed with zinc to slow down the growing of moss. There were also things that had to be done inside the house, including our bathroom, but this would be taken care of in the late fall.

Frank really surprised me this year by picking flowers out of the yard, putting them in a vase with water, and giving them to me for my 84th birthday—something he had never done before was pick flowers like this.

Frank and the bouquet
of flowers he picked for me

141

Frank and me in summer 2006

AT THIS POINT, IN summer 2006, Frank had really improved health-wise in many ways since he had given up the sleeping pills; however, his PSA had climbed to 217.32. His doctor gave us a warning on what that meant. Frank had trouble with his legs and got tired more easily when he took his walks. He had to stop and rest several times before finishing his mile walk around the local grammar schools, stopping along the way at SPD to buy some groceries. And I noticed he was experiencing trouble remembering what he had done during the day. He also got a little dizzy at times, but he still read the papers and took care of his puts and calls. He also had more trouble with his hearing, so he lost interest easier.

Health-wise I was feeling much better, mostly because the pain behind my right ear had not returned.

In July, we learned from X-rays that Frank's prostate cancer had spread to the bones of his shoulder, collarbone, the head of his humerus, scapula, and upper ribs; but, at this time, he did not complain about pain. He was still taking his daily walks, but he needed to rest more often along the way. He was still in good humor and didn't seem to let the cancer bother him. He was still getting his PSA shots every three months, and in the evenings, we continued to play Hand and Foot, or some other card game before going to bed around 10:30 p.m. He was still sweating a lot during the night, to the point that we had to change his pajama top four or five times a night; at the same time he still used an electric blanket. As for me, I threw the covers off and put my feet out the bed.

The only thing that really was bothering Frank at this time in life was his lack of memory, which did foul him up at times, but then again, I was having the same trouble. One day he had a date to see Dr. Harris at 11:30 a.m., followed by a luncheon date with Brayton Hahn. Frank had forgotten both appointments, even after I had reminded him in the morning before I left to go do some things. I called home at 11:45 a.m. to see why he wasn't at the doctor's office; I reached him at home eating his lunch. He said he forgot, but he went anyway to get his PSA shot and ended up having pie with Brayton.

CABPRO had a party at Julia and Mark's place to honor Frank. Seventy or so guests showed up, along with all our family and the grandchildren. Julia and Mark had done a great job of setting up the yard, and everyone really enjoyed walking around outside. After an excellent barbecue dinner, time was given for people to say things they remembered back in the earlier years of our life in this community. Some of them shared stories about how badly Frank had been treated by the press and the community, even up to now. All was said in high regards to him, for his honesty and straightforwardness in all his dealings. I gave a little history of his earlier life, and his children had things to say as to what they remembered growing up. Terry McAteer thanked Frank for all the charity work he had done all through his life and in his later years here in this community that would be remembered for many years to come. It was wonderful seeing so many old-timers who had been in and out of our lives all these years.

All that was said gave a rather nice end to Frank's working life. And with the help of Karen Wood, the "Performing Arts Culture Center" had already started to get the ball rolling, which Frank and I were very happy about.

In July, Tom Barney, who has worked for me off and on all through the years as a painter, wallpaper hanger, repairman, electrician, or anything else we needed done in the way of fix-it jobs, started working on all the projects that I had lined up for him a couple of years earlier. He was finally able to come and start working on them, including washing down all the bricks and getting rid of all the moss on the bricks and the shingles on the roofs of the houses. Once the outside projects were finished, he would start work inside the house. However, if the work continued into the fall, he would have to take a break and go do some work he had set up to do for Laurence on the SPD property. I also wanted to redo our bathroom, for the tub shower and sink both had cracks and needed to be replaced, and mildew had gotten into the back of the shower tile.

Frank's health was about the same and he still went on his daily walks. I went with him most of the time. I had been having trouble with my eyes and forehead, so an MRI was done. They found I had a small tumor, or growth, between my eyes on the inside. Dr. Cobb said it had been there for about twelve years. Compared to the test that had been done five years earlier it hadn't grown very much, but enough to give me a mild headache. It wasn't exactly a headache; Dr. Cobb called it a meningioma. He said he would call me back to see him in five years for the next test.

I was told that in time the headache-like pain would get worse, and by the time it does, I hope the good Lord will say it is time for me to go home to Him.

A new pickup

ON AUG. 15, I shopped for a Ford F-150 pickup at Ford Motors in Grass Valley. I also looked at the GMC pickups at Weaver's new location along Highway 49. Julia went with me to help me look. After sitting in many pickups and not being able to see over the steering wheel, I finally found one that would work, but I didn't buy it yet. This was after several hours of looking. Finally, we gave up around 6 p.m. and said we would look again in a few days. After Julia had left the dealership, I drove down the wrong road in their parking lot and had to back up the hill with brand-new pickups and cars parked on both sides. The driveway is situated on a steep hill with no place to turn around. After I got to the end of the hill and was ready to make a turn to go forward, I had a minor mishap; I accidentally ran into the back end of a new, small white car, breaking its tail light and scarring the paint job on the back right side of the car. Luckily, it did very little damage to my old pickup. So I told the people at Ford Motors to have the shop fix the car and that I would pay the bill, rather than put in a claim on my insurance policy. Now it was time to wait for the bill, for the car wouldn't be taken to the shop until the next morning to get repaired.

On Aug. 19, we celebrated Spence's 50th birthday party at Gloria and Laurence's place; both adults and kids were present. There were around 75 people at the party. It was a nice evening with plenty of food and everyone had a good time. The party was held down on the lower end of the yard where Laurence and Gloria had spent a lot of effort and money to flatten the old stump dump to make it into a nice area for parties of any kind. Laurence had even put in two lanes for the game of bocci, which is a very fun and popular game.

On Aug. 22, we bought a Ford pickup in which I could see over the steering wheel. We decided not to get a shell for the bed. The truck is gray in color and has an automatic four-wheel drive, which is something I was really after so I could drive in the snow. It also has all the other automatic things that go with trucks these days. There are steps on each side, so I can get into it easily, and I bought an insert for the trunk that makes it possible to add more room in the bed with the tailgate down if needed.

I sit high up in the cab and can see over the hood, which I like. I bought a personalized license plate and called it, "4 MY Yard." After explaining to people for several days why I wanted a pickup and Frank didn't, I would say, "It's for my yard," so I decided why not call it that?

Dinner parties in September 2006

IN SEPTEMBER, WE HAD two dinner parties in the yard. Tom was busy working on the outside of the house and in the yard, leaving the house with dirty windows and the yard not too tidy, but the weather was great for Tom and the parties. One party was for Frank's old-time business friends, some called them "the war horses." They were here for the first time in more than 40 years, and it turned out to be a great "forgiving party." Why I hadn't done it years earlier, I'll never know. We invited Bill and Monique Pendola, Harold and Mary Ann Berliner, John and Clara Casey, and Lowell and Wanda Robinson, along with our children who had known these people all their lives.

Frank, me, Mary Ann Berliner, Wanda Robinson, Laurence, Lowell Robinson, and Mark

Gloria with Bill and Monique Pendola

Clara Casey, me, Harold Berliner, Frank, and Mary Ann

It turned out to be a wonderful evening, bringing back many old-time memories. The flowers in the yard were one of the best showings I'd had in years; everyone seeing the yard enjoyed it, for the good Lord really outdid Himself this year.

I say to Frank, at least once a week, "The good Lord has really been nice to us, for we are able to see so much beauty and color surrounding all the green lawns, and we're still here to enjoy our life that He has given us."

Hospice of the Foothills fundraiser

ON SEPT. 10, 2006, we attended a fundraiser for Hospice of the Foothills. It took place outdoors at a private ranch in Penn Valley. Frank was feeling good that day and even did some dancing. We all had a very good time. This was among the last fun outings like this we would have with all of us together.

Me and Frank dancing in boots

Julia and Frank on the dance floor

Laurence and Gloria enjoying the evening

145

Aunt Edith passes away

ON SEPT. 21, 2006, Aunt Edith, my mother's youngest brother, Uncle Burt's wife died. That was the last of her siblings, but we would still keep in contact with their children in Minnesota. About the same time, my brother Nick's wife, Ollie, who had remarried in May, was found to have a fast-growing cancer in her head, and she was electing to go through chemotherapy in two weeks; however, her daughter Holly was not so sure. I could see why Ollie would want to do treatment, seeing as she had just married and wanted to enjoy as much of her new life with her husband as she could. We would see in a few weeks which route she would take.

During this time, Frank had had some setbacks with his health, and we found out he was low in iron and, therefore, anemic. The doctor believed Frank might be bleeding a little internally, so now we were dealing with that, along with blood tests and a colonoscopy; but we felt, as a whole, that he was doing fine, and we continued to go on his walks.

Now that all his commitments had been met on his donations, he was feeling better on that score. Hospice had signed the deal on the land. The hospital's Diagnostic Imaging Center was almost completed, and Foothill Theatre had continued matching Frank's fund and was collecting from other people. So he felt much better about all of that, and now he said, "No more," and I said, "For now."

Julia and Mark's housewarming party

ON SEPT. 30 AND Oct. 1, Julia and Mark had their Nyumbani (house) warming party with 50 people attending. Father Tom, a long-time friend of Julia's from her college days, performed the blessing on the house. Afterward, there was a sit-down dinner out on the patio. Father Tom spent the night at our house, and we took him for a tour around the yard before leaving for Julia and Mark's place at eight in the morning for Sunday Mass. Anyone who wanted to attend from the party the night before was also invited to attend. Mass started in the living room around 9 a.m. and then moved to the dining room for the Host. Afterward, a wonderful breakfast was held out on the patio, along with the remains of the previous night's dinner party.

Those of us who were there in the morning for the Mass stayed to help take down all the tables and chairs so Mark could take them back to the rental place. He used my new pickup to take care of the job.

That Sunday, fall set in. I told Frank summer was gone, for it felt like rain was in the air.

Many of Julia's friends from the Bay Area came up for the Nyumbani warming, as did many of her pilot friends and local church friends. Scott Kellermann was home from Africa and joined us at the party. Laurence, Gloria, Spence and his friend Roxanna Cohen were also at the party. Gloria and Laurence did not attend the party on the second day. They had their hands full, for they were in charge of their dear friend Lois Anne Snow's memorial service that was held in the afternoon. I am sorry to say I had forgotten until it was too late, otherwise Frank and I would have gone to the service.

A new woodstove

A DAY OR TWO after the housewarming party, Julia and Mark flew us up to the ranch to see the new kitchen woodstove that was put in to replace the old one that was full of holes. I had been afraid for two years that it might burn the house down, and I told them they should get a new woodstove for the kitchen. On our last trip there, we got the old stove ready to be taken out when the new one arrived. I was very glad to see a brand-new stove on which I could now bake an angel food cake in, wondering if I could still do it the way I had in Camptonville in the 1940s. The stove really put out the heat, even with very little wood in it. It kept that end of the house real warm, including the rooms upstairs.

Remodeling

I WAS BEGINNING TO redo my bathroom and would try to get it done some time before Christmas. I hoped I could get the right people together to get the job done, as much as I hated to tear up that end of the house. I finally got the cottage done, except for painting the inside. We would be able to sleep down there if we had to.

Laurence and Gloria were finally getting "Eddie the Elf's" new house finished for the Christmas holiday season. It should be nice and warm inside, as he sits and talks to the people who come to visit and talk to Eddie. They had also put in new walkways, so it wouldn't be so slippery during the snow season. This would also make it easier for people in wheelchairs to get around.

The "Performing Arts Culture Center" continues ahead

KAREN WOOD HAD CONTINUED working on the "Performing Arts Culture Center" (the name might be changed) with a new group that had been made up from the list she had developed earlier. There seemed to be a lot of interest in having it progress on to the next stage.

Along with that, she was helping me with this book. I was now looking for pictures to use in it.

Frank's PSA climbs

IN OCTOBER, FRANK'S PSA had climbed from 217 to 500, so things were not looking too good, and the blood test and colonoscopy he was scheduled to have were canceled. Hospice had moved in to keep an eye on him.

The family at the Silver Ball fundraiser, 2006

We attended the Silver Ball, which is a fundraiser for the hospital. Everyone was well dressed, and the setting was wonderful, all done in Chinese décor. The tables were done in black, with silver centerpieces on each table. As usual, Laurence and Gloria were on the committee. They did a very good job. And we had our picture taken as a family, realizing this would be our last Silver Ball together, with all of us dressed well for the occasion.

After dinner, Frank had a few dances with Julia and me. Gloria's knees were bothering her so she was not dancing. After a few dances, he was getting tired, so we came home around 11 p.m. During the night I came down with a high fever and wasn't able to make it to church on Sunday. By 9:30 a.m., I was at the Yuba Docs clinic. The doctor took an X-ray of my lungs and found what she thought was a spot, so they called the hospital for me to get a CAT scan done from the lungs down on Tuesday. By the time she was done, it was running close to 1:30 p.m. We went and had a light lunch at Perko's and then went home for me to rest. Frank took off to go to the Amaral Center to see the afternoon concert, even though he was late. It was a good thing though because they now knew it was me who was sick and not Frank.

In the meantime, things were getting done outside by Tom, and the bathroom crew came by to recheck all the details, for they plan to do everything as efficiently as possible once they start. They planned to be in and out as fast as they could in five weeks for Frank's sake. As I've said, I was hoping it would be done before Christmas. And I had to redo the plumbing in the bathroom off the kitchen that was put in during the 1950s or earlier. The pipes were badly rusted, and I would sure hate to have them break or crack during the time we were using that bedroom while our bathroom was being fixed.

I had some plumbing people over and thought I was getting the job done, only to find out that after two hours all they had accomplished was turning off the water. This meant the cleaning women had no water and nothing had been done. They said they couldn't do anything until the boss made another bid on the job, so I blew my cool and they may never come back. I wouldn't blame them. But with the pressure I was having trying to help Frank, who was having more stool problems and bloody noses, along with the continued left arm bone giving him some pain and his left hand giving him trouble, I lost my cool. And yes, I owe the men an apology.

As I said, Frank's blood test and colonoscopy checkups were canceled. The doctors said no to them. I was told that time may be running out, so I hoped to have the bathroom project done as soon as possible. I told the kids what I had been told. After hearing the news, Julia came over and played Hand and Foot with us that evening. She wanted some fun time with him, and she wanted to help Frank surprise the doctors by being around a lot longer. I hope so, for I want to get this book corrected and completed. I am now working on putting the pictures together so he can see what it will look like when it is all done.

The flowers were still holding out in the yard, even though it was now Nov. 9. A photographer from the hospital was over to take pictures of Frank and me. They wanted pictures of us to hang in one of the rooms in the Diagnostic Imaging Center in recognition for the help we gave to get the ball rolling on their fundraising campaign. And I was glad that Frank was able to attend the opening to see where he had put his money.

On Nov. 17, a big party was held at the new center to show the completed interior to the people. We cut the red ribbon for the grand opening and had our pictures taken of us cutting the ribbon. After it was done, Frank quietly went up and cut off six inches of the red ribbon and put it in his pocket to bring home and keep, so that tells you how he felt about the whole thing. One thing I have learned from our big donations is that if you say you will match whatever the public puts up to a given amount, things do happen. The project gets done, rather than getting dragged out over a long period of time. You also come to learn to overlook the negative comments that are made about you.

A few days later, we were invited to go down to the Air Force base and see the unmanned Global Hawk take off for the first time and return a few hours later. We had lunch between those times, and then we went through a few different buildings and saw how the spacesuits look close up, how they put them on, and how heavy they are. We also got to see how the pilots are checked out before they go up in a plane. Julia tried on the helmet and said it was indeed heavy.

Thanksgiving 2006

IN 2006, THANKSGIVING WAS at Gloria and Laurence's home. We had a wonderful feast with everyone there, except Brad and Lisa who couldn't make it. The outside Christmas lights were almost all done and would be turned on Dec. 1.

Sunday, Nov. 26, was our 64th wedding anniversary, which we celebrated at our home. A crown pork roast was served instead of turkey, along with all the other goodies the family had brought over. Laurence, Gloria, Julia, Mark, Brad, Lisa, Spence and his friend Roxanna were here to help us celebrate. It was very nice to have all the family together.

On Dec. 6, everyone would be at our house to put up our Christmas tree and lights. This would be our last Christmas together with Frank, and at my age, I might not be able to do it many more times. Christmas Day would be at Julia and Mark's place.

Ending the Amaral story, November 2006

FRANK AND I, AS of this writing in November 2006, are into our 65th year of married life together. This story has found the Frank Amaral family going from developing and buying businesses and properties, starting in 1944, and continuing all through the years, to turning them over to our two children in their adult years. In turn, they are trading some of them off as they reach their retirement age.

After leaving behind a very active life, and slowing down to a lower gear, Frank and I are able to see the many changes that have taken place in our lifetime. We have gone through wars and changes in attitudes of the culture, including how children are being raised and not being raised. We have lived long enough to see our children carry on into other adventures. We realize that we are among the few parents of our age whom God has blessed with so much in life, including gracing us with our two loving children, their spouses, and our step-grandchildren, and living to see all the things they are doing.

Frank and I are still active people, even if we are in low gear, with Frank still playing the market and me supervising the care of this big house and yard. We do our walking and exercise, but we do realize change can come about at any time. And along the way I didn't think I would ever get to this point in the book!

I started out writing this book as Frank's biography, but it has ended up as a story of our life together, with small and major, sad and happy things happening to us throughout our 64 years together. But most of all we are not alone, for our two children have been with us all the way. And for this I thank the good Lord for making everything possible. As I re-read this, I realize what a wonderful life we have had together, through sickness and good health, the great changes in our lives and in the world. And above all, I appreciate the patience Frank has had with me, correcting the "there and theirs," the "then and thans," along with the spelling, as writing this story goes from "Nothing to Riches" in our lifetime. And we are still able to love and enjoy each other every day to the fullest. Surrounded with family and friends, we go into what we call our twilight years, leaving a little of ourselves to be remembered down through the years with Music in the Mountains; Hospice of the Foothill's new home being built; the Diagnostic Imaging Center that is done and had the ribbon cutting by Frank; and the "Performing Arts Culture Center," which is starting to take hold under Karen Wood's direction; along with helping the Foothill Theatre move forward — these projects were all done in our later years.

We made contributions from the 1940s forward, but in the earlier days, Frank and I wanted to keep what we did quiet, for we were in the newspaper so much for other things in the business world.

At this time, we are finding Frank's health going downhill a little.

PART VI

Twilight Years

December 2006 to July 2011

PART VI INDEX

The diary of Frank's last days, December 2006

(Some of my dates on things may be a little bit off. I am now writing this after Frank has left us, but I do have notes that I made at the time. As far as I can remember, Frank was still thinking clear most of the time, right up to the very end, even though he couldn't talk very well. The medications also made things difficult for him.)

Dec. 1, Fri. On the evening of Dec. 1, we were invited to a Christmas dinner with Bev and Al Erickson, along with some of their other friends. Frank's mind was sharp that night; he was able to run a good conversation with the men and enjoyed himself. He talked to his friend Howard Epstein who had left Bear Stearn and had gone into business with Friends of Larry (FOL), which is an adventure that Frank had taken some interest in, so they really had something to talk about that night.

Frank spent his latter days as he had for the last few years. During breakfast, he would read the local paper and watch the Wall Street ticker tape at the kitchen table. He'd fall asleep while sitting in his chair, or he'd put his arms on the table, lay his head down, and fall to sleep. He'd say he wasn't sleeping, so maybe that was how he would think out what to do in the market that day; this is just a guess on my part for he never said, nor did I ask. He would also look out at the gardener or anyone else that was there working and complain about how they were not doing anything and walking around too much. Quite often I would tell him that the person outside working was doing exactly what I had asked them to do. Not having anything to do with the yard, Frank never understood some of the things I had done, but he loved the results. He was still going into the art room to sit and do some reading, and he'd spend some time looking out the window at the yard. He would often rest his head on the top of the desktop and fall asleep on his arms.

In the past, at around 11 a.m., Frank would go to town to get the mail. He would then go into his office to read the mail and the *Wall Street Journal* to see how his stocks were doing. He would be out there for a few hours doing this, and Ina said he would quite often take a nap out in the office. When he had to put things away in his safe and use the bottom drawer, he said he could not get up off the floor. I happened to be out there at the time, so I helped him up and said I would do it for him from now on. He was also having trouble pulling out the heavy drawers on the counter in the office. I told him I would move all the folders out of the bottom drawers and put them in drawers that were easier to get to; but he didn't say much at the time, and as time went on, he no longer put things away as he had before. He would leave them out for Ina to take care of.

By this time, Frank was no longer driving a car because he was getting weak in the legs. I told him if he had to slam on the brakes, he would not have the strength needed to stop in time. If he got into an accident, it would be his fault, even if it wasn't, and we would be sued. In the end, I don't think he really cared, and he had no trouble with my driving or handing the keys over to me.

Given the way Frank had recently gone downhill, I asked him if he wanted me to go ahead with remodeling our bedroom on Dec. 14 or wait until summer. He said summer, so I cancelled the job until then. (I think he knew he would not be here in the summer.) The weather would also be better, so he could go outside when the noise got too bad inside the house, and it will make the holidays much easier, not having that end of the house all torn up.

The two of us by our Christmas tree

Dec. 5, Tue. Around 3 p.m., Julia, Mark, Gloria, and Laurence came over to put the lights on the tree. After that was done, it was time to have dinner. We had a chicken stew and biscuits, which I made using Maryann Berliners recipe. We also had salad and ice cream in the living room, among all the boxes of ornaments yet to be put on the tree. After we ate, we put the ornaments on the tree and had it all decorated by around 9 p.m. I was able to climb the ladder and put the small ornaments on the top of the tree for the first time in years, due to the dizziness. By 10 p.m., the empty boxes had all been put away. During this time, Frank spent most of his time just sitting in a chair watching what was going on and saying he was cold and had very little energy. We had put lots of blankets on him, and he didn't get into the action at all, which was not like him. We had also turned the heat down for the rest of us while trimming the tree but did have the fireplace going for him. At this time he was still eating regular meals and would eat whatever you gave him; he was never one to complain about what you served him, but he was not eating as much.

Dec. 6, Wed. Frank went to see Dr. Harris. He had Frank go to the hospital to have blood drawn so they could get a match. On Dec. 7, Frank went to the ambulatory treatment center for his first blood transfusion. He had to lie down on a bed for this, and he had a half sandwich and a banana for lunch. He left feeling much better, and that night we went to Foothill Theatre. He did fine but started feeling tired toward the end. He was feeling so good the next day that he went back to walking. He also started helping with the cooking and doing dishes; he was more like his old self again.

Dec. 9, Sat. Anna Marie and Ron, Frank's sister's daughter, came to visit us and to see Laurence and Gloria's lights. We then left their place and went to see Julia and Mark at their new home. Afterward, we took them out to dinner before they left for Princeton. We had a wonderful visit. Anna Marie pointed out that I had some corrections to do on the family tree. I said that after all these years of having it, why wait until I have already given it to someone to correct and put it to print? At this point, I don't know if it can be corrected. (In the end, the corrections were made.)

Dec. 10, Sun. We went to the M.I.M. Christmas program held at the Amaral Festival Center. The performance was very good, and by the time it was over Frank was too tired to stay for the goodies. It was at this time that Paul announced he was retiring in 2008.

Years back Frank had refused to pay on a charge on a New York Bank statement that he said he didn't owe, so during the last four years he had incurred a lot of late charges. Given the state of his health, I knew that one of these days it would fall on me to take care of. It was also in my name, and how that got there I will never know, for Frank has always handled the business end of things out in the office, not me. I ended up calling Judy Hess at the Grass Valley branch and asked her for help. She had us come in to see her on Dec. 1, and after looking things over and many phone calls later, she said it was going to take some time and she needed a few days to work on it. Several days later, we finally got the credit agent to help us settle it. I hope that is the end to these kinds of problems.

With Frank's health the way it was, many things were becoming a problem for him, and I was now becoming aware of it. After leaving the bank, Frank took me to two jewelry stores to look at three large ruby stones that he and Julia had the stores order for me to see. He told me I could pick one out for our 64th anniversary. I ended up selecting a nice red oval ruby stone from Schwarz Jewelers. It was the smallest of the three, but I felt it was the nicest one. I had to wait until after the holidays were over to have it mounted for a pendant. That, along with working to get my rough draft of my book done, made for a very fruitful 64th anniversary day for Frank and me. I was hoping the book would be done for Frank to read, for I really wrote it for him. He had read all my finished notes and said I'm a good writer, but the spelling is another matter. I told him what Janice said many years ago that anyone can correct the spelling, but writing and telling the story, that's another thing and that's where I come in.

Dec. 13, Wed. Hospice had moved in to take care of Frank early in October, with Diane Miessler serving as his head nurse. Today she came to see him and ordered haloperidol 2mg/ml liquid to help him sleep. And he was still changing his pajama tops at least four times a night because they were so wet. For a while, Frank was sleeping in bed about as much as he was sleeping sitting in a chair or sofa at night. Several times during the night, he would get up and go to the chair or sofa, and then he'd get tired and come back to bed. When I woke up during the night, I would reach over to see if he was in bed and if not, I would get up and go cover him with blankets to help keep him warm, and we always kissed each other. I didn't know what else to do for him. He would say he couldn't sleep, but he wouldn't really complain. He always tried not to wake me up by not turning on any lights until he got into the den, living room, or kitchen. He would seldom turn on the TV, and when he first started getting up at night, he spent the time reading. It was during this time that he finished reading the initial draft of my story, "What a Wonderful Life." Sometimes he would heat a cup of soymilk in the microwave and drink it with a cookie. At this time, he was able to get up and walk around without stumbling or falling into things, as he later did. When that started happening, I put nightlights in the foyer so he would not fall over anything.

Dec. 14, Thur. Howard Epstein and his family came to visit and to talk about changing some securities into another interest, one that would be easier for me to handle when the time came. They stayed for a couple of hours as we spent time talking over things in Frank's office. Frank was very alert at the time and could still do everything in the office, except for getting down in those drawers at the bottom of the safe. Julia and Mark joined us for the meeting; Laurence and Gloria were somewhere else, so they weren't able to be there.

Dec. 15, Fri. We had a dinner date arranged at the home of John and Madelyn DiMugno, and somehow we never made it. She called that evening and I felt bad; however, time and everything going on sort of started to run together. She said there were enough people that it was all right if we didn't come.

Dec. 16, Sat. My niece Cheryl, her husband Tom, and their children, Thomas and Analisa, stopped in to see us on their way home from Lake Tahoe. They enjoyed seeing the Christmas tree, and we had a nice visit with them. They said there was little snow up-country.

Dec. 17, Sun. Frank and I were on the Eucharistic Ministry, and at the time, he said he didn't know how much longer he could do it. From there we went to the Trolley Junction restaurant for breakfast and met up with and joined Martha and Deiter Juli. This is something we have done often throughout the years.

Dec. 18, Mon. We had Betty and Brayton Hahn over for a Christmas crab feed and a game of bridge. This turned out to be our last dinner with our friends here at the house. During the entire last two months, Julia was working at our house putting together a memorial movie for her dad. She was using all my pictures from my photo albums, so she was here a lot each day, sometimes until after 6 p.m. However, we really didn't get to visit with her because she was very busy sorting out pictures, and at that time she was seeing if she could do it on her own. Frank was taking an interest in all the photo albums that were now in the dining room and in Laurence's old bedroom and the pool table downstairs. I had them all out so I could easily find pictures for my book and Julia's movie.

Julia and Frank working on pictures in the art room

In time, Frank asked me to get the dining room cleaned up. He was beginning to want the house back in order, so I moved them all to Laurence's bedroom and put them on card tables. This is where they were when he died. He wanted things neat and orderly at the end. He was also getting tired more often. (On this day, Frank wrote a special note to the kids that I did not know about. It wasn't until two years later, Dec. 7, 2008, that I found a copy of the note that was stored away with all my Christmas cards and notes.)

Frank's handwritten note to the kids and me

Dec. 19, Tue. Carol Kellermann came over to visit with me, while Julia was busy on the computer and Frank was lying down on the sofa or trying to sleep in the living room, which he did a lot of during the day. At this time, he was still going to the office and taking care of his business and the market. But when he went out to the office, he would fall asleep at the desk several times before coming back in. I now wonder how much he was able to comprehend in regards to what he was doing and how he was able to follow through on the things he did do.

Dec. 21, Thur. Michael Sion came down from Reno to go through the pictures for my book. I had Frank pay him for his job, and at the time, Frank didn't know where to put it in the books or what to put it under. Around noon, Kimberly Parker came over to see Frank and me about the sign at the Diagnostic Center. That night we went up to Laurence and Gloria's for dinner and saw the Christmas lights and Eddie the Elf.

159

Frank at Julia's place, Christmas Eve 2006

Dec. 24, Sun, Christmas Eve. We had dinner at Julia and Mark's, and then the four of us went to ten-o'clock Mass. After that, we drove over to visit Laurence and Gloria, but the tree lights were not on, so we drove around looking at other Christmas lights in Grass Valley. However, by this time, most were turned off, so we went back to Julia and Mark's place where we spent our first night in their new home. Frank wasn't able to sleep and was restless, so he spent most of the night sitting up on the sofa or chair in the living room. This was something he had been doing for months at home. I got up and put a blanket over him, so he wouldn't get too cold as he moved around from one place to another. At least he was able to see the Christmas tree all during the night. On Christmas day we had our crab feed and then came back home that night.

Dec. 31, Sun. We went to a play at Foothill Theatre but stayed for only the first half. Frank was not hearing what they were saying and had lost interest, so we came home early.

For the last few years around 9 p.m., Frank would get ready for bed and then we would always play some kind of card game. We mostly played Hand and Foot. This kept his mind active and relaxed him before going to bed around 10:30. I would follow him in an hour or so later, only to have him get up out of bed an hour later and heat up a cup of milk and eat a cookie. His nights were very restless. He could not sleep very long, and he had been that way for several years. In the past, I would not get up every time he got out of bed, but I would reach over to see if he was in bed. By this time, I was no longer sleeping soundly, and somehow I knew when he was not in bed. I would often get up and put a blanket on him, and this would happen several times during the night. I would find him sitting in the kitchen, living room, or den reading my book or some other book. Sometimes he would sit on the loveseat in the foyer. And he was always cold. Even in bed, he would have two pairs of wool socks on his feet, wool pajamas, and the electric blanket set to 6. He had a blanket and a comforter on top of that, and he would still be cold. I even had a soft down pillow at the end of the bed.

Our evenings together in the places where we usually sat

At this time, I felt he was here with us longer than I thought he would be. For a while, I didn't think he was going to make it to our anniversary. His blood transfusion helped him for a while, and somewhere along here, Hospice had ordered a cane to help him walk, just in case he should need it. However, he never used it very much, and when he did need a cane, he used the one I had for my dizzy spells.

Months earlier, Frank was still driving his car, which was in bad need of repair. If he planned to continue driving, we would need to fix it or get a new one. He didn't want to give up the car, so I said, "Get it fixed." It ended up costing a lot, and yes, he drove it for a few months until I saw he was too weak to drive safely. I would like to drive it, but I sat rather low behind the steering wheel, so I didn't feel comfortable driving it any distance. I have had offers from people who want to buy it.

Frank always got me a new car about every five or six years, for he was not one to take a car in and have it serviced, unless something went wrong with it. To him it was easier to go buy a new car and get rid of all the trouble of getting the old one fixed. But with his health, he did not have the energy or desire to buy one, nor did he care to go out to look at one. I did not press him on the matter, except for the Ford pickup, and on that I didn't take no for an answer. I knew if we got deep snow, I would be in trouble, if in no other place than getting in and out of our driveway.

All through the years, Frank and I would weigh ourselves each morning, and we kept a running record of it, so I'll give a general idea of where he was starting on Nov. 11, 2006. His high was 156 lbs, which was what it had been for many years; mine was at a high of 118.5 lbs, and that worried me. On Nov. 13 he went to 155, and I went to 114.5 lbs. From then on Frank continued to fluctuate a little, going down to 152.5. I can remember him being concerned about that. On Dec. 3, he weighed 150.5 and continued to fluctuate, and on the 12th he was at 149.5. My weight was at 115. At this time, we continued going on our mile-long walk, and if I didn't go with him, he would still go on his own. When he didn't get back when I thought he should, I would start to take the car out looking for him, only to have him show up in the driveway about that time. It was at this time that he needed to take more rest periods. From Dec. 13 to 25, he kept his weight around 150.

(In four days, he dropped down to 149, and on Jan. 5, he was at 146.5. From then on, he continued to fluctuate, and I remember he began to get more worried about it. His weight loss was bothering him, for he couldn't understand what was going on. At this time, I still weighed around 116. Around the time of his 2nd blood transfusion in late Jan. 2007, he was back up to 150, and then he would be down to 146 by Feb. 4. The last time he would check his weight would be on Feb. 6; he weighed 148.5, and I was 116. I continued to check my weight, but he never checked his again. I have a loose paper book that we kept our weight in, and I had torn out all the pages up to Nov. 2006. I now keep the last pages of Frank's weight log in with all the other papers I have of him.)

Pictures of our whole family

Frank, me, our son-in-law Mark, our daughter Julia, our daughter-in-law Gloria, and our son Laurence

Our grandchildren and great-grandchildren

Spence

Stephanie, Evan, Collin, and Jeff

Brad

The diary of Frank's last days, Jan.–Mar. 2007

Jan. 1, 2007, New Year's Day. Frank wasn't too interested in the Rose Parade this year. He would watch some of it and then fall asleep. He did the same with golf. It was getting so he would spend a lot of time sleeping on the sofa in the living room in the daytime, with pillows under his head and covered up with blankets.

I think his blood transfusion was wearing out at this time, for he just didn't have very much energy. The daily walk he had been taking for the last several years took him from our house, down Reward St., over to Seven Hills School, and up Doane Rd. In June, we would eat the ripe cherries off the trees and then walk down Zion St. and back to home. The walk was about a mile and included both uphill and downhill stretches. Along the way, he would stop three or four times to get his breath, but by this time he was stopping more often. And he always stopped at the bench across from the SPD store to rest and watch the people come and go. Sometimes he talked to me about how he had bought the SPD property. And he would look out over the three mountains east of Nevada City. In time, it got so he could not do the walk, but he would try to walk to the store and buy some groceries. By Feb. he was unable to do even that.

Back in Oct. 2006, Frank and I had gone in to see Dr. Tomlin because his left shoulder and arm were hurting. The doctor had some tests taken, and we found out his PSA was 500. He told Frank it was time to get Hospice in the picture and that it was time for our lawyer, Richard Keene, to make sure our Will was in proper order, so we did.

Jan. 3, Wed. Diane Miessler, Frank's nurse from Hospice, came by. She and Frank got so they enjoyed each other. Frank's left hand would hurt him, so he would soak his hand in a hot wax bowl and then wrap it in a towel for a while to keep the heat in. This did help him. This was in Laurence's old bedroom, which was now being used for an exercise room, a sewing room, and as a place for having easy access to all the photo albums Julia was using on the video project. Diane and I had gone in to join him and got to talking on all kinds of things. Frank would give her a bad time, but she knew how to handle him, so they got along fine. This was right about the time I received my printed books of Volumes I and II of "What a Wonderful Life" in the mail from Michael Sion in Reno, NV. Frank was happy to see how it would look once I had it all done. He was able to read all of it and kept telling me what a good writer I was, and he said to not let anyone change what I said.

Jan. 6, Sat. Frank went over to Ford Motors and paid off my pickup. I was relieved when that was done. Somehow, they had talked Frank into paying most of it off when we bought it and then make four monthly payments to pay off the balance. This would save him money, and in the end, it did. However, it created a big headache for him until it was fully paid off. He no longer knew or remembered what he had done on the deal.

Jan. 7, Sun. Our Godchild Kellie and her family came up to see us. Frank always enjoyed seeing them and the two kids. The kids would always give him a report on how they were doing in school, and they would play a musical instrument or a game for him.

Visiting the new Diagnostic Center

Jan. 8, Mon. Julia went with us to the new diagnostic center at the hospital to take a picture of Frank and me in front of our name at the sign-in desk. Right after that, I noticed that Frank had to sit down, for he had little energy to stand for very long. I'm glad we did this, for these are the only pictures I have of him at the center. I know that when the center was opened for the public to see, they took pictures of him cutting the ribbon, but we never got any of them. At the ribbon cutting, Mark said he saw Frank go up and cut about 8 inches of ribbon and put it in his pocket. I never saw that piece of ribbon until after his death. Frank was never one to talk about the things he had done.

Rest time at the Diagnostic Center

Jan. 9, Tue. Around 1 p.m., the Weibe's came over, and we had our last bridge game with Dick and Alice. Around 5 p.m., the four of us went out to dinner to the place that took over Lyons. It wasn't very good, so we will not go there again. And I think it was the following day that Julia and I took the Christmas tree down. Frank was no longer able to help.

Jan. 12, Fri. We received a phone call and a visit from two of Frank's distant cousins that are grandchildren to his Aunt Gertrude. Their names are Arlene Leal and Irene Block. This was a nice surprise, and they brought some pictures with them. One was of Frank's Mother's parents, Maria Julia and Manuel Mendes Pereira, married around 1850. Irene lives in Alta Sierra, which is about 12 miles from Nevada City, so I'm sure we'll be seeing more of her.

Jan. 16, Tue. Frank had been going to a woman barber for a couple of years who had been cutting his hair too short and would cut off the wave out of his hair. I couldn't get him to change from her because the price was right. No doubt, he paid her no more than $10, and it was obvious she did not know how to cut to a wave. The kids had been after him for so long that I decided to make a change and took him to Hairline. It took three visits to get his wave back in his hair, but by now, time was beginning to run out for him. I'm glad he had the wave back in his hair, for it looked very nice.

Jan. 18, Thur. Frank had been complaining about his vision and had an appointment to have his glasses checked, but it turned out that his vision was all right. I began to notice he was using a card or a strip of paper under each line of text whenever he would read something; however, the eye doctor said his glasses were fine.

Jan. 19, Fri. I had been having trouble with my hearing lately, so I went and got a hearing test done. I found out I had trouble. Hearing aids had to be made for my ears and were ordered. I got them a week later. I could hear so much better that I even wore them at night, so I could hear Frank when he got up or made any noise of any kind. It was around this time that Diane and other people from Hospice started coming by more often. The visits often took up so much time that it interfered with things I had to do. I noticed it was beginning to wear me down. They now had Frank on Lasix for the swelling in his legs and ankles. He was also taking potassium chloride, thyroid tablets, and bisacodyl. Then at bedtime, he took melatonin and trazodone, which is a serotonin modulator. For pain control, he took acetaminophen, ibuprofen, and hydrocodone as needed.

Frank had a doctor's appointment with Dr. Harris and found that his PSA had jumped from 500 in Oct. 2006 to 1,787. This is when the doctor told Frank to come back in six months, but on the side, he wished me luck. I knew then there wasn't much time left. That night we had dinner and played bridge at Betty and Brayton's home. Frank was able to play, but he was asking me questions about how to respond to certain things. Before going over to their place, he had spent most of the day sleeping so he would be alert. And I found myself closely watching what he was doing.

Frank was beginning to stumble during the night. He needed to be watched more closely when going to the bathroom, which he did several times every night because of the trouble he was having with his bladder. I now put nightlights in the hallway so he would not trip and fall.

Jan. 21, Sun. We went to Mass at 9:30 a.m. Julia joined us, which she did on most Sundays, unless it was her turn to be a lecturer at the 8:30 Mass. In that case, Mark would go with her. This Sunday we were on the Ministry, and I had found someone to replace Frank. I knew he would not be able to do it anymore. During Mass, at a time when we were all seated and then had to get up, Frank was unable to get up on his own. This is the first time this had ever happened. I told him to remain seated, and I then burst out in tears, for I knew the time had come when he would really need help, and I realized his time was short. Well, everyone around us in church was also crying, men as well as woman, for we all saw it happen and knew the time was near. I finally got a hold of myself in time to go up to the altar to help with communion. I had communion served to Frank at his seat. I often wondered what he thought, for he never talked about how he really felt during this time.

That afternoon I called Hospice and Diane stopped by. After checking him out, she said she would call Frank's doctor, Dr. Tomlin, to set up a blood test in the morning to see about getting Frank a blood transfusion. A few days later, we got word that the hospital had set the date. Frank was now having bloody noses, something he often had, but now they were much worse. He was also bleeding when he went to the bathroom. One of the things I am sure our whole family will miss is seeing him blowing his nose and clearing his throat to get the clots out. He did this in the kitchen sink with the hot water running, which he used to help clear things out. We could never get him to do it in the bathroom, and he didn't care how much we complained.

Jan. 22, Mon. I got my new hearing aids today; what a difference they make! And Hospice was here and gave me a list of some of the medicines Frank needed to be taking at this time, in addition to the pills he had been taking for years. Some were vitamins, and docusate was also added for a stool softener. At lunchtime, he took half a Lasix pill and half a Vicodin with his food. He took docusate at bedtime to help him sleep and Ativan if needed. He was also told to increase his dosage of Mirapex at bedtime and to increase it a tablet each day for three days if needed. And he needed to stop taking his fiber pills.

During this time, Frank's nails and finger turned a little blue, and there was not much color in his face. He continued his Pilates exercises with Roxanna three times a week. Even if an exercise wasn't very hard, she would help him with his breathing and tried to open his chest area. She had him do easy exercises that would help him, and they would end the time with his legs up on the wall to help take down the swelling in his ankles and legs. It was through this exercise that we began to see he was having trouble with internal bleeding.

Jan. 26, Fri. At 7:30 a.m. I took Frank to the outpatient center at the hospital for his second blood transfusion. It took about four hours. He had to sit up this time and got tired. Julia stopped by to be with him during the time I was at exercise class. She gave him a banana and some custard for lunch, along with his Ensure, the nutrition shake he was now drinking at least twice a day. We hadn't had breakfast before going to the hospital, so I knew he would need something to eat. When he was through, she brought him home. He wasn't too happy with the whole process, nor did he think he got the results he had with the first one. However, it did bring him back to life. Color returned to his face, and his fingernails and finger were pink again. He had more energy and was more alert, and he didn't sleep as much during the day.

The skin on his fingers had started to crack, and his mouth and chin area on his right side had gone numb. He had a hard time breathing out of his right nostril, and he could no longer chew his food very well. I hoped the transfusion would help for a while, but he said he would never do it again, for he didn't like how he felt after the one he had just had.

How long the transfusion would last before he needed another one remained to be seen, for we knew he was going downhill fast. In July, the X-rays showed the cancer had gone into the bones of his shoulders, collarbone, scapula, upper ribs, and the head of the humerus. But at this time, he was in no pain, or at least he never complained about it. We didn't know if he had pain anywhere else, but the Hospice people seem to know more about these things than we do.

As I've said, Frank had a little more life after this last transfusion. He slept better on Friday and Saturday but not as well on Sunday. He slept a lot in the day and said he got physically tired but not mentally tired. He said his brain didn't get tired, and maybe this is why he couldn't sleep very well. But he never said what he was thinking about even when we asked him. He was still having continual night sweats and needed his pajama tops replaced throughout the night, which kept him awake, along with the trouble with his bladder and stools. Somehow, even with all this going on, he still had his good humor.

Jan. 28, Sun. We went to church on Sunday, and Frank was able to get up without any trouble. He had more energy than he had had in a while. He even went for his walks.

Jan. 29, Mon. Frank weighed in at 150. He had gained 2 ½ pounds, which I think was all water gain. I weighed 117.5.

Around 5:30 p.m., Dr. Tomlin from Chapa-De came over to the house to see Frank. He stayed for over an hour, checking Frank out and asking us all kinds of questions. At this time, he was thinking about having Frank get another blood transfusion. After he left, we went over to Julia and Mark's place for dinner and then played Mexican Train. We left for home around 10, for Frank was getting tired.

Jan. 30, Tue. Diane from Hospice came over to check on Frank. His health was continuing to go downhill. We were both still going to Roxanna for our exercise routine. I would drop him off at Julia and Mark's place at 9:30 a.m., and then I would go back for my exercises between 10:45 to 11:30. As I did my exercises, Frank would lie on a pad with his feet and legs up the wall to help get the blood out of his feet, or he'd end up taking a nap. Usually by this time Mark would be back from town with the mail; he would bring ours home with him, so I wouldn't have to get it. Looking out the big window in Julia's exercise room, we always saw a big crow that would fly in the wind currents. Frank loved to watch it. (Now that he is gone, Roxanna says she thinks of Frank when she sees a crow soaring in the wind.)

Feb. 1, Thur. It was a nice, warm day, so around 11 a.m. I put the chaise lounge out on the driveway by the redwood tree so Frank could sit out in the sun. After a while, he lay down on it and tried to sleep. By this time, I was keeping a close eye on him wherever he went, and I could see he was trying to get warm. I took two blankets out and tucked them around him. He stayed that way for a couple of hours. I went to do something, and when I saw him again, he had gotten up and was walking up the steps to the back of the house.

Frank tripped on the step outside the kitchen and fell toward the sliding glass door. Fortunately, the glass didn't break and kept him from falling on the cement step, and I was able to catch him as all this was going on. I checked his leg and saw no broken bones, so I helped him up and got him in the house. His left ankle didn't hurt too bad. He later wanted to go to the office with the mail, so I helped him. As he walked up the steps, he sort of stumbled. I told him to do whatever he needed to do in the office because this would be his last trip there. From now on the books would be brought to him in the house as he needed them. He stayed in the office for about an hour, and, yes, I think he took a nap.

Frank was scheduled to have a colonoscopy this morning, but the doctors cancelled it and said it was too late.

Feb. 2, Fri. I dropped Frank off at Julia's place for his exercise routine and when I came back for mine, Roxanna told me that Frank should see the nurse about his ankle, so I called the nurse after we got home. I had an appointment later that day for my heart checkup, and my heart was fine. I also had a hearing aid checkup and needed to go back on the 5th. At this time, Frank was still able to be by himself for a while. Father McKnight came over later in the day and anointed Frank and gave him communion. Julia was having work done on her movie for Frank's memorial service. The project had been going on all along for the last two or three months. At this time, she had a man by the name of Greg Whatley from Mountain Event Productions doing a recording of Frank telling his life story. Frank's voice was hardly loud enough to hear. The recording sessions were done at our place, while Frank sat on the sofa in the living room. I was too busy to keep any tabs on what the two were doing, but every so often they would have me sit down with Frank and help him recollect some of his memories for the recording. He didn't always know quite where to start, so I would remind him of the place, time, etc. and then he would recall the details.

My days were already too full for me to pay much attention to what Julia or Greg were doing with the movie. Between going through all the 50-some-odd albums for pictures and talking to Frank, who was tired most of the time, the house was full of activity. Julia and Mark took off that evening to go skiing for the week, which I'm sure she needed. (Later, after Frank's death and at the reception at St. Canice Hall on Sat. March 24, Greg told me he felt right at home all through these months. He would come and go through all the doors as if he were at his own house. This made the job much easier for all of us. He said he had never had that happen before, and he thanked me for giving him that welcoming feeling. And let's face it, he and Julia really did an incredible job on Frank's memorial movie. I thank them for a job well done.)

Feb. 3, Sat. Around 10 a.m., Lowell Robinson came over to visit with Frank. Frank was sitting in a chair by the sliding glass doors in the kitchenette, so he could see everything going on outside. While Lowell was here, someone from Hospice came by to check on his ankle and bladder. Lowell took it all in stride, and Frank had long since gotten used to no privacy when it came to that department. The two continued with their conversation, and as I recall, it was about all the things they had done together many years ago. Lowell wanted dates when some things happened, so I got my book out and looked up the dates for him. Frank's mind was still good most of the time, but he was not always talkative. However, he was very talkative today with Lowell.

About this time, the nurse decided that Frank would need a raised port-a-potty chair with arms to put on the toilet in our bathroom. The side supports would help him get up and off the toilet. Up until now, he had been using the towel rack that really was not strong enough to support him. I knew that if the towel rack broke off while he was using it, he could really hurt himself.

Feb. 4, Sun. After coming home from church, I called Hospice to see about Frank's ankle, for the swelling had now gone up to his knee. I needed to know if he should see a doctor. Diane was here around 9 a.m. and told me to put an icepack on it and to elevate it as needed to see if the swelling would go down. We did what she said, but Frank was not about to do it very often. I think the ice packs made him too cold. He was also told to take one or two Vicodin every four hours for pain.

As I've said, for the last several years, Frank had been getting up at night and would go from the chair to the sofa in the living room, and to the kitchen to warm up a cup of milk in the microwave and have a cookie. He would also read my book, along with other material. He was not one to waste time reading casual things. He would sometimes watch TV but not very often. When he came back to bed, he tried not to wake me, but as time went on it got worse and by January I was up a lot during the night covering him with blankets. When he got tired of sitting, he would come back to bed. But by now he was not able to move around as easily without stumbling around, so I would have to really listen to him, so I could help him and keep him from falling. At first I kept the light on in our bedroom closet, but he said it was too much light to sleep, so I now added two more nightlights in the foyer to help him see where he was going at night. And I had earlier put one in our bedroom.

Frank weighed himself today and was down to 148.5. (Frank never weighed himself again after this.)

Feb. 5, Mon. Hospice came over in the afternoon to check on Frank's ankle and leg. They told me to take him to Yuba Docs, rather than the hospital, so he would get faster service, and this is what we did. By this time, Frank was using my cane for support in case he happened to lose his balance.

We also wanted to check out why the Social Security checks we were getting for Frank weren't as much as they had been. We found a deduction on his that was making his checks less, so around noon I drove the two of us to Auburn. We didn't have to wait to see someone and got waited on right away. They told us that the cost of Frank's pills were being taken from his checks. We left with the idea of them telling us he should drop his medical plan with Humana since all the bills were being picked up by Hospice at this point. The next day we checked in with our insurance man, and he agreed with us. I stayed on the same plan and Frank's was changed.

We checked in around 2 p.m. at Yuba Docs, and it wasn't until around 4 that Frank was called into the exam room. By this time, he had sort of lost his patience. We were planning to have a dinner date later on with Gloria and Laurence, but by this time, I knew we weren't going to be able to make it. I tried to let them know, but I wasn't able to reach them on the phone. By the time he got to see a doctor it was closer to 5; there were so many people ahead of us. When we finally did get to see a doctor, it was Dr. Yamato. He insisted on taking X-rays, which they can do in their office. This took us past 6 in the evening. After getting the X-rays developed, Dr. Yamato found no broken bones. He told me to get Frank a pair of support hose that went up to the knee. He said they would help cut down the swelling in the leg and ankle. Frank needed to put them on both legs because his right foot and leg were also swelling, just not as bad as the left. He also put Frank on an antibiotic, for he was afraid Frank's left leg was going to get inflamed. They checked Frank's blood pressure and found it was 94 over 48.

The doctor told me to go to Albertsons to get the support hose and antibiotics. By this time it was after 7 p.m., so I told him, "No," in no uncertain terms. I would not go there at that hour with Frank, who was really getting weaker and needed some food. I told him to find what he could in the office supply cupboards that would take care of Frank until the morning. So the doctor and a few other people in the office went looking for something. They came up with 6 pills to get Frank through the night, and I thanked them for doing this for us. (Three and a half years later, in 2010, I had to go to Yuba Docs for help with having cut off the tip of my finger. I thanked them again for helping Frank that night. I also returned the unopened medicine they had given me and told them to use it for someone else who may need it, as I did that night.)

Yuba Docs is just a few doors down from the Asian Garden Chinese Restaurant, so we walked there and got soup and some food that Frank could eat. As I've mentioned, he was beginning to have trouble swallowing food by this time. This was the last time he got to go to the restaurant.

I went out the next day and got the medicine and support hose for Frank. The only color of hose I could find was white, and I really had a hard time getting them on his legs. For at least the last three years up until now, he had been wearing two pairs of wool socks to go to bed in to help keep his feet warm. However, he found the support hose were warmer, and from then on he never wore his wool socks again. And, of course, the salty food he ate didn't help him, but at this stage in the game, he enjoyed eating it. It really wouldn't make that much of a difference in the end.

Feb. 6, Tue. Frank was still having trouble with swelling in both of his legs and ankles, especially the left. When Lynn from Hospice came over to check on him and take his vitals, his blood pressure was 90 over 48, his heart rate was 68, and his oxygen was 93. This was when I started to write the numbers down, so we would have a record in case one was needed.

Feb. 7, Wed. Diane from Hospice came in to check Frank's leg and his pill status, along with everything else they do when they come over. She was here for a couple of hours. We ended up in Laurence's old bedroom, while Frank soaked his hands in the hot wax, which he said helped with the pain in his fingers and the palms of his hands. I think it was during this visit that she told me she would be switching over to night shift in a few weeks. She said she would be our nighttime nurse and told me she was planning to quit Hospice in order to work on another project of her own. However, she assured me she would remain with us through Frank's time. At the same time Frank was sick, so too was her father. Her father passed away sometime in the first week of April. I know she and Frank really enjoyed each other's company.

Feb. 8, Thur. Frank was still having many heavy nosebleeds that lasted a few minutes. He was really going through the hankies, so I started keeping a glass full of Clorox water to soak the hankies in to get them clean. For a while, I ended up buying a half a dozen new hankies a week. He also had a couple of nosebleeds at night that would cover a big area, covering around 2 feet on his side of the bed. When he woke up in the morning, he didn't know it had happened. I would have to remove all the bedding and the mattress pad and do a good washing.

He was having a more difficult time staying in bed at night and had become even less sure-footed in finding his way to the closet. I would turn my light on for him to see where he was going, and he was still changing his pajama tops several times during the night to stay dry. He was also beginning to have trouble finding his way to the bathroom at night and was stumbling into things.

His body was passing more blood at this time, and he was having a hard time urinating. It was getting harder for me to help him, and I was really getting worn out from not having much sleep. When we got up in the morning, I would make the bed, get Frank bathed and dressed, and then get him to the kitchen, where I would put the support hose on his legs. I would sometimes put my weight on his thigh while doing this, and he would tell me not to because it hurt. Otherwise, he never complained about it hurting. I would tell him I was sorry and would try not to do it again, but I would sometimes forget. After a few times I began to be very careful how I got up off the floor, so I wouldn't hurt him by putting my weight on his thigh. By this time, an hour and a half would have gone by, and I would still have to get breakfast. One of the things I kept telling Frank over and over was what a good patient he was, for he never complained about all the things I had to do for him or around the house, nor did he ever complain about having to wait as I took care of something, even if he needed my help at that time.

After getting Frank dressed, I would fix him a plate of different kinds of fresh fruit. Up until now, he was having a lot of protein with his meals, so I had been making two poached eggs, turkey bacon, and a piece of toast with strawberry jam that I had made. All along, I had been telling him that he was a very good patient. As I've said, he never complained about anything I did, and if he didn't like it, he never let on. I loved him very much for it. I told him he had taken such good care of me for so many years without complaining that I would do the same for him, and I did.

Feb. 9, Fri. Today was Frank's last time to go to his exercise class with Roxanna. While I was doing my exercises, he was getting really tired and having a hard time going through the mail that Mark had picked up for us. He was no longer reading the Wall Street Journal or any of his other magazines as he had before, but he would glance at them and maybe read an article or two.

Feb. 11, Sun. We went to church, but it was hard for Frank to walk very far. I had a feeling he wouldn't be going to church again. We went to breakfast at Perko's restaurant with Julia. She had already had breakfast but wanted to talk to us about the pictures she was working on for Frank's movie. We both knew it would be our last breakfast outing together with Frank. We usually had Sunday breakfast at the Trolley Junction Restaurant, but we knew it would be too much food and would take too long to be served.

After we got home, Frank was having a great deal of pain urinating. Diane from Hospice came by and told Frank he would have to have a catheter put in because he was not urinating and too much urine was staying in his bladder. This was why he was having so much pain and trouble. So the three of us went into Julia's bedroom where he laid down on the bed. She got him all squared away and said he may not have to keep it in if he could drain all right. But that night he was having continual trouble even with the catheter, so we knew he would be stuck with it.

Feb. 12, Mon. Throughout the day Julia and Mark, along with Laurence, came over to help me. We knew I would have to have more help to take care of Frank, so they contacted Hospice. Someone was sent over to talk to us, but Hospice could only give short-term hours of care. So they called *Home Instead.* They sent a person out to see us, and it was arranged for someone to come in to help me every night from 9 p.m. to 8 a.m., with Hospice doing the bath and a few other things for Frank. So I agreed to that. I still didn't want someone around all the time, for I knew Frank would not like that anymore than I would. However, I was also beginning to notice that when Frank saw how tired I was getting, he wouldn't complain when we brought in outside help. It was the same when different things were brought in for him to use. He would wonder why they were brought in, so I would explain it to him and tell him he may never need it.

On the *Home Instead* report, under *Health* they wrote: "Prostate cancer that has gone to his bones. He bleeds out of every orifice, gets bloody noses, diarrhea comes with bloody nose. He is deaf, has hearing aids that help. Wears glasses, has respiratory problems. He is mostly alert, has a dry sense of humor, intelligent." Under *Background* it read: "He is clean and tidy, no facial hair, lived in same house 56 years, has lots of friends, and family, and Hospice is involved." *Daily Routine:* "Under ambulation, he shuffles, so give him an arm, wanders around, you have to go with him, ask what he needs. He is weak, so be sure to be with him. He carries a cane but doesn't use it. He is a high fall risk, weight 145 lbs, and has had 2+ falls in last six months." *Personal Care/Bathing:* "He has a catheter and there is blood in it, has had two transfusions, have to empty bag. He has total bowel incontinence and has BM 2–3 times per night. Check him every hour on the hour."

Around 1:30 in the afternoon, our God Child, Kellie, and her two children, Katie and Michael, came up to see us. They brought a real nice orchid for Frank, which was still in bloom all the way into late April. Michael had learned how to play guitar and was learning how to do acrobatic things, so he demonstrated his new talents for us. More than anything, he wanted to show what he could do for Frank. They left around 3 p.m.

Around 4 p.m., I got a call that Hospice had ordered a hospital bed to be delivered to the house for Frank to use. I had to rearrange the furniture in our bedroom before it arrived, and when I saw it, I thought Frank would never sleep in it. But that was what they wanted, and I wasn't going to argue with it. I took the drawers out of Frank's dresser, so I could move it over by mine. I put the hospital bed at the foot of our bed, so I would be near him. This left plenty of room to get around. I also thought that if he had to use the new bed, I would move my head to the foot of our old bed so I would be closer to him. When he saw it, he wondered why they had brought it, but by this time, I was beginning to see that just before things were needed, they would be on hand. The bed was one of those things.

During the last several days, Frank was not able to get in the bathtub to take a shower, nor did he want to take a shower in the small bathroom off the kitchen, so I started giving him sponge baths. I also washed his hair, helped him brush his teeth, washed out his mouth, and helped him get rid of the blood clots in his throat and nose. I helped him to the toilet, which made him tired, and he would still have to be dressed. Hospice called and said a man would be at the house at 9 in the morning to give Frank a bath. I was really relieved to be free of that.

Feb. 13, Tue. A man from Hospice by the name of George came by and brought a supply of all the things that were needed in the mornings to help Frank. Frank's dresser was now full of all kinds of things: incontinence products, bed sheets that hold water, towels, liquid soaps, hair shampoos, cream lotions, and bedpans. And now Frank would have his first bath while lying down on the hospital bed. Before I left the room, I laid out all his clothes he would need: shorts, support hose, shoes, T-shirt, outer shirt, and a dress sweater to go with the shirt and dress pants. And he always had a nice sweater that would help keep him warm every day. I did this morning routine every day for the rest of his life. I also laid out bath towels and washcloths so George would not have to go looking for anything.

I did not go in to watch what went on while they were giving Frank his bath, but I had one madman on my hands when he came out all dressed and clean. Even his hair was washed and combed. He thought it was outrageous to spend an hour and a half getting a bath, especially while lying down. Frank has never been one to hold any bad thoughts for very long, and by the time George had cleaned everything up and put things away, and came out to say goodbye to Frank, Frank had gotten it all out of his system and was in good humor. The two got to talking about where they were from, and it turned out George was also Portuguese. I got the feeling the two of them ended up having a good conversation, despite all the grumbling.

George told us he would be gone for a week and would not be around to give Frank a bath in the mornings. So we called *Home Instead* and asked if they could change the morning hours from 8 a.m. to 9 a.m. and told them the reason: I wanted Ken to give Frank a bath, clean him up, and dress him in the morning. They said they could do it and told me they were looking for someone to fill in for Ken Lauer on Sunday night. I told them I could take care of Frank that night if they couldn't find someone. (I did not take into account that Frank would become weaker in the meantime.) They said Ken would be back on the job on Monday. Frank was rather tired, so I helped him to the living room so he could sleep on the sofa. He hadn't heard my conversation with *Home Instead*.

Word had gotten out that Frank was getting worse, so friends started calling to drop in and to bring by food. Karen Wood brought over bedding for Frank's hospital bed, and Carolyn Dean brought us an electric blanket. Later in the day, the kids and I were having a business talk on what to do about the help, along with other stuff going on, when Jack Moorehead arrived with some cookies. He took one look at me, saw the tension on our faces, handed me the cookies, and started to leave. I gave him a kiss and tried to hold back my tears as he left. Frank was sleeping in the living room at this time. I later called Jack and said Frank would want to see them. I asked if they would stop by, and they said they would. Netta Kandell also stopped by and brought us a nice white azalea plant. And so this started a whole new schedule for Frank and me.

Frank was still eating some regular foods, just not as much, and he was always cold. He was taking naps and could walk with help. I went shopping for Valentine's Day cards that would say what Frank would want said for each of the kids. I spent some time making sure the cards said what he would want them to say, and when he read them, he said I had done a good job. He wrote something in each one and gave their cards to them.

I had a dentist appointment at 12 noon, so Julia stayed with Frank. Later, Frank's nephew, Milton, and Mimi from Oregon came to see him. They had come south to be with their son in Sacramento. Frank and I always tried to have dinner around 6 p.m. if we were home, and I was still doing it at this time. Ken came by tonight at 9 p.m. and got Frank ready for bed. Diane also came by to flush out his catheter. She found out she had to replace it with a larger one, for the one they gave him kept plugging up and that was one of the reasons he was having so much trouble all night long. It was around 10 p.m. by the time they were through with all the things they needed to do, including checking his blood, heart rate, and oxygen level. By this time, Frank was no longer getting any real good sound sleep of any kind. He was up several times every night and wouldn't always come back to bed right away.

Feb. 14, Wed., Valentine's Day. After Frank had his breakfast, sometime around 10 a.m., Betty and Brayton Hahn came over and brought some soup for us and visited awhile. Ina, Frank's secretary, came in to see him after she was through with her work in the office. She told Frank she would take care of anything I needed in the future. I talked to her later and told her as long as Frank was alive, she was to follow his rules, but after he was gone, I would want her to work more days and would give her a raise, which I did. Jack and Beth Moorehead came over later in the afternoon and had a nice visit with us in the kitchenette where Frank spent most of his time. He liked looking at the yard and being around me, and he liked reading the paper in this room because it was so light. While they were here we shared old times and memories together. Frank talked a little, but he mostly sat listening to us, for he had started having trouble talking for very long. It used up a lot of energy that he was short on.

Some members of the M.I.M. choir in our living room for a special performance

That evening Mark had cooked dinner and brought it over for the four of us. He made enough for Laurence and Gloria, but they had to be in Sacramento. The four of us were sorry they couldn't be with us because at 6 that evening, Music in the Mountains had arranged a group of around 20 singers to come over to our place and sing about 20 old-time songs to us in the living room. Julia, Mark, and the M.I.M. people all took pictures. During the performance, the four of us sat on the sofa. Frank's catheter bag was in view, but that didn't bother them at all.

The four of us enjoying a special M.I.M. performance at our house

175

Frank really enjoyed the show, and after they had left, he wrote a note to them on a piece of paper that I had written some notes on from what the Hospice workers had told me earlier. It wasn't until after he passed away that I found what he had written. I took it over to the M.I.M. office. His handwriting shows that his thinking was not all too clear and that his hand wasn't very steady.

Frank's handwritten comments about the Music in the Mountains serenade on Valentines Day 2007:

To Valentines Day performers at Amaral Home on Feb 14, 2007 we wish a very fond welcome and appreciation for their wonderful performance and friendly atmosphere involved by all the singers and musicians. This was a very unusual performance in our own home for a select group of people who along with the performers all enjoyed each other immensely and all enjoyed a great evening of music.

Right after they left here, they had to go and practice for the performance that was scheduled for the next M.I.M. program. Julia and Mark left to go home a short while later. This was one full day. Frank really enjoyed the evening with them, and around 9 p.m. Ken came by for the night. Frank was in his pj's and had played a little Hand and Foot with me before getting ready to turn in around 10:30 p.m., the time that Sharon from Hospice would stop by. His blood pressure was 98 over 40, his heart rate was 100, and his oxygen was 89. It took her about an hour to take care of Frank before getting him to bed. After she left, I took a shower and got ready for bed myself.

Each night while going to bed, we would say our prayers and kiss each other goodnight. Frank would always say, "I love you very much," and I would say the same to him. He always managed to say it first. Even though we had someone here to look after Frank at night, I still slept in our bed with him. At night, Ken would be in the kitchen, or some other part of the house. He had a room monitor set up in our bedroom that allowed him to hear what was going on, regardless of where he was in the house.

When I went to bed, I would turn the furnace down to 68, so they had to wear warmer clothes for the night, but they always came prepared for that. I also had plenty of blankets and pillows around the house for Frank that they could use if they wanted to lie down on one of the sofas or chairs. They started most of their evenings by doing some reading or taking care of whatever else they needed to do, and somewhere along the way, they would eat their dinner. Frank kept them fairly busy all night long.

The first few nights that Ken was here, he found that Frank needed support to keep him from falling down. Frank also needed help carrying his drainage bag into the bathroom to empty it. The bag got to be a problem by making it difficult for Frank to get in and out of bed. And Ken needed to help Frank put on his bathrobe, for he no longer had the strength to use his arms to put it on. Frank would get up at least six, seven, or more times each night. When he was in bed, he tossed and turned a lot, while I did my best to keep him covered.

Feb. 15, Thur. Ken decided to see if Frank could handle the shower in the bathroom off the kitchen if he helped him. I had had a support bar installed in this shower and had added a light and a new showerhead with the hope he could use it. I also removed the drain cover in case he had accident. Hospice had also brought in a shower chair for him to use. He did all right, but Ken felt he was too weak on his own and there wasn't enough room for two to be in the shower at the same time. However, he shaved Frank and did all the things he had been doing in the bathroom, but this was the only time they used the shower. After they were finished, they came into the kitchenette for his breakfast. Just after that, Victor, our gardener, came in to talk to Frank and told him he would always take care of the yard for me and anything else I needed to have done. He more or less said his goodbye to Frank at this time.

Hospice had to come in and clean Frank's catheter tube again. It was all plugged up, and we knew it was because nothing was moving down the tube. Frank was in misery by having such a full bladder. They found a lot of clots had plugged up the openings and had a hard time getting them out. He always felt so much better when it was working right. Later that day Lowell Robinson came over to see Frank and to say goodbye. He and Wanda were leaving on their trip and would be gone for at least 10 days. And Betty Hahn came over with some goodies and to visit with Frank. The Hospice nurse came by later that afternoon to clean and drain his catheter tube again. Frank was now showing more signs of tiring and wanting to rest more. He was reading less, but he still went through the mail. I took care of getting the bills paid, and Mark continued to pick up our mail.

Feb. 16, Fri. After getting Frank bathed, dressed, and fed, we received a nice bouquet of flowers from the florist given to us from Bev and Bill Riddle. Bev later delivered a nice plum cake, and the family enjoyed it very much. Maria Durr brought over a big dish of custard that Frank really liked. By this time, I was fixing him Jell-O and other soft foods for him to eat. I continued giving him Ensure for protein.

We had to have Diane from Hospice come in and check Frank's catheter because it had plugged up again. This time they took it out and put a larger one in, hoping it wouldn't plug up as easily. Frank was very tired after that, so he spent the greater part of the day in the living room lying down on the sofa, covered with blankets and pillows under his head. He found he could breathe a little better with pillows under his head. Laurence came over in the afternoon and sat with Frank for over an hour. I left them alone so they could talk to each other. I never asked what they talked about. Carlos Astesana came over later to see Frank, and after visiting with him and talking about things in the past, he said some prayers with him. He then left, for Frank was getting tired. Dr. Tomlin called to see how he was doing.

By this time, Mark was bringing me the mail every day, and if he didn't, Laurence did so if he was coming out our way. If not, I would go get the mail. Mark was coming by several times a day to see Julia, who was still working on her pictures at our place for the movie, and to see if he was needed.

In the past, Frank would turn on the TV in the morning to watch the ticker tape and to watch the golf tournaments when they were on. He would watch the news in the evening and then turn to Jeopardy. He really enjoyed watching the TV. He watched a little TV now, but I noticed he would soon get tired and turn it off. I have never been a fan of TV, nor do I watch any movies. However, I would watch the news and some of the golf with Frank, and when he had Jeopardy on, I would sometimes watch that as well. We usually watched TV while having our meal at the kitchen table.

Our evenings were more or less the same as they had been in the past, although by the time a Hospice nurse came by, which was almost always between 9 p.m. and 10 p.m., it had been a long day for Frank, and an even longer one for me. Ken was still coming in at his regular time each night. Frank's nights were getting more restless. He was having to get up more often and was also getting weaker. By now I was beginning to hope they would find someone to help Frank on Sunday night since these were Ken's nights off. I was beginning to wonder how I was going to handle Frank when he kept getting out of bed.

Sometime today, a wheelchair and a stool for the shower were brought in for Frank. The wheelchair was folded up and kept out of sight, placed by the den near the big window. The stool was put in the shower. As I've said earlier, things seemed to arrive at the house a few days before we needed them. Hospice must have a very good record of knowing when to anticipate when such things will be needed.

Feb. 17, Sat. My alarm has always gone off at 7 a.m., and it continued to do so every morning during Frank's sickness, until the last two days. By 7 he was usually ready to get up anyway. This was after I had said the Rosary. In the past, he used to help me make the bed, but that had stopped a few months earlier. And he always used to turn the bed down before we went in to go to sleep. He continued doing this when Ken was with us and did so until his first catheter was put in; after that, he never did it again.

During this time, other than the one shower that was attempted, Frank's baths were done on the hospital bed. He had gotten used to having the bed reclined upward, which allowed his head to be higher than his feet and legs. He rather liked this position, and I was inwardly hoping he would like it enough to sleep that way at night. I knew he would have to sleep on it the night I wouldn't have any help, and I knew he wasn't going to like that. Each morning, except for Mondays, Ken would clean up the bathroom and sleeping area. They were always a mess this time of day, and I had a lot of laundry to do each day. Ken would then bring Frank out for breakfast, write up his report, and then leave for the day. He said he would be back for the night but not for Sunday night.

Frank's days were always much easier on him than the nights were, and he was now getting very little sleep. Along with getting up so many times, he would toss and turn all night long, which also kept me awake at night.

Around this time, Julia and Mark's new furniture had finally arrived. They had waited about a year. They wanted Frank to see it while he could still walk, so I got him in my car, locked up the house, and went over to their place for the day. We also had dinner with them. Their furniture looked very nice in the living room, and Frank spent most of the day sleeping on one of the new sofas. He also spent some time sitting out on the patio in the sun looking out at the snowcapped mountains to the east. We had a nice dinner prepared by Mark that consisted of corn beef and cabbage. After dinner, we played a few hands of cards and then came home. I brought the leftovers home with me.

Up until now, Frank had been trying to walk up the basement steps at least twice a day to help keep his legs strong and to help with his breathing. We talked about how long he would be able to climb the steps. Ken came by for the night around 9 p.m. and helped get Frank ready for bed. The catheter, bag, and tubing made it impossible for Frank to do this by himself. Everything had to go up and be secured to his left leg before he could even get dressed.

Feb. 18, Sun. Ken got Frank up after the alarm went off. I continued with the Rosary and then got dressed to go to church. I had asked Mark if he would come over at 9 a.m. to be with Frank while I went to church, and he said he would. Ken said he would stay at the house until Mark got there, and he told Frank he would be back Monday night. The office still hadn't found anyone to take care of Frank on Sunday nights. This meant I would continue taking care of Frank on Sunday nights by myself. Mark later told me that Frank had asked him to bring the wheelchair into the bedroom this day. He started using it and never stopped. Mark also told me Frank was having fun raising and lowering the head of the hospital bed, and he hoped this would prove to be a good sign for the upcoming night.

Sometime back in January, Laurence, along with some of the Hospice people, said I would need to take up the rugs because Frank would trip and fall on them. Frank made it clear that the rugs would not be taken up for the wheelchair and that he would not fall on them because he never had. Frank loved the rugs on the floors throughout the house, and he found the wheelchair light enough and easy enough to operate that the rugs were not a problem. Frank himself wasn't very heavy either; his weight at this time was about 148 lbs.

The nurse came by today and took his blood pressure, which was 122 over 60. His heart rate was 70 bpm. She didn't take his oxygen this day, but she did clean his catheter and empty the bag.

Julia had gone to church with me, and when we got home, we fixed breakfast for ourselves. I think she and Mark stayed for the day, for I was going to need help now that Frank needed the wheelchair to get around in. This meant he was no longer steady on his feet and that his legs were weaker. We took him into the living room where he remained on the sofa or in his wheelchair for the rest of the day.

Shortly after Frank was in the living room, he said he had to have a bowel movement. Mark was still here, and thank goodness for that. I ran to the bathroom to get some plastic blankets to put on the floor by the sofa and got the potty chair out of the bathroom and then ran downstairs to get a bucket to set it on—now we were in business, in the living room! While I am doing this, Julia and Mark are getting his clothes down, and by this time, Mark had to help him get up. By the time he was ready to sit down on the potty chair, Mark said Frank could no longer hold his weight. Well, it took time, but he had a good one. After all the things that Hospice was giving him, it should be. About this time, the Hahn's had come over to see Frank. Mark had gone to the kitchen while we took care of Frank, so Mark kept them company while Julia and I got Frank all cleaned up and dressed again. And, of course, I got the living room ready for company. Frank had taken this in his stride, but he, along with the three of us, were exhausted, and Frank was ready to lie down on the sofa. He was very cold, so we covered him with a blanket, and then Betty and Brayton came into the living room to visit with him.

Around 2 p.m., John and Clara Casey came by to visit with Frank, and a little later Amy and Harold Schuler stopped in, followed a short time later by Rena and Dick Marundee. Laurence and Gloria also came over to spend some time with him. I think I went in and took a nap on the bed, for I was getting tired from the lack of sleep. I also think other people dropped in to see Frank while I was asleep. I tried keeping a record of all the things that were happening, but everything was beginning to move much faster. I don't remember, but I think Julia cooked pork chops and an apple dish for our dinner this night. Frank was able to eat some of it; he was still eating meals, just not as much as he used to. After dinner and getting the dishes done, we went into the living room and played Hand and Foot. When it came time to get ready for bed, Mark went home and Julia stayed to help me out.

I told Frank he had to sleep in the hospital bed tonight, so we could put up the sides and keep him safe. If he ended up falling out of bed, I don't know if we could've helped him. We got him in the bed and tucked the blankets around him. I could see this was going to be tight quarters for him, and I hoped he would try to help us. I showed him how to use the electric blanket and how to use the switch to adjust the bed. I then put up the sides of the bed. This really wasn't making him happy, but at the time, all he said was the bed was too short and there wasn't enough room to move about, and on that score he was right. But I knew I would not be able to handle him in our bed. I also knew I wouldn't be able to get him up, walk him around, and do all the things he needed to do all night long by myself.

Julia went into her old bedroom for the night, and I got ready for bed. I have to admit I felt guilty having him sleep in the hospital bed, but it was at the foot of my bed, so I would be able to hear him when he needed me. He was sort of a different person once he got to sleep; he tossed and turned and moved around a lot, just as he had in our bed, but now he couldn't get up. Well, this became a nightmare for both him and me. He kept telling me he had to go to the bathroom, and I kept telling him the bag would take care of it. I would have to get up, uncover him, and show him that the urine was going down to the bag on the floor. To make this story short, I'll simply say this went on all night long, all the way up until seven in the morning. He tried crawling out of bed many times, and his legs always got tangled in the steel spokes on the side of the bed. At no time during the night was he rational enough to talk to, so there wasn't much I could do. He did not understand why he couldn't be in bed with me. But I knew if he were in our bed, he would be getting up all night and would fall before I could get to him. I never did get much sleep, but at least I was lying down and that helped. I kept telling him how sorry I was that I had to do that to him, and I reminded him it would only be the one night he would have to sleep in that bed, and I meant it.

If he had been thinking right, he could have figured out how to lower the side and get out of the bed. But his thinking at night had changed, and in a way, he was not my Frank. I never called Julia in from her bedroom, but in the morning, she said she had gone in to check on him three times, and each time he was asleep. This could have been right after I had gotten up to help him. I also remember I emptied the catheter bag at some point in the night. And at one time he had his knees jammed between the bed spokes. I had a hard time getting them out. His bones would hurt him when I pushed too hard to get his knees back through the spokes. I got up at 7 a.m., dressed, made my bed, and took care of him. He never said a word about the night, and it was never mentioned again.

As I write this I still can't say I did him wrong, for I know I could not have been able to handle him, even with Julia's help. He would have gotten out of bed before I could get to him, and by this time he was too weak to do it on his own. You could not rationally explain this to him, for he would not have understood any more than he did with Ken. And it would end up getting worse as the nights went by. He never talked about his night episodes; it was as if they hadn't happened. I wonder now if he knew what was going on.

Feb. 19, Mon. I was one tired gal from this time on. I spent the morning getting Frank ready for the day. I got him undressed and into the bathroom, which always took time. I brushed his teeth and helped him clear out his throat and nose, and then made the small bed he had slept in. I gave him a sponge bath, washed his hair, got him dressed, and out to the kitchen. I didn't get him shaved, but he said he would do that in the kitchen. It was now around 10 a.m. and Julia had our breakfast ready. I'm sure all his tossing around all night didn't add to his health. From this day on things started going downhill faster for him. But he was always good-natured during the daytime and was a very good patient. He was very loving to me and never complained. He would tell the Hospice nurses that I was the better nurse.

I noticed today that his skin was bluish. He was cold, especially in his hands and feet, so I had a Hospice nurse come by to see him. She said it was caused from a lack of blood getting to his heart. Laurence was over so I asked him if he would go buy his dad a warm pair of gloves to wear to bed. He got a pair and brought them over the next day.

Julia had to leave after we had breakfast, so I cleaned up the kitchen, and by that time, Frank wanted to lie down. I pushed him in the wheelchair to the living room and had a hard time getting him out of the chair and onto the sofa. He was so cold I had to put several blankets on him. I was so tired that I pushed the coffee table up to the sofa so he couldn't fall onto the floor. I then took a pillow and lay down on the floor with his head near me. I would only dose off for a few minutes, for I was afraid he would try to get up as he did during the night. I'm not so sure, but it could have been the medicine they gave him at night when he went to sleep that made him that way. We stayed this way in the living room together all morning. I was still alone with Frank and didn't want to leave him alone at any time.

Whenever the phone rang I would run to the den, and from there I could watch him. I would tell the caller I couldn't talk very long, and at one time, I had to hang up on someone because I saw Frank trying to push the table away to get up. When Hospice came, I told the nurse about the problem. I think they changed his medicine, and they cleaned out his catheter and emptied the bag, along with all the other things they did. I fixed lunch for Frank and myself, and Laurence and Mark came over around noon. I told them I needed a cordless phone, so I wouldn't be leaving Frank when the phone rang. My phone system was changed, and to this day, I don't know if it was Mark or Laurence that did it. But it sure saved me a lot of walking. I also knew by now that the only way Frank was going to get around during the night was with the wheelchair. So I had Mark and Laurence help me move my bed closer to the dressers to make room on Frank's side of the bed for his wheelchair, so they could get him in and out of our bed. We were also beginning to put a table and a big chair next to his side of the bed, so that when he got up to get out, he would have to move them. This kept him from getting out of bed without our help. Frank and I have slept on an elevated bed for many years. And because there were blocks under the head of the bed, I needed help moving it, otherwise I could have pushed it myself.

In the afternoon, people started coming over to see Frank. I think the first couple was Netta and Joe Kandell, and a little later Father McKnight stopped by. After he left, I told Netta I wanted to go take a nap. She said they would watch Frank. And about this time, Julia and Mark were here. I left to go to my bedroom and closed the hallway door, so I would not hear anyone while taking a nap. Jayne Clare and Ed Robinson came by and brought some food, and then right after that Alice and Dick Weibe stopped by. I understand that both of them sat down on the coffee table to talk to Frank. The coffee table was used by many this day and ended up becoming a good bench for people to sit on while visiting with Frank. Roxanna also stopped by, and about this time I woke up as Martha and Deiter Juli came to visit.

After everybody had left, Julia took Frank for a ride in the wheelchair out in the yard. While they were out there, Frank picked me a bouquet of Daphne. I found a vase and put the bouquet in the living room. It lasted for two weeks. I was fixing soup for our dinners, and Frank had started not wanting any meat, for he was having a hard time swallowing it, but he could eat fish and chicken. Now that I think about it, I am pretty sure this was his last ride in the yard. I wasn't able to move the wheelchair out the kitchen door and down the step, nor could I bring him in the house on my own.

Ken showed up around 9 p.m. and got Frank ready for bed. He would be with us for the night and leave at 10 a.m. He put Frank in our bed. And because Frank had gotten worse, Ken really had his work cut out for him getting Frank in and out of the wheelchair and the bed throughout the night. Sharon came in around 10 p.m. to check on Frank.

I was still sleeping in our bed with Frank, even if he was up half the night, and tossing and turning in bed the rest of the night. And he was always so cold. We would heat a heating pad in the microwave to get it hot enough and put it at the foot of the bed. Sometimes I would have to get up and find more blankets to put on him, even with the electric blanket turned on.

Feb. 20, Tue. Ken took care of Frank in the morning, and I had noticed when I had taken care of him the morning before that areas of his skin were real scabby and looked like they were going to crack. I showed the Hospice nurse and was given salve to put on it. They also told Ken to do the same. After his catheter bag was cleaned, Ken brought him out to the kitchen area. As I've mentioned, by now Frank was having a hard time getting food to go down, so he wasn't eating very much. Sometimes I would fix Cream of Rice for him to have with the fruit I would give him. And he would stay in the kitchen with me as long as I had work to do, for he could never be left alone anymore.

I haven't said very much about the weather, but all through Frank's last few weeks of sickness, we had fairly nice weather. Sitting in the kitchen and looking out at the yard was always enjoyable. At this time, the snow flowers were really showing their white colors along the patio, and the lawns are always bright and green at our place. The tall camellia trees along the back fence were really beginning to show their colors—whites, reds, and pinks of all shades and sizes. These were in bloom for Frank to see, along with the yellow daffodils, crocuses, and hyacinths. He could see these flowers and the cherry trees that were ready to burst while sitting in the kitchen area. And today while sitting in the kitchen, Paul Perry came over to read Frank a letter he had written about Frank. While Paul was here, Genevieve Phillips stopped by on her way from St. Canice Hall.

I took Frank into the living around noon, and shortly afterward Lynn from Hospice, who had replaced Diane for daytime care, came by. She brought a board with her to go over the arms of the wheelchair that could be used as a table to make it easier to feed Frank. Up until now, I had been using a large cookie sheet. Frank would sometimes put pillows on top of it and lay his head on it to sleep. And it was around this time that they brought a strap that we could use to strap him in the wheelchair. At first, I wondered why, but in a few days the strap would come in handy.

Lynn cleaned his catheter and talked to him about the things that were going on; she always took time to help Frank understand what was happening to him. He was having a lot of trouble with his blood at this time. And his feet, ankles, and legs were continuing to swell, right up to the point where he could no longer get into his shoes. So he wore a pair of slippers that had long lost their shape and had an open back, which made it easy for him to get his feet into. (Later, when I got rid of all his shoes, I kept the slippers. Mark found several pairs of shoes he liked, for he and Frank wore the same size, as did many of the relatives.)

Laurence brought the new pair of gloves over today, and Frank wore them all day and night. Over the next several days, Frank would be hot or very cold. I had finally gotten around to bringing out all the spare pillows and blankets I had on hand that we could use to keep him warm during the times he got so cold. And because the weather was nice and warm outside, I hadn't turned up the heat in the house, for if I did, the rest of us would be way too hot. During the time Lynn was here today, Netta and Joe came over to see if they could help, and around 2 p.m., Tom and Sharon Seck from our church came over to see Frank. Betty and Brayton also came over and brought some eye drops for my eyes, which were giving me some trouble.

Frank spent the rest of the day in the living room trying to keep warm. The nurse had changed some of Frank's medicine, but he was still restless and cold while lying down. I piled the blankets on him during the daytime, and we had to watch him to make sure he didn't overheat, which he never did.

I have no notes as to what we did for dinner, nor that night, but I do know that Ken came in at 9 p.m. Did Frank and I play cards? I don't remember. But I know we were still playing cards around this time, and Julia sometimes joined in before leaving to go home for the night. She was still spending a good amount of time at our place in the evenings working on the pictures for Frank's movie. I do know that when Ken put Frank to bed, I got a large heating pad, heated it in the microwave, and put it on Frank's feet. Ken reheated it throughout the night to keep it warm.

Diane now works the nightshift, even on the days that Sharon is off. When Frank was getting ready for bed, Sharon came over, cleaned up the catheter, and took care of any sores. She always took extra care when cleaning the catheter, and if she saw any sores, she would always put salve on them. The *Home Instead* people did not do this kind of work, so the Hospice nurses always watched that at night.

Later that night, around 3 a.m., Frank was still having a hard time keeping warm. He had been up and down many times during the night, and Ken couldn't keep him warm. I noticed that Frank was ice cold at some point in the middle of the night and that really made me worry. So I called Diane at her home to ask her if I should call the kids to come over, for I thought he was dying. She said no; she didn't think it was necessary at this time. The reason I called her was we had become good friends and she knew what was going on, so I called her as a friend, rather than calling Hospice. Then, ten minutes after talking to her, my phone rang. It was Diane. She was at the kitchen door calling from her cell phone, waiting for me to let her in. She came by to see if anything was needed — in the middle of the night and on her own time. She checked him out and said he would be all right. Although it was in the middle of this night, this was during her normal working hours, so at least I hadn't gotten her out of bed. What a jewel!

Frank remained cold the rest of the night. Ken kept taking care of him and put blankets on him when he was in and out of bed. I did the same. When he was not with Frank, Ken spent time in other parts of the house. The room monitor allowed him to hear Frank and me talking, and if I thought I needed Ken's help, I'd simply call out for him. Otherwise, he was very much in tune to Frank's movements and would come on his own, which allowed me to rest.

Feb. 21, Wed. The alarm went off at 7 a.m., and I noticed Frank always seemed more at peace at this time of day. I said the Rosary and then got up, took a shower, and got out of the bathroom before Ken came in at 8 to get Frank ready for the day. After breakfast was over, the cleaning women showed up. I had them clean our bedroom and living room while we were in the kitchen area. The girls always turned the heat down when they were there, so the house got real cold and I had to keep putting blankets on Frank. After they had cleaned that end of the house, I took Frank in and he lay down on the sofa, and I covered him with a lot of blankets. Up to now, he was able to go to his office on their cleaning day, where he was able to stay warm when they were here.

Right after lunch, Harold and Mary Ann Berliner came by with a loaf of sweet bread, and we enjoyed a nice visit together. Then right after that, Maria Durr and her friend, Gertrude, came with a nice, big bowl of custard. Clara and John Casey also came by, and while we were all visiting and sitting around the kitchenette table, Mark arrived with the mail. Maria and Gertrude said goodbye and left. After a few minutes, Mark asked everyone if they would like a scotch and water, and the four said, "Yes," so he fixed everybody up. Even Frank joined in with them. Mark left right after that.

We continued to talk, and Frank was alert to everything being said. They got to asking Frank about the business and who would be handling it or something to that effect, for now I don't remember the exact words. And he came right out with it, in no uncertain terms. He said, "LaVonne can handle it with Ina's help." He stated it very directly, leaving no room for dispute as to what he meant and who would take care of it. This made me feel good. It was now out there publicly to where other people knew the plan besides me. Julia came over about this time and joined us.

Frank had been telling me this all along, but until now he hadn't told anyone else, except Ina, who had known the plan for years, and of course, Howard Epstein, who had also been told this many years ago when it came to the market. Frank had also told me that Julia, Laurence, and Mark would be able to help me whenever I needed it. He also said that Laurence knew how to handle the books the way he did, in case I needed help. Laurence had done the books years earlier, and Julia and Mark could help me out with the market. And that is what has happened.

After a while, Hazel Shewell came to give Frank a card that she had written her thoughts in. She had no intention on staying because she was still having trouble with the passing of her husband, Paul, who had passed away earlier. But Julia had her stay while she read Hazel's card to Frank. I knew this was hard for Hazel, so I held her while Julia read it and then she left. A short while later, Betty Hahn came over with some food, which was greatly appreciated. After everyone left, we went into the living room for Frank to rest. Lynn from Hospice came by about this time to check on Frank. She and Laurence went into the kitchen to set up full-time care without Frank hearing about it. Then about 2 p.m., we had an appointment with a person from *The Union* newspaper who wanted to do an article about Frank's history while he was alive.

Both Frank and I were very leery of news people, for they have never been very kind to us in all the years we have lived in this area. We were sitting down on the living room sofa, and Frank was leaning on me when Jill Bauerle arrived. Laurence brought her into the living room to talk to us. She started to ask Frank some questions, but he would not answer her. So I said, "I have no idea why you are here to ask questions since *The Union* has all the information dating back to 1945 or so on us, and all you have to do is remove all the negative stuff and you will have his history." She said she was new to the area and didn't think she could find it. She really wanted to write the story while Frank was alive, so he could enjoy reading it. She asked questions about where he was born, his childhood life, and how he got started in business. I was not too happy answering the questions and was very careful how I answered them.

Laurence finally came in and sat down beside me on the sofa. He started to give her information. Even he was very careful as to what he said, for he knows about the negative things that have been printed about us. Julia came in towards the end of the interview and talked to Jill about getting some pictures to use in her story. Julia helped her with that, and two days later, a very good front-page article came out in the paper. It was a long story and, yes, a very positive story. Jill did some additional research and put out a very positive story that included everything about Frank's life, things that most local people did not even know about. Throughout this whole conversation, Frank never said a word. When the article came out, Frank wasn't in a condition to thoroughly enjoy it. Julia had to read it to him, for he could no longer concentrate or read very well. I think his sight might have been giving him trouble, but he never said so. We started getting letters and phone calls from people after the article came out saying what a good story it was, and that they didn't know anything like that about him.

Laurence, Julia, and Mark were a great help all day long. One of them was here whenever I needed them. I hadn't written any notes about the evening, but during this time Frank was still able to come to the kitchen, have dinner, and play some cards at night before going to bed. Ken would then take over. Frank's nights were up and down, and he was very cold. He was also beginning to spend more time sitting in the wheelchair during the nights in the living room, and sometimes Ken would turn on the TV for him.

Feb. 22, Thur. After the alarm went off, I said the Rosary, got up, got dressed, and went into the kitchen to prepare breakfast. I also put out a load of wash — something I was doing every day. Frank was still able to eat some Cream of Rice, papaya, and a piece of banana. Earlier on, I was able to fix eggs, bacon, and toast with strawberry jam for him. He needed protein, but in time he couldn't eat bacon or meat of any kind because he started having trouble swallowing food. So I changed to Cream of Rice. And I sometimes made him oatmeal and once in a while, cold cereal. I tried to make his food look good by having several kinds of small pieces of fruit to go with it. He could only eat a little of each, but I wanted it to look appetizing to him. The last three weeks he ate very little of anything.

I had a hair appointment around 2 p.m., so I asked Laurence if he would stay with Frank while I was gone. While he and I were sitting on the sofa in the living room visiting, Laurence was telling his dad that he was proud of him as a Father, and as a man. Frank asked Laurence what he (Frank) should be proud of, and Laurence said the elimination of the "carry all" and pond. (These are Laurence's notes that he was taking at the time, and I don't know what he meant by "pond".) Frank said to Laurence and me that he was most proud of the way his wife and children had been able to live their lives because of him, and he said he wanted to say that to Julia, Gloria, and Mark. He said more than that, but I was not taking notes, so I don't remember what else he said. I left for my hair appointment shortly afterwards. I'm sure that Frank and Laurence did more talking between themselves when I was gone.

While I was gone, Frank got a real bad bloody nose, and when I got home, Laurence said he had a hard time finding the cotton balls. He also said Frank had trouble with his bladder and that the catheter bag had filled up with blood and urine and he had to empty it. During the entire time Frank had the catheter, I always tried to keep the bag in its own container in case the bag started to leak. It did so a few times, and I had a towel to cover it, but most of the time it sat on the floor because Frank moved around on the sofa so much. But this was our life at the time, so we lived with it, even if the red blood in the bag might disturb other people.

I showed Laurence where the cotton balls were in case he needed them again in the future. I got Frank a clean hanky and cleaned up the area for Laurence. Hospice came by and gave us a list of the medicines he would be taking, which included: Lasix, potassium, Levothyroxine (morning and noontime), Vicodin/hydrocodone, docusate, and lorazepam for sleeping (I hope I've spelled them right at this late in time). And because Frank's legs were so restless during the nights, Dr. Tomlin, of Chapa-De, had given him some medicine for that as well. Frank was taken off fiber tablets and was told he needed to get an electrolyte panel and Complete Blood Count CBC lab test done. A lot of his restlessness was due to lack of oxygen in his blood, and he was losing a lot of blood through his nose, stools, and bladder. He had been coughing up blood, and a few days later, he began coughing up lung tissue. He was now having a hard time swallowing things and did not always want to eat because of that.

Laurence had his hands full while taking care of his dad. And I'm not sure, but I think that while the nurse was here, she told Laurence we would have to get more help. Somewhere about this time Betty and Brayton came over to see Frank, and Netta and Joe Kandell came by.

Up until now, I haven't said much about our dinners. For Frank I cooked anything I thought he could eat. At first, he was able to eat any type of meat, chicken, fish, shell fish, and tuna. Our lunches always consisted of some meat, and for many months Frank liked his tacos and would have them with sliced ham or turkey, lettuce, cheese, and his hot salsa, along with a cookie or a piece of cake, whatever I had on hand. By early February, he was eating half a taco, and then it got to where he couldn't eat that kind of food at all. (In time, it would be soups that were pureed, for I don't think he could chew his food towards the end, but he never said. During the last two weeks he said couldn't swallow anything that was stringy.)

I usually had brown rice of some kind and a green vegetable for dinner, along with some type of protein, which might consist of fish, beef of some kind, lamb chops, spareribs, chicken, pork chops, or any kind of fish. We often had salad and seldom had dessert or bread. Sometimes we would have stews and soups of all kinds and make a meal of them. I continued to cook meat or fish that he would ask for, but in time, this would all change.

I had started Frank on Ensure a few weeks earlier to help give him protein. He was now drinking two or three bottles throughout the day and into the night. I always made sure there were two different kinds of bottles in the bathroom each night, and I would open one to make it easy for him to drink when he went to the bathroom during the night. He did not have the strength to break the seal and open them. I would open the second bottle when I got up to help him in the bathroom. There were four different flavors of Ensure, and I would buy a carton of each so he would have variety.

The nurse told us this evening that Frank would be getting some Ambien during the night. He was still getting cold and was tossing and turning all night long. He was also getting up often and needed his pajama tops changed at least four times each night. It was getting harder and harder for Ken to handle him, for along with all of this, Frank was beginning to lose his ability to help himself get up and out of bed, or in and out of a chair.

Feb. 23, Fri. I want to repeat how our mornings started, for they were almost always the same. Frank's day started by going into the bathroom, getting his pajamas off, and taking his bath. His hair was washed and dried, and then his catheter bag was emptied. He would get dressed and shave himself using an electric shaver. By the time this was all done, a couple of hours will have gone by. In the meantime, I will have started to put out a wash, started getting his meal, and will have brought in the *The Union* newspaper. And today the paper had the article on Frank. I showed it to him when he came out to the kitchen. He looked at the pictures, but I don't think he read the story. I noticed he was having a hard time reading anything by this time, but he never said his vision was going. Maybe he did not have the power of concentration he used to have, for he no longer spent much time on his mail or the *Wall Street Journal*. He continued to glance through *Forbes* and other magazines he had been taking for years. Anyway, I showed the article to him, for it was on the front and second pages, and there was a picture of us on the front page. He liked that. I then gave him his breakfast, and Ken left for home. Julia came by later and read the article to him.

Around 10 a.m., I received a phone call from my cousin Lorna in Minnesota (she is the oldest daughter of my Aunt Eva). She told me her husband Duane had died during the night from pneumonia in the hospital. He had come down with a cold that never got better, so he went to the hospital for the last couple of days when it turned to pneumonia. He was in his mid-70s. She told me when the funeral was going to be held, so I had flowers sent to them from my mother Nellie's family in CA. She later called and said how nice the flowers were; I told Frank about this.

As I've said, because of the article in the paper, more people started calling and wanting to come by to see Frank. Some didn't know how bad he was, and those that did wanted to tell him how much they liked the story. I took Frank into the living room after lunch, and while he was resting, Netta and Joe came by and brought some food. Betty and Brayton came over, and Dale and Bob Peterson came by and stayed awhile. They asked if they could do anything, so I said if they were going to Grass Valley, I'd like them to pick up a dozen papers with the story on Frank. They did so and were at my door half an hour later to give them to me. I really appreciated that, for it kept me from having to leave Frank to go get them. After they left John and Phyllis Hazelwood called to see if they could come the next day to see Frank, and I said yes. Around 3 p.m., Father McKnight came over and brought communion. Frank was lying down on the sofa and not very alert, so Father said he didn't think Frank should have a whole wafer, in case he might choke on it. So he split it in three ways and gave a piece to Frank and a piece to Julia and me. It was always nice to have him come to see us, for I needed his visit as much as Frank did. Carol Hamilton called to say how much she liked his story, and Roxanna Cohen later came over to see him for a few minutes.

Lynn from Hospice came to take care of Frank. She usually showed up between 2 p.m. and 3 p.m. and would take care of all the preparations Frank needed for the evening. She would sometimes change the support hose for Frank. By this time, most of my thumbs and fingers had cracks by the nails, and I was having them bandaged up to cut down the pain. Frank's legs and feet had gotten so big that getting those support hose on him was really a job and took some time to do. He was continuing with the medicine he had been on for the last two days. Lynn told us that Frank's blood pressure was 120/60 and his heart rate was 72. On the 22nd it was 112/40 and 64. She was never in a hurry to leave and would answer any questions we had. As she did so, I noticed she would observe Frank.

Julia was here every day, for she was still working on the pictures in the art room for Frank's movie. And Mark would be in and out all day long doing any errands I needed. He brought me the mail since our place was on his way. When he didn't, Laurence would bring it up to us, but doing so was always out of his way. Nevertheless, he was over most every day and sometimes twice a day.

Today Frank was sleeping more in the daytime and had become more restless due to the lack of oxygen in his blood. We had to watch him while he was awake so he wouldn't try to get up on his own and fall.

I had made up my mind that he would not have any broken bones, so I had to watch him very closely, which I did. After I noticed I couldn't hear him very well, I didn't wait to have my ears checked. I got hearing aids, and I have never been sorry. I wore them at all times, for I needed to be able to hear him even when I was in another room.

Starting around five in the afternoon, Frank's personality began to change. While sitting on the sofa together, I held his head on my shoulder. He kept asking me about every five minutes what time it was and if it was time for Ken to come to put him to bed. This continued for the rest of the evening. Ken wasn't scheduled to come in until 9 p.m., and I told Frank that, but it didn't register. I was having a hard time keeping his mind at rest, and I was holding him the whole time. Frank was very loving and gentle to me all throughout this ordeal. He would often tell me he loved me, and he never wanted me very far away from him.

After dinner, I began to get Frank ready for bed. We then played cards to keep him occupied until Ken showed up. He was happy when Ken came at 9 and took him to the bathroom to get him ready for bed. Hospice came during this time, and I think Frank was hoping he would sleep when he got to bed. This must have been the reason he wanted to go to bed so early.

Julia was often here when we had dinner and would stay until around 8 or 9, but tonight no one was here. I remember Frank telling me during this time that she wasn't spending enough time with Mark. So Mark, I hope you forgive her for that.

As I've said earlier, Frank's personality changed at night. He became very restless during the night and didn't want to stay in bed. Ken would get him back into bed, and then within 5 minutes Frank was ready to get up again. He kept saying he had to go to the bathroom. The catheter really gave him a bad time, and there was nothing we could do about it. Even when Ken had him sitting up in the living room, it was the same way. Ken would even turn on the TV to see if that would quiet him down, but it didn't help. And Frank continued to be very cold and needed lots of blankets wrapped around him. The two medicines they had given Frank for the night were morphine and Ambien, and he needed to take them five times during the night. I now wonder if that is what upset him all night; instead of putting him to sleep, it seems to have kept him awake.

This was Ken's last night before taking a break. He works five nights on and has two nights off. Fortunately, *Home Instead* had found a good woman to take over for the next two nights, allowing Ken to get some rest. Her name was Maria Quimby, and I wondered how Frank would take to that. She was rather small, about my size, and I wondered if she could handle Frank and his physical weakness and get him in and out of bed and out of the wheelchair.

Feb. 24, Sat. I was up before 7 a.m., took a shower, washed my hair, and got dressed. Frank had kept me up most of the night, even though Ken was there. I was kept awake by Frank's tossing and turning, and I needed to keep him covered with blankets. Ken was still spending most of his time in the rest of the house, and if he did sleep, it was on the sofa in the living room or foyer. He didn't know when Frank was uncovered. In the morning, Ken told Frank he would see him in two days and that he was going to Reno for a day. He also told Frank about Maria and said she was a highly rated and a capable person. And from there I took over.

Mark usually dropped in around eleven to bring me the mail and to see if I needed anything done. He would usually spend some time talking to Frank, and today he helped Frank to the living room.

Lynn from Hospice came in a short time later and, along with taking care of him, the catheter, and checking everything else, she said she had to leave and would be right back. It turned out she had gone into the office and ordered a big oxygen tank with 90 feet of tubing and a smaller portable tank. The Hospice office is about a mile and a half from our house; it was delivered while she was here. The men put it in the foyer, so it would be in the center of the house, and they made sure there was enough tubing to go from the big machine to our bedroom, the kitchen, and living room. After checking everything over, they felt he was well taken care of and they left. Lynn showed Frank how to use it—if and when he needed it. He wasn't so sure he would use it. But as I have said before, Hospice was always a day ahead of things that would be needed. I had already learned that. And somewhere about this time, they had given us something to swab out Frank's throat.

None of the kids were here, so I was alone with Frank. I didn't feel I wanted to leave him for very long, but later Julia and Mark came over and had dinner. Julia worked on the pictures, while Mark sat in the living room so I could leave.

I'm sorry that I didn't keep better notes, but one doesn't think to write down conversations they have with a sick person. First off, you don't have time and are very tired, and secondly, your thoughts don't keep reminding you that today could be the last day.

Maria came by at 9 p.m. She is a very strong woman and not much taller than I am. She wasted no time in taking command of Frank; I wondered how far that would go with Frank. I took her into our bathroom and bedroom and showed her where everything was, including all his medicines and their instructions. As I said before, that end of the house had now been turned into what looked like medical rooms, filled with all the things Frank now needed. I showed her where she could find his pajamas and underclothes and then left her to take care of him.

Maria was very gentle with him and really knew more about how to take care of him than Ken did. She was very good with him in the bathroom and at helping him get ready for bed. She also observed all the things that were going on with Frank, including his sore bottom end. After the nurse came to check on him, they helped him get in bed and put a chair and a table against the bed to keep him from getting out. If he tried to get out, she would hear it on the monitor. I was now very tired and went to bed at 10. Maria had gone into the kitchen to do her paperwork. She or Ken usually had their meals there around 10.

Shortly after Ken had started staying with us, I kept several lights on dim so the caregivers could see their way around the house at night. And as I've said the thermostat was set at 68 at night, however they both told me they were used to working in cold homes at night. Maria kept better records than Ken, mostly dealing with the medicine Frank needed to take and when, so I now have those to work with. By her record, Frank was up at 12 a.m. and she helped him walk to the living room. At 12:25 a.m., he wanted to go back to bed. This went on every two hours, and before going back to bed, he would always go to the bathroom, wash his face, and would put water in his nose and mouth to clear out his throat and spit out some blood. He would then drink some of his Ensure and take his medicine if it was time. Her notes say he was confused, and she changed his pajama tops four times during the night. He tossed and turned in bed most of the night. She would tell him to lie quietly so he wouldn't wake me up, but during this time I don't think he understood much of anything when he was in bed. I was up at 6 a.m. and Frank slept until 9; he was upset when she made him get up. As I've pointed out before, it seemed to be toward dawn that he would really get to sleep. He was really becoming a different person these last few weeks, and as he got sicker, he became a different man at night once he was in bed.

Feb 25, Sun. Maria got Frank up at 9 to get him bathed and dressed for the day, and she cleaned up our bedroom and bathroom. I always had the bed made when I got up in the morning, so they wouldn't have to do it. And I always got things ready for them. I put out clean towels in the bathroom and would lay out clean clothes for Frank for the day. This being Sunday I had a nice shirt and slacks for him to wear. Maria would take care of Frank and his needs using the hospital bed at the foot of our bed. By this time, Mark had come over to stay with Frank, so I could go to church and then out to breakfast with Julia. Maria later told me that Frank kept asking where I was. Maria stayed to feed him his breakfast and then left at 10:30. Mark took over after that. As I write this, I now wonder if he knew or remembered what his nights were really like.

When Julia and I got home, Frank gave me a big smile and said he was glad I was home. He was sitting by the sliding glass door in the kitchen when I got home. This has been his favorite place in the kitchen all through the 57 years we've lived here, even to watch TV, read the *Wall St. Journal,* or to relax and take a nap with his head on the table. Betty and Brayton had dropped in for a minute from church to see him; Laurence and Gloria were here with Mark to help keep Frank company.

The Hospice nurse gave Frank Mirapex with a little bit of food for his restless legs, and she cleaned and flushed out his catheter and emptied the bag. We went into the living room after she left, so Frank could rest for a while. I saw that he tried to sit up more often because the kids were here. They stayed for most of the afternoon.

Venus, my niece, called in the afternoon from Eureka to ask how Frank was doing; she said they were all doing fine. Frank continued having trouble with his bladder, and his catheter kept getting clogged up. It was always a relief when the Hospice nurse would come to clean it, and this being Sunday, you never knew who the relief nurse would be that would come in to take care of him. She changed his support hose for clean ones I had washed by hand; it takes them a couple of days to dry. And I was glad she did since it's very hard on my fingers for they are so cracked. She emptied the catheter bag, flushed out the tube, and watched to see if any clots came out, and there were some. When she was done, she cleaned out the bag again. This was all done in the living room with the kids in there too. Most all the time the nurses came in the afternoon to check on Frank, they took care of him in the living room. And if they came in the morning, it would be done in the kitchenette, even if company was there.

The kids left around 5; they had dinner dates with different people. When it came time for dinner, Frank and I went into the kitchen and I fixed us some fish, a vegetable, and a Jell-O salad. He was able to eat a little bit of everything. We were in the living room by the time Maria came over at 9 p.m. After she got him ready for bed, the Hospice nurse came in and gave Frank Thorazine for his restless legs. Up until now, the nurse had been coming by so late that it was after 10, sometimes even 11, before he was able to go to bed. I had been asking them if she could come earlier, but it was always at least 9 or later by the time they got here.

Frank had finally gotten to sleep, but a short time later he woke up and found I wasn't in bed. He told Maria he wanted me in bed with him. He was having trouble getting back to sleep and was tossing and turning in the bed, so Maria called the nurse to see what she could give him to calm him down. The nurse called back half an hour later and said he could take some morphine and that should help calm him down. But again, he was up at 11 to go to the bathroom and wash his face. Maria had to put his bathrobe on him each time, help him get out of bed, make sure he had the bag in his hand, and help him walk to the bathroom. He was up again by 12 a.m., went to the bathroom, washed his face, and coughed stuff out of his throat. It was at this time he asked Maria to take him to the living room in the wheelchair. Her notes say he was very confused. She changed his pajama tops 15 minutes later, for they were wet and he was very cold. He stayed up until 3 a.m. and went to the bathroom. Maria said he was still very confused. I hadn't slept much by the time he came back to bed. After he got back in bed, he didn't sleep much and tossed and turned the whole time. I kept having to put blankets on him.

Now that we had two people taking care of Frank I had them change the hours and had them come at 6 p.m. and stay until 10 a.m. And the reason for the early evening time was Frank was wanting to go to bed earlier, and needed more care in the morning. Up until now, he would help put on his clothes but now it was getting harder for him to do so.

Feb. 26, Mon. Maria tried to get Frank up at 7:30, but he was very tired, so it took a while before she got him out of bed. She had to get him up, bathe and dress him, and clean things up before leaving at 10 a.m. Frank came into the kitchen a little while later, all cleaned up, dressed, and shaved. Maria finished cleaning up our bedroom and bathroom and left at 10. Frank began to move around better in the mornings once he had been up for a while.

Along with all the other things going on, it looked like it might snow within the hour, and it did. Frank had to go get his hearing aids fixed, and by this time, I was now doing all the driving. So we took Frank's car and went over to the ear place, which is right across from the Nevada County Golf Course. When we went in for his appointment, it was just starting to rain, and by the time we came out, two inches of hail was covering everything. I helped Frank into the car, and we could see cars sliding out all over the road. I told Frank they shouldn't be using their brakes. I can't quite remember, but I think he said something about me driving in the snow. I got in the car, sat behind the wheel, and backed up to get out of the parking lot. As we got onto the road in front of the golf course, I told him we would be all right, and I would not use my brakes. I shifted down into low gear and kept it there all the way home. I hoped we could get up our driveway. I didn't use the brakes the whole way. Surprisingly, the stop light at Sierra College Drive turned green as we approached it, and all the other lights along Nevada City Highway were green as well. Frank told me I was a good driver and that he was not afraid of me driving anywhere. He has said this to me many times through our married years, and on many of our long trips together, he would read or sleep while I drove.

Frank had trouble getting in and out of his car because the seats were so low, so I knew he would not be riding in his car again. We would be taking my car from now on that had seats higher off the floor. We made it into the house, and Frank slowly walked up the steps holding onto the railing. He had been walking up these steps at least two times a day to keep his legs strong, but I could see he was having trouble breathing and had to stop several times before reaching the top.

When we got home, Julia and Mark came to see if we were all right. It continued to get colder, so I started a fire in the fireplace, put four bricks in it, and got a grate out of the barbecue to lay on top of the bricks. I was now ready to heat water or make soup for Frank if the power went out. I was thinking of Frank this whole time and knew I had to keep him warm. In the meantime, Gloria and Laurence had lost electricity at their place.

Mark came by and brought us the mail. There were a couple of checks that needed to be deposited in the bank, so I wrote it up in the books and took care of it. Mark took them to the bank and deposited them for me.

A short time later, the electricity went out at our place, while it was still daylight. Julia and I got all the oil lamps out of the closet to make sure they were full of kerosene, only to find that I needed more. So Mark went over to SPD, but the store was closed due to the power outage. In the meantime, I got Frank bundled up and added more blankets around him, but he was still cold. Mark took off in his car to go home and see what was happening at their place. On the way, he called and told Julia not to drive up to their place in her car. He told her if she had to come home, she needed to drive very carefully in low gear. They still had power, so if we had to we could go to their place. However, our power came back on in a couple of hours and remained on. So Julia went home, and I took care of Frank.

Several people called during the day to see if we were all right. They were Netta Kandell, Ruth Cramer (whom I hadn't heard from in years), and Alice Wiebe and Dick Cramer, who is not related to Ruth. He called and asked if he could come see Frank on another day, and I said yes. Once the electricity was back on and we got the house warmed up, I put Frank in an armchair in front of the fireplace so he could keep warm. Later we had dinner, and I kept the fireplace going. Frank liked looking at it.

Ken Lauer was in at 6 p.m. to take care of Frank. We were having dinner when he arrived. Frank hadn't eaten very much, but he ate a little of everything and said he wasn't very hungry. Ken drove up in a four-wheel drive and had no trouble getting up our driveway. He helped get Frank ready for bed at 8. Frank seemed to get weaker as the night came on, so it was taking longer and longer to get him into bed. I was nearly always very tired by the time the Hospice nurse came in to take care of Frank's bladder. I got ready for bed right after we got Frank into bed.

Ken was in the kitchen when Sharon from Hospice called after 9 p.m. She said she was stuck in the snow and would have to find a way to get to us. Ken came in to tell me, so I had Ken ask her where she was and told him to take my pickup and go get her. I said I'd take care of Frank until they returned. It was an hour later by the time they got back, but she took good care of Frank and that was all I cared about. By now, Frank was really getting restless and I was having a hard time keeping him in bed. After they showed up, Sharon now had no way to get home, so I had Ken take her home. I think it was in the Chicago Park area. When he got back an hour later, he said he drove through a lot of snow and loved the way my pickup handled it. It went through it without him having to shift to the lowest gear, which I was happy to hear. By this time, Frank was sound asleep.

Frank didn't stay asleep for long and kept getting up. Ken would put him in the wheelchair, which was now no easy chore to do. Frank is weaker at night and to get him in the wheelchair, you had to put on his bathrobe, making sure not to step on the catheter bag. You had to secure the bag to the chair or get Frank to hold it, and then you had to cover him with blankets to keep him warm. After a while, I got up to see how he was doing and put a log on the fire. He and Ken were in the living room by the fireplace.

Tonight there was a good moon out and all the snow was lit up from the moon. It was really a sight to see. So I opened all the curtains and turned on all the outside lights, so Frank could go from the living room and look out all the windows on his way to the kitchen. He got to see the snow on the azalea shrubs, the red maple, and the cherry tree branches. The lawns were blanketed in snow, and at the back fence, the Camellia and Rhodies were drooping heavy with snow. Frank really enjoyed seeing it. I knew he would. We had snow on the ground for a few days.

Around 11:30 p.m., when Ken was trying to help Frank out of the bed, one of them stepped on the catheter bag and opened the tube valve. The bag's contents started to flow in the basin and some got on the rug before I had time to close it. This was one of the things that always interfered with getting Frank in and out of bed.

During this time, Frank was having Ken get him up many times throughout the night, sometimes every half hour, so he could go to the bathroom and help relieve the pressure on his bladder. He was told the catheter was not doing it. Up to now, he had to put pressure on his bladder to help him urinate, but even this was not enough to take care of the problem. It was getting so that even Ken was having trouble handling him during the night. He would have Ken take him to the living room, and he would rest during the night on the sofa. Tonight, while lying on the sofa, Frank started to slide off it and onto the coffee table. Ken got to him in time. A little later, when Ken was not watching him, he pushed the coffee table away and ended up on the floor. Ken came in to get me out of bed and told me what had happened. He asked what we should do. This was the one thing I had kept telling both Maria and Ken—don't ever let him get on the floor, for we wouldn't be able to get him up. And Frank had been trying to do just that for the last few days, not only in the daytime, but at night as well. Ken said he couldn't get him up because Frank was too heavy for him to lift and said we would have to get help. I told him, "Not at this hour of the night," and said, "Let's put the coffee table to his back and between the two of us let's get him up on that, and from there we would see what we could do." In a stern voice, so it would register, I told Frank he would have to help us get him up, and he did. We got him into the wheelchair and then to bed.

We still didn't know what was happening with the tube in his bladder at this time. He kept complaining about being cold and had to have lots of blankets on him to keep him warm. During this time neither he nor I were getting much sleep. But sometime during the night he did get some sleep, maybe it was toward morning when that happened. Many times I would lie close to Frank's body to help keep him warm, but his body could not handle any pressure for any length of time. Even when we held his hand for any length of time, he would pull it away. This was always during the night. At this time, Ken was taking his rest breaks in the living room to take advantage of the heat from the fireplace.

I now decided I would need day care during the daytime hours to properly take care of Frank, and I set it up to start the following day. Ken and Maria were scheduled to work from 6 p.m. to 10 a.m., so I arranged to have someone here between 10 a.m. to 6 p.m. This would allow him to have the same person that put him to bed at night on shift in the morning to get him up. This would help cut out any confusion for him.

Feb. 27, Tue. I was up around 7 to make the bed, take a shower, and clean up the bathroom from all the night's mess, so Ken would have a clean bathroom for Frank. I continued to notice that Frank was getting a little weaker each day, and I knew it was going to require more time and energy to take care of him. So I started using the time when Ken was taking care of Frank to take a load of wash to the kitchen and start the machine. I would then go down to the carport to get *The Union* newspaper. After that was done, I'd start making our breakfast. Today it was Cream of Rice, which he liked, with lots of honey and butter. He needed protein. I also prepared several different kinds of mixed fruits. He liked papaya, bananas, and berries. I made them into a few small pieces, so he wouldn't get overwhelmed by the size. I was beginning to see if you gave him a little, he would eat it, but if it looked like too much, he might not touch it. I also gave him a piece of toast with strawberry jam that I made. And he always liked his Roma coffee with breakfast.

The schedule I had worked out made it so I had breakfast ready when Ken finished taking care of him. Ken's biggest chore was getting Frank to the bathroom, which was the first thing that needed to be done each morning. Frank was always happy to see me when they brought him into the kitchen. While having breakfast this morning, I noticed his fingers and nails were bluish and that the area around his mouth was white. I saw that he didn't have much energy and had lost quite a bit of weight.

Frank was sitting in the wheelchair, which put him high up at the table, so I got a large cookie sheet and put it across the arms of his wheelchair. I then put a nice napkin over the tray. This helped him eat his food easier. The board that Hospice brought in earlier just wasn't big enough to do the job. Frank was also using a colorful bib given to him by Maria that helped keep food from getting on his clothes. (I found that bib a month and a half later after he had passed away. It was tucked under a shelf in the kitchen; I don't know how it got there.)

As I've mentioned, daytime care was scheduled to start the next day. Julia and Mark had been helping on and off during the last couple of days, but today they both had meetings to attend. Today I was alone with Frank and felt really tired. He required me to be with him, so I just sat by him most of the day or laid on the floor by him to keep him from falling off the sofa. I would tell him not to move when I had to answer the phone. When I needed to go to the kitchen, I strapped him in the wheelchair and took him with me.

Gloria from Hospice came around 1 p.m. and changed out Frank's catheter for a new one because the one he had kept plugging up. And I think it was at this time that she started the morphine drops and changed some of his medicines. She and Julia were talking about a lot of things that I don't remember; I was very tired. She checked his blood pressure, which was 108/50 and his heart rate was 67. She had also ordered and got him on prochlorperazine, which is used for nausea and vomiting, and Hurricane Spray for external pain and itching. I wonder if the medicine she gave him is what made him sick later in the afternoon, or did she have a sense of what was going to happen?

Looking back now, I wonder how much Frank was really with us during the nighttime, and I remember he was always very cold, even with the electric blanket and two blankets on top of that. Someone from Hospice came over this day to take care of his catheter tube.

Around 2 or 3 in the afternoon, Frank and I were sitting in the living room with no one else here when Betty and Brayton stopped by for a short visit. Betty was sitting on the coffee table talking to him, and after a while, he motioned for me to sit there. I never knew why. Shortly after they left, Jayne Clare and Ed Robinson came by and brought some food. While they were in the living room, Frank began to throw up. I grabbed the basin with his catheter bag in it and put it in his hands and up to his mouth. I asked them to take care of him as I ran to the bathroom to get some water and towels. When I got back he was really sick and throwing up. It was grayish mucus, and while he was doing it, they left, and now I had no one to help me if I needed help, but I continued to take care of Frank and after he was through he said, "no more company." He was really weak after that, and he just laid down on the sofa, and he was so cold. I covered him up as best as I could and put pillows under his shoulders and head hoping that would help him get some air in his lungs so he could rest. I asked him if he wanted some oxygen and he did. He never really liked using it, but it did help him. He looked colorless around the mouth and was so weak that I wondered if this was the time he would leave us. But toward evening, he improved in health, as well as in spirit.

Julia and Mark had been here on and off earlier in the day and came back around 4 p.m. after everyone had left. I told them that Frank said he wanted no more company, and I think she told Laurence and Gloria, who then passed the word around.

Because Julia and Mark were here off and on for most of the day, she fixed dinner. It was her specialty—pork chops for the four of us. At dinnertime, Frank sat at the table in the wheelchair with Julia at his right with her good ear to him. She kept giving him things to eat off his plate to make sure he kept eating, and Mark got him some wine to drink. At 7 p.m., he said he was ready to go to bed, so Ken took care of him. I stayed in the kitchen and did the dishes after Julia and Mark had left to go home. This night was a repeat of what had been going on the previous nights, but now Ken was staying more in the foyer and living room, so he can get to Frank faster. And I kept having to put blankets over him and tried to keep him from getting out of bed on his own. One time during the night, I called Ken to come in and help me, but he didn't respond. I finally got out of bed to get him, and he was fast asleep on the sofa. He came to help Frank, who was really getting weaker by now, and it was getting harder and harder to get him into the wheelchair. Frank kept trying to get out of bed, wanting to go to the living room. After that, Ken kept a closer watch on him and began putting a strap around him in the wheelchair, so he could not fall out. Frank had started sleeping in it while sitting in it, and he liked being near the fire in the fireplace.

Feb. 28, Wed. This would be a busy day for me, so I got up, dressed, made the bed, and laid out the towels and Frank's clothes. Ken got him up and did the usual morning routine with him. Frank loved to wear nice sweaters, so I picked one out for him to wear. The new day-care woman, Janet, came by at 10:30 a.m.

In the meantime, Ina had arrived and around 8:30 a.m., Kelly from the CPA office in Sacramento came to see Ina and go over the books. I had to be in the office, so Mark and Julia stayed with Frank while he had his breakfast. After we were done in the office, we came into the house to show Frank what we had done. Kelly was taking the books back to her office in Sacramento to finish things up. She said the books would be back in 2 weeks. I asked her to make it a week if she could, for I was sure Frank would hang on until they were back. She thought for a while and said she could have them back within six days, and she did.

After Kelly left, I went back into the office with Ina; she needed to show me some things, now that the main books we used were gone. As Ina was going over things with me, I got a call on the phone in the office from Mark. In a distressed voice, he told me I was needed to help clean up Frank, for he was getting ready to have a movement in the living room, and neither of them knew what to do. They needed my help. So I ran into the house and found all three of them over by the TV. The kids had gotten a plastic sheet on the floor and were trying to get him on the potty chair that was on top of the sheet. Mark was trying to hold him up, using every ounce of strength he had. Frank was unable to help. Julia was trying to get him ready to sit down on the potty chair. And this is what I saw when I came into the living room, so I ran and got towels and a bucket of water. Working together, we got Frank taken care of. As soon as we got Frank on the potty chair, Mark left the room—he had had it!

About this time, Janet Weddle from *Home Instead* arrived around 11:00 a.m. at the kitchen door. Mark showed her into the living room for the first time. She went to work without asking or saying a thing and found a place to empty the dirty bucket and clean it. She then took everything that was soiled and put it in the garbage. Julia and I continued cleaning up in the living room, got Frank dressed, and wheeled him to the sofa to rest. And if I remember right, he told Mark, "Gee, I feel so much better."

Someone from Hospice arrived about this time and brought in special hand washing towels that had soap in them. These were now added to his care. After cleaning and checking the catheter and bag, the Hospice lady checked Frank's health and said he needed more thyroid pills. She then sprayed his throat with Hurricane Spray, which he would need every 6 hours. She also added Pyridium, which he needed to take 3 times a day; it would help him with his urinary pressure. And this was along with all the other medications he was taking. She had him use his oxygen and then left. And all of this happened before we had lunch!

We had lunch around 1 p.m. with the kids in the kitchenette. It was chicken soup. Frank ate a lot of soup and some crackers. He also drank his Ensure. It sure was nice having Janet there to clean up the mess and do all the dishes for us. She also helped us take Frank in his wheelchair to the living room and helped us get him on the sofa. By now, Frank had very little energy to help us lift him, and he sometimes had very little control of his body.

I took a nap. As I slept, Brad and Laurence came over to visit, and Julia was also here. Janet was watching Frank. When I woke up Brad, Laurence, and the Hospice nurse were wheeling Frank into the bathroom so the nurse could take care of him. I didn't know what the problem was, but when I went in to see what was going on, I could tell Frank wanted a basin of water. I tried to get it for him to spit up in. Laurence was standing close to the toilet, and Brad, a big fellow, was standing by the bathtub. The nurse was kneeling in front of Frank who was in the wheelchair. She was trying to clean out his catheter bag and empty it into the toilet. Julia was in back of the wheelchair, and the cabinet and sink were only a few inches to the left of Frank. Our bathroom is fine, but with that many people taking up the space, it doesn't leave much room to move around in. So Julia left to give me room so I could help Frank. Not having seen Brad for some time, I said hello to him and to Laurence, and then Brad told me that if I needed help during the night or day, I could just call 911 and someone would be there to help me.

The nurse continued flushing out the catheter and bag, and we saw there were a lot of blood clots coming out. She did this until all the clots were gone. In the meantime, Frank had asked me to help him clean out his throat and nose. The nurse said she would do it. She then gave an order to make sure that *"that woman,"* meaning me, didn't come back into the bathroom. I could tell Frank was upset about that. So while she was finishing up the job, I checked the card to see who she was and went to the phone in the kitchen. I called Hospice and said *"that nurse"* was to never come back to this house to help Frank again, and she never did.

And yes, I know who she is but will not use her name. Brad brought Frank back into the living room after they were done. I don't remember when the nurse or Brad left, for I don't remember saying goodbye to him. Laurence stayed to be with his dad for a while. Frank told me later that the nurse never did wash his face or help him clean out his nose and throat.

Janet was sitting in the living room, finishing up on a small quilt she had been working on. When I came back to the living room, Janet told me Frank had been restless all afternoon and kept changing his position on the sofa. I could have told her he would be that way until I was back in the room with him, for he did seem to miss me if I wasn't with him. When I came back from my nap, after everyone had left, he told me he did not need pain medicine. For the rest of the afternoon it was just Janet, Frank, and me. I spent most of the rest of the day sitting beside Frank with his head on my shoulder, with his eyes closed, holding my hand, except for when he was lying down.

Janet and I visited off and on during this time, but Frank didn't say much of anything. He mostly just wanted me to hold him. If you asked him something, he would answer, but I did notice that when the day care people were sitting in the living room with us, he wouldn't say much. And I noticed that sometimes when Frank got a bad nosebleed, it would be followed by him having a movement; it seemed they were beginning to always happened together.

Janet was scheduled to leave at 6, so I had her help me undress Frank and get his pajamas on. I then had her change Frank's support hose, for doing so always hurt my fingers that were now covered with Band-Aids most of the time. Ken came in right after she left, and I got dinner for Frank and myself. What helped a lot was there was always someone bringing us food during this time; I want to thank all of you for your thoughtfulness.

Frank was ready to go to bed by 7:30, so Ken took him into the bathroom. I haven't said this before, but when Frank started needing help, he wanted me in the bathroom when he brushed his teeth, washed his face, and put water in his mouth and nose to spit up the phlegm that was in his throat and the blood clots that came out of his nose. I helped by holding the small washbasin close to his face, which made the job easier for him. I did this for him until we got more help. We were now beginning to see that what he was now coughing up was very bloody and had clots or pieces of lung with it. That concerned me and made me wonder if he was doing this during the night without Ken or Maria noticing it.

Ken put salve on Frank's skin, and as he did, I noticed how sore it was and told Ken to put a lot on. He then changed Frank from under pads to adult diapers, which ended up making it easier to take care of him. I don't know why we hadn't used them earlier, but I didn't know about them, and I don't think Frank did either.

As I've said, Frank was getting weaker. Even I noticed it, and he could barely stand on his own. It was taking Ken more work and effort to get him into bed, even with me helping him put Frank in bed. And we always needed to have at least a foot of empty bed along the side to keep Frank from falling out; this made it even harder. And as we did this, there was the catheter tube and bag to deal with. The biggest trouble I had was that I thought the tube should be at least two feet longer than it was so it would give more room to maneuver with, especially when getting him into and out of bed.

Frank went to sleep but was very restless until the nurse came. This was one of those rare nights that the nurse showed up early, around 9 p.m. She gave Frank some Ambien and morphine for his restless legs, along with Thorazine. And Frank now needed to have morphine at more regular intervals than in the past. This seemed to settle him down a little. I also noticed he didn't have his pajama tops taken off during the night, for they weren't wet. But he continued to toss and turn all night long, and I was really having a time keeping the blankets on him. He was still getting up several times throughout the night to go to the bathroom. Ken would sometimes take him into the living room.

When Frank wanted to get up, Ken would first have to get him to sit up on the edge of the bed and hold him as he got Frank into his bathrobe. He then needed to get Frank in the wheelchair, and I could see that was a problem for Ken. After several nights of this, I sat up in bed and told him to put the wheelchair up by the pillow so he wouldn't have to take a step before sitting down on the chair. That made a big difference, and they were not as apt to step on the catheter tube and bag in the process. It also made it easier to get Frank back into bed.

Ken was now staying more in the living room, so he could get to Frank more quickly when he needed to. If it looked like Frank was really trying to get out of bed, I would call out to Ken to help me. We continued placing the chair and table against the bed, so he would have to move them to get out. This gave Ken, Maria, and me a warning. And if I was awake, I could tell what he was up to by how much pressure he put on them. And, as usual, Frank slept the best as morning approached.

Mar. 1, Thur. I woke at the usual time and made the bed, showered, and got ready for the day. I have never been one to wear a bathrobe and slippers in the morning; I don't even own a pair of slippers. However, I do own two silk bathrobes that were made and bought in Japan sometime in the '60s. I use them only when I have to, and most of the time it's when I have to go to the hospital. Nevertheless, I have used the pink robe all through this ordeal with Frank whenever I had to get out of bed for him.

Because it was taking Ken and Maria more time to get him ready in the morning, I had more time to do chores in the mornings before Frank was brought into the kitchen. I would sometimes have three washings to do. I'd start one, and then check on our gardener, Vic, who always came on Mon., Tue., Thurs., and Friday, unless it was raining heavily or snowing. I'd also check in with Ina when she came in to work.

By this time, I would have now gotten the paper and started breakfast for the two of us. Ken would bring him into the kitchen around 9 in the wheelchair. And around this time, Hospice had now supplied a tabletop that fit over the arms of his wheelchair, so he could rest his arms as he ate. Or he could put his head down on it, and with some pillows, he could take a nap in his wheelchair. This morning, we had oatmeal, fresh slices of different fruits, toast with strawberries, and he had his Roma coffee, but he only drank half a cup. That was unusual for him, for he usually had at least two cups, or close to that. I drank my standard hot water.

After Ken got the bathroom and bedroom tidied up, he came out, did his paperwork, and left at 10. Lois, our day care provider from *Home Instead*, had arrived before 10, and they sat at the kitchen table with us as Ken told her how the night went, and then he left. As I said, Frank really liked looking out the kitchen window at all the camellia trees. They were now in full bloom, along with all the other spring flowers. So he stayed there in the morning until I finished my work. I knew he rested better on the sofa, so as soon as I was done I took him to the living room where he could sit or lie on the sofa. Ever since his sickness began, I have kept the sheer curtains open in the living room so he could see out those windows. Some of the tulips were beginning to bloom, along with the grape hyacinth and other spring bulbs. He liked looking at them and could see them from the living room.

We spent the afternoon in the living room with Frank sleeping more or less throughout the day with his head on my shoulder or lying down on the sofa. He kept moving from one place to another and didn't lie down very much. He mostly held onto my hands. Lois said she learned a lot by watching us. She said whenever I had to leave the room, he became very nervous and agitated, and as soon as I came into the room, he was peaceful, quiet, and would smile. She said he did that all day long. And he wanted to kiss often. I made sure he took his medicine and drank some water, and he now needed thickener for his water so he wouldn't choke on it. He also had some Ensure, which he was now drinking through a tube. Lynn from Hospice was by at 2 p.m. to take care of him. She flushed out his catheter and cleaned out the bag. There were a lot of blood clots, but at least he always felt much better right after they did that.

Wylene Dunbar dropped by in the afternoon and gave me a card and left. I then returned Ruth Cramer's call. Julia, Mark, Gloria, and Laurence came by much later in the afternoon. They brought dinner and we ate around 6. Frank didn't want to join us, so he sat in the wheelchair with his head on a pillow in the kitchen where he could hear and see us in the kitchenette. He said he was very cold, and this was after we had already put lots of blankets around him. Maria was in at 6 to get him ready to go to bed, and Lois helped her out, which I thought was nice. The kids said goodnight to him and then the two ladies took him to the bedroom and got him ready for bed. They gave him his medication—morphine, Thorazine, and Mirapex, then Lois left. Frank slept for a while but was restless. The kids did the dishes and left around 8. Frank went to bed without eating anything, and he didn't care.

Sharon from Hospice came around 10 p.m. to flush out his catheter that was full of clots. It again took several times of flushing before she got it all out. In the process, some got all over his pajamas and everything else. So they had to undress him and put clean clothes back on him. You can't imagine how much time this takes. He had to sit up while they changed him, and as they did, I helped hold him up. He was very confused. By the time, they got his catheter tube up his pajama leg and then got the pajamas on him, half an hour had gone by. And they still had to put salve on his sores, which were dry and ready to crack. Sharon gave him his medication and put him into bed. He was one tired man. They also gave him some oxygen, but he didn't use it very long.

After Sharon left, I went to bed. And I told Maria if she wanted to, she could lie down on the hospital bed that was at the foot of our bed, which she did so she could be near Frank. He ended up keeping both of us awake all night long, for he didn't sleep much the rest of the night. I had started to say the Rosary, and Maria said she had left hers at home, so I got up and gave her the one I had in my purse. Frank kept tossing and turning and throwing blankets off, and around 3 a.m. he said he was too hot. He was now wanting the electric blanket turned off, and even a sheet was too hot; however, his body was ice cold. We kept trying to cover him because he was so cold, and his pajama tops were no longer wet. His body had completely changed in the last day and a half. Maria told me he should be sleeping by himself so he wouldn't keep me awake; she said I would get sick if I didn't get some sleep, and I agreed.

Mar. 2, Fri. Frank finally dropped off to sleep around 6:30 a.m., and it was at this time that I started the morning Rosary that takes me about half an hour to say. Afterward, I got up, used the bathroom, and got dressed. Frank wanted to get up by this time and have breakfast, so Maria helped him up and took him to the bathroom and brought him back into the bedroom. I made him his breakfast and brought it to him in the bedroom where we fed him, while he sat on the side of the bed with me holding him. He drank two cups of his Roma coffee, ate half a bowl of Cream of Rice with honey and butter, had a few slices of banana, some papaya and blue berries, and a cup of water with thickener in it. He was now using a straw to sip his liquids. Maria fed him while I held him. After he had eaten, he wanted to lie down and go to sleep, so she washed his face, gave him his medication, and we put him back in bed. Maria then cleaned up the bathroom. In the meantime, I laid out his clothes, a dress sweater, and clean washcloths and towels. He could no longer wear shoes and had worn out his slippers, but they are easy to get on his feet, so that's what he wore. I then left for the kitchen with his dishes.

Frank finally got up, so Maria got ready to bathe him, and while he was in bed, he had an accident. She cleaned him up, gave him a bath, and put lots of special cream on his sores. She then dressed him and brought him into the kitchen where I was, and then went back and made my bed, cleaned up the area, and put things in the garbage. When that was done, she wrote up her report and left at 10 a.m. Hospice showed up about this time to take care of Frank. When they were done, he asked me to take him into the living room so he could lie down on the sofa.

Lois Cabbage also showed up at 10. She sat in the living room and looked after Frank, while I went to the kitchen to make some tapioca pudding for him. Frank's niece, Anna Marie, her husband, Ron, and their daughter, Amber, arrived around 12:30 p.m. as I was making the pudding. Julia also showed up about this time. After everyone had some pudding, they went into the living room to visit with Frank. He also had some pudding. I then left them so they could visit with him. I went back to the kitchen and cleaned up the dishes and then went and took a short nap in Julia's old bedroom. By what Lois said, he went to sleep right after he saw them.

I was up by 1:30 p.m. and saw that Frank was getting tired. Jack Cramer came to see Frank sometime around 3 and stayed a very short time. Anna, Ron, and Amber left about this time. Shortly after that, Father McKnight came and gave Frank communion.

Maria arrived early at 5:30 p.m. to relieve Lois. She found us in the living room where I was giving Frank some Ensure with warm, thickened water in it to keep him from choking on a pill he needed to take to kill the pain around his bladder. Frank was in a very agitated state. He also needed to take .05 mg of morphine and his other medications, but he only took two or three sips of liquid and that was all. Lois visited with Maria and told her about the day as I held Frank's hand. Maria sat on the edge of the coffee table; Lois was on the granny rocker next to it. As I've said, Frank has been a very good patient all through this ordeal. He hasn't even complained about all the things we have to do for him and to him. Then, as we were all in the living room, and out of the blue, Frank became very agitated and sat up straight at the center edge of the sofa by me. He started to talk in a very strong and dictatorial manner. He spoke in a way that I had never heard him talk in all our married life together.

I remember he was upset by the new cordless phone lying on the coffee table. He couldn't understand what it was, nor did we understand what he was trying to tell us, for he acted so confused, and all this upset him further. He kept talking about the table and somehow he was talking as though it had become round. He was using his hands and arms and talking about a round table, which wasn't there. I remember he said to me, referring to the cordless phone, "What is *that* thing, what's it for, and how did it get there?" He said other things, but I don't remember what they were. Speaking to the girls, in a very strange voice, he said, "Don't sit on the table!" He said this when Maria was still sitting on the left end of the coffee table facing us and the sofa. Finally, he said, "I don't want to see your ass on there again," meaning on the table. He said other things that had no meaning to any of us. So Maria looked at me and said, "I think we should get him ready for bed."

The girls and I took him into the bathroom to get him ready for bed. It took about two hours. As his sickness got worse, I would put a bowl of water on his lap while he sat in the wheelchair and help him clear his nose and throat. He had now been coughing up blood, and tonight he coughed up a chunk of lung about the size of an egg yolk. It was dark red. Once this was over and his catheter bag was emptied, Maria wheeled him into the bedroom where the two of us took off his dress clothes. She put salve all over his sores and then put a patch over them. It did help but he still needed to use the special cream. We then got his pajamas on him.

Diane from Hospice came by and flushed out his catheter tube and bag, which had plugged up. This night there were many clots that had to be flushed out and it took several times. I wondered how this felt to Frank, but he never complained. Until the catheter got flushed out, his bladder would be filling up. I knew it was painful for him. Frank and I had eventually begun to watch his tube to see if blood was running down it; if not, we knew he was not urinating. Cleaning the catheter always took time, and by the time it was done, he was one tired man. Tonight my bathroom had blood everywhere. This had happened many times before, but tonight it was worse. It was at this time that I knew I was glad I hadn't remodeled the bathroom. Frank never complained when they cleaned the catheter, except when they had to wake him up at night to do so.

Frank was not able to sit up very well by himself tonight. I held him up at the edge of the bed to keep him from falling while Maria took care of him. He drifted off as this was going on, and I knew he had really left us. This all happened around 8:45 p.m. He started to mumble and said something that didn't make any sense. He then seemed to be having a horrible nightmare, or so we thought. This happened as he was sitting up on the edge of the bed; he hadn't even gotten into bed yet. So I had to hold him to keep him from getting up and falling over. He was rigid and then grabbed and held me very tight. Maria asked him if he was having a nightmare. He started to talk. *He was very happy and said he was four years old, so I asked him if he had red hair and could he talk, and did you see your father that you wanted to know. He paused and did not answer, but he also said something about seeing all four.* I don't remember what else he said, except something like, "there was no more business." Then he changed to a commanding voice and said, "Forget it, I don't want to talk about it again." He then became very peaceful and relaxed and lay down and went back to sleep.

Up to now, I was still sleeping in bed with him, however he didn't want me too close to him. He told me he was too hot, even though his body was cold. He kept throwing the blankets off himself, even though he had wanted the electric blanket on. He later had Maria turn it off.

Maria was now lying down on the hospital bed to rest, stay warm, and keep an eye on Frank. (Maria and Ken did this each night of his final week.) During the night, Maria and I kept putting blankets over him, being careful not to disturb him. But in a short time, he would have them off again. He would toss and turn and fling his arms and legs all over the bed. We kept a close eye on him, for we were afraid he would fall out of bed and hurt himself. For several nights now, he had been really tossing, turning, fighting the blankets, and wanting to get up. When it came time to get him up at 8 a.m., he was ready to go to sleep, but we had to give him a bath. By the time we got him dressed, he was ready to get up; he was now nothing like the man that was fighting, tossing, and turning all night. By this time, he could no longer stand or walk on his on, and he didn't know where he was during the night.

Mar. 3, Sat. In the morning, I asked Frank about seeing the four people, but he had no comment about it. Either he didn't remember, or he did not want to talk about it. Never during the day, except starting with the round table episode the day before, was he irrational like he was at night. After he began to talk about his past, we began keeping notes of what he was saying.

I was now beginning to get real tired, even exhausted, for I hadn't really been getting any sleep for several weeks. Even though I needed to, I didn't want to sleep in the spare bedroom away from him because he would reach over every so often to make sure I was in bed with him.

Today, nobody from *Home Instead* was available to fill in the hours from 10 a.m. to 6 p.m., so Maria got him up and made sure to take care of his sores. She said they would not split open with the pad on it, but we decided to leave him in his warm pajamas, for he was bleeding from the catheter tube and was in pain because no urine or blood was coming out—pressure was building up in his bladder. Maria then took him out to the kitchen in the wheelchair where I fixed him breakfast. He ate very little of it; I ate what was left. It was at this time that he told me he could not see me very well, even when he had his glasses on. Frank and I talked a lot, but it was mostly just about everyday things. Maria left and we had the Hospice nurse coming in at 11 a.m. However, it was more like 1 p.m. when she showed up, and all the while Frank kept looking at his catheter bag to see if any blood was coming out, and, of course, it wasn't.

In the meantime, I had wheeled Frank into the living room in his pajamas where he spent the rest of the day on the sofa. He waited there for the nurse to come. All the kids were here when Mark brought the mail in to Frank around noon. He was lying on the sofa while I sat on the coffee table where he could see me. Mark sat on the sofa at his feet when he handed the mail to him, and in the mail was a contract from Howard. Somehow Frank knew it would be there. He tried to open the envelope but couldn't, so I opened it for him. There were some papers that had to be read and signed and then faxed back to Howard. It took Frank a long time to look at the sheet of paper, and I could tell he was having a hard time seeing where he had to sign, but he said nothing. Laurence was standing behind me and observed this, as we all did. He said, "Dad, I have the power to sign if you can't," but I could tell Frank wanted to sign it. Mark held the papers for him, and after a great deal of effort, he finally signed it. It didn't look much like his signature. That would be the last time he would sign his name. Mark went right out to the office and faxed it off to Howard, just in case something happened to Frank before it got sent off.

The nurse arrived at 1 p.m. and cleaned out the catheter. There were enough blood clots to fill a cup. We then gave him a sponge bath and put on his dress pants, shirt, a sweater, and his support hose. He liked to dress nice and the dress pants kept his body warm. Mary Grace stopped in for a while in the afternoon to see Frank and then left to go to Sacramento on business.

I noticed that before the week was over he no longer needed the sweater, nor any of the blankets we had been putting on him. And he could now get into his shoes very easily, for the swelling had gone down in his legs and feet, and he had lost a lot of weight. His legs and feet were very thin. His slippers, the ones that had lost their shape long ago, were now so loose that he could easily get into them, now hoping to keep them on.

Sometime after the nurse left, Frank ended up having his third episode in the living room by the sofa. Julia, Mark, and I were there to take care of matters. I finished cleaning up the living room; no one would know that anything had gone on. I then sat down and rested by Frank. I think I even had a catnap while doing so. And so our living room has now been put to use as a bathroom three times in our lifetime; I wonder how many other living rooms have been used the same way.

Not having any day care help today, members of the family were taking turns being with Frank. For most of the day, I was sitting and holding Frank's hand—he never wanted me far away from him. He would also put his head on my shoulder and try to sleep sitting up. Maybe he could breathe better that way; I'm not sure, and he never said. And he would often kiss me and say he loved me. Frank and I would talk a little bit about different things, and as we did my eyes would often water up. I don't remember what we talked about, nor did I take any notes, but I remember I did most of the talking. I could tell he preferred not to talk, but he did look at me a lot and smile and would kiss me. The only time we did take notes was when he said things that were unrelated to what was going on. There was always paper and pencils on the coffee tables for the nurses to jot things down.

Sometime during the afternoon, while Julia and Frank were sitting together on the sofa by the TV and I was in a chair nearby, out of the clear blue, he said, "Nothing is of no mean." "We all received a call from them." "It's done. The goal is completed. I'm not going to worry anymore." "When someone is into you, like now, they should say so." When asked what he meant, he replied. "You know… they owe you money. They are always owing money." So who was he talking to in his mind? We asked him, but he didn't answer. Julia wrote down what he said.

Frank's last comments as recorded on March 3, 2007:

"Nothing is of no value."

"We all received a call from them."

"It's done. The goal is completed. I'm not going to worry anymore."

"When someone is into you, like now, they should say so." When asked what he meant, he replied, "You know….they owe you money. They are always owing money."

As you know, Julia was at our place a lot during these days working on the pictures and story for Frank's video. She would sometimes sit in the living room as she did this and would share with Frank what she was doing. It was nice that she was next to him when he said these things on this day. He spent most of the whole day moving from one sofa to another.

Frank was ready to have something to eat, and it was time for him to take his medications. I remember he had told me he never wanted to take them again because it did things to him. But we knew he needed them for the pain. I called to have the Hospice nurse come by early, for Frank was again having trouble with his catheter draining properly. Once again, it took two hours before he was ready to go to bed.

Frank ended up having a very bad night. At some point, he took off his pajamas, which is not easy to do with the catheter in the way, but somehow he did it. Maria once again said I needed to sleep in the spare bedroom. She could see I was very tired and was going to get sick if I didn't get some sleep. So I listened to her and went to bed in the spare bedroom. I woke up around 2 a.m. or 3 a.m. and got back into bed with him. However, he continued to toss and turn the rest of the night, throwing off the blankets. And, as usual, we tried keeping the blankets on him, for his body was so cold.

Mar. 4, Sun. After a very fitful night, Frank was ready to get up and have his bath. Somehow he didn't remember anything he had done during the night. During the day, he was always so calm and good-natured and wanted to sleep, even sitting up in his wheelchair. Maria cleaned up the bedroom, while I made some breakfast for him. Then at 9 a.m., I left for Sunday Mass; the Mass was said for him. While I was gone and after Maria left at 10 a.m., Mark and Laurence came over and stayed with him. The day nurse from *Home Instead*, Sofia Marzan, also came over.

After I got home from church, I picked three white and purple crocus flowers and showed them to him, but his interest was short, so I put them in a small water glass. I can't remember who put Frank in the living room on the sofa so that I wouldn't have to do it, for he was now very weak. I spent most of the day sitting with him in one sofa or another, holding him when he wanted to sit up. After everyone had left and we were in sitting on the sofa, I asked Sofia if she would leave us alone in the room for a while, which she did. I had brought home communion for him and gave it to him. Then Betty and Brayton came by to see him right after their church service was over, and the kids came by about this time. Around 1 p.m., Laurence and Gloria left to play a round of golf. Mark was in and out for the rest of the day, and Julia was around but needed to work on the funeral program.

Roxanna and Spence came to visit around 2 p.m., and it was time to give Frank his medication, along with his Ensure and thickened water. I then went to the bedroom and took a nap. Spence said he was shocked at the change in Frank from two weeks earlier.

Frank was taking more time between breaths, and his fingers had started to turn bluish-purple. He was very restless and not able to get comfortable anywhere he sat. When I got up from my nap, I went into the living room. Before Spence and Roxanna left, she had given Julia her check. Julia brought it in to show to Frank; he looked at it, got real mad, and pushed it away. Julia asked what was the matter, and he said, "It's no good." So I took it, went out to the office, and checked it out. As I got ready to put it in the accounting book, I saw what he was mad at. She had written Feb. 4, instead of March 4, so I called her at her home and told her to come and correct it right away, which she did. I knew Frank would be upset, so when she came back, I later told him she had made it right.

Sofia was in the living room with us later in the day. Frank and the family spent the rest of the afternoon on the sofa by the TV, with Julia sitting next to him. She was asking him things for the funeral story, and then out of the blue, he took the paper and wrote *"Frank has lost his voice, will anwer (answer) voice only by letter, ask what you wat (want) to know and I will tell you."*

The following are Frank's last written words:

"Frank has lost voice, will answer voice only, by letter, ask what you want to know and I will tell you."

March 4, 2007 -- Frank said his bones hurt.

After a while, Julia went back into my art room to work on Frank's video, and I continued to sit by Frank. He held my hand even when he was lying down. He was now no longer cold, nor did he need a blanket or a sweater.

Mary Grace Tassone came over close to 3 p.m. to sit with Frank. He had been very restless all day and was being moved from one sofa to another in the living room. He liked sleeping on the sofas, maybe because he could breathe easier sitting up at an angle. Mary Grace was sitting on the rocker by the TV where she could look at and talk to Frank, who was sitting on the sofa by the window that looks out to the cottage. I took advantage of her being here and did some work around the house. Many towels had been used and needed to be washed, along with his pajamas and other laundry. I took several loads down to the cottage so I could also have that washer and dryer to use. I told them what I was doing, but I guess Frank didn't remember. After I was gone for a short while, Mary Grace said he started asking where I was. She had him look out the window, and he saw me coming back from putting a load in the washer. She said he then relaxed a little.

I really needed a break by this time, so I took in the fresh air and looked at the yard, and yes, I said a prayer, for I knew he might not be here the next day. I remember looking at the yard, saying that to myself, and wondering what it would be like when he was no longer here.

I spent the rest of the afternoon with him. He was very restless all day and went from one sofa in the living room to another. He liked sleeping on the sofas, and he always liked being in the living room where he could see everyone and look out the windows. I think the elevation of his arms on the sofas helped bring his chest up high enough that he could breathe better than when he was in bed. He had refused to use the hospital bed. It was too short for him and had no room for him to toss and turn around in. And he didn't like to use the oxygen, but there were times he had to have it and didn't complain.

209

She spent the rest of the afternoon with Frank, and I continued to spend the day holding his hand, or his body. I remember at one time while we girls were visiting, he was holding my right hand and put it to his lips and kissed my ring finger. I wondered what he was thinking. I smiled and didn't say anything, for he was no longer talking by this time. Mary Grace and I continued to talk about what was going on at St. Mary's school. Frank listened to what we said, and I think he was showing me that he approved of what I had said to her.

Later that afternoon, Frank was very nervous and kept pulling on his catheter tube. Around 5:30 p.m., he started to have a lot of blood coming onto the floor and sofa, for he had worked something loose, so I gave him some medicine, which we were now doing about every two hours. Between Julia, Sofia, and Mary Grace, the three of them tried to take care of the accident, along with me going for the stuff to remove bloodstains. At this time, he wanted to move to the chair nearby, and even with our help, he almost fell to the floor. We really had trouble getting him up and into the chair. I then called Hospice to have a nurse come by to see what was wrong with him. In the meantime, we had to remove all his clothes that had blood on them, along with needing to empty the catheter bag. Despite all of this, he did not complain at all about the things that all we women were doing to him. However, I do remember that sometime during the day he told me "his bones hurt." He really was a very good patient all throughout this whole ordeal. Sharon finally came and found where the blood was coming from. Somehow the snap to the tube that went to the bag had been opened. My guess is that through all his moving around to get comfortable, he had stepped on the clip and opened the bag.

After we finally got him changed and got salve on his sores, the nurse came and really flushed out his catheter, which was full of blood clots. Mary Grace left about this time and Judy Kenny came to see him; but, by the time that was done, he was more or less out of it, and we were cleaning up all the blood. After seeing the trouble we were having, she knew too many people were around, and seeing the confusion, she said she'd be back later. Sophia, Sharon, and Julia finally got him in the wheelchair and took him into the bathroom. There was more blood on that end of the room by the toilet, for in moving him, the clip came open again. By the time he had brushed his teeth and cleaned out his nose and mouth, more blood clots from his throat had come out. The bathroom was not only full of different kinds of medicines, but also buckets and wastebaskets full of paper towels used to clean things up, and there were three washbasins used for bathing him. A lot of this stuff was stored in the bathtub. After he was done being taken care of in the bathroom, Julia left, for she and Mark had a dinner date.

When we finally got Frank all cleaned up, Sharon took him into the bedroom to get him ready for bed, only to get more blood on the bedroom carpet. By this time, Ken had come in, and the three of us got Frank onto the hospital bed. Maria had earlier put a patch over his sore, but the area around it was now getting bad, so they creamed it up good and put an adult diaper on him and got him into his nightclothes. He was now ready to lie down. A couple of days earlier, Hospice had brought over a big, heavy 4ft. x 4ft. rubber sheet to put under him and they now used it to move him into the center of the bed.

They had Frank lie on it and then Ken got on the bed from my side, and the two of them lifted him up and got him into the center of the bed. For the last few days, it took more than one person to take care of him; he was now getting much weaker.

It was around 7 p.m., or later, when they finally did this, and by this time, Frank was one tired man. They put chairs at the side of the bed. I then reached over, covered him up better, and kissed him on the forehead and told him I loved him. I don't know if he was still with me or not. I left the room. Ken stayed in the room, and the nurse came out and made her report before leaving. I had to get something to eat and decided to read a little, and by the time I got ready for bed, it was 9 p.m. In the meantime, Julia and Mark came by to pick up Julia's car. She came in, kissed her dad, and said goodbye to him and told him it was all right for him to leave. He knew it was Julia. I was in the bathroom off the kitchen and didn't know she had done so, but I did see her car drive out. So she was the last one of the family to talk to him. (She told me about this later.)

When I was ready for bed, Frank was sound asleep. I refused to wake him up for he was so tired. I went to bed in the spare bedroom, for I knew I had to get some sleep for the next day. However, I did pause and look at my side of the bed. My subconscious mind told me to crawl in bed with him, but there was so much stuff on top of the bed to keep him from rolling out on my side that I went into the spare bedroom. I knew I needed some sleep. Looking back at this, I will tell you to pay attention to what your subconscious mind tells you, for this is your guardian angel talking to you. During the last several nights, he had tossed and turned all over the bed all night long and kept pulling the blankets off saying he was burning up, even though his body was cold. During the early part of this night, he was restless. Then later Ken tried to give him some water, but he did not drink any. Ken had given him some morphine and Frank said he didn't want any more. This was just before I came back to get in bed with him.

Mar. 5, Mon. In the very early morning, around 1:00 a.m., I left the spare bedroom and crawled into our bed to be near Frank. Ken told me that at midnight Frank refused his medication; he didn't want any more medicine. Frank had said many times that he did not like taking morphine, for he said it affected his brain. When I got in bed with him, I could tell he had tossed a little, for the blankets were not completely over him; but, when I got in bed, he was no longer moving and tossing as he had been for the last few nights. I also saw that he had a peaceful look on his face. The electric blanket was off and his body was still. His right arm and hand were up by his head, and his hand was cold, so I tried to cover it with the blanket. His left arm was warm and down by his side, and he was breathing softly. He never moved all the while I was in bed with him. When he got that way, Ken didn't tell me, nor did I ask.

From the time he started having cancer problems, Frank didn't like me sleeping too close to him. He said it hurt him, but he would reach over and touch me many times during the night, so at this time I put my arm and hand along his left arm and lay very close to him and remained very quiet. I did not want to wake him up; it was time for him to go on. I remembered that some of the nurses said you can bring them back, but doing so only prolongs the death process. I didn't even try to kiss him or tell him I loved him or say goodbye, even though I wanted to.

Then around 3 a.m., I noticed his breathing was erratic, and he started to have fluid in his lungs. I think I then called Diana at her home and asked her if I should call the kids. She said there was no point in getting them out of bed at that hour, for it could be a few hours or even a day. I got the Rosary and said it. At times, I think I did dose off a little but never for long. Then at 5 a.m., I noticed a change in his breathing. And during all this time I was with him, he never moved his body, and I never wanted to wake him up. It was time for him to go. Then at 5:30 a.m., I felt something very heavy, like 50 lbs, lift out of his body and knew his soul had left his body. His face was peaceful, as it had been all the while I was with him. That lifting occurred in two stages, one following right after the other. I knew then that we really don't die; we just move up to another world, leaving this one behind. No, I didn't cry. I looked at the clock to see the time and it was 5:50 a.m. I reached over to the phone and called Hospice and then called Laurence, and then Julia. Mark answered the phone right away, for he was awake and in his office.

I then got dressed, except for shoes, and told Ken to leave the room and take a break. I crawled into bed on Frank's right side, under the blankets. His body was nice and warm. I stayed that way and did not cry, for he was now at peace. I kissed him several times, and several times I would close his mouth for it was ajar. At 7 a.m., Laurence came into the bedroom and that is where he found me. We talked and he stood in the room for a while and then left to go to the kitchen. Later, Julia came in and also got into bed on his other side. While we were looking at his face and shutting his mouth, Julia lifted his eyelids to look at his eyes and noticed the color real close up. We then closed them back down. I can't remember now, but I think she said they were hazel. In time, we had his mouth closed, and he looked very peaceful. I don't think he was ever afraid of dying.

Around 7 a.m., we got up, and Laurence came in a little later and spent some quiet time alone with his dad. In the meantime, Mark and Gloria had arrived but did not come into the bedroom. When I got up and out of bed, I opened the blinds in the bedroom and looked out the window and saw the cherry trees starting to bloom. Spring was really in the air when he left, as it had been ever since the snowstorm.

Sometime around 7:30, I told Ken that after he wrote up his report he could leave, for there was nothing more he could do. I went outside about this time, and it was a very nice, warm morning. I had Mark go and put our flag at half-mast. I walked around the yard and over to Nicole, my neighbor, to tell her what had happened so she would know why there was so much traffic at our place, but she was not out of bed. It ended up that Victor, our gardener, told her, for she eventually came over to see what was going on. Sometime around 8 a.m., along with Mark and Gloria, Netta and Roxanna arrived and they made breakfast.

It was around 9 a.m. when I motioned Laurence to come out of the house and join me near the barbecue. I showed him Frank's watch and asked him if he would like to give it to Mark, and he did. I think they were both happy it was done that way. And before the day was over, several big bouquets of flowers had arrived from different people.

Around noon, Diane from Hospice came by and did their checkup and notified the mortuary. I asked her if she could remove the tube, and she said yes. I then had her take off the tight stockings. By this time, his legs and feet were beginning to get cool, and we covered him up to his shoulders. I also told her to take all the medicine, diapers, anything on the dresser in the bedroom, and anything in the bathroom that she could use, and she did. She said she would take them to Mexico on her next trip there. When she was done, she had a few full bags of things, for a lot of stuff had been brought in for Frank. They never wanted him to run out of diapers, pads, or towels, and among the stuff were bottles and jars of salve, creams, shampoo, and many kinds of pills. Both rooms were sort of back to normal by the time she was done. I then moved Frank's dresser back to where he had always had it.

We wanted Frank to be with us until each of us had had some time with him. Father McKnight came and blessed him, and Julia, Laurence, and I had communion with Father. We later called some friends that we thought might want to say goodbye to him. I now can't remember all who came, but I do remember Brayton came by, followed a little later by Karen.

The mortuary people came by, and just before they took Frank away, Julia and I cut off a wave of his hair to save. I have my piece in with his picture, along with his hearing aids and glasses. I had the mortuary people take him out the bedroom door. They took him down the patio, past the kitchenette windows that he liked to look out, and past his office, where he had spent many hours each day, and where many a deal had been made and money had changed hands over the phone for 57-some-odd years. He was taken down the walkway to the hearse parked in the circle driveway, near the flag at half-mast. He was put into the hearse for his final drive around the driveway and yard. They went out the gate, leaving the home where he had spent the last 57 years of his life. He was taken down Reward St., right on Zion St., and up past the SPD store and property that he had owned and which is now his son's—the property he loved to look at when he went on his walks. He was 88 years, 9 months old.

Frank and I were in the habit of saying our prayers every night asking the Lord to forgive our sins and to look after the world. We would then kiss and Frank was almost always the first to say, "I Love You." He almost always said it before I could say it to him. In all our life, we never went to bed mad or upset with each other.

After Frank left us, I had all the stuff that had been brought in through the months removed by Hospice, including the hospital bed, toilet, oxygen, wheelchair, and many other things. The bedroom was put back to normal so that the day would end as Frank would have wanted it to, for he hated all the stuff that had been brought in for him to use.

Around 6 that evening, I said that I didn't want to cook and said lets go out to dinner. Julia, Mark, Gloria, Laurence, Spence, and I went to Friar Tucks for dinner and had it on Dad. Julia stayed with me that night, and I slept on Dad's side of the bed. And no tears—I guess I was too tired to cry.

(I decided to give more detail about the things that we as a family went through when it came to taking care of Frank. I have done this, thinking it may be able to help other people down the road. If you know what to expect, it can make things a little easier when you have to deal with them, and to know that you are not the only one. Whatever you have to do to take care of your loved one, it's all right.)

Mar. 6, Tue. The paper carried a long story on Frank's death, and another story ran the next day, so he was well covered. Flower and cards started coming in right away, along with food from different people, which was very nice.

I decided I had to start living on my own. So on Thursday night, I went to the prayer and soup supper at St. Canice Hall, and I walked to church on Friday morning. Mass was said for Frank and again on Sunday. Julia did the reading at the 8 a.m. Mass; she is very good at it. Afterwards, she, Mark, and I walked from church to Ike's for breakfast. I spent the rest of the day around the yard and started working on this part of the story on Frank. Laurence and Gloria dropped in, but at that time, I was out having breakfast with Julia and Mark, so I didn't get to see them.

Up to now, we had received many deliveries of potted plants and flowers, and there was so much mail, at least 75 cards in just 3 days. Articles in the paper were favorable. And along with missing Frank, we had wonderful sunny, warm days. And there was the paperwork that had started to come in. The first was the death certificate, and then insurance policies came in the mail for us to take care of. These didn't require too much work, which was very nice. Frank bought one of the policies in 1932, when he was about 14 years old. It was for $1K and his mother and brothers were the beneficiaries on it until he married me. He bought another one when he was 18 for $3K, and years later, he bought one in 1944 and one in 1966. None were very large. But the one at 14 when saving was hard tells a lot about Frank and where he was headed. Also, by the time he was 19, he and his brother George had saved enough to build a home for their mother Rosa in Stockton on Bristol Street, which I talked about earlier in the story. It had two bedrooms, a living room, kitchen, sunroom, and a garage off by itself. They put in a nice yard with lawns, and she had a garden and flowers.

In the meantime, and with a fuzzy head, I was trying to take care of the office mail and getting checks deposited in the bank and posted into the books. All this was with the help of Laurence, Mark, and Ina, who was coming in on Wednesday morning to work and to take care of the things she had always done for Frank. Laurence came to help me with the books when Ina wasn't here. Julia was also around working on the funeral arrangements and finishing up Frank's movie. So life will go on with tears, laughter and loneliness, but we had a good life together, so there will be many good memories of our 64 years together and our 57 years here at Reward St.

As I was on my way to Julia's for dinner, the Casey's brought over a wonderful dinner in a basket, so I ended up taking the food with me to Julia and Mark's place, where I spent the night. Again, no tears. Since then I stayed home, and, yes, sometimes with plenty of tears.

Wed. Mar 7. Flowers kept coming to the house, along with food. People were dropping in and calling. There were phone calls and flowers, and I stayed home this night.

Thur. Mar 8. Today was another full day of calls and visits, and in the evening I went to the soup supper at the church hall; I decided I had to start making the change and that was the best place to begin. If I cried my eyes out they would know why, but I did all right and stayed home that night. Betty Hahn took Julia and me out to lunch this day.

We were not able to have Frank's services right away. Brad was back east on an assignment and would be gone for two weeks, and then we ran into no services in the church during St. Patrick's day, so that took us into another weekend, the 23–24. And then we ran into M.I.M. spring season. We knew that this would affect many people, but there was nothing we could do about it. However, M.I.M. did give Frank tribute at the programs.

In the meantime, Julia continued making the arrangements for Frank's memorial services, and Paul Perry came over to help us select the songs that some of the choir would sing at St. Canice Church on Friday the 23rd and at Mass at St. Patrick's Church in Grass Valley on the 24th. And there were the arrangements to be made for food at St. Canice Hall after the funeral service Mass. In the meantime, I had calls to make to all the family, notifying them of Frank's death. A few days later, I was calling them again to let them know when the funeral service would be and to let them know about hotel reservations. And let's face it, I was not very good at this time, as far as being good help. And Julia had been very busy trying to get all the pictures sorted and organized to get the video on Frank ready to show. Along with getting everything else ready for Frank's funeral, notifying the newspaper, and getting people to help with the services, she was really showing the strain.

In the meantime, I have been going to church every morning for I'm awake by 6 a.m. and can't sleep. When the weather was nice I would walk to church, otherwise I would drive. I must also say that Mark and Laurence have really been a great help for me in the office. I have been making the deposits as the checks comes in, and I have been using any spare time I have to write down the details of what has been happening so I won't forget.

Mar. 15–16, Thur.–Fri. Karen Wood and I went out to dinner at New Moon Cafe and then to Foothill Theatre to see a play. Frank had already bought season tickets, so he already knew I would go if he weren't here. On the 16th Julia and Mark had me over for dinner and we played Mexican Train. I then drove home. All during this time, I have started writing down all the things Frank did and went through near the end. I have discovered it has helped me, and it also keeps me from crying so much. I think the reason is that I don't have to remember it anymore, for I have written it down.

Mar. 17–22, Sat.–Thur. Our time has been filled with getting ready for the services and answering all the phone calls that continue to come in, along with getting the cottage ready for the Tatmans to stay in while they are here for the M.I.M. performances. Months earlier I had gotten out all the photo albums and had taken pictures out of them for Michael Sion to use in this book, and then later for Frank's movie. Before I did this I had marked each album and numbered each picture so I'd know where I had taken them out of, but when Frank started getting worse, Julia started working on his movie, and in the process things got all mixed up. The pool table and benches in the basement were full of photo albums and pictures, and now they had to be put away quickly so we could use the space to store huge flower arrangements and other things for Frank's service. We didn't have time to get the pictures back where they belonged. Julia and I had to put them together as fast as we could, so we could move everything up into the spare room. When I get done writing the things I want to remember of Frank's last days here with us, I will go back to get the pictures ready for this book that I started with Frank seven years ago. I know that will bring back even more memories.

There was going to be a lot of families on both sides coming and going, and they would not all know each other, so I asked Toni DeRego if she would watch the house and take care of the food. She said she and Karen Wood would help prepare a meal for all of Frank's and my family to have dinner here at the house after the services on Friday night. We had tables and chairs set up for 40 people or more, and I had flowers from the yard in the center of all the tables. They prepared two kinds of lasagna, French bread, and salad for everyone. They made enough food so that we had leftovers for Saturday evening. Anyone staying after Saturday's service could come back to our place to eat, and quite a few ended up doing so. And there were cookies that other people brought, so I could forget about needing to make a dessert. All this really helped me out, for I was not up to it, and Julia did not have the energy, nor the time to think about that end of things. Laurence and Gloria would be taking care of the bar and drinks at the hall and here at the house. They didn't have to serve the drinks at the hall, for all the churchmen wanted to take care of that and anything else that needed to be done, including handling the parking. In the meantime, many friends kept bringing in meals for us to eat.

The day has been full of phone calls and I'm still not too clear all the time. I still have trouble sleeping at night, and may get only three or four hours of sleep. And I try to keep up with all the mail. Today, three of the insurance policies came in, so I signed them and posted them in the book, and then Mark took them to the bank to deposit them for me. And that night Julia and Mark took me to the M.I.M. concert.

For the next three days, I walked to church each morning, and after coming home I spent the day writing to all the people that sent flowers and brought food during the time Frank was here, and afterward. I sent out close to 70 cards at this time. So many people have had Masses said for Frank that some weeks there are at least three of them said during the week and also on Sundays.

There are times I have a hard time keeping the tears down. On Sunday, March 18, Julia was with me in church and all of a sudden it hit that in all the years that Frank served wine, she never went to him to receive it, but instead received it from me, for he was on the opposite side of the church from where she sat. She said, "Why didn't I just go over to his side?" So that is something she feels bad about. On Tuesday Betty Hahn, Julia, and I walked to Daddy's Little Grill to have lunch. We had a nice time, and then we walked back home. And it was another day of lots of phone calls, along with doing the other things that have to be done.

The cleaning women always come on Wednesday, so this week I had them go down to the cottage and give it a good cleaning for the Tatman's who were coming in from Arizona and would be staying at the cottage while they were here for M.I.M. They came in around 4 p.m., just in time to go to their practice rehearsal that evening. They came up to the house and asked me if I was free Thursday night so they could take me out to dinner, and I said yes.

During all these days since Frank passed away, Julia had been very busy trying to get everything done for the services. She had been in and out all the time, along with taking care of all the other commitments she has. And this had been a full day for me, for I had to also make sure the flower arrangements for all the tables at the hall were taken care of by the girls from the Altar Society from St. Canice Church. I also had to make sure I had everything I needed for here at the house too. Karen and Toni came over around noon, bringing tables, chairs, and a lot of things they would be using the next few days to host everyone.

Mar. 22, Thur. Today was another full day for me. After getting home from church, I had to rearrange all the furniture in the living room, hallway, den, dining room, and art room in order to set up ten card tables and get the chairs around them. I also had to put colorful tablecloths on all of them. I then went out and cut fresh flowers to put on the center of all the tables. I did this in the late afternoon, hoping the flowers would stay fresh for Friday evening's meal. Mark and Laurence were busy arranging wine and drinks for both the hall and here at the house. The local florists were bringing in flowers that people had ordered for Frank. And I had people calling to ask what they could bring, and I said cookies. There were lots of phone calls, and I was needing to keep up with the yard and get things in line for the next few days. And as I've said, I still wasn't steady in the thinking end, and I had lots of tears along the way.

The Tatman's did not have rehearsal during the day, so they left early to go to their new cottage up at Lake Tahoe to spend some time doing carpentry work on it. They came back in time to take me to dinner, and we enjoyed a nice evening together.

Mar. 23, Fri. It was a beautiful day for Frank's service. I went to Mass and then had a hair appointment at 10:30 a.m. Toni and Karen arrived in the afternoon, and several members of Frank's family came to visit before the services at St. Canice Church in Nevada City. For the last several days, I had gone through all of Frank's clothes and sent anything out that needed to be cleaned. I put the clothes in the spare room on hangers and on two clothing racks, along with clean sweaters, shirts, sport clothes, and shoes. Earlier, I had Laurence go through all of his dad's clothes. He took what he wanted, and then I had Mark do the same. He took several pairs of Frank's shoes, for they wore the same size. If I recall, nothing fit Spence or Brad. Then, when Frank's relatives came by, I had them do the same, as well as the in-laws. I then let my side of the family do the same. This all took place after everyone came back to the house after Friday's service for dinner. All the families had a wonderful time here at the house. It was around 11 p.m. when people left for the night and Karen and Toni had cleaned up and left to go home. Everything was served on plastic plates, using plastic forks, spoons, knives, and throw away cups.

That evening, when we arrived at church, there were many people that came for the Sharing of Memories. I tried to say hello to as many people as I could before the service, but I also wanted to enjoy the songs that were being sung before the service started. Both Frank and I had relatives that came quite a distance, and I wanted to say hello to all of them, but there were also many locals I felt I had to pay attention to. Some were real old timers that we hadn't seen for some time. Frank would have been pleased and surprised at how many people had come for his honor.

Father Simon Twomey did the honors, and I have to admit he enjoyed doing it. Frank's nieces, Anna and Carol, and his nephew, Chris, helped with the services. The church was filled with so many people that we had attended church with every Sunday for 57 years, and some of the men helped usher people in. And Father Simon mentioned how we always sat in the same fourth pew in church (but it was really the 3rd pew) and how Frank helped serve communion for many years.

Many local friends that knew Frank through the years went up and talked about him. They told stories about what he had done for them, or what they remembered him doing. Afterward, more members of his family and mine talked. Many people on my side of the family talked, mostly about the ranch. Many of them knew him best from all the get-togethers at the ranch through the years, which they knew were made possible because of him.

The youngest one to talk was his godchild's youngest child, Michael. He said how he loved to crawl up on Frank's lap when they came to visit. He talked about how he would fall asleep on his lap when he was little and stay there until they left to go home.

The church had very large bouquets of flowers that surrounded Frank's picture and his urn of ashes on the altar. The songs that were sung included Hosea, In the Garden, Amazing Grace, and the Our Father. At this time, I had all of my family sitting on one side of the aisle and Frank's on the other side, so that the local people would see who belonged to whom. My sister LaVena was also there and she did very well with her handicap. Mark's mother also joined us on Frank's side of the family. Frank's side was much smaller, but he did have two cousins that he had met for the first time two months earlier who also attended. I introduced them to all the relatives on Frank's side. I have to admit I held up better than I thought I would and had no tears.

Ilene and Denise Dodini, Randy and Kelly (Dodini) Valdez with their daughter Katie and son Michael, and Frank's picture. Kelly is our godchild.

Me with Frank's niece Carol Wrolstad and her son Christopher

Afterwards anyone who wanted to come to the house for dinner was invited to do so — about 40 people showed up. This was also opening night for M.I.M. at the Amaral Family Festival Center, so many left to go to that. I was told that for all three concerts M.I.M. placed white roses on our seats that we always have.

218

Me, LaVena, her daughter Barbara, and Barbara's grandchild in the morning before church service

Mar. 24, Sat. Several members of both sides of the family came and stayed at the house until church service. Before we left for Grass Valley, it was understood that I was not to stay around after the service to talk to people, but instead go right away back to St. Canice Hall to meet people there. So Frank's nephew, Milton, saw to it that I went right to the car, and I have to admit I wanted to stop and say hello to many of our friends after the service.

We arrived at St. Patrick's Church early, but even so, there were already a lot of people standing around outside enjoying the wonderful spring weather. I greeted all of them and there were some people I hadn't seen in years. It was very nice seeing them, even if I didn't get to say more than a short greeting. As I walked into the church, there were many people already seated and listening to the music and singing that we knew Paul Perry and his group would be doing. After putting my purse down in the front row, on the left side of the church that was on the side of the pulpit, I noticed that on the right, in the first three rows, there were about 18 or so M.I.M. women from the choir sitting. I went over and greeted each one of them. I was trying hard to hold my composure for this was rather touching. Then one of the girls said don't forget the boys, and I have to admit at the time I hadn't seen them. So I turned around and there were 20 or so men facing the audience, so I started to greet each one of them. Along the way, the tears came, but I got a hold of myself and they waited for me to do so. I then continued to greet the rest, along with Terry who was to sing the Lord's Prayer as the service started. Then I threw a kiss to Paul, for he was already playing the organ. I wanted to greet each one of them, for I knew that right after the service they would have to head right back to the Amaral Festival Center to get ready for the evening performance that night. And all these people were doing this just for Frank. On the altar close to them was a big picture of Frank, along with his ashes and all the flowers that had been at St. Canice Church the night before.

When I turned around and looked back, I saw the church filling up. Many more people were seated and coming in, so I went and greeted as many as I could. Many of the people were relatives that had come just for the service and the reception. I think this church holds around 400 people and it was full by the time the service started. Just before the service started, Frank's nephew, George, who is the son to his brother George who was with us at the Winchuck Ranch and had died earlier, arrived and sat in the front row with us. I'm sorry that we really didn't get to say more than a few words to each other. He drove up from Fremont in time for the service and went back during the time we were eating. He didn't even get to see the movie of Frank's story. There were others who did the same.

Paul started playing the Our Father when the altar boys and Father James McKnight started walking up the aisle. Terry sang the words to the Our Father; he does such a good job of it. Both he and Paul also did this at Julia and Mark's wedding 13 years ago, so we knew everyone would enjoy it. After Father was at the front, the altar boys sat down. Laurence, who is a tall, handsome man and gets better looking as the years go by, gave the welcome talk. I was very proud of him for wanting to do this. He talked about the opening and closing of doors and if you have a choice or not. I now can't remember what all he said; I will say he left the pulpit very tall and straight and sat down at the edge of the seat next to Gloria and me. Father then introduced the liturgy. He has always done a very good job at explaining our Mass to everyone, for he knows that many people will not understand what we do. I was glad to hear many people saying "thank you," for the introduction helped them to follow what was going on.

Frank's niece, Carol, gave the first reading. When she finished, Laurence helped her down the steps from the altar. My grandniece Kristen gave the second reading, and when she started to leave the altar and come down the steps, she went back up to the pulpit to say "Thanks Be to God." We all laughed and Laurence helped her down as everyone said, "Praise to You Lord Jesus Christ." Father read the gospel and the Homily. Then we sang the Old Rugged Cross. When it came time for presentation of the gifts for communion, our godchild, Kellie, her husband, Randy, and their two children, Katie and Michael, brought the gifts up. Everyone sang Christ Has Risen, and later we sang the communion song, Be Not Afraid.

At the eulogies, Father announced who was going to speak and in what order so there would be no confusion. Each speaker spoke on a complete different aspect of Frank's life. People who listened that day got to hear things that they never knew about Frank and what a real person he was inside. Most knew him as a hard, tough person, for he did not like to have someone side track him or interrupt his thoughts, which really was his front, for he really was a soft-hearted person once you got to know him.

Frank's nephew, Milton, told the story about Frank starting from when his father and mother met and passed away. He told a lot about Frank's history, including how they lived in a three-room house with a dirt floor. He talked about how the boys milked cows while they were in grammar school, with the money coming in being mostly how his mother lived. As a relative, Milton was able to touch on many aspects of Frank's life, and he shared what he himself learned and got out of it. I have a copy of his story so I'll leave off here.

The next speaker was Father McKnight. This was a surprise for it was not on the list of people that were to talk. I don't have a copy of his story but will try to say it as I remember it. He gave a little talk about Frank and how he really got to know him. It was about the parking lot that the church wanted to have which had to go through the local planning department. He thought that by having Jerry Frey, a pillar of the community, go with him, he would have no trouble. This was until the Board of Supervisors started to lay down what Father would have to do to get the parking approved. He was told he would have to give up three lots for public parking and pay for a year. I can't remember what he was supposed to pay for, but it didn't take long until Frank got up, hammered on the table with his fist, and said, "No deal!" Father said to himself, "There goes my parking lot," but when Frank got through, he had the parking lot, with no restrictions added. He said he could see that Frank talked their language and their attitude changed as soon as Frank got involved. They listened to what he had to say. Father said he himself was a "just a babe in the woods" when he saw how Frank handled them.

I hope I have Father's story right, for I told Father afterwards that with him telling the story there could be no shading to it because it came from the pulpit and from him, with no deviations or false sayings.

Lowell Robinson was the next person to speak. He talked about his relations with Frank, both business and friend, and how long the relations were, going all the way back to 1952. He also spoke of the North Star and their relations on that project, and his word was good. Most of all he considered Frank a good friend. I have his written speech, but he said more than what he had written down.

Howard Epstein, who was Frank's stockbroker, was next to talk. They knew each for over 20 years by phone, talking each day at 8:30 a.m. about stocks and bonds, five days a week. He said Frank stressed, "Double check your math," and know what you are talking about. He said Frank never bragged about what he did or had and that he loved his family enough that Howard plans to do the same with his family. He said he learned this just by listening to what Frank was saying. I have his speech so will say no more, as this is reminder enough, except to say that Howard has kept his word to Frank and does help me when I need it, along with when the kids need his help. The outcome of his talk is that Lowell asked him for his card so he could also do business with him.

The next person to speak was Paul Perry. He had written a letter to Frank a few weeks before Frank died. He had planned to mail it, but at the last minute decided to bring it over to Frank and read it to him, for he wanted Frank and me to know how he felt about what we had done. He gave the same talk in church and was very nervous and just short of tears. And I should add that it was Paul who told us we should let it out publicly about our donation, so others would do the same. It has worked, so we no longer keep all of it quiet. We hope others continue to do the same as we did. Again, I have his speech so will say no more, for I can remember what he said, and when I need to remind myself, I can go back to all these nice speeches.

Julia gave the closing thoughts. And it is here that there are a few things that I want to share first. Julia was on my left and Mark was next to her; she was very nervous and afraid she would cry while giving her talk, especially after listening to Paul give his talk. As she got ready to get up, Mark grabbed her hand and hung onto it for a few minutes and did not let go until he felt Julia relax. She then got up and did her talk without a quiver in her voice, not even once throughout her long comments. I must say that Julia is a very good speaker and knows how to use a microphone to its advantage. She acknowledged that although she may have sympathized with people and their grief before, it wasn't until now that she really knew how. She described her dad and her loving feeling about him. She then told a story about a man asking a doctor about what was on the other side. The doctor opened the door to let the dog into a room he had never been in before, but his master was there. And so her father, Frank, has gone to his master. And as she looked out at all the people that had come for Frank, she saw a church full of quiet angels. She also shared all the things that people had said in the many notes we had received. She then thanked all the people for coming and invited everyone to the hall afterwards.

As she came down the steps, Laurence stood up to help her. Then they gave each other a very long, loving, and close hug that everyone in church saw, which touched them.

After Julia finished, there was a meditation prayer, followed by Robin Mayforth playing Ave Maria on her violin. She was one of Frank's favorite players in M.I.M., and she knew it. She later said she had a hard time keeping the tears away as she played.

Father then gave the closing prayer and blessing and came down to talk to me and the family. I told him I wanted to say something to the people, so before he gave his last blessing, he announced it. I stood up, turned to face everyone, and thanked them all for coming and invited them to the hall. I did not have a quiver in my voice, nor did I cry during the service. We then had the recessional song with everyone singing "How Great Thou Art."

There was music and choir singing as Father and the helpers left the church. Then Robin Mayforth played as each row left their pew. And, of course, I dropped my Celebration of Frank program folder with his handsome face smiling up at me. I had to stoop to pick it up, so I held up the first row. As I was walking down the aisle, many people wanted to say hello and shake my hand. I really wanted to say more than I did, but there just wasn't any time. When I got outside the church, Milton was there to get me to the car and off to the hall. He just pulled me right along.

At this time, I want to say that I received a very nice letter from Carol Hamilton, which she wrote, had printed, and mailed to the press. It was very touching. I have kept her letter, along with the rest. I also received an e-mail letter from our friend Mohammad, who is in Iran. He wanted to know if I was going to sell Frank's car, and if so, to keep it for him.

We went back to Nevada City to St. Canice Hall for Frank's farewell to all his friends. The hall is on Reward St., just a short ways down from our place. The girls from St. Canice Guild had done a great job at setting up the tables. The main tables had the food set up in way that everyone could be served as fast as possible, so they could sit down to eat. Frank's movie would be shown for everyone to see when it came time for dessert. There were about 30 round tables with white table clothes and a colorful centerpiece with all kinds of mixed flowers in them that made the room look very nice.

Me and Julia at St. Canice Hall

At the entrance to the hall, there were all the big flower arrangements and pictures of Frank and his life. The place was full of friends and relatives; about 250 people were in the hall. It was very quiet when the movie was shown of Frank, so they could all hear his soft voice. By the time the film was made, Frank could hardly talk very loud. People got to see Frank's life from his grandparents, up through his whole life, to the last few weeks of his life. It ended with Frank kissing me and showing the empty swing at the ranch that he loved. At the end of the movie, there were very few dry eyes in the hall, and that included the men as well. Julia, along with Greg, who did the editing, narration, and detail work on it, had done an excellent job. I now have it on tape to help me remember our life together.

The people at Hooper & Weaver Mortuary handled all the transportation of the flowers and the picture of Frank and his Urn for all the comings and goings. Due to Lent Season, we could not leave the flowers in the Church, so when everything was done for the day, my basement was full of huge flower arrangements. And I decided to wait to bury the urn until maybe it's my turn, and then the kids can do so, but then again I could change my mind. To this day, I have Frank's picture on my kitchen table, and on the frame, I have his hearing aids and his glasses. I like looking at it and give it a kiss every so often. I also say goodbye and goodnight to it also.

After everything was done at St. Canice Hall, the kitchen staff sent all the extra food here to the house. That evening anyone who was staying around or overnight was welcome to come to the house for leftover dinner, and quite a few were staying over and going home on Sunday after church. All the card tables and chairs were still up from the night before, and before leaving for Mass at St. Patrick's Church, I had put fresh flowers in the bowls on the tables that needed them, so they would be ready for the evening. Toni was here to keep an eye on the house for me, and to help anyone who might happen to drop by to see what was going on and where.

The living room ready for the relatives and guests

I did not have anyone staying here in the spare bedroom, for I knew that if anyone was in town staying overnight without reservations, they would not have a place to sleep. Gloria did the same. It ended up that she did have some at her place, but I did not. I will have to say it did give me some quiet peace, and I am not afraid to stay alone.

All the people that ended up staying until Sunday ended up having breakfast at the Trolley Junction Restaurant after going to church. And again, Mass was said for Frank that day. We had to wait so long at the restaurant that Laurence and Gloria had to leave before the food came. They were on a committee to decorate for something else and had to leave. After eating breakfast and paying the bill, I said my goodbyes to everyone and to my sister, LaVena, who was 83 and not in good health. However, she was so glad she came for both services, and all the families on my side got to see her. I then came home because I was so tired. Everyone else ended up at Mark and Julia's place. After I got home, I took a nap and then started to put all the tables and chairs away. Later in the afternoon, Karen and Toni came by to pick everything up and take everything home that belonged to them. For several days afterwards, I was very tired and found I had a hard time sleeping.

The first week after Frank died I was crying a lot, but once I started writing down what happened to him, I found I was much better because I didn't have to go back over everything again and again in my mind. Then in

April, Julia and I joined a bereavement class that lasted for 12 weeks. That also helped, hearing what the others say, and I'd think to myself, as I listened to what they were saying, "I've been there." There were about 16 of us, and I'm guessing the ages were from the 30s to maybe 65, with maybe one or two in their early 70s. I feel they will all come out of it fine; they just need time, and yes, I'm not supposed to say that. However, age is to my advantage in this course. If I can help any of them, so much the better for me, as well as them.

A nice group of people going through bereavement

Mass was said for Frank the next two days I went to church. It continued like that even until the end of April, and not only on Sundays, but also two or three times during each week. And Masses in May are already set up for the next three Sundays.

After Mass was said for Frank on Tuesday, Father McKnight invited me to have coffee with him and several others at one of the restaurants here in town. But I didn't go because I had too many other things to do at that time, including my exercises I do every Monday, Wednesday, and Friday, and did so right up until the last month Frank got so sick and I didn't want to leave him. He asked me since, but we haven't gotten around to it yet.

I went back to doing my exercises again after Frank passed away. I am also walking downtown to get the mail and walk to the bank to make my deposits. I have taken in a luncheon for Allegro Alliance and have gone to dinner with Karen at the Asian Gardens. I have played bridge at the Wiebe's with Betty, where I was the bidder, and while playing my hand, I had what they call a blackout, or loss of memory. Right away, I told them what had happened, and after a minute, I was all right. That was an awful experience, and I have been told I will have many of them before the year is over. And I have, along with those instant tears that pop up at the oddest moments.

Mar. 30–Apr. 1, Fri.–Sun. I attended the M.I.M. Concerts with a flower in Frank's seat every night. On Friday afternoon, Roxanna Cohen had her grand opening of her new studio. Frank would have loved to have been there for that, for he was instrumental in her going into this adventure.

Apr. 5, Thur. It has been one month since Frank left us. Julia and I went to church, and they did the "Washing of the Feet." Julia and I helped with this by pouring the water from pitchers over the feet while Father washed them. This was the first time I had seen it done in our church; in the past, it was "Washing of the Hands."

Apr. 12, Thur. Julia and Mark left for Kona, Hawaii, and stayed a week. They were both so tired they just rested, read, did some walking and sleeping, and came home rested up. In a way, Julia was in far worse shape than I was. She had to do all the work that went into the pictures and movie, and helping me out took its toll on her. She really took her dad's death very hard; in a way, she says it was her first real experience of death.

During the next few weeks, people have asked me out to lunches and dinners, and a couple of times Paul Perry was asked to pick me up, so I wouldn't have to drive late at night. A few days later, I had dinner at Lowell and Wanda Robinson's place. I had a nice time playing Hand and Foot with them, only to get lost coming home on different roads; however, knowing the area, I finally found a street that got me onto Banner Mountain Road and that got me home just fine — after an hour of driving around dark residential streets! This happened late at night, and a lot of the houses had their lights turned off, so if I had to go ask them how to get on the right road, I'd of been in trouble. So I told the kids I will have to learn the new cell phone and carry it with me in case I have to call one of them or 911.

Before Frank died, he told me to go to things, and if I needed a ride, he gave me a name of the person to ask. He was well in touch with what I would be doing and what I'd need. He also told me not to sell the house because it was part of him and me, and whoever buys it will never keep it like I have, and he was very proud of the yard. He just loved to sit and look at the yard on the square rock post by the redwood tree in the driveway. He also knew before he died that the SNMH Foundation Board had asked to use the yard in May to host a Red Rose Social Reception sometime in May. The date was finally set for May 20, 2007. I have set June 1 for the remodeling of our bathroom. And on May 10, I'm taking Ina to a Foothill Theatre play; she has never attended one, so that will be new to her.

I continued receiving many, many cards with Masses that are and will be said for him going into several years. I think one was for five years every Sunday. I have not counted the cards that I have received, but they have filled two big shoeboxes stuffed full. I would guess there are at least 300 of them. When I get to the tail end of writing about the things that happened to Frank, I will start to answer all the letters and cards. I had sent out around 70 cards to people who brought flowers, food of all kinds, and to those who have helped. There have been many donations to Hospice, M.I.M., and Foothill Theatre. I will have to answer all of them, and they are still coming in. When I finish sending out Thank You notes, I will call and ask how much came into each organization.

I had a checkup with Dr. Newsom. She was surprised to see me looking like I did and asked me how I was doing. So I told her what I have been doing about putting things on paper. I also told her that since the pain behind my right ear had left my head that I was in better health than ever, other than the problem in my forehead and between my eyes, and only to have Frank go in the reverse and not have many years with me in good health. But because I was doing better, I had no trouble taking care of Frank, other than being tired all the time. I had strength in my legs, arms, and back. For all our married years, I had something going wrong with my head, and now my head is clear, not dizzy, floating, or hurting. He knew it too, for I kept telling him how much better I was.

As I come to the end of the notes on Frank, I feel his loss, yes, and I can cry easily when I think about it. But I find I have been able to write this, and I feel it helps a lot and has cut down on a lot of emotion that I would have had otherwise. I can talk about him most of the time and hold my own in conversations about him, but if you say to me, "I want to give you a hug, because you need a hug," then the tears will come. Because, yes, I do need that hug, because Frank would give me many, even out in public he would do so, and even kiss me, and think nothing of doing it in front of people. Frank was a loving man, only most people did not know him that way, nor did they know his sense of humor.

Mark, Julia, Laurence, and Gloria have all had their birthdays since Frank has left us. Mine is in a few days and none of us got together to celebrate our birthdays. Julia and Mark were in Hawaii, and I think Laurence and Gloria spent it with friends. So each major holiday is continuing to go by. And Frank's birthday is on June 19.

As I look out and walk the yard, I think of him not with me to see all the lovely spring flowering shrubs of all kinds that are all over this yard in their bright and radiant hews. As I have mentioned, it was this time of year that he picked the last bouquet of flowers for me for my birthday. He had also given me two very nice cards for my 84th birthday and Mother's Day that fell on the same day. He had written some very touching words in them that I read every so often. That was to be my last birthday with him.

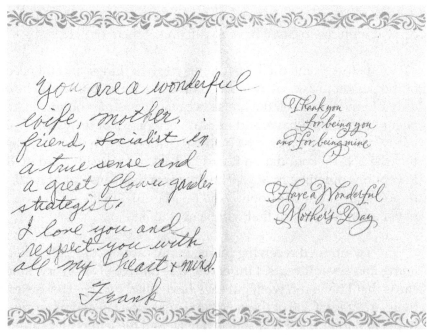

Frank's birthday and Mother's Day card to me (2006)

As 4 myself

My birthday balloons from M.I.M.

May 12–14, Sat.–Mon. I spent my first birthday without Frank working in the yard all day until late. A group from M.I.M. decided I needed a gift, so they had a huge bouquet of balloons that ended up being about ten feet high delivered to me. And Howard and Tami sent me a big bouquet of flowers. Later that day, Lowell and Wanda brought by three crates of strawberries for me from Marysville, so I spent Mother's Day morning making strawberry jam before going to church. After church, I canned 21 pints of jam and then spent the rest of Mother's Day at Gloria and Laurence's place with Julia, Mark, and Spence. Brad and Lisa were not able to be there, but our friends, Hazel, Roxanna, Netta and Joe were there. We had a good time sitting out on the deck until 10 p.m. We had a very nice time.

On Monday my godchild, Kathie, and her daughter, Katie, drove up to spend a few hours with me. This was a real treat.

I have had many friends take me out to luncheons since Frank has left me. This has really helped fill in the gap during the daytime. I have also taken up playing the game Mahjong, playing in the evenings with a whole new set of friends. And some people see to it that I have some meals that they bring to me already cooked, which is a real treat.

May 29, Tue. Milton and Mimi drove down from Oregon to see their family and new grandson that live in Sacramento. They drove up here to have lunch with all of us. I had set out plates and silverware for eight people on the patio table, and Mark said, "There are only seven of us." That brought the tears, for I had included Frank with us.

May 30–June 1, Wed.–Fri. I hadn't been feeling too good for several days, so I called the doctor. She said to go the emergency room at the hospital to find out what was wrong with the pain I was having in my chest. I was also having trouble walking any distance without losing my wind and feeling faint. I came to find out it was not my heart but trouble with my esophagus. I was able to stay on the treadmill for 15 minutes, so my heart is still in top shape. The doc told me to stay on the Prilosec for the rest of my life and drink lots of fluids. They think it is the acid that is giving me the trouble. They also said Frank's death has a lot to do with what is going on in that area. Now I wonder what that doctor and hospital bill will be like! That could give me another set of pains.

June 4–5, Mon.–Tue. It has been three months since Frank has left us. Today the crew started to work on the bathroom, which Frank had me put on hold back in November. They tore out the outside wall and took all the debris out that way. Later, by June 18, they had the new bathtub in place, the closet back in shape, the new vanity in place, and were ready to paint in the closet. They did not work on the place on Frank's birthday. Everything is now more or less ready for the tile man. I'm not too happy with the drain board that I had selected as a last-minute choice to hurry the job in November, so I just may have to live with it now. I forgot I had done so, and I forgot to get it changed back to what I wanted. However, with some talking, Gary ended up making the change for me.

In July 2007, I went to my first real public outing since Frank died. Music in the Mountains was putting on a big performance for the Fourth of July. I wanted to go to this, but I didn't want to have lots of people asking me how I was. To avoid this, I volunteered to sell tickets. That way everyone could see I was doing OK. A couple of days later my body froze up on me.

After the Fourth of July, I started having some trouble with my colon. The doctor gave me some metronidazole and ciprofloxacin, and that really sent my spine from neck to tailbone into a spasm. The next two nights I had trouble getting out of bed. During this time, one night while I was sleeping in Julia's old bedroom because of the remodel, it was real dark, and Frank came and stood at the side of the bed. The room was dark and so was he, but I knew it was him. He had on black clothes and a black hat. I then had trouble getting out of bed to go to the bathroom. I ended up putting my feet over on the dresser, finally slid down off the bed to the floor, and then got up on my hands and knees. The next night I brought in the cushion off the patio chaise lounge and slept on the floor in the dining room, for the pain was so bad, but I could get up on my hands and knees. This did not affect my arms or legs, and once I was up I was OK. I just couldn't bend over or pick anything up. I took some Aleve for pain relief, and I also saw Dr. Greenlee, Tucker, and finally Sievert, who said I wasn't out in anyplace. After seven days I ran out of pills and hoped it would leave my system and clear up, which it didn't.

Gloria took me to see Dr. Newsom. She concluded I might be allergic to the Cipro and it was affecting my nervous system, but she was not sure. For the next five weeks, my body was in very heavy pain, from my waist to my neck. If I cried, it hurt worse, so I didn't cry if I could help it. Finally, a doctor took a blood test and my SAD rate was at 85. At this time, Gloria had taken me to see Dr. Newsom and she gave me prednisone. Both doctors said I would be out working in the yard the next day, but no such luck. The next day it really got worse and entered my legs, ankles, wrists, hands, fingers, and neck. Doctor Newsom and her staff worked hard for the next week to get me in to see Dr. Carolyn Dennehey, a rheumatologist in Sacramento.

Dr. Dennehey took blood tests and X-rays of my hands and chest area. The results were that my SAD rate was indeed 85. Things continued about the same for the next several weeks, and in time, my SAD rate dropped down to 48. Every 10 to 12 days I needed to change the number of pills I was taking, and in time it was cut down to half. Along the way, I hoped the pain that was now in my chest, neck, and face would go away. And the doctor told me I would not be able to drive. She also said it was the result of Frank's death.

Aug. 1, Wed. I still have the pain and trouble, but it is not as bad. My last SAD rate was 27, and it has to come down below 20 to reduce the prednisone. In time, I reduced the pills and then cut them in half. It took a few months before I could get off them, and when I did, I still had the side effects from them and didn't really feel very good.

Along the way, I had been seeing Dr. Seivert on Mondays for therapy because my body was so stiff, and, yes, I cried, for it was so painful. I saw Dr. Tucker on Fridays for acupuncture treatments. My head has not been very clear and I make all kinds of thinking mistakes. For seven weeks, I did not drive and depended on my friends and the kids to take me places. And I thank them all for doing so. As of this last week, I can finally drive again, and as of today, maybe my bathroom will be finished next week. I hope all this mess in my body will have cleared up by that time. In the meantime, I miss Frank very much; but I don't let this pain keep me from going and doing things, including "Starry Starry Night," which is put on by Laurence and Gloria and their crew. I danced at the event, although not too well, with some of the younger men who have known us all their lives. I'm also going out to lunches and dinners. I am playing bridge and Mahjong, going to church, and attending Music in the Mountains programs. Life does go on. And the kids think I should buy a new car, so I'm looking into that, but it will have to wait until I am over this problem I have.

2008 to January 2011

AFTER FRANK PASSED AWAY, and even though I wasn't feeling well, I held dinner parties here at Reward St.—one during each summer from 2007 to 2010. I've also held several Christmas dinner parties. Frank had told me to continue having catered dinner parties, and this is what I did. I also hosted a tea get-together with 40 or so some-odd gals.

On March 4, 2008, I gifted Frank's car to the Sierra Adoption Agency for a fundraising project they were doing. As it drove out of the driveway, I realized it was only one day short of the anniversary of his death. I hope it has a happy new home.

Saying goodbye to Frank's car as it was being towed out of the driveway

M.I.M. party at Reward St. for Paul Perry

Three months later, in June 2008, Music in the Mountains held a surprise party in the yard for Paul Perry. The party was celebrating Paul's 25 years of work for M.I.M. and was given by Bev Erickson, the chorus, and orchestra. About 150 people attended. I don't remember many of the details because I had nothing to do with it. I gave them the yard to use for the party. At the end of June, Music in the Mountains held their summer program at the fairgrounds.

Music in the Mountains summer program, 2008, under the shell we helped buy many years earlier

On Aug. 23, 2008, I held my first dinner party since Frank's passing. I had 20 people over and everyone had a good time. My toast was the dinner itself, which was from Frank because he told me to have parties. Carol Hamilton and her husband, Bob, took pictures.

Putting name tags on the tables

230

In Nov. 2008, I was about to have a tree fall down that was at the edge of the heart lawn and driveway. At the same time, two other trees were also in trouble, the one in the lawn by the walkway coming up to the house, and the one closest to the house off the kitchenette. I had the tree by the kitchenette cut down to about three feet above the ground and put a flat rock slab on top of it, using it like a tabletop. The other trees had their stumps and roots dug up.

Me in front the house after the trees had been removed

The crane getting in position to remove a tree by the house

In Sept. 2009, I finally did buy a new car for myself. It's a Mercedes E550 sedan with the extra 4-wheel drive added. The license plates says, "4 Myself." It's a smaller car than what I had been getting in the past, and I love it. It did take me awhile to get used to getting over not having all that roomy space inside the car.

In 2010, I spent some time in and out of hospitals for the same things — getting over all the things that went on after Frank had left me. My sister Helen and her husband have since passed away leaving only my younger sister LaVena and myself. Frank's sister-in-law, Edna, has also left us. I have my ups and downs, but I think the doctors have finally figured out what's wrong with me. I finally have a steady body, I am no longer lightheaded in the mornings, and I feel better than I have most of my life.

Because my health has improved, mostly in 2010, I am back to being active in the yard, and I'm walking down and up the steep hill from our house to Reward St. about four times a day. And in the summer of 2010, I had Tom Barney and his son remove the stump that the big flower urn sat on in front of the house next to the art room. The stump had rotted away and it was time to get rid of it. The brick walkway had to be torn up to get the job done, so I had a brick man come in to re-lay the brick that was taken out to remove the stump. The brick man re-laid it a couple of times, but it just wasn't coming out right. I wound up having Victor, my longtime gardener, help me redo it. It was a big job, but I was getting better and could hold my own. Victor really took pride in the job he did with the brick, and I am very pleased with the results.

I received a couple of awards in 2010. One was a Rotary Award, and the other was an award from Hospice of the Foothills.

Me receiving the
Rotary Award from Dick Landis

I went to the Clarke Ranch four times with Julia and Mark during the years 2007 to 2010. I fell once at the ranch by missing the bottom step of the stairs inside the main house. I think this happened in 2008.

I had another fall at home in Feb. 2010. About eight in the morning, I decided to go out the kitchen door to walk down to the carport to get the paper. On the way, just before the walkway going up to the front door, I felt an odd pain on the back of my head and knew I was going to fall, but I couldn't stop it from happening. (It was just like the fall I had about a year ago in the foyer when I was all dressed and getting ready to go to church on Sunday.) I even had the cane with me too, but it didn't help. It acted like it had turned to rubber on me, and I even said that out loud just before I fell. I fell hard on my right elbow, which started to really bleed. The fall really affected my shoulder and did some damage to my neck. I landed hard on my right hip. So I decided to see if this little, white, life-saving *Life Line* button that I had been wearing around my neck since Frank died really worked. I pushed the button, and then right after doing so, I got up and used my cane to finish getting the paper in the carport. I then walked back up to the back door and started to get my breakfast.

In the meantime, I had decided that the button didn't work, so I called the *Life Line* company to let them know. They replied, "Yes ma'am, it does work, and we have already called Julia. We didn't get her, so we left a message." (She and Mark were headed for Sacramento to catch a plane to Africa.) Then they called Laurence, and about the time they were telling me all this, an ambulance drove into the driveway. When they got into the kitchen, they would not let me finish making my breakfast, but instead pushed me into a wheelchair, took my pulse, and did all the rest of the things medics do. There were around four of them and they got right to work on my elbow. I didn't know it was bleeding so badly. It was obvious they knew me well enough to take command. In all this commotion, Julia called from the airport to say goodbye to me and one of the medics answered the phone. That is how she found out I had fallen.

In the meantime, Laurence had arrived. As I left in the ambulance, he locked up the house for me. It's always nice having children around. I'm not going into any more details, other than the end results. It was discovered I needed fat in my bloodstream. So I was put on a gluten-free and sugar-free diet, along with vitamin B-50 and lots of water. It has taken several months, but I do have more energy and feel safe to drive. And my age does come into play.

In the fall of 2010, I had to have an old two-inch steel water line replaced. It ran from Reward St., just as you enter the property, on up the hill alongside our driveway and joined in with the two-inch line we had installed 25 years ago that went to the pump house. The old steel line had filled with rust and was only about an inch in diameter. This was causing some problems with our water. For one thing, in the summer of 2009, the sprinklers weren't getting enough water to do their job, so I cut down the size of the sprinkling system and added a second large water tank hoping that would do the job, but it didn't. We also found out that the electric bill was very high because the pump was working overtime. I had Tom Barney come in and do all the work of replacing the water line going from the two-inch hook up down to the water meter on Reward St. I will know this summer if I've wasted my time and energy. And now, other than shingling the house, I hope to have all the projects done, at least for a while.

I helped Julia at Christmastime with her tree as I have done in the past, and she, Mark, Gloria, and Laurence helped me with my small seven-foot silvertip tree that I get each year. We also enjoyed some special dinners together, including a soup dinner at Gloria and Laurence's where we got to watch people come to see "Eddie the Elf." There are always so many people that come to see the lights and Eddie at this time of year. It sort of ties them up, but it means a lot to the kids, and Laurence and Gloria enjoy going out to talk to all the people. Julia and Mark had me and a few other people over for Christmas dinner.

We had some real cold weather that brought several inches of snow, so I had some shoveling to do in order to get to the office. I also cleared the walkway from the kitchen down to the driveway. I use my pickup to open up the circle driveway; I simply drive around it several times. I also drive down the road to Reward St. to open it up too. After I open up the driveway with the pickup, I can then get in and out with my car if I need to go anywhere.

Now, in 2011, I can see I have a couple of lawns that need to be turned over. This will probably get done in April, before the shipment of plants and live flowers arrive in May and need to be planted. I always look forward to the yard looking nice for the dinner parties that I have in the fall. Along with my improving health, I am finally seeing my way through this book with my children's patience and the persistent and dedicated help of Mark Bancroft.

My twilight years

As I think about my life and heading into my twilight years, I know I haven't finished everything that the good Lord has put me here to do. For most of my life, I have had many ups and downs with my health, but I am still here, so He must have more work for me to do. And I am feeling much better health-wise than I've felt most of my life. The doctors tell me I have the body of a 68-year-old as I go into my 89th year; however, I will be having open-heart surgery as I go into my twilight years. My heart doctor and long-time friend, Dr. Mallery, said if I were his mother, he would have already had me in surgery. I know the good Lord has more work for me to do, and as Frank said, if I were on Hitler's side, the Germans would have won the war.

As I look back on my health, I notice that the pain from my kidney went away a few years before Frank died. I believe my Pilates exercises with Roxanna is what really solved the problem. After the pain stopped, I stopped going to Pilates, but I may go back to keep my waistline in shape. I am not interested in golf and don't think I'll ever take up golfing again, but I did enjoy taking the golf trips around the world with Frank.

I get good exercise walking up and down my steep driveway four or five times in a row without stopping. My heart really gets going on the first trip but then subsides. It takes me about 20 minutes to do five trips.

Charity work is still an important part of my life, both publicly and privately. I feel it is something both Frank and I were put here to do. I am not afraid to say what I think should be done. Time is on my side when it comes to giving advice. And I am not into hurting other people's feelings, either. Frank and I were hurt too many times by others. We both found ways to take care of that, mostly by keeping busy with traveling and our businesses. After Frank left, I've been keeping myself busy with this book and with doing work that will help other people. As I do that work, I try to always remember that the left hand is not to know what the right hand is doing.

Now that I am thinking back on my life, I have come to discover something interesting about myself that I never realized before. I notice that I have never been a person to ask "Why?" nor have I cared to find out. I now wonder why I never asked Frank what he meant by so many of the things he said. Even at the end, I never asked him what the pills did to him. I think the reason I don't ask "Why?" is because I know that God is in control and looking after things. I suffered so much as a young person and I really feel God won't let you suffer twice. I feel I will leave this world peacefully.

I accept my weaknesses and don't let them bother me too much, for my strong points out number them. I feel very comfortable with whom I am inside. I also feel that by just being myself I can really help people who have lost someone. I don't need or look for praise, but I do need respect. I speak my mind and find I can be very blunt.

Art has always been a very important to me, and I strongly feel that the future of Nevada City and Grass Valley lies in the arts. I can see the area really heading into the arts down the road. I very much feel that land should be bought so a new performing arts center can be built. Everything happening in the arts in this area is leading up to that; it's the next step that the community needs to take. It's too bad that as a group all the local organizations cannot get together to see that a community arts center is viable for everyone. And it has to be an organization that brings it together to make it viable, so that money can start being put into the project. The money is here. The people just need a trusted organization they can put their money into, knowing that a center will get built with their contribution. Having many little organizations fighting against each other doesn't work, not for the community, nor for the artists. A large building could give each smaller organization its own space and could also be used as a convention center. Art lessons, teaching, and instruction would also become more feasible. The first step is buying the land.

Once I finish this book, I look forward to maybe getting back to my own art. I have always wanted to make a painting "walk" — to make it appear that the subject is coming out of the painting. I think that by working at it I can make it happen. I once saw a picture like that in our travels, and I remember telling Frank I would love to go to the teacher who taught the artist the technique. If I ever go back to painting, that's what I'd try to do. I don't know if my eyes will hold up, but I'd like to try it. No matter what I do, my yard is like a painting to me, so I always have that to work on and enjoy.

As far as living at 211 Reward Street, I want to stay here as long as possible. However, I never want to become a burden to my children. They, too, are no longer so-called young. If it gets to the point where I can no longer take care of myself, I'd rather go someplace where help is available 24 hours, rather than relying on the kids day in and day out.

I continue taking care of the business end of things with outside help. This helps keep my mind from moving in other directions. I find I no longer want to collect things. I now think about the things I need to give away and how best to do it. I am very aware of how my children and their spouses think and how they respect each other. Above all, I notice how they have mellowed in their 60 years and take care of each other. Frank and I have been truly blessed with four fine people.

I will say I am not very happy about what is going on in our country. It is very much a repeat of the late 1930s and early 40s. I went through that time as a child; I hate to think I'll go through it again before I leave this life. If things keep going the way they are, young people will not have a good life to look forward to. That makes me sad and also a little angry at those in charge that don't care and are causing it to happen. Above all, I say my prayers to God and give thanks to the values that have made this country so great. The community is full of many fine friends, and as time allows, I plan to get more involved with charity work and helping other people where it is necessary. I am so very grateful and say my prayers to the good Lord for all He has given to Frank, who, in turn, gave to me and the children so we could enjoy such a wonderful life.

I hope you have enjoyed our family's life history.
It is now 2012 as I complete this book and look forward to my twilight years.

APPENDIX A

The Clarke Ranch

APPENDIX A INDEX
<u>The Clarke Ranch</u>

241

APPENDIX A (continued):   **Page**
The Clarke Ranch

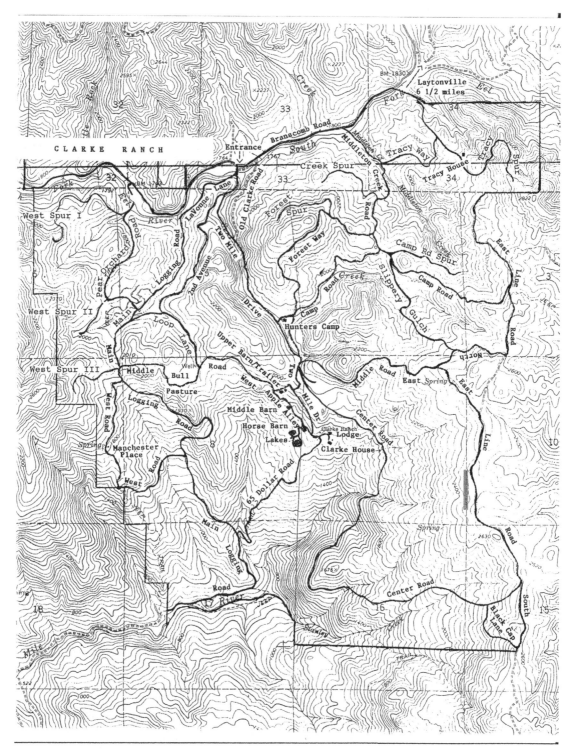

Topographic map of the Clarke Ranch

The Clarke Ranch: a great investment

View of the Clarke Ranch

Frank's story

FRANK RECALLS THAT HIS purchase of the Clarke Ranch—a 5,000-acre property in Mendocino County—in 1967 was one of the very good deals he made. In fact, the ranch is still in our family and is now owned by our daughter, Julia, to whom we sold the ranch to in January 1990. Frank sold 8 million board feet of timber off the property from 1968–70, and by doing so got the entire price back that he'd paid for the whole ranch. While owning the ranch, he leased sections of the land to a cattleman for grazing and to clubs for hunting, fishing, and recreation. This has allowed the ranch to generate income and carry itself.

After the price of timber went sky-high between 1990 and 1991, Julia sold small amounts of timber. She still has a lot of timber on the ranch, which keeps growing every day. Frank believes she has sold less than 10 percent of the volume he sold in the earlier days, and she still got more out of it than he did because, instead of getting $35 per thousand square feet, like he did, she received almost 10 times that amount. This just shows what has happened in some of the businesses we've been in, and the Clarke Ranch investment was one that worked out very well and continues to do so.

The year Frank bought the Clarke Ranch, 1967, was a rather full year for us. We had the Winchuck Ranch in Oregon going and were involved with other projects and adventures as well; including the trip to Europe and Africa with the Morrises that summer. In November of that year, Laurence and Julia threw us a surprise 25th anniversary party at the Alta Sierra Country Club. Still, the purchase of the Clarke Ranch was the biggest development in our lives that year. It marked a milestone of sorts in our family history since the ranch has, and continues to play such a big part in our family's life.

Ariel view of the ranch

We buy the Clarke Ranch, 1967

Sign at the entrance to the ranch

WHEN WE BOUGHT THE Clarke Ranch in 1967, there were three livable houses on the property. One was called Manchester House, built sometime in the late 1800s, which had long since seen better days. It had turned into a transient house of sorts being far enough away from the main houses that nobody knew if anyone was in it. The Manchester House was accessed by going up from Ten Mile River. It also had a garage that was in better shape so it is likely the garage had been built years later. The Manchester House was on the west side looking southwest down the canyon, a little near the middle of the ranch. To reach the house meant going through an area called the "bull pasture." This place had a good orchard, large English walnut trees, a nearby creek running year-round, and a great view of open grasslands and canyons, hills and distant trees. However, the house was low enough down the canyon to get shrouded by fog when it rolled in.

The two other houses—the so-called Upper House and Main House—each had a garage, and there was a garage between the two houses used for tractors and other equipment. The houses and three barns were built during Joe Clarke's and his son Frank's time.

The Upper House was built about 1917 and is just above the Main House, about 400 feet away up on a hill. It is on a hillside and sits high enough to overlook the Main House. The Upper House was built by Joe Clarke and his son Frank in order for Frank and his new wife, Catherine, to have a place to raise their family. There is also a working-man's shed at the foot of the hill alongside Maple Creek between the two houses; it has its own outhouse. This shed looks like it was built in the early 1870s. In all the years our family has had the place, the shed was used as a "bunkhouse" for Frank Sagehorn to stay overnight in when working his cattle. As of this writing, the shed is just "hanging in there." No one goes inside for fear it will collapse.

At the time we bought the ranch, a nice couple lived in the Upper House. They rented the ranch to raise sheep and continued to stay there for a couple of years. There were many old things of value in the house. They invited us in to visit them and showed us all the things that came with the house. One was an authentic crank telephone that was still in use; it was left behind when they moved out.

A beautiful 5,000-acre ranch

THE CLARKE RANCH STARTED out as a cattle ranch that years later became a sheep ranch during the era when the pioneer Clarke family owned it. It also has timber that grows very well on it. The ranch has meadows, rivers, mountains and valleys, and different kinds of fruit trees, including apples, pears, plums, cherries, and figs. The trees are English walnuts and black walnuts, fir, pine, cedar, redwood, hemlock, madrone, and many other kinds all planted during Thomas Clarke's time. There are blackberries, salmon, and red berries, and different kinds of grapes, bulb flowers, and wild flowers of all kinds all over the hills, mountains, and valleys. There are springs and creeks everywhere. There is also a large, special tree on the ranch in the area we call the bull pasture; it is a California bay or pepperwood tree. I understand it is considered the largest one of its kind found anywhere, and Frank's favorite madrone tree is found in the same area.

Frank and his favorite madrone tree

The Thomas Clarke family
began their ranch in 1868

THOMAS CLARKE (born May 23, 1818 England, died 1886), WIFE ELLESA (July 3, 1815 to Dec 8, 1893), and their son William (died Feb. 2, 1912) came to America from England sometime around 1840. They brought with them nursery plants that included different fruit and nut trees, seeds to start a vegetable garden and flowers, shrubs, roses, grape and berry vines, and bulbs of various kinds. They were in Utah for about three years where they had some type of episode that held them up, and along the way their sons William, Alfred, Frank, and Joe were born. Joe was born in 1853, followed sometime later by daughter Eliza.

The Clarkes came to California by horse and wagon. Thomas Clarke was a nurseryman looking for good land for raising crops and planting his trees and seeds that he brought over from England. They traveled through the central valley of California toward the coast and arrived in the Mendocino area in, or around 1867. They ended up traveling south on the Cahto Road and on their way saw lots of mountains with open space. The Cahto Road was the main road at that time going north and south. Thomas Clarke fell in love with the area and bought land. What became the Clarke Ranch borders the west side of Cahto Road going south, and runs for three miles from the Cahto Road going west on what is now called the Branscomb Road, with the Eel River running alongside to the ocean.

Thomas and Ellesa built a home there sometime around 1868. I think it was near where the houses are today. His family ended up buying several thousand acres running along and on both sides of Cahto Road and Branscomb Road. His son William, in 1867, acquired 1,000 acres along the Cahto Road and could have been the one to live in what we call the Brown House, which is on one of the nicest spots for viewing the ranch. The place is warm and sunny with hardly any fog. The view overlooks canyons, mountains, ridges, a valley, rangeland, streams, and trees. This spot also has underground springs that can be tapped. In the far distance, the ocean can be seen on clear days, and sometimes a ship can be seen going by. This is also near the highest point on the ranch, which we call "Lookout Station," or "Station A," and where the grass has grown very tall. It was in this area that Julia and Mark built their airport strip around 1994 so they could land their plane.

Thomas Clarke settles on the ranch

STILL STANDING ON THE ranch are two tall posts that mark the entrance to the property that was called the Brown House, which is where the Brown family lived. I understand that stagecoaches would stop there for food, water, or an overnight stay. This was also the entrance to a road that still goes down the canyon through the center of the property, past where Thomas Clarke settled with the rest of his family around 1868.

To get to the site they must have gone west off the Cahto Road and continued going west on what is now called Branscomb Road and entered somewhere near the pear orchard that has the last entrance to the property. This part has a rather large, flat area that can be used to raise a good garden. The Eel River runs through it providing plenty of water. This is part of the area the Clarkes saw as they traveled along on Cahto Road and branched off onto Branscomb Road with their horses and wagon. They are no doubt the people who later planted the trees that are there.

From there the road continues to the bull pasture. Continuing to the left brings you to the Main House, and to the right brings you to the Manchester House. There are still traces of the road going down the canyon and on towards the Union Lumber Co., the property west of the ranch. There is no doubt that at one time the road went on to the ocean.

The Clarkes built their first homestead around 1868—where, I am not sure—and around 1900–1905 they built where the Main House is today, and some years later they built the Upper House. The flat area there is protected by mountains and trees on the north, east, and south sides, but gets the fog from the west coming in off the ocean and 100 inches of rain a year. You can still see where large gardens were planted. In later years—and this could be when the Model T Ford cars came into popular use—the ranch residents entered from Branscomb Road, just as we do today. Cahto Road is no longer being used. However, you can see where the entrance was; it borders along our east line to Branscomb Road and continues south towards Willits. During the early years, Strong Mountain Road came through the Clarke Ranch property and the stagecoaches would stop at the ranch house. When we bought the property in 1967, there were six entrances to the ranch off Branscomb Road, and the first entrance was where Cahto Road entered the property. The last entrance was at the far west end of the property where we enter the pear orchard. At the orchard, there are two old Bartlett pear trees that still bear lots of good fruit. At one time, the orchard included apple trees and crops of some kind.

The Clarkes were industrious

AS THE YEARS WENT by, we talked to people who worked on the Clarke Ranch when they were young. They remembered how hard they worked and told us what hard workers the older Clarkes were. As I understand things, Cecile Clarke (Joe's daughter) and her younger brothers and sisters were raised and schooled by their mother, Annie, and when the time came for them to enter high school she rented a house in Ukiah and moved down to be with them. They came home for the school breaks. We were told that the mother did not like ranch life and she preferred the social life, which she missed. I think all the children, except Annie, attended college and some graduated from the University of California, Berkeley. The family was known at Stanford and also in San Francisco. Some of the girls were married at the ranch, and there are pictures of these events at the Clarke Museum in Eureka, where Cecile donated a great number of items from that era. We also have a lot of magazines and papers that were left behind and stored in the attics of the Main House and in the Upper House attic. The bunkhouse shed between the two houses had even more items, and some of these dated back to the mid-to-late-1880s. Someone in the Clarke family played the piano, for there was sheet music found with the magazines. The magazines were all good reading material, some dating back to the 1870s, and a lot pertained to sheep and wool.

The Clarkes became very well known for their sheep and wool. The Main House has a parlor that looks as if it was used only for weddings, funerals and entertaining. There is a sliding panel door that goes between the walls (I think it's called a pocket door), and it can be pulled out or closed off as needed. There are also sliding doors that separate the living room and the dining room the same way. The doors are made of redwood and I think each panel was made from one big piece of the same wood. The door openings are at least eight feet wide.

The Clarke Ranch is shown on maps of Mendocino County. We have maintained the historic name under our family's ownership, despite having owned it for so long that all the younger people in the area have grown up knowing that the Amarals are the ranch owners.

Building of the Main House

THE MAIN HOUSE WAS built on one acre of flat land, with an underground cellar to store food and canned goods. The main floor has a kitchen over the cellar area; on one side of the kitchen is a good-sized dining room and beyond that a good-sized living room. Off the kitchen and to the right is a service hall that goes upstairs and beyond the stairs is a small hall that leads to a maid's bedroom and a door leading out to a private porch. The bedroom also joins a bathroom with an extra-long bathtub held up by four animal-claw feet. Anyone who enjoys taking a bath and soaking in water loves the tub. The room has a toilet and basin, and there is another door leading into the bathroom from the main hallway so others can use it.

Off to one side of the kitchen, a door opens to another hall that goes to the main entrance to the house, and to the living room on the left of the hall and on the right a parlor and the main hallway leading upstairs. The second floor has four bedrooms, two on each side of the stairs. There are two smaller rooms, one at each end of the rather wide upstairs hall. I understand one was used as a sewing room and the other a nursery. From what I can tell, the nursery was the room facing the front end of the house with two large windows that are four feet high and go the full width of the room to let in lots of light. Today we use the room to store bedding, and it serves as a spare bedroom for a single guest. On the other side of the hall is the second small room that might have been used as a washroom of some sort; it had a toilet and a basin. We turned it into a bathroom and added a second toilet and shower to accommodate all the people we knew would be visiting. In this room is a door that leads to a hall going up to a full-sized attic that can be used for a playroom on rainy days.

The house is still heated by wood, but over time, electric heaters in the upstairs bedrooms replaced the two wood heaters that were in the bedroom located over the dining room and living room. The openings in the walls that lead to hidden chimneys have since been covered with fancy lids. The heat from these two rooms, along with heat coming up the two stairways, warms the other two bedrooms and the bathroom.

The main floor had a wood heater in the dining room and parlor. The wood heater was removed when the Clarkes brought in electricity. The living room still has a fireplace. The kitchen was and is heated by a large wooden range stove for cooking and heating water, and helps heat the house. Later, we added an electric stove that has two ovens, which come in very handy. The firewood stoves in all the other rooms were removed by the time we got the house. Electric heaters are used in all the upstairs rooms when needed and downstairs as well. I understand coal was never used to heat the house.

The other structures on the ranch were built sometime from 1867 to the early 1900s. I understand that the lumber used for the structures came from the redwood and Douglas fir trees that grew on the ranch on little Stanley Creek, which enters the Ten Mile River that makes its way to the ocean. These structures include a shed that is just off the porch of the main house and is divided into three small rooms. One room was a washroom; the middle room had a gas stove, and was where they cooked and canned foods in the summertime; and the third room was and is used as a shop, and for storing supplies, including ladders and garbage barrels. Another shed that was a little ways from the porch was a chicken coop. It was filled with things from the past, including coal and old dynamite that had lost its charge due to moisture coming in through open doors and broken windows.

Two garages, a horse shed, a tool shed, and a barn filled with old buggies and things from an earlier era were still in good shape when we bought the ranch. However, through the years, Miss Clarke had let the place go. By the time we got that acre of her estate the years had done their damage and she ended up giving away many things that were, in fact, good. The Clarke family sold all the land and everything on it to the Union Lumber Co., except the one acre, which included the main house, barns, shed, and garage that she reserved as a lifetime estate on the property. It is through the Union Lumber Co. that we bought the Clarke Ranch.

Barn that had two buggies in it at one time

Bathtubs for troughs

WHEN THOMAS CLARKE AND his son Joe had the ranch, it was in cattle, but later Joe and his son Frank went to raising Rambouillet sheep. The ranch has underground springs everywhere, which are easily tapped into with a pipe and then run through a trough. This type of water system works just as well for fruit trees and gardening.

The troughs were made from big redwood planks that came from trees off the ranch when the Clarkes owned it. Through the years, the wood was getting waterlogged; this was okay for sheep, but horses and cattle were a different matter, and in a short time the planks were busted up. In the late 1980s, we came upon bathtubs of different sizes and shapes around the ranch, and as time went on, we found more and more such tubs. One time, Frank and I were riding the ranch with Bev and Jack and we commented on the tubs; Jack then told us he had brought them down. He had access to many of them due to his contract work with schools, hospitals, and homes. One day Jack and Frank Sagehorn, the cattle rancher, were talking about the damage to the troughs, so Jack told him about all these tubs and said that Frank could have them and it would save him money. So Jack brought them down in his truck when he came to the ranch. He and Sagehorn ended up becoming good friends through the years.

That is the story about how the tubs got on the ranch. In those days, anything free was better than spending money on troughs, especially since the cattle were also doing a lot of damage to the redwood picket fences that were used for sheep. Sagehorn had to replace the fences with barbed wire, but he was able to use the old posts. I think we helped him out by splitting the cost on the wire and labor.

The Clarkes started farming and raising cattle, ended up sheep people

THE THOMAS CLARKE RANCH started out as a nursery business of trees and seeds that Clarke brought from England. He was also into cattle. He, along with sons William and Joe, and later, grandson Frank, became well known for raising sheep and wool. The fencing was put in using redwood stakes that were placed so close together that sheep could not get out, nor could coyotes get in easily, and if they did, there were coyote traps set in fenced-in areas.

The three barns away from the main house were all made and used for shearing sheep, and chutes were put in to push the wool down from the top floor and into a place on the first floor where the wool was bundled up for shipping or hauling to market. Each barn had two stories. I understand that during the Frank Clarke era, a great deal of work on the ranch was done by manual labor. Horses were used sparingly on the ranch. We have been told that most everything was done by hand and walking; horses were mostly used for riding or to pull the horse buggies or a wagon for transportation to other places, such as for shopping, social functions, transporting wool, weddings, etc. When we got the ranch, we saw several carriages that must have been quite nice back in their day.

Laurence kills his first deer

AFTER FRANK AND I got back from our trip to Europe and Africa with the Morrises, we spent a lot of time at the Clarke Ranch. There was so much that had to be done, and while we were there, the kids would come to visit. Once Laurence was back in school, he would bring some of his buddies on weekends or during vacation. One time he brought a young fellow during hunting season and they wanted to go hunting, so Frank and I took them up to the east end in my big white Lincoln; at this time I didn't have a pickup. Laurence killed a deer but we had no way of getting it back down the mountain other than to put it over the hood of the car, blood and all. I held on to one of the front legs out the window on my side while I drove with my right hand and Frank held on to the other two back legs by putting his head and arms out the right front window.

Down the mountain we went—slowly, you can be sure!—or maybe I should say, slow for me, for in those days I was a rather fast driver; that's because there was never enough time in the day to cover all the things I *thought* I had to do. I couldn't drive back the way we drove up, so I had to go another way back to the main house; I didn't know that an earlier wash had taken out a small area of the road that I finally decided to go down. When I got to this spot, I could not back up the road nor turn around. By the way, these were logging roads and were neither wide nor smooth. So I had to drive off the road and went down a small hill and onto a flat area that was like a meadow that wrapped around several trees, and came back out onto the road a half-mile or so father down and ended up on the road going to the hunting lodge. Of course, the deer didn't seem to mind. This was really a "hairy move" on my part, but it worked. I have since tried to see how I did it, and to this day, I can't find the route, for none of the ways seem possible to navigate in a car. To both Frank and I, a car has always been nothing more than a means to get from here to there, with no worry or thought about how you got there, you just went.

We finally made it back to the hunting camp, and the boys wanted to clean the deer but were hungry and needed to eat first. This was a long day and I suspect they wanted to enjoy talking about the fun they'd had. They washed the car before cleaning the deer. After the car was cleaned up and they had their lunch, they hung the deer in a nearby tree and cleaned it. Then, they wrapped a sheet around the deer, put it in the trunk of the car, and took it to town to the butcher to be cut up, packaged, and frozen so we could take it home later. At this time, the deer shack was not in good shape. I think that was the only deer that we as a family ever killed. I take that back—a few years later, when we were in the pink trailer, Frank killed one when just the two of us were there. The deer was near the trailer porch; it was too close for Frank to miss. It had a nice set of horns. He had to clean the deer by himself and hung it from a tree near the trailer. He later said, "Never again."

Quail dinner

IN FALL 1967, WE had fresh quail for dinner.

Frank and I were driving around the ranch in our car and had a gun with us. We were over at the far northeast part of the ranch where there were lots of oak trees and very few firs in this rather steep and rough terrain. We noticed that the trees were loaded with acorns and the ground was covered with them. This year there were lots of quail everywhere, especially in this area among the trees, so we shot at least 10 to have for our dinner that night. The quails' throats were so full of acorns I don't know how they could fly.

We enjoyed the dinner very much and have never seen so many quail since then. Maybe it's because we haven't been there at the right time of year.

1967—Laurence as a log scaler

LAURENCE SPENT THE SUMMER of 1967 as our scaler at the Clarke Ranch, and one of the first things we did was move the little trailer that he used at Jackson Meadows up to the Clarke Ranch and set it up near the hunter's shack, where it stayed for a couple of years. The hunting shack was just that; it had a potbelly stove in the center of the room used for heat and boiling water for coffee and for cooking chops, bacon, eggs, and hotcakes on its top. There was a sink with cold running water at one end of the room, a shower, a few chairs and tables, and electricity—and that was about it.

We added a septic tank that is still there today. There is an outside john that is up the hill; it is a "two-holer," one for adults and one for children. It is still used today.

There was a small shed screened in on four sides and sealed off so no flies or animals could get in, but by this time, it was in bad need of repair. The shed was made for hanging wild animals the hunters killed and had not yet cleaned and gutted. The shack and shed were near Section Four Creek, which runs to the highway and joins into the south fork of the Eel River that starts on the ranch and runs to the ocean. This is a nice cool area to spend the summer and a bitterly cold place in the winter. Laurence stayed here by himself for a couple of months in the summer of 1967 when we started cutting timber on the ranch. The evenings were very lonely since he was the only person on the ranch after everyone left for the day. He was the log scaler and his job was to keep an eye on all the trucks that went in and out of the ranch. In the fall, he left to finish his senior year at the University of San Francisco. We ended up logging at the Clarke Ranch through 1971.

Our family members enjoy the ranch

Frank, me, Julia, and Laurence sitting on the porch at the trailer, 1973

IN 1968, OUR DAUGHTER and son came to the ranch as often as they could. This would be when school and Julia's job schedule allowed them to visit the ranch when we were there. The kids would bring friends and really enjoyed themselves along with the rest of us.

Frank and I were at the ranch a lot on weekends. We worked all day doing what had to be done, and then in the evenings, we'd have fun driving the ranch in a truck that had a bed large enough for a group of people to ride in. Later in the evenings, we enjoyed playing card games of some kind when it was too dark to do anything else. We did this for many years.

In the 1970s, when we were all there together, young Henry, my brother Jack's grandson, whom he adopted years later and was not in school yet, played with us "old" people in our forties and fifties, and he learned to count points playing the card game Hand and Foot and would try to beat us. And sometimes he did.

Witch hunting for water

WE WENT WITCH HUNTING to find a better water system on the ranch because the water supply to the area was not too good, and we had to do something about it. We went looking for a place high enough to have gravity flow and that would be good for many years giving enough water to install a cistern system. We found a spot that had lots of water. It was able to supply the campground and provide sufficient water to an area on the opposite side of the hill. We later moved a pink trailer from Nevada City to that spot for our family to live in.

By using a witching stick, we found a spot near the top of a steep hill that ran opposite the main road and down to the campground area. We were not sure if it would be good water or enough water, so we had a person from Laytonville come out to check the water and the well. It ended up being a very good well, and it is there that we get our water for the campground area and the pink trailer. My brother, Jack, who was a building contractor, and his two sons, who were in training to do the same line of work, along with local workers helped us put in the well. A fence was put around the well to keep deer and cattle from contaminating the groundwater. The water for the trailer ran into a large wooden storage tank that we put in up on the hillside and piped down. This did not happen overnight, and, if I recall, Frank had a few headaches over this, but it is a very successful cistern.

Jack and his family at the hunting shack

IN 1969, MY BROTHER Jack and his family started coming to visit us at the ranch on weekends. They stayed in the hunting shack, and before long, he was fixing it up so he could come down for the weekends more often, which he did for many years. He installed more electrical outlets and put in running water, a refrigerator, a kitchen sink, a new table, and chairs. He also brought in an electric stove, lights, and a shower. He made places for beds and added on a porch. He repaired the screened shed used for hanging game.

Over time, this area came to have a larger trailer on it used by managers of the hunting club that contracted with us for use of the ranch. All the hunters check in at this area when they come to fish, hunt, or camp. It's a half-mile from the county road and the entrance to the ranch and works perfectly as a check-in station.

After we contracted with a hunting club, the club's on site manager took care of the club members and looked after our interest.

Good camping across the creek

ACROSS THE SECTION FOUR Creek is an area good for outside campers, tents, and trailers; it has trees surrounding a flat open space for camping and playing games and is a popular place to camp. We put movable outhouses in this area to provide closer restrooms for the people camping there. We also put in tables, benches, and a water faucet. (After Julia bought the property, she did more of these types of upgrades.)

Moving the pink trailer

View from the pink trailer looking out over the ranch. Morning fog is common at the lower elevations and usually burns off by mid-day to reveal a spectacular view of the Pacific Ocean.

IN 1969, WE MOVED our pink trailer to the ranch. The trailer had sat on a parcel of our land in Deer Creek Park, in Nevada City. Jim Frey, a local boy and friend of the family, piloted the trailer to the ranch. The trailer was well furnished and had a pink refrigerator and a pink stove. It was ready to move into as it was. We moved it to a flat area that overlooked part of the ranch to the west, under a big shady oak tree, alongside and about 10 feet from one of the barns. The barn acted as protection and shelter from the wind. It furnished shade for the trailer and provided good storage space and an additional place for people to sleep in if necessary. After the trailer was in place, the wheels were removed and it was put up on jacks. A skirt was added to keep animals from getting underneath it. We had a septic tank installed along with water from one of the springs that was high enough above the trailer. We also brought in a butane tank that was larger than the one we brought in for the small trailer. Electricity was already available.

Frank Clarke brought electric power to the ranch in 1935 and had it hooked up in all the buildings, including the houses, barns, shacks, and sheds of all sizes that Thomas and his son, Joe, had built years earlier. I do not believe that Joe lived to see the electricity come in; he passed away in 1932. So we hooked our trailer into the meter at the barn. This was a good-sized barn and was built of redwood lumber from the property, as were all the other buildings on the ranch. There were, and still are, three barns in this part of the ranch. (Most of the information I have about the Clarke Ranch came either from reading material left at the ranch, from stories from locals, or from local history stories put to print.) Many years later, the roofs of the barns, which were made out of wood shakes, were replaced with corrugated iron.

From the week the trailer was moved into place, Frank had me set it up so we could move into it from the little trailer that Laurence used. By this time, Laurence was working in Alaska. The pink trailer was 60 feet long and 10 feet wide; it had two bedrooms. The larger bedroom was at one end, with a closet and a vanity built in, and this was our room. A hallway ran along one side of the trailer from our bedroom past the bathroom and a small closet that held a heater and hot water tank. I used the smaller bedroom as a storage room for the spare mattresses and a trunk full of bedding, sheets, and so on. The bedroom closet was used to store extra coats and clothes. The hallway ended in the living room.

The exterior wall of the hall faced the barn and there was a door with windows leading to the outside. The living room, with windows on both sides, opened to the kitchen area and had a door that went to the porch. There was a full window over the sink and drain board that went from one side of the trailer to the other. The view from this window looked out over the lake, the ranch, and the vast land toward the ocean. Cooking and doing dishes was never boring.

Me looking out the kitchen window toward the ocean

A large deck is built

LaVena, me, and Jane Marcus enjoying the deck's vast views that look out over the mountains to the ocean

SHORTLY AFTER MOVING THE trailer to the ranch, we built an eight-foot-wide deck that ran the length of the trailer and alongside the barn. A short time later, we extended it out and in front of the trailer for about 20 feet and included the width of the trailer. Benches were installed along the sides of the railings to seat many people. We had room to put mattresses down on the deck for those who preferred to sleep outside, as well as room for a large table and more benches. We barbecued and ate out on the deck. It became a busy place for many years.

Alongside the deck and facing the barn were steps going down to the ground and to the barn. In this area, I had an outside washtub with cold running water installed and a mirror above it to cut down on the congestion inside the trailer. We used this tub for everything, from cleaning fish to putting makeup on, washing hands and faces, washing hair, and shaving. I also had a washboard hanging nearby so we could wash clothes there. I had three clotheslines running the full length of the trailer. These were on the porch side next to the side of the barn, which helped cut down on the dust when clothes were hanging out to dry. For the first several years, I went into Laytonville to wash clothes, and then I would bring them back and hang them up to dry on the deck. I would do my ironing out on the deck as the clothes dried. There was always a pleasant, cool breeze on this side of the deck, even on hot days.

Traveling on Highway 20

FRANK AND I WENT to the Clarke Ranch almost every weekend we were free. It was about a four-and-a-half- to five-hour drive. As the years went by, Highway 20 kept getting improved and in time this cut our driving time down by half an hour. We drove there in our big Lincoln that was always loaded down with things for the ranch, along with food I would buy at SPD Market in Nevada City because it was cheaper than buying groceries in Willits. Frank and I took turns driving to keep from getting too tired; we would always stop in Lucerne and have a milkshake, and sometimes a hamburger.

During these earlier years, we did not have the roads that we have today, so traffic was always slower. Somehow, Highway 20 always seemed to be under construction. Through the years, Frank and I had some harrowing experiences on these trips. One time the Lincoln's radiator ran out of water and started to overheat; all we had was a cup to get water from the river to fill it up. And we had our share of flat tires where there was no one to help. Many other troubles also arose.

We were lucky most of the time in getting help from people. Some helped fix our car, while others gave us a ride to the nearest town. It always seemed to be on very hot or very cold days when such mishaps happened, and it was usually on Highway 20.

Selling timber to Bud Harwood

DURING THIS TIME, WE were cutting and selling timber to Bud, who owned Harwood Lumber Co. To get the logs off the ranch and to the mill, we had to build roads and the workers used large logs as bridges to cross over streams and canyons. Red rock, which we have small mountains of in several places on the ranch, was used to gravel the roads. By the time it was all done, we ended up with about 30 miles of roads inside of the ranch. During this time there were about five or six gates for entering and leaving the ranch to reach Branscomb Road. The Clarke Ranch is seven miles due west from Laytonville on Branscomb Road, and from the front gate it is two miles to the ranch house. The ranch runs three miles along the highway. Harwood Lumber Co. was about another seven miles west down the road past our gate. The road also leads to Highway 1 and the ocean. At this time, the road was narrow and graveled. It was a slow drive and took an hour to go 20 miles or so. (Not true today—now, about 30 years later, you can go the whole way on paved roads in a half-hour, from our place to Highway 1).

Renting grazing rights, coping with mice

FRANK RENTED GRAZING RIGHTS to a cattleman for six years. The cattleman moved his small trailer to the other side of the barn and out of sight. He and his wife stayed in the trailer. I remember his wife telling me she always had so many dead mice to clean up when they came up to stay, but the mice didn't seem to bother her husband when he came up alone. I had to laugh, for I had to do the same thing. Sometimes the mice made a nest under the burner lids of the stove, and I would have to clean it up before I could do any cooking. The termites also seemed to have had a very fine time for there would be piles of wood powder on the floor when we arrived.

I've often wondered how long those walls would hold up with what the termites were doing, but as I write this, they are still standing. This particular rancher was not a good cattleman—too much a city man. But he was on the ranch and was helping look after our interest, so to speak.

Building the upper lake

IN 1971, FRANK HAD our first lake at the ranch built by Homer Helm. Homer dug out a low area fed by a natural spring. Thus, a lake was made which we call the upper lake. We could now enjoy going swimming and fishing in the summer right on the property. Over the years, we've spent many hours on hot days down at the lake. My brother, Jack, and his wife, Bev, often came down from Eureka on the weekends. In addition to doing other things, Jack did odd jobs on the ranch, as well as contracting work in the Ukiah area. He stayed at the hunting shack at night rather than staying in a motel in town where his men were staying. In the evenings, he and Bev enjoyed driving around the ranch and taking a swim in the lake.

Enjoying the lake, picture taken in 1976

Catching fingerlings

WHEN JACK WAS OFF doing his thing in the day, Bev and I would go fishing and catch fingerlings together. We would walk down to the Eel River, two miles from the entrance to the ranch from the trailer. We would have someone drop off a cooler down by the bridge when they went that way earlier in the day. Once there, we put our lines in the river with a very small hook and would snag tiny fish. We then put them in the cooler with water. The fish were quite sturdy and survived in what little water we had. We would then walk two miles back up the hill with this one-by-two-foot cooler to the lake and drop the fingerlings in and away they would swim. In time, some of these fish got really big. Yes, I know, "illegal," but it was on our property, so I didn't think much of it at the time. It wasn't until later that I became aware of the legalities.

Frank proudly showing the results of
the fingerlings planted years earlier

A few years later, my sister Helena was down at the creek catching little fish by herself. She was near the highway where cars were going by and where people could see her. A Department of Fish and Game employee saw her, and he came over to talk to her. He asked her who she was and she said she was on her sister's property and that it was all right for her to fish there. He then told her it was illegal and made her put the fish back in the creek. That was the end of stocking our lake from the river. After that, we began buying 10-inch fishes by the thousand each year to stock the lake for the hunters and ourselves.

Jack moves into Upper House, 1971

IN 1971, JACK AND Bev moved into the Upper House from the campground shed and stayed there until 1989. The Upper House had become vacant after we fired a ranch employee who'd been living in the Upper House with his wife and two small children. Things didn't work out and we ended up having to terminate his employment.

Unfortunately for us, Cecile Clarke hired them on as caretaker, and they then moved into the Main House which was still owned by Cecile. She taught school in Eureka and only came to the ranch for summers or on vacation. But as she got older she simply stayed in Eureka and rented the Main House on the ranch to our former employee. He did not receive rights to use the ranch other than the road to the Main House, but he didn't observe this law. Frank finally got fed up.

This man's pig was roaming free range and getting big and fat on the ranch. Frank shot the pig. Then he enlisted the help of Jack and Jack's son, Randy, and brother-in-law, Les. They drove down to the bunkhouse between the Main and Upper houses where there is a big oak tree with large branches. They used a pulley to pull the pig up by its hind legs, high enough in the branch to clear the ground by four feet. Next, they built a fire under it and set a barrel full of water on rocks over the fire to get hot. After the water was hot enough, they lowered the carcass into the barrel. When the carcass got hot enough for them to shave the hair off the skin, they pulled it out and laid it on a board that was once an old door. They shaved the carcass and gutted it on the back end of a pickup. When that was done, the men took it in to Laytonville to the butcher to have him cut it up and freeze for us to take home.

Getting ready to clean the pig

I'm sure our former employee was not a very happy man seeing this. Frank did it in full view of the Main House so he could see it happening. But it still didn't get him to leave the ranch.

Cecile's contract inherited

WE INHERITED CECILE CLARKE'S contract when Frank bought the Clarke Ranch in 1967 from the Union Lumber Co. of Fort Bragg. Cecile had maintained a "lifetime estate" on one acre. That meant she could stay there as long as she lived (with certain conditions, though, including that she took care of the place). This acre of her estate included the Main House built by her grandfather Thomas and parents Joe and Annie Clarke. The Main House was built between 1910–15 and had a porch that went along three sides of the house. I am not sure, but I believe the main house was built in the area where Thomas Clarke built his first home around 1868 when Joe was a boy. This area included a barn for the horses and is where the wagons, buggies and carriages, along with other farm equipment, were housed. It joined horse corrals, and off to the side and on higher ground on the south side was the chicken coop. These structures were built of redwood lumber from the ranch all around the same period. The little shack they built by Maple Creek is still standing, and, after many repairs, is still being used by cattlemen as of this writing.

The Clarkes must have had some kind of a band mill and planer to make the lumber for all these structures.

Going to court

BY 1975, IT WAS obvious that the Main House was getting run down and needed to be jacked up and a new foundation put under it. In addition to this, the shingles were coming off the roof and we could see areas where it looked like water was getting into the house. We were unable to get Cecile to do any repair work on the house, and she was unable take care of it herself.

Pictures showing the rundown condition of the main house

So, in 1975, we took pictures as evidence from outside of the fence area. We took Cecile to court and the judge ruled that she was not able to adequately care for the place, and the acre with the house on it was rewarded to us.

Cecile loses in court

Pictures used in court to show the rundown condition of the Main House

WHEN WE WON OUR suit on Dec. 8, 1975, against Cecile Clarke, we were awarded the Main House and the surrounding acre right after the first of the year. As soon as she had moved out, we took possession of the place and started doing the needed repairs on the house.

Jack and his crew, along with his sons Johnny and Randy, started to fix up the house. The first thing was to take down the garage that was near the house—they found rattlesnakes nesting under the floor. When the men were working under the house putting in a new foundation, they also repaired the cellar to keep water from seeping in. As this work took place, they had to deal with rattlesnakes. It took a few months to get the job done, but when it was done, the house was level and the snakes were gone.

The next job was to remove and replace the shingles on the roof and the shingles on the siding of the house. Next, they repaired the windows and put in new window cords to replace the old pulleys so the windows would work like new. The window glass was also re-puttied. We kept the original glass from that era with all its blemishes and character. After that they re-leveled the doors, both inside and out; everything needed to be adjusted.

Jack's crew worked long, hard hours, under the hot sun. It can get very hot at the ranch in the spring and summer, and it can get very cold in the winter. The ranch can get as much as 100 inches of rain in a season, and heavy winter winds are not uncommon. Because Jack and his crew were staying in the Upper House during the time they were at the ranch, they would start work early in the morning, and when they got back from their jobs in the local area, they would continue the work in the evenings to avoid the heat. Bev nearly always came down to the ranch when Jack did. While there, she would have dinner about 5 p.m. each day, leaving their evenings free for doing whatever they wanted to do. The Upper House is more protected and always cooler than the Main House. During this time, they also replaced the old brick with new brick on the top of the fireplace chimney on the outside, so the Main House now has a character of its own—and it leans slightly to the south.

Jack also did the chimney on the Upper House and put a screen over the top to help stop sparks from coming out. It was during this time that most of the renovation and repairs were made on the outside of the house, including the porch on three sides. We also brought in and installed a large butane tank for the Upper House.

On the outside of the house, Jack built a small shed to hold three hot-water tanks. I commented that we could have a family reunion now that we were finishing the house. I knew we would need lots of hot water available for showers, cooking, and washing dishes. Having three hot water tanks proved to come in real handy. This was one of the major improvements we did to make the family reunions possible.

The interior floors also needed to be fixed up. Bev and I worked on that job by scrubbing and cleaning all the corners of each room. Jack rented an electric sander and floor scrubber to remove the grease and refinish the floors, both upstairs and downstairs. Grease had been building up for a long time so it was quite a job. Later, we oiled all the wood floors.

Hunting for arrowheads

IN 1971, MY SISTER-IN-LAW, Bev, and I hunted for arrowheads from the edge of the lake. She would leave her fishing rod next to the lake with the line in the water and then go searching for arrowheads. When she saw her pole move she would run back to catch the fish, hoping it was still on the line. Bev did a lot of arrowhead hunting and had a great deal of fun. While other members of the family went swimming, we would fish instead. Bev and I caught some very large fish out of the lake that we stocked years earlier with the fingerlings from the Eel River.

Bev and me fishing at the lake

In the evenings, Jack's family would go down to the lake to go swimming and then take their baths. At this time, they were still living at the hunting lodge and having a nice bath was a treat.

Living in the pink trailer

IN 1972–73, FRANK AND I were living part-time in the pink trailer. When we would arrive there, I would put all the food away, and then I'd pick up dead mice and sweep out cobwebs, dead flies, and termite dust, and give the floor a good mopping. It was a small trailer, so this didn't take too long. It was just part of the normal routine of going to the ranch in those days. After it was cleaned up, it was easy to keep clean.

We had a good time whenever we were there. It is so enjoyable looking out over the ranch from a wonderful view, seeing the birds and wild animals as well as the cattle, and driving around the ranch and checking on what was going on with the removal of timber.

The kids came up whenever they could and brought their friends. In 1966, Julia became a World Airways stewardess and came to the ranch whenever she was off and we were there. Laurence was back from his job in Alaska and working for Frank in Nevada City, at Deer Creek Park.

We had a great time with Jack and his family driving around the ranch in a pickup truck with the kids all riding in back. They had even more fun trying to shoot the ground squirrels as the little animals ran for their many holes that were everywhere in the ground; the squirrels were always the best targets—they were hard to hit. Going to the lake to relax, swim, and catch fish added to the enjoyment.

Fire at the ranch

SUMMER 1973 WAS A hot, dry season and a fire broke out near the Bartlett pear orchard, on the northwestern part of the ranch. We were sitting out on our deck at the trailer having dinner when a helicopter flew over, went to the lake, dropped a big bucket down, and scooped up a bucketful of water, then flew off. When we saw this, we got into the pickup and drove over to the pear orchard. We drove through the ranch because the highway was closed to traffic. One of the pilots flew too close to a telephone wire and hit it. He crash-landed and was killed at the pear orchard. The helicopter crash stirred up a lot of local excitement for a while.

Wild pigs and turkeys

IN 1973, WE BROUGHT in wild pigs and turkeys to run free on the ranch for a few years, to multiply, and make a nice addition for the hunters. In the meantime, whenever Bev and I were out in the hills and found some pigs, we would try chasing them toward where we knew the men were, hoping to see if they could kill one to eat. The meat on wild pigs, or so-called boars, is very tasty. It's not fat and is very lean. Bev and I got quite good at going up and down the hills on the ranch.

Wild pig free ranging on the ranch

Railroad flatbed cars replaced log bridges

IN 1973, FRANK BOUGHT several railroad flatbed cars, two 40-footers, four 60-footers, and one 90-footer. We used the flatbeds to replace the old log bridges used for crossing the canyons and streams. The 90-foot car was used to bridge the Eel River and the main entrance road to the ranch. The two 40-footers were used to cross small streams on the main road to the house. The others were used for crossing rivers and creeks on the ranch. Frank bought another used 90-foot flatbed and had it hauled to Oregon to cross the Winchuck River on our ranch there.

The rail cars cost $150 to $250 each and were purchased from Southern Pacific Railroad Co. They are still in good shape today. Frank had Homer, or maybe it was Robinson, haul the cars up to the ranch.

Most of the redwood logs that the Clarkes used for crossing the Eel River and canyons had rotted away and could not be safely used anymore by cars or logging trucks. The main entrance into the ranch was getting to the point where we had to find a way to forge the river to get to the road on the other side, in order to get to the trailer or anywhere else on the ranch. The river was just inside the entrance to the ranch and made it difficult to access the property.

Prior to putting the 90-foot flatbed in place, Jack and his crew made large cement footings to hold each end of the flatcar. These cement pads are at least 10 to 12 feet high from below the riverbed to the top of the bank, and maybe 2 feet wide at the top of the roadbed. This job took a few weeks because the cement had to set properly. Since being completed, the new bridge has proven to be a great asset to the ranch. Big logging trucks can now safely come onto the ranch, which they frequently do. Even the shorter 40- and 60-foot bridges have proven their usefulness. As of this writing, wherever you cross a river or stream on the ranch, you do so by going over one these railroad car bridges.

Laurence brings Gloria to visit

IN 1975, LAURENCE BROUGHT his friend, Gloria, to see us while we were at the pink trailer. They had been camping with friends in Mendocino. When they got ready to go home to Auburn, they decided to take the long way and come north up the coast and then east on Branscomb Road to the Clarke Ranch. This was Gloria's first time to see the ranch. She, with her children, joined our family through marriage in October that same year.

Cattle return to the ranch

Cattle walking through snow in front of the Main House

IN 1975, A CATTLEMAN from San Francisco, who had run cattle on the ranch for six years, left when his lease was up. We then leased it to Frank Sagehorn, who lived in the area and did not need a home on the ranch. He was a cowboy and his wife, Mary—I think she was called a "cow belle"—could ride herd out there with the best of them. They knew the ranch very well and leased from us for a good many years. Sagehorn operated his herd with some outside help from time to time, such as when branding cattle or getting cattle ready to ship to market; he would then get some real cowboys and gals in to help.

After we moved down to the Main House, we were able to hear and see him operate, and we saw how he got his cattle ready for market. It was not only a noisy time for us while trying to sleep, but also a very interesting experience to watch them brand, cull, and separate the cattle and put them into trucks to be shipped to market. Many years later, sometime around 2000, Sagehorn brought in a younger partner and ended up phasing out his interest in the cattle at the ranch.

Improvements included an 8,000-gallon water tank

FRANK WAS MAKING A great many improvements to the ranch, and among them was buying an 8,000-gallon used butane tank that he had placed on two large cement stands above the apple orchard. The tank is on a hillside surrounded by trees and about a mile from the lodge and the Main House. He did this in 1975. This tank is used to store our water for the Main House and the Upper House. This was just about the time we decided to move into the Main House.

There was a big redwood water tank from the Clarkes' era that served both houses and the surrounding buildings. It sat higher up on the hill just above the Upper House, and no doubt, had been there for many, many years, for some of the planks had rotted and were falling out.

Frank devised a cistern system for the ranch. He has a very good mind when it comes to such matters and knows how to find the right materials to make it all work. His only trouble is he hates working, so he finds others to do it. Jack used to laugh about that.

The water for the Main House and Upper House comes from a cistern that is below the pink trailer and on the same hill that the other cistern is on, but on the opposite side of the hill, and much lower. The well is above the tank, and water is fed to the tank by gravity. The gravity causes the water to flow through a pipe for about a mile to the two houses being served, as well as anything along the way between the tank and the houses. Once in a while, an airlock develops in the air valve pipe that extends about three feet above the ground. When this happens someone has to open the valve on top of the big tank, and then the water will flow again. The tank fills up in about eight hours, but it can start being used sooner than that if necessary.

It is a good system and supplies enough water, but not enough to be wasteful. At one time, I had Jack pipe water down to the lake, but the cows and horses kept damaging the pipe, so we let that go. However, the cattlemen also use this same water for their animals and have it piped to the barns as well as the troughs. Everyone on the ranch drinks this water. I have had as many as 60 or more family members at the ranch for several days, taking showers and baths, washing clothes, doing dishes, cooking, and so on; and no one has ever had trouble with the water system—except the time when someone decided to water the so-called lawns and forgot to turn the water off and the tank emptied.

Blowing up the shed

THERE WERE OLD RANCH houses, barns, and sheds throughout different parts of the ranch, and some may have dated back before Thomas Clarke's arrival in 1867. One shed that was hard to see was so well camouflaged by shrubs, vines, undergrowth, trees, and dead logs that you could go right by it and not even know it was there.

My brother Jack loved to go horseback riding, and through the years, I'm sure he covered the whole ranch. A lot of this was done with my daughter, Julia, when she was there visiting the ranch. Most of the time, they would go riding early in the morning. One winter day in 1975 or '76, with snow on the ground, he went riding and came across the shed by accident. He went to see what it was and what it had been used for. He found all kinds of explosive materials, such as dynamite and powder; it was all old, wet, and of no use anymore. Since the shed was over in the meadow area, and not too far from the hunting campground, he got to thinking that the hunters' kids might find the shed, and they might get into it and get hurt. So he went into town and got a stick of dynamite.

Knowing Jack, it actually could have been a dozen sticks to make sure he got the job done properly. He fixed it so he could set it off by shooting it, and then he set the whole thing off and burned everything up, and that took care of the problem. In the spring, grass covered it up, and you couldn't even see where it had been. Frank and I never knew about the shed until Jack told us about it, and we had been all over that area several times.

Vistas on the ranch

OLD BARNS, HOUSES, AND sheds stood in an area from Old Cahto Road that runs along the eastern side of the ranch. From this area of the ranch, you can see the ocean, and if a ship is out there, you can see it. Looking west down the canyon to the center part of the ranch you can see where the Manchester House and garage were located. During the time, Thomas Clarke and his family owned it, vast amounts of grazing and timberland stretched all the way toward the ocean. It is this land and timber that the Pacific Lumber Co. bought from Cecile Clarke and Frank Clarke's widow, Catherine. As years went by, some of the old houses and sheds have gone by the wayside, along with some of the barns.

Some of these buildings are down where the Manchester buildings were. In springtime, with the old fruit and walnut orchards, this is one of the nicest views on the ranch. You look out across a vast amount of open rolling hills full of spring green grazing grass, and spring flowers scattered among the grasses going up and down the canyons and mountains, along with oak trees putting on their new leaves. In summer and fall, this same area has different shades of dry grass surrounded with the same green trees, which opens up another great span of scenery.

The ranch in springtime, looking east

At close range, and scattered on the hills, you can see and look down on rivers and streams, wild animals, pigs, birds, cattle, and all the spring wild flowers including California poppies. Surrounding the grasslands are vast amounts of timberland that go up to the skyline and down the canyons to the ocean. Looking up the canyon and to the east you can faintly see the ranch house. (Looking farther up and to the southeast, you might be able to pick out where Julia and Mark put in the airport in 1994.) Occasionally, you will see the results of a jet that has gone by overhead.

Sagehorn dismantles the Manchester House

The Manchester House before it was dismantled

BY 1988, THE MANCHESTER House had finally seen its better days. Frank Sagehorn dismantled it and removed all the redwood boards of all sizes and lengths that were made on the ranch in the 1870s. A lot of these boards were 1 inch thick, 12 inches wide, and 8 to 10 feet long. There were also 2 x 4's. Whoever did the work at that time was a real craftsman. Sagehorn

My oil painting of the porch at the Manchester House

put the lumber into the house he was building for himself. What was left of the Manchester House was burned down. He did the same with the garage that was built in the 1940s and was in a little better shape. Now, all that is left in this area is the round galvanized water trough, several walnut trees, and many old pear trees, along with a purple fig tree that is still putting out. Down by the spring that runs all summer long are grapevines that go clear to the tops of the oak trees.

When we first bought the ranch, I painted the broken-down porch of the Manchester House. The painting is in my home today. It helps me with memories both wonderful and sad. This is one building that should have been restored, if for no other reason than for its location.

The rest of the buildings on the ranch, through the years, have continued to be used and kept up, thanks to Julia. Frank wasn't into keeping up the old things. That would be too much like work. His comment when asked about restoration was typically, "What for?" Two main homes, the hunters' shed, a couple of other sheds, two garages, three large barns, and maybe a few smaller sheds are still kept up and are more or less in the center of the ranch. They are all that is left of structures from the time of Thomas Clarke, son Joe, and grandson Frank.

Just keeping the road up and cleaning out culverts was all the work that Frank wanted to do after taking care of the business end of the ranch operation. There are several hills of red rock on the ranch that are easy to get to, and, as I mentioned earlier, the rock is used to make roads and repair them. This rock makes a wonderful roadbed, and, of course, it is free for the taking.

Keeping the culverts clear

ONE OF THE TASKS that Frank and I would do was drive the roads and open any culverts that were plugged up from storms, so the roads wouldn't get washed out. This was one thing that Frank was "dammed" about, and he hated every moment he had to do it. Sometimes we would have to get down on our knees and shovel out rock and dirt to clean the culverts. We would also have to remove branches and debris. Frank would leave the fallen trees for someone else to take care of. In time, Jack was down at the ranch so often that he was able to handle that task; whenever he saw that something needed to be done, he did it, including removing trees that were blocking the roads. In time, he cut up wood and took it to his home in Eureka, so he got lots of firewood free for the taking. At the same time, he cut up wood for us, trying to make it easy for Frank. Jack was also free to take a deer (with a license), fish, and hunt anything else, and he seems to have enjoyed the ranch more than we did.

Snowy wonderland at the ranch

Snow at the ranch, looking at the Main House

WHEN IT SNOWS AT the ranch, it is quite a peaceful sight to see. There is pleasant quietness to it as you look out over the mountains and valleys and see all the tall green stately trees dotted with white, and the bare trees with their bowed, leafless branches covered with snow. The old sheep redwood picket fences and posts become capped with snow; they stand out in long lines that wander up and down the open space and mountains. There is not a foot or animal print to be seen anywhere in the vast stillness.

It is, indeed, a spiritual experience to see and feel the peace and stillness that comes with the snow, in this great God-given world.

1977—the first hunting club

THE AMERICAN SPORTSMEN'S CLUB was the first hunting group to come on to the ranch, and they were with us through 1983. They had the camping ground area and hunting rights to the whole ranch, which included fishing in the lake. After a short while, however, we started to see bottles, beer cans, papers, cigarette butts, and packages littering the roadways. We were picking this trash up, so I told Frank we would have to put a stop to it. So one of the rules that I made for the club was no bottles, beer cans or any other cans, nor cigarette butts, paper, or anything of the sort was to be found anywhere on the ranch. We made it clear that if we found club members littering that would be the last time they would be on the ranch. This still holds true today, and such activity is closely monitored. The way it is done is that each group is sent out in a different area to hunt. The next time, when a different group of hunters was in any area, if they found anything, they were told to pick it up and report it. We soon did not have any trouble. Yes, there were some members who did not get invited back to the ranch, and the club enforced this. In their monthly brochures, the Clarke Ranch is called a "pristine ranch". The women like to come to the ranch because it is easy to walk with so many roads and easy hunting. They usually get their first deer on the ranch.

We've had hunters tell us they have enjoyed watching Frank and me from the bull pasture, which is quite a distance away and looks down at the lake area, as I fished while Frank read in his lounge chair. I loved fishing at the lake, but Frank couldn't care less. With this club, it was almost always the same guests who visited the ranch year after year, so they got to know us pretty well.

I get moved into the Main House

IN 1978, UNBEKNOWNST TO me, Jack and Bev (and maybe Frank had something to do with it) intended to move me out of the pink trailer and into the Main House as soon as possible, so I could be down near them on the ranch.

The distance between the Main House to the trailer is about a mile, and it is all uphill. I had no desire to move. I didn't want or need the amount of work it takes to properly keep up a large place like that when I visited the ranch. Keeping dust, spiders, mice, flies, and other insects and vermin out of the trailer was enough for me.

I started planning the Kruger–Evenson family reunion that would be held on the Fourth of July, 1979, at the ranch, with the reunion running several days after the Fourth. I expected 50 to 70 people would attend. As for the Main House, my real intention at the time was to turn it into a museum.

In the meantime, I started to make the Main House livable for the family reunion. I really wanted a used electric Tappan stove like I had at home, and I wasn't yet ready to give mine up. So Frank and I were driving around Grass Valley and found a sign on a house that had a stove for sale. We went in to look at it and were surprised; it was something like I had at home, except it was an Imperial model. The Imperial had one large and one small oven side by side, and a long, narrow four-burner that pulled out, just like the Tappan. So we bought it and took it to the ranch and put it next to the woodstove. It is still in use as of this writing.

The Imperial stove is to the right

Frank got a big truck, I think from our friend, Robinson, which had a good-sized bed to haul all this stuff to the ranch, along with all the other stuff I got together the previous few weeks from home. I don't think I bought anything new. I got an electric refrigerator from the Deer Creek Park office; Laurence was replacing it with a larger one.

We took all of this stuff to the Main House, along with a table and several chairs that I had bought from a used goods store in Nevada City. I looked around for the things we needed, shopped, and picked up a few items, including an antique woodstove at an antique store on Highway 101 that we saw on our way to the ranch. I took with us two large barbecues to cook on outside. Our friends Ad and Jack Thomas were buying a new sofa, and we happened to be at their place at the right time. I asked her what her plans were for the old sofa. It turns out she was planning to sell it. Her price was right, so it went with us to the ranch and is still there today. I also bought a used Tao rug from a store on Commercial Street in Nevada City for the Main House's parlor room. All of this was going on before the house was ready to be moved into. It ended up taking a year to put it all together and required many trips back and forth to the ranch until everything was complete. All the while, I simply intended to use the Main House for family reunions, and maybe as a museum.

Jack and Bev, Les and LaVena, and maybe Frank, too, conspired to get me into the Main House. And they succeeded.

The first Kruger–Evenson family reunion was set to begin on July 4, 1979. On the morning of July 2, I was moved out of the pink trailer. It all started when my sister LaVena and her husband, Les, came down from Eureka. He came into the trailer about eight in the morning and said something along the lines of, "You're moving out and we're here to help. We would like to use the trailer, and with all our kids coming I've got to get it ready for them by the time they arrive."

LaVena, Robert, Mark and Barbara Faustino, Olive and Nick moving me out of the pink trailer

Well it was obvious to me that this move had been planned by Frank, as well as the rest of them; however, Frank has never said anything about it in all these years. So I was moved out of the pink trailer and into the Main House within an hour or so. It was made clear that I was not to bother myself with carting anything down whatsoever. I was told to simply stay put at the Main House and put things away as they were brought in. The house was nice and clean, and, looking back, I have to admit, it was a move I would not have made on my own. But, once I was settled in, it was OK. So between LaVena and Les, Frank, and all of Jack's family, I was moved out mighty fast and LaVena was quickly moved into the trailer. In the couple of years leading up to this, Les and LaVena were coming down often from Eureka to visit us, and Les was around quite a bit helping Jack do work on the place.

Frank deep in thought

There were maybe 15 or more members of the family sharing the trailer and area, including grandchildren. My brother Nick and his family came down a few days early for the reunion to help and put up new screens on the doors and windows on the Main House to keep the bugs out.

As I write this, Les, Jack, and then Nick have passed away, and I'm sorry they aren't able to read this, for they all loved the ranch and all the fun we had there through the years.

Helena, and all the members of her family, used the camping site along the river, as did Nick's, for he had a camper and they shared the hunting shack. There were 15 or more people at the camping site sharing the hunting shack. This was no doubt tight quarters for so many people to share a stove, sink, tables and chairs, refrigerator, shower and outhouse. My only regret is I was not able to get Helena's family involved with the rest of us except for evening meals, going on walks, and a few other activities. The next day was the beginning of our first family reunion in the Main House that would run for four days, and this put Frank to thinking about our move that was to continue for many years.

I took a great deal of time getting things ready for the reunion. The idea for a reunion came to me when our son Laurence told me he did not know his relatives, and I thought, "He is right," so I did something about it and set things into motion.

Planning the first Kruger–Evenson family reunion

PREPARATION FOR THE FIRST Kruger–Evenson family reunion began soon after we took possession of the Main House.

First off, I had to get all the names and addresses of my brothers and sisters and their children and grandchildren. They were asked not to bring friends, for this was to be a "get to know your relatives" affair. I wasn't too popular after setting that condition, but I was serious about it and stuck to the request as best I could. Most of the relatives hadn't been to the ranch, so I had to write up directions and guidelines. I didn't want anyone to get lost or hurt, so I

From left to right:
Helena, me, LaVena, Nick, and Jack

wrote some material about the ranch—its safety, and how, if anyone got lost, they could find the ranch house. There were plenty of "do's" and "don'ts" along with, "No riding on the ranch except on roads."

At the reunion, the relatives did get to know each other. I had pins made up with peoples' names on them and how they were related to the rest of us; parents' and grandparents' names were printed on each pin. So there was no excuse not to get to know each other. (I must say that through the years, at each reunion, without me saying anything, the relatives have obeyed the ground rules and have intermingled.)

I also had to find out how many people would be coming and for how many days; when they would arrive and when they would leave. I had to make sure everyone had the combination to the lock at the ranch gate along with rules to the lock and keeping all the gates closed for the cattle. I also included the checkout time for leaving the ranch on the last day. (As I recall, checkout time was noon, for Frank and I had to leave at that time to drive home. On our way out, we closed everything up and changed the combination lock.)

One large chore was determining where everyone would stay while there, how many days they were staying, and what the food requirements would be for everybody to have three meals. I don't remember all the food details, but I do remember something about 50 chickens, lots of fruits and vegetables, corn on the cob, tomatoes, pots of beans, strawberries, raspberries, and melons of all kinds, cakes and pies and buns and breakfast food. Anyone coming north to the ranch could shop at Safeway in Willits; buying vegetables at Laytonville was always "iffie." Somewhere I'm sure I still have the original list of everyone who came and what we ate.

Frank the chef and his helper

Each person or family was given a list to indicate what they would bring in the way of food and how much, as well as what games to bring. The cooperation was great, and remains so to this day when we have our get-togethers. At that time, though, we were starting from scratch.

Frank and I bought two aluminum boats, oars, tables, chairs, and umbrellas for the lake, along with plenty of fishing gear. We also got items for the yard at the house to play games with, including badminton, horseshoes, and whatever else we had available from the time the kids were young and still living at home.

Floating dock at the lake

We ended up with 14 people inside the Main House, with some on the porch, and some around the outside. It was all the Kruger and Evenson kids.

Frank preparing 50 chicken halves

I wanted everyone to know what area they would be camping or staying at before they arrived. I did this so nobody would feel left out or end up wondering where they would be camping. They also needed to know what they would need to bring depending on where they would be staying. The area covered about two miles. I would walk from one camping area to another to visit them each day. In future reunions, we changed this so everyone would be closer together.

I furnished all the paper plates, silverware, paper cups, mugs for hot drinks, pots and pans, spices, flour and sugar—you name it, we had it—and above all, plenty of great homemade ice cream. We all got together by six o'clock each evening to say the family prayer before the main meal. Some people came earlier to help with meals and to get everything set up; this included the younger generations that helped out the adults. At this time, we didn't have many tables but we had lots of benches, so we used the eight-inch board that went all along the railings on the porch as our tables. The benches were pulled up to the railings and this worked pretty good for meal time.

Enjoying dinner on the deck at the first reunion

274

After dinner, it was time for cleanup, playing games, and visiting in the Main House after it got dark outside. We even danced and sang songs. Jack said that seeing the Main House from the Upper House at night was like looking down on a hotel, given there were so many lights on. I have always been sorry that I didn't go up to Jack's and look down on the Main House to see this when all the lights were on at night.

We had a blackboard on the porch, and it was used as a notice of things that would be going on for the day. This came in handy for everyone. Keeping 60 to 70 people busy and having a good time became one of Julia's jobs, and she did a great job of it.

The first trip to Ten Mile River, and keeping attendees busy

Walking down to Ten Mile River

ONE DAY JULIA AND her friend she brought to the reunion (against my rules, but I put him to work!) organized a trip down to Ten Mile River. It was an all-day outing. We walked down to Ten Mile River, hiking through the woods, grasslands, over and through creeks.

It was mostly all downhill and when we got there, some people went swimming, some went fishing, and some simply enjoyed relaxing by the water. It was quite a jaunt downhill to the river and some people got tired along the way. A few drove down in pickups to bring food for lunch and to bring some little kids and older ones back up the hill.

Everyone resting on a log in the shade
to cool off on our way down to Ten Mile River

Frank getting dunked at Ten Mile River

275

After the reunion,
rolled carpet was used on the dock, and rails were added

On another day, we all went to pick blackcaps up on the far southeast end of the ranch. To this day, it is a popular and rewarding trip. The blackcaps are gathered and then used for making pies, cobblers, and homemade ice cream. The blackcap gatherers all have a cup, pan, or something to put the berries in. After a container is filled, the blackcaps are put into big salad bowls. Then, of course, it is time for fishing and swimming at the lake, along with games and cards on the dock.

To make sure everyone was kept busy at the reunion, Julia had them bring wood that was cut and piled out on the ranch, put in pickups, and brought down, and had them pile it into the shed. This was both fireplace wood and kitchen wood that would end up being used year-round. If the fog comes in or the house is slightly chilly, the kitchen stove and fireplace are started; we heat water, cook meals on it and sometimes cook breakfast on it. Right next to it is the electric range, and many times the two are used at the same time

This is the only heat we have in the house, except for the electric heaters in Julia's and our bedroom and in the bathroom. It is very hard initially to get the house warm, but once we get it warmed up, we can keep it warm by using the woodstove or fireplace in the early morning and evening. That is, unless it's a hot day; then it's too hot even to cook any more than you have to. Most days will bring in fog either in the morning or at night.

I'm glad to say that every family helped clean the house, not only with the food and meals, but also setting up and cleaning up after each meal. As I recall, every family had to take care of their own lunch. Breakfast was held at the Main House.

I did not ask for any help from my family to get this started, and I've ended up handling the planning and logistics and execution for several reunions. It was quite an undertaking, but I got the necessary cooperation from all the families, including my own, in sending back their sheets on what they would bring, and on what days they would do a project or help with the cooking. My family helps with everything once they arrive at the ranch.

Brad, Laurence, me, Spence, Julia,
Gloria, and Frank

Ice cooler storage area

However, this was not a problem, for most everyone helped, and it didn't take long to find out who was trying to slack off. I soon learned that others would take care of that, and somehow everyone got along fine. You must remember that at the first reunion, in 1979, this was the first time for everyone to be at the ranch house, and I was the only one who knew where everything was, so I was kept busy all the time. I was 57 at the time, but quite able to keep up.

After everyone arrived at the ranch, the west side of the porch, which is in the shade most of the time, was lined with ice chests full of food, drinks, and ice. Whenever anyone went into town it was, "Check the ice coolers to see if anyone needs ice"; if so, you got it, regardless of whose ice chest it was.

Making homemade ice cream

MAKING HOMEMADE ICE CREAM the first time at the ranch was a great deal of fun. As I recall, Helena's girls were in the kitchen with the rest of us and we had a wonderful time. Nobody knew where anything was, so my job was to find the things we needed. We mixed enough ingredients to fill two ice cream makers. As we were doing this, the boys and men were outside having a fit that we weren't ready for them to put the containers in the ice cream makers so that they could fill them with ice and start turning the cranks. This was a big project. It all started by going into town to get enough ice and making sure you had plenty of rock salt. Then, you had to make sure you would have enough hands around to turn the crank, even after the fun had worn off.

Making homemade ice cream.
Frank and me, with my brother Jack
churning out ice cream the old-fashioned way.

Rowdiness in Laytonville

SAY WHAT YOU WILL, when you get my side of the family together, there is no such thing as relaxing—too many people and too many things going on, but we do have a good time. As an example, at our first reunion, we had lots of teenagers and people in their early twenties; it was a young group of kids. So, some of them decided to go into the nearby town of Laytonville to go to a bar. Some in the group got rather polluted and out of line; the more sober ones had to keep the peace and bring them home.

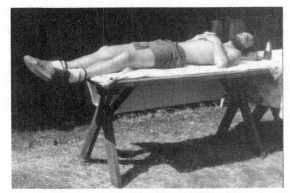
James sleeping off the night before

We never got the whole story, but those who are reading this and were there will remember, and they can tell the story of what happened. I do remember that it took one of the boys a day or so to sober up.

On the last evening of the reunion, we got everyone together and took a family picture on the front porch of the main house. We have continued doing this at each reunion ever since. Looking back, the first family reunion was successful. Everyone had a good time, and I am happy I was able to put it all together for all of us.

The first family reunion.
This picture was taken early Saturday evening just before dinner.

The Frank Amaral family reunion, September 1979

Manuel, Marie, me, Frank, a friend, and Julia

WE HAD FRANK'S FAMILY reunion shortly after the Kruger–Evenson reunion. The Amaral relations were also given a royal treatment. There were only about 15 people at Frank's reunion, so it was much more relaxing. We went on the same walks taken at the Kruger–Evenson gathering, and we did many of the same things, including spending time at the lake, which, of course, was a big hit. My brother, Jack, and his family were down for Frank's reunion, and Jack took us around in his pickup, in addition to ours, which made it easier to get around and do things on the ranch. When it came to meals and other reunion events, Jack's family didn't join in; they spent their time at the Upper House.

It was nice having Frank's sister and her family at the reunion. This was their first time coming to the ranch and we had a very pleasant and relaxing time together.

Me, Marie, and Frank

Frank and Marie

Marie and Manuel

Using the shed rooms

The shed and two barbecues, with a door in between used as a table

THE THREE-ROOM SHED off the house that the Clarkes used had a roof over the porch. They used one of the three rooms as a washroom; we use it today to store many big logs for the fireplace. They used the second room in the middle of the shed for canning (left side of the picture, the window goes to the second room). It is used today for storing kitchen wood on one side of the room, and the other side is used for storing all the things that go down to the lake, such as folding tables, chairs, umbrellas, rugs to roll out on the deck at the lake; you name it, it's in that room. Nails, screws, paint, and other supplies are stored there. The third room (large door on right side of picture), which the Clarkes used for maintenance, is still used that way. Wheelbarrows, shovels, axes, ice cream makers, and assorted garbage cans for different uses can be found in this room. On the porch and under the roof are two large barbecue units that are used to do all the cooking when we are all there. The units are kept at the ranch year-round and are covered while not in use. There are also plenty of electrical plugs and lights in this area which make it easy to barbecue after the sun goes down. The porch wall has become an area of historical interest. On the wall are license plates and other signs of years gone past.

Me bringing wet laundry down from the Upper House to the Main House

A few years earlier, Jack's wife, Bev, put in a clothes washer in the room off the porch in the Upper House for her use. So, back in those days, I would go up and use it to wash clothes. After the clothes were washed, I would bring them down the hill in a wheelbarrow and hang them out to dry on the clothesline located under the porch roof. I have a picture of me pushing the wheelbarrow doing this. This made life more convenient for I no longer had to go into Laytonville to do laundry. I later gave Bev money to put in a dryer.

The new GMC pickup

ABOUT THIS TIME, FRANK bought a new, full-size, four-wheel-drive GMC pickup truck, on which he had an extra gas tank installed so we could drive from home to the ranch with one stop in Laytonville for gas. We now had a vehicle that allowed us to do a lot of packing and hauling of things between our home and the ranch. I liked the truck because I was higher up in the seat and could see more as we drove along the highway and while driving around the ranch. I also found that the new truck didn't cause my neck to snap while driving over bumps, which oftentimes would give me a headache.

Tired legs

DURING THIS TIME, JULIA would visit the ranch on her days off, when she knew we would be there. She is a great person to take long walks with, and I liked going with her, but one time she asked me to walk to the bull pasture and back. It required at least an hour of fast walking, both uphill and downhill. I told her my legs hurt too much to walk that far, which they did in those days. What I didn't tell her, and didn't have the heart to tell her, was that I was too tired to walk after getting the house and yard ready at home and then packing the pickup before leaving for the ranch. Then there was the four-hour drive, unpacking to do, and the work involved with getting the place ready to live in after we got there. To this day, I am sorry that I didn't go walking with her anyway.

The Upper House porch addition

The Upper House. Jack built an extension and roof over the deck off the front porch and around the side for his family.

ABOUT THIS TIME, JACK added an extension to the front porch on the Upper House so that his kids could sleep outside on the porch on those unbelievably hot days that can happen at the ranch. Most of the time, the fog rolls in either in the morning or in the evening, but when it doesn't, it can get hot, and the heat spell can last for a few days. It was around this same time that Jack took the storage room off the kitchen and turned it into a bathroom and put in a shower. This made the place much easier to accommodate large groups of people.

Earlier, Jack and Bev added a woodstove, an electric stove, and a refrigerator that was never quite large enough when all the members of his family came to visit. The ranch is about nine miles from the closest town, and, back in those days, the road was not easy to drive on. So an ice chest became a "must have" item to have on hand when friends and family members visited.

Pilings for the deck at the lake

Frank standing on the new dock overseeing progress

FRANK HAD HOMER HELM come in and put some pilings in the lakebed, so we could add posts and build the deck to extend out into the lake to the shutoff valve; the deck would be about 20 feet long and 8 feet wide. We have a picture of Bev having a hard time waiting for the lake to fill up with water so she could go fishing. We were gone while it filled up with water, but they were there to see it.

Jack and his family helped us construct the deck by putting the posts down and laying down heavy planks and nailing them into place. Railings were installed so no one would fall into the lake, and we added a ladder down into the water. Jack also put a floating platform in the center of the lake, and anchored it down with a heavy cement block at the bottom of the lake for the platform to stay in place. The platform is still there today, although it has had major repairs throughout the years. The lake became a favorite place for me, and whenever I went fishing, the hunters did not come down; they all knew the reason the lake was there was because Frank made it for me.

Bev and her dog waiting for the lake to fill up with water (the barn with the white roof up near the left is where the pink trailer is).

The upstairs bathroom and leaky pipes

IN MAY 1980, WE took on the project of improving the upstairs bathroom in the Main House. Frank, Jack, and his sons put in a shower and an extra toilet. After the first family reunion, we knew we had to do something about the bathroom. Jack cut a hole in the corner of the room for the shower, and he was able to save the antique linoleum that was on the floor. Frank vacuumed 80 years of dirt from the area that was cut out, and we have a picture of him doing this.

The upstairs bathroom renovation was not easy. The bathroom is directly above the kitchen. We needed to install two sewer lines going down the outside of this two-story house and out to the main sewer line leading to the septic tank in the backyard. Jack had to take up a lot of flooring so that he could put pipes between the floor joists and the ceiling of the kitchen. When that was done, he had to take the sewer line pipe out the side wall to the outside.

Preparing the bathroom

Frank vacuuming

Installing the new shower floor

Putting the shower in took a little while, but the second toilet was easy to do. The hot and cold water pipes had to come up through the kitchen, behind the woodstove. This took a few weeks because we were not always there. When it was all done, I took up a bunch of 17-by-29-inch remnants of different patterns and colors from the carpet stores at home, and put them together with glue tape and a hot iron and made my own carpets. I made them for both bathrooms. They are a colorful patchwork job and are holding up well and are being used to this day. I also made runners for the areas in front of the electric and wood stoves and the area in front of the sink. I took two paper pie plates that said "girls" and "boys" on them, and whoever went into the bathroom was to turn them over so there would be no mistakes.

By doing this, two people could be accommodated. Any privacy? Not much.

A few months later, we started having water leakage problems with the new shower, and water was coming down into the kitchen ceiling. Jack tried everything he could think of to fix it; he even removed some boards off the stairway wall going down to the kitchen. For the time being, we put a small pail there to catch the drips. He could not figure out what to do and why it was leaking. It kept getting worse, and one day Laurence and his family were up visiting us and were using the shower; with so many showers being taken, the water was really coming down into the corner of the kitchen ceiling. I kept emptying the pail of water. I guess I was talking to myself, as I sometimes do, as I came down the backstairs into the kitchen, and Spence was there at the table doing something, and he said, "What's the matter?" So I told him what had to be done and where the problem must be coming from. I didn't want to tell Frank, for he would botch up the job, and it was too big a job for me to do by myself.

So Spence said, "Tell me, maybe I can do it." So I told him what I thought the problem was: the pipes behind the shower must be loose and in need of tightening. The only way to get to the pipes without taking out the shower wall was to remove the wall in the upstairs hallway next to the shower. However, a major concern was to not damage the wall panels in the process of removing and putting them back. By getting to the pipes this way, we could get in there and tighten them without removing the shower. I believed that if we did this it would end the problem. So Spence said, "I'll try," and he removed the panels without even leaving a mark on them. It turned out that all the plumbing was loose, so he tightened the fixtures that went to the shower, and that did the trick. He put the panels and trim back in place, and, I must say, he did a very fine job. We haven't had any water troubles since. So, thank you, Spence. You may not know it, but you left a very soft spot in my heart for you.

I think what happened was there were too many people doing too many jobs that were not completed when they left at the end of the day to go home. Quite often, a few weeks would go by before we or Jack got back on the job again. Therefore, the pipe joints simply didn't get checked and tightened down before the shower walls were put up.

Salvaging goods from the O.C.S.C.

THE ORANGE COUNTY SPORTSMAN'S Club was a property in Anaheim with a building that had been a restaurant for a few years and eventually was turned into a sportsman's club. Frank had acquired it, mostly because he knew its land was valuable. I will discuss this property in more detail later in the book.

When we left home in 1980 for a big trip, we knew that we would have to fly to Los Angeles on our way back from Israel to see what had to be done with the restaurant in order to get it rented again. When we got there, we ended up walking into a very dirty building. There had been a big party there, and the people left all the food, et cetera, as it was, including half-eaten watermelons. We also saw that rats had gotten into a lot of things.

The gist of this is that we had to do a grand job of cleaning it all up, and we finally ended up getting some help to finish the cleaning. How this applies to the Clarke Ranch is that we rented a U-Haul and filled it full of anything I thought would help out at the ranch for family reunions. We moved a large chest (now in our bedroom), a sofa and two chairs, several captain's chairs and covers, one large coffee table and several small ones. I also took a booth table that is now used in the kitchen as a table. Extra rolls of new carpet that had never been used, dark brown with birds on it, were in the storage room in the attic. I took the rolls home and had the edges seamed, and I took most of the carpet to the ranch and put it on the floor in the living room. I think some went on the floor in what we call the bunkroom. Some remnants went into our basement at home, along with a nice chair that is now in my bedroom at home in Nevada City. We also got 60 items of the LeRoy Neiman Collection, and they went home with us, along with some silver trays. All the rest went to the ranch, including the chef's clock that rings at the darnedest time when Frank winds it up.

The nitty-gritty things taken from Anaheim

ALL THE THINGS I wanted for the ranch were loaded into the moving truck. Among the items were 36 pieces each of dinner plates, salad plates, bread and butter plates, large and small soup bowls, cups and saucers, oval spaghetti plates, oval brown baking dishes for small pies of sorts, butter cups, maybe a dozen salt and pepper shakers, cream and sugar dishes — all the things that are used in restaurants. The dishes were white and of good heavy quality. The plates have been used in the wood oven, and on top of the woodstove at high heat, and have held up very well through the years. Along with everything else, there were several serving trays, very large and medium-sized salad bowls, and all sorts of cutlery, as well as all kinds and sizes of glassware from the bar, which are on the heavy side, but hold up well with all the kids.

I believe I got 36 each of all the silverware pieces, and a tray to hold them. I got a chopping block and a large dishpan. What else there was I can't remember, but I do know it all came in handy at the ranch through the years. There were large containers of pepper, salt, sugar, spices, oils, canned cherries, olives, pickles, mustards, catsup, and many other things like this. We also picked up lots of paper napkins, bread and butter baskets; the list can go on and on.

All these things went to the ranch and are used every day we are there, along with all the cast-off things that I brought to the ranch from home. Among these items are apple-pattern dishes and a yellow poppy platter that were wedding gifts Frank and I received when we got married. I have visited the antique shop along Highway 101 between Ukiah and Willits and bought many things from them. It is at this shop where we bought the woodstove and the copper boiler to hold the wood for the kitchen stove, the secretary desk in the living room, and the vanity that is in the upstairs bathroom, as well as one in Julia's bedroom. The vanity in Laurence's room is Frank's first desk that he used in Camptonville. The dresser in the storage room came from one of the houses we got in Camptonville; the one in the bunkroom came from an antique store, as did the phone on the wall in the hallway. One rocker belongs to Mark and one large chair in the living room belongs to Laurence; it was in his bedroom. The large chair with hassock was Frank's from years back, and, at one time, it was covered in leather. The table and chairs that are in the game room were things that we picked up in different homes that we have collected through the years. The table was redone by a Hispanic gardener whom I hired earlier, and it used to be in the gardener's house. He liked it and it needed redoing, so he fixed it up in his spare time in the winter.

Most of the finished and unfinished paintings hanging around the Clarke Ranch are mine. Since the first family reunion, all the beds have been replaced from the ones that were there when we first moved into the ranch house. When the time comes for the next reunion, it will be much easier for everyone.

"Living Images" photo group

Julia getting dinner ready for her guests

IN EARLY 1981, JULIA had the "Living Images" group from her photo workshop up at the ranch. About 15 to 20 people showed up and they all had a very good time—going on long walks, taking pictures, and enjoying the ranch. There are many things to see and take pictures of at the ranch. Julia was great for having groups come in and enjoy the ranch and the things there are to do there. Being with other people gave her the chance to see different parts of the ranch that she may not have seen by herself.

Julia ringing the dinner bell

It snowed the first day of February that year, 1981. It can get really cold at the ranch in the winter, but when the sun comes out on the snow it is a delightful time, and for photo taking it's really great. Julia did the major part of the cooking, which at this time of the year means that the meat would be cooked outside on the barbecue and the rest of the meal cooked on the woodstove, unless you are baking; then, the electric oven comes into play.

Julia warming up in front of the fireplace

The woodstove and the fireplace will be going full blast just to keep the place warm. Upstairs, the electric heaters will be going full blast and warm clothing needs to be worn. The evenings are spent around the fireplace playing games and visiting.

Second lake started

FRANK STARTED CONSTRUCTION ON the second lake in 1981 and when it was done, he had Homer and his crew put in the deck at the same time. This lake was deeper than

the upper lake but not as big. We were not inclined to go swimming in the second lake but it came to have much bigger fish growing in it; although, the fish were not as easy to catch. The hunters liked going down to this lake, which is about 300 feet below the upper lake; but when they had their families with them they preferred the upper lake.

The second lake had a good stream going into it. There was one drawback: every year we would have to repair damage done by one side of the lake slipping down the side of the hill after a big rainstorm. The two lakes were located between a fruit orchard of apples, figs, plums, and cherries that were planted during the Clarkes' time. Wherever there was water, the Clarkes had vegetable gardens and had planted fruit trees and nut trees, mostly walnuts, blackberries and red caps. At the upper lake, a big green fig tree had been planted.

The lake trying to wash away

On Memorial Day 1981, Jack's family, LaVena and Les, ourselves, Julia and some of her friends were visiting at the ranch, and we wanted to have a toilet facility at the lakes. We had an old outhouse not being used by the Upper House, so the men decided to move it down the hill to the upper lake. We managed to get it onto a pickup, and with a lot of help we got it down to the lake in one piece. Les and Jack dug out a pit hole on the top rim of the lake facing west and

we set the outhouse over the hole. We tried to secure it so the wind wouldn't blow it over. The new facility got a lot of use all season long, and everyone was happy it was available. We get a lot of heavy winds at the ranch, and the lake is highly vulnerable to the wind. The outhouse stood for the season, but during the winter, it went over the bank with the first windstorm. The following year, we had an outhouse built and put down by the fig tree, and it has been there for several years where it is protected from the wind. It gets a lot of use by many people and keeps the area clean.

Moving an outhouse down to the lake

American Sportsmen's lease ended

THE AMERICAN SPORTSMEN'S LEASE, which was in effect from 1977, ended in 1983. As a result, we ended up going a few years with no hunting on the ranch.

One thing I remember well is that when we first got the ranch, the grass was hip-high and we were always afraid of fires. We were very careful not to have cars drive off the roads, and that still holds true today. I have not seen the grass that high since those first few years, and it could be because of the cattle.

July 3, 1983 — Second Kruger–Evenson reunion

Setting up picnic tables for the second Kruger–Evenson reunion

WE HAD OUR SECOND family reunion in 1983 and all the major work to prepare for a large gathering had been taken care of earlier in 1979, so this time around it was much easier. The house was better equipped with everything that came from the restaurant, and this also made things easier. The bathroom upstairs was fixed up and better equipped to handle more people.

Earlier on, Julia took a trip to Mexico where she bought a table and six chairs she especially liked. The table and chairs were shipped to her home in Mill Valley. When they arrived, she was very disappointed, for the top of the table was warped and the set was not the one she thought she had bought. So she brought it up to the ranch and we put it in the dining room, where it fits in very nicely. We use it all the time and it comes in very handy for reunions.

When it came time for a reunion, Frank and I would go to the ranch and stay a week ahead of time to get everything ready. We would wash the windows inside and out; sweep all the walls down inside as well as outside; and, mow the so-called lawn by hand that covers the acre of land that is fenced in. Jack and Bev would come down and help when they could, and as a rule, they would arrive a week early to help get everything ready.

There is a lot of work that must be done the week before a family reunion that not all the family knows about. We make sure the place always looks nice when people arrive to enjoy it and we clear the roads to make driving on the ranch easier. This includes cutting brush along the roads, trimming branches on the trees, and so on. I have to say, we workers are usually tired when everyone arrives, but it is worth it, for everyone has a good time.

Although a lot of the work that needed to be done for the second Kruger–Evenson reunion had been dealt with earlier, I still had to send out all the invitations. I did this early enough—in February—so that everyone would have a chance to take the days off from his or her jobs. After confirmations came back, I sent out the food and beverage notices letting people know what they could bring to help out. By this time, I had received a lot of input that made it easier to work out all the details. The only difference between this reunion and the first one is that we now had some young married people who had been in their late teens and early twenties five years before. So we now had couples, and if I remember, babies, and I had to figure where they would stay.

We had a good turnout. Everyone enjoyed themselves and had time to do the things they wanted to do. One difference between this reunion and the first one was that we did not take as many walking trips as we had five years earlier. Some of the older people didn't feel like taking long walks, so they traveled around the ranch in pickups along with the babies and toddlers who were too young to walk. Older people, babies, toddlers and everyone in between got out and thoroughly enjoyed the ranch. I noticed we had more pickups at the ranch this time. As before, nobody was allowed to drive off the roads. We told everyone to watch out for cattle and asked that they keep a close eye on the gates to make sure they remained closed.

Swimming out to the floating dock

People stayed at the same camping places, and we found they were more relaxed this time and would freely go from camp to camp to visit each other more often. By now, there were two lakes to enjoy, along with plenty of games to play in the yard. If the upper lake was full of swimmers, people could go down to the lower lake to fish.

Also, there were always two horses to ride; we never used Frank Sagehorn's horse. Years earlier, Jack had gone up to the Winchuck Ranch in Oregon and brought back our two horses that we had up there. They were really just two old plugs but they were on the ranch for many years. Julia and Jack used to go riding all over the ranch. She got to know the ranch better than any of us, and as time went on, she replaced the plugs with better horses.

The riding horses at the ranch

289

I think this was the year we had a room full of used clothes for everyone to try on and take whatever they wanted. Helena ended up taking the unwanted items to her church. I remember Barbara's girls took a couple of pairs of my shoes and some of my clothes.

My family members represent many religions, and getting together a group of this size can be a little touchy. Fortunately, we get along very well together. We try to have food at the reunions that appeals to everyone's taste buds. Overall, I think we have done very well and everyone is able to get his or her fill and have a good time. At the second reunion, I found that the mixing of people was a little easier and there was more kidding around. Looking back, I guess I accomplished what I set out to do, which was to "learn our relatives." The second reunion started on Wednesday and was scheduled to go through the weekend up until Sunday afternoon. I found that half the people came early during the week, and the rest arrived Friday morning and stayed until Sunday afternoon, which is when we leave for home ourselves.

I remember one day Randy said that at the next reunion, we should bring in two port-a-potties for each house, and that he would pay for them to be delivered and picked up. This made me feel good, for others were now taking an interest in trying to help keep the reunions going.

We took family pictures together on Saturday evening, as we had done before at the previous reunion. This is always a fun time. Sunday is a rather sad time for me, for I wonder who will be there for the next reunion, and if I will be there. On Sunday morning, some of the people come down for breakfast; others have already left. Those who are still there remain for lunch and we divvy up the remaining food for people to take with them. The fun time together, once again, eventually comes to an end.

After the family reunion, Jack took the first shed by the Upper House and made it somewhat livable for Helena's family in case they wanted to use it next time. Staying at the shed would put them closer to the rest of us. By this time, Jack had finished tearing down the other two sheds that were already on the ground. After the reunion, we found that some people had brought their own campers and stayed down by the house to be closer to us. This is what Nick's family did.

The ranch is in full working order

I HAVE NOT SAID much about all the work that was done on the ranch during the years; but, by 1981, the ranch was in full working order. Frank and I would go there almost

The Main House as seen from the cow pasture

every week and stay for a few days. There are about 45 miles of roads inside the ranch, and about this time, we closed off all the exits leading into and out of the ranch, except for a few, including, of course, the main road into the ranch that everyone uses. The roads used by the rancher and loggers go to the pear orchard on the far northwest side of the ranch, and the road on the far northeast side along the main highway is used by the cattlemen. We kept these roads as they were.

In addition to the ranch itself, we also own several acres of land across the highway from the pear orchard. We ended up selling one piece of land that now has a nice home on it and we still have one nice piece left that is along a stream. The ranch runs along Branscomb Road for three miles. The main entrance to the ranch is roughly in the middle of that section of road. There is a big sign that says, "The Old Clarke Ranch," and in smaller words under it is, "The Amarals." Jack and his boys made the sign for our first reunion.

Sign to the Clarke Ranch

The ranch is seven miles due west from Laytonville. On one particular day, we were out cutting brush around the sign and entrance to the property next to the highway. It was still a dirt road at that time, and the county crew was out working on the road near our driveway entrance. An officer on the job asked us if we would help with paving the road along our property, and we said yes. So we ended up with a paved road from town to the ranch. Several years later, it was paved clear to the coast.

The $65 road

I WOULD LIKE TO tell the story about the "$65 Road" that goes from the area of the ranch house down to the middle of the ranch.

Construction of $65 road

One winter Jack took his pickup down the canyon to Ten Mile at a time when the weather was really bad. One of the rules on the ranch is that you don't drive down any roads in bad weather that are not rocked well, for the roads will not hold up during a rain. Well, Jack came back up Center Road from Ten Mile and got stuck. He had to get home to Eureka that night, so he called the tow truck from Laytonville to come and help him get out, which ended up costing him $65. So that is how the road got its name and it is called that today. Through the years, there have been many other drivers that have gotten stuck on this road.

The road named LaVonne

HOW LAVONNE'S ROAD CAME about, in September 1987 or 1988, is this way.

Frank and I were at the ranch driving around in the pickup gathering firewood for the woodstove and fireplace. Jack had already made firewood from the trees that had fallen across the roads and in other places during the winter months, but he had not been able to get to one particular area with his truck.

Frank and I were on the north center area of the ranch on a hillside that went down to Eel River and the highway. A few years earlier, we had closed off the exit to the highway below us because the logs that crossed the river had rotted away. The exit would have taken us to the main road from the area we were in. Although it would have been easier to take the pickup off road and drive over the land, we didn't want to make any opening for highway traffic into the ranch. So that meant we would have to backtrack to another road inside the ranch and go through the bull pasture to get back to the ranch house.

Frank said, "It's too bad we have to backtrack to get to the ranch house; if only we could make a loop inside the ranch without leaving it," and I said, "There is." He argued with me. So I said, "Leave the pickup where it is and follow me." I walked him along the north side of the hill, going west through small creeks, trees, brush, poison ivy, and so on, with the Eel River and highway between us. We came out on the side of the main bridge and entrance road into the ranch. We walked back to the pickup, and Frank drove as I walked the same path we had just taken to make sure the truck wouldn't get stuck or hit any boulders.

Frank had Homer drive the Caterpillar over it the next day. Now the road is called LaVonne's Road, and it makes a complete loop from the middle section of the ranch to all areas east, west, and south of the houses. You can drive all around the entire ranch without leaving it or backtracking, unless there is a tree down or some other act of God intervenes.

Wilderness Unlimited leases the ranch

IN EARLY 1988, A man named Jerry Wetzel, with Wilderness Unlimited, came to the ranch when we were there and wanted to make a lease with us for hunting, fishing, and other activities. If I recall right, one of the men in Wilderness Unlimited had also been with American Sportsmen, and he was branching out into another aspect of the hunting and wanted to have the Clarke Ranch be a part of it. He knew us and knew how to get a hold of us. The men were out of Hayward, which is where their headquarters was going to be located.

We told Jerry to meet us at the ranch. He came with another man who was going to be a partner with him. We made our first lease with them. In time, it grew into a rather large hunting group. The rules that applied with American Sportsmen's also apply to Wilderness Unlimited. The members are always allowed to fish in the lakes; however, when I'm at the ranch the lakes are out of bounds to them if I am at either lake fishing or if there is a family reunion going on. As I said earlier, the lakes were made for me by Frank. The lakes are stocked each year for their members with 1,000 trout averaging 10–12 inches in length. The members and their families enjoy the lake, which is open to them year-round for fishing, swimming, and boating, except when we're at the ranch, and I should really say, when we are down at the lakes.

Third Kruger–Evenson reunion, July 1988

IN THE FIRST HALF of 1987, I was doing a lot of work for the upcoming family reunion. I started getting things ready by sending out the invitations early. I sent them out with the Christmas cards to save time, and this gave everyone a good chance to set up their vacation schedules. After each reunion, I mail out an 8-x-10-inch picture of everyone together to the head of each family. I also send out 4-x-6-inch pictures to each of the second-generation members, along with pictures that go with any particular family. This is a big job and I have continued doing it.

Jack finished fixing up the shed that he started back in 1983. It is located across the road from the upper lodge. He finished everything except for the windowsills, sink, and stove. He put in electricity, insulated the walls and ceiling, painted it, and did the floor. The room looked nice. He also put in two large sliding glass doors that lead out onto a large deck on which they could eat, visit, and sleep outside on if they desired.

The shed was now livable for Helena and some of her family. The rest of the people planned to bring campers. However, with the shed fixed up, there was now room for all of them to be together during the day if they wanted to; they could now visit comfortably. Nick's family are campers, so they would park in the shade under the trees between the two houses. Now, we would all be close together, except for LaVena's family who would be staying up the hill in the pink trailer that looked down on the lake and the deck. From there they would be able to see when everyone was down at the lake. LaVena has a lot of family and they needed all the space they could get.

This ended up making the reunion much easier. I felt we would enjoy being together much better and that we would all get better acquainted.

I continued to plan for the reunion and hoped to have a good turnout. We did end up with a good turnout, and there were now more married couples and very young kids. The horses are always a big hit with the little ones on up to the teens at every reunion, even though the old plugs don't go very fast (but they are safe for the little ones). The lake has always been a big hit for fishing, boating, swimming, or just sitting on the deck and visiting, reading, playing games, picnicking, or getting a suntan—especially on the hot days. It became a popular place for lunch where people ended up staying until it was time to go and start dinner for those who were on the cooking committee.

We found that having different people on cooking committees each day helped make it easier to spread the work around. The younger ones took care of all the paper plates. The plates were set atop wicker mats to make them stronger for holding food and cutting meat on. By this time, we now had tables set up on the grounds. Tablecloths would have to be cleaned and salt and pepper shakers would need to go out.

People having fun on the big rock

Julia trying out the swing

Then there was a group in charge of making salads (both green and fruit salads), husking the corn, and, above all, preparing the hors d'oeuvre dish large enough to feed everyone until dinner was ready. During this time of the day, the men and other kids would be outside playing horseshoes or badminton, swinging in the swing, or climbing the big rock in the yard while waiting for dinner.

At dinnertime, each family brought and took care of the meat for their family. They would barbecue it on the two grills, which were always started well enough in advance to have hot coals ready when the time came to cook the meat, chicken, pork, hot dogs, steaks, ribs, hamburgers, or whatever they brought. Strange as it may seem, the longer-cooking meats, such as chicken or steaks, would go on first. Room was made and set aside on the grills for the easier to cook items so they could be cooked at the same time. Everybody good-naturedly waited their turn. The hot food dishes, salads, bread, and so on, came out of the kitchen. Every family was required to furnish one hot dish; their dish could be made at the ranch or brought ready to put in the oven from home. Each family was given a day when they were put in charge of the food. Each was told what it would be so that there was enough food for each day. Depending on the day you got, you might find yourself cooking beans, a large casserole of some kind, vegetables, spaghetti, rice, you name it. Whatever it was, you can be sure it was good and all of it was eaten at that meal or for lunch the following day.

After dinner, everyone took care of their own plates, placemats, and silverware and put them in the correct bins, along with the garbage. Next, volunteers would go to the kitchen for cleanup duty. By now, everyone knew where everything went, which made things a lot easier for me. Each item had its own place which never changed from year to year. This made it possible for anybody to help put food away, clean up dishes, wash, and wipe them. Someone would put things away, and along the way, she or he would be relieved and someone else would come in and take over. We have continued doing it this way because people really do help out to make it work for everybody, and each time it gets better.

Getting well acquainted at the ranch:
Ray, Ella, Pat, Elmer, and Frank

After everything is done, everyone stays at the ranch house and plays cards, talks, looks through the photo albums together, and above all, enjoys eating desserts of all kinds. Around 10 p.m. some people start to leave, while there are those in the game room who could well stay until midnight. I must also mention that it is at night when those who are camping out, or sleeping outside around the house, take advantage of the bathrooms to enjoy a shower.

Those of us staying in the house have to wait to get to one of the bathrooms. This is a rather busy place every night, but things do tend to run quite smoothly. You should remember that there can be anywhere from 40 to 60 or more people in the house during this time. I'm sure that at the trailer and upper house something along the same lines took place. It just comes down to patience and learning that "you wait your turn."

Camping on the ranch between the houses

There are always some relatives who come only for a day and then leave to go home. Some others go to a motel in town for the night, for they elect not to camp out, now that they have grown up and have left the "kid stuff" behind.

Picking berries, going for walks, riding around the ranch in pickups, visiting, and just plain relaxing, besides all the other things I have mentioned, are activities that everyone does at the reunions at the Clarke Ranch. And, as I mentioned earlier, there is always the Saturday night picture taking. This activity is a must; you just don't miss it. If you do, you will miss seeing yourself when you come to the ranch for the next reunion. The group photographs are all on the wall in the dining room for people to look at and to see who was there and who wasn't, and above all, what people looked like and how they have changed over the course of time.

As I've said, Sunday is always a little bit of a sad time for me. I think of my mother, for these are all her children, grandchildren, great- and great-great-grandchildren, and we are still seeing each other.

While at the reunion in 1988, Jack's younger daughter, Mary Ann, who is very good with horses, and Julia got to talking about horses. Julia asked Mary Ann if she would find a good riding horse for her to have at the ranch. Mary Ann said she would look around to see what she could find, and she did. A few weeks later, she brought to the ranch a much smaller horse than what we had, and it was definitely the right size horse for Julia. Mary Ann said the horse had never been on a ranch or on steep hills, and she would have to be broken in slowly on the ranch or she would spook. Her name was Pockets.

Meeting Mark Strate

JULIA MET A YOUNG fellow named Mark Strate in June 1987 on a boat outing on Lake Shasta. She brought him to the ranch in July. Julia bringing people to the ranch or home was nothing new to us, for she was always doing that, but this time it was to turn out different. She had flown her plane up to Shasta Lake to be with a group of friends for the weekend. She took some of them up in her plane for a ride, and one of them was Mark. It was by taking the plane ride that they got to know each other. At that time, Frank and I had a lot of business going on at the ranch, so we were going there often. Julia knew we would be there, and she knew that Pockets had been brought in earlier.

I think it was on a Saturday morning when Julia and Mark decided to take the horses out for a ride, and when that happens with Julia, it's an all-day ride, going all over the ranch. This time she told us that they were going toward the bull pasture, so I said, "Stay on the roads until the horse learns the ranch before taking her across hills, or she will buck you off." I really thought that she would be careful but I should have known better. Frank and I had just started to take our walk together, just around 10 a.m., and here they came back, and not in a happy mood. Julia was sort of slouched over the horse, and Mark was not very happy either. So I said, "What happened?" She said that Pockets had gotten spooked on something and had bucked her off. Whatever Julia hit when she landed must have been either a big rock, a hole in the ground, or the horse's hoof, and she got it full-force in the right rear cheek.

I said, "Let's take you into Willits to the hospital to see if you have hurt your kidney or have any broken bones." Both she and Mark said no, she was OK in that regard. I guessed that between themselves they had already come to that conclusion. So I said, "Come in the house and let's look to see what was done." Julia lay down on the living-room floor in front of the fireplace, on her stomach, and pulled down her jeans and underpants. She was in real pain. What I saw was not pretty; it was the size of a great big grapefruit, and it had already started to swell and turn black and blue. The injury covered the whole right side of her butt. I started in with ice packs and did so for the rest of the day.

When it came time to go to bed, I could see that I would be staying down on the sofa to sleep for the night and said so to Mark. He said, "No, I will take care of the ice packs, you go up to bed." So I did. It was only the second day that we knew Mark. It is strange that I let him do it, too. The next day was Sunday, and they left in the afternoon to go back to Julia's home in Larkspur in Marin County, California. This in itself was a surprise, for Julia always stays late into the day before going home. Mark was living some place south of San Francisco at the time. At this point, Julia was having a hard time sitting; how she managed to get home and get around on her own afterward, I don't know.

Over the next few months, Julia saw many different doctors to see if they could get that big bump to go down. She said it felt as if it would pop at any moment. She also went to a Chinese acupuncturist. They would draw out the dark blood, but as all the doctors said, it would heal in time, and it did, but it took over a year. (During that time, she would not hesitate to show you her rear, for the bump was really something to see.)

This tells the story of our introduction to Mark Strate. Little did we know at that time he would stay around and end up being part of our family. He and Julia will surely tell you a little different story than the one I have told here about needing to keep Pockets on the road. I think they just didn't hear me say the words, but I know I did.

Burls

Frank checking out some of the burls getting ready to leave the ranch

FRANK HAD A BURLWOOD man, who was interested in the burls that we had on the ranch, come to see him around this time. The fellow wanted the wood burls to make veneer panels for the dashboards and trims on big, expensive cars. The man was out of Marysville, and when he came to the ranch, he saw the walnut trees and was also interested in them to make stocks for guns. As I recall, they planned to ship the stumps to Germany, and it was there that they would go through the process of being made into finished product.

This continued for a few years; removing the big stumps took quite a bit of time. At this same time, we had Bud Harwood looking at some oak trees to cut up at the far northeast side of the ranch. These are just a few of the enterprises we had going on at the ranch.

Frank thinks about selling the ranch

FOR SEVERAL YEARS, FRANK said he wanted to sell the ranch, and I kept telling him no, but he actually did go as far as to talk with brokers in Laytonville two or three times throughout the years, but it didn't go anywhere. Then one day, without saying anything, he moved forward, and the ranch was listed on the market. He received an offer of $1 million, but he had to turn it down. First off, it was not enough; and, second, I did not want to sell the ranch. I have always felt it would become more valuable as the years go by. Large parcels, such as the Clarke Ranch, will not always be available on the market.

About this time, Julia was more or less winding down with the Winchuck Ranch in Oregon. She was still involved with real estate work in Larkspur, where she bought her home and was currently living. She had always liked the Clarke Ranch, and she knew how I really liked the ranch, so she said she might like to buy it if possible.

During this time, many things were going on at the ranch that was taking a lot of Frank's time, and he was not too happy about all the things that needed to be redone. Frank is not one to spend much time on repairing anything, let alone having to do it over again once he has done it the first time. Frank was very busy at home with all his other business projects. Taking time out to deal with the Clarke Ranch was becoming a problem and was taking up too much of his time. So far, he has held onto the ranch land longer than anything else, and to him it was time to move on.

A boy falls off a horse

IN 1988, JULIA HAD her church group at the ranch for a week in August. It was their second year visiting the ranch, and they always had a good time. If I recall correctly, some of the kids wanted to go horseback riding, and Julia had warned them that a parent had to be with them. Well, I don't have to tell you how well that goes over.

Anyway, one of the boys decided to get on a horse all on his own. I don't know what all happened, but he ended up falling off the horse and breaking both arms. The parents took him to Willits to get them set. I am pretty sure they returned to the ranch and enjoyed the rest of the week as best as they could.

Frozen water pipes, 1989

Dining room ceiling and cupboard

More damage in the dining room area

IN WINTER 1989, WE had a freezing water pipes disaster at the ranch from January to February. Just before the disaster, we had been up at the ranch and the weather was really hot for that time of year, and I remember we forgot to turn off the outside water line to the house when we left to come home.

A few days later, after we left, the weather turned very cold and stayed that way for some time. Even at home, it got really cold, but I didn't think much about things freezing at the ranch.

At the ranch, on the back porch, there is a double washtub that has a cold-water faucet. It is on the outside wall that goes to the dining room. On Feb. 8, the temperature really dropped and the pipe froze and broke. Later, the weather warmed up and the broken pipe sent a lot of water all over the wall and into the kitchen. Then, it froze again and stayed really cold for several days, and all this time water was running.

The Sagehorns called us to tell us what had happened and said it was still frozen. They told us it froze so bad that there was six inches of ice that went clear through the wall and into the dining room wall and into the cupboard. They said there was even frozen water in all the dishes. The Sagehorns happened to come down to the house to check on the horses just before they took their trip to Europe and saw the damage that had been going on for several days. They turned the water off, disconnected the broken pipe, and then called us to let us know what had happened.

Damage was everywhere

I told them I would not be able to get to the ranch right away. They pointed out that when the weather turned warm, water would be all over that end of the house. However, there would not be any more damage than what had already been done. We were not able to get to the ranch for another month-and-a-half. It turned out to be sometime in late March. I told Frank I would have to go up and see what had to be done. Frank had a trip scheduled to New York and said I would have to go without him. I told him it was OK, that I was not afraid to stay at the ranch alone.

I check frozen pipe damage; Frank follows

IN LATE MARCH 1989, I took off in my car for the ranch to take care of the water damage. Frank left to catch his plane to New York a short time later. I think that this was the first time I had ever gone to the ranch alone. It takes about four hours to drive to the ranch from our home if you stop to eat lunch, but I drove straight through. I am a very fast driver and didn't waste any time getting there. The weather was nice and warm, even at the ranch. I took enough food from home so I wouldn't have to stop to buy groceries at Willits. I got to the ranch about noon.

Dishes stacked on the dining room table

What I saw when I opened the door to the kitchen was enough to break your heart. The kitchen wall to the dining room was white from where the water had run down it. Everything in the dining room either had or did have water in it. The floor was sopping wet, and the old linoleum on the floor that I have tried to save for the pattern on it, was loose. The varnish on the walls and ceiling had turned a whitish color.

I turned on the main water to the house and started up the hot water tanks. After putting my food away, I got something to eat. It was too warm to start a fire, so I opened the cupboard to get a plate and found that every dish had water in it—even the salt and peppershakers were full of water. I finished my lunch, and then I started from the top shelf, took every dish down, emptied the water out, and put the dishes on the dining room table. I had to dump water out of every plate, saucer, bowl, cup, glass, and everything else that could hold water. The water didn't miss a thing; even the pictures on the walls had gotten wet. The towels and tablecloths in the lower drawers and cupboards were also full of water.

I had just taken everything out of the upper cupboard and had emptied the water from each item, when I heard a car drive up. I wondered who it could be, for no one can come into the ranch without knowing the gate combination. I looked out the window and saw Frank in his car. I had not been at the ranch much more than a few hours. He said that I hadn't left home 10 minutes when he canceled his trip and was on his way to join me. He said he could not leave me at the ranch alone; he knew that I had planned to stay until I had everything cleaned up, and he didn't want me up there by myself.

I was one surprised and happy person when I saw who was in the car; I was delighted that he had come to be with me. He was as shocked as I had been when he saw the dining room.

That night, we started up the fireplace and the woodstove and kept them going. We also put an electric heater in the dining room. We kept the heat going the whole time we were there, even on the hot days. I washed all the dishes, put them back on the table, and covered them with a sheet so they would not get dirty until the cupboard dried out and was usable again; even the shelves were all warped. We spent the rest of the day cleaning up water, which was in everything; even Julia's bedroom that is above the dining room had water in it. I thought, just where *does* one start, with a mess like this?

Somewhere along the way, I must have thought about my mother, and if I didn't, I should have. She went through the flood when she lived right near the edge of the Illinois River, and her house was full of water that was three feet deep. She never really recovered from it. (This story is told in the earlier years in the 1960s).

Water damage inside the kitchen

All we did on this trip was empty water, pots and pans full of water; and, we dried out all the wet clothing and linens. We kept the fires going night and day so we could live in this mess. There were some real nice days, but we still kept the fire and electric heat going. Frank cleaned up the kitchen the best he could so we could live in the place. The dampness went all through the house.

We went back to the ranch several times after this first cleanup operation to build fires to help dry things out and to try to put some things away.

Marking 10 years at the Main House

IT WAS THE WEEKEND of the Fourth of July 1989, and 10 years after we had moved into the Main House for our first family reunion, when I started washing down the cupboard in the dining room and found that some of the varnish was coming off. But I continued washing down the cupboard anyway. I started on the wall with the most damage, and, as I cleaned, I started to do some scraping. It didn't take me long to discover that years of lamb or mutton grease had accumulated on the wood casings around the doors, windows, and on the baseboards. It turned out to be one big mess, and I knew I really had to clean to get the job done. What I thought was not bad at first turned out to be a lot of work. It took the whole day just to do one wall. I realized I needed some professional help and advice on how to clean up this mess.

I finally went into Laytonville to the hardware store to find out what I would need to clean the walls, and I told the owner, who was an old timer, what had happened. He knew the house and knew the kind of panels that were on the walls and ceiling. He said I should use steel wool, sandpaper, soap, and hot water, and when I got the walls all clean and after they were dry, to use Danish oil by Watco. I was told to use two or three coats, and to put it over everything, including the ceiling, window frames, doors, wall panels, and so on. The wood was so dry from years of not having any treatment of any kind that it would absorb the oil really

Frank cleaning up the
service area off the kitchen

fast, and it did. So I went back home loaded with things to work with and used the "elbow and gut process" and started to work.

One thing that I will tell you is that you don't think about how long a project like this is going to take; *you just do it.* I don't remember how many days we were there, but that weekend, or maybe it was during the week, Julia and Mark came to help. Julia took pictures of the rooms and of Frank vacuuming the floor in the service room. We did the ceiling and most of the walls in the dining room; then it came time for Julia and Mark to leave to go home. I don't remember if they even stayed for dinner. After they left, I finished the last wall in the dining room, and I guess we had dinner.

At this same time, there were other things going on at the ranch that took Frank's time, for this deep freeze had done other damage besides what had happened to the house. The next day, I started to wash the kitchen wall behind the stove; this wall is next to the dining room wall, and it had also gotten really wet. It was requiring a lot of hard work. This area is where the woodstove is, and always has been, and is where we also have the electric stove. All the grease from so much cooking of fried lamb, mutton, and other meats over the years was caked on the wall and ceiling. There was also grease all over the spice cupboard that is in the corner of this same wall. We had cleaned the house well before we moved in, or so we thought, but we were not aware of any of this until the water damage. This same sticky film was also on the other walls in the kitchen.

More water damage in the kitchen

I can remember that by this time I was very tired, and the muscle on my right side was really bothering me from all the scrubbing and hard work that I was doing. I was at it for a couple of hours and hadn't gotten very far. As I recall, I was still working on the wall and ceiling over the woodstove and electric stove area when my right side started hurting badly.

Frank was in the living room reading, and I said to him, "Would you please come and help me? If this room isn't done when we leave for home, I will never come back." I knew I would not come back knowing the mess I would have to come back to again. I said that I had about reached my limits on my right side, after all that scrubbing and lifting for several days. As I am writing this, I can still feel that pain!

Asking Frank for help

WHY I HADN'T ASKED Frank sooner for his help is beyond me, but I hardly ever asked him to do things like that for me. When he came out to help after expressing his thoughts, he took one look and assessed the matter, as he does with anything that he has to do. Then he started on the wall to the hallway by getting a second ladder and all the things that were needed to do the job, and he went to work scrubbing and splashing water everywhere. When he got to the top of the doorjamb to the hallway, and saw this mess of glob, he took a knife and really scraped. He ended up doing this to all the doors, window frames, and cabinets in the kitchen. All the while he was doing this, he was "expressing his thoughts to the Clarkes."

It took the rest of the day and into the evening to work on the room and ceiling. Frank did all three walls, doors, windows and frames, and three-fourths of the ceiling, while I did that one wall, the spice cabinet and about three feet into the ceiling. We took time out for lunch, but otherwise we did not stop until it was done. I tried to save the floor while I was doing my work, but when Frank got into it, "forget the floor" — water, soap, lamb grease, and Clorox went everywhere. But we sure had one clean kitchen when we got done! Frank is a very good worker when he has to work, but most of the time he avoids any hard labor of any kind. The floor was made of 1-x-4-inch finished Douglas fir boards, and in fairly good condition; but, after Frank got done, I knew that it would have to be sanded down and refinished.

I believe we left for home the next day, but I'm not sure. We had to come back often to build fires to help dry out the wood, and when things dried out, I put them away in the cupboards. It wasn't until sometime after mid-July or August that I started varnishing the dining room, and when I did, I started with the china cabinet so I could get the dishes put away. Over a period of time, the dining room got done, and then the kitchen. Each room got two or three coats of varnish. The cabinet has one panel that didn't get completely dry; it has a whitish streak on it yet. After I got done, things looked so good that I went on and cleaned and varnished the living room.

Every time that we went to the ranch, we would stop at the hardware store and pick up two gallons of Danish oil, for the wood was absorbing it so fast.

Believe it or not, I ended up having all the other rooms in the house done because of how nice the three finished rooms looked. It took a year to do everything. This was such a traumatic thing that happened that I don't remember the exact dates when everything happened. I do know that by late summer the three rooms were done. And I have to thank Mary Sagehorn for all her help.

The GMC pickup at the ranch

IT WAS ABOUT THIS time that Frank and I drove a car and the GMC pickup to the ranch and left the pickup there. We bought a new Ford pickup in August 1989, which we still have today. I missed the two gas tanks that were on the GMC because now we had to stop twice before getting to the ranch. When we first got the GMC pickup years earlier, Laurence backed it up to Frank's office at our home in Nevada City, and in so doing he drove it into a hole that turned out to be the septic tank for Frank's office. That was the first time we knew that the office was on a septic line, so we made a change, and ran a sewer line clear down from one end of the property to the other end where the main sewer line to the city runs through our property. The septic tank was probably put in during the 1930s, and it had gone unnoticed all this time because it had been covered with a lot of dirt. The wood on top of the tank had rotted away and had seen better days. Luckily, only the left backside of the pickup fell in. Laurence, Frank, and I were certainly surprised!

Julia takes more trips to the ranch

JULIA STARTED TO COME to the ranch more often after she and her dad had made an agreement on her acquiring ownership of the ranch. She was bringing her church friends, the Ninety-Nines group, and other people to the ranch for weekends. She decided that she needed to hire someone to come in and clean the clean house after we leave for home, rather than having to clean everything ourselves before leaving. This way the house would always be clean whenever any of us came for a visit.

Sometime in 1988, she was able to get Mary Sagehorn to do the work, and I will have to say it surely was a nice feeling having the house clean. Of course, there were always the dead mice, flies, and cobwebs to greet you whenever you arrived.

I can tell you that after that episode with the water, we never left the ranch again without turning off the main water line to the house—summer or winter. We also turn off the gas to the hot water tanks and the electricity to everything except the refrigerator; we also lock all doors, whether it is summer or winter. There are no exceptions.

Mark's parents

THE HOUSE WAS STILL a mess from the water damage when Mark's family, Curt and Kay, Julie, Cheryl, and Chelsea, came to the ranch in July 1989. Despite the mess, we all had a good time. On Saturday, Cheryl's husband, Michael, flew into Willits, and someone went to get him and drive him to the ranch for the day.

Mark's parents gave the ranch a guestbook. Mark was the first to write in it. I started making notes in it, and so did Julia and anyone else who wanted to leave a few nice words. I found that the guestbook helped me finish writing the story on the ranch. (Through the years, I have kept notes on the ranch and on what we did and what went on while we were there, as did Julia and Mark. Those notes also helped tell the rest of this story.)

After Mark's family left, I did some oiling on the walls and came back a week later and finished oiling the two rooms. This project took two more gallons of Danish oil.

Still oiling walls

DURING THE WEEK OF July 27, 1989, I finished up one coat of oil on the two rooms. The first thing I wrote in the guestbook that evening was, "What a relief to come to the ranch and have the water damage no longer facing me as I come in the door and knowing how much hard work had been done, and I mean, hard elbow work."

Julia and Mark came up on Saturday and brought a very firm king-size bed up with them. They moved Julia's queen bed into the dorm and put the king-size bed in her room. I didn't approve, but because she would soon own the ranch, I found I didn't have much say on the matter.

At this time, we moved the kitchen table, which was damaged from the water, into the parlor to sand and varnish it. Mark did most of the work, and I put the second coat on the next time we were at the ranch. It sure looked nice when we were done!

We enjoyed this trip. We drove all over the ranch, picked blackcaps, blackberries, and any other fruit that was ripe. We also checked on the water line and new water tank for the hunting lodge to make sure they were working.

As I mentioned earlier, the deep freeze did a lot of damage in February, and it included damage to the lakes, the pink trailer, and the water supply. The copper water lines that went into the shower in the trailer were broken in several places. To fix them, we had to take off the inside wall to the bathroom and put in all new lines; this included the toilet and the sink. If I recall right, I think we also had to replace and put in a new hot water tank. My brother Jack took it all apart and tried to fix the line, but he didn't have time. We called the local plumber and all-around-fix-it man to finish things up (at this time I don't remember his name, so from here on he will be referred to as Jeff).

Then, for pleasure, all four of us trimmed the walnut tree over the shed and in the front yard. With lots of bosses, we had Mark do the major part by sawing and pruning branches on the walnut tree, while we told him where to prune. We picked up all the cuttings and hauled them to the burn pile, and, once finished, it ended up being a good job. We had fun and later had dinner, and then it was time for Mark and Julia to leave. Frank and I stayed on for a couple more days, and I put the second coat of varnish on the two rooms.

Both lakes needed stuff put in them to kill the weeds and cattails that take the pleasure out of fishing. This is an ongoing project that has to be done once every year.

Mary, oiling rooms

WHILE WE WERE AT the ranch, I asked Mary Sagehorn if she would wash and clean the rest of the walls and ceiling and oil the rooms in the house. She said she would. She planned to start right after we left for home. Sometime later, she told me that on cold days in the winter months she had her Frank come down to the house to start the fireplace, to take the chill out of the rooms. It would get so cold that it was hard for her to work many hours at one time. As I've said, it can get very cold at the ranch and it can rain 100 inches in a year. She would come to the house to work whenever she had a few hours to spare.

After she finished doing the rooms downstairs that I had not done, she went upstairs and did the four bedrooms, hallway, bathroom, and the small storage room. I had her keep track of her time and any expenses she had. When I returned to the ranch, she gave me the bill and I paid her. She bought a lot of Danish oil, sandpaper, soap, steel wool, and other things needed to work on the job for the next several months. Mary did an excellent job, and as of this writing, the rooms still look good. Down the road, Julia will have to have someone do the Danish oil job again. The next time it is done, it should only take one coat of oil applied with a brush.

Pickup sliding down a bank

ON SEPT. 4, WE left Nevada City to go to the ranch, and on the way there, we ran into trouble. The weather was good; then, near Highway 101, the road was under repair and closed to traffic. Therefore, we had to take the Redwood Valley Road cutoff and go on a very narrow dirt road for several miles. Part of the road ran along a river. It was on the muddy side and the traffic was heavy in both directions from all the cars and trucks traveling between Highway 101 and Highway 20.

We were following a big pickup, and as we did I saw his back right wheel spin and drop toward the narrow bank that slid down to the river, but he corrected and came out of it all right. However, Frank did not see what had happened, so he was not so lucky. When we got to that place in the road, the two wheels on the right side of our pickup slid off the bank and we were pulled off the road, down the four-foot bank to the river. We landed with my side of the pickup one inch from the river. A few tall willow trees kept us from ending up with my side in the water. Other motorists stopped and helped pull Frank out from under the steering wheel; the driver's side was high off the ground. Several men tried keeping the truck from sliding down the slope any further. Other men pulled me up and out the driver's side door, hoping in the meantime that the pickup wouldn't plunge into the water.

When the pickup started sliding down the hill, Frank and I tightened our seatbelts and this kept us from sliding on the seat. The accident turned me into a true believer in seatbelts, for mine kept me from leaning on the passenger door, which could have put us in the water. All traffic on the road in both directions came to a standstill until Frank and I had gotten safely out of the pickup.

The people at the scene were very helpful. One couple drove us into Ukiah to get a tow truck. Several hours later, the tow truck took us back to our pickup and pulled it back up and onto the road. No major damage was done but we lost a lot of food. There were a dozen broken eggs, which were a real mess to clean up. I took care of the egg mess right there before they dried up. After about four hours, we continued on our way to the ranch.

Julia and Mark picnicking
on the ranch, photo taken by Mark

Julia and Mark were at the ranch when we arrived. We did a lot of leisure work needing to be done, such as getting firewood for both stoves for the winter months. Collecting firewood is not something you do in the winter months, for the roads are not that good to travel on at that time of year. Julia and Mark also picked pears and brought home several boxes for us to make pear butter, pear chutney, and pear-tomato chutney.

Some of the best pears in the area are at the ranch; the secret of getting them is to beat the bears to them. Getting the apples is a different story. The crows go after the apples when they're ripe, and it's hard to beat them. I think they must go by the smell of the fruit. In one day, many trees will be stripped of apples.

The ranch in bloom

SOME OF THE DELIGHTFUL things you will find at the ranch if you are there at the right time of season are the wildflowers, then lots of bulbs in the spring. The backyard is full of narcissus, daffodils, hyacinths in blue and some white, and muscari or grape hyacinths, along with many other flowers. In the summer are irises, then in the fall the backyard is full of amaryllis. There are so many bulbs that they push up right out of the ground, but those "naked ladies" do look good at the ranch. Over the years, I have brought some bulbs home that are so far out of the ground that they will not bloom anymore; they need to be planted five inches deep or two inches below their tops so they will continue to bloom. I am sure the bulbs were put there by the Clarke family.

Early spring at the ranch

Then, late summer to early fall, there is lots of fruit of all kinds: grapes, nuts, many kinds of apples including crabapples, many kinds of pears, plums, cherries, purple and white figs, and wild berries of different kinds. The Clarkes planted a large berry patch with different kinds of berries and raspberries that we took out. Why? They were in the wrong place and had no one to take care of them. The Clarkes did a lot of canning, and we found a few jars of jam in the cellar when we got the Main House. They had a large garden, and the remains of the garden are still there. Wherever there was a place to make a water system, the Clarkes had some type of food growing there. We now have horses eating the grass in that area.

I am sure that if you looked into it, you would find that the Clarkes had pigs, cows, and chickens, along with cats and sheep dogs. This is in addition to their livelihood, the sheep that Thomas Clarke's offspring introduced to the area and were successful with.

Fixing up the two lakes

IN SEPTEMBER 1989, WE went to the ranch to check on the lakes and knew we would be there several days. When we got there, we checked on the two lakes. On the drive to the Main House, you pass the lakes that are about a block to your right and down the hill off the main ranch road. When coming to the ranch, we always look to see if everything is all right. Homer Helm was there working on the upper lake to try to fix the slide that resulted from the deep freeze in February. He sealed it from leaking with gray clay that acts as a sealer; we have this clay on the ranch. To do the job, we had to lower the water level a lot, and while we were doing it, grass that grows in the lake was removed. He still had the lower lake to work on, and it was a very hot day. After he finished with the lakes, he started working on the roads, getting them ready for winter by putting water breaks every so often. This job is done every year.

The club closed hunting season two weeks early that year; the game limit had been reached. Because of this, we knew the roads would not be traveled on much more for the season. The hunters have a field day going all over the ranch, and they are not ones to miss a single road. They don't care how hard it is to get to a road, by wintertime all the roads on the ranch are in need of repair.

Wilderness Unlimited rents the Upper House

JERRY OF WILDERNESS UNLIMITED came to the house the morning of Sept. 15. He was there for several hours to talk about the sports end of things. His group decided to rent the trailer and the Upper House. (This was going to be a problem for me, for Jack and Bev had been going to the house for years, and I knew I would really miss them and this would hurt their feelings.)

To get things ready for Wilderness Unlimited, Mary and Frank Sagehorn came in with Danish oil to do the hallway in the Upper House. Harwood was given the job of cutting the downed wood on the property, which included a tree that had fallen over on LaVonne's Road. They were not able to use that road, and the main road was tied up with all the people using it. Harwood was sort of upset about that and wondered what could be done for him to get out, so we had to come up with a way for him to be able to leave, which we did.

Big tank out of water

THE BIG WATER TANK was out of water, and no water had been going into it for at least three or four weeks. We were using the reserve water and didn't know it at the time. So we called Jeff, the local plumber and all-around-fix-it man, and he told us what to do. He said to blow into the pipe attached to the standing pipe outside of the water reservoir. It worked, and we had water within an hour.

It turned out to be a busy day. And the stock market did all right by Frank; he always called Howard, his broker, even when we were at the ranch. So this was an average morning at the ranch with things humming along, and it starts while eating breakfast and sometimes continues on into lunch. Such business always takes place in the kitchen, sitting at the table near the woodstove. In the mornings, I always had the woodstove going with a cast-iron teakettle full of water on top. Yes, it gets rather warm for the others, but I was always cold. Also in those days, Frank always had coffee going on the woodstove. I don't know if Julia has continued this, but I do know that if there is any business needing to be done, it's usually done in the kitchen.

Thundering and lighting

IN THE MIDDLE OF the night, we had thunder, lighting, and fog. This really helped to settle the dust from the new roadwork that Homer had just done. We woke up to a heavy, cold rain, and I fixed breakfast on the woodstove. About 10 a.m., Sagehorn came over with vegetables from Mary's garden. Jeff, the plumber, came over to talk about finishing the water job to the trailer and hunting lodge and to also do repairs on the Upper House. I don't remember what he did. All these things were discussed while we were having our breakfast.

Later, we went down to the lake and got the umbrellas and fishing gear. While we were at it, Frank worked on pulling weeds out of the lake and in front of the deck. Earlier, we had drained the lake so the leak could be taken care of. All the grass that was pulled out of the lake at that time was piled up along the rim of the lake and had to be removed.

Sad news for Jack and Bev

ON SEPT. 17, JACK and Bev came to the ranch while we were there, and I had to go up to the Upper House and tell them that they would have to move out of the house. I think Frank was with me and I don't remember what I really said. This is one of the things I still live with today. I knew Jack and Bev would be hurt, and that was not something I wanted to do. I told them that Julia was taking over the ranch and that Wilderness Unlimited had asked for the trailer and the Upper House so they could rent it out to put families in it. It was clear that Julia would have to rent the trailer and Upper House to bring in enough money to help pay the bills.

In the meantime, Frank and I went to the lake and worked on getting all the dead grass removed from the sides of the lake. Then we went up to the trailer to get all of the things out of it that were left by LaVena's family, but most of it was my stuff from when Frank and I lived in it. I wanted to take out whatever I wanted to save before the hunting club took over. A couple of the items that we removed before someone could walk away with them were Frank's mother's blanket and bedspread.

After that job was finished, we drove around and checked on the roads. After getting back to the house, I put sheets on the beds in the dorm. I wanted to get my work done before going up and visiting with Jack and Bev, for I thought they were going to stay through the weekend. I wish they had because Frank and I could have visited with them and helped them with the move. We did not know they would pack up and leave that day.

When we got back up to see Jack and Bev, they had already moved everything out and into the truck and were ready to leave. I almost missed saying goodbye to them. I did not expect them to do it so fast, nor to take so much out at this time. I still wonder how Jack handled the big heavy iron woodstove they had just gotten a few months earlier from Bargain Lane to replace the old one with. They moved the beds and refrigerator and disconnected the phone. The muscles in their bodies must have ached that night when they went to bed.

We did not go into the house and thought they must have left some things behind. They always used the Upper House when they came to enjoy the ranch. It was in a rundown state before they moved into it, so little time had ever been spent on any so-called fixing up, except what they wanted or needed to do for themselves. They sort of became used to keeping an eye on the ranch which made us happy. I know I will miss having them around when we come to the ranch.

The phone at the Upper House was Jack's and the phone line was the only one we had coming into the ranch. Jack was there more than we were, so we eventually had a secondary line run from that house to ours. This gave us phone service at the Main House, and we had our own phone number. However, when they disconnected their phone, we no longer had any service at our house.

Running a business at the ranch without a phone became a big problem, and the phone at the trailer had been disconnected years earlier.

After Frank and I had all our work done, we left for home.

Mary starts cleaning both houses

I CALLED MARY SAGEHORN on Friday to arrange for her to clean our house and the Upper House. In the meantime, we spoke to Tom Barney, our local carpenter, about whether he and his crew would come in and do some repair work to the shingles on the outside of the house and the roof, and then oil the shingles to help save them and the wood on the outside of Main House for a few more years. It was arranged for him to stay in the Upper House, but when he saw there wasn't anything left in the house, I had to get busy and find things for the house to be livable so Tom and his crew could stay in it. Tom said he did not want to stay in our house with his men but would use the Upper House while the repair work was being done.

The Upper House had long since seen better days; it needed work, and the kitchen, which was in bad shape, needed a lot of work done on it. So, we knew that having several men living in it was OK, for it would no doubt be in no worse shape when they left. I brought in the old relic refrigerator that was on the back porch; it took a half-day just to clean it up. Then, it took the rest of the day to clean the cupboards and walls in the kitchen. While doing that I discovered a cupboard that turned out to be a cooler storage area. It was neat setup. It was constructed in a way that there was storage room consisting of two shelves made of slats. The bottom shelf had a heavy screen to let in cool air and no bugs, with slats over the screen to hold things. Cold air from under the house came up into the cooler, which could keep butter, eggs, cheese, and, no doubt, milk cool all the time.

However, it was so dirty that I am sure it had not been used since refrigerators came into play in the 1940s. I still say it is a neat idea even for today. I don't know if Jack and Bev even knew about this closet.

Julia making changes to the ranch houses

JULIA SORT OF BEGAN taking over some of the things she wanted to change at the ranch. She knew that to make the Upper House pay off, she would have to do some major repair work. So she asked Tom if he would do the work on the Upper House after he finished working on the Main House. She also asked him to work on the shed next to the Main House. The first thing he did was take off the porch that Jack added onto the front porch and go back to the original porch. Then he shingled the house and did all the other things that needed doing on the outside.

We had to find a woodstove for the house; in the meantime, they used an electric stove. I had to get pots, pans, dishes, silverware, towels for both the bath and kitchen; also soap, sugar, spices, flour, salt and pepper, and so on. I had to furnish the place with everything except for the beds. Fortunately, I was able get most of the needed items from our house. It was late by the time I got all this done. I ended up fixing dinner and then went to bed. Tom was due in at 8 p.m.; he didn't make it until 10. When they got to the ranch, they went straight to the Upper

House and went to bed. They didn't sleep too well that night. Frank Sagehorn had earlier worked over his cattle, and, in the process, about 70 calves were separated from their mothers and were crying their heads off. Every so often, the mothers would join in and the whole ruckus went on all night and the next night as well. This ordeal all happened down at the corrals, which is near the Main House and below the Upper House.

Sagehorn and his men separating the cattle

Work continues on the ranch houses

BUD THE BURL MAN showed up around noon on Sunday. He wanted to show us the trees that were going to be dug up and the different kinds of oaks. This took most of the day, for it meant going all over the ranch. As a result, many things we were going to do didn't get done, including checking the water system.

On Monday morning, Tom came down at 7 a.m. to start work on spraying the roof of the house to get rid of the moss, so we hoped. Calvin Harwood also came and delivered wood for the kitchen stove, but it was too long, so he had to take it back and find shorter wood. In so doing, when he left the ranch, he locked out our lock on the chain that held the gate closed. This was a long, thick chain that was wrapped around the post and then to the gate. Several locks were locked onto this chain. One was ours, and he mistakenly locked it out. Therefore, we couldn't get out, nor could anyone else. We ended up removing the entire gate by lifting it up and off its hinges.

Each lock has its own combination. We had no telephone, for it had been disconnected when Jack left. This made it so we could not call out to check on where the stuff was at that Tom had ordered for the job he was working on. Frank was unable to contact his stockbroker, nor could his broker call in. As this was going on, Frank had blown a 220-watt fuse at the Upper House, and he couldn't find all the parts to the homemade ice cream maker. He had to go into town to buy an electric fry pan for Tom to cook hotcakes on for breakfast. An early morning delivery of the things Tom needed to work on the job was attempted, but the deliveryman couldn't get through the gate. So in addition to finding a fry pan, Frank also went to town to look for Tom's missing goods. He went from store to store, and even to the gas station in town, hoping to find where they could have been dropped off, but no such luck. Later we found out that the items had been dropped off at Gary's Lumber and Paint Store, the one place that Frank did not go to.

Frank also went to see what could be done about a phone. He called the phone company, and they said they had a man scheduled to be in Laytonville the next day, and that he could come to the ranch after he was through with his appointment. Frank also called Pacific Gas & Electric. While still in town, he bought ice to bring home to make ice cream. By this time, it was late in the afternoon. Frank was not a happy man by the time he got back to the ranch.

Mike, who was working for Tom, had finished getting the windows covered so they could spray the sides of the house. Tom was scheduled to quit working at 7:30 that night, but, without the delivery, he was unable to get any work done at all. So Frank's temper got rather out of control. We ended up having dinner at 10 p.m. that night. We also had Tom and Mike down for a dish of ice cream before going to bed. We left the gate to the ranch open all night just in case the delivery truck came in the early morning, and we hoped and prayed that no cattle would get out. We planned to leave for home in the morning.

Laurence called about lost delivery

THE NEXT DAY WAS another long day with everything going wrong once again. Added to this was the frustration of not getting much sleep due to the cattle crying all night outside our windows. Tom showed up again at 7 a.m. to get to work. Frank Sagehorn came out and told us that Laurence had called him, passing word that the trucking company called him and told him that Tom's materials were in Laytonville—but the company hadn't said where. They told Laurence they would send somebody to the ranch to let us know because they had not been able to reach us by phone. So at noon, Tom and Mike went into town. They knew there was only one place the materials could be. They went to Gary's Lumber and Paint Store, and there they found Tom's missing delivery.

In the meantime, Frank was still hot under the collar. To get our minds on something else we went down to the lake to spray weeds, thistles, and cattails. His temper was still going strong on all the things that were going wrong or not getting done. So I left him down at the lake. I got in the pickup and went up to the house to do some house cleaning, as well to do some work outside while waiting for the telephone man to show up. I needed to make sure someone was there to tell him what to do. He had not come by the time Tom and Mike got back from town. So I went back to the lake to see if Frank needed any help.

Frank was all done spraying around both lakes, and he had enjoyed his fill of white figs from the tree next to the upper lake. He was feeling OK and sort of enjoying the fruits of his labor. This was about two hours after I had left him to go up to the Main House to do some cleaning. One thing I have to say about Frank's temper is that it never lasts very long, and if you remind him of it five minutes later—he won't even know what you're talking about!

Installing new telephones

THE TELEPHONE MAN GOT to our place around 4 p.m. and spent about two hours working on the phone lines. He put in four jacks at the Main House and arranged for a pay phone to be installed in the Upper House. He also worked on installing outside boxes so phones could be used outside. It was around 6 p.m. when he finished the job.

The PG&E man came out to fix the damage that Frank had done, and Tom put in a new meter box. We now have 220 volts in both the Upper House and the little house next to it. Mary decided to wait until Tom was finished before she continued working on the walls in the house. Work was still being done to the trailer and the water line. It was getting close to 7 p.m., and I was already packed and ready to go home. Frank decided to pick figs and other fruit to take home with us.

313

By this time, Frank and I both needed to take a shower. Tom and Mike had quit for the day, and it wasn't until after 7 p.m. that we left for home. It had been a long day and a lot had happened. We still had the long drive home, but at least at this hour there would be little traffic. Later that evening, before leaving for home, we drove to Williams and went to the Auction House Restaurant. The Auction House is a place we sometimes go to for dinner, only it was closed this night. We ended up having hamburgers at one of the other places in town. Then we got on the road and made it back home around midnight, a far cry from leaving early in the morning and getting home by lunchtime.

One of the reasons we were able to leave home whenever we had to is that we always had a live-in gardener who took care of the yard and looked after the place, and in those days, live-ins could be trusted.

Julia and Mark pick pears

IN OCTOBER, JULIA AND Mark went to the ranch to pick pears. I can't remember exactly, but they must have left their plane in Laytonville or Willits. Julia brought home boxes of pears from the ranch for me to can. When they were there, she also checked on the work that was being done.

I think Tom and Mike had finished their oil job on the outside of the house. Julia reported that Mary was back to doing the interior walls and ceiling.

Locked gate on Highway 101

WHEN WE LEFT HOME to go back to the ranch, it was raining, but once we got to the ranch on Oct. 27, we had nice weather. The San Francisco Giants were playing the Oakland A's in Game 3 of the World Series. We heard the broadcast over the car radio but eventually lost it due to the mountain ranges, so I didn't know how it turned out. (The A's did win, on their way to a series sweep.)

As we were coming up Highway 101 out of Ukiah, I remembered seeing a gate that looked funny and had many locks on it. So I said to Frank that there was a gate coming up on the right side that had a lock contraption on it that we should stop and take a look at. I remember thinking it might be something we should have on our gate. When we came to it we stopped, and Frank really looked it over. When we got to the ranch, Frank told Homer about its design.

Homer knew what we were talking about, for he had also seen it. We asked him if he could install one for us. (This is funny, because Mark and Julia ended up doing the same thing, and Julia took a picture of Mark looking at the long row of locks, 10 of them in a row, to see how the mechanism worked.)

Mark investigating the lock mechanism

New oil job; truckload burls; earthquake

Bud and Frank at the burl shop in Marysville, CA

AFTER WE ARRIVE AT the ranch, we always drive to the hunting lodge to let them know we are at the ranch. This time, on our way down to the house, we saw lights on inside the pink trailer. We drove down that way and met the new patrolman and his wife, Santos and Mary Punados. They moved in three days earlier and told us they had no water. Unfortunately, it was too late to do anything about it. One of their jobs was to check the loads of logs and burl logs going out of the ranch; they told us about a load that went out that day.

We drove down to the lakes and then on to the ranch house. Frank said, "Gee, the house looks nice with all the fresh oil on the outside wood," referring to the job Tom had just finished. The oil job being done inside was going well. Mary still had the downstairs bedroom to do, but everything else inside was finished and looked great. After seeing how things were turning out, Frank decided the ranch house looked great, despite all the trouble we had on our last visit to the ranch. Amen!

A big dump truck load of burls went out of the ranch that day, no doubt headed for Marysville, California, where they have a big yard to store them before they go to market. Frank and I have been to the place where the burls are stored. Anyone looking at it would say, "What are all those stumps doing there?" A great part of our time spent on business at the ranch took place on weekends. One of the reasons for this was because we were not there when most people worked for us. They came by on the weekends when we were there to visit and tell us what they had done. They would also check to see if there was anything else we wanted them to do. Along with the good news or bad, we did enjoy the ranch.

The Loma Prieta earthquake, which struck just after 5 p.m. on Oct. 17, 1989, had registered 7.1 on the Richter scale. The epicenter was about 200-plus miles from the ranch. This "grand old lady" of our ranch house stood up well under all the rolling and shaking. There was not a single dish out of place.

Frank Sagehorn talks business

ON SATURDAY, FRANK SAGEHORN came down to the Main House to talk business and have his cup of coffee with Frank. This is something he always did when we came to visit the ranch, and I'm sure he continued to do so after Julia took it over. (But by the time Julia became the owner, he had given up drinking coffee and had switched to Roma, which was what my Frank was drinking.)

I went fishing and caught two good-sized fish while the two Franks did their talking. Tom came down for the weekend with his son Boyd and Boyd's girlfriend Daisy. They also went fishing. Tom was there to give the outside of the houses one more coat of oil. From then on, the Upper House has come to be called the lodge. He also fixed the wire mesh covers used to cover the tops of the fireplace chimneys. In the afternoon, he worked on the foundation of the shed at the Main House, constructing wooden forms used for making cement blocks to serve as the shed's new foundation.

Talking about fireplaces, Jack made the fireplace racks that hold the firewood, and he used old horseshoes off the ranch for the decorations on the front of the racks in both houses. Thank you, Jack, for the memory!

We went up to the trailer to talk to Santos and Mary about all the things they wanted to discuss. They wanted to know about the burls being shipped out. We pointed out where their water tank was, along with the water line coming down to the house. We also showed them where our dump for the garbage was located. Now that Mary and Santos would be living there for three years, they, and the lodge guests, would need to use it. I removed the rest of the stuff out of the trailer that they did not want.

Harwood cutting trees

SATURDAY WAS A BUSY and productive day. In addition to everything else going on, it was also Calvin Harwood's first day of cutting trees above the hunting lodge. By the time we got back, it was 5 p.m., a long time since breakfast. No wonder I was dizzy; I was hungry. We had a light snack and then went to help Tom with the cement before it got dark. After dusk, we came in and heard that the A's beat the Giants and won the World Series in four games. I guess Tom must have heard about it on his radio, for we didn't have one at the Main House. We fixed a light dinner, and while it was cooking, I played Hand and Foot with Frank and beat him. After dinner, we went to bed at 11 o'clock. Days at the ranch were always long.

On Sunday, Tom worked on electrical projects at the lodge. Earlier, while staying there himself, he learned what needed to be done for us to rent it out to Wilderness Unlimited. Later that day, he came down to finish putting cement pilings under the shed.

Frank and I were able to spend a little time checking out the lake. While we were there, I did some fishing, but no luck. Then we went up to Mary and Santos's place to see about the water problems at the trailer. Jeff, the plumber, came down earlier around 9 a.m. to talk about putting in a new water tank for the trailer; the wooden one just wasn't holding water anymore, and we needed to put a new tank in. He needed to know where the water line was. I remembered its location, and we walked the line right up to the old tank that was put in about 1969. While at the trailer, they said there was a leak in the bathroom. Jeff said he would fix it right away. In the meantime, we told Mary and Santos to go down to the lodge to take their showers. Furthermore, Santos did not have any tools to work with. We told him to go down to our tool shed, and he could use tools from there as long as he put them back and locked the door to the shed when he was finished.

I remember we saw an eagle down at the lake that day. We also saw eagles around the middle barn. We learned a long time ago that they really don't need trees. We also picked apples to bring home before the frost or birds could get to them. At 6 p.m., we went back to the house to help Tom finish working on the shed. He told us not to burn any of the lumber behind the shed, that he might need it for repair work. Therefore, we piled the lumber along the shed so that no cattle would walk on it and damage it. Tom planned to finish putting the rest of pilings in when he came back to the ranch on his next trip.

All the while Frank and I owned the ranch house, we let Sagehorn use the fenced-in area for his cattle and horses to eat down the grass so we wouldn't have to mow it. Mowing grass was not one of Frank's hobbies. However, once Julia took things over that method of yard care was eliminated. No more animals or cars were allowed in the yard.

Daisy had dinner waiting for Boyd and Tom up at the lodge. They ate, cleaned up, and left for Nevada City. He let us know that the shed was now ready to store firewood, but Frank said he wanted all the old wood used up before putting freshly cut wood in the shed for the winter.

Cleaning the Upper House; fixing leaks in trailer

ON OCT. 30, 1989, we set the clock back one hour. On that day I had to go up to the lodge and take out all the things I brought there for Tom to use. The stuff had to be returned to the Main House to get things ready for hunters to come in and use the lodge. I gave them an electric heater to use for a few days, and told them that Julia would need it for the weekend.

Before leaving the lodge, Tom pulled out the old wooden box that held wood in the kitchen. It left an opening to the porch that had to be covered. The woodstove would go there, but Tom didn't have time to put the wall back, nor the floor, so he fixed it temporarily. In doing so, he accidentally broke a water pipe just before he left, so the Punados went into town to get the parts needed to fix it, for they wanted to take a shower that night. They were also going to be leaving for their home in Sacramento for a few days to get some of their belongings to bring back to the trailer.

Jeff did not show up to fix the water tank, so Frank asked Homer if he could push it over when he wasn't loading trucks, but he was too busy. So Mary, Santos, Frank, and I pushed over the redwood tank and removed the boards and cleared the area of brush so Gary could get in with his truck with the new water tank. We ended up getting the job done faster than we thought we would. Frank called Gary to see if he could deliver the new plastic tank that afternoon. In the meantime, Frank and I went to check on the loggers' work, and along comes Jeff with the tank. He said, "I guess you got someone to take my job." Frank said, "No, we're doing it; after all, the tenants are out of water." Jeff didn't think we were in that big of a hurry. Anyway, he got the message and quickly got the new tank hooked up and working.

The trailer still had several leaks in the copper pipes from the frost, and water was still running down one wall in the bathroom. This was supposed to have already been fixed by Jeff. He said he had been down to fix the leaks in the morning, and we thought he got the job done. I hoped he understood Frank's language. He should have put in new copper pipes on the first go-around, but he didn't.

Logs going to Harwood

TWO LOADS OF LOGS went out that day from the area above the hunting lodge, and three more loads would be going out first thing the next morning. Santos's job was to get log tickets for each load that went out. The club asked him to get the price of four loads of firewood right away, so I guessed they had people coming in to stay at the lodge. It turned out they were having twenty people coming in that weekend for winter pig hunting.

While Frank was driving to the dump area, one of his tires started to go flat, but he was able to drive it into town to get it fixed. While he was gone, I went fishing and caught two nice-sized fish for dinner. I used a two-pound weight to get the line down past the grass to where the bigger fish were.

We were now able to use the telephone to receive and place calls. We now had two working phones, up from none. Having two phones put in might have been overkill, but it sure was nice to be able to call when we needed to. Frank really missed being able to call his broker the first thing in the morning.

Burl stump at Marysville

BUD WINERWIG, OUR BURL man, was at the ranch at 9 a.m. Oct. 31, and he told us our share of the two burl loads that went out the day before came to $1,800 plus loggers. We got far less for the three loads that went out that morning. We were planning to leave for home sometime that day, but Bud wanted to check the east side of the road, and he wanted to see Frank when he got back. He said it would be a few hours.

It turned out to be late in the afternoon by the time Bud got back. Frank wanted to go over everything with him in person, so they went back out to where he would be cutting. While waiting, I went fishing again and caught one more fish to add to what I'd caught the day before. That night's dinner was taken care of, and we decided to stay at the ranch one more night. I only took so much meat to the ranch to cover the days I thought we would be there, so if we stayed any longer, I would have to go fishing or go into town for us to have something for dinner. Laytonville is a very small town on Highway 101 and just doesn't have many eating places.

I got back just as Frank and Bud were returning from driving around the area where he would be getting the burls. And, of course, we would leave early the next morning, I hoped. I knew we had to stop at the Auction House or Bargain Lane to check on a woodstove for the lodge. Then, on our way through Marysville, I knew we needed to stop at Hardwoods Unlimited to pick up our burl check.

318

The boards on the bridge to the hunting lodge had rotted and caved in, so the loggers replaced it with a nearby bridge that was made earlier in the season and was ready to be used for that location. They also put rock on the road going down to the trailer.

Two sets of hunters came in for the weekend. It turned out to be a long day. That night I beat Frank at three games of Hand and Foot again, so he quit and went off to read.

I called Julia that evening. She and Mark would be the only ones at the ranch that weekend, besides the hunters. We had nice, warm days all the while we were there. I hoped we didn't have any children come by for trick-or-treating at our home in Nevada City that night. Mary Sagehorn continued to oil the walls and ceilings. I paid her about once a month or whenever she was at the ranch when we were there. She was a good worker and did a fine job keeping the house clean for us.

Leaving the ranch for home

ON WEDNESDAY, NOV. 1, 1989, believe it or not, we left the ranch on time for home. As we left, we dropped off the camera at the trailer at 8 a.m. for Mary and Santos to use for taking pictures of the burls going out. All in all, it had been a long six-day week, with long hard days, lots of disappointments, pain, being mad, activity, excitement, fun and pleasure. When things finally go right, you feel like you have accomplished something. In my notes, I have thanked the Lord for all the things that happened, good and bad.

Julia and Mark were up for the weekend of Nov. 3. They didn't leave a note for us at home, but I know they were planning to talk to people while they were there about trimming the fruit trees. And I'm sorry to say the Punadoses were still out of water.

By now you can no doubt tell that Mark's name had become quite familiar around the ranch.

Checked burls in Marysville

ON NOV. 7, WE left home at 8:45 a.m. to go to Marysville to check the burls. We stopped to vote before leaving town. In Marysville, we drove over to the plant called Hardwoods Unlimited. Fred Edler, the owner, showed us the burls that came from our ranch. One was sure big, about 10 feet tall, and as big as a small car. He gave me a burl candy bowl made out of California myrtle. I took it to the ranch and left it there, feeling that it was part of the ranch.

Burls at the wood shop in Marysville

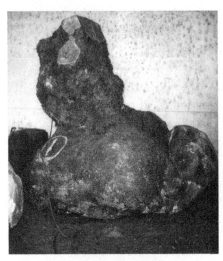
A burl from the Clarke Ranch

On our way to the ranch, we stopped at Lucerne for our pit stop, milkshake, and hamburger. It is at this stop that we usually change drivers. Then it was on to Highway 101 and a visit to Bargain Lane to pick up the woodstove. Mr. Blacklane already had it loaded into his pickup and was ready to take it to the ranch for us. We had to stop at Willits for groceries and gasoline, then on to Laytonville to stop at Geigers' to get a new stovepipe and other parts for the stove, then on to the ranch. Mr. Blacklane got to the ranch before we did. He helped us put in the woodstove at the lodge. He also installed the stovepipe and put in the damper control the right way so everything would work properly. This was an old, restored stove, not a new one.

He took some old iron bedsteads and other stuff that was lying around that we didn't need any more that he could sell in his store.

Jeff still fixing pipe damage

JEFF STILL HAD NOT fixed the water pipes in the trailer, so we called him and he came out and fixed it. After Jeff said the repairs were done, I gave Mary some insulation that I had left over from the attic of the Main House and told her to put it around the pipes before putting the wall back. At around 6 p.m., we went up to see how they were doing, and she had water all over the house. So we went back to the house and called Jeff. Frank had a few words with him. Jeff said he would fix it in the morning, rather than having Frank getting someone else to fix it. We told him to put in all new pipes, which he should have done in the first place. We called the telephone man to come out and put a phone line in the trailer, and he said he would be there in the morning.

We then went to see the loggers and Bud the burl man. We picked up logging tickets from Santos, and then we went back to the Main House to make dinner and clean up the kitchen. Verl Wetzel from Wilderness Unlimited called and said he would be there in the morning. I finished making my notes and it was time for bed. Frank had long since been asleep. Despite a couple of setbacks, it was a beautiful day.

Verl talked about the club

ON NOV. 8, VERL came to talk about the club at 9 a.m. The telephone man came and said he would have the line in for Thanksgiving; new lines needed to be brought in for service at the trailer. Jeff also showed up, and at last the Punadoses finally had water. They really had an ordeal with the water. Verl got settled with us on what was going to happen with Wilderness Unlimited; he was with us until 3 p.m. Then we went up to see Calvin about cutting wood. We were having a little trouble with him, but, to his credit, he was trying to do what was right.

Mary Sagehorn came by to oil the house, but we were too busy with Verl to be interrupted, so the Sagehorns burned leaves down at the shack instead. At 5:45 p.m., we were packed and ready to leave for the long drive home.

We ended up getting many things done, and again they were long, busy days. The day was beautiful. It was much warmer the next day, so I was somewhat glad we were leaving, for it can get very hot at the ranch. There is no such thing as air conditioning at the ranch; that's when the lake comes in real handy, even at night.

As long as our family has owned the ranch, whenever we leave to go home, I feel I leave a little bit of me behind. It's really a nice place to come to; it's so quiet and peaceful most of the time, and you can see for miles around. There is different scenery to look at, and it's all yours. It really is God's country. It's only when the cattle are brought into the corral that things get noisy; but then you have another interest to keep you going, just watching all the things the cattlemen do to handle the animals, including tossing the bulls' balls to the dogs—who catch them on the fly to eat. I can watch this from the porch.

Thanksgiving 1989; our wedding anniversary; Mark's family

Laurence, Gloria, Mark, and Curt in front of the shed

ON NOV. 20, WE left home early to go to the ranch to celebrate the holidays and our anniversary. I bought a whole 8-pound salmon, a 25-pound turkey, and all the trimming for a Thanksgiving dinner. All the Amarals, as well as Mark and his parents and family, joined us at the ranch for the Thanksgiving holiday.

On our way there, we stopped at Bargain Lane; this place is just past Junction 20 on Highway 101. I remembered seeing an old antique platter with roses on it that was extra-large on our last trip in the store. I thought it would be good for holding a large fish or a turkey; we didn't have a big platter like that at the ranch or at home. So we stopped and bought it, along with a small antique secretary desk with a roll-down top and an old-fashioned telephone that cranked. We put the phone on the wall in the hallway. Over time, I came to buy many nice pieces for the Main House that sort of fit in with its surroundings. (I took the big platter with us when we left for home after the holiday.)

Next, we stopped at Willits to buy regular groceries, milk, butter, eggs, and so on, and anything that doesn't travel very well. From Willits it's still over a half-hour drive before getting to the ranch. We stopped at Mary and Santos's and discovered they were still having water problems. On the way to the trailer, we saw that the lake had risen six inches since we were last there.

On Tuesday, we drove around the ranch and checked on the loggers and the stump man. Julia arrived in the late afternoon and helped me make three each of apple and pumpkin pies, and she helped me get stuff ready for the next few days. Frank Sagehorn showed up to talk business for a couple hours.

Wednesday. Laurence and Gloria showed up around 4 p.m. A few minutes later, Curt, Kay, and Chelsea arrived (Mark's parents and his niece). We had a wonderful dinner that included the barbecued salmon, which I had covered with a lot of mayonnaise, both inside and out, before wrapping it in tinfoil with all the trimmings. We had a wonderful evening, and it turned out that the weather was pretty good all three days. Around 11 p.m., our step-grandchildren, Spence and Brad, arrived just after we had gone to bed. When the boys came in, they said the gate was left unlocked and the combination was set to 7-0-9-1. Several hunters had come in for the holidays and we would have to report the unlocked gate to the club in the morning.

Me, Frank, Kay,
Chelsea, Curt, and the salmon

Thanksgiving Day. Sharon, one of Helena's twin daughters, and Harold had just gotten married Wednesday evening around 7 p.m. in Santa Rosa and showed up at the ranch in the morning for a lively breakfast with the rest of us.

It was an active day with a lot of energy flying around. After breakfast, it was time to

start working on the 25-pound turkey. After it was stuffed and in the oven for the day, we were free to enjoy our time together. I don't know if I have said this before, but one of my faults is that I have a lot of energy that rarely stops or sits still for very long. I move faster than I can tell someone else to do something, so I usually just do things myself. Good or bad, that's the way God made me and He does a good job of looking after me. Nevertheless, it can "tick off" other people!

Kay, Brad, Spence, me, Mark, Frank, Gloria,
Laurence, Curt, and Chelsea (Julia took the picture)

About this time, Mark's sister Julie arrived. My Julia, with all her energy, decided to remove the big dirt pile and clean up the yard. Spence and Brad decided to bring in sand and fix the horseshoe pits so they could play the game. I went fishing, but there were too many hunters down at the lake fishing, so I came back rather than have them leave.

In the afternoon, it started to rain just about the time the ice cream crew got ready to make homemade ice cream. Kay brought Christmas ornaments for each table setting, which made the table look really nice and decorative for the holiday season. This was something Julia and I have done for years when we have dinner at our homes, and she wanted to do it this time. It was really nice. Kay also brought some potted plants of different kinds to set around the house, and she brought homemade breads of all kinds. We had our turkey dinner with all the trimmings. The "boys" did the dishes. Julie left after dinner to go see her boyfriend, who, I believe, later became her husband. She left her daughter, Chelsea, with her parents, Curt and Kay.

We spent the evening playing Hand and Foot and other games and sitting in front of a hot fire in the fireplace and eating all the goodies that were sitting around. It rained all night long. All in all, it was a very nice Thanksgiving Day at the ranch.

It rained off and on most of the day on Friday, so everyone stayed in and played games, looked at pictures, and did what they wanted to do. Most of the roads were too muddy to drive on, except $65 Road, or so it was thought. This road is also known as Center Road, and I should add that it is on the crest of the mountain that starts in the area of the ranch houses and goes all the way down into the canyon. It is usually on the drier side due to its makeup of so many rocks and boulders. Anyway, Gloria and Laurence wanted to collect moss off the trees to take home, so they, along with Julia and Mark, took the pickup out to look for moss, and they did find some nice pieces. Coming back, however, they got stuck in the mud up near the house on $65 Road. They got Sagehorn and his friend who had a tow truck come and pull them out. I wonder who else besides Jack has gotten stuck on this road throughout the years?

Getting the truck unstuck on $65 Road

Mark is a very good cook and made dinner Friday night. It was a barbecue and shish kebab meal. We have sure had some fine meals at the ranch. We spent the evening visiting, playing games, and enjoying each other's company as it rained outside. On Saturday, after breakfast and while it was still raining, Brad left for home around 9. At 10, Laurence, Gloria, and Spence left. Then around 11, Curt, Kay, and Chelsea left for home.

Before lodgers leave the ranch, they change the sheets and remake the bed, so it will be ready for the next person who visits and stays for the night. Julia, Mark, Frank, and I spent the rest of the day being lazy, eating leftover food, taking naps, playing cards, reading, and relaxing.

On Sun., Nov. 26, Frank (age 71) and I (age 67) celebrated our 47th anniversary. We took our time getting up and had a leisurely breakfast. The four of us still at the ranch chopped and piled wood, cleaned up the yard, and put things away. We had a turkey soup dinner. Then Julia and Mark left around 7 p.m. It was a clear evening. We could see Venus, which was very bright in the night's sky. Frank spent most of the day reading, and we both turned in early.

Monday was a full day at the ranch. It was a bright, sunny, windy day. Tom was supposed to be there, but he didn't come, although he did show up the next day. We put more wood in the shed and removed tools on the shed wall so it could be oiled sometime the following week. A man was scheduled to come by with his backhoe to fix the cistern at the lodge. I spent a great deal of the day cleaning up the house and getting ready to go home in the morning. The pickup was packed except for leftover food and a few other essentials.

Tue., Nov. 28, we left early to go home, and on our way, we made a stop in Marysville to see about the burls. It had been a long week and a nice 47th wedding anniversary.

Tom and Mike were now staying at the Main House, now that the lodge was being fixed up and used by the club. Tom and Mike were using the downstairs bedroom; they cooked their own breakfast, and if we were there, I would cook dinner for all of us.

A week later, on Dec. 6, we left home once again for the ranch. It was a beautiful day and we arrived about 5:30 p.m. We drove up the road and went by the hunting shack area so we could check on the logging. As we did, we got stuck in the mud and had to back down for about a mile until we were able to turn around and drive back to the hunting lodge and then to the Main House on another road. Tom and Mike had been there and had oiled all the windowsills, put new pulley cords in the window sashes, and placed the windows back in the frames and the glass panes were washed, the screens were oiled and restored. The foundation to the shed had also been done.

I like cooking pork chops in a cast iron grill on the woodstove. It gives the right kind of heat and makes them taste exceptionally good. We had pork chops and all the trimmings to go with it, along with freshly made hot applesauce also cooked on the woodstove.

On Dec. 7, Pearl Harbor Day, Tom and Mike came up early from Nevada City and finished putting the roof on the shed, blocks under it, and screen doors on the house. Mike put two coats of Danish oil on the outside shed walls. I put all the tools back on the walls on the inside, and I hung all the antique tools on the wall on the outside of the shed under the porch roof. The shed looked nice, and it was a nice day to work on it.

Tom spent the day working up at the lodge. Jerry, from Wilderness Unlimited, came in to stay for the night while he was up visiting. We called the plumber before we left, but he had not come, so we had to call him again to get rid of the roots that had gotten into the toilet line that was in "the toilet room," which is between the kitchen and the bedrooms at the lodge. Also, we had to replace the new water tank top with a new one because it had a crack in it. We called Alan Geiger to come and replace it.

We had Jerry in for a chuck roast dinner with Tom. We invited Mary and Santos to join us, but they had to go into Willits to pick up their son at the Greyhound bus station. Mike had left earlier to go to Nevada City. After dinner, we had a very nice visit.

Friday, Dec. 8, was an overcast day. Tom sprayed the posts under the shed with preservers and fixed the shower and bathroom pipes to get rid of the odor in the Main House. Frank and I put more wood in the shed. Tom went up to do some more work at the lodge, and we went up to put a fire pad in place on the floor where the woodstove would sit. We also put in a fire-protection sheet on the back wall behind the woodstove, and Tom laid down linoleum on the floor. We fixed the cupboard doors so they would open and close easily, fixed light fixtures, and removed all extra telephone wires. We taped windows closed for spring replacements as this is an old house. Tom left for home.

Frank and I had dinner, played a game of Hand and Foot and then went to bed. The work that Tom did at the lodge and on the shed was under Julia's instructions. Tom was supposed to work even when we were not there, and during this time, the weather was really cold.

Monday was a beautiful, clear day to drive home. The toilet by the window in the upstairs bathroom of the Main House was plugged up, but I fixed it. We cleaned everything up, turned off all the outside water and electricity, and left for home. In Marysville, we stopped to check on the burls and then went on home. Mary continued oiling the walls and ceilings.

Mark and Julia at the ranch, January 1990

ON FRIDAY, JAN. 5, 1990, Mark and Julia arrived at the ranch around 11:30 p.m., and the house was really cold. The first thing Mark did was build a fire, but the house still wasn't any warmer by morning. After breakfast, they checked out where the loggers had been. There was still some debris left over from the logs cut by Calvin, and they found where Bud took out burl wood just east of Middleton Creek along the road. Julia and Mark were not able to get out through that gate, which is on the far northeast part of the ranch. This is the first gate entering the ranch off Branscomb Road, the area where the old Cahto Road entered the ranch in the early 1800s. Mark and Julia found that the combination on the gate had been changed and the roads were too wet to go back the way they came. It is a good two- to three-mile walk from the Middleton gate back to the house. Mark and Julia walked back to the Main House and found Frank Sagehorn was there. They got the new combination from him and eventually made it out. After quite a delay, they made it into town to buy some parts to fix the hinge on the driveway gate at the house. After dinner, they caught up on reading and went to bed.

Julia said it rained all day on Saturday and continued raining all the way through until Monday evening. They weren't able to do much but enjoy the house and walk out on the porch. On Saturday, Marvin's gardeners pruned the walnut tree in front of the house and cut the small oak in back. Mark worked on the backyard fence and Julia talked to David, the guy who lived across the way, about repairing Santos's water and cutting burls. Marvin also pruned one pear tree before the rain got too heavy.

On Sunday, Mark and Julia relaxed, played cards, walked in the rain, and Julia pulled some weeds. On Monday, the rain was still bad. She had long, separate talks with Calvin, Santos, and Bud. Slowly, she was getting the big picture of the workings of the ranch. Mark says the truth is somewhere in the middle. (I guess there had been some trouble that happened when we were not there, and they were taking care of it. This could no doubt be over the locks on the gate and the tree slash that was everywhere in the areas they were working.)

On Tuesday, Marvin worked on the apple orchard. He planned to have Santos let him in to finish, weather permitting. Ken Smith, a local welder that Mr. Geiger recommended, worked on putting in a new gate and lock system. Hopefully we would be able to monitor things better now. (This is the lock system we saw on Highway 101 a few months back that had a string of 10 locks on it. We have six on ours. After a lock is used, its digits are set back to 0000 so no one can try guessing the combination of a lock. Each lock has a separate owner and its own unique combination. The gate can be opened by unlocking any one of the six locks. Once a lock is taken off, a long locking lever can then be removed without interfering with the other locks on the gate.)

Bud and David worked on the burls in the meadow, which were now ready to be trucked out. David also worked on the water for Santos and it still wasn't completely fixed. He would have to do a permanent job in the spring. Mark continued working on the fence by the house and got a load of dry firewood. The house was working fine, and Mark and Julia had a nice, five-day stay at the ranch.

Burls are trees that have big stumps that grow deep into the ground. They require a tremendous amount of work to be dug out of the ground without damaging the stump, although some do grow above ground. The roots can run from 4 to 10 feet deep and wide, and some are as wide as a car. It takes a lot of time to get just one of them out of the ground. When the burls arrive in Marysville, they are washed and the dirt is removed. If I remember correctly, they receive a thick coat of wax over the whole stump before being shipped to Europe.

Julia buys the Clarke Ranch, January 1990

ON JAN. 27, 1990, Julia bought the Clarke Ranch. Now that she owned it, she took over her dad's interest in running the ranch. With Frank's help, she had already started doing some of these things. She was involved with the logging and the selling of timber, and she was involved with redoing parts of the Upper House (now called the hunting lodge) that Jack and Bev lived in for many years. Julia also supervised some of the work done on the Main House, knowing she would come to own it and she wanted the Upper House, or hunting lodge, brought back to its original structure.

While work was being done on the hunting lodge, Wilderness Unlimited had already rented it as a lodge and was using it as a place for families and groups of people to stay in. Weekend staff meetings were also held in it. Understandably, many women don't mind going hunting if they don't have to camp out and rough it. The rules of the lake were the same as always: If I was down at the lake, they left, for Frank made the lakes just for me to fish in, for I love to fish and I do not swim. Julia also made a deal that whenever she hosted the family reunions, the lodge and the lake would be made available to her for that week. In addition to the lodge, Wilderness Unlimited also got the pink trailer to use for the winter months. The main reason for this was so the manager would have a warmer place to stay during the winter months.

The campground on the ranch is right down on Section Four Creek, an area that is very nice in the summer but gets downright cold in winter. The same rules for things tossed out and left on the grounds at the ranch still hold today. To make the transition of ownership a little easier, from the time Julia took over the ranch, she ran it with her dad's help until she felt confident in handling it alone.

Snow at the ranch; water damage from 1989

Wintertime at the ranch

IN FEB 1990, FRANK and I left home to go to the ranch. The temperature was 24 degrees outside, the roads were icy, and the weather forecast called for snow. It was a slow trip to the ranch. It started raining at Junction 20 and rained the entire way along Highway 101 to the ranch. When we arrived there, it was very cold. Fortunately, there were no broken pipes. We turned on the water and electricity and lit the lights under the hot water tanks, then started the wood fires. By this time, it was dinnertime, and then time for bed. The electricity went out at 1 a.m. Frank got up out of bed and put a lot of wood in the fireplace. He also started up the woodstove in the kitchen, which we kept going for the rest of the night. We put more blankets on our bed and went back to sleep. In the morning, we woke up to snow on the ground. The power came back on at 7 a.m., and the fog was rolling in.

I was very pleased with the work Mary Sagehorn did with the oiling of the house while we were away, including the kitchen sink area and the china cabinet. It was now a year after the water damage from the burst pipes in 1989, and Mary was just about done with the job of oiling the rest of the house. I spent some time fishing while Frank worked on taking care of business. Julia and Mark arrived at the ranch around 6 p.m. They said the weather was really bad in the Bay Area, and that Highway 49 was closed and Highway 80 to Reno was closed from Auburn over Donner Summit. At 7:30 p.m., Laurence called us and said they had 27 inches of snow at their place in Nevada City and the electricity was out. In the morning, we woke up to four inches of snow on the ground. This was our first trip to the ranch where we had snow of any depth while we were there. It snowed and rained, and the sun shone off and on all day long. Julia took pictures of the snow on the sheds, fences, houses, lakes, cattle, and Mark with his snowman. I was glad we were at the ranch because with the electricity out at home it would be impossible to get the house warm with the one fireplace.

Frank Sagehorn came over in the morning to talk about buying the 160-acre piece of land on the northeast corner of the property. Afterwards, Jerry and Kelly from Wilderness Unlimited came in to talk and to work on getting things cleaned up; they were having a large group coming in to stay at the lodge. We knew the kids would really enjoy getting out and playing in all the snow.

Wilderness Unlimited's members quickly recognized that the lodge is a great asset for them, and everyone so far has been happy with the arrangement.

Four feet of snow in Nevada City

WE CONTINUED STOKING THE woodstove and fireplace with wood. At 4 p.m., we called Laurence from the ranch and he said they had four feet of snow in Nevada City and that we should stay put. The weather report said it was a "100-year storm". Laurence said they had enough food to be all right for a while, and he told us the electricity kept coming on and going off, but they had a generator that would help them through the ordeal. Here at the ranch, toward evening, Mark went out and built a good-sized snowman.

Julia, Mark, and the snowman

Sunday night it froze, and Mark's snowman was one stiff man. The sun came out Monday, but it was very cold and there was snow in most places. We cut firewood and brought it into the house. We burned a lot of firewood keeping the place warm. Frank and I went fishing, but no luck. Later, the four of us went out and cut branches along the road and piled them up to burn later. All the roads that have trees and brush alongside them have to be cleared just about every year. While we were out doing this, we ran into the group from the lodge. They were all in their thirties and were out enjoying a long walk. They told us they were having a great time.

Monday morning turned out to be nice and sunny. We went down to the upper lake and opened the valve to start lowering the water level in the lake to prepare it for the winter runoff. We also wanted to see how long it would take to go down from its nine-foot, two-inch water level. Harwood came by around 10 a.m. He, Frank, Julia, and Mark went to check on the logging works up east past the hunting camp. I went fishing, but I didn't have any luck. I came back to the Main House and tried to locate where the septic tank was in the backyard that we had installed years earlier. I was looking in the right area, and when Julia came back, we did some more digging and found the right spot without too much trouble. At 5 p.m., we went down to the lake and closed the water valve. The water level went down 18 inches. We had dinner together and then Julia and Mark left at 7 p.m. to go back to the Bay Area.

The following day we found out that the lodge people were having trouble with the sewer system, so Frank and I went up to locate where that septic tank was located. After some digging, we found it. The top of the tank had collapsed; so we called Joe, the man who installed it, to come and replace it. Later, we went back down to the lake to check on how much it had filled since five o'clock the night before, up to 4:30 p.m. this day. The water had risen 10 inches in just under 24 hours. Knowing this would now give Jerry and Julia some idea as to how long they could plan on the product called Reward to do its job on the weeds.

Later that day, Julia called and said they had trouble with the pickup just as they got to the airport in Willits on Monday night. They had been flying up when visiting the ranch for a long time, rather than driving. As a rule, they left the plane at Willits. The pickup was left at the airport so they would have a way to come and go to the ranch. If the weather was right, they would fly to Laytonville, and Sagehorn or Santos would go into town to pick them up. Before Frank and I left to go back home, I found someone in town to fix the lawnmower. In the meanwhile, the lake had risen three more inches in 24 hours.

Amazingly, we were still having trouble with water at Santos's; now it was in the road. We went up and found that the pipe crossing under the road was plugged up, so we opened it and that took care of the problem. Furthermore, at the hunting camp, the cement cover over the septic tank had caved in, so we would have to fix that as well. Come springtime, we may have to put in a whole new system there and at the lodge as well. As you can tell, we were having septic problems. Frank and I went fishing and caught two good-sized fish; one was 16 inches and 2 pounds; the other one was a little smaller. Later, we went out in the boat, and I caught another fish while Frank read. We had caught enough fish for our dinner.

Frank and Fred had a few words exchanged between them later that night. I don't remember now what it was over. Laurence called and said the road to the house was open, but it was very icy on Reward Street. The worst of the storm apparently was over, and we would be able to get home in the pickup. We would leave for home in the morning. On Thursday, Feb. 22, it was Washington's Birthday, and there was still snow on the north facing slopes. The weather warmed up to 74-degrees outside, and Mark's snowman was melting away fast.

Tom Barney remodels the Main House and lodge

IN 1989 TO 1990, Tom Barney, from Nevada City, and his crew worked on remodeling the Main House and the lodge. It took him and his crew several months, but they got it finished on schedule.

They started with the Main House; while they were doing this, they stayed at the lodge. They put a new rail on the wall going down the steps to the kitchen and all the windows got fixed. They washed down the house to remove moss and stained the outside. The tool shed was raised and got a new foundation; the south wall was re-shingled, along with the west wall and part of the north wall; new windows were put in and stained to match the house; and, new septic tanks were put in.

A summary of work done at the lodge includes: the outside north wall facing the hill repaired; a drain put in between the road and house; a new roof put on; upstairs windows fixed; kitchen and surrounding area repaired; and, new floor coverings in the kitchen and bathroom. The outside of the house was stained to match the Main House; the small outside building received a new foundation and was roofed and stained to match the lodge. The front porch addition at the lodge, put on by Jack, was removed and put back to its original size. The back porch was made smaller to original size; a new septic tank was put in; electricity and a telephone were put in both houses.

When repairing the Main House, Tom and his men stayed in the lodge. Frank and I didn't go up as often while they worked on the Main House.

On Feb. 14, 1990, Julia and Mark flew to Nevada City and picked us up, and we flew to Willits where the pickup was parked. We drove to the ranch to check on the work that had been done. It snowed again while we were there. We stayed for the day and flew back home that evening.

Drain the lake, kill the weeds

ON MARCH 9, 1990, Mark and Julia went to the ranch to drain the lakes so they could take care of the weeds in both lakes. The water was down four feet in the upper lake and five feet in the lower lake, but then it started to rain and continued raining the rest of the day, so they decided to abort the job and wait until April.

Mark went fishing and caught a 14-inch fish. Saturday afternoon, the temperature dropped from 40 degrees down to 30 degrees and it snowed for a few hours. The sky cleared in the evening and a full moon came out, and what a sight! So they went walking, and it was like daylight outside, with the reflection of the moon on the snow. It rained again Sunday, so not much work could be done, except that Mark worked on his fence project and Julia pulled thistles in the yard in the rain. They also started on a jigsaw puzzle that Julia gave to me last Christmas.

Julia talked with Jerry to reschedule the lake job for April. She spoke with Frank Sagehorn, and he wanted a three-year lease. She also talked to Calvin Harwood and David Ferrell about the logging, and Calvin would complete the plan for the fir and clean up. David would wait until Julia talked to Fred Edler about the burls. It was sort of a busy but slow weekend. Three trees fell across the main road; Jerry saw them first and cleared the road before Julia even knew about it. Nice!

Julia's accident; discovery of a pot farm

AS PLANNED, JERRY AND his crew came up in April to help Julia take care of the weeds that were in the lakes. And that's how she celebrated her 48th birthday on April 10, 1990.

During their trip to the ranch, Julia had a run-in with a tree, which ended up leaving some bad scars on her back. She and Mark were out riding in an all-terrain vehicle, going over to the northeast line. While trying to climb up a steep hill, the ATV wasn't able to make it and fell backwards onto a tree, sandwiching Julia back up against the tree. Luckily, no one was seriously injured. Between that and Pockets, her horse, she's gotten some bad black-and-blue scars on her back and rear end. I hope nothing else like that happens to her!

Mark and Julia were going up to the northeast corner of the ranch to check on the property line. They discovered that someone had apparently been growing marijuana on the ranch under the trees. Mark and Julia accidentally found it and wanted to be sure it was what they thought it was, so they called the sheriff's department. Later, we all went up to check out the plants. Their cultivators really had a fancy way of growing them, including fixing a small dam to collect water for the drip system that went to each plant. The plants were in black pots so they could not be seen very well from a distance. Everything was well camouflaged so it couldn't be seen from the air. It was even hard to see the farm if you were walking right up to it.

Julia notified the sheriff's department and told them they could fly over the ranch at any time to check things out and catch the growers. I think they used a helicopter, for I remember seeing deputies in a chopper many times going over the ranch after that. Julia certainly did not want to be caught with marijuana growing on her ranch. She opened the road in this area and that stopped the problem.

In the late 1980s, Frank and I saw some pot growing on the northwest corner up past the Manchester Place. I thought it was wild tomatoes growing there. In time, we didn't see it anymore. Whoever was growing marijuana decided to quit growing it. We asked Jack to check on it whenever he was up in that area. He figured whoever was growing it would come in off the highway and climb over the fence to get to it. During our time, we also saw lots of it growing on the banks of the Eel River. In later years, we have not seen any.

A full weekend at the ranch

IN LATE APRIL, THE four of us were at the ranch for the weekend. Julia took care of some ranch business and met with Homer. It turned out to be a full weekend. We got David to bring in his backhoe to work on putting in new septic tanks at the Main House. We had

previously dug down and found three lids, so he knew where to put the new tanks. He finished making the boxes to cover them, and he also put together large culverts to fit over the holes so we could find them more easily when they needed to be pumped out in the future.

Frank locating the septic tank   Frank finds the lid to the septic tank

David also took care of some jobs that needed to be done at the trailer and the lodge so we would be done with septic troubles for another 10 to 20 years, we hoped. We took pictures of where they are located so we can easily find the holes again when we need to. The pictures are kept at the ranch in the roll-top desk.

I re-stained and oiled everything in the dining room and put a second coat of Watco oil on the inside of the china cabinet, so we could put the dishes back in the morning. This would allow Mary to come in and put a third coat of oil on the walls and ceiling in this room.

The newly oiled china cabinet
filled with dishes from O.C.S.C.

Wheel comes off the pickup

ON MEMORIAL DAY WEEKEND at the ranch, Julia and Mark and the Gralys—Jane, Tom, Joseph and Marcus—were up at the ranch for the weekend. Frank and I came up on Sunday and it rained all the way to the ranch. Monday, the Gralys left about noontime to go home. The four of us that remained spent some time cutting branches off the trees that were hanging over the central road.

The weather turned nice, so Julia and Mark took off before dinner for Willits, hoping to fly home. My niece, Barbara, and her daughter, Cheryl, came in from their trip to Eureka. They went to visit my sister LaVena, who'd had a stroke on May 17. LaVena was coming along all right, but she was in a convalescent hospital needing to learn to talk and to use her body on her entire right side. She could still see, hear, and understand what was said to her most of the time, but she couldn't talk.

Frank and I went up to Eureka in the pickup to see her, and on our way there, the right front wheel and tire came off the pickup and went sailing up the road ahead of us on the right-hand side of the road. Luckily for us, it was at Myers Junction. Frank walked down a hill into a town and got help putting it back on. Earlier, he'd had a flat tire at the ranch and fixed it, but I guess he didn't have the lugs on tight enough. It was a good thing that this did not happen while driving around the ranch, we really would have been out of luck! We continued on our trip to Eureka and saw LaVena. She was still in the convalescent hospital and still couldn't talk, but she could understand what we were saying. Later we saw Les, Jack, Bev, and their families.

We stayed in Eureka for two days, and then went home to Nevada City by way of Blue Lake, Weaverville, Redding, and Marysville. There was cold weather the entire way.

Cost of the oil job

HERE IS THE COST of the oil job for the damage done by the frozen pipes to the Main House at the ranch: Mary Sagehorn's labor at $10 an hour and materials came to $4,306.50. It took 19 gallons of Watco oil. The water damage was $6,283.50. Julia's materials and labor were $1,162.50, and Frank's totaled $1,265.00. This does not include our labor and the cost to drive up and take care of the problem, nor all the other things that went with it.

But by now, it was all over with, and it did help the wood on the inside of the house and made it look much nicer. We chalked it up as part of owning the ranch. As written earlier, this is a job that will need to be done in another 20 years.

Work on the upper lake

JULIA AND MARK WERE at the ranch for a few days in early July 1990 to take care of some business and get some work done on the upper lake. They had David put new planks down on the dock and had him put in a stepladder extending down to and below the water line. Frank and I joined them and helped put new planks on the bridge down in the canyon that had to be crossed to come up $65 Road. We weren't able to get the boards all nailed down because we ran out of long nails. Later, we picked blackcaps and caught some fish; Julia and Mark took some home with them. After dinner, they left for home, and I froze what was left of the blackcaps for Mark to make mixed drinks with.

We drove to the ranch in the big Mercedes, for we planned to go up to Eureka again to see LaVena. We left on Monday and saw her later that day. LaVena was doing much better than when I saw her earlier. I sat in on one of her lessons on how to count money. This "lesson" made her mad; it was obvious that she knew how to count money, she just couldn't tell them, so she refused to play with the money. She could walk and throw beanbags with little trouble, and had fairly good balance. She had to eat with her left hand, and that was not too easy, for she was right-handed. Later we took Jack, Bev and Les out to dinner.

The next day, around 2:30 p.m., we left to go back to the ranch, and on our way we drove over the bridge to Ferndale. In all the years we have traveled up and down this road, this was our first time to go out of our way to see this area. It is really a delightful place to see and to spend some time at. There are lots of old homes with gingerbread works that have been restored, and the homes are painted in all kinds of different pastel colors. I can understand why people go there to have a little vacation. From there, we drove on to Benbow, where we had dinner, and then we went on to the ranch for the night.

On Wednesday, Frank and I lopped branches off the trees along the road going to the dump area; the chore took almost three hours. We went back to the house for lunch, and then to the lake where we caught some fish. One of the fish was two pounds, just the right size for dinner for the two of us. We also went to Laytonville to get some groceries and vegetables, but the items were in very short supply, so we didn't get any. This was a very hot day, 90 degrees in the shade. Frank mowed while I got dinner prepared and I vacuumed the carpet and rugs. Later, we played cards for a while, and then went to bed.

The next day, Thursday, we continued to lop trees. We worked at it for about five hours. We piled the branches along the side of the road so we could burn them in the winter months. That night, while Frank and I were playing Hand and Foot, around 11 p.m. Julia and Mark showed up. They bought food in Willits, so we put the food away and all went to bed.

Friday was another hot day. We mowed the rest of the grass around the house. Both lawnmowers broke down, as well as the weed eater. That's what happens when you bring your castoff stuff down to the ranch and buy new ones for home. The four of us continued to lop branches along the roads for another four hours or so. We then stopped to get some lunch and went down to the lake to cool off, fish, relax, swim, and play cards together.

On Saturday, Dave came over to finish fixing the ladder down at the upper lake, and he put more long spikes in the planks to the bridge that is down in the canyon. He then came up $65 Road to put in more culverts. While he was doing that, we drove to the main gate and lopped limbs off the trees all the way up to where we were working on Thursday. The road grader man came in and did some more work on the roads and put in water breaks as he went. This was a hot, hot seven-hour day for all of us, and I was tired, so we relaxed by picking blackberries. From there, the four of us went down to the lake to swim, and while we were playing cards, I caught six nice-sized fish. I caught one fish that broke the line and got away, and then I caught a big one, so we had plenty for dinner. It was so hot all night that it was difficult to sleep.

I have mentioned that we do not have air conditioning at the ranch. I think I have forgotten to add that we do not have TV, and radio reception is very poor, so we play cards, read, put puzzles together, go for walks, swim, and so on, to pass the time when we are not doing whatever it takes to keep this place going.

Sunday morning was great because a nice breeze came up the canyon around 9 a.m., so it was going to be a nice day. A big family came in to the lodge that morning and was soon having one great time. When we were out sitting on the porch or on the swing, we could hear them. They were there for a week and there was no caretaker on duty. They would no doubt be all over the ranch, for we were leaving that day and they would have the place to themselves.

Mary and Santos decided to leave the ranch. I don't know why for sure, but I know they really had a lot of water problems while they were there. If they left for that reason, I can't blame them. They may have left though because it was the end of their contract with the hunting group. The glad bulbs that Mary planted in front of the trailer bloomed shortly after they left.

Fifth-generation Clarke family members visit

THOMAS CLARKE'S TWO great-great-great granddaughters and their husbands came to visit the ranch this day in 1990. Their names were Kathy (Taylor) and her husband, Neil Quakemeyer, of Security, Colorado; and Jeana (Taylor) and her husband, Jerry Schorr, of Mission Viejo, California. Kathy told me who they were and her history. They were the fifth generation of Clarkes, and the daughters of Marge (Clarke) Taylor, who is the third daughter of Frank Clarke. Frank Clarke was the son of Joe Clarke, born in 1853, and Joe's wife, Annie. Joe was the son of the original Thomas Clarke people who bought the ranch sometime around 1867; Joe left the ranch to his children. Joe and Annie's six children were Cecile, who was born in 1885, Frank, Bill, Annie, Bell, and May.

Frank Clarke and his family continued to live in the Upper House that his dad, Joe, helped him build after he married Catherine. Some 30 years later, Frank's daughter, Marge, and her six children came to stay with them until he died in 1958 and the ranch was sold. It was Marge's two girls who came to visit us; they also had young children. The two girls did not say anything about their father.

Frank and I were at the ranch at the time, but he was not around when they came, so I met the girls. They came to Laytonville hoping they could find Frank Sagehorn, whom they remembered as children. They were able to find him. They asked him if he knew who owned the ranch, and if they could come and see it. He said yes, and he took them to the ranch and let them in at the gate. He found me and introduced them to me, and then he left to do some work on his cattle. I had a very nice chat with them, and they told me a little bit about themselves.

As little children, they lived in the lodge (the Upper House). They told me how they would climb out the window above the steps that came from the back bedroom area to a small landing that went to the two bedrooms upstairs that are like dorm rooms. The window could be opened, and they would climb out through it and be on top of the back porch roof; from there, they could get down to the porch and onto the ground without anyone hearing them, or knowing where they were. The window also helped put circulation into the upstairs bedrooms. They said that the hallway steps made too much noise. Their grandfather, Frank Clarke, had the bedroom next to the hallway and would complain about the noise. They did not mention anything about a grandmother.

They explained to me that the lower bedrooms (which are on the main floor) and the one near the living room was their mother, Marge's bedroom. She was Frank Clarke's daughter and in the fourth generation of Clarkes. The bedroom was no doubt for many years Frank and Catherine's bedroom, after the house was built in 1917 (I maybe be off a few years). The middle room was for the small children, and in his old age, Frank Clarke had the end bedroom next to the bathroom and stairs that went to the upstairs; the rest of the children slept upstairs.

They said that the middle bedroom was called the "spider room," and I told them it still had spiders in it. They said that they lived at the ranch until their grandfather, Frank Clarke, passed away. They agreed this was about 1958 or when the ranch was sold to the Union Lumber Company. This is the company we bought the ranch from in 1967 — 100 years after the Clarkes arrived and settled down at the ranch.

I asked them if they knew the name of the creek that runs between the two houses and down by the shack; they said no, but they called it Maple Creek after the big maple tree that was there. This happens to be the tree Frank hung the pig from. However, that "maple" tree is really an oak tree and there are two of them.

They said Cecile Clarke lived in the Main House, and the house had been built much earlier than the Upper House. Therefore, our date for the Main House is much older, and it was built by Thomas and his son Joe for Joe's family around 1910. It was in this same area that Thomas built his first home for his family in 1868. Cecile never married and she ended up with the house that Thomas and Joe built. As mentioned earlier in this book, Cecile was a schoolteacher in Eureka. She ended up spending the last few years of her life at her home in Eureka.

They said that their mother, Marge Clarke Taylor's garden was in the place where we have the upper lake and near a bay that extended out from the lake (which we later removed). The water for her garden came from a spring above it, and this same spring feeds into the upper lake today. This spring produces a lot of good clear, cold water, and it has watercress that grows there year-round. Marge Clarke Taylor also had a cherry and a walnut tree in this area, and a little farther down are apples, fig, pear, and plum trees that are near another spring below which feeds into the lower lake. Both springs produce a lot of water and run year round.

"Miss Clarke," as they called her, never allowed the girls in any room other than the kitchen in the Main House. They did not know what the rest of the house looked like. The girls showed very little respect for Cecile Clarke, nor were they interested in seeing the house. They only wanted to see the Upper House, and they really went through it.

They said that their mother didn't want to see the ranch, for she had been told that the houses were all rundown and in ruins, and that all the timber was cut. The girls told me they were elated to see the Upper House in better shape than they remembered it, and that the timber was still growing on the property.

We talked outside at the Upper House, standing on the road that is below the porch. As we spoke, I saw several dried amaryllis bulbs growing on the hillside by my feet. Two of the bulbs were easy to remove from the dirt, so I reached down and pulled them off the clumps they were in, and gave one to each girl for them to plant in their yard right away so that they might bloom in the fall. I hoped it would serve as a good memory, in years to come, from their childhood life at the Clarke Ranch.

My guess is that Kathy was about 14 and Jeana was about 6 when their grandfather died in 1958. Therefore, Kathy would have a good memory of what it was like in her youth.

It was Catherine or her daughter, Marge Clarke Taylor's, grape jam that we were eating that week when the girls came to see their home. I found the jam in the basement of the Upper House, in a far corner and out of sight, when we were there cleaning it out. When I saw anything like that, I would save it and use it, for I knew that anything canned and kept cool would be good as long as it wasn't opened or exposed to heat or light. I did the same thing at the Main House with some of the items I found in the cellar. None of the jams had turned to sugar in all those years. The basement at the Upper House was well built and had a cement floor, along with shelves and good storage places. It was and still is used to this day as a working place where somebody can work on his or her tools, repair things, and store wood. The basement in the Main House is of dirt and is not a functional place. Nevertheless, it is good for storing winter and summer foods and canned foods. It stays cool the year round, however we do not use this cellar.

I have to admit I was surprised that Bev did not find the jam in the storage area, for she did a lot of canning when she was staying there. She canned a lot of grape jam from the grapes that she got from the Manchester place, and no doubt, that is where Marge got hers, too.

When Jack and Bev moved into the Upper House, they found down in the basement a large old-looking crate that had never been opened. When we opened it, there was a large icebox about 4 feet tall and wide, and two feet deep. There were two cupboard doors on it. One side was big enough to hold a 12-by-24-inch block of ice, and the other cupboard had shelves to hold food that could be kept cold. The outside of the cabinet, I think, was made of oak and had a high gloss finish on it. This "old-time refrigerator" would be from the period of about 1934–35, and we found it in 1977. Frank Clarke no doubt ordered it from a catalogue, and before the shipment arrived, electricity became available. He had electricity brought into the ranch and had it put into all the buildings including the houses. When the icebox arrived, it no doubt was put down in a far corner of the basement in the Upper House and forgotten. When the family moved out in 1958, the icebox got left behind. Maybe they didn't even know what it was. Because it had never left the shipping box that it came in and had never been exposed to air or light, the wood was still like new when we opened the crate. Laurence and Gloria took it home and used it as a piece of furniture in their game room downstairs.

The girls told me that Frank Clarke had three sisters, but there were really four: Miss Cecile, Annie, Bell, and May Clarke (Winchester). There were also two boys, Frank and Bill. I got the feeling they didn't really know much about the rest of the family. In all the years at the ranch, I have never heard the name of Bill or Annie mentioned. I've heard the name Bell at times, so maybe they moved away or died at a young age. The girls talked more about their mother, Marge Clarke Taylor, and about themselves. Kathy was 46, married to Neil; Jeana was 38, married to Jerry. Each girl had a child. The men more or less stayed in the background and let the girls do the talking, and it was Kathy who did most of the talking.

The date of their visit was Wednesday, July 11, 1990. I took down notes and hope I got it all straight. They gave me their addresses and telephone numbers. A few months after their visit to the ranch, Julia and I went up to clean the attic that's off and to the side of the upstairs bedrooms. We were getting things ready for Tom to do some repair work on the windows and the roof that looks down toward the Main House. I found a letter in the far northwest corner of the attic with other things, and I thought it was to their mother Marge, from her mother Catherine, so I mailed it to Kathy. She called me and thanked me for sending it. She told me the story, but I have forgotten what she said, and I have not heard from them since, nor did I read the letter I sent her. Then in 1993, I received a letter from Betty Sumrall, Frank Clarke's oldest daughter, and his youngest daughter, Virginia Harrington, thanking me for forwarding the letter to Kathy. Kathy had mailed it to her mother Marge, who forwarded it to Betty, who then mailed it to Virginia, whom the letter was originally written to. The letter was written some 66 years earlier, so she said it was a real gem for them to get it.

I understand that none of Frank's daughters married farmers. In addition, all of his children went to high school in Berkeley, California. His wife, Catherine, would rent a house for them to live in, and they came home for vacations. Frank graduated from Cal in 1911, and got a Master's Degree in Parasitology (the study of parasites and their hosts). Joe's son Bill was killed in World War II. She said she remembers the Upper House was built in 1911, the year her dad got his degree, so now we know the year the houses were really built. The Main House was built somewhere around 1900 to 1905, and not in 1917 or 1920 as others have said.

The Ninety-Nines spend the weekend

The 99's enjoying dinner at the ranch with Mark's workshop in the background

IN LATE JULY 1990, Julia had her group of Ninety-Nines at the ranch for the weekend. Among them were Cathy, Jeff, Dixie, Rosario, and another LaVonne. They all had a good time and made notes in the guestbook. They mentioned great hospitality, great time, great scenery, great food, great ranch, and great company, and that the weather was good. The rest I'll leave up to your imagination.

Julia and Mark are good at taking care of their guests, and they enjoy showing everyone a good time. What they may lack in entertainment, the ranch will make up for on its own. One thing is for sure, if you don't have a good time at the ranch, it is more or less your own fault or lack of imagination.

Enjoying fine wine and dinner as the sun sets

As we arrived at the gate entrance on Aug. 4, we found someone had left a duffel bag at the ranch gate. A short time later, Mark and Julia came by, and Mark called the police to see if it had been reported as missing, but no luck. We thought it might belong to one of the hunters, but no one ever claimed it. What happened to it? I don't know. We came to the ranch to be there for the museum people from Eureka who were coming to see the ranch the following day. We wanted to make sure the roads and everything were all right. I find it strange that they were to arrive right after the Clarke girls were there.

Visit from museum people

ON AUG. 5, 1990, Raymond W. Willman from the Clarke Memorial Museum in Eureka came to the ranch, and he brought a group of people in a full-size charter bus. This was the first time the museum group had visited the ranch. The trip celebrated the museum's 30th anniversary. They called themselves the "Ranch Pilgrimage." It was a very nice day, on the warm side, and around 1 p.m. when the bus got to the narrow dirt road that winds up to the Main House. It was something to see watching that big bus on the ranch roads coming down to the house. They left Eureka early that day and were tired when they arrived. When they got to the gate and saw the bridge that they needed to cross, I'm sure they had second thoughts. Three narrow bridges need to be crossed to get to the Main House.

The bus entering the gate coming down to the Main House

The bus could not get to the Main House on the main road, but Julia knew that they could make it by going down to the trailer and coming down that way. When they got to the trailer, some of the passengers got out and walked the rest of the way to the house. Julia and I were at the gate to greet them, and she rode down with them in the bus while I came back in the car ahead of them. One of the first things they asked was, "where is the bathroom?" And luck had it that there were two. While they waited their turns, they signed the guestbook. It took two pages by the time each signed it; there were about 40 of them.

The group of visitors brought their lunch with them and were ready to eat when they got there. We had tables and benches set up for them so they could picnic out in the yard. By the time they were through with their lunch and did a lot of chatting, it was 3 p.m. and they still had not seen the house. The Yukoms, who were part of the group, arrived earlier; they used to live in the Laytonville area and knew the Clarke family when they were still living on the ranch. Mr. Yukom was telling them some of the history that he remembered from back when he was a young fella. The museum people had never been to the ranch, even those who knew "Miss Clarke" (as they called her) for many years. "Miss Clarke" not only had the Clarke Museum, she was also well known as a schoolteacher for many years in the Eureka area. I have been told she was very strict. I understand she was also the schoolteacher to my sister-in-law Bev. Now, they were ready to see the house that "Miss Clarke" was raised in and later lived in as an adult.

The bus made it down the narrow road
to the Main House, which was a surprise

Julia showed them around in groups of six so they could all see and hear her. She took them upstairs as well as downstairs, and I think she even showed them the attic. She pointed out the two big sliding doors that separate the living room from the dining room and parlor room, and how smoothly they slide after all these years. She also showed how wide the panels were on each door and how each were made of one piece of redwood board. The windows have the same type of glass as the doors, but new pulley cords had been installed to the weights to make the windows move more easily. The glass windows still have the rippling and wavy look to them. The original linoleum is still on the dining room floor, and there is similar linoleum on the bathroom floor upstairs. We keep that covered with a make-do carpet to protect it from getting wet.

Julia showed them the rooms where there are holes in the walls. The holes are where the pipes from the potbelly wood heater went that helped heat the rooms; the holes are now covered with decorative lids. She also explained to them how the rest of the upstairs rooms over the parlor and back bedroom were heated from the rooms that had heat, and from the heat that came up from the front and backstairs.

The director of the museum, Raymond Willman, said it was a thrilling experience to visit the ranch and to see where the founder of the museum was born in 1885. He said the day's experience fulfilled a dream he'd had since 1988. The ranch was even more wonderful than he imagined. He presented Julia with a framed picture of the ranch from the museum collection. In his own research he established that the Main House was built about 1911–1914, and the lodge in 1925. However, the Taylor girls said they thought the lodge (Upper House) was built in 1920, and on this score, I am inclined to believe them. (We have since learned that the Main House was built in 1900–1905, and the Upper House was built in 1911, as I've pointed out earlier.) Mr. Willman was going by the lumber in the walls and how the planks were applied, along with the cut, finish, and pattern of the wood, and the style of the houses. They were surprised to see it in

Frank, Mark, me, and Julia
saying goodbye to the Clarke group

such good shape. They were all having such a good time. It was soon 5 p.m., and they had not even gotten to see the Upper House—time ran out on them. They had the four of us stand on the porch to take a picture, and then Julia rode with them on the charter bus back to the main gate. I left ahead of them to open the gate so the bus would not have to stop until they were over the bridge, through the gate and past it. Julia thanked them for their interest, and then got out and said her goodbyes and locked the gate. We drove back to the ranch together.

Raymond was the last person to go through the house with Julia, and she taped what he had to say about the "Grand Lady's House." Julia was sure glad she had gotten the road graded and all the lopping of the trees done beforehand, otherwise the bus may not have made it down to the house. After they left, we had a quick dinner, packed, and left for our homes at the same time.

We hit traffic between Laytonville and Willits, and it ended up taking us an extra hour to get home. At one point, we were held up for 20 minutes. In all our years of traveling this part of the road, this had never happened to us before. Julia and Mark were six cars behind us when we had to wait. She got out and ran up to our car to have a chat about all the things that had happened. When we finally started moving, and once we reached the turnoff to the airport they would be taking, we waved goodbye to them; Julia and Mark would be flying home. It was a long trip home that night for Frank and me.

A new patrolman

ON LABOR DAY WEEKEND, Frank and I left home to go to the ranch. On our way there, we encountered a lot of traffic on Highway 20 heading west to Highway 101, and it got worse at Willits. It was almost impossible to get gas—so many motorcycles—and we found out that there was some kind of a jamboree going on in Garberville. We finally got to the ranch and settled in for the night.

On Sunday, we met with Wilderness Unlimited and the new patrolman, Ken. We drove around the ranch with him and met his wife, Josephine. By this time, the water problem at the pink trailer had finally been solved. Later, Frank and I went picking pears at the pear orchard, but they were not quite ripe—maybe they would be next week. We went fishing and caught three trout and played Hand and Foot down at the lake. When the weather is hot and there is no breeze, it is nice to play cards at the lake. The lodge had two nice families in from Sacramento and Santa Rosa for the week.

On Monday, we cut dead branches off the walnut tree in front of the house for a couple of hours and cleaned up the yard. Then we showered and took a ride to Fort Bragg for the rest of the day and went over to Mendocino. It was a real nice day and we had a nice dinner along the waterfront in Mendocino. We enjoyed a beautiful sunset over the Pacific Ocean on our way back to the ranch. It's 17 miles from the ranch to Highway 1. The road is no longer gravel, but half of it is oiled and the other half is paved; it takes 30 minutes to drive it. It's one hour from the ranch to Fort Bragg. This is a trip we do not take often, even though we are so close by. There are so many things that have to be done at the ranch, along with enjoying just being there, that we don't go out much when we are there. When we got back to the ranch, we ended up playing cards in the evening.

On Tuesday, we brought in two loads of firewood. Someone by the name of Tom came by to check on stumps, so we waited for him to come back from doing his thing. Around 10:30 a.m., Julia called from Washington State, from one of the islands, and said she would leave for home in the morning. Frank and I also planned to leave for home in the morning as well.

More remodeling

JULIA HAD A GREAT deal more remodeling work done on the ranch in January and February of 1991. The job included finishing up the work that was being done on the Main House. Julia's cousin, Robert Faustino, did the work and continued additional remodeling projects off and on from January into November.

A new tractor for the ranch

ON APRIL 26, 1991, Julia and Mark bought a small Kubota 1630 tractor with extra parts to do all kinds of little jobs on the ranch. She and Mark had a ball with this "new toy" and

Julia and her new machine

quickly found many uses for their new machine. They used it to mow the grass down in a hurry, dig up dirt and rocks and haul it away to other places, as well as haul hay, manure for the iris bed, and wood for the fireplaces. Somewhere along the way, I'm sure Mark became fed up with cutting an acre of grass with lawnmowers that kept breaking down. I call the tractor his "toy," but Julia drives it as much as he does. It was a real time saver in helping us get ready for the next upcoming reunion.

With Mark's help, Julia has really improved the ranch since she has owned it. She has put a lot of effort into remodeling the houses and barns. This keeps Mark on the go, but I think he likes it. I hope she can hold out, for I know this ranch is a lot of work.

Me stacking hay

Around midnight, this "Old Lady" was really on a roll, but no damage was done; we had an earthquake of 6.5 on the Richter scale. It caused damage in the town of Scotia, where a fire burned down the shopping center. Eureka, Arcata, and Ferndale got the brunt of it. Both Jack's place and LaVena's place in the Eureka area had some damage to the houses, as well as broken dishes. The quake also cracked and raised the cement patio in Jack's backyard. The following day we left for home.

In June 1991, we went back to the ranch to clean up all the grass that had grown a foot or so tall, and to work on getting the grounds ready for the family reunion. Mark handedly

Fixing up the fence by the Main House

mowed the grass down with his toy. Their friends, the Morsheads, from the Bay area came up. Kathy, Julia, and I worked using rakes and pitchforks to gather up the cut grass into piles for it to be put into the wheelbarrow for Frank to take to the compost pile behind the shed. Jeff and Mark had to make it a bigger compost site to hold all the stuff we were putting into it. Mark also had the men working on the picket fence that surrounds two sides of the house. We got everything done that we could ahead of time, before the reunion.

Julia's first Kruger–Evenson reunion, 1991

1991 Kruger–Evenson reunion, group photo

FROM July 24–29, 1991, Julia had her first Kruger–Evenson family reunion, and 45 family members attended. She has taken charge of the reunions now that she is the owner of the Clarke Ranch; I helped her in every way I could.

The planning was the same as when I did it, so I will leave out all those details.

That year Ella and her husband, Allen Harris, came to the reunion; they are on the Evenson side. Ella was my brother Jim's second wife until he died, and she was the mother of his son, Raymond, and his daughter, Jennifer, along with all the other Evensons. LaVena had recently suffered her stroke, but she was there. Of course, she had changed. She could no longer talk and she used sign language whenever she could. She and Les stayed at a motel in town; the rest of her family and grandchildren were at the lodge, as were some of Helena's. By this time, the pink trailer was rented to the hunters. Nick's, and Jack's, and all of our family, except Stephanie and her family, were there. Julia did a great job, but found out that it was, indeed, a lot of work.

At this time, Julia was having trouble with her hearing in her right ear. She wondered what was going on in her head, and she was concerned whether or not she would have the problem the rest of her life.

Julia got a lot of willing help from many people at the reunion, but they were not quite sure what she wanted done when it came to the cleanup job, such as putting away the clean dishes. I think the reason is they had gotten used to doing it for me. Now, it was Julia's ranch, and they wanted to do things the way she wanted them done. I saw what was going on, so I said, "Give everything to me, and I'll put it away." By the end of the reunion, it was going smoothly, and everyone was getting used to doing it her way. All the people that attended the reunion had a good time, and we took the usual family pictures on the last evening. This is always a great hit. As mentioned earlier, everyone likes to look at the pictures and compare them from year to year to see how each person has grown and changed, or how silly they were.

Barbara, Kristin, Mark, and Laurence
getting meat off the barbecue

A few of the relatives said they came up for a vacation at the ranch and really didn't want to do a lot of work, but in the end, they also helped out. I got this when I was doing it, and I had a hard time telling them that it really is a lot of work putting on a reunion of this size. I wondered who they thought was going to do all the work for so many people. Fortunately, this is the exception. Most people will help do anything you ask them to do. To continue the reunions, everybody will have to help. It is hard for them to realize that we do not live there all the time, and it is a good deal of work for us to get the place ready. Furthermore, when it is over, everything has to be put away on the last day. We usually leave for home right after everybody else has left on the last day. The last thing we do as we leave is to change the lock numbers at the gate.

This reunion was an eye-opener for Julia. I had done everything at the previous gatherings, and she did not realize how much work went into putting one on until she did it herself. When the reunion was over, it made her think that if the reunions were to continue, she would have to get help from other family members.

Ending Julia's successful family reunion

Jim, Kitty, Gloria, Frank, Laurence, Brad, and Mark
enjoying the feast

Planting irises

The Main House with me planting irises next to the work shed

ON OCT. 1, 1991, we came up to the ranch for a few days, and I bought a variety of nice irises to plant in the area by the shed and the old grapevine. Mark brought up a big scoop of horse manure from the horse shed down by the lake in his new toy tractor and put it on the ground; we spaded it in and then planted the irises. It is really a sight to see in the spring when they are in bloom — they stand on tall stems and have big flowers in all colors, and they come back every year.

Julia and I put in a drain foundation made of flat stones between the flowerbed and the shed, and to my surprise, it is still in good shape. No gophers have raised it up or filled it with dirt. We also planted some grass seed in the bare spots that were created by the remodeling projects in 1990–91; but it didn't take.

Robert got back to work on the kitchen floor that Julia was having him do. Over a period of time, he sanded down the floor and reset nails, puttied the nail holes, filled in cracks, and then let it dry for several days, perhaps even longer. Before we left, we moved the wood and electric stove and refrigerator to the outside porch, so he could do a good job on the floor. He sanded the floor again, then stained it and put on a good sealer. When the floor was dry, he waxed it. He did a really good job over a period of time. This is the Douglas fir floor that Frank and I ruined when cleaning up after the 1989 water damage in the kitchen. Nothing had been done to the floor until now.

Julia's recovery from her acoustic neuroma surgery

DURING THIS TIME, JULIA was recovering from her acoustic neuroma surgery she had done Oct. 13, 1991. Mark came to the ranch by himself every other weekend to check things out for Julia. On the weekends Mark was at the ranch, I stayed with Julia at her place. In addition to making sure everything was okay at the ranch, Mark's weekend trips also gave him a break from Julia, who was very sick at the time, and provided him a chance for some much needed relaxation.

On the weekends Mark stayed with her, I went home to Frank. It was during the time Julia was recovering from her surgery that I came to inwardly accept Mark as part of the family. Because of Julia's recovery, it turned out to be some time before the four of us we were able to get back to the ranch.

346

Memorial Day Weekend, 1992

The Upper House

JULIA AND MARK WERE up at the ranch for the Memorial Day Weekend in 1992 with Julia's friends the Gralys, and the Greenes and their children. Julia has known these people for many years; they are from the Mill Valley area. It was a wonderful holiday for the kids, and the adults had a great time as well.

On June 6, Frank and I went to the ranch to help Julia and Mark get ready for the upcoming Amaral reunion. It was a clear and warm day. Julia took pictures of us around the ranch house and lodge. The place looked really nice after all the staining that was done to the buildings. The lodge was full of hunters for the holiday, and they are also in some of the pictures. During this time, Julia was working on getting someone interested in cutting some of her timber on the ranch.

The Main House

Frank sitting on the hay rake
enjoying a relaxing afternoon

On one of their trips to the ranch around this time, Mark and Julia had a little extra energy and decided to bring down the old hay rake that was left under the trees when last used opposite the trailer area by the Clarkes. This had to have been in the early 1950s at the latest. There is a lot of open space in this area where grass can grow, and it's just as you make the turn to come down the road toward the ranch house. Mark and Julia removed all the brush and shrubs that had accumulated around the area and they pulled the hay rake down at least a quarter-mile to the ranch house yard, where it sits today under the American flag that Frank puts up whenever some of us are there.

Julia's first Amaral reunion, 1992

Julia hosting Frank's family at the ranch

JULIA WAS BUSY GETTING things ready for her first Amaral family reunion scheduled to be held at the ranch July 8–14, 1992. She, Frank, and I had gone up a day early to get the place ready. The next day, Laurence, Gloria, Frank's sister and her husband, Marie and Manuel, their daughter Anna Marie, her husband Ron, and their two children, Amber and Jordan, arrived. While they were there, we got a phone call from Mark saying he had just passed his flying test and he would soon be on his way to join us. So we got our heads together and made a big sign to congratulate him on "Happy Flying." We hung it above the front door so he could see it when he came down the road to the house. One of the things he said after he got there was that I must have said the Rosary for him, because he should not have passed it. We were all glad that he passed, and now we knew that Julia would have someone able to fly the plane with her. This was important because she was having a lot of trouble with her balance and hearing after her surgery.

Manuel, Anna Marie, Ron, Jordan, me, Amber, Frank, Gloria, Marie, and Laurence ready to congratulate Mark.

Later Frank's sister-in-law Edna and her husband Ed, her daughter Carol and her husband Ken, with her three children, twins Debbie and Donna, and Donna's two children, and Chris with his wife Lisa, Edna's son Milton, and his wife Meme, all came. Frank's sister-in-law Marie and her boys were planning to attend, but she got sick and they were unable to come. The weather was good the whole time.

Me and Frank with our gift

We spent time down at the lake; some fished, some went swimming, and we all visited with one another. With the two little ones, we were busy keeping an eye on them at the lake. Some went for rides around the ranch; some enjoyed walking. Because it was such a small group, we later made ice cream; it was not too much work, nor as big of a production. In the evening, we older people played hearts, while the younger generation visited. Marie and Manuel gave Frank and me our 50th anniversary gift; it was a plate and on it is an inscription wishing us a happy anniversary. They knew that they would not be seeing us on Thanksgiving, so they gave it to us at this time.

Meme, Milton and me making ice cream

Everyone enjoying the lake

Manuel and Marie Souza playing hearts with Edna and Ed Marchese

Donna and her two sons flew in from Philadelphia just to be at the reunion, which made it special for all of us. Donna was also expecting in another few months. A month later, they moved to France; her husband got a job overseas, near his family, and the baby was born in France. Everyone left Sunday afternoon except Marie and Manuel, who left Monday at the same time we left to go home. Thank you, Julia, for making all this possible. This sort of gathering has turned out never to have happened at the ranch again.

Julia was still having trouble with her head and balance issues from her surgery, which, along with having business problems with her Anaheim property, did make it hard for her to think straight. She decided to have her lawyer go ahead and serve the tenants notice to evict them from the property.

In summer 1992, Julia started logging on the northeast section of the ranch. This is the section where she was having trouble with the neighbors raising marijuana; by cutting the timber, she eliminated the problem altogether. This logging project was ongoing and lasted for several months. In cutting the timber, she made enough money to cover the cost of buying the ranch from us.

Fire in the bull pasture

ON OCT. 10, 1992, a fire started in the bull pasture and burned three to five acres of grass. It also went a little into the timber area. A helicopter came in along with California Division of Forestry personnel and responders from the local fire department. The copter made three borate drops and flew over the trailer to go to the lake to scoop up water and return to douse the flames. This was the second time a fire of this sort broke out at the ranch in all the years that we have had it. We know there was a big fire in the lower-west part of the ranch several years before we bought it, and another one on the upper-mid-eastern end of the ranch. You could see traces from the spots where the fires had been.

CDF Helicopter getting water at the upper lake

CDF airplane fighting the fire on the upper ridge

Fire is the one great danger we are all aware of when we are at the ranch. There is only one real way out with a car, a dirt road that you cannot drive fast on. If there were a fire in the center of the ranch near the houses, you would not be able to get out to the highway.

Roads inside the ranch going to where the fire was at

Mark's Christmas surprise of 1992

Christmas tree at the Clarke Ranch

MARK AND HIS PARENTS, his two sisters and their husbands, and his niece joined Julia, Frank, and me at the ranch for the Christmas holiday.

I shall try to tell this story as closely as I remember it. Frank and I spent a few days at a hotel in Larkspur to be with Julia and Mark, taking in all the Christmas singing and church activities for three days and evenings. We really enjoyed going to the different churches and seeing the different activities. We went to the cathedral for a Christmas evening performance; the place was packed with people. We went to St. Vincent de Paul Church and saw a Christmas concert the night before. We also did some shopping, and how could anyone pass up doing that at Christmastime in San Francisco?

I believe it was Dec. 24, the morning before Christmas Day, that we were having breakfast at Julia's condominium. Mark and his parents were there. After breakfast, Frank and I planned to leave early for the ranch; it was about 9 a.m. and Curt was to leave a little later. The pickup was loaded with things that I had brought from home, and now it was really loaded with things from Julia's place. These included all the things needed to finish decorating the tree that had been put up the week before by Julia and Mark. I had poinsettias to decorate the house, and all the gifts, along with most of the food that was needed to feed nine to fifteen people for three to four days. The pickup was loaded from top to bottom and from front to back. The last things put in were gifts and the flowers, and these would be the first things unloaded and taken into the house.

This wasn't a very good morning for me. I was sort of, as I recall, plugged up, and was having trouble with my head, which in those days was not unusual for me. I was a little late getting out the door by 9 a.m., but Frank and I did get on our way soon after that. As we were getting ready to leave, Julia gave me a last-minute grocery list of things to get in Willits, and Mark gave me some last minute instructions.

Now, you must remember, Mark had been around our family long enough to know our weaknesses. He said the first thing I was to do when I got to the ranch was to start a fire in the fireplace and kitchen stove, so the house could start to warm up while we were doing everything else. After that was done, I was to put the gifts under the tree and arrange the flowers around the house. Furthermore, I was to put together some decorations with greenery and red ribbons, and so on, on the entrance to the stairs and upstairs bathroom before I did anything else. In addition to this, dinner was to be at 5 p.m. My job was to have the table set and I needed to make a big salad for everyone. Mark's mother, Kay, would have the French bread. I agreed to all of this, for I had no problem with what he asked me to do. I knew we were going to have a crab feed that night, and Mark would be taking care of things on that end. (He didn't say it, but I guessed he wanted the house to look nice for the arrival of his parents, and the rest would take care of itself. Looking back, I realize that Mark had never said things like this to me before; I should have guessed something was going to happen.) The pickup was loaded accordingly to make it easy for me to do the things I was supposed to do when we got to the ranch.

When Frank and I got to Willits, we stopped at Safeway, bought the groceries that included the salad makings and the rest of the stuff on Julia's list, and put them in the front of the pickup with us. I knew Mary had cleaned the house, and that there would not be any need to have to wash windows, pick up neither dead mice nor dead flies, so that job was out of the way.

On our way to the ranch, I told Frank I did not want to unload the pickup until I got the fires started. Then, as we unloaded the pickup, I would take care of putting the gifts under the tree and place the flowers and decorations where they needed to go before doing anything else. Doing things this way would make it so I would not have to backtrack, nor would I have to go looking for things later. I told Frank if he backed the truck up to the front porch, I could take the things out as they were needed, which would make it much easier for me. We arrived at the ranch about 12:30 p.m.; it was a nice, crisp day.

Frank backed the pickup truck up to the front porch. While I was starting to get the fires ready, he unloaded the pickup and put everything into and around the hallway, parlor, living room, and steps. Once he was done, he had all the things that I needed to come out first completely out of reach. It was not possible for me to do the job as I had planned. All the groceries were sitting where I would get to them last, and all our luggage was in the hallway. There were a lot of heavy boxes and ice coolers; he was just trying to keep me from lifting them. I told him he could have done it, but only as I needed the items.

At this point, I was so mad I could not see nor think straight. Frank said it was warm and we didn't need a fire. In a way he was sort of right about that; however, I knew we would need the fire for later. I was trying to do exactly what Mark had asked me to do.

About this time, Mark's dad arrived. He put all his groceries and food containers in the middle of the kitchen for me to put away. This set the stage for Frank and me to have our first and only real fight in 50 years. Curt heard just enough that he left the house and went for a walk and didn't come back for a few hours. By this time, I was so tired and all I could see was all the work ahead of me that was not called for, and we still had not had lunch. You must remember that Frank thought he was helping me, and he could not see what he had done wrong. My problem was that he hadn't even paid attention or heard what I said to him on our way to the ranch. I finally got Curt's groceries put away.

Kay, Julie, and Chelsea came in about 5 p.m. By this time, Curt was back from his walk. I got everything done that needed to be done and was just starting to get the salad ready when Mark came in about 6 p.m. with his crab and all the makings. He came in by himself, and said, "Where is Julia? She was right ahead of me in her car." He was worried when he saw Julia wasn't at the ranch. At this point, I was worried too, for I thought she might have had trouble with her head. He told us he was going out to the gate to wait or go out looking for her. She should have arrived by this time, and it was now rather dark out. I think Mark went back to the gate, and Julia showed up about that time. We came to find out she was daydreaming and drove right past the turnoff at Laytonville. She was on her way to Garberville when she realized she didn't recognize where she was. At that point, she said she got scared for a few minutes, and then turned around and drove back to Laytonville and then to the gate, where I think Mark met her.

I had the table set for nine people, and sort of on the crowded side, but it would do for that night's dinner. Everyone had a drink or cocktail in front of the fireplace. At this hour, the fire felt good, and I was still in the kitchen finishing up my end of the meal. The living room was beautifully decorated, and along with the Christmas tree, it was very festive. We were all in good spirits and enjoying each other's company. We finally sat down to dinner. I can't remember if it was Curt or Julia who led us in prayer; then we went to it. Remember, this was a crab feed, and Mark is good at having all the goodies that go with it. We were all in the deep of eating crab, our hands and faces sticky with the juice. Frank and I were sitting at the end of the table, and Mark was to my right, closest to the kitchen. Kay and Curt were to Frank's left, so was Julie, and at the other end of the table was Chelsea. Coming up the right side of the table was Julia, Thomas, then Mark; this is how I remember it.

So we were in the deep of the crab, salad, and warm buttered French bread, when Mark got up and said he had something to tell us. He had proposed to Julia that morning before breakfast, and they'd decided to tell us at the ranch. It was very good timing, Mark. All I know is that Frank and I were speechless and lost for words. So were Curt and Kay, but they finally came alert, along with Julie, Mark's sister, and said, "Well, I guess it's in line to say congratulations." It took Frank and me longer to recover. However, we were glad that Mark had finally popped the question and that Julia had accepted. It was so far from my mind that they would be getting married. Needless to say, we were happy!

This explains why they had wanted us out of the house by 9 a.m. in Larkspur. And Julia getting lost in her driving—she said she was thinking all about it on her way to the ranch, and she just flew by Laytonville. She didn't want to tell us why she drove past the turnoff, so she came up with other excuses. This explains the last-minute details that Mark gave me; he really wanted everything perfect and in a holiday mood when he told us of the engagement. He did such an outstanding job! It was only *me* who got out of whack. We continued with the crab dinner, along with a lot of talking. By the time we had finished eating and it was time to clear the table, I had finally recovered and said, "Well, now that we are all family, you men can do the dishes." It was Curt who said, "That's a good idea," and the men got to it. You have to remember this is washing dishes the old-fashioned way; there is no dishwasher at the ranch. Curt remembered and knew how tired I was. I really wanted us to always be together as a family, and at the same time let Mark and his family have their times together, too.

So Frank and I had our first big fight—and to Frank it wasn't a fight; he had already forgotten about it, and, oh, yes, I got over it in a few hours—and Mark asking Julia to marry him, all on the same day, is rather a nice memory to have. That is why I remember the story so well.

Julia and Mark newly engaged

The next day, Curt, Kay, and Julie made a great turkey dinner. While they did that, I went fishing, and everyone else scattered over the ranch. Mark's other sister, Cheryl, and her husband, Mike, came to spend the rest of the holidays with us. Julia and Mark had a picture taken in front of the Christmas tree— their first picture after their announcement. The next day Julia took a picture of Frank and me by the tree.

Me and Frank standing by the first and only Christmas tree at the Clarke Ranch

After Mark's family left on Sunday the 26th, Frank and I, along with Julia and Mark, decided to burn piles of brush at the landing. That is one thing that Frank really enjoys doing—burning the piles and clearing up the area—and I enjoy doing it because I get warm. This is an ongoing project every year, and it is done in the winter months, usually when it's raining or has snowed, to keep the fire in check. Piling brush is a continual project, and it will be as long as we own the ranch or for whomever else owns it.

Me and Frank burning brush

The next day we left for home and did not get back to the ranch until the following summer.

Lower lake slipped

SOMETIME IN LATE DECEMBER 1992 and early January 1993, the lower lake slipped again. This lake continues to give us trouble every year. This time it slid into the lake putting more dirt into the lake rather than opening it up and going down the canyon as it has in the past. So it really didn't need too much work done on it this time. (see lake, 3-287.)

The chicken coop

IN FEBRUARY 1993, THE old chicken coop, which could well have been built during Thomas Clarke's time, and was up by the Main House, finally collapsed.

The chicken coop collapses

This was the shed I mentioned much earlier that held some unused coal and rusted tools, pots and pans, along with broken glass, and anything else a farmer would store to get things out of the way. About this same time, the horse barn in this same area started to give way. Clarke, himself, may have built these buildings sometime around 1868. He may have built his home along with the chicken coop and barn, which were used for horses, wagons, yard equipment and then buggies and the real nice carriages that were there when we bought the ranch and had seen better days. It wasn't until the late 1920s that cars came into play.

Somewhere along the way, and during our time, different sizes and shapes of bathtubs that were scattered around the ranch had been replaced with regular galvanized water troughs for the cattle. Julia couldn't stand those white bathtubs scattered around 5,000 acres of land, and of course they really didn't fit in with the landscape, even if they were practical and free. They did add character and something to talk about, but I will have to admit they were completely out of place, although they reminded me of Jack. A lot of wire fences have replaced the redwood picket fences and were put up along the property lines, as well as all new gates throughout the ranch.

Julia helped Frank Sagehorn split the cost of these projects, and she helped put new corrugated roofs on the barns that replaced the redwood shakes that were made on the ranch. Julia did far more to bring the ranch up to a better working place than her father would have done. While doing this, she also replaced the "Amaral's Ranch" sign at the entrance, back to reading "Clarke Ranch," which is what it is called on the county maps. But now the local people more or less know it as the Amaral Ranch, for we have had it for so many years.

Horse barn down; view opened up

Burning the old horse barn

Opening up the view

ON MAY 31, 1993, Julia and Mark came up to check on the logging and saw that the horse barn had collapsed. At the time they were there, the yard had lots of spring flowers in bloom; the grass everywhere had that rich green color. The weather was cool and damp, so

James and the giant oak

Mark, Julia, and my nephew James, who was visiting them at the time, helped burn the pile down, and what a view it opened up from the ranch house looking south! All the piles of old wood and junk were gone, and Frank Sagehorn was replacing all the broken fence posts and boards in the corral area; the place was looking really nice. The next day, a big old oak tree fell down across the road near the apple orchard and had to be removed. James tried to do the job, but it was just too much without a Cat to push it out of the way, so after some effort, he gave up.

Irises put on a big show

JUNE WAS OUR FIRST time at the ranch together since Christmas. Julia and Mark were also there checking on the logging and some other things. The irises we planted in front of the shed were in bloom and had some of the largest flowers I have ever seen; I think the horse manure did it. We had to cut and pull a great deal of grass by hand that had grown very tall around the flowers. With so many irises in bloom in the side yard and the front yard, it was just breathtaking.

Irises blooming in the side yard at the ranch

More flowers in bloom at the ranch

This yard is one beautiful place in the spring, and the flower bulbs have been in the ground for many, many years—long before we bought the ranch back in 1967. I wouldn't be surprised if the bulbs came with the Clarke's from England. The bulbs keep right on multiplying and putting on a great show every year.

Anaheim property is rented

JULIA FINALLY GOT HER Anaheim property rented. Once it was rented, she and Mark rented a U-Haul and brought back the piano and bench that were not going to be used by the new tenants. They also brought back some chairs, and I think a nickelodeon or a game machine, along with a bunch of kitchen utensils and some nice wine glasses.

Logging and fishing, summer 1993

ON JULY 21, 1993, I went to the ranch by myself—a rare thing for me to do. Frank was in Bakersfield, California, checking on an oil well. Mark was at the ranch by himself, so I joined him there. He was checking up on what the loggers were doing on the logging plan that Julia had going on in the northwest section; the cutting was about all done. Next would be the skidding and hauling the timber out.

Mark was also checking up on a man called Bob, who was cutting down wood and making it into firewood to sell, with some of the firewood being set aside for use at the ranch. The logging that was done made a very small dent in the number of trees that come down every year at the ranch. This would no doubt be something that could go on for several years and still hardly make a dent in the downfall trees.

I later went fishing and caught two fish big enough for our dinner.

Iron pipes to the house are changed

ON THE MORNING OF July 21, 1993, Mark found the old cast-iron water pipeline that goes from the house, and he followed it to a break in the pipe near the culvert. He was able to get the ground ready for a new plastic pipe to replace that section of galvanized pipe. This would give us clean water and put an end to all the rust from the old iron pipe. There is still a section of galvanized pipe from the culvert to the bunkhouse.

No doubt, the original pipe was put in around 1910 or earlier. While Mark was doing this, I worked in the yard pulling weeds and trimming irises and other flowers, then I went picking blackcaps. After that, I went fishing and caught three fish big enough for Mark and Julia's dinner that night. He left at 5:30 p.m. to go home. It was a beautiful day. In the evening, I cut back the hybrid irises, now that they were done blooming.

Frank called about 9 p.m. from Bakersfield and said he was not sure about the oil well deal he had gone down to look at. He said he planned to spend more time the next day checking it out further. He said that Julia didn't know it yet, but she had a new tenant for the property in Bakersfield.

I spent a quiet evening by myself in front of the fireplace. I took the time to read and got caught up on reading the guestbook, then I went to bed around 11 p.m.

The next morning was foggy. I slept in until 10 a.m., and then did some yard work and went fishing at noon. By 2:30 p.m., I had caught four fish to take home with me. After fishing, I did some chores around the house. It was an overcast day with fog trying to come in. I had lunch at 4 p.m. and then left for home.

I planned to take a leisurely drive home and stop in Lucerne, California, to look at the big hotel that Mother used to go to for her church conventions. I had never taken the time to go out of the way to see it, so I did on this trip, and it brought back memories of my mother.

Oh, yes, in the guestbook at the ranch I'd written that Wilderness Unlimited's people had brought in more pigs for the hunters, and that I had seen turkeys that day. (We had been wondering if we had seen any.)

Newlyweds at the ranch

JULIA AND MARK WERE married on Oct. 9, 1993. That November or December, after coming home from their honeymoon, they came to the ranch to check on Julia's logging plan and take care of both lakes that started leaking from the winter rains. After the logging job was finished, Julia ended up making more money on what little she sold than Frank made on his big logging job in 1967. She was able to pay off what the ranch cost her and even make a profit. She also paid off the 10-plus acres in Bakersfield.

Julia and Mark were coming to the ranch often. They did additional work on the ranch and continued finding more work to do. The ranch gave them more space to breathe and move around in than what their condo in Larkspur gave them. Julia said that when she bought the condo, she thought it was going to be her home for the rest of her life. Little did she know, she would be getting married and would outgrow it!

For many years, when coming to the ranch, Julia would fly to the small airport at Laytonville, rather than drive. Mark started coming with her, and many times in the past she would fly over to Nevada City and fly Frank and me to the ranch. Flying over and landing at Laytonville airport was a little hairy, for there were electric wires right in line as you flew in to land. Julia always notified someone from the ranch to meet her when she was flying in to visit. If somebody wasn't available, a person at the ranch would drive the pickup and leave it for her at the airport. The Willits airport was larger and had a gas pump in case you needed to fill up, as well as someone on hand to do airplane repair. Julia and Mark could fly in and land in any kind of weather, and there was a fenced-in parking area for cars.

Laytonville airstrip

Julia and Mark got so they used the Willits airport more and just left the pickup there because the Laytonville strip was deteriorating and not as safe. This way, they could also buy their groceries at Willits before going to the ranch. Julia would fly out of the San Rafael airport, where she had her own hangar for her plane, and would fly from there to Willits or Laytonville.

After Mark passed his flying test, it helped Julia come up more often, for after her surgery on her ear, she had trouble feeling comfortable flying by herself for any distance. For years, she and Frank kept looking for a place to put an airstrip at the ranch. Frank even thought of trying to buy the airstrip in Laytonville. After Julia got married, they were flying to the ranch so often that she and Mark started looking in earnest for a spot to build an airstrip on the ranch.

Airstrip at the ranch

IN MARCH 1994, MARK and Julia found a place to put in an airstrip and, if I recall right, they had Homer come and look to see if it was viable. The place is up on the far eastern line, along the Old Cahto Road, near what we call A Station, more or less in the center area. It is a rather flat area at the top of the mountain and is above the fog belt most of the time. From this spot, you can see for miles in all directions. You can look down to where the ranch houses are, and on a clear day, you can see the ocean. The only problem in this area looked to be the underground springs, some trees, and big rocks that would have to be removed.

Homer thought it would be okay for an airstrip, and he thought he could take care of the springs. Therefore, they started moving dirt and using big rocks to fill in any low spots. A lot of dirt was moved to make a long enough strip for their plane to land; in the weak spots in the ground, they used the gray clay on the ranch as a stabilizer. Work on this part of the construction project continued until it was done. During the rough gravel stage in July, the new airstrip was ready for them to fly their plane in on and use. Next, it would need to go through a rainy season before being used again to be sure it was safe. They took pictures of this project.

When we have the family reunions, this is the area we visit to fly kites and sing songs. It is also in this area where we pick blackcaps and find rattlesnakes, and you can be sure someone has a gun handy. The berries are ripe in July, so whoever is at the ranch during that time is given a small pan to put them in and a big salad bowl to dump them into when the small pans are full. You can also eat your fill while picking them, and everyone helps pick the berries. We try to pick enough to have cobblers and pies, and enough for homemade ice cream, and yes, some to freeze for Mark's special drink that he makes.

Constructing the new airstrip at the ranch

In April, while the landing strip work was going on, Julia and Mark started looking for a home in Nevada City. They found one on Loma Rica Drive, very close to the Nevada County airport. They fixed up the guesthouse on that property and moved into it while they remodeled the main house. The remodeling took about a year to complete. They also built a hangar on the property that is close enough for them to pull the plane out of and run it out to the airstrip so they can fly out from there. Now it would take them one hour to travel from their home in Nevada City to the ranch, whereas by car it takes at least four hours of hard and sometimes slow driving.

First landing on the airstrip takes place in 1994

Julia coming in to land on the new airstrip

ON JULY 15, 1994, Julia and Mark landed at the ranch for the first time. They did so without any trouble on the first attempt and took a picture of it. Right behind them, their friend Sara Shapiro flew in and landed her smaller plane with ease. As Sara flew in, they took pictures of her landing. Julia and Mark were very happy about the new airstrip.

On July 22, Julia and Mark flew Frank and me from Nevada City to the ranch to show us the new airstrip. We flew over it but couldn't land because of fog, so we landed in Laytonville. The next day, the skies cleared, so the four of us went into town. Julia drove the pickup back to the ranch and up to the airstrip to pick us up when we got there. Mark flew us to the ranch so we could have the experience of landing there. I found it exciting flying over the ranch and right over the houses and actually seeing the ranch from the air. Both Julia and Mark are good pilots, so I am not afraid.

Sara coming in for a landing at the Clarke Ranch

During this time, three big cats—cougars—had recently been spotted on the ranch and were killing the deer and their fawns, along with the baby calves. So no doubt, something would have to be done about that.

Julia has done a good job at keeping the ranch in good shape and this is obvious when you see the ranch from the air. To protect the cattle and the planes she had Frank Sagehorn fence in the airport area to keep cattle out of it. When someone wants to land, they can do so without having any trouble with cattle on the airstrip.

Mark and Julia getting ready to take off from the ranch

Overrunning the airstrip

Overrunning the airstrip

ON OCT. 15, 1994, some of Julia and Mark's friends tried to land on the airstrip, but the pilot didn't give himself enough runway to land and stop his plane in time. The plane went over the edge of the runway and down the hill a little ways, and, yes, I think it totaled the plane. No one was hurt other than maybe a little pride.

On a different occasion, another plane overran the runway by just a foot and we were able to pull it back with no problems. These two incidents caused us to change the landing pattern, so we now land uphill to the south, rather than downhill to the north. No more overruns.

Cathy and Jeff, and Don and Cindy were at the ranch during this time; I don't know who else was there. They always have a good time at the ranch. The oversized bathtub in the downstairs bathroom becomes a hit to warm up the body when you're cold, tired, or just want to relax. It is big enough for two people to get in and soak all their cares away while sipping on a glass of fine wine. It makes a good setting for a picture of two.

The plane that didn't make it

Thanksgiving 1994 at the ranch

Celebrating Thanksgiving 1994 at the Clarke Ranch

FROM NOV. 23–27, THE four of us celebrated Thanksgiving at the ranch. Laurence and Gloria and their family did not come; they had other things planned. Mark's parents joined us, along with Julie and Thomas, Chelsea, and Cheryl, who was staying in Fort Bragg at their cabin. Cheryl's husband and dogs did not come. Julia invited Jim and Ellie, the caretakers for Wilderness Unlimited, to join us. Jim was doing side work for Julia and Mark when not patrolling the ranch. He cut and trimmed down branches and did other needed tasks; he also opened the house, turned on the hot water heaters, and got the woodstove and fireplace going for Mark and Julia so that on cold days it would be warm when they got there. This way they don't even have to turn the water on or start up the hot-water tank when they arrive. Jim also did this for Frank and me when we went to the ranch by ourselves, and it was really nice. I can thank Julia and Mark for arranging that for us.

Julia's second Kruger–Evenson reunion, 1996

1996 family reunion group picture

FROM JULY 30 TO Aug. 3, 1996, Julia hosted her second Kruger–Evenson family reunion with 45 relatives attending and 40 staying for picture taking on the last day. This time Julia got Kristen, her second cousin, to help her out. Kristen was glad to help and did whatever she could, for she wanted to keep the reunions going. Kristen sent out the notices for the reunion before February and kept everyone posted. At that time, she had recently left her husband. I told her if she helped Julia with the reunion, I would pay for the mailing stamps. She was surprised to find out how much the postage added up to before she was through sending out the last notice in May. The stamps alone came to $200, and there was the cost of the phone calls as well.

Kristin continued to follow through on things when she got to the ranch, helping Julia with the organizing of food, games, and all the cleanup chores. That took me off the hook. I really thank her for all the work she did. Kristin is a natural organizer and enjoys doing it, so I hope she will be around to help Julia in the future.

On Tuesday, July 30, Frank and I drove to the ranch in the afternoon; Mark and Julia flew up in the morning. Frank was sitting out on the back porch enjoying the sun, cleaning out the barrels of his guns, and I was working in the iris bed pulling out all the dead leaves to make them look nice for the holiday. While doing this, I heard a loud cry like a child.

I knew there were no children on the ranch. I went running toward where I heard it, at the same time calling to Frank to get his gun ready to shoot whatever it was. That was like talking to a blank wall, for he didn't hear a thing. When I finally got his attention as to what was going on, a cougar was in fast pursuit of a deer that was crying and running for its life. As the deer went up the hill and behind the back part of the house, it made a fast left turn going uphill and into the wooded area. This big cat looked to be eight feet long from head to tail when in full stride, and was chasing the deer for all it was worth. Then I saw and heard no more; the cat was out of sight by then and I don't know if it made the turn or not. Did the cat get the deer? I don't know.

This was just a few yards from the house and our backyard. That cat was too close for comfort. If the cougar's den was close to the house, that was something serious to worry about. After all the families arrived, I told them to keep a close tab on the little children at all times.

The guests arrive for the 1996 reunion

MY OLDER SISTER HELENA did not come that year to the reunion, nor did her husband Dick, who seldom came to the reunions. But all of Helena's girls and many of her grandchildren were there. Pat and husband, Elmer, Sharon and husband, Harold, Sandy and husband, Duane, and Wanda and husband, Marvin, all arrived early in the day and set up camp. Afterward, the girls came to the house to visit.

Julia and I had a great time visiting with them before other people arrived. We had such a good time that Wanda asked that we have the reunion every two years so that we could all get to know each other better. Hearing this from her made me feel like I really did the right thing back in 1978 when I started with the first reunion.

On Wednesday, their children and grandchildren arrived—Pat's oldest daughter, Ramona, and her husband, Gary; Sharon's daughter Wendy and her husband Bud and their three girls. They all stayed until Sunday. Sometime during the day on Thursday, Sharon or Harold fell in the lake with clothes on while riding in the canoe; no doubt, someone was trying to be cute. They didn't have a change of clothes, so they left early for home, which was not more than two hours away. If I recall right, they came back the next day.

James and Frank spending time together

The rest of my family arrived that evening, and it was always good to see them come to the ranch. Laurence, Gloria, Brad and his girlfriend arrived; Spence came in later. On Aug. 3, we celebrated Spence's 40th birthday. His "birthday cake" was two fat candles stuck in a pie that he made; Spence makes very good pies.

Spence's 40th birthday party

On Thursday, LaVena and her husband, Les, and their children, Barbara and husband, Lynn Ray and their girls, Kristen with her new friend Scott, Cheryl and her husband, Tom, and their children, all arrived in the afternoon. After that, the others started coming in. Venus and her three children, Bob and his wife, Ellen, were there; Paul, his wife, Karen, and son Brad did not make it. This reunion turned out to be Les's last time with us at the ranch. (He died Jan. 8, 1998.) LaVena was not too well, but she had a lot of attention, with all her grandchildren to help her.

Bev, Jack, Julia, Spence, and half of Lynn Ray

My brother Nick, his wife, Olive, nor any of their children were there. Jack and Bev came on Friday and stayed for the day. The four of us took a ride around the ranch and had a good time talking about old times; they stayed for dinner. That evening, we took pictures of the two of them and the four of us together in front of the fireplace. None of their children were there. This also was Jack's last time with us at the ranch. (He died Aug. 20, 1998.) On the Evenson side, my brother Jim's two sons James and Ray, were there, but not his two daughters, Kitty and Corinda. By now, James had outgrown his young habits and he, who never missed a reunion, and Ray, with his daughter Jennifer, camped out behind the house close to where Randy's outhouses were located for the campers.

Jack, Bev, me, and Frank

They all helped out and had a good time visiting as they worked preparing food and setting up tables. The younger kids all had a good time as well. Wendy's oldest girl and Venus's oldest boy had a great time together; this was the first time they had met. Seeing this made me glad to know that what I set out to do with the reunions was working a few generations later.

Playing cards while the kids enjoy swimming

The weather was very hot the first three days, so the lake became the center of everything. This is when the lake comes in very handy, especially as a way to keep the younger ones happy. It cooled off for the rest of the days, which made playing games and taking long walks easier and more enjoyable.

Several family members made notes in the guestbook. We did the usual things that I have mentioned before.

Les, LaVonne, Lynn Ray, Frank, with LaVena & Kristin sitting. Brad Angove is leading the horse ridden by Nicole.

The younger generation playing a lasso game

The older folks enjoying mealtime

Replacing shingles on the Main House

Working crew removing the 22-year-old shingles put on in 1975

IN JUNE 1997, JULIA once again had the shingles removed and replaced on the roof and sidings of the Main House. When it was finished, it was sprayed with a sealer.

Me standing in front of the Main House after the shingle job was done

A lady hunter shoots her first deer

IN NOVEMBER 1997, ONE of the lady hunters in Wilderness Unlimited went to the ranch to spend a week there. On her visit, she shot and killed her first deer; it was the thrill of her life. Jim Powers, the caretaker for the club, helped her get the deer out of the creek, where it finally landed. He got into the jeep and took it to the hunting shack to hang. The woman then had to skin and gut the deer before taking it home to be butchered.

Pristine snow falls at the ranch

A quiet, peaceful setting after a snowfall

IN JANUARY 1999, IT snowed at the ranch while Julia and Mark were there. Everything was covered with snow as far as the eye could see. This time there were no cattle around to mar the snow. Standing on the porch, you could look out and enjoy the snow on the bare tree branches and boughs bent to the ground, loaded with the weight of the snow. The redwood picket fences stood out against the white snow.

Everything was so quiet and still, you felt like you were the only one around in God's country. It was like the snow we had in 1975–76. It is not often that we get so much snow when we are there, so it was a real treat to see the crystal glitter on the snow in the evening when the moonlight shone on it.

Flying friends at the ranch in 1999

IN MID-MAY 1999, Julia and Mark were up at the ranch for a few days; joining them were their Marin 99's friends—the Morsheads, Pittelkows, Picketts, and Brooke Austin. They always have a wonderful time together enjoying each other's company and driving around the ranch. Julia and Mark's friends have been to the ranch many times, so they knew their way around. And they know the pleasure that comes with seeing the ranch in many kinds of weather.

Lunchtime time with Julia and Mark's fly-in friends

These are the same people that Julia and Mark do a lot of flying with to different places in the United States, Canada, and Mexico.

Julia's third family reunion, 1999

1999—my how those little kids have grown up since 1996, they are now in the back rows

FROM JULY 14–17, 1999, Julia hosted her third Kruger–Evenson reunion. This was the family's sixth reunion at the ranch. This time 53 people attended and Julia had it down rather well, with the help of Gloria and Kristen. Upon Kristen's arrival, Julia had her bulletin notes ready to post on the side of the refrigerator as to what everyone was to bring and on what day. Kristen brought in her new boyfriend, Scott.

The rest of the gathering went more or less like the other ones. One of the things that had changed was the lower lake. It had been decided to let it go, so the water was really low in that lake, and, yes, there were still fish in it, but it would be hard to get them from the dock. Bev took advantage of this and went hunting for Indian arrowheads down by the lower lake.

Bev searching the abandoned lower lake for arrowheads

The big rock by the Main House was busy this year with the younger ones. This was also the way it was back in 1979. I've noticed that as the kids get older, the rock sort of takes a backseat.

Nichole, Brittany, Andrew, and Jessica on the big rock

We had a lot more tents behind the east side of the house this year. We also brought in an outside toilet to put in this area, and it really came in handy. All of Helena's family and a few

Tents along the side of the house

grandchildren were there. This was Sharon's last time with us at the ranch. My family was all there, and Brad brought his new wife, Penny. All of LaVena's family came to the reunion, except Venus and her family. In Nick's family, their daughter Holly and son Todd, with his wife, Sherry, and daughter Katelyn, joined us; it was also Nick's last time at the ranch. This year was Holly's first time. Bev's family was all with us, except her daughter Francine and her family.

This was Bev's first time to a reunion after Jack's death. It was so nice that her family was there to help see her through this period, for there were so many memories for her. To help out, I put her in the house in the big dorm room. This room was for Bev and anyone who wanted to stay with her, but most of the family went into town to spend the nights at a hotel. My youngest brother Jim's families were there. James brought his girlfriend Elaine; Kathy brought her new husband, Dave. Corinda (her husband Rick died in August 1998) came with her two children, Chad and Kristen; and Ray (his wife, Mary, has never been to the reunions) came with his daughter Jennifer. The Evenson kids had a great time together; they don't get together very often, so they really enjoyed the reunions.

Olive and Nick Kruger family,
three generations down by the lake:
Sherry, Katelyn, Todd, Holly, Olive, Nick

Pictures were taken of couples standing by the old walnut tree by the house. This is a very old tree and has seen better days. Mark and Julia planted two new trees close to it, so there will be trees there when the walnut tree is gone. At this time, Frank was recovering from his colonoscopy surgery in June, so he was not very spry at this reunion. Julia took a picture of Frank and me standing by the tree, and I think that is what started the picture-taking spree.

Me and Frank at the old walnut tree

The lake was very popular all three days this year. In addition to the lake, the men kept from getting bored by helping Mark with one the work projects he had going on. The project consisted of bringing in and piling up firewood. Mark decided to get that job out of the way and found he had many hands to help get the job done fast.

The lake got a lot of action at this reunion

Todd, Laurence, Sharon, Jim, Ollie, Penny, Bev, Melissa, Henry, me, Nick, Frank, Olive

Jim Evenson family: Kristin, Chad, Corinda, James, Elaine, Dave, Kitty, Raymond, and Jennifer

This year we had the piano that Julia had brought up from the Anaheim restaurant along with the game machine, so along with cards and puzzles in the evenings, this room was kept busy until late at night. Anyone trying to sleep in the dorm bedroom upstairs before midnight was out of luck.

Spence had to leave a day early for one of his sports-announcement jobs that he does on weekends. He really enjoys coming to the ranch and we love having him there with us.

The family enjoying a nice evening together

Pat, Sherry, Helena, LaVena,
and Bev looking at photo albums

Todd, Gloria, Holly, Brad, Sherry, Nick

The Frank Amaral Family: Mark, Julia,
Spence, Frank, me, Laurence, Gloria, Brad and Penny

Sagehorn makes a change

IN 1999, FRANK SAGEHORN brought in a younger partner; he was finally thinking of making the break from his business. Frank Sagehorn would be phasing out of the cattle end on the Clarke Ranch in a few years. He was going into his eighties, as were my husband and I. He was ready to retire, so he says, but he will have a few cows on his place where he lives. He bought 85 acres of ranch land from Julia, at the far northeastern corner, and built his home on part of it. During his time on the ranch, we leased the property to hunting clubs, and that brought in more rent. As time went on, the clubs brought in more rent than Sagehorn's cattle operation. To make the ranch pay off you have to keep using your imagination for income sources, for the upkeep on the roads and buildings is constant. A good deal of the upkeep is due largely to the fog and the 100 inches or more of rain the ranch gets each year.

Before selling the ranch to Julia, Frank put the property under the protection of the California Williamson Act to save on taxes; this prevented it from being subdivided into parcels of less than 160 acres.

stock Man of the Year

Service in 1991. He is also a member of the Laytonville Chamber of Commerce.

In announcing Sagehorn's selection as Livestock Man of the Year, the directors of the 12th District Agricultural Association said that Sagehorn embodies the spirit of the award, "committed to his community through service and faithful to his life's vocation through his industrious application of self to it and his accomplishments in his chosen field."

Frank Sagehorn

Frank Sagehorn was with us for years

Bull pasture drive to the large bay tree

Another picture of Frank
and his favorite madrone tree

ON MAY 28, 2000, Mark and Julia were with their friends at the ranch and took a drive over near the bull pasture to show them the largest bay tree in California. From there, they continued towards the Manchester place, and on their way came to Frank's favorite madrone tree.

Mark and Julia had someone take their pictures in front of both trees. This is always a nice drive and from here you can continue going down to Ten Mile River. On your way back, you can take a short cut and come up the center of the ranch by crossing over the bridge and coming up $65 Road. There is another tree—I think it is a pepper tree, or it could be a maple—that is also worth looking at. Frank would not let the burl people take it. This tree is at the landing just as you go down to the upper lake, on the left side of the gate. This is the area where the hunters park their cars and walk down to the lake.

Julia and Mark at the world's largest bay tree at that time

Julia's fourth Kruger–Evenson reunion, 2001

We have all gotten older, including the teenagers

FROM AUGUST 12–19, 2001, Julia hosted her fourth reunion and had 44 people attending, with 43 in the picture. It's always a circus getting all the people together for the big moment when the picture is taken. Kristen did all the paperwork and got all the new addresses that had changed. She followed through with everything and that proved to be a great help for Julia in making the reunion possible.

The four of us arrived at the ranch early to get things ready. Julia and I washed windows, inside and outside, using ladders to get to the tall windows. We did all the usual things to get the Main House cleaned. Once the house, the yard, and the deck at the lake were done, we went up to the lodge to do what we could to the kitchen and the refrigerator, which takes forever to clean. (The hunters do not clean up very well.) This place is reserved for LaVena's family.

Then we went out and cleaned the annex for Helena and Pat and part of her family; some of them liked to camp out under the trees. This year we had Bev and her family in the dorm room with us again, along with a few others; the rest stayed in town. James and his new wife, Elaine—we were all happy he found someone after all these years—camped out by the bull pasture near the garage. Ray and his daughter slept in their double-room tent in the back of the house in the shade, along with several others.

The east side of the house was tent haven this time around. I believe Ella (my brother Jim's second wife, and Ray's mother) and Olive were staying at a motel in town. My family stayed in the house, and I think Brad and Penny were in the downstairs bedroom. I think Spence used the bedding supply room upstairs.

At this year's family reunion, we noticed a big change. To start with, we were minus Les, Jack, and Rick (Corinda's husband) in 1998; then Sharon, Allen (Ella's husband), and Nick were no longer with us in 2001. Harold, Sharon's husband, joined us this year, and it was good to see him. Then we noticed many of the young kids from the first reunions had grown up and now had children of their own. Other than two who were small, the children were getting near or were in their teens. Somebody would be needed at the next reunion to take over that young group to keep them busy; it would be more or less like it was in 1978. It didn't seem possible that so many years had gone by since the first reunion!

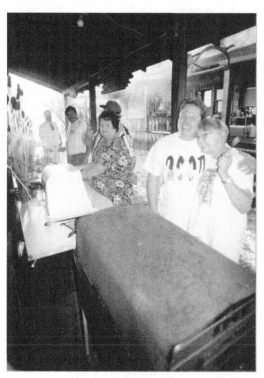

At the barbecue area
Gloria and Scott, Pat and Elmer, Paul and Tom

We enjoyed wonderful food for all our meals. Each year the food got better, and everyone really pitched in to make that happen. We spent more time at the lake fishing and visiting, and some just drove around the ranch and went up to the airport to fly kites.

This was one of the smaller family reunions we've had and was rather different than before—there were more people in their late fifties and sixties and very few in their late seventies and eighties, along with having lost some relatives along the way. It was strange to look at the pictures and see the changes in all of us.

On the last day, Sunday, everyone ate breakfast outside in the picnic area on the south side of the ranch house under two big shady trees. After breakfast, we said our goodbyes; this tradition started after our first reunion in 1978. However, this year it was different.

Mark began cleaning up and putting away all of the barbecue stuff, including the makeshift tables that are made of old plank doors that are not used anymore; we sit them on old sawhorses, and they make great working tables around the cooking area. He started putting them in the storage room. It was not long before I noticed the younger married men getting in and helping him fold up all of the outside tables and putting them in storage, and putting all the benches back up on the porch. Meanwhile, we girls were doing the same kind of work in the house. The men even went down to the lake to help bring up the boats that needed to be stored in the garage at the lodge. They also rolled up the rugs on the deck that we use to keep slivers from getting in people's feet. They put the rugs in the truck along with the folding chairs, mats, tables, fishing gear, and umbrellas, and brought them back up to the house to put in the center storage room.

These were tasks that we had always done by ourselves, and what a difference it made to have this new, unexpected help! An all-day job was done in a couple of hours; this made our last day so much easier.

We were ready to leave right after noon. We pulled down all the blinds and locked the windows, shut the water off, turned off the electricity, and locked the house. The four of us then drove up to the lodge to have lunch with Barbara and some of her family and help clean up their leftovers. They had their cars packed and were all ready to leave. While we were visiting, they said that they didn't realize all the work that went into getting things ready. They also had a couple of suggestions to help make the next reunion easier; even one of the younger girls said she would take on the project of entertaining the younger people so they would have things to do. She said she noticed this year that her age group needed more games and things to do to keep them busy. It was nice to see the interest the younger people were taking.

Julia and Mark really put themselves out for all of us at this 2001 reunion, and I want to thank them for doing so. It takes a lot of energy to get the ranch ready for the reunions. You have to make sure that everything works and that things are convenient, and this takes a lot of advance preparation.

At this reunion, LaVena fell off the last porch step onto Barbara, but did not get hurt. Later, Wanda fell and sprained one of her ankles. I think at all the family reunions we've had, Wanda's sprained ankle was the worst injury that has happened. We put her foot in the salty ice left over from making homemade ice cream, to help take the swelling down. She said, "It's sure cold," but I saw that she soaked her foot a few more times, so it must have helped her ankle feel better. She came out of it OK. I called her a few days later at her home to make sure everything was all right and she said her ankle was fine.

I am sorry that my mother didn't live long enough to see the ranch and all her children, grandchildren, great-grandchildren, and great-great-grandchildren enjoying themselves together for several days at a time, with little discontent, as we did when she was alive when we all got together for Christmas at the Winchuck Ranch in Oregon.

Saying goodbye
Me, Teri, Maryanne, Bev, Helena, Elaine, Cheryl, Ella, Jim and Pat

Frank's business in Garberville

ON AUG. 30, 2001, on our way up to Garberville, California, where Frank had some business to take care of, we stayed at the ranch for two nights. As we drove down the hill to the Main House, we saw how rich the brown color stain on the houses looked and how much sharper all the buildings looked, just as if the buildings were new. Julia started this job in June and it took a few months to get it done. As I have said before, the ranch is an ongoing project. You have done a great job, Julia! The place looked nice inside and blended very well with the new outside color.

Around this time, Frank had invested a good sum of money into the hospital in Garberville, but the directors filed for bankruptcy rather than pay him off. For over a year, Frank worried about this, but he didn't say too much to me; however, I knew he wasn't receiving any payments. The money Frank put into the hospital went towards computer equipment, so we went there, picked it up, and brought the equipment home. One of our stockbrokers, Richard Grossman, was there with us to help us through the process. It was through him that we made the hospital investment, so he felt partly to blame.

I decided to go with Frank on this trip mostly because he had recently broken his left little finger and it was in a cast. He fell off a ladder while picking peaches in the side yard here at home. This limited what he could do, including driving. Rich drove up from the city in his pickup in case he would be needed to help bring some equipment back in his truck. There were 19 computers and all the parts that went with them. I took one look and figured out how they could all go into the back of the pickup; however, the men started to load them in, and I could see that they didn't know what they were doing. After they had loaded six or seven of them, I got into the back and repositioned them. Seeing the progress I made, it wasn't long before they decided to follow instructions from me. We got everything in the back of our pickup and even had enough space left over to put our stuff in from the ranch when we were ready to drive back home. I remember several of the men were quite surprised to see that all 19 big computers fit in the back of one pickup. They had obviously not counted on LaVonne. I packed everything so tightly that nothing could move as we drove home over all the curves on Highway 20.

In the meantime, the men at the hospital were talking as if no one would want the computers and that they might have to go to the dump, which would cost a lot of money.

Being married to Frank, one thing I learned to be good at was putting puzzles together of all kinds; but I became even better at packing the trunk of a car or a pickup. Anyway, Frank, Rich, and I had lunch in Garberville and then left for the ranch. Rich followed us to make sure everything was all right. I was doing the driving and wanted to make sure I had the pickup balanced. It was a little too heavy on the left side, which made the pickup pull to the left on the highway, so I couldn't go too fast. Later, I was able to fix the problem using the stuff we would be taking home with us from the ranch. After that, the pickup rode like a jewel all the way; even going fast on the curves, it held its own.

After we got to the ranch, we had Rich leave his pickup at the gate area so it wouldn't get dirty by driving on the dirt roads on the ranch. Rich rode with Frank and me to the Main House and enjoyed seeing the ranch; he was happy we invited him to see the place that he had been hearing about for many years. After a few hours, Frank took him back to the gate so he could leave for home, and I set out to go fishing at the lake by myself. I didn't catch anything, but I enjoyed it anyway, and it was a nice day.

This was on Labor Day weekend, and we planned to stay at the ranch from Thursday through Monday. We had picked the load up in Garberville on Friday and gotten to the ranch about two in the afternoon that day. Then Saturday morning Frank said, "We're going home"; I didn't question him on it, for I give him enough hassle at home, not to add to it at the ranch. He drove from the ranch to Lucerne with his hand in the cast, for there are not as many curves on this stretch of the drive. In Lucerne, he had his milkshake that he always gets when we go that way, and he used the bathroom, for the town is halfway between home and the ranch. I drove the rest of the way.

After we got home, Laurence and Gloria had us over for dinner, and Laurence started talking to Frank about the computers. He said that Frank was wasting his time, that they should have gone to the dump. Frank, in no uncertain terms, told his son that he didn't want to talk about it. His rudeness was uncalled for, and then I thought, "Now I know why we didn't stay at the ranch." Frank was upset about the computers and that maybe he had made a mistake. So that's why we came home early.

I had guessed it right, and the next day I called to tell Gloria about it. Laurence had told his dad earlier before going up to get the computers that he didn't think it was a good idea to pick them up, for no one would want them. And he said Dad would have to pay a big fee to take them to the dump and that it would be very costly. And if that were to happen, "we as a family" would hear about it for a long time. So all along, this was on Frank's mind, but he was still going to see what he could do with them. The local hospital had already told him that they did not want them.

On Monday, Laurence and Gloria had us over again for dinner with some of their friends, and while there, Spence showed Frank one of the latest computers, how it worked, and so on. Frank later called Terry McAteer, the superintendent of the local schools in Nevada County, to ask if he could come over and talk to him, and Terry said yes. When Frank got to the office, Terry invited him in and Frank said, "No, you come with me." Terry did and took one look at what was in the back of the pickup. He was elated with what he saw, and said that it was really a great gift. They drove over to the Imaginarium building across the highway from the Superintendent of Schools' Office and unloaded the computers right then; Frank said Terry was really glad to get them.

When Frank got home, he told me what happened, then he said, "You really did a good job at packing that pickup, for it was done very neatly and you could see what was in it and where." Frank was not happy about losing so much money, but he would be able to get a tax write-off from donating the computers. That would help a little, and above all, relieved his mind of one more headache that he had. So ended one more chapter in Frank's life, and it would teach him to be leery of hospitals when it comes to investing.

A week later, I began noticing that Frank was not so, shall I say, bitchy about what I was doing in the yard with redoing the brick walkways. I began realizing that the deal with the hospital in Garberville had been bothering him for almost a year. Even David, the gardener, who was doing the brickwork, noticed the difference. It was like a load had been taken off of Frank.

Hunting family at the Upper House

AT THIS TIME, THERE was a family of four and a grandmother staying at the lodge to hunt, from Wilderness Unlimited. I got all my fishing gear and started walking up the hill, and as I got halfway up the hill, a woman came out and joined me and we walked down to the lake. I am sorry I don't remember her name. She told me they had been coming to the ranch for 12 years, and they loved it very much. She said that when she saw me with the fishing gear, she wanted to come and talk to me and tell me how much they loved coming to the ranch. She knew she had to go down to the lake and have her family come back to the hunting lodge. She said she had always known that the lake was mine when we were there, and she thanked me for the lake. The hunting club members are told by the patrol officer that the lake was made for me; otherwise, there would not be a lake. Her two boys had spent every hunting season at the ranch. This year was her mother's first time at the ranch, and she was enjoying it very much.

From the ranch house, you walk up the hill past the hunting lodge, and then downhill all the way to the lake. Coming back, it can sometimes wear you out. However, I am used to walking it, sometimes two or three times a day. It's about a quarter-mile one way. I find it a great challenge for the legs and lungs. When we have the family reunions, I find that I get in great shape walking the hills; simply walking up and down the hill to the lodge can do it.

Frank and I spent the night and left for home in the morning. I always sort of hate leaving to come home. I feel that I leave a little bit of me behind.

Thanksgiving 2001 at the ranch

FROM NOV. 22–27, 2001, Frank and I went to the ranch to spend Thanksgiving Day by ourselves, and later to celebrate our 59th wedding anniversary. We were there from Thursday through Tuesday. Not having a gardener to look after our home in Nevada City, we hired Nancy Donahue to housesit. Julia and Mark left earlier to go to Ukiah to visit his family for Thanksgiving Day, and then came to the ranch later that night. Laurence and Gloria were spending Thanksgiving with their friends at home.

On our way to the ranch, Frank and I planned to stop at our regular place, the Foster's Freeze in Lucerne on Highway 20, only to find that it was closed, so we had to find another place to eat. By this time, it was now 2 p.m. so we turned around and headed back to look for a place to eat in town. Only a block away from the Foster's Freeze, we found a place that was open. It didn't look like much from the road, but we stopped and went in and found out that it's the place in town where the locals go for a nice Thanksgiving dinner.

They asked if we had reservations, and we said no. We asked if we needed reservations; they said yes but it was all right. All we wanted was a sandwich, but we ended up having our Thanksgiving dinner at the restaurant, and it was very good. We also had pumpkin pie, but it was far too much food, so we ended up taking enough leftovers to the ranch with us for our evening meal that night. The day was very nice and the weather could not have been better. There was very little traffic on the road, which made for a pleasant drive. Later that night, Mark and Julia came in, but Frank and I were already in bed.

On our way to the ranch, we noticed the Sutter Buttes were the clearest in color we had ever seen. The following day, Julia and Mark said the same thing about them. We always take a close look at the Buttes when we drive by them because at one time we owned property going up into them.

On Friday, Mark and Julia went to Ukiah for the day to visit with his family and one of his sisters who had come in from Washington. Frank and I enjoyed a very nice day together doing only what we wanted to do, which consisted of taking it easy and simply enjoying the ranch.

Saturday was cold and hail came down in sheets, leaving the ground white for a few hours. We also got a lot of rain that day. There was so much water down by the shed that it starting to look like a lake. Mark went outside and tried to divert the water down to the creek. He ended up doing a pretty good job, but he really got wet doing it.

A wild tom turkey for dinner

AROUND NOON, JIM THE caretaker showed up with a big year-old tom turkey he had just shot in the head for Julia, who had been on him to get her a wild turkey. So here the turkey was; now what do we do with it? It was too cold to clean it outside, and the body was still warm. Looking back, I am sorry we didn't take pictures of this rather strange and unusual situation.

We got two large plastic tablecloths and laid them on the floor in front of the fireplace in the living room. We then put the tom in a large plastic bag so the blood and feathers would not get all over the room; the bird was still warm. Frank, Julia, and I started to pull feathers as fast as we could, and they came off rather easily. We did a good job of it, and when we were done, we took the turkey to the sink, poured hot water all over it, and got the rest of the fuzz off. Frank cleaned up the mess on the living room floor. As a kid, I had killed and cleaned many chickens and some turkeys, so I remembered how to do it.

The tom was about 10 pounds dressed and was far too heavy for me to handle. So Julia really got into the spirit of things, and with me "telling" her what to do and her heart in the project, she ended up doing a very good job, even if I did get a little on the dictatorial side. We got the guts out, and she got the lungs out, then she washed it inside and out really well and dried it. She then hung it head-down in the back spare bedroom downstairs where it was very cold, hoping that would help take some of the "game" taste away.

On Sunday, Mark cooked the wild turkey in about two hours. We had it with all the leftover trimmings from Mark's family turkey dinner, and a pumpkin pie that Julia made. The turkey was a little on the tough side, nonetheless we enjoyed having the first wild turkey killed on the ranch for ourselves. I told Frank that, at 83, he was still enjoying the fruits of the ranch.

While the turkey was baking, Julia and I decided to take a two-hour hike up the canyon, across some of the open country going up towards the airport area. We stopped every so often to turn around to take in the spectacular views behind us of the ranch, the valley below, on out to the coastline and ocean beyond. It rained a little, but with our umbrellas, we did fine.

Our 59th wedding anniversary

WE HAD A VERY nice leisure time during that Thanksgiving weekend of 2001. The weather was good, and we went for another walk. This time, in our rubber boots, we went more under the trees and over the river crossings, and ended up in the hunting lodge area. Later, Frank and I took our own walk down to the lake and back up the hill by the horse pasture. The four of us ended the day playing Hand and Foot, with Julia and Mark the winner.

The next morning, we cleaned up the house and did some packing, then after breakfast we got ready to leave the ranch by 11 a.m. and then headed for home. The weather was nice, and as we drove by Clear Lake, the lake was calm. We came home to a very messy pine needle yard, for there had been a storm, and the yard told the story; nonetheless, it was good to be home. As Frank says, the good thing about our home in Nevada City is that it's within walking distance of everything. On his own, Frank would just as well prefer to live in a complex; all he needs is a place to live where he can call his broker. For me, it's about working and having different things happening in the yard. However, I am sort of thinking that maybe I should just think about him and what he wants, in case I should go before he does.

The second repair job on Canyon Bridge

FROM OCT. 18–20, 2002, Mark was at the ranch to fix the bridge down in the canyon that you cross to get to $65 Road that comes up to the ranch house. That road branches off the road that goes down to Ten Mile River. The timbers that we put on the bridge years earlier had rotted away and needed replacing. Mark and Julia bought new 2-foot-by-12-foot planks and had them creosoted so they would not rot out as easily as the old ones. They had them delivered down the canyon to the bridge. Julia and Mark had to remove the old ones and remove all the — as she says — "gunk," and put the new planks in place.

Jim, the caretaker, helped, but the planks were too heavy even for him to lift by himself. Julia said each plank was so heavy that she could hardly lift one end of the new ones. They worked all day at it. They were so tired by the time they got them in place, they could hardly do more than hammer in a few nails, and what few nails she hammered in she said went in crooked, so they finally called it quits for the day.

The next day, they were so sore and tired that they didn't go down to finish the job; however, cars could go over the bridge. On their next trip to the ranch, they would have to buy more big nails and go down there, and Mark would have to pound them into place. Julia said she couldn't get a nail to go in straight. I knew what she was talking about, for I helped Jack and Frank years earlier when the first planks went down, and she had been there to help. In those days, I was in very good shape. I put nails in the boards using a small sledgehammer, putting the nails in at an angle, and yes, I bent a few of those long nails myself. I don't think Frank nailed any in place; Jack did most of them.

As the years go by, if Julia and Mark plan to keep the ranch looking sharp and in working order, they may have to hire extra help to do the heavier jobs. Age does take its toll on people, just as it does on lumber or anything else.

The pink trailer is on its last legs in 2002

THE PINK TRAILER WAS still in the same location in 2002, and was being used by the hunting club's manager, Jim Powers, during the winter months. In the summer months, he went back to the hunting lodge area, where he had his own mobile trailer. The pink trailer has definitely seen better days, and it is just a matter of time before it will have to be replaced. Julia will no doubt put another trailer or small modular home in the same spot, for it is a very good location and has all the facilities right there.

In time, Jim, who is getting old, will retire and be replaced. No doubt, it will be at this time when a change in the living quarters would be made. Jim served Julia and Mark very well, and I hope that whoever replaces him will serve them just as well.

Frank and I celebrate our 60th anniversary

NOV. 26, 2002, WAS Frank's and my 60th wedding anniversary. We now each were octogenarians; Frank was 84, I was 80. I felt we had done all we are going to do to contribute to the growth of the Clarke Ranch. Julia was doing a good job running it, along with the help of Mark, who had taken a real interest in the ranch. This made us very happy. So, a business that Frank started in 1967 had, in time, turned into a wonderful family place to come and enjoy along with family and friends under Julia's care.

I knew we would continue coming to the ranch, for Frank and I both love it there very much, but it was time to step down. This last "repeat job" on the bridge told me it was time for me to let go of keeping notes, so this entry comes from the last of my notes on the Clarke Ranch. And with Julia and Mark now owning the ranch, Frank didn't have to do any work. He could sit in the swing, enjoy the view, read the paper, or just sit, look and dream. And that is exactly what he did.

Kruger–Evenson reunion, 2004

Julia's 5ᵗʰ reunion at the ranch.
Attendance really tapered down, mostly to the 1ˢᵗ, 2ⁿᵈ, and 3ʳᵈ generations.

IN SUMMER 2004, WE had another Kruger–Evenson family reunion at the Clarke Ranch. Julia and Mark, along with Frank and I, flew up in their plane on Aug. 31, and stayed until Sept. 7. We wanted to be there early enough to clean up and put tables and other things out for the family reunion, and then stay long enough to help put things back after the reunion before coming home. Most of the families would be coming in on Friday and leaving on Sunday, but a few would come earlier to help us out.

When we arrived at the ranch on Aug. 31, we had the plane so overloaded that Mark was on pins and needles for an hour until he set the plane down on the ranch runway. There's always a pickup at the airstrip so we could simply drive down to the ranch house. Mark landed us safely, and we unloaded the plane and put the stuff in the pickup, then we covered and tied the plane down, drove the mile to the house, unloaded the pickup, and put things away. Earlier, they had the caretaker for the hunters open the house so the electricity and water were turned on when we got there. After everything was unloaded and put away, Julia and I washed the windows inside and out and cleaned up the house from all the dead flies and mice.

Frank with some family members by the big rock

Looking down on the ranch from the airport area

While Julia and I were doing this, Mark was getting things out of storage to take down to the lake. Once at the lake, he put down the rug on the deck to keep slivers out of our feet, and then arranged all the tables, benches, umbrellas, and chairs. By the time this was done, it was dinnertime. Julia and I had also taken time to go up to the hunting lodge to make sure everything was clean and ready to go up there as well.

About 10 that evening, around bedtime, Barbara, Lynn Ray, and Kristen, with LaVena, arrived at the lodge. When they arrive at the ranch, they always plan to do a lot of cleanup before going to bed. However, for the first time, it was so clean when they got there that they didn't have to do anything but put their food and things away and make up their beds and go to sleep. They even commented that all the rooms smelled clean. They said it was a real gift having the place clean, including the refrigerator, toilets, and shower; they went out of their way to thank the caretaker and his wife for doing such a terrific job.

The next morning, Kristen came down to the Main House to help Julia organize the food and meals, and to make any phone calls that were needed to those who were coming. It takes a lot of phone calls to make sure of what everyone is bringing, in the way of food, and to find out if any changes have to be made as far as what each family needs to bring.

Later in the day, Olive arrived, and she stayed upstairs in the dorm room in our house. On Friday, her family, Todd, Sherry and Katelyn, showed up and stayed in Laurence and Gloria's bedroom, since Laurence and Gloria were not coming this year; they were just too busy getting the yard ready for Brad's wedding that was going to be held in their yard. In the afternoon, Tom and Cheryl and their two children came, and they stayed up at the lodge. Pat and Elmer came and stayed in the annex up at the lodge. James and Elaine arrived in the afternoon in a brand-new white pickup with wide fenders; they were so proud of their first brand-new pickup. They stayed in the bedroom downstairs.

Later in the evening, Kristen's husband, Scott, and their two girls arrived, and they were all in the hunting lodge. By this time, both our houses were full of people. When it came time for breakfast, lunch, and dinner, it was quite a beehive. On Saturday morning, James's daughter Marilyn and friend Nelson and their two boys arrived. They brought tents and set them up on the northeast side of the house, and I believe they were the last ones to arrive.

With 30 people, this was the smallest family reunion on the Kruger–Evenson side that we had ever had. It was also one of the hardest reunions when it came to the workload in the Main House; maybe we were just getting older and it was harder to do all the things that had to be done. The other relatives all have younger generations to help them out, but Julia and Mark do not. Besides myself, there was no one to help them, unless her second cousins volunteered. That is what Kristen did, in addition to helping her own mother, Barbara, who is six years older than Julia is.

LaVena was getting weaker and more or less gave very little trouble, except someone had to be near her all the time, so she was never left alone for very long.

The family picture was taken Saturday evening before dinner; the event is always a fun time for all of us. By late Sunday afternoon, some people had left, and by Monday evening, everyone had left except for James and Elaine.

On Sunday afternoon, two strange men in their mid-twenties came walking up from $65 Road to the Main House. We were out on the front porch. One of them had his shirt off and they were each carrying a light backpack. When I saw them, I called Mark, for no one should be on the Clarke Ranch without the hunting club's approval, and this was hunting season.

Mark asked them where they had come from, and I think they said the Willits area. They said they went out for a walk in the woods and got lost. According to their story, they had spent the past two days and nights walking the canyons, trying to find their way out. Mark asked if they had anything to eat. They said they were all right; they had water from the creeks and each had a bottle of water, so they were all right that way.

James said they were looking for a place to grow marijuana, and no, they would not need anything to eat. Having been there himself years earlier, he knew what they were looking for, and one such thing was for a place that would have water the year round. He said they would be looking for a place where green ferns grow in September, for this means water runs in the area year round and is a good place to set up and grow a patch.

Anyway, the men asked Mark if he would give them a ride to Willits, from there I think they said they could get a ride. Mark said no, but he would take them out to the highway and off the property; they could walk the seven miles to Laytonville, then 20 miles south to Willits. So Mark took off in the pickup with the two men. All of a sudden, it dawned on me what could happen, and I said someone had better hurry up and follow Mark out to the gate. The trespassers could hit him or kill him and take the pickup, and we did not even know who the two men were.

Julia and Kristen quickly ran down to the only pickup left, which was James's brand-new pickup. As Julia started up the truck, James got into the front right seat, and as they went around the corner to get onto the main road out of the ranch, Julia turned the corner too sharply. With the very wide back fenders, she took out the corner post that holds the gate that comes down to the Main House. And there went James's first brand-new pickup that he had ever owned, and was so proud of. Additionally, someone else also went out, but by the time all the commotion was over, Mark was on his way back.

Mark said that the thought had also come to him while they were in the pickup, and he had made up his mind to give them the pickup rather than have anything happen to himself. After he left the two men on the other side of the gate, they walked off toward Laytonville, but Mark didn't know what they did after that because he didn't stick around to find out.

That was the biggest excitement that went on at the ranch that year, and Julia had the task of seeing to it that James's pickup got fixed up to looking like new again. Julia sort of wiped herself out thinking how she could have hit that post, knowing how many times she had gone around that same corner throughout the past 30-some-odd years.

Me and Frank outside the
Main House at the last family reunion

It was now Monday, after lunch and all the extra food either had been eaten or would be taken home by someone. All the tables, benches, and chairs that were outside in the backyard under the trees had been put back in storage. We were saying our good-byes. I then said that this was the last family reunion I would work on, of the many reunions I started many years ago. I said if anything were going to take place in the future, they would all have to help Mark and Julia. Frank and I would not be able to help put the gatherings together. At this reunion, I was not able to help Julia as I used to, I was sort of dizzy all the time.

After everyone had left except for James and Elaine, the six of us drove down to the pear orchard (which consists of two old pear trees), taking boxes, ladders and buckets to pick at least 10 boxes full of Bartlett pears. There were so many pears on the two trees that we just picked the largest ones. James and Elaine took two full boxes and left for home from the pear orchard. We took the rest of the pears to the ranch house and put them out on the side porch to keep cool until we left for home on Tuesday morning. After we vacuumed the entire house and packed everything that had to go home, and we finished cleaning up the kitchen and bathrooms, it was around 11 a.m. We then moved all the pear boxes into the darkest and coolest part of the back downstairs bedroom and left to fly home after having enjoyed a full week at the ranch.

Mark and Julia enjoying the view up by the airport that looks out across the ranch and out towards the ocean

A week later, Mark flew up to get the pears and they had all turned ripe. When he got the pears home, there was no choice but to get to work; by 2 p.m. he and Julia were deep in making pear chutney. That night Julia called and said, "Help!" So the next day I went by to make eight pear pies for the deep freeze, and Judy Kinney helped Julia make pear butter. By 5 p.m. the pears were all gone, and all that was left was to continue cooking the pear butter and put it in jars, which took Julia and Mark until at least 9 p.m. That was the most expensive pear chutney, pear butter, and pies you could have, with Mark having flown the plane to and back from the ranch just to get the pears.

This is a good place for me to tell about my two pear trees here at home. I picked my pears and put them in the refrigerator down in the gardener's house before we went to the reunion. They stayed on the green side for the next eight or more weeks. However, the story I really want to tell is that these were the biggest Bartlett pears I had ever seen. One was 7 inches tall and 13 ½ inches around and weighed a pound-and-a-half. There were many that were 6 inches high and 12 inches around, and most of the others were larger than regular pears. There were no worms in any of them. This is also true of the ones that we get at the ranch, and they are never sprayed except with the crows' and other birds' droppings; I like to think of that do-do as plant calcium—these pears always need a good wash job!

2004 was the year of the big pears

The Pink trailer is hauled away

IN 2004, A NEW patrolman came on board and the pink trailer saw its final days sometime during the winter months of that year. It was pulled out, crushed, and hauled to the dump, along with the pink stove, refrigerator, the kitchen sink, the pink bathroom sink and tub, and the woodstove in the living room that was used to heat the place. Many other things inside the trailer that served at least 50 years or more during its lifetime were also retired to the dump.

The porch, deck, and benches remain, and it is a great place to stop to rest and enjoy the breeze and the vast scenery all around you; it's even better on a moonlit night.

My regrets about the ranch

I REGRET THAT MY mother didn't live to see the ranch and all of her offspring of five generations getting together and enjoying each other's company. I also regret that we didn't turn the Main House into a museum, but by the time we got the house, too many things had disappeared. As the years have gone by though, the results suggest that the house has better served as a family ranch home. I really regret that Laurence, Gloria, and the grandchildren didn't come up more often.

I have loved the ranch from the beginning, with all the fun we've had with our kids, and with Jack and Bev in the early years, and later with all the families. And, I remember all the hard work that Frank and my brother Jack put into the place to make the ranch viable, and later all the work Julia has done to continue making it a viable, working ranch.

Through the many years, the Clarke Ranch has been a wonderful stopover place for a night or two on many of our trips, on our comings and goings while looking at our businesses, leaving home, and making a loop from the north end of California into Oregon and back home.

The Clarke Ranch is just one phase of many in Frank's and my life; however, it is one of several businesses that has given us a lot of enjoyment to our family and friends, and it continues to do so. It will also continue being a timber-producing ranch along with cattle and hunting, which is why Frank bought it in the first place.

I have turned the guestbook over to Julia and Mark for the keeping of good notes. It will not only be Julia and Mark's continued history of the ranch, but will help them in their old age to remember the when, why, what it cost, what they did, with whom, and all the good times they've shared there with friends and family. And the ranch will be a good place for Mark to be by himself and let his hair down, so to speak.

This story about the Clarke Ranch is my story as I remember it. The dates given might be different from somebody else's story. But this is as I remember it to be based on the materials, notes, the magazines and papers that were in the buildings when we got the ranch house, and what people have told us through the years.

Me and Frank enjoying the view

Mark, I got to know you as one of my own. You fit the ranch so very well!

Julia, you have always loved the ranch very much; it shows in what you have done and continue to do. Frank has turned the ranch over to you and into good hands.

In time, know that there may come a day when it is time for you too, to say "goodbye" to the ranch.

May God bless you, and look after you in health and everything that you do!

One of Frank's "should've deals"

THE CLARKE RANCH WAS a big success for us, but there were some properties that Frank learned about and did not buy. In other words, looking back, they were his "should've deals." Some of them were pretty big things.

The biggest property Frank ever bought was the Clarke Ranch, which he bought from the Union Lumber Company in 1967. After he bought the ranch, Frank became acquainted with the Union Lumber people, and they were talking with the fellow who had a sawmill seven miles away from us; his name was Bud Harwood. Bud ultimately wound up buying and cutting the timber Frank sold. Bud said, "Gee, now that I know who you are, and some of your background, why didn't you buy the company?" Frank said, "What are you talking about?" Bud said, "The Union Lumber Company. You bought this 5,000 acres from them, but I know your connections with American Forest Products, and so on, and wondered how come you didn't buy the whole company? It is for sale!"

Well, that was the first Frank heard of that! So over the next few days, he went over to the Union Lumber Company in Fort Bragg, California, and talked with some of the officials there. I guess he talked to the right person, because the guy said, indeed, the company was for sale and, yes, Frank could buy the company if he wanted to. He was glad to meet Frank. They had sold us the 5,000 acres of the Clarke Ranch, yet the Union Lumber officials themselves had not personally met Frank. The entire transaction had taken place through a broker. So the guy gave Frank a price for which the Union Lumber Company could be purchased for. The purchase price was not only for their properties — but the entire company, everything it owned. And it turned out that they had quite a bit of lumber and log inventory, and accounts receivable — even a very large note receivable, as Frank recalls. This was a big operation.

Union Lumber cut something like 160 million board feet a year. They had a total of 300,000 acres of land. And they wanted to sell. So Clyde Renfrow and Frank checked out the land for about an entire week, which was very easy to get to and look at. Frank specifically asked them for information on this. He wanted to know what their first timber was that they had cut back in something like 1885, when they had first started operations. They gave Frank maps and, in fact, the guy said there was approximately 60,000 acres of owned property in an area of easy ground and very close to Fort Bragg; the area where they'd started their first sawmill.

Frank particularly wanted to look at this first land they had cut, to see what it looked like in 1967, roughly 80 years or more after they had first started cutting timber. The land looked even better than Frank thought it would. They had done a pretty darn good job of cutting their timber. They left trees behind that were now pretty big. Scattered throughout the whole area, they left big old-growth trees for seedlings that had to be very old, even back in the time when they were doing cutting on the land. Clyde and Frank went through this whole area of 60,000 or so acres, and it all looked very much alike. It all had a good 50,000 to 60,000 board feet of cutable timber per acre, which was a tremendous amount of timber, and would be even today, let alone back then on land that had been cut 80 years before.

Frank's calculations showed that the timber on that land alone would pay for the whole price of the company. With this information, Frank went to see Walter Johnson and told him all about it. He told Walter he thought it was something we should buy. Then he got Charlie Gray into the act, and Charlie, being the highly conservative person that he was, decided that he didn't feel he wanted his company (American Forest Products) to put anything into a $30/thousand redwood operation. Well, actually, Frank wasn't pricing the timber that they saw at $30. It's easy to make a calculation to show that the values were tremendously there, but Charlie just wanted to turn it down. He said they had bought the mill at Jackson (actually at Martell), got a lot of timberland with that, and paid about $17 million for it, and they had that load on their back yet.

American Forest Products just wasn't ready to buy anything else. Frank thinks Charlie simply took a very dim view on what he told him, and just didn't want to open up his mind to something new like that. Walter Johnson just decided to go along with Charlie. That company could have come up with the money, or at least enough to do the deal, and then borrow what was needed to buy the Union Lumber Company in 1967. And Frank didn't go any further than that. He was scared to death to go to other big lenders. Looking back, that's what he probably should have done—gone to big lenders, such as insurance companies. Maybe he could have done the deal that way, but he didn't.

Frank did go to his bank, Crocker Bank, and was told that the most the bank could loan any one person wasn't enough to cover the price, so they couldn't even handle the deal even if they wanted to. He thought of maybe going to famous, well-known people that he knew had that kind of money, but then the thought occurred to him that if he did that, the information would start getting out to other people, and they could go ahead and make the deal without him. So he didn't do anything.

As bad as it all looks today, Frank just backed off and did nothing but hear about the news two years later. In 1969, the Boise–Cascade Company, from Boise, Idaho, purchased the property from the Union Lumber Company, and they didn't have any money either. Boise–Cascade bought it with Boise–Cascade stock. They gave the Union Lumber Company owners shares of Boise–Cascade stock, which subsequently was worth a whole lot less, for whatever reasons Frank won't mention. But, at any rate, the Boise–Cascade people, whom Frank knew well and who had bought out his mill that he had in Meridian, Idaho, freely told him all about it. They said they were sending money to Boise on a daily basis. That was just fantastic. In fact, the guy told him, "Have you ever been in an old J.C. Penney store and seen where you go to pay your money?" (You bought merchandise and then you paid the money and someone stuck the money into a receptacle, pulled a lever, and it went flying up on a wire to the head office, which was usually upstairs.) He said, "That's just like what we were doing. We were pulling a lever every day and sending money to Boise."

Boise–Cascade owned the Union Lumber Company from 1969-73. During those four years, Boise–Cascade received from the operation far more than the value of the stock paid for the property. After that, they sold it to the Georgia Pacific Corporation. Well, the real kicker here is that Georgia Pacific itself knew Frank quite well, and he talked with one of the executives at the company a year or two later. The executive said, "You know, Frank, we've made a lot of deals for Georgia Pacific over the years, and some awfully good ones. This is probably the best one we ever made right here. We know about your history of trying to buy this company and not doing so, and always wondered how in the hell come you didn't buy this company. We assumed just what you already told me, the reason you didn't was because Charlie Gray talked Walter Johnson out of it and, consequently, American Forest Products, who should have bought it back then, didn't. It's too bad you weren't able to buy this yourself. This has turned out to be just one hell of a deal for us, even at the price we paid!"

So there's the biggest "I should've" that Frank never did!

I tried to tell Frank to buy it on his own, but he could not get past the "I can't" stage. Years later he said he could have done it; he just didn't have the nerve.

Frank meditating over the market

APPENDIX B

<u>Over 50 Years at 211 Reward Street</u>

APPENDIX B INDEX
Over 50 Years at 211 Reward Street

211 Reward Street: the beginning

I HAVE BEEN ASKED by several people over the years what our place at 211 Reward St. looked like when we bought it and what changes have been made over the years. Therefore, I spent some time putting the story together to pass out on our 50-year anniversary of our family in the home. I called the story, "Garden Party Notes of 50 Years at 211 Reward Street to August 5, 2000." However, the notes ended up not being used because Julia gave us a surprise by having two couples come in and perform a Viennese waltz dance program for us, which everyone at the party loved watching.

Reward St. house in 1954, now painted white

I will now go into a more detailed story of our move, and I'll share what has happened to the house and area since we have lived here.

In July 1950, we decided to look for a house in Nevada City to move to so that Julia could go to school at Mount Saint Mary's Academy in Grass Valley. Frank said he was going to get a house so big that I would have to have a cleaning lady come in and do the work. It turned out not to be an easy task to find such a place. There were lots of old places in Nevada City, but none that you could move into without doing a lot of work on. We took a close, hard look at the red brick house, out on the (at that time) old highway, which had a swimming pool out in front (today it is a lodge). I remember it had one shower with seven showerheads, and as I recall, the showerheads were on three walls. I thought that was a bit much. It sits across the street from the Humpty Dumpty restaurant. Back then Maury Pontius's sawmill was just down the road, and with the noise it made, it would've been a little too close to home for me. I had spent a lot of time living near a mill in Camptonville, so I knew what that would be like. We put the brick house on the back burner and kept looking.

We looked at several houses over by the Pioneer Park area. The Lawrence Painter family, of S.P.D. Market, who at that time had a store on Broad Street, was living in the area. Then we saw an ad in the paper for a place on Reward Street. We took a look at it and thought it might be closer to what we were looking for. It was getting close to evening, so we asked the people if we could come back the next day, which we did.

The owners of the place were Kent Walker and his wife. After taking a very close look at the house, we asked if we could stay in it overnight. This was on a Saturday. They said yes, so we went back to Camptonville, got an overnight kit, and came back. We looked the place over and found that it would do. It was in need of some work, but not bad, or so we thought. We forgot to look under the house or up in the attic; just as well, for we would no doubt still be looking for a house. On Sunday, we bought the house. The pool table came with it. We moved in the next weekend, on Aug. 8, 1950. We rented the house in Camptonville to our mill superintendent, Ed Lemon, and his family, and later sold it.

The first thing I did on Monday was order a truck full of sand to be delivered to the back yard behind the office and by the big rock that is still there today. This was to take care of Julia and Laurence, who were six and four at the time, while I cleaned the house, which was on the dirty side. I also had to get work done on unpacking all the things we brought with us from our 1,000-square-foot home in Camptonville to this 3,000-square-foot home in Nevada City. Of course, the kids would bring in a lot of sand, but at least they were where I could keep an eye on them. The furniture we arrived with was rather lost in this big house. I remember having very sore legs after a week from walking on so much hardwood floor, which was everywhere except in the kitchen area.

The kids in our new living room, seen with the contoured chair I used to relieve the pain from my kidney surgery.

At the time, I remember the living room looked like a skating rink; it looked so big after coming from a small living room. Our four-foot sofa, big brown leather chair, nice chair, and coffee table were all the furniture we had for that room. (The leather chair is now at Julia's home. She has since had it reupholstered for her bedroom. The upright chair is in our exercise room and still has the original upholstery. In time, the sofa went to Mount Saint Mary's Academy, and the coffee table went into the gardener's house.)

We were not in the house more than a couple weeks when the Walkers asked if we would buy the rest of the acreage, which had the big swimming pool at the far end of the property. At that time, I was not very well, and I said that I could not take care of it, with all the kids in the area, so we said no—to Frank's regret to this day. He was too close to the forest to see what we could have done. As he says now, he could have brought down the bulldozer and covered the pool up, but that is past history.

Two months later, Walker started to build the house that is there now. He then lived in it for about two years. The Walkers sold it to the Spillers, who added on a room that was a garage and put a bedroom above it. The Spillers also extended the kitchen and added on a fireplace, and then added on a carport and a washroom, and then a guesthouse down by the pool. They lived there about 10 years.

They sold it to the Heilmans, who added on a room off the left side of the house and made an upstairs room in the area that was an attic. They also made the living room and dining room into one room. Somewhere along the line, they added on a bathroom and made the guesthouse larger. Their daughter, Barbara, ended up living there. Then, years later, they turned the back three acres into a subdivision and called it Heilman Court. The main house and guesthouse were sold a few years later to new owners by the name of Oros. They have been doing nothing but repair work since—along with having a tree fall across one end of the house that split one end of it right in two. This happened in January 2000. And so the adventure of all this property we should have bought continues on.

The Walkers were not the best builders but they sure did have good ideas.

Johnson helps fix up 211 Reward St.

AFTER WE MOVED INTO 211 Reward St., we realized that the house was in a run-down condition. After taking about two bucketfuls of cigarette butts out of both air vent returns, where the Walkers had placed tables with phones and used the vents for ashtrays (at least that is the explanation I came up with), I decided I would have to have some help to clean the house. At the same time, I would need a man to do some painting—I would also need a gardener.

As it turned out, the painter became my part-time gardener between his painting jobs. He stayed on with us for 11 years. He was sort of like a grandfather and a babysitter for the kids whenever I had to leave to go buy something. His name was Axel Johnson; he went by Johnson. Within a short time, he made a tree fort in the backyard. The kids would get pinecones and throw them back and forth at each other. He made a teeter-totter and a swing. Those, and the sand pile, were all there until after the kids came home from college. We also got a dog and called her Queenie. She was with us for a couple of years, and Johnson made a doghouse for her. Her doghouse stayed around for many years. One winter Queenie got out on the highway and was killed by a car. We also had a cat; I don't remember its name.

Johnson also made a small swimming pool out of the big fishpond. He raised it up two feet with bricks, put a ladder in it, sealed it in cement, and painted it a teal-blue color inside. This was in 1952. There were about 17 kids in the neighborhood, and they all came over just to be in the pool on a hot day. In those days, no one had air conditioners in their homes.

Frank and I enjoyed the pool on hot days

Johnson taught me how to take up and re-lay used bricks. Used brick that has been on the ground for a while will curl down on each end and rise in the center. If you turn the brick over and lay it down, it will break in the center. This has been a hard thing for me to get across to our workers. This kind of brick is hard to come by, and I really try hard to keep even half-pieces on hand that can be reused in any way. Having Johnson teach me this has helped me through the years. I have re-laid many a used brick, and have had to teach many a gardener how to take up and re-lay brick. (A lot of patchwork was done by taking up broken and cracked brick that was damaged by tree roots and re-laying them for our party in 2000 celebrating 50 years at 211 Reward St.)

What 211 Reward St. looked like in 1950

AS YOU DROVE UP a slight hill into the yard, you first saw the garage and the granny house (the gardener's house today). To your right, you saw the main house that was dark brown and covered with ivy. Then further to your right, at about the three-o'clock position, you saw the guesthouse, which is our office today. At the four-o'clock position, you saw the barbecue house. A closer look revealed five fishponds and a tennis court that had basketball hoops at each end.

Farther down the hill was a large swimming pool that was put in by the Walkers that we did not buy. The layout of the yard is very close to what it was when we moved in, and it is the layout of the yard when the original owners, the Jacobs, lived here. I think they were the ones who laid out the grounds in the late 1920s and early '30s. The main difference in 1950 was that the whole yard was overgrown with shrubs and in need of a great deal of work.

The original property went from Zion St. between Brock and Reward streets and back to what is now the Seven Hills School. The original entrance to the property was at the corner of Zion and Reward streets, and it's still there. The rock entrance that is there is of the same type of rock that is used in this yard. We retain the Reward Street name (although on some maps our driveway is now called Amaral Lane). Our house was the original house on all the property. I have traced the property back to Sara Jane Johns, who sold it to Edward C. Jacob and Bessie Jacob, on Aug. 8, 1933. The Jacobs sold the property to Roy E. Stowe and Elizabeth Stowe on Nov. 8, 1944. Stowe sold to Kent E. Walker and Grace R. Walker on April 10, 1946. Walker sold to Frank and LaVonne Amaral on Aug. 8, 1950.

This property was the only one on the hill that had any buildings on it. They were built by the Jacobs and finished by Walker. As I've said, by the time we got the property, the yard was more or less overgrown. This is Lot 3, Block 43, in Nevada City.

Lot 3 included parts of Brock Street that turned left onto Zion Street, which was in those days our main highway. It went past Reward Street, which was a short lane at that time, and continued past what was then called Miners Hospital. A few lots past that, it took off from Zion, went left down to Woodpecker Ravine, and from there turned left again and went uphill between where the school and Heilman Court are today, and then left again and back onto Brock Street.

Jacob sold off some of the land. The rest of it he sold to Stowe, who sold to Walker, and he sold property along Reward Street. There were several homes along Reward Street. In 1950, Walker sold the corner lot to Del Schiffner and moved the entrance road that came to this house, which was at the corner, and put it along the back of Schiffner's property line. Walker made a 40-foot easement and called it 211 Reward St. Walker later sold the rest of the land we did not buy to Spiller. When we moved to Reward Street, there were not many homes in the area; today, as I write this, it is a different story.

As I understand, Walker and his two boys are the ones that added onto the house at 211 Reward St. and did the work. They put in the living room over the basement, put in a furnace room and storage area, and put a fireplace in each room. The basement was joined to the old outside stairs. In the living room area, a hallway was added to the foyer; they joined this to the old bedroom and added a hallway, a closet and storage area, and added what is now our present-day bath and bedroom to the old house. They also added to the foyer from the living room to the dining room. It was joined to the old house. This is the shingle part of the house. The original house was a bedroom off by itself, with steps that went down to the outside and to an outhouse that also had a walkway leading to the granny house, which was on the other side.

Originally, I think the granny house at that time was just one room with a porch. Walker turned that room into a kitchen and added on a bath and a bedroom. When we bought the property, we redid the kitchen in the granny house, and also did the bathroom and put in a shower in the bathroom. We did other work in the house and used it as a gardener's house. Then, in 1995, we cut down the size of the kitchen, took the extra space, added it to the porch, and made a large bedroom. We added a storage room on one side of the porch in front of the bedroom and now had a very nice gardener's house, or guesthouse, with three rooms large enough for someone to live in. At this time, we also added insulation to the walls, redid the bathroom, took out the shower stall, and put in a tub-shower. We also added a heat and air-conditioning unit, redid both bathroom and kitchen floors with linoleum, and covered the bedroom and the living room floors with carpet.

I'll now continue with the story about the grounds of 211 Reward St. In the backyard was, and still is, the garden that had a water fountain, dated 1936, that ran from a fishpond, across the walkway, and down to a rock garden that had a lady fountain. The lady is still there and so are some of the plants surrounding her and a lawn. The willow tree that was there has long been gone. In my time I put a Blessed Virgin Mary statue in what was the pond, filled the pond with dirt, and I plant impatiens in it. You can also find, in some areas, dates embedded in the rocks. The walkways are the same; some are of rock and some are of brick. The rock walkway had a grape arbor, and the top of the arbor was covered with old wagon wheels. These were covered with grapevines that had seen better days and were past being able to save. I would like to have saved the old wagon wheels, for even at that time, I realized they were going to be keepsakes of the past.

Also under the arbor is a bench made of petrified wood, which has a table with a lady sitting on it (with no date). It is still there today, along with a round, rock tabletop on a rock stand, dated 1937. This is in the flowerbed area. About 1990, redwood branches fell on the tabletop and broke it in half. We had it fixed. In 2001 it happened again and we fixed it again; this time I hoped it was fixed for good. This is the area I call "the horseshoe lawn." In front of the carport, as you go toward the flower garden, is another stone wall that was made from volcanic ash. It is dated 1935. You will also find a brick oven and/or a barbecue or a smoking oven on the other side of the rose arbor. Above this area, the Walkers put in a tennis court with basketball hoops at each end. Volcanic ash rocks were used for stone walls and also for the foundation to the house.

In the area where the 1935 date is found, there were steps to an outside porch that went to a bedroom that was off the ground and stood by itself. The bedroom connected to an outside door that went to a walkway that went to a door to the living room. The living room had a big fireplace that was also made of petrified wood. This room was long and about 14 feet wide, a good-sized room. The area took in what are today my den and Julia's bedroom, closet and bath. We removed the fireplace. Next to it was the kitchen and a dining room that is now our dinette area. The floor is slightly higher where Walker joined the foyer to the bedroom hallway. He did this rather than make a slight rise in the two rooms. Walker joined the outside bedroom to the hallway that led to a coat closet, a bath, and our master bedroom. These you enter on the left; on the right, it went to the foyer, which went into the old living room, now a den, and also to the new dining room. From the foyer, you go to the big living room that is above the basement. From there you go down the stairs that were the original steps that went along the outside wall leading to the old bedroom and old landing, which has a door leading to the outside and to a walkway going to the gardener's house. Going down another flight of steps takes you to the basement which is 19' x 26' and has a big rock fireplace, a furnace, and a storage area. This room is a wonderful area for parties for the young and old alike.

The area between the main house and the guesthouse (or Frank's office) off the kitchen had a fishpond and a rather large patio area of nicely laid brick in a diamond-shape pattern. The brick walkway extended over to the barbecue house and large fishpond. (We later made a small swimming pool by raising it two feet above ground and, years later, took off the two feet and made it into a flowerbed). This makes a good area for having parties; no doubt the Jacobs used this area a lot.

The Jacobs originally laid all the brick walkways. They used "con" (convict) labor to do the work. When we first moved here, I found several balls with chains lying around the area of the barbecue house. I didn't pay much attention to them and my gardeners eventually walked off with them through the years. (After we moved here, Frank found out that some of the men who worked at the mill had also worked for Mr. Jacob on the grounds.) From the barbecue house area, you walk toward the front of the house and come to another fishpond, dated 1933. Sometime in the 1970s, Frank put the figure of an Oriental woman in the center of it, but it has never worked very well as a fountain.

One of the first things I did was have Johnson get rid of the ivy that was all over the outside of the house. This got rid of the ants and all the bottles of poison that were everywhere. The next project was to do some paintwork, and later the main house was painted white. Until now it had always been stained brown.

Some fixes and remodeling
at 211 Reward St.

THE FIRST YEAR, THE basement filled up with water that had to be mopped up after each rain. Many a night I would lie in bed thinking about how to correct the problem. I came up with a solution, which is still in use today. We put a two-inch drainpipe under the house, in the area over by our bedroom. The pipe was wired to the joists under the floor on that side of the house so it would never fall down. It was placed at an angle for the water to run down and exit by the basement walkway, then run down the side of the house and down the main walkway. And if water happened to get into the basement again, I had Johnson drill a hole through the cement and lay a pipe under the carport entrance for water to drain. This proved to be a good solution, for several years anyway.

Christmas 1950, George, Manuel Amaral and Manuel Souza playing pool in the basement

In 1952, we redid the kitchen by tearing out the old brown cabinets, which were later put in the gardener's house, and some in the garage. (They are still there today.) We next installed white metal cabinets that were in vogue at the time. We put a wall in the middle of the old living room (now my office), took out the fireplace, and made a bedroom for Julia. I think when Walker lived there they put in a bathroom between the living room and the kitchen.

About 1957, Ralph Childers raised the guesthouse two feet and Frank turned that building into his office.

In 1963, I completely redid the kitchen and Julia's bedroom and we remodeled the bathroom. One of the Ramey boys did it. The tile was done so well that it's still there today. We also added a closet in Julia's bedroom. (This was the year she went to Europe with the Experiment in International Living Group, her first trip alone out of the country.) While she was away, I did her bedroom. I also redid the dinette room from what used to be a service room for ironing, sewing, a storage space, and so on. We tore out the old walls in the kitchen and found that they were put together with boards taken off orange crates. No wonder our house was so cold! We added my art room off the kitchen where there used to be a porch. This work was done by a fellow named Ed Nygard. He did all the cabinet works, and so forth, right on the spot. I was the first to put all the drawers on rollers in this area, including the drawer under the sink.

At that time in my life, I had a very difficult time getting into cupboards to get things out, so I asked Nygard to see what he could come up with to make drawers pull out more easily, and he did. We did the same thing to the kitchen drawers in the houses we built in the subdivision in Deer Creek Park. In time, Nygard moved to Europe after he found out he had a daughter living there that was from his service days, and if I recall right, at the time he was alone and nearing his seventies. He did excellent carpentry work which I still have around today, and I remember him often.

In 1965, we tore out the walls in our master bathroom, took the tub out, added that space to the closet in our bedroom, and installed a Jacuzzi tub. I did the finish work on the cabinets, while the Nunnink boys did all the other work, including the tile job.

In summer 1993, the family was giving a party for Julia and Mark to announce their engagement. While we were getting the yard ready, along with the flower arrangements and everything else, I noticed the basement floor by the steps kept filling up with water. I was constantly mopping the floor and could not figure out what was going on. It was too late to get a plumber. On Monday I had a septic man come over to check and see what was going wrong. He used a camera device hooked to a wire that he could put into the sewer line. We found out that our line was an old hollow log that was used for a sewer pipe. No wonder I had so much trouble with water getting in the basement! Hollow logs had been used all over the city in the early days. We had to dig up the dirt before the plumber could do his job, so he left. This became a very big job. We had to dig out an area that was about six feet long, wide, and deep, in front of the outside door leading to the basement stairs. My gardener at the time was a man named Leonard Caskill, who had been with us for seven years. He and I started to dig. This became quite a job, especially when we hit a big chunk of cement about 18 inches square or so. The cement had been put there to hold the joints of the logs together. We got the dirt all out, but the two of us were unable to move the cement.

Whenever I'm in a tight spot, I always go to Frank. When he gets into the act, things happen, one way or another. This time he decided to get in on the action and help. Even

Charlene Appleton, who worked for him for years, got her camera out of her car and took a picture of Frank in on the action!

She said, "This I have got to see." Frank sized up the job and said, "Let's hook a pulley around the redwood tree and get the cement block out that way." This took a few hours. The hole he had dug was about six feet deep and there were roots from the redwood tree to deal with. When the concrete slab was finally out, Frank decided he had had enough. Now we were ready for the plumber to come back.

Frank, out of exasperation, got
a sledgehammer and started clearing the concrete

They ran the new sewer line attached to the joists running under the house so it would be easier to get to if any more problems should arise. As soon as the plumbing job was done, back went that big chunk of cement, and I sure do not want to be the one to dig it out on the next go-around. Leonard and I then proceeded to lay flat rocks with cement around the area as a walkway. We then re-laid the brick walkways in that area. There should never be any water in the basement again, and now maybe we can enjoy that room knowing there will not be any more water to deal with.

In 1995, we had all the kids over for our last dinner before the next big remodeling job. This was on the Saturday before the remodeling which was scheduled to begin on Monday. As I washed the dishes, they decided to take everything out of all the cupboards and drawers, and so on, and store everything in what had been Laurence's bedroom. What a time I had finding things after that! They set up the basement for us to have a make-do kitchen, and we had to wash dishes in our bathroom. By midnight, I was ready for the contractors to come. On Sunday, Laurence and some of his friends came over and removed all my cabinets to use over in one of the houses at the North Star property, rather than have the contractors rip them out. On Monday the remodeling of the kitchen area began. In the art room, we added the washroom, ironing room, and computer room. The cabinetwork turned out to be not as good of quality as what I had—the cabinets that were made in 1962—but the layout is better. The entire project took about six months and ran into our Music in the Mountains fund-raising party scheduled to be held in our yard in June. (Music in the Mountains is a program in Nevada County in which an orchestra performs classical music, pops, Big Band, and Broadway songs in concerts scheduled throughout the year. The program also offers educational opportunities for children and adults in music appreciation, performance, and composition.)

Through the years, we did many inside wallpapering and painting jobs that were mostly done by Tom Barney. He has gone from a young kid to a man in his middle years while working for me, and for the family.

Changes in the yard made through the years

WHEN WE MOVED INTO 211 Reward St., brick was on all the walkways and patio areas leading up to the front door. There was also a walkway along the house near the basement windows that led to the front door. The front area had, and still has, two holly trees, and between these two trees was a fishpond that you would see as you opened the living room door.

So much water was coming into the basement at the time that I had to find a way to stop it. So the walkway by the house was covered with cement and made into a drain and the fishpond was removed. Johnson put a walkway in its place. It is still there as I write this and the rest of the walkways are the same. Then, over by the walkway that is in front of the dining room and towards the kitchen area, and in front of my art room today, another change was made around 1958. I removed the brick and had cement put down. The short walkway that was there was removed, and we extended the lily-of-the-valley patch into this area, making the lily patch bigger. I have no idea how old the lily bed is; it could go back to Jacob's time. The lilies really seem to like where they are. It was around this time I realized I had to start finding ways to save brick to be used in other places. This short walkway was one place where I started saving the brick.

Ina and her family in Frank's office, 2005

By this time, Ina Gibson was back working for Frank and we had Brunswick Timber Co. (Ina had a baby girl who would sleep under one of the desks in the office while she worked.) Ina would laugh, for she saw me cut out a root as big as 18 inches around! It took me several days to cut it out because every time anyone came to the office, Frank told me to stop. And in those days we didn't have chainsaws. He could not stand to have anyone see me doing this.

(In 2005, I took a picture of Ina with her daughter—the one who used to sleep under the desk while she worked—and her granddaughter, with Frank in his office showing the two pictures of his Idaho and Camptonville mills.)

All the other walkways are the same in this area. The area between the house and the office had, as I mentioned, a fishpond. It was removed a couple of years after we moved in. The bricks were laid in a diamond shape, and I tried to keep that shape after the pond was removed, but through the years, the tree roots made it impossible to keep in shape. Around the pool were many small box-hedge shrubs that I removed and put around the yard. I have trimmed some into different designs.

Then, sometime in the early 1970s, Frank decided to have all the slate and brick removed from the back patio and have color cement put in its place. I could not get Mr. Joerschke to put the garbage can in a hole on the porch, so I told him I would do it. While he was working to get the ground ready to pour cement, I dug the hole and put the liner in. He was one surprised man. Those were the major changes to the brick areas, other than the walkway going to the gardener's place that was replaced with cement in about 1955. I'll never forget when the cement man came and poured the cement in one pile in that area and I had about 45 minutes to spread it and take the kids to school. I sure worked my fanny off on that job. Now, when I say, "I," I mean myself, not a gardener!

Low water pressure

THE FIRST YEAR LIVING at 211 Reward St., we discovered we had only 14 pounds of water pressure. This resulted in a battle for water in the house, as well as for the yard. To fill the little pool was another story. We were higher than the city reservoir which made it impossible to get the water we needed to even run a washing machine. I don't know how other people were able to operate this place with so little water. So the city let us install a pressure pump to bring enough water in for us to operate the washing machine. This was about 1951. After that, we had 60 pounds of pressure and I was then able to do what was needed to keep the place going.

Watering the yard at that time was done by moving a hose from place to place, until 1975. That was when we had a bad drought and you could not use water on your yard. Knowing rain would someday come again, we hired a contractor to come in and install a sprinkler system, but his crew didn't do a good job. I have often thought that this was their first job. They laid a two-inch line all around the property and put in the system. When I saw that they were fumbling around on the job, I decided to make a rather crude map of the job they did. That map has become a rather handy piece of paper many times since. I also had a drip faucet put in alongside each regular faucet so the yard can be set up for a drip system if it should ever be needed.

The lawn you see today by the pump house used to be all shrubs when we moved here. I had the shrubs removed and placed along the property line, and then turned that area into a lawn.

Fences, the barbecue house, and more additions

RIGHT AFTER WE MOVED in, the Walkers started to build their house, and it was built rather close to the swimming pool that Johnson made for Julia and Laurence. The Walkers lived in the place for about two years, and then they sold to the Spillers around 1954. They also had children and wanted a fence between our places. So they had Johnson, who was our gardener at the time, put the fence in. We did this job together.

Years later, after the big trees had to be removed, we finished the fence from our gate entrance to the property line using picket fence stakes and posts. Those stakes are made of redwood and came from the Clarke Ranch.

The heart lawn has not been changed. The flagpole stands in its original place and the sundial is on its original cement post. As years went by, Mark, Julia's husband, has supplied us a flag whenever it needs to be replaced. I should also add that when we first moved in, there were more trees around the edge of the lawn, as well as on the pump house lawn. These were mostly poplars, a silvertip tree, a spruce tree, and cedar trees that were removed over the years.

I'll always remember the time around the early 1960s when the Heilmans lived at 213 Reward St. Their son, Jeff, who was about 14 at the time, had just cleaned the roof of all its pine needles — that was a big job — and had finished cleaning up the yard. A big wind came up, and all the yellow leaves from our poplar trees blew over the fence into his clean yard. He was just at that age that he came over and told me about it in a very matter-of-fact way. I respected his courage enough that those trees came down within a few days.

There were also two cedar trees in front of the barbecue house, which is a hexagon-shaped building. After many years, the tree roots lifted the brick walls off the foundation, leaving the wall with the fireplace the only one still standing straight. The other walls were at

all angles, and were in bad need of being replaced. Through the years, I spent many hours wondering how it could be repaired back to its original shape. When I finally decided that I had figured it out, I called Tom Barney and told him what I had in mind. He said he thought he could do it, but it would not be an easy project and would cost around $50,000. This was done in 1996. The two cedar trees were gone years earlier and now the roots were dug up to make room for the new foundation.

The barbecue house that has been
used for many different things over the years

Tom worked many years for us doing house repairs, wallpapering, painting, carpentry, brick and cement work. He understood how I worked, and he also understood Frank and knew that he would gripe about the price all the way through it.

The first thing Tom did was raise the roof and secure it in place. After that, he dug out the tree trunks and the roots of the old trees that had raised the walls and destroyed the brick floor. He found a way to secure the walls, and proceeded to dig out the old floor and then put in a drain. He brought in underground electric and water lines. For a deep, strong foundation, he put in a lot of rock and then covered it all with cement.

None of this happened overnight; by this time, a few months had gone by. When the cement was dry, the walls were pushed and pulled into place. They only needed to be repaired where the old cement had broken away from the brick. After that was done, the roof was put back into place. The next job was to replace the windows and shutters, for the old ones were beyond repair. The windows had four-by-four-inch stained glass of all colors; to get this job done proved rather expensive.

After the roof and sides had been re-shingled and the place painted like it had been, the project turned out to be quite successful. I had the barbecue fireplace cleaned and put back into working order. I also installed a sink area that is hooked up to the city sewer. When Tom put in the floor, I had him put in a floor drain to the outside for washing down the floor. We added more electrical outlets and put in hot and cold water. It is now a good working addition to the place and a good place to store things during the winter months. And, yes, I still had an unhappy Frank. We finished the flowerbed area and re-laid the rock wall. The people of Music in the Mountains were pleased to see how well it turned out. They were always asking what I planned to do with the building.

From the time we moved in, the barbecue house went from a playhouse to a woodshed, then to a place for storing shingles left over from repairing the big house roof to use for starting fires in the fireplaces. The barbecue house stayed that way until I finally figured out how to save the building, starting right after I had the kitchen done in 1995. Tom did not do the kitchen job, but after it was done, I had Tom do the barbecue house job. About this time, I did not have a very "happy husband," but I had the work done anyway. It would have been cheaper to start from scratch, but it would have looked out of place with the rest of the property.

I should mention a little more history here about the tulip bed. It started out as a fishpond built around the 1930s, under Jacobs. As mentioned, I was told he had used convict labor to work in the yard, and they laid a lot of the brickwork throughout the yard, including the fishpond. I found this out because of the convict labor balls and chains I found in the yard.

In 1952 my gardener, Johnson, raised it two feet and turned it into a mini swimming pool. It stayed that way for about 30 years and was then turned into a flowerbed. I started by planting 300 tulip bulbs in the fall, which bloomed in the spring. I then planted impatiens, which I did for years, until the cedar tree by the garage had to come down. Once that happened the flowerbed no longer had shade; it was getting direct summer sunlight. The impatiens could not tolerate it, so they were replaced with tuberous begonias and many other types of summer flowers that could take the full sun. And that's what is there today.

Me and Frank standing by the tulip bed that was at one time a fishpond and then a swimming pool

About this time, Music in the Mountains held their first "Some Enchanted Evening" party at our property. To take care of this fund-raising party, which was during the time I was having the kitchen done, I had the electrician put in many electrical outlets on their own circuit all along the tennis court and the rose arbor. I also had additional power put in behind the office for the caterers. Before the job was all done, it cost us close to $5,000, but we did have a very nice party, and a year later, it was held at our place again. Any weakness that needed to be corrected was taken care of. This included a new toilet and shed that was put in behind the garage for anyone to use, including the gardeners. The yard was now set up for almost any kind of outside party. We later added another light post along the driveway coming up the hill to our place to match the one we had put in for the first party. The one thing that really needed to be done now was to re-do the tennis court.

As you entered the property on the left side, there used to be several big pine trees like a small forest, but in the 1990s they were hit with some bugs and we lost the trees. They might have been saved if I had known early enough about the infestation, but I wasn't aware of it until it was too late. After the trees were gone, I turned it into an acid-loving shrub area. It is a very nice spot in the spring when you drive into and out of the place.

I hope you enjoyed the history about 211 Reward St. You should now have a good idea what it looked like when we bought it and the changes that have been made over the years.

APPENDIX C

<u>The Gardeners Story</u>

APPENDIX C:
The Gardeners Story

The gardeners

SEVERAL PEOPLE HAVE ASKED me to write a chapter about my gardeners, saying it would be interesting to read about them, so here goes. As with the rest of the story, what I am writing is as I remember it and as close to the truth without hurting anyone; I do not intend to hurt any of them in writing this. My memory may not be exact, but I will try to come as close to the details as possible. My years may be off a little on some of the gardeners, for I have not kept a complete record on all of them. I may unknowingly leave out a few names, but if so, it's because they had only worked for me for a few weeks to a few months.

I have always been a very strict person that knows what I want, and all of my gardeners soon learned this. I also knew what they were doing and when, and about how long it should take them to do any given project. I would tell them not to try to fool me, for I would know in a very short time if they had tried. I would not take any nonsense from any one of them, even if I had to prove it by showing them, and sometimes that was necessary. And I can work along with the very best of them. I was more than fair with them and would always help them whenever they needed help. If there was anything they needed to do any given job, it was provided, for no one can work without good tools. They all got praise, for that is the best reward you can give others, besides pay.

During the times when there were no gardeners around, and this happened many times over the years, I would have to do all the yard work myself, including mowing the lawns in the summer and shoveling the snow in the winter months. Mowing lawns was and still is a hard job for me, for I have never been able to use my right side all that well; there just isn't any strength on that side. So when it came time to start the lawn mower, after trying several times, I'd often have to go to the office and get Frank to come out and pull the cord to start it for me. Then back to the office he would go. There would be little conversation, for no doubt he was deep in thought and didn't want to lose his train of thought, and, no, he did not resent me asking for his help to start the lawnmower. I would only be in his way for a few minutes, and then off I'd go to mow the lawns. I tried very hard not to kill the motor too often.

So when there were no gardeners, there was always *me, myself, and I.*

1950 to 1962 — My first gardener was Axel Johnson

BEFORE I GO INTO Axel's story, I would like to tell a little history of the gardener's house on our property that he moved into. I'm sure I have talked about the gardener's house before, but I'll share it again here because I feel it will sort of help you understand why it was easy for me to get gardeners.

First off, the building was old when we moved here. It started out as a one-room building and was used as a granny bedroom, and in those days you went outside to the "john" that was between the two houses. Then sometime in the early 1940s, a bathroom and living room were added on, and the first room was made into a large kitchen and dining area. There was a porch and a shed on the side and electricity was added. There was a wood heater in the kitchen that we took out right away, and we added gas heaters to both rooms. The house has always been painted white on the outside. To dry clothes, the laundry was hung on a line behind the house, so as not to be seen by anyone. This is the guest house that Axel moved into sometime in the fall of 1950. He came to live here for 11–12 years, and he was already in his mid-sixties when he started.

When he took sick, and I never really knew from what, he went to Miners Hospital, which is right at the foot of our hill. He stayed there for several weeks. Dr. Frey told me not to let him move back in, saying he would die on me if he did. So I went into the gardener's house to pack his things. When I got inside, I saw about two inches of dirt caked to the bathroom floor that had rotted away. No doubt, he had never swept the house all the while he lived there! I knew I would have to rip out the floor and put in a new shower and a new toilet. I also ended up redoing anything else that had to be done, including painting the inside. This all took some time, and by the time Axel got out of the hospital, the bathroom was all torn up and the rest of the house was under repair. There was no way he could move back in.

He moved to a nearby hotel where there were rooms you could rent by the month. It took some time before he could work at his painting, which is what he mostly did for a living, even while he lived here as my gardener. By this time, he was in his late seventies and not in good health, and he didn't take very good care of himself. He gave me some of his old paintbrushes when he left; I still have them and take very good care of them, for the bristles are made of pig's hair.

About a year went by before we put anyone back into the gardener's house. It was from this experience that I learned about what gardeners will and will not do.

(I have written about Axel back in the first part of my story that pertained to the yard and what it looked like from 1950 and on through the years. I will try not to repeat myself too much here.)

When Axel first came here, he was doing some painting for me, and he asked if he could live in the house. He said he would do yard work for me whenever he had any free time. That is how he came to live here. He became like a grandfather to the kids. He was a short, wiry fellow and was nice. He never used any foul language and was always clean in appearance. He was very good to the kids and could be trusted at all times. He was a religious person and used one of the closets in his house for praying in each day.

He showed me how to take care of my bricks and how to lay them back in the ground after they had been pulled up. Bricks have a curve in the center where they have been lying on the ground for years. They have to go back the same way or they break in half, and you need to lay them on a bed of sand.

Axel turned the oblong fishpond into a small swimming pool for the kids in 1951–52 and laid brick all around it. He made a tree fort, put up a swing, and made a teeter-totter for the kids. He also put in a basketball hoop for them. He changed the walkway going up to the front porch, and it is the same today. When he put this walkway in, the kids would ride piggyback on him. He really had fun with the kids and they had fun with him.

In order to put the new walkway in, he had to take out a round fishpond that was between the two holly trees. The fishpond was never put back. There were actually two fishponds removed. The other one was in the patio between the office and the kitchen. He replaced the area with brick. At the time, he was able to keep the bricks in their original diamond pattern, but through the years, I have not been able to keep it due to the tree roots that keep moving it out of position. As the years have gone by, I have replaced many of the same bricks that he laid, and, yes, I put them back in the same way again. Axel also turned the garage into a tool shed, and he did the walks that have the round rocks laid in cement.

I took care of the yard work during the week, and when Laurence got older, he helped after school. Axel would always work on Saturdays and on weeknights after he got home or when he wasn't working on a painting job.

Frank was gone so much during this time that Axel, whom we really called Johnson, was a good man to have around. I always felt safe with him here, and when I would have to leave to get something, he would look after the kids for me.

Axel has always been a little gem in my life, and regardless of who comes to work for me, they hear about him, and I always tell them about how I learned to lay brick.

I took care of the yard work myself after Axel left and did so until the gardener's house was fixed, which took about a year or so. Through the years, there have been times when a year or so would go by before I would have a new gardener move into the house. It was during these times that I would get outside help that worked by the hour.

1963 — I can't remember his name

I CAN'T REMEMBER THE name of the gardener who started working for me in 1963, but he was what we would call a first-class Okie in those days, which wasn't saying much for him. He was with me for less than a year. While we were on a trip one summer, I think it was to Idaho, he forgot to water the two shrubs that we have always had in the two green planters that were here when we moved in. The planters are in the area going up the steps to the back patio. One died for lack of water, and it was right next to a faucet! We had to replace it. I lost other plants that also dried up from lack of water.

This gardener was the one who helped me plant the dogwood tree that I brought down from Deer Creek Park in the "blue bomb" pickup, so I guess you could say he had his good points. And he was also one to throw a temper and would never take orders from me. I moved him—lock, stock, and barrel—out of the gardener's house after he refused to plant the lawn seed the way I asked him to on the heart-shaped lawn after it had dried up. I remember I had a cleaning woman who really enjoyed helping me do it. She really went to work with her broom sweeping the cobwebs down and giving him hell for not keeping a clean house; she could hardly wait to get him out. He just sat in a chair on the lawn watching us do all the work. Yes, we did move his stuff, which we put in boxes, out on the lawn that night. This was during the summer of 1963.

Pitchfork

I DON'T REMEMBER WHERE this story fits in, but I will tell it anyway, for it would fit in during any of the years of the late 60s.

One time when I was home alone, at a time when I had no gardener, I was out by the garage doing yard work. During the early years, I had a real nice vegetable garden and a strawberry patch in the lower yard, which I had right from the 1950s on up until the kids left home. I was working in that area when a young man about my age, maybe in his late thirties, came walking up towards the garage with a look on his face like he belonged here. I was alone, so I went up to the garage, and as he walked up, I backed up into the garage door and reached for the pitchfork that was hanging inside the door. I walked right toward him with the tines facing him and said, "What do you want?"

He said, "I'm going back of that house (pointing to the gardener's house) to climb the fence to go to Brock Street." I said, "Oh no, you're not," and I went right toward him with the fork in front of me facing him. He said he did it all the time. I told him this was the last time and that he had better not do it again. He walked backward to the gate with my pitchfork right at his heart level, and, yes, I would have used it. I don't think he ever came back again.

That corner behind the gardener's house has always been a trouble spot for me through the years.

About 1963 to 1964

A YOUNG FELLOW CAME to work for me and was here about a year as I recall. One day in the summer, we were laying a rock wall by the two redwood trees that are near the horseshoe lawn. He said I didn't need him on Saturdays and asked if I would let him work for someone else to make extra money. Now, I was neck-deep in cement laying the rock wall with him, and this was a Saturday, and he was already being paid for it. So I said, "You're right, I don't need you. You may move out and leave right now." He said, "Oh sh*t," and that was that.

I finished the rock wall myself and went on to do another one. I don't remember getting anyone right away. (This same rock wall came down and was replaced in 2002, so I guess I did a good job.)

1965 to 1966 — Mario, a Hispanic man

EVERYBODY KEPT TELLING ME to get a Hispanic man to move in and do the gardening, so I finally did. His name was Mario. He was good and left his "trademark" on the flowerbed area down in the lower garden. He did this by laying rocks at an angle and they have held up very well. He also laid rocks in cement that outlined the borders around the flowerbeds; this made it easier to have walkways between the beds. We put small white rocks in the walkways that are still there today.

Mario was a small, frail man. He was the man who helped me with the apartments in Oroville that I have told the story of — pouring cement all along the backside of the apartments to keep water from getting into the building.

Mario was also a good woodworker. I had an oak dining table in the kitchen in the gardener's house that would easily seat six to eight people. It was in need of being refinished. Mario did that during the winter months. He did such a good job that it is now in the music room in the house at the Clarke Ranch. It is still in excellent condition. He stayed on for a year, and then one day he said it was too lonely for him and that the house had ghosts in it. He didn't have any friends in the area and wanted to go back to Stockton, so he left us.

Every good gardener I've had has always left a mark somewhere on the property, and that is one way I have been able to remember them throughout the years. I may not remember their names, but I can see them in my mind.

1966 to 1967 — A married couple; I forget their names

I DON'T REMEMBER WHY I put them in the gardener's house, but I remember he was a good gardener, or so he said. He wife was an invalid, and I think Frank found them through some organization that had asked us if we would help them out any way we could. At that time, I was completely furnishing the house, providing everything except for the dishes and the bedding. The house had a full-sized poster bed in the living room. I remember she did not like the bed, so they put in another bed for her. She had a habit of staying in bed most of the day, and the rest of the time, she would sit around and read. I never knew what was the matter with her. He did the yard work, but I don't remember how good he was. I do know that they didn't stay long.

I would like to tell a story about them, one that has always stayed with me because of the scene it made as it happened. We live very close to the hospital and she had to go see the doctor at his office in downtown Grass Valley. How they got there, I don't know. I do know they had to get from the downtown office back to the hospital near our house. The doctor was Dr. Bern Hummelt, a good friend of ours, and after he was done with whatever he did for her at the hospital near our house, the couple wanted the doctor to get an ambulance to bring her home.

Well, when Dr. Hummelt found out where they lived, he said, "I know those people and you don't need an ambulance to take you up there. I'll take you up." So they came up the driveway in a wheelchair with Bern pushing it all the way up the hill. I was out in the yard working. He saw me and said, "I'll be damned if I was going to spend my tax money on such a foolish thing as that." He hated the "welfare freeloaders" who used his, and our, money so wastefully. He said all she had to do was get out and do some walking and she'd be fine.

They moved out shortly after that.

1967 — John, who was about 35 and was from Downieville

I THINK JOHN'S FATHER was a judge, and John used that claim to get the gardener's job with us. After several months, I let him go in the fall, for I found out he was on probation. He was one of those fellows who was always drunk and young enough to always have a group of people in and party up half the night when I was gone. He would try to sneak them in by going down below the garage and into his house.

At that time, there were two older gentlemen living in the house just below ours. They would always look after my place and could see everything that went on up at my place. They told me that when we were gone, a lot of parties were going on. During that time, Frank was not home much and I was going away a lot with Frank, so we let John go.

I was sorry when the two elderly men took their own lives within a few months of each other. They were kind gentlemen and were my "watchdogs," so to speak. We had many conversations across the fence. Fortunately, the people in the houses below mine today are still my watchdogs.

I did all the gardening work after this for a while; I even mowed the lawns. I also became good at mixing three parts cement to seven parts sand and adding water to make a mortar to lay bricks and rocks. Axel taught me how to do this back in the 1950s.

When I didn't have a gardener around, it was not unusual for me to do all the work in the yard, even bringing in the firewood and removing the snow from the walkways in the winter. So being out a gardener was not something that would upset me for long.

1969 to 1977 — John Acher

JOHN ACHER WAS SOMEWHERE in his seventies when he came to me. He was really nice. He came to me one day while I was doing books in my den inside the house. He came to the sliding glass door that was open and talked to me through the screen. At this time, I was doing the gardening work by myself and had been for a while. How he found out about me, I never knew. He asked for the job and I said, "No, you are a wino." I looked at his face and he had a big red nose, so I knew he was a wino. I said I didn't need that around. He said, "Yes, I was, but I'm not now, and I need this job to stay sober." He said he would take good care of my yard.

Well, I ended up hiring him, and he was true to his word—he never did drink. He was with us until one day Frank asked him to do something, and he told Frank, "You are not my boss," so Frank told him to leave. I had to go down and talk to him, and he was really sorry he had said that to Frank, but he did leave.

During the time he worked for us, John took art lessons from me. He often took care of the house and would lock it up after all the students had left the art class I was teaching. There were quite a few times when Frank would come down to the basement while I was teaching an art class, with six to eight students, including John. Frank would come down and say it was time for us to leave for some trip we had to go on, and the students would all stay and finish up what they were doing. John took good care of everything. I did a portrait of him, which now hangs in the hallway of our house. He would often have me come down to visit him in his house to show me a painting he was working on. He kept a very clean house and was a good cook.

My portrait of John

After he left, and because of the drought in 1975, I didn't have a gardener for a few years, but I had other people coming in to do odd jobs.

About 1977 to 1978—Ralph Heath

RALPH WAS WORKING FOR Frank, so I had him come over and do some work for me. I had him redo the garage and put it back into shape; he leveled the building and put in a cement pad for the floor. He also put in shelves and fixed it up to what it is today. He also re-laid the brick between the office and the house, but he laid the bricks upside-down, so I ended up re-laying all the brick that he forgot to turn over. Frank was fit to be tied with me for redoing it, but I knew the bricks would only wind up all broken in half if not re-laid.

During this time, Ralph did many odd jobs for me, as well as for Frank.

Summer 1977 to 1978 — A couple of young fellas broke their eyeteeth putting in my sprinkling system

I HAD A COUPLE of young men come in that were so-called contractors; they were here to put in a new underground sprinkling system throughout the yard. To do the job, ditches had to be dug, electrical wiring needed to be put in, and a new 2-inch main water line was needed to circle the whole yard. I still think they broke their eyeteeth on this job because of the way they went about it. I knew I would have to do a drawing of some kind of the yard, for they worked with no drawings or plans of any kind. The yard was tied up for at least a year and a half before I could even start putting landscaping in of any kind. It ended up that in order to have electricity to the garage, it would have to come from the gardener's house. So, electrical power for the sprinkling system ended up on that meter, as did the controls to that end of the yard. This meant I could no longer turn off the power to the gardener's house when it was not in use.

And to this day, many years later, I have little respect for their workmanship, and I don't mind saying so.

1978 to 1979

I HAD KEVIN DODINE working for me about this time. He was the one that plowed the grounds that were to be put into lawns, and he did a very good job. He was going to school at the time and lived at home with his folks.

He worked off and on for me for several years, and his youngest sister is our godchild. After he finished taking care of the soil, I planted the lawns myself, did the watering, and watched it grow.

1979 to 1983 — An elderly gentleman

ABOUT THIS TIME, AN elderly gentleman came to work for me. He was a good man and was never in a hurry when it came to quitting time. If I was doing some work with him in the yard, he would stay with me until it was done, even if it was six at night. The next day when he was doing something, and I felt things could wait until the next day, I would tell him to take the rest of the day off. Not many of my gardeners would work the way he did.

I found he was really easy and enjoyable to be around. I'm sorry I can't remember his name, but somehow the name John keeps popping in my head. He helped me put in all the plants that are around the pond in front of Frank's office.

He stayed a little over four years, and as I've said, he was on the older side. Then one day he told me he was leaving. When he left, he asked me if he could have one of the old lanterns that were hanging on the tree near the office, and I said yes. He fixed it up so it worked. At that time, I had two of them; now I don't have any. He said he had no home or family to go to, so he was going to go out into the hills and spend the rest of his life there. He had an old car, and it was full of all the things he owned. He no doubt lived out of his car and made a bed in the backseat. I never saw him again, and I'm sure he ended his life living off the land. I have very good memories of him. May he rest in peace.

1983 to 1984

WHO CAME NEXT? I don't remember, but no doubt they came and went and left some part of them with me. I remember I had other gardeners here, but I can't recall the years or their names; however, I can see their faces.

One was a young couple with a very small child, and they would throw darts at the closet door in the living room. And this was not too long after I had just had it painted. I installed a full-length mirror to cover up the damage. They left on their own after a few weeks.

I've already said that there were times that maybe a year or so would go by without a gardener and I would do the work. Frank and I had an understanding when we first got married that I would take care of the house and everything therein, and he would take care of me. And I've tried to keep it that way.

I always considered the yard my business and I knew I could handle most any problem that came up. This has helped keep me in good health and kept me from ever getting lonely. As I've said, Frank was gone a great deal in our early life, and after that, the kids left home.

Nov. 13, 1985 to 1993 — Leonard M. Caskill

LEONARD CASKILL WAS WITH me for about eight years and was a really nice fellow. Toward the end, he got so he was going to Reno a lot, so I had to let him go.

Leonard knew a great deal about yard work, but he did not like to do it the way I wanted it done. I would often have to go out and do it the way I wanted it done. But he was a loyal person, dependable, and likable. He had many personal problems and felt he had to take care of them himself. I remember he was worried about a sister who was giving him trouble. He asked me if she could live with him until she got on her feet, and I said yes. He then had a younger brother who also came to live with him. Leonard sure had his hands full!

Where they slept in that two-room house, I will never know. And how they could move around and do anything kept me wondering. I was sure the house was getting all banged up. The electric and water bills really went through the roof at that time. But Leonard would put in extra time, and he made his younger brother do yard work with him to keep him out of trouble and out of the house. This let up after a few years.

I had Tom Barney paint the house inside and out. Somewhere along the way, I think Leonard brought in a waterbed and put it in the kitchen, and if I recall right, he also brought in a girlfriend, but she didn't last very long. The bed, however, did. I overlooked a lot of what he did because he was a good worker and could be trusted; he was never one to lie to me. It got so that when we went on long trips, he would drive us to the airport in Sacramento and then bring the car home. He would then come and pick us up when we got back.

Leonard's handiwork is all over the yard. It's hard for me to walk around without seeing something he did, for he had many good ideas. Some of the things he did have since been redone by me or replaced with something else.

A few things changed after he left, including no more fires to burn pine needles and a blower to blow the needles into piles. We now take the pine needles to the dump, which cuts down on a lot of hours spent burning. And I still don't know if the blower was such a good idea.

One of the things Leonard said I taught him was how to take up and replace old brick, but then again any gardener who works for me and stays around this yard for any length of time will learn this trade from me. He also re-laid the brick around the tulip bed, but when he was done, I redid them. He learned not to get in too big of a hurry.

One of the last major things he did was replace the sewer line from under the house. We had to take out a lot of the walkway in front of the door leading to the basement steps. We also had to remove a big piece of concrete that held the old wood together that was used as a sewer line. This was buried underground. In the old days, old logs were hollowed out and used as pipes for sewer lines, and that was what was under our house. No wonder I had so much water getting into the basement!

We had to dig a big hole at least six feet deep and at least as wide before we could have the new pipes and drains put back in. Even Frank got into the act by helping us with that piece of cement. After everything was done and we were ready to re-cover the line, back went that cement into the hole. I hope I never have to redo that job again. After it was finished, Leonard helped me replace the rock slate with cement, and we replaced the bricks in the walkway that had been taken up to do the repair job.

Leonard came over to see me in November 2001. It was good to see him. He enjoyed just walking around the yard. He also wondered if I could use his brother to work in the yard, and I said yes. I used his brother once but have not been able to get him since. I believe Leonard has a good job up around the airport, and I have an idea he is still living by himself, as of this writing.

In fall 2004, he called and asked me if I had enough work for him to work two days a week. I told him Victor was able to do all the work in three and a half days each week, for he is a real gardener and knows just what to do. But I told him I'd keep him in mind, for he does know how to do brickwork. I always enjoy seeing and visiting with him when he drops in.

December 1993 to November 1995 — John

JOHN WAS WITH US for a couple of years and was a good worker, but he hated doing some things and would not do them. So I had to tell him my priorities came first, and if they were not done by 4:30, he would have to continue until they were done. It took several months for this to sink in. I finally told him to do what he hated to do first, to get it out of his hair, so to speak. Once he learned that method, he was fine.

His ex-wife kept coming over and harassing him on the job. So one day Frank called the Department of Corrections and had a restraining order put against his ex-wife, to keep her off our place. She hollered, and Frank could hear it in the office — all kinds of things, and she used a lot of four-letter words when she came in the yard. This took place around the heart lawn. John was a hard worker and was clean in every way, including his housekeeping. But in time, she succeeded in getting him picked up by the police.

I didn't put anyone in the house after he was picked up. I started thinking about remodeling it, and it took a while before Tom Barney was able to get to it.

John came back after he had been gone for a while, but I had already started the remodeling job. I should add here that anybody who has worked for me for any length of time has learned a trade that will put him to work anywhere in the local area if it pertains to gardening, for most people know what I do to train my men. And that is how John got a job with a local landscape firm and ended up working for them until about 2000.

He called me one day and asked me what he should do about being tired with the kind of work he was doing. I suggested maybe it was time for him to move on to some other kind of work. I told him to remember to do the things he hates to do first, for if he did, he would have any job covered.

I tell all my new gardeners that it takes me just a few minutes to find out what they like to do and what they procrastinate on doing. I'm an old pro when it comes to this yard and no one fools me for a minute, even about how long it takes to do a job. I've done all the jobs many times over throughout these 50-odd years.

In 2001, John was working a good job in Reno. I later found out in reading the local newspaper that he had been put back in jail for the same problem he had here.

1995 to 1997 — Time out to remodel the gardener's house

IT TOOK OVER A year to remodel the gardener's house. During that time I had no gardener, so I did the gardening work myself with the help of Glen Cooper, Paul Faahs, and others who could do what I couldn't. In all the years we have lived here, I have always worked right alongside the gardeners, and many more hours on my own after they would quit when their workday was done.

Around this time, I added a full-sized bedroom to the gardener's house, which had originally been built around 1927. Tom Barney knocked out the kitchen wall and extended that area into a new large bedroom. Before we could do that, we had to dig out a lot of dirt and lower the ground; part of it was below ground level. We put in a full-length closet, and in doing this, we cut down the size of the kitchen. We enlarged the bathroom, put in a tub-shower to replace the shower, and removed the hot water tank and put it outside in a shed of its own. We installed a new air-conditioning unit, insulated the whole house, added a washer/dryer unit, and put in a new refrigerator. We still had a good electric stove. We then put new linoleum in the kitchen, bath, and hallway. The bedroom and living room were carpeted and drapes were added. We also made a nice storage room on the porch.

After everything was finished, the cottage ended up as a nice small home of about 600 square feet.

May 1997 to 1999 — Sonya

SONYA WORKED FOR ME until giving notice on Jan. 1, 1999. She left a month later on Feb. 1. Sonya was a tall, heavy-built woman, and when she got the job, she said she had wanted it for several years but was never able to get it, for we preferred men, and she was right.

Sonya was a good worker and did most of the weeding and working the ground while sitting down. She did not want to do heavy work like trimming the English laurel plants, and so on. She said she would not do them, so I would have to either do it myself or get someone else to come in and do that work, including other things.

One day she asked for a raise. I said not as long as I had to get outside help to do her work. So she decided to leave. She left the house clean, and she did clean it every weekend, which most of the gardeners did. She had some birds that kept her company; she was not one to have a lot of people in. She was also quiet with her radio.

I got a call a few years later from someone that wanted to know if she had worked for me, and, if so, if she was all right to hire. I said yes, she was fine.

Feb. 6, 1999 — Ralph

RALPH WAS A GOOD worker and a nice enough person. He worked for me for about a month. On getting his first paycheck, he and his girlfriend went walking down the hill of our driveway to go to the bank to deposit the check. He was picked up by the police and put in jail; this was during his lunch break. I waited all afternoon for him to come back and help me with the job we were doing on the heart lawn; finally, his girlfriend came back and told me what had happened, but she didn't know why they'd picked him up.

Ralph had borrowed $100 from me earlier in the month and was going to pay me back after he cashed his check. It was obvious he was not going to be back for some time, so that weekend I went down and packed up his belongings in boxes and stored them here for more than a year. He wrote me a note and to thank me for what I had done for him.

Then one day in fall 2000, he came to see me in the yard and told me what had happened. He had stopped by to see if he could work for me to pay back the money he owed. He did some odd jobs and brickwork for me until he had me paid off. He had also come by to tell me he was married, had a baby, and had found a good job. He said he was living in the area.

In summer 2004, he came over and asked for some work so he could have some money to help him get a ride to Los Angeles, so I put him to work washing the cars. That was all he needed; I haven't seen him since.

April 1, 1999 — Charlie

I DON'T REMEMBER CHARLIE'S last name. He moved in at the beginning of April 1999 and was out on June 1, 1999. He moved out on his own. He loved the house but didn't want to work very hard.

He was short and slender and a nice enough person.

June 1999 — Nathan Hank

NATHAN WAS A QUIET gentleman of about 57. He was with us for a year, left a clean house, and was a good gardener. However, he wanted to go on a bicycle trip from Los Angeles to New York with a group. When he left, he said he liked living and working here because of the relationship that Frank and I had with each other. I would have kept him on the job. He was like an old man for his age, more like 70, except that he went everywhere on a very expensive bicycle. He was a very thin, wiry fellow.

He left us a note when he left, saying he had learned so much in such a short time. He also felt privileged to have our worlds meet. He was in awe of the bonding that Frank and I showed for each other. I feel he did not lack for money and was an educated man, but maybe he was trying to find himself. I hope he did.

Jan. 1, 2000 — Richard

RICHARD MOVED IN RIGHT after Nathan moved out, and when Nathan left, the house was clean. He did not smoke or drink and had very little company.

It was a real nice January when Richard moved in, and it was at this time we started to redo the tennis court. So Richard got a good dose of different kinds of gardening work, and I also found out what he could and could not do. He became good at laying brick and took great pains to do a good job. Like Nathan, Richard was a tall, wiry man. He had just joined Alcoholics Anonymous and was going to the meetings, as well as to his church. He was really working on that. He would cry at the drop of a hat and would have to go see his pastor all the time. He told me he did not drink and was quitting smoking, which he never did.

One of the things about the gardener's house was that I never allowed anyone to smoke in the house. It had a very clean smell about it and I wanted it left that way. That was the one thing the rug-cleaning people always commented about—how clean the house smelled, and no animal smell, either. In a very short time, he was having his five kids in. I noticed the blinds were always pulled. This should have been a warning, but it never occurred to me that they were smoking inside the house. And he was having his kids in at all hours of the day, which interfered with his job, and they were staying with him at night.

The house was meant for only one person, and sometimes gardeners would try to fool me, but never for long. Richard had fooled around with not paying his child support, and it caught up with him when he came to work for me. This became the reason he left.

He was a good worker and tried to do anything I asked him to do. One of the things he learned very early is that when I say turn the dirt over, I mean a whole shovel-full turned over, and to take out all the roots. I had him do the lawn in back after the tennis court was done. When I got ready to seed the ground, I found he had not turned it over yet. So I started at one end of the lawn and turned every inch of the ground over. I took three small truckloads of roots out of the ground before we planted the area. This job took me over the weekend to do. Then on Monday, he helped me rake and level the ground. This was the one major job we did while he was with us.

He was a good learner and I would have liked to have had him stay, but he could not tell the truth, and his family overran the place. He and Frank sure did not like each other; they had a few words and that ended that. He took a month to move out, and he had destroyed the stove. The house was so full of smoke that the walls had to be cleaned before I could put a new gardener in the place. The smell did not leave for three months. He was the first gardener to do that to me. I had to spend a lot of money to clean it up, so he never got his last paycheck, and he never even came to get it.

Feb. 14, 2001—Scott

SCOTT CAME TO WORK for me on Valentine's Day, 2001. He was a good-looking blond fellow on the husky side and stood around 5-foot-6. Earlier, his father had dropped by to see me and asked if I could use a man that he knew of, someone who would be good and was single and was not on drugs and did not smoke and had no girlfriends.

All this was true when Scott started to work for me; he went to church every evening and was a good worker. He worked for me for a few weeks. He moved in on Feb. 15, and that evening I had a new stove delivered for the gardener's house. His dad was there to help him move in when the stove arrived. I always have the house clean and expect to have it that way when they move out; if not, then I take it out of their paycheck when they leave.

This was the case with Scott; he was a clean housekeeper. After being with us for a few weeks, we had to go to the ranch for several days and left him to take care of the place. On one of these days, it was raining when he walked to the store to buy groceries. When he got ready to walk home, he had someone bring him home in a car. The guy's car had poor brakes and could not stop, so it ran into the rose arbor and broke a section of the fence. This caused the neighbors to call the police. Scott called Laurence who came and took care of the problem until we got back.

When we got home and got out of the car, Scott was right out there to let us know what had happened; he thought for sure he would be fired. He told us the whole story, and, of course, we did not fire him, which later was a mistake.

After a while, when he worked, he would sweat so much that it ran off of him like water was poured over his head. I later learned that was caused from methamphetamine or vodka.

The next time we took a few days off to go somewhere, I can't remember what for, something else happened. It was nothing bad, so I've already forgotten what it was. He was always out of money, but that was OK, for I'd loan it to him and would take it out of his paycheck, so it wasn't a problem.

Then one day I went down to the garage to do some cleaning and found an empty bottle of vodka hidden in the far corner over a cabinet. I sort of thought that it might have been Richard who had put it there, so I thought no more about it. Then later, sometime in July, we were told that Scott was taking vodka bottles from some of the stores, so I knew I would have to do something about it.

I then noticed there were a lot of garbage bags in one of the waste containers. I decided to check to see what was in them to see what was going on in the gardener's house to make so much waste. It was then that I discovered six empty vodka bottles. And Scott started having a lady friend over and staying overnight, and she was smoking in the house. That was a "no-no." A few days later, something came up in the yard that really made it possible to let him go. He used an electric edger to trim an arbor after I had told him to do it by hand. He got so he did not like taking orders.

He got the electric edger out after I left to go to the store and started to trim the arbor. Somehow, he ended getting a bad cut on his arm, so he left to go to the doctor to get some stitches in his arm. This was on July 25. He did not come home for a couple of days and did not tell me about what had happened until a few days later when he came to work. I asked him about it, for I had put all the tools away. I knew something had happened. I then told him what I had said about not using the edger and he agreed with me; he also said he forgot to be careful when using it.

We had a Kruger-Evenson reunion planned at the ranch and needed someone to stay at our house to keep things watered, so I told him I trusted him to look after the place, and he did. I will admit I asked other people to come by and check on the place, but when we got back, everything was OK. About a week later, I told him he would have to leave, that he was drinking and had women in the house and they were smoking in the house.

He left a week later, but not before he had cleaned the house. He cleaned the stove, refrigerator, washer-dryer, and shampooed the rug, but he forgot to move the refrigerator and clean behind it. When I had the cleaning girls go down to check on things, they found another empty vodka bottle behind the refrigerator; they had fun with me and said, "Now we want you to know this is not of our doing." Scott was a likable person and very good with equipment, but had to be taught about gardening.

He left behind a nice set of roasting pans, along with a few other things. I lost more shrubs under Scott than any other gardener I had ever had. I don't know what he did to them. Maybe he didn't know either if he was on vodka. He left the house clean, but again, full of smoke.

Over a year later, on Sept. 11, 2002, Scott drove up in the yard in a nice car. He came to the kitchen door and gave Frank the key to the cottage. This was a surprise, for gardeners do not usually return the key. I wish him luck in whatever he does or is doing.

Frank still had the list of names from his last ad that he had put in the paper, so he went to work calling people on the list. Shane Kenny, Michael Brenner, and Mark Cooks' names came into the picture. I ended up having all three working for me. After a while Mark got married and that took care of that, but he didn't want to burn any bridges, so he said he would work on Saturday if I needed extra help. He was good at washing cars, so he is still doing the job. Michael was only interested in working by the day instead of on a regular schedule. After some thought, Shane was given the job.

Sept. 12, 2001 — Shane

SHANE WAS AGE 28 going on 18, which should have been warning enough. He was a good worker, knew a lot about plants and bugs, and knew how to operate the sprinkling system and the drips, and so on. He was also very good with equipment. But he was very cocky and acted like a kid; little did I know he was on methamphetamine, or "speed" for short.

I had called the police before having Shane move in. I wanted to see if they had a record on him, and they said no. He moved in and was with us for three weeks. He asked twice if he could use the phone in the office and I said yes; he had not yet had time to have one put in the gardener's house. I had done this for all the gardeners all through the years with no trouble.

One day Ina, Frank's secretary, noticed a blank check missing among the pile of blank checks she needed to make out that day, and she called it to Frank's attention. She asked him what he had done with the check and gave him the check number. He said he hadn't done anything with it as far as he knew. The next day Ina was going through the canceled checks and found the missing one. It had been forged and was for the total of $402. Someone had written out Frank's full name in longhand. The check was made out to our neighbor, whom we later found out was a friend of Shane's. She made the check out in her name and cashed it for Shane at her bank.

432

As soon as Frank saw the check, he knew it was a forge. He took it right to our bank and they knew it was forged. Frank never writes a check out longhand; he does it by using the typewriter.

The officer at the bank called the police; in turn, they went to the neighbor. She told them that Shane had given her the check and said it was OK for her to sign her name and to cash it for him, which she did. She then gave him the money. In the meantime, our bank had reimbursed Frank's account. Her bank reimbursed our bank and took the funds out of her checking account. While all of this was going on, we received a visit from the police department and were told that Shane had been named the one who'd taken the check.

Neither Frank, nor I, believed this; we were sure it was Scott who had taken it. In the meantime, the officer had come here to the house and wanted to see Shane. I said, "He is right out in the horseshoe lawn fixing the sprinkling system." He was there just a few minutes earlier with all the equipment. So we went to see him and he was gone. I said he might be at SPD getting his lunch, even though it was 1:30. He sometimes ate late. So we waited, and he did not show up. But of course, what had happened was as soon as he saw the police car drive up, he beat it out of the backyard over the fence on his bicycle.

The only way I can figure out how he slipped out was by putting the bicycle over the fence between the gardener's house and the neighbor's place, and then taking off from there; otherwise, I would have seen him leave. When we couldn't find him, we proceeded to gather up as many of his handwriting samples as we could find, including notes he had written that were in the garage. The police needed to verify his handwriting. At this time, I asked the officer to go into the house with us, for we were looking for anything that had his handwriting on it. There wasn't anything there, so we locked up and left.

The officer said he wasn't sure he should go in, but I said, "You are with us, and if he has left, I have the right to enter and secure the house." We were told that if he showed up to call them, and we said we would. This was on a Thursday, Oct. 11.

Our neighbors, Kristin and Paul, came over on Friday afternoon to talk to us. They told us her side of the story, and I think she was hoping that we would take care of her check. This was the first time I had ever really met her in person. I learned that Shane had lived with her at one time and that he would also jump the fence and go through her yard to go to the SPD store, which was much closer than going down the road.

I took mental note to make sure no one else did that in the future. She also said she had called Shane from across the fence and gave him hell about the check. I told her that by doing that it had given him the one notice he needed to know he was in trouble. That had kept us from getting to the bottom of the story, and it made him able to leave in a hurry when he saw the police were here.

By Saturday, Oct. 13, he hadn't shown up, and I was getting worried about the garbage left in the house. So I went down and entered the house, something I don't do as a rule. I'm not one to bother the gardeners once they move in.

I noticed how dirty the house was but went to work to do what I had come down to do, which was to empty the garbage, close the windows, and pull up the blinds. I noticed a lot of other stuff was all over the floor, except the living room, which was clean. A lot of one-gallon plastic jugs were all over the bathroom and in the tub, and some had this reddish stuff in them. Some had plastic tubes coming out of them, and some had things you could whiff things out of by your nose. I put some of this in a box and stored it in the garage; some went into the garbage barrel, along with the garbage and food that was around the house. I also washed a few dirty dishes.

I checked inside the closet in the living room and found two boxes, one on top of the other. They were covered with a sheet, so I looked inside the top one to see what he was hiding. I saw the words "Muriatic Acid" on a gallon container and thought, "Oh, he's gotten some to clean the brick with." I did not check the rest of the boxes because they were covered with a small sheet. I wondered what was behind them, and that is what drew my attention to look.

There was a quart container in the deep freeze with a plastic tube coming out of it. There was a lot of other stuff in the refrigerator and a lot of red stuff had been spilled. But at the time, I didn't pay too much attention to it.

He had clothes all over the bedroom and kitchen floors, so I picked them up and put them in the basket that was on the bed. I sort of tidied up the house and noticed that nothing was hanging up in the bedroom closet. The house smelled of smoke and stale food. I opened the blinds to let some light in; he always had them closed. I didn't leave the windows open because I didn't want anyone trying to break in.

Frank and I locked up the house and then fixed the fence between the two houses so it would not be easy to climb over. In doing this, we saw Kristin and let her know what we were doing. Also in doing this, we ran across some wire going from the living room window and underground to the fence. We removed it and got it out of the window that was leading to some fixture in the living room. After that, we left to go golfing, and when we got home, we noticed everything was as we had left it.

At 6 a.m. Sunday, I went to the bathroom and saw a light on in the kitchen of the gardener's house. It was easy to spot because I had pulled the blinds up so that if he did come back and put the blinds down I would know. I got Frank out of bed to call the cops; we did, but they didn't show up, so we called two more times. By 8 a.m., he had left, for the lights were out. Before going to church at 9:30, I went down to check to see what he had taken. I had hoped it was his clothes and everything else, but all that had been moved was one box that was on the shelf in the living room closet and one jug from under the sink that had been removed. Later, I got empty boxes and took them down and put them on the porch, sort of hoping he would come back and fill them up, but no such luck.

We left and went golfing about 1:30 p.m. and were back by 5:30. While we were golfing, he had come back and left a note saying he did not know anything about the check and that he would be back later that day to see us. We had not seen him, so we wondered how he knew we knew about the check. We went in the house again, and I told Frank what he had taken: the two boxes of muriatic acid that were in the living room closet, the bottle that was in the deep freeze, the gallon bottles of stuff under the kitchen sink, and a pair of shoes that I could see was missing. He had also taken some of the plastic tubes that were lying around in different places in the house.

On Monday, I had Frank get a locksmith to come out to put an extra lock on the door so Shane could not get in again. I went in the house again and put all his pots, pans, and dishes in one box. I put all the loose things on the tables in plastic bowls, put lids on them, and put them in another box, along with other things. He had some radios and other small equipment that had been dismantled, so they went into another box. I put his bedding and pillow in a plastic bag. I put this box of stuff out on the porch. Shane still had his key, but now he could not get into the house. I put all the food that was in any sealed containers in a box and put it inside the shed.

I didn't do anything more until Thursday, when I knew the girls would come to spend the day cleaning the house. The food in the refrigerator went to the dump barrel, along with two bottles of good-looking punch, or so I thought. After the girls spent eight hours cleaning the house and mopping the floor, I left a note on the outside door giving him time to remove his stuff. If he didn't remove it, I would give it to the Goodwill and the rest would go to the dump.

I got concerned that all this "stuff" didn't look right, so I talked to Julia about it. She said to call the police, so I did. One of the girls washed down all the walls and ceiling in the bathroom, it was so bad. We concluded that that was the room he smoked in. The police came right after the girls had just cleaned up the house; the floor was still wet when they walked in and did their inspection. This was after I had shown them the box in the garage. They took one look at it, carried it outside right away, and said that it was very explosive. The girls had done such a good job of cleaning the house that, after the inspection was over, all they found that had to be removed was the 5-by-8-foot floor cover by the kitchen sink, and a few other little things.

In the meantime, they had really gone over the grounds around the gardener's house to see if anything had been dumped on the ground. Fortunately, I got a good bill of health on that.

We now came to the boxes that were outside, and I was told to throw all the food away. Then they went through the other box that had all the "stuff" in it and threw away what had to go. From there we went to the garbage barrels. They wanted to see the stuff we had thrown away that was in the refrigerator. They couldn't find the bottles I had told them about, and I said, "It's in there because I put it in the barrel." They finally found the two bottles and said, "That's what we're looking for." It was the real thing, methamphetamine. To me they looked like bottles of different kinds of punch, but the police were real careful how they handled them.

The police took some pictures of the house before they left and said they would get back to me, which they did. They also said it would have to be reported to the paper. The next thing I would have to wait for was a letter from the Department of Environmental Health, which I soon received. I could not put someone in the house until they gave me the clearance. It cost me about $500 to remove and replace the flooring in the kitchen. In the meantime, Shane's things were still in boxes on the porch, and I was sure he would never show up again.

He never did come to get his check, and, of course, it was less than what it cost me to clean the house, do the rug, and pay the $100 that the Department of Environmental Health charged me for the report. I disposed of all his things on Jan. 1, 2002.

I also had to have a plumber come in to clean out the sink drains, and the smell in the house was so bad that I would have to have the rugs shampooed. So it ended up being a rather expensive experience.

I decided next time that I would try to get an older man and have him really checked out by the police.

This has become a good story on me. The locals, who know me, know all the gardeners whom I have had all through the years, and my ups and downs with them, so they were having a good laugh, for I did hit the local paper. Frank and my two kids hit it often, but never me, unless it's the social section. So now I had hit the scandal section, and it was giving them a good laugh. My kids thought it was terrible; it was bad enough for the three of them, who hit the papers on business stories all through the years that we have lived here, but not "Mother."

Some of my gardeners are real good people and others need a little help. I have always thought that the good Lord put me here for something, and maybe it's to help out the gardeners whom I've had all through the years. These are usually men with nowhere to go, and they usually know very little about gardening, but they want a home to live in, and that has always been my draw. Frank, who hired them, never thought beyond filling the job, for he knew I could train anyone. Up until the past few years, I have really had very little trouble with drug users, and so on. I have had good men most of the time. I have yet to be afraid of any of the people who have worked for me; the first thing I tell them is that I trust them and that they are to trust me. They get the house, water, electricity, gas, garbage disposal, and wages, along with two weeks paid vacation in December.

One of the things that I have always been easy with is helping my gardeners with some money in the first few months that they are on the job, and they all, except Scott, have paid me back on the first paycheck. With Scott, I took it out of his next check, and that is something I really do not like to do. I like to feel that the men who work for me are good men and are worth trusting. Also, if they needed any doctor care, of any kind, I would try to get a doctor to take care of them. I would try to get them to pay at least half of the bill so they didn't feel dependent on me.

A year later, Shane was put in jail, and we received a call asking if we wanted to make him pay for some of the bills, and we said no.

November, December 2001

AFTER SHANE DIDN'T WORK out, it was back to square one on gardeners. Michael Brenner was working Mondays and half-days on Fridays; Kathy Laible was working Mondays and Fridays. On Saturdays, Mark Cook came in for four hours, washed the cars, and did any other handiwork that was needed. About the middle of November, Leonard, an old gardener, came over to see me while I was out working in the yard with Kathy. He asked if I could use a handyman to help in the yard. He then said his brother was out of a job and was living with him, and he asked if I could I use him? I told him I could, so he came and he was on the slow side, so Frank was not too impressed with his work.

For a few weeks, I continued doing some raking of pine needles that never stop falling during this time of the year. I would fill the back of the pickup with them, and then Frank would haul them off to the city dump, or over to Laurence's place. He would dump them down into the big ravine that Laurence has in his backyard that we call the stump dump, which never seems to get filled up. And Laurence was not very happy about that.

For the past two years, Frank had been complaining about the yard giving us too much work. He said it was time to move, but that did not fit in my plan very well, for I had planned to sort of live my life out here if at all possible. We can walk to the store, the doctors, get the mail, and walk to church from where we live. But Frank said it was too much work and too many people around working. So I finally reminded him when we moved here on Aug. 8, 1950, that he said he was going to get a place so big that I would have to hire help to do the work. I told him the work had not changed, other than in the earlier years up until the late 70's when we could burn the pine needles and yard waste. After that, we had to haul it away.

Now, the only trouble is that Frank has nothing to do other than play the market and golf. So he was now, for the first time, really seeing all the work that has gone on around here for over 52-plus years. I had always taken care of it, and all those needles have always come down in November and December.

Frank had been "bitching" enough that it was getting to me, so I asked for a "little help from above," and I got it. I told Frank that the negative complaints were getting to me more than the problems of the yard that I had been taking care of for 52 years with little problem. And I told him I am not a negative person and would not have made it up to now if I had been. I said all he had to do was keep to his word and hire help to do the work when I was too sick to do it. "Thank You Lord" for Your help; I used the right words, for I didn't hear the negative out of him since. He might be saying it to himself, but not to me.

In his later years, Frank had become a pretty good cook and helper in the kitchen, even trying to cook rice and other foods. He was also learning to use the washer and dryer.

January 2002

THIS WAS MY YEAR of replacing the brick walkways. I had three college fellows come work for me who said they really knew yard work and knew how to work with brick. They did a good job. Most of the time it was only the two of them, for three do have a tendency of getting into each other's way. I intended to use them until I got all my brick walkways redone in the places where the roots were trying to come through and force the bricks up.

They were doing work on the walkway next to the two redwood trees near the horseshoe lawn. The walkway was done in 1963-64, and now the trees roots had moved the rock wall out of place and raised the bricks making it dangerous for people to walk on.

The job finally got done after a month of working on that section. Charlie kept laying the same 5 feet of bricks over and over and would break them. He would tap them in place with a hammer, which you shouldn't do. So once all the roots were removed and the rock walls were in place, I told them I would finish laying the brick, that they were breaking too many bricks by putting them in upside down. As I've said, you have to put old brick back in the way they were laid in the ground to begin with, or they will break. So I finished the last 10 feet of the brick walk, working from 8 a.m. to 6 p.m. I got the job done and cleaned up the area. I put them to work on other things for the last few days. While I was doing this, my dear friend, Hank Maxwell, and a few other men came to visit me to talk about M.I.M. He saw me putting the brick down.

I found they were nice 22-year-old boys, good talkers, knew how to charge and kill time, but when it came time to do the brick job, they were all fingers and thumbs and no thinkers when it came to brick. They were all right on garden work. So I'd now have to look for another brick person to do the job.

Frank lost his patience with the boys and wanted them fired, but I told him to leave them alone, that I would take care of it. I just wanted them to get all the big roots out of the ground, which is a very hard job for me. And the day before, I had found out that my blood pressure was 90 over 60; no wonder I had been so tired and dizzy when I first got out of bed for the past two months.

Kathy was doing fine. She is a good worker and does a very good job removing the moss off the walkways and pulling the weeds in the flowerbeds. Michael was also doing good on his jobs; he was good for doing anything I asked him to do without my having to say much to him. My trouble with him was I could only get him a day-and-a-half a week. I had hoped the boys would work out the same way on the brickwork, but they knew it all. They were too young to take orders and didn't want to be told how to do the job, even if it was not what I wanted done, so I let them go. By this time, Mark had not been coming on Saturdays, and I hadn't heard from him, nor could I call him, so I guessed he'd moved on.

February to April 1, 2002

THE WALKWAY GOING TO the BBQ house really needed to be taken up, and the roots from the redwood and fir trees needed to be worked on. In order to do this, I had to take up the old brick and put in new sidewalls. My friend, John Simon, called and told me he knew of a man who needed a job. He asked if I could help him out, and I said yes. The man came to work; his name was Jeffrey. So with Jeffrey there to help me, I started removing the brick and having him dig up the roots. But he did not want to use any electrical equipment to cut the big roots; he was afraid he would cut a pipe or something, so he was doing it by hand, the hard-elbow method.

It was starting to take too long and the bad weather was coming on. This started to get to Frank again, but Jeffrey finally did get all the roots out. As soon as the weather got better, I started putting the right side of the wall in place with brick, and I had Jeffrey make the mortar. He knew nothing about cement but was willing to learn. After about 6 feet of wall was up, I started laying the brick down on the walkway and had Jeffrey work on the rest of the wall. He did fine, but he did not understand that you had to take care of cement and finish it up while it is wet. Instead, he left for the weekend. By Monday, the cement was hard, and we now had a rough surface to work on, so we had to remove that part of the wall and start over.

Frank decided to run an ad for a gardener, and by Saturday, I had several men here. I started putting them to work in the yard doing different things. Along with these men was a young man by the name of Mac who was in his early twenties, and his mother was with him. After Frank had talked with him, Mac told me he could lay brick and knew how to work with cement and had done a lot of it, and his mother agreed. So I put him to work right away, and, yes, he did know brick and cement, which was great. I then put Jeffrey to work doing yard work and let him go that night, for he was married, had a child, and couldn't live in the gardener's house.

Well, this new, young boy, Mac, was used to getting his way with his mother, and he started to do the same with me, but I was willing to hear what he said. After doing a particular job, the weather got bad so he had to stop. He came back a week later to do some more work, didn't show up the following day, and I didn't see him for another week after that. A man by the name of David was also here that day from the ad; I put him to work. One other man worked for two hours and left a note in the garage as to how many hours he had worked and left his address. He then left without talking to me. I found the note in the garage, so I sent him his check and that was that. He was one that if it had worked out I could have put in the gardener's house.

After Mac had not shown up, I put David to work helping with the cement and laying the rest of the wall. I then put him to work on the left side of the wall. By this time, Frank and I had been to Carefree for a week and the job at home still had not been done, so as soon as I got back from the trip, I started back to work on the brick walkway.

While David and I were working on the cement and I was laying the walkway bricks down, the police drove up and had a little visit with me and asked about the old gardener Shane. They wanted to know if he had ever come back, and I said no. (This was on the day that Friar Tuck's restaurant and the old Elks building in Nevada City burned down.) The police told me they had just introduced the new sheriff to my kids, Laurence, Spence, and Brad, who were down at the fire, and so they introduced him to me. About two hours later, here drives Mac up in a car with three girls. I said, "What happened to you? Why didn't you finish this job?" And he said he had been in jail.

Well, I didn't ask any more questions, but I gave him what money he had coming, and as he left, I said, "Remember what I said about the 'frosting on the cake.'" His mother had told me he didn't have any girlfriends and was a good boy. She said he wouldn't have any girls around in the house, but he also thought he knew more than she at this stage of the game. So when we were working in the yard earlier he started to tell me how to do something. I told him he had the "frosting on the cake" but "not the cake" and it would take about four years before he would have the cake, and he would then tell his mother she knew more than he thought she did.

Anyway, now I knew why the police were in my yard; they'd come to check up on Mac, and, of course, he wasn't here. While in jail he must have had to tell them whom he worked for, and I was the only employer he had. So much for Mother's Good Boy!

David finished the brick wall, with me laying the rest of the brick walkway. When he got ready to finish putting in the details with cement, he got fouled up at the entrance and took out a few rows. He then had to re-lay them, only now he couldn't put them back right. So I had to go back and start from the entrance again and show him how to re-lay about 10 rows of bricks until we had taken up all the space between the bricks. This took an extra day with some prayers and help from the good Lord above, and, yes, He came through with the help we needed to finish the job.

David did a good job for someone who hadn't laid brick before. Thus far, he had turned out to be a good worker, and I hoped he would continue working for me. He would have to be trained for the yard work, but he was a good learner. His main problems were he smoked and could not drive a car; he did have a wife, so I was slow to think about putting him in the gardener's house.

I next had a stump removed from a flowerbed; I continued with the new brick wall around the flowerbed and joined it to the old border wall. The rest would have to wait until after the M.I.M. party in June; we would then take it to the pump house.

I was glad to get this done before I left for Holland with Julia to see the tulip show that is held once every 10 years. We would be gone April 18-28.

I would still have Michael and Kathy working for me part-time while I was gone. I was leaving Frank home by himself, and (as I wrote earlier in this book) I didn't know if I was doing the right thing by him or not, but I was looking forward to being with Julia for that time. In the meantime, Frank was busy learning all the little details about running this place.

Frank had been busy picking up pinecones that had been falling for the past few weeks. It was keeping him in shape, bending down to pick up hundreds of them. I told him to be sure to spend some time enjoying looking at the flowers and tulips as he worked on the pinecones, which he had been picking up by the sackful one day, only to do it all over again the following day. He said he hated the trees and wanted to cut them all down, even if he had made his livelihood from them. This was one of the worst years for pinecones we'd had since living here. It seemed to me, even now, it was late in the season for the cones to keep falling. This had also been a big cedar tree season, for new cedars were coming up everywhere, so no doubt we would be seeing little cedar trees everywhere in a few months.

Michael had given me notice that he would be leaving May 1; he was taking a full-time job working on a farm. So after I got home from Holland, I'd be going full speed ahead to plant 22 flats of flowers that would arrive on May 1.

I got back from my trip to Holland with Julia and put the flats in and a great deal more. I did this with the help of Kathy and Michael. David was doing a lot of brickwork, including finishing the wall to the pump house. He removed more brick where roots had raised it up. Because there was so much to do, I hired another man named Kevin to help with the yard work while David spent his time on the brick. It took him awhile to catch on how to lay the bricks without breaking them, but he learned and was now a little faster with lifting them and re-laying them. This was the year I had planned to do it, and it was getting done, and we were now in August and still had more to go.

Music in the Mountains had their performance here in June; it was a success. But a few days before, a storm came through and really played havoc with the yard. I needed fast outside help, so with Julia and her friends, Laurence and Gloria, Jim Maxwell and his pull at M.I.M., I was able to get all the help I needed to take care of their wonderful event.

I still had the same people working in August 2002, with David doing most of the work. As I've said, his trouble was that he smoked. He also had a very sick wife who kept him from showing up for work. Therefore, I had to have Kevin come in to help out, but he did not know gardening work. The girls kept coming to pull weeds, which was a job I would mostly do myself. I also had to look after the flowers and make sure things got done right, and I needed more time to finish this book for Frank.

I still had David working for me in December 2002. His wife continued to be sick, so he was gone most of the time, but he kept me posted. Kevin filled in on weekends, along with Mark, who was back to work on Saturdays if I needed him. On Dec. 16, we had a bad windstorm with gusts up to 85 mph. It took down a big pine tree that was growing in the pump house lawn. (I wrote about this earlier.)

In falling, the tree ripped up and broke a street lamppost. The tree fell across and broke the new hour-time ornament. It ripped up power lines, water lines, sprinkler systems, and telephone wires. It broke a PG&E pole, ripped out the office power box, tore down fences, hit the side of the barbecue house, and smashed part of the roof. It also hit the neighbor's car and took out my new brick walkway. So this was going to be a project for 2003.

In the process of getting the fence put back, a fellow by the name of John came over to help. He asked if he could do gardening work for me. I said yes, and he began doing odd jobs for me. The fence was finished in March 2003.

2003

ON JULY 12, 2003, Frank counted the trees left on our property and tallied 35 pine, 11 cedars, 4 redwoods, and 2 Douglas fir—a total of 52 trees. The large trees averaged 100 years in age. And Frank, whose business it was to know the board feet of trees, accounted 200,000 board feet of total estimated volume.

On Labor Day weekend, we were at the Clarke Ranch. While we were there, a big lightning storm struck Nevada City. (I also wrote about this earlier.) Lightening hit our big pine tree that had our antenna wire nailed to it. The electric current went clear to the base of the pine tree, which was in front of our carport. The top 30 feet of the tree exploded and shattered all over the yard, putting out a couple of truckloads of branches, limbs, and bark. It took a few days to clean it up; John did the job. He was a good, hard worker but knew very little about gardening, yet he was willing to learn. However, he didn't want to learn from reading books; he said it was easier to learn by me telling him.

As time went on, it got so I was losing too many plants because he didn't know how to take care of them, or he would wait until it was too late to tell me. He was inclined to throw a fit whenever I asked him to rake the lawns. If he did he wanted me to pay him more money, and he wasn't worth what I was paying him now. He was still learning, and he didn't always understand why I wanted him to do things a certain way.

Then one day after we had been working on the lawns, I asked him to raise the blade on the lawnmower the next time he cut the lawns. He asked me how to do it. I told him it was the same way he lowered it, but he still didn't know how, so I told him to get the book out and read up on it, for I didn't have time to do it for him. This happened to be the same day Frank and I went to see his doctor. Frank dropped me off out front while he parked the car, and I went inside to sign him in at the office desk.

As I entered the door, sitting across from the entrance was Victor Charnett. He lit up like a Christmas tree and said, "LaVonne, will you hire me?" I have to admit I felt like the good Lord had entered the distance between us. I said, "What's it going to cost me?" So he told me, and I said, "Give me a few days to talk to Frank." At this time, I knew I no longer wanted to spend so much time in the yard because my right shoulder was really giving me fits whenever I used it. I couldn't really golf with Frank anymore, and I wanted to be able to do that again with him.

October 2003

NOW, VICTOR IS A professional gardener. For years I had wanted him to work for me, but he was with the big landscape firms. I knew he wouldn't want to leave them. But as we talked he said he was tired of repairing and redoing other people's mistakes and had been thinking about quitting the firm he was with. We got together on Saturday, and he ended up telling his current employer he was quitting on Monday. I said I would have to give John two weeks or until the end of the month.

John had been doing carpentry work for other people a few hours in the mornings and a few hours after work. So on Monday morning, when I told him about letting him go, he sort of went off on a tirade saying, "I've got to go home to think about it." I knew then that I would not see him again, for I knew where he was going, right back to work.

I told John I would hire him if I needed a carpenter and said he was a good worker but that he didn't know gardening. I knew he wanted to learn gardening so he could go into landscaping as a profession. After he'd learned, I knew he would be asking me for more money, and that was all right with me. I was willing to teach him, but I soon knew he was not a gardener. He was honest but spent too much time smoking and killing time. So now I had Victor, and he doesn't kill time or do wasteful movements. I now hoped this would be my last gardener.

After two weeks, I hadn't spent more than an hour with Victor in the garden. Other than telling him where things were at, what needed to be done, and what had been done in the way of fertilizing things, he didn't need much attention. I really hoped Frank saw the difference in men who don't know about gardening but are willing to learn, and one who does know what he is doing.

Victor knew nothing about brick but said he was willing to learn. So that would be my next project, and it would be an ongoing one.

We were now in mid-November 2003 and approaching Frank's and my 61st anniversary. We were heading to the ranch to celebrate it.

2004

VICTOR WAS STILL WITH us a year later. He was very happy he'd made the move he did. He said if he was tired, he could sleep in an hour later and still have a job when he went to work—all he had to do was work an hour later that day.

There was no heavy burden on him to make sure other people working under him knew what they had to do, nor did he have to follow up to see if they did a good job. That burden was now gone. All he had to worry about was when a tree fell, which one did this year. He now had a big job on his hands to clean up the mess, but that just meant labor and not too much brainwork was needed to repair the damage done to the yard.

What Victor was really good at was keeping the whole yard and all the grass looking nice. For many years, I had been known for my green lawns the year round. I had worked very hard over the 54 years in this yard, learning my soil and finding out what it took to make that happen. He was willing to do whatever I told him, as to what needed to be done, if he hadn't already done so. Above all, he was organized and kept notes as to when and where he worked and did things.

Victor had the yard in very good shape when M.I.M. came for their June party. Everyone commented on how good the lawn looked. And it was the lawns that always got the biggest comments.

Having Victor doing the yard work kept me from having to worry that if things didn't get done right away, they would soon get done. He was good about listening to me and took my advice, for there were things he was still learning about the place. Furthermore, there were things about plants and bugs that I did not know and I listened to him, so we both learned. He started learning how to replace brick and rock walls and took great pride in what he did. When he got a job done, it was done right and looked good. And as he said, he could now do some brick and rock work in his yard because he knew he could do it.

All the while I was helping Victor lay the brick, I would get dizzy when I bent over and got up. This had been a real bad two years for me with the dizzy problem, and it seemed to be getting worse. I had had it for so many years, but it had been far worse the past two years. No one knew what to do about it. All they said was I'd live to be 100, but I thought, "Who wanted to live that long being dizzy?" (And I was dizzy all along doing the work on this book for Frank. I just hope it reads fine.)

Many a man has learned how to lay old brick under me. I get out there on my hands and knees with them and get as much cement, mud, sand, and dirt on my hands and clothes as they do. I take time to show them how to make old brick work together and how to use pieces to fill in bad spots. Once they learn, I find I don't have to be around them as much. However, it may take a few times doing the same job over before they gain their confidence. One of the main things I tell them is to learn that the bricks have to follow each other in the same size and to remember not to turn an old brick over. If they must turn one over, I tell them they need to make sure the ground is lower in the center and higher on the edges, so it doesn't rock or break the brick. Above all, I tell them to use plenty of sand because it moves easier and once the bricks are laid, they stay put.

December 2004, Victor was still with me as my gardener, and he seemed to be happy. He didn't have to be told much, and that part I liked. He didn't need me standing over him and did what he thought had to be done without asking. If in doubt, he would ask right away. He had already replaced a few bricks and had learned how to do that without my being around.

Victor was still working 3 ½ days a week for me. He got as much work done in that time as anyone else I'd had working 5 days a week, those who were not gardeners but good workers. If they weren't good workers, they wouldn't be around very long, for one thing I do know is how to work. As I've said, when someone thinks he can fool me, he has another guess a-coming, for I have no trouble giving them their walking papers.

January 2005

   VICTOR REPLACED THREE FEET of wall that the cedar tree roots had pushed over. He did a very good job of it and took great pride in the fact that he had learned enough to do it and have it turn out as well as it did. He made it blend in well with the 2-foot wall that was there. This was on the patio area between the office and the house where it is noticeable.

   He knew garden work very well and did not need a lot of direction, so I was not out in the yard as much, which allowed me to spend more time on this book. My problem was with Frank; he just didn't like paying much for labor. He was still living in the past when labor was cheaper. But Frank did enjoy the yard and really didn't mind what I did or spent on the yard, for he liked the surroundings he lived in.

   Victor was still keeping the yard in very good shape and continued keeping up on everything with each passing season. However, he learned one thing this year, which was that you can and do burn the lawn when you put dolomite on the grass and don't wash it in real good. He wouldn't be doing that again. He was quick to recognize his mistakes and quick to try to correct them. And now the lawns and soil were ready for the light spring seeding that gets dressed with topper. I hoped that would take care of the lawns for a few months.

   The rhodes, azaleas, and camellias had already been doing their thing, along with the tulips that stand very tall each year, mixed in with the grape hyacinth and other bulbs. Maybe next year I would add more tulips to what were left from the big planting I did a few years back.

   Victor was already getting the ground ready for the May shipment of plants I had ordered back in March to put in the ground for a good display the first week in June for M.I.M.

   I am hoping Victor stays with me for the rest of my life here at 211 Reward St., for we got along well and understand each other's wants and issues. I thank the good Lord for getting us together at this time in my life.

   We were going into another season for Music in the Mountain's Board of Directors. They wanted to thank their special supporters and were calling it, "An Appreciation Garden Party," held in the Amaral Gardens on June 5, from 4-6 p.m. So for the past few weeks, Victor, with the help of Kathy, were very busy getting about 30 flats of different flowers planted. And all this was between rain, cold weather, and the pine pollen that had laid me up with a bad sinus infection. Victor had also been busy shaping the two large holly trees in the front yard at the main entrance, along with a lot of other tall shrubs and the azaleas, rhododendrons, and camellias that were now getting ready to be deadheaded.

   It was going to be a very busy two weeks before the party, and he was well tuned into what had to be done during the past week, such as washing down the houses for the pollen and really cleaning the tennis court to remove winter dirt and pollen. And, of course, he was making sure the lawns were all in good shape. I have always been very fussy with my lawns, for they are like green carpets the year round and with very few weeds at any time. Through the 50 years or so, I have learned how to treat the grounds surrounded by pine trees, and the lawns are of Manhattan Rye. We make sure they are not watered for two nights before a party.

All the moss on the brick walkways are scrubbed down, along with all the driveways. The rest of the yard is raked to get rid of pinecones, needles, and any other debris that nature may drop. Then, when all is done, the place is ready for the M.I.M. people to come in and set up a place for their food, bar, tables, chairs, and a place for the music.

And with God's help, we prayed that a windstorm wouldn't come in on Saturday to undo all the hard work that had been put into the M.I.M. event.

January 2006 to February 2011

ON JAN. 1, 2006, two more cedar trees came down. Counting the pine tree that fell from the previous year, we were left with 49 trees and hoped that ended the trees falling for the rest of our lifetime here at this place.

I have already mentioned the damage that was done before, so I will not say any more about it here. I will say that the summer of 2006 would turn out to be the best display of flowers I have ever had in the yard, and it lasted all the way into November when the frost came.

Victor Charnett

And here I will end the story of my gardeners who have been with me from August 1950 up to now as I finish writing this in 2011. They have been my right hand all through the years. And I hope that the M.I.M. people—who have liked coming here to enjoy talking and visiting with other people, enjoying drinks, food, music, and walking the surroundings that are like a masterpiece of art in itself that I have created through the years—will continue to use the yard when needed as the years go by.

At no time have I ever wanted to hurt any of my gardeners that have been with me, nor do I want to do so now in writing this, for each one has left a mark in the yard, as well as on the growth of my life in living at this place. I thank every one of them, along with Victor, who is still with me, and I hope will be to the end of my time.

May God bless all of them and look after each and every one of them wherever they are now. I thank each and every one of you.

Feb. 2011. Victor is still with me and continues doing a very good job. We had three trees fall in Jan. 2007 and since then have taken three more trees out in 2009. He has seen me through Frank's death and up and down through sickness. He has also become my driver who is there to take me places when I am unable to drive. He's still laying brick for me and continues to do a better job each time. Now, as we head into spring, I'm hoping we'll have time to work on getting the moss off the bricks. And a few of the lawns are due to be turned over and reseeded again after 15 years. We have this scheduled for April.

- La Vonne

APPENDIX D

Family Tree on LaVonne's Side:

1798 to 2010

Head List of the Different Generations

*Peter Voshell, born 1798, Baltimore, Baltimore Co., Maryland. Died Apr. 1, 1874, Volga, Clayton Co., Iowa, buried at Stone School House, Taylorsville, Volga, Iowa. Married, date unknown, to Mary Miller, born 1800, Maryland. Died June 7, 1873, Volga, Iowa. Buried at Stone School House. (They had 5 children and 45 grandchildren.) Francis, Jesse, Killian, John Miller (my grandmother Martha's father) and Elizabeth.

- John Miller Voshell, born Sept. 16, 1930, Delaware. Died June 15, 1917. Married Edna Martin on June 18, 1857. She was born Jan. 18, 1842, and died Jan. 27, 1901. John and Edna had 11 children, including Martha Amelia Voshell (my grandmother).

-- Martha Amelia Voshell, born Oct. 25, 1869, Arlington, Iowa. Died Aug. 3, 1946, Hubbard County, Minnesota, buried at White Oak Cemetery, Chamberlain, Minnesota. Married April 30, 1889, to Charles Henry Andress. He was born June 16, 1866, Oelwein, Iowa. Died Sept. 20, 1949, Hubbard County, Minnesota. (They had six children, including Nellie.)

--- Nellie Fanny Andress, born Oct. 8, 1897, Arlington, Iowa. Died June 21, 1965, Arcata, Calif. Married April 10, 1920, to Nicholas Francis Kruger, born Aug. 30, 1894, Hammond, Minnesota. Died April 7, 1927, Akeley, Minn. (Nellie and Nicholas had 5 children: Helen, LaVon, LaVena, Nick, Jack.) Nellie married again on Nov. 12, 1932, to Julius Cornelius Evenson, born Dec. 25, 1885, Holstead, Minn., died May 19, 1943, Franklin Hospital, San Francisco, Calif. (Nellie and Julius had one child, James Andress Evenson.) (Julius had four children: Evelyn, Joe, Agnes, and Art by his first wife Anna Lagergren, born, Jan. 22, 1891, Minneapolis, Minn., died July 12, 1925, buried at Akeley, Minn.) Nellie's third marriage was in 1947 to Victor Hilton, he died June 15, 1976.

---- Gertrude LaVon (LaVonne) Kruger, born May 12, 1922, White Oak Township, Minnesota. Married Frank Viera Amaral, born June 19, 1918, Orland, Calif. Married Nov. 26, 1942. Frank died March 5, 2007, Nevada City, Calif. (They had two children: Julia Rose and Laurence Viera.)

----- Julia Rose Amaral, born April 10, 1944, Stockton, Calif. Married Oct. 9, 1993 at St. Helena Catholic Church, St. Helena, Calif., to Markus (Mark) Brent Strate, born Mar. 25, 1953.
----- Laurence (Lance) Viera Amaral, born Apr. 27, 1946, Nevada City, Calif. Married Gloria Ann Morrison (Spencer, Angove) Oct. 26, 1975, Miners Foundry, Nevada City, Calif., born May 3, 1936, Pasadena, Calif. (Gloria had three children previous: William (Spence) Spencer, Stephanie Lynn Spencer, and Bradley Lawrence Angove). Laurence adopted Gloria's son, Bradley Lawrence Angove, in 2000. Bradley changed his surname to Amaral.

------ **William (Spence) Spencer**, born Aug. 1, 1956, Pasadena, Calif. Married Tracy sometime in the 1980s and divorced same year.

------ **Stephanie Lynn**, born Aug. 4, 1958, San Jose, Calif. Married May 19, 1984, Sacramento, Calif., to Jeff Clark. (They had two children.)

------- **Collin Jeffson Clark**, born July 31, 1986, Sacramento, Calif.

------- **Evan Spencer Clark**, born Nov. 17, 1988, Sacramento, Calif.

------ **Bradley Lawrence (Angove) Amaral**, born April 6, 1967, Roseville, Calif. Married Penny Kathleen Marsh, Feb. 7, 1998, at American Victorian Museum (also known as the Miners Foundry), Nevada City, Calif. Divorced, 2003. Married Lisa Marie Brown at his parents' yard in Deer Creek Park, Nevada City, Calif., Sept. 25, 2004. Divorced in 2009.

Extended notes on Peter Voshell-Mary Miller Family Tree, 1798-2010

Note: The names of direct ancestors to me, LaVonne Kruger Amaral, and my children are shown in boldface. Although Peter Voshell was the first of six children, I will start with him as being the first. His father, William Voshell, was born 1772 in Kent, Delaware. He married Mary (last name unknown). William and Mary Voshell had six children: Peter, William, James, Levi, Susan, and Elizabeth.

The Family Tree of
Peter Voshell and Mary Miller
1798–2010

*Peter Voshell, born 1798, Baltimore, Baltimore Co., Maryland. Died Apr. 1, 1874, Volga, Clayton Co., Iowa, buried at Stone School House, Taylorsville, Volga, Iowa. Married in Kent, Delaware, on Jan. 1, 1824, to Mary Miller, born 1800, Maryland. Died June 7, 1873, Volga, Iowa, buried at Stone School House, Taylorsville, Volga, Iowa. (They had 5 children and 45 grandchildren. The five children are: Francis, Jesse, Killian, **John Miller**, Elizabeth.)

- Francis Frank Voshell, born Feb.18, 1822, Maryland. Died Jan. 15, 1906, Arlington, Iowa, buried at Arlington Cemetery, Fayette Co. Married Nov. 30, 1853, to Alimena Smith, born Apr. 7, 1832, New York State. Died June 1, 1896, buried at Taylorville Cemetery. (They had 8 children: Dan, William Bill, Alfred James, Harry, Hannah A., Sarah, Elizabeth, and Amelia.)
-- Dan Voshell, married Ella.
-- William Bill Voshell, born Mar. 19, 1853, Brush Creek, Iowa. Buried at Arlington. Married Mary Smith.
-- Alfred James Voshell, born Nov. 16, 1872, Wadena, Fayette Co., Iowa. Died Nov. 2, 1927, buried at Otis, Washington Co., Colorado. Married July 3, 1903, to Nellie Rosa Crawford.
-- Harry Voshell, born Fayette Co.

-- Hannah A. Voshell, born June 11, 1860, Fayette Co. Died June 8, 1928, buried at Taylorsville Cemetery. Married Will Seward.

    -- Sarah Voshell, married Mar. 14, 1885, to Jim Cordin.

    -- Elizabeth Voshell, married Rodney Cline.

    -- Amelia Voshell, married Apr. 4, 1889, to Perry Smith.

* * * * *

- Jesse Barber Voshell, born Apr. 27, 1824, Maryland. Died Jan. 16, 1923, buried at Arlington Cemetery, Arlington, Fayette Co., Iowa. Married Oct. 20, 1853, to Annaple Muir Dempster, born Apr.16, 1837, in Scotland, died Feb. 4, 1904, Arlington, Iowa, buried at Taylorsville Cemetery, Fayette Co. (They had 9 children: Elizabeth Mary, John Dempster, Ella Loretta, Jesse Thomas, Margaret Lavena, Susanah Josephine, Peter, Ellen Jennings and Eneans.)

    -- Elizabeth Mary Voshell, born Jan. 21, 1855, Arlington, Iowa. Died Aug. 25, 1861, buried at Taylorsville Cemetery, Arlington, Iowa.

    -- John Dempster Voshell, born Feb. 7, 1857, Arlington, Iowa. Died Nov. 27, 1949, buried at Taylorsville Cemetery, Arlington, Iowa. Married Mar. 2, 1887,to Effie Parson.

    -- Ella Loretta Voshell, born Feb. 21, 1860, Arlington, Iowa. Died Sept. 19, 1867, Arlington, Iowa, buried at Taylorsville Cemetery, Fayette Co.

    -- Jesse Thomas Voshell, born Jan. 22, 1862, Arlington, Iowa. Buried at Taylorsville Cemetery, Fayette Co. Married, Carrie.

    -- Margaret Lavena Voshell, born Mar. 25, 1865, Arlington, Iowa. Died May 22, 1950. Married on Apr. 9, 1886, to Edward Smith.

    -- Susanah Josephine Voshell, born May 8, 1868, at Arlington, Iowa. Died Mar. 2, 1940, Arlington, Iowa, buried at Taylorsville Cemetery, Fayette Co. Married Aug. 8, 1890, to Thomas Hulroyd.

    -- Peter Voshell, born Oct. 12, 1870, Arlington, Iowa. Died Jan. 18, 1946, Arlington, Iowa, buried at the Taylorsville Cemetery. Married July 2, 1898, to Rose Warner.

    -- Ellen Jennings Voshell, born May 3, 1873, Arlington, Iowa. Died Aug. 5, 1909. Buried at Chamberlain Cemetery, White Oak Township, Hubbard Co., Minn.

    -- Eneans Voshell, born Nov. 4, 1875, Arlington, Iowa. Died Mar.16, 1962, Volga, Iowa, buried at Volga Cemetery. Married Mar. 22, 1898, to Bessie Biesel.

* * * * *

- Killian Voshell, born Feb.14, 1829, in Maryland. Died May 2, 1909, buried at the Taylorsville Cemetery, Arlington, Fayette Co., Iowa. Married Mar. 1851 to Hanna Taylor, died Dec. 7, 1901. (They had 1 child, Mildred.) Killian married his 2nd wife, Thankful Perkins, and they had 8 children.

    -- Mildred Voshell, born 1853, Fayette Co., Iowa. Died 1940. Married Dec. 1, 1875, to Melissa D. Glidden.

    -- Cam Calvin Voshell born Feb.23, 1864, Arlington, Iowa. Married Dec. 30, 1888, to Minnie Lockard.

    -- George Voshell, born May 8, 1865, Arlington, Iowa. Married Eva Hall. Died Jan. 28, 1936.

-- Nancy J. Voshell, born June 17, 1867, Arlington, Iowa. Married Apr. 19, 1888, to John Tripp.

-- Cindy Lucinda (Lucindy) Voshell, born Oct. 23, 1869, Arlington, Iowa. Married Mar. 5, 1891, to William Burgett.

-- Henry Voshell, born Jan. 13, 1873, Arlington, Iowa. Married Mae Oldfather.

-- Liza Eliza Voshell, born Sept. 18, 1875, Arlington, Iowa. Married Ed Crissman.

-- Mable Voshell, born Arlington, Iowa. Married Sept. 7, 1900, to Ed Corbin.

-- Ira Voshell, born Arlington, Iowa. Died Mar. 6, 1964, buried at Taylorsville Cemetery, Arlington, Iowa. Married in Mar., year unknown, to Alice Cummings.

* * * * *

- **JOHN MILLER VOSHELL**, born Sept. 16, 1830, Kent, Maryland. Died June 15, 1917, Akeley, Minn., buried at Taylorsville Cemetery, Arlington, Iowa. Married June 18, 1857, to Edna Martin, born June 18, 1842, in Fulton Ill., she died Jan. 27, 1901, in Fairfield, Iowa. (They had 11 children, including **Martha Amelia** (my grandmother), and 25 grandchildren.)

-- George Washington Martin Voshell, born, Apr. 21, 1858, Arlington, Fayette Co., Iowa. Died May 15, 1859.

-- Albert Sylvester Voshell, born June 7, 1859. Died Dec. 27, 1861, Arlington, Iowa.

-- Andrew James Voshell, born June 28, 1861, Arlington, Iowa. Died Apr. 1942, buried at Akeley Cemetery, Akeley, Minn. Married Jan. 20, 1889, to Anna Elizabeth Wallenbough, Fayette Co., born Nov. 11, 1873, died 1920. (They had 1 child (Lester), 10 grandchildren, and 8 great grandchildren. *All are listed, so stay with me.*)

--- Lester Voshell, born Feb. 28, 1891, Fayette, Co., Iowa. Died Oct. 1947, buried at Akeley Cemetery, Akeley, Minn. Married Sept. 26, 1918, to Josephine Katzenberger, born Mar. 6, 1891, Ashby, Minn., died Dec. 16, 1972, Akeley, Minn., buried at Akeley Cemetery, Hubbard Co. (They had 1 child (Robert), who was adopted in 1934.)

---- Robert Mastny Voshell, adopted, born Mar. 12, 1918, at Two Harbor, Lake Co., Minn. Married Sept. 26, 1939, to Helen Thelma Kastner, died at Larimere, North Dakota. (They had 10 children, including twins Anna Mae and Edna May.)

----- Clair Richard Voshell, born Nov. 2, 1941, Akeley, Minn. Married Sept. 12, 1961, to Sandra Grover, born at River Falls, Wis. (They had 3 children.)

------ Cheryl Lynn Voshell, born Mar. 5, 1968, Wabasha, Wabasha Co., Minn.

------ Steven Voshell, born Aug. 25, 1969, Spring Valley, Fillmore Co., Minn.

------ Jeffery Virgil Voshell, born Aug. 30, 1971, Spring Valley, Fillmore Co., Minn.

----- Anna Mae Voshell, born Feb. 4, 1944, Walker, Minn. Married Sept. 2, 1967, to John Richards, born Apr. 29, 1943, Minneapolis, Minn. (They had 1 child.)

------ Jesse Noland Richards, born Oct. 7, 1970, San Francisco, Calif.

----- Edna May Voshell, born Feb. 4, 1944, Walker, Minn. Married June 20, 1964, to Ivan Imm, born May 7, 1939, Jeffers, Cottonwood Co., Minn. (They had 2 children.)

------ Pamela Beth Imm, born July 3, 1968, Madison, Dane Co., Wis.

------ Nathan Adam Imm, born Apr. 2, 1972, Madison, Dane Co., Wis.

----- Beverly Jean Voshell, born June, 11, 1946, Park Rapids, Minn. Married Aug. 20, 1966, to John Beck, born May 17, 1945, Lansboro, Fillmore Co., Minn. (They had 2 children.)

------ Todd Robert Beck, born May 18, 1964, Spring Valley, Fillmore Co., Minn.

------ Joan Mary Beck, born June, 2, 1970.

----- Alan Edwards Voshell, born Apr. 26, 1950, Park Rapids, Minn.

----- Bonnie Jo Voshell, born Jan. 13, 1952, Rush City, Chicago Co., Minn. Married Sept. 18, 1971, to James Helvorson.

----- Dana LeRoy Voshell, born Feb. 25, 1954, Rush City, Chicago Co., Minn.

----- Mary Helen Voshell, born Oct. 17, 1956, Rush City, Chicago Co., Minn.

----- Tina Marie Voshell, born May 25, 1959, Harris, Chicago Co., Minn.

----- Peter Michael Voshell, born Apr. 27, 1965, Harmony, Fillmore Co., Minn.

-- Edward Wilson Voshell, born Apr. 13, 1865, Arlington, Iowa. Died July 24, 1930, Delurin Hospital, buried at Volga Cemetery, Volga, Iowa. Married Dec. 21, 1890, to Martha Ann Porter, born July 10, 1869, died Oct. 20, 1902, (Had 4 children with his 1st wife: Cora Mae, Ethel Bell, Alice Grace, Leo). Married Dec. 26, 1906, to Bertha Bleuer Leuenbegor. (Had 3 children with his 2nd. wife: Paul Floyd, Forest Edward, Leona.) (Total of 7 children, 23 grandchildren, and 50 great grandchildren.)

--- Cora Mae Voshell, born Aug. 24, 1891, Volga, Iowa. Married Apr. 23, 1913, to Oscar Hinkel, born Aug. 22, 1893, Wadena, Iowa, died Dec. 29 (year unknown), Moorehead, Minn. (They had 11 children and 28 grandchildren.)

---- Donald Dale Hinkel, born May 30, 1913, Moorehead, Minn. Died Oct. 22, 1957, Wadena Minn., buried at Wadena Cemetery. Married Jan. 9, 1937, to Vera Hicks. (They had 5 children.)

----- Donna Mae Hinkel, born July 26, 1937, Wadena, Iowa. Married Roger Candy.

----- Pattie Ann Hinkel, born July 15, 1940, Wadena, Iowa. Married Cornelius Yearous (a cousin—his mother was Ethel Bell Voshell.)

----- Mary Hinkel

----- June Hinkel

----- Jerry Hinkel

---- William Lewis Hinkel, born July 28, 1915, Wadena, Iowa. Married Jan. 17, 1942, to Gladys Schroder, Maynard, Iowa. (They had 1 child.)

----- Phyllis Hinkel, born Mar. 5, 1942.

---- Russell LeRoy Hinkel, born Aug. 27, 1916, Wadena, Iowa. Married June 27, 1942, to Maxine. (They had 1 child.)

----- Beverly Lewis Hinkel, born July 19, 1943. Married David Shakhouser.

---- John Pershing Hinkel, born Nov. 7, 1918, Wadena, Iowa. Married June 1, 1946, to Ruth Iris Hughes. (They had 5 children.)

----- Tammy, adopted, born Dec. 4, 1944. Married Vernon Wilding.

----- Russell John Hinkel, born May 5, 1947.

----- Jim Daniel Hinkel, born Jan. 1, 1949.

----- Gary Dean Hinkel, born Aug. 26, 1952.

----- Kathryn Rae Hinkel, born Jan. 29, 1955.

---- Alo Martha Hinkel, born Dec. 12, 1920, Wadena, Iowa. Married July 21, 1945, to Leonard Church. (They had 1 child.)

----- Carol Lee Church, born Apr. 3, 1947. Married Jerry Majer.

---- Ona Hinkel, born Jan. 30, 1925, Wadena, Iowa.

---- Robert Albert Hinkel, born Mar. 15, 1923, Wadena, Iowa. Married Jan. 25, 1946, to Kathryn Tayke. (They had 2 children.)

----- Bruce Hinkel, born Aug. 6, 1947.

----- Richard Lee Hinkel, born Apr. 8, 1949.

---- Delmar Hinkel, born Nov. 25, 1926, Wadena, Iowa. Married Apr. 16, 1949, to Jean Peder, born Dec. 30, 1931. (They had 4 children.)

----- Charles Oscar Hinkel, born Oct. 7, 1949. Married Oct. 15, 1971, to June Halverson.

----- Sharon Kay Hinkel, born Nov. 13, 1950.

----- Robert Duane Hinkel, born Sept. 28, 1951.

----- Donald Delmar Hinkel, born Dec. 12, 1957.

---- Robert Oscar Hinkel, born Jan. 27, 1929, Wadena, Iowa. Married Sept. 20, 1948, to Warenita Brauham, born Oct. 30, 1928. (They had 2 children.)

----- Larry LeRoy Hinkel, born Apr. 23, 1949.

----- Janet Marie Hinkel, born Jan.9, 1951.

---- Bernadine Mae Hinkel, born Dec. 14, 1934, Wadena, Iowa. Married Rev. Ronald Ginter, born Oct. 22, 1933. (They had 4 children.)

----- William Davis Ginter, born Apr. 15, 1953.

----- Linda Lee Ginter, born Aug. 5, 1955.

----- Ronald Mark Ginter, born Jan. 30, 1958.

----- Steve Ginter, born Sept. 5, 1959.

---- Betty Hinkell, born Oct. 21, 1930, Wadena, Iowa. Married Sept. 15, 1956, to Robert (?) (They had 4 children.)

----- Donna Lee, born Aug. 26, 1959.

----- Lori Ann, born Nov. 22, 1960.

----- Lyna Marie, born Feb. 11, 1962.

----- Heidi Elizabeth, born Mar. 7, 1969.

(These are all of Cora Mae Volshell Hinkel's children and grandchildren.)

--- Ethel Bell Voshell, born May 11, 1894, Volga, Iowa. Died Mar. 17, 1917. Married Dec. 12, 1912, to Jacob Yearous, Jr., born May 23, 1890. (They had 2 children and 12 grandchildren.) Married second wife Bertha Malberry, Jan. 2, 1920. (They had no children.)

---- Cornelius Yearous, born Oct. 18, 1913, Wadena, Iowa. Married Aug. 11, 1934, to Gladys Severive. (They had 8 children.)

----- Cornelius, born Nov. 6, 1936. Married Patty Hinkel (Cora Mae's daughter.)

----- Patricia, born Aug.8, 1938. Married Gene Berry.

----- Donna, born Mar. 7, 1941. Married LeRoy Richards.

----- Paul, born Apr. 28, 1942. Married Nancy Price.

----- Ronnie, born June 18, 1949. Married Kathy.

----- Ricky, born Oct. 6, 1952. Married Joan.

----- Vicky, born June 28, 1954.

----- Kirk, born Apr. 11, 1956. Married Anita, born Aug. 18, 1957.

---- Gladys Yearous, born Mar. 25, 1917, Wadena, Iowa. Married June 4, 1940, to Hugo Hapkenan. (They had 3 children.)

----- Rachel Hapkenan, born Feb. 7, 1943.

----- Stanley, born Aug. 19, 1945. Married Dianna Olson, Oct. 23, 1971.

----- Mark, born Feb. 11, 1957.

--- Alice Grace Voshell, born Sept. 27, 1897, Volga, Iowa. Married Dec. 21, 1915, to Otto Popenhagen, born July 7, 1892, died Jan. 27, 1969, Fayette, Iowa. (They had 3 children and 12 grandchildren.)

---- Lucille Arlene, born Dec. 9, 1919, Wadena, Iowa. Married Feb. 3, 1941, to Harold Tope. (They had 3 children.)

----- Roger Dean, born Feb. 8, 1943.

----- Roland I., born Apr. 30, 1944.

----- Barbara Ann, born Dec. 14, 1945. Married Jan. 9, 1966, to Richard Earle.

---- Otto Dale Popenhagen, born Jan. 2, 1924, Wadena, Iowa. Married May 1, 1949, to Helen Henrick. (They had 3 children.)

----- Sandra Kay, born Feb. 2, 1951, West Union, Iowa. Married May 25, 1972, to Richard Solheim.

----- Linda Sue, born Apr. 19, 1953, Hawkeye, Iowa.

----- Steve Dale, born June 12, 1955.

---- Robert DeWayne Popenhagen, born May 9, 1928, Fayette Co., Iowa. Married Feb. 23, 1957, to Kattie Guinan. (They had 5 children, all born at Cedar Rapids, Iowa.)

----- John James, born Oct. 1, 1957.

----- Michael John, born Jan. 15, 1959.

----- Robert Joseph, born Jan. 25, 1961.

----- Mark William, born Aug. 8, 1967.

----- Lisa Marie, born Mar. 12, 1970.

--- Leo Voshell, born 1902, died 1906, Volga, Iowa.

--- Paul Floyd Voshell, born July 9, 1907. Married Oct. 15, 1939, to Ethel Elizabeth Numan, born Sept. 14, 1911, Iowa. (They had 3 children.)
---- Duane Paul Voshell, born Dec. 15, 1940. Married Jan. 11, 1969, to Carolyn Nordeen. (They had 1 child.)
----- Valarie Ann, born Aug. 2, 1971, Cedar Rapids, Iowa.
---- Gary Edward Voshell, born Feb. 21, 1946, Iowa. Married July 10, 1972 to Barbara Ann Prosek.
---- Lowell Dean Voshell, born Nov. 1, 1946. Married Oct. 12, 1974, to Hareas Smith.

--- Forest Edward Voshell, born Feb. 2, 1909, Wadena, Iowa. Died June 14, 1970, Mainland, Florida, buried at Glen Heaven Cemetery, Winters Park, Florida. Married June 17, 1931, to Bernise LaVerne Schleny, born December 31, 1909, Chicago, Ill. (They had 3 children, all born in Chicago, Ill.)
---- Robert Charles Voshell, born June 7, 1932, Chicago, Ill. Married Dec. 28, 1951, to Joan Marie Finch.
---- Joyce Jean Voshell, born Aug. 13, 1935. Married May 14, 1965, to John Joseph Heary.
---- Janice Marie Voshell, born Nov. 5, 1947, Oak Park, Ill. Married Nov. 5, 1967, to Joseph Edward Glynn.

--- Leona Voshell, born Apr. 24, 1911, Wadena, Iowa. Died, unknown. Married Jan. 26, 1934, to John Wayne Cunningham, born July 24, 1911, Hubbard Co., Minn. (They had no children.)

-- Marion Markeley Voshell, born Sept. 2, 1867. Died Mar. 23, 1902, Arlington, Iowa. Married Sept. 2, 1890, to Lide Eliza Ann Lockard, born Sept. 29, 1873; died Feb. 25, 1955, Arlington, Iowa.

--- Myron Henry Voshell, born Apr. 24, 1895, Wadena, Iowa. Died Dec. 29, 1960. Married July 27, 1921, to Flossie Delilah May Wilcox-Fink, born Dec. 12, 1899, Fayette, Iowa. (Fink had 2 children: Fern and Donald. Myron and Flossie Delilah had 8 children: Marian, Harley, Verna, Bernice, Hazel, Laura, Martin, Melvine.)
---- Fern G. Fink, born May 17, 1918, Oelwein, Iowa. Married Jan. 19, year unknown, to Stanley H. Franks, North Dakota. (They had 3 children.) She later married: 2nd Gee, 3rd Thomas, 4th Semraw, 5th Hoag.
----- Maxine Franks, born July 29, 1934. Married Wayne Miller.
----- George Franks, born Aug. 12, 1935. Married Maureen.
----- Roger Franks, born May 15, 1936, Lansing, Mich. Married Sharon Graves.
---- Donald Clarence Fink, born Nov. 19, 1918, Oelwein, Iowa. Died Jan. 18, 1920.
---- Marian Maxine Voshell, born May 10, 1922, Wadena, Iowa. Married Walter Peterman. (They had 6 children.) (Fox was her 2nd husband; they had no children.)

----- Lewis Henry Peterman, born Mar. 20, 1939. Died Dec. 10, 1940.

----- Beverly Jean Peterman, born July 2, 1941.

----- Sharon Kay Peterman, born May 26, 1950.

----- Debra Sue Peterman, born Nov. 3, 1951.

----- Patty Lou Peterman, born Dec. 30, 1956.

----- Dan Peterman, stillborn.

---- Harley Clarence Voshell, born Oct. 16, 1923, Wadena, Iowa. Married Myra Kidney. (They had 7 children, all were born in Staten Island, New York. Note: 3 or 4 of them are married but I do not have their names.)

----- Harley James, born July 15, 1944.

----- Mary Verinica, born May 2, 1946.

----- Martin George, born Apr. 19, 1949.

----- (twin) Patricia Ann, born June 9, 1951.

----- (twin) Geraldine Ann, born June 9, 1951.

----- Paulette, born Jan. 12, 1959.

----- Jeannie Maria, born June 6, 1967.

---- Verna Imalien Voshell, born Dec. 9, 1925, Wadena, Iowa. Died Mar. 12, 1926.

---- Bernice Isabelle Mae Voshell, born Jan. 26, 1927, Wadena, Iowa. Married Jan. 19, 1946, to Eddie Aksamit. (They had 6 children, all born in Fergus Falls, Minn.)

----- Dennis Edward, born Mar. 24, 1947. Married July 19, 1970, to Rita Pelletier.

----- Donald Alvin, born Sept. 12, 1948. Married Aug. 11, 1970, to Adrese R. Purefoy.

----- Steven Larry, born Mar. 24, 1950. Married Patricia Stokka.

----- Ronald, born July 8, 1952.

----- Barbara Anita, born May 27, 1958.

----- Julia Ann, born May 13, 1964.

---- Hazel LaVerle Voshell, born Mar. 10, 1928, Wadena, Iowa. Married Merlyn Kissee, and divorced. (They had 3 children.)

----- Merlyn Wilson Kissee, born Feb. 11, 1960. Died, Feb. 12, 1960.

----- Ronald Gregory Kissee, born Mar. 2, 1961.

----- Sandra Diane Kissee, born Mar. 5, 1961.

(There are only 3 days between Ronald and Sandra. Can this happen? The dates are right by my records.)

---- Laura Mae Voshell, born Aug. 2, 1930. Died several days later on Aug. 4, 1930, buried at Arlington Cemetery, Iowa.

---- Martin Henry Voshell, born Aug.17, 1932, Oelwein, Iowa. Married Donna Haush. (They had 7 children.)

----- Kathy Jean, born Jan. 21, 1960, Eaton Rapids, Mich.

----- Tamie Marie, born May 21, 1961, Eaton Rapids, Mich.

----- Cheryl Lynn, born Aug. 26, 1963, Eaton Rapids, Mich.

----- Gail Ann, born Aug.12, 1964, Eaton, Mich.

----- Roxanne Louise, born May 19, 1967, Hastings, Mich.

----- Allen Lee, born July 29, 1969, Hastings, Mich.

----- Steven Martin, born Jan. 29, 1970, Hastings, Mich.
(It looks like Donna was a very busy, tired lady, along with a few other people.)
---- Melvin Leroy Voshell, born June 27, 1941, Iowa. Married Sally
Affen.

-- **Martha Amelia Voshell,** my grandmother, was the 6th in line of the 11 children. She was born Oct. 25, 1869, Arlington, Fayette Co., Iowa, and died Aug. 3, 1946, at the age of 77 at Hubbard Co., buried at White Oak Cemetery, Chamberlain, Minn. She married Apr. 30, 1889, to Charles Henry Andress, born Jan. 16, 1866, Oelwein, Fayette Co., Iowa, died Sept. 20, 1949, at the age of 83 and buried by his wife Martha. (The family tree was started by my mother Nellie's cousin, Edith, who was married to Harley Moore from Fayette, Iowa, about 1973, and she sent me the list. I have taken over since then for my mother's family.) (Martha and Charles had 6 children and 26 grandchildren.)

--- Allie Bell Andress, born Aug. 31, 1890, Arlington, Iowa, died Feb. 20, 1913, Akeley, Minn.

--- Arthur David Andress, born Jan. 6, 1896, Sioux City, Iowa, died Feb. 5, 1983, Akeley, Minn. Married Jan. 1, 1920, to Ethel Sutliff, born Nov. 26, 1896, New Richland, Minn., died Mar. 18, 1959, buried at White Oak Cemetery, Hubbard Co., Minn. (They had 6 children.)
---- June Deloris, born Nov. 26, 1920, Akeley, Minn. Married Mar. 14, 1942, to William Ernest Hemp, born June 28, 1923, Watertown, So. Dakota, died Apr. 27, 1981. (They had 6 children.)
----- Gloria Suzanne Hemp, born Feb. 26, 1943, St. Paul, Minn. Married June 10, 1961, to Allen Mike Murphy.
----- Nancy June Hemp, born Feb. 16, 1945, Park Rapids, Minn. Married to Smith and divorced. Married Mar. 31, 1963, to Robert Trever.
----- Charlene Marie Hemp, born July 24, 1946, Little Falls, Minn. Married Dec. 30, 1967, to Ray Zipper.
----- William Ernest, born July 3, 1947, Bemidji, Minn. Married Dec. 28, 1968, to Helen Sevenson.
----- Kenneth Alan Hemp, born Mar. 15, 1951, Bemidji, Minn. Married June 27, 1970, to Lee Ann Wilcox.
----- David Arthur Hemp, born Feb. 11, 1956, Bemidji, Minn.
---- Ramona Evelyn Andress, born May 30, 1922, Akeley, Minn. Married Nov. 24, 1943, to Stan Van Canneyt, born May 6, 1923, Burtrum, Minn., died Dec. 4, 1989. (They had 2 children: Robert (adopted) and Charles.
----- Robert Steahnke Van Canneyt, born July 15, 1951. Married to Judy, born Feb. 19, 1950. (They had 3 children.)
------ Robby, born Apr. 28, 1975.
------ Joe, born Mar. 19, 1978.
------ Crystal, born Dec. 25, 1981.
----- Charles Van Canneyt, born Nov. 6, 1960, divorced, no children.

---- Charlotte LaMae Andress, born Aug. 5, 1924, Akeley, Minn. Died June 28, 1961, buried at White Oak Cemetery, Hubbard Co. Married Clell W. Steahnke. (They had 1 child)

----- Robert (Robby), born July 15, 1951, St. Paul, Minn. He was adopted by his mother's sister, Ramona, as I understand, just before his mother died.

---- Charles Morris Andress, born Sept. 21, 1926, Nevis, Minn. Married Mar. 20, 1948, to Jane Buck. (They had 2 children.)

----- Chuck.

----- Jean Ann.

---- Virginia Andress, born July 4, 1928, Barkowa, Hubbard Co., Minn. Married Eltin Hensil. (They had 6 children, but I have no names.)

---- Myrna Jean Andress, born Feb. 7, 1939, Park Rapids, Minn. Married Sept. 1, 1961, to Frank M. Whitcomb. (They had 2 children.)

-----Lucinda, born July 21, 1968.

-----Jonathan, born Dec. 27, 1970.

--- **Nellie Fanny Andress,** my mother, born Oct. 8, 1897, Arlington, Iowa. Died June 21, 1965, Arcata, Calif. She married Apr. 10, 1920, Akeley, Minn., to **Nicholas (Nick) Francis Kruger,** my father, born Aug. 30, 1894, Hammond, Minn.; died Apr. 7, 1927, age of 32, Akeley, Minn. Nellie and Nick married Apr. 10, 1920, in Akeley, Minn. (They had 5 children, all were born at White Oak Township, Hubbard Co., Minn.: Helen (Helena), *LaVon (LaVonne)*, LaVena, Nick, and John Jack.)

After my father died, Nellie ended up marrying two more times. Her second marriage was on Nov. 12, 1932, to Julius Cornelius Evenson, born Dec. 25, 1885, Holstead, Minn.; died May 19, 1943, Franklin Hospital, San Francisco, Calf. (They had 1 child together: James Andress Evenson, born Apr. 30, 1933, in Akeley, Minn.) Julius had 4 previous children (Evelyn, Joe, Agnes and Art) from his first wife, Anna Lagergren, born Jan. 22, 1891, Minneapolis, Minn.; died July 12, 1925. Nellie's third marriage was in 1947, Eureka, Calif. to Victor Hilton. Nellie died June 21, 1965.

[In Calif. 1938, my mother Nellie received a package of pictures from my grandma Gertrude Kruger-Kelley of her family that included my father's brothers, their wives, and their children, with names and notes on the back of the pictures. So most of my information comes form that and what I remember my mother telling me. There were many postcards from Helen Shoecard to my dad and from him to her. On one of the postcards to Helen was the name of Klug from Zumbreta, Minn., so this had to be her stepfather. I was 18 at the time Mother received this and my cousins were about my age.]

* * * * *

My father's side

-- **Gertrude Elgin and Joseph Kruger,** my father's parents, were born sometime around 1866. Gertrude was born in Germany and Joseph was born in Minnesota. They married in 1892, and their wedding picture was taken at Mazeppa, Minn., at the Studio of A.R. Hawkinson. Some of the pictures were later taken at the Stearus studio in Rochester, Minn. Some pictures were from East Hammond, Minn., and some from South Dakota. Grandpa Joseph died in 1899.

(I know that Gertrude and Joseph had 2 children: Nicholas (Nick) and Pete. Genealogy records show they may have had 5 additional children: Catherine, born Apr. 1888; Helene, born Aug. 18, 1898; Paul John, born Dec. 21, 1896; Leo, born Aug. 19, 1890; and Mathias, born Aug. 6, 1889. I have not been able to confirm this.)

Gertrude's second marriage was to John Kelley. At the time they lived in the area of Hammond and Rochester, Minn. (Gertrude and John Kelley had 3 children: Earl, Charles, and John. Genealogy records show they may have had 2 additional children: Leo, born 1901; and Edward, born 1907. I have not been able to verify this.) Gertrude died sometime in 1947.

--- Peter (Pete) Joseph Kruger, born Aug. 11, 1892. Married Kate in 1918. (They had 1 child.) He died Aug. 7, 1969, Plainview, Minn.
---- Lucillia, born around 1922, . She was my age. At that time they lived in South Dakota.

--- Earl Kelley, married Lena around 1917-18. (They had 2 girls.)
---- Two girls, about 1 and 2 years old, names unknown, born in 1920 and 1921.
--- Charles F. Kelley, born 1905. Married, name unknown. (They had 3 children, and I have pictures of him and his three children, but no pictures of her.)
---- Arlene Kelley, no other info.
---- Arthur Kelley, no other info.
---- Johnny Kelley, I think he was killed during WWII.

--- **Nicholas (Nick) Francis Kruger,** born Aug. 30, 1894, Hammond, Minn. Died Apr. 7, 1927, Akeley, Minn., age 32. He married Helen Shoecard. She died within a year, about 1918. His second marriage was to my mother, Nellie Fanny Andress. (Nick and Nellie has 5 children together: Helen (Helena), *LaVon (LaVonne)*, LaVena, Nick, and John Jack.)

* * * * *

---- Helen (Helena) Marie Kruger born, Feb. 14, 1921, White Oak Township, Minn. Died Feb. 22, 2010, at Santa Rosa, Calif. Married Jan. 1, 1938, to Floyd Bert Anderson, born Dec. 11, 1916, Arcata, Calif. He died Jan. 22, 1964, Arcata, Calif. (They had 4 children: Patricia (Pat), twins Sandra and Sharon, and Wanda; all born in Eureka, Calif.) Helena married again Oct. 21, 1970, to Richard Holten, born Sept. 22, 1925, Sioux Falls So. Dakota; died Mar. 5, 2009, at Santa Rosa, Calif.
----- Patricia Anderson, born June 18, 1938. Married Jan 31, 1960, to Elmer Kelley, born June 27, 1938. (They had 3 children.)
------ Ramona Kelley, born Mar. 3, 1961. Married May 20, 1990, to Gary Clyde Wilkerson, Centerville, Calif.
------ Rochelle Louise Kelley, born Oct.8, 1965. Married Nov. 24, 1984, to Clifford Eugene Salver, divorced. (They had 1child.)
------- Andrew Lawrence Salver, born Aug. 28, 1987, Chico, Calif.
------ Sean Kelley, born Mar. 20, 1971. Married May 24, 1992, to Lynette Ruth Gayton, Windsor, Calif. (They had 3 children.)

------- Kayla Rochelle Kelley, born Sept. 3, 1991.

------- Kristen Kelley, born Oct. 22, 1994.

------- Matthew Kelley, born June 18, 1997.

----- Sandra Marie Anderson, a twin, born Feb. 2, 1944. Married Dec. 3, 1962, at Napa, Calif., to Duane R. Smith, born May 21, 1942. (They had 2 children, both born in Redding, Calif.)

------ Daryl Duane Smith, born June 26, 1966.

------ Darren Alexander Smith, born Dec. 3, 1967. Married Jan. 4, 1997, to Carol Ort, Angwin, Calif. (They had 1 child.)

------- Alexandria Paige Smith, born Oct. 31, 1998.

----- Sharon Lee Anderson, a twin, born Feb. 2, 1944. Married June 8, 1961, Clyde "Bud" Davis, born Feb. 28, 1939, later divorced. (They had 1 child.) Her second marriage was Nov. 25, 1989, to Harold Truman. She died on Mar. 22, 2001.

------ Wendy Lynn Davis, born July 14, 1962, Eureka, Calif. Married Dec. 13, 1981, to Charles Lloyd at Carson City, Nevada. (They had 3 children and later divorced.) She later married Jay Cramer.

------- Krystal Lynn Davis, born Aug. 1982. Married Dec. 2003.

------- Mandy Davis, birthday unknown. Married Nov. 11, 2003, to Tony.

------- Karrie Davis, birthday unknown.

----- Wanda Jean Anderson, born June 26, 1946. Married Sept. 13, 1964, Lodi, Calif., to Marvin James Hansen, born June 4, 1943, Dinuba, Calif. (They had 2 children.)

------ Vernon Russell Hansen, born May 15, 1965, Lodi, Calif. Married Nov. 20, 1988, to Donna Grace Bates. (They had 2 children.)

------- Heather Ranae Hansen, born May 13, 1993.

------- Tyler Austin Hansen, born Aug. 4, 1994.

------ Gregory Lynn Hansen, adopted, born Nov. 15, 1967, San Jose, Calif. Married Apr. 12, 1998 to Shelly Bohlman.

---- *Gertrude LaVon (LaVonne) Kruger,* born May 12, 1922, White Oak Township, Minn. Married Nov. 26, 1942, Stockton, Calif., to *Frank Viera Amaral,* born June 19, 1918, Orland, Calif; died Mar. 5, 2007, at home in Nevada City, Calif. (They had 2 children.)

----- Julia Rose Amaral, born Apr. 10, 1944, Stockton, Calif. Married Oct. 9, 1993, St. Helena, Calif., to Markus Brent Strate, born Mar. 25, 1953.

----- Laurence (Lance) Viera Amaral, born Apr. 27, 1946, Nevada City, Calif. Married Oct. 26, 1976, Nevada City, Calif. to Gloria Ann Morrison-Spencer-Angove. (Spencer died; they had 2 children: William and Stephanie.) Married Larry Angove, divorced. (Gloria and Larry had 1 child, Bradley.)

------ William (Spence) Spencer, born Aug. 1, 1956, Pasadena, Calif. Married Terry and divorced.

------ Stephanie Lynn Spencer, born Aug. 4, 1958, San Jose, Calif. Married May 19, 1982, Sacramento, Calif. to Jeff Clark. (They had 2 children.)

------- Collin Jeffson Clark, born July 31, 1986.

------- Evan Spencer Clark, born Nov. 17, 1988.

------ Bradley L. Angove, took the name of Amaral in 2000, born Apr. 6, 1967, Roseville, Calif. Married Feb. 2, 1998, Nevada City, Calif., to Penny Kathleen March, divorced 2003. Married Lisa Marie Brown, Sept. 25, 2004, Nevada City, Calif.; later divorced.

---- Martha LaVena Kruger, born Sept. 1, 1923, White Oak Township, Minn. Married Jan. 11, 1941, Bayside, Calif., to Leslie Joseph Faustino, born Sept. 26, 1920, Bayside, Calif., died Jan. 8, 1998, Bayside, Calif. (They had 4 children.)

----- Barbara Jeanne Faustino, born July 8, 1941, Eureka, Calif., married July 23, 1960 to Lynn Ray Carter, born Oct. 16, 1938, Manila, Ark. (They had 2 children.)

------ Kristen Lynn Carter, born Dec. 5, 1964, Eureka, Calif. Married Sept. 29, 1984, Livermore, Calif., to Martin Reese. (They had 2 children.) Divorced Sept. 1993. Later married Scott DeAraujo on Sept. 18, 1999. (He had one child, Brittany).

------- Nicole Carissa Reese, born Aug. 24, 1987, Livermore, Calif.

------- Jessica Jeanne Reese, born Feb. 15, 1989, Manteca, Calif.

------- Brittany Renee DeAraujo, born Dec. 22, 1989.

------ Cheryl Lynn Carter, born May 29, 1967, Woodland, Calif. Married Feb. 22, 1992, Livermore, Calif., to Thomas Burr Honour. (They had 2 children.)

------- Thomas Joseph Honour, born Mar. 25, 1993, Concord, Calif.

------- Analisa Marie Honour, born Apr. 5, 1995, Walnut Creek, Calif.

----- Robert Leslie Faustino, born May 14, 1945, Arcata, Calif. Married Sept. 4, 1965, Arcata, Calif., to Ellene Frances Grace, born June 12, 1946, South Dakota. Divorced. (They had 2 children.)

------ Marc Robert Faustino, born Sept. 14, 1970, Santa Rosa, Calif. Married Sept. 25, 1999, Windsor, Calif. to Janya Bennett. (They had two children.)

------- Benjamin Marc Faustino, born May 10, 2002.

------- Owen Bennett Faustino, born Apr. 4, 2005.

------ Shari Ellene Faustino, born Apr. 3, 1973, Santa Rosa, Calif.

----- Paul James Faustino, born Sept. 20, 1951, Arcata, Calif. Married May 26, 1973, Lake Tahoe, Nevada, to Karen Ruth Garrison, born Sept. 18, 1953, Eureka, Calif. (They had 1 child.)

------ Brad Allen, born Sept. 19, 1979, Santa Rosa, Calif. Married Christina Anne Plume on Sept. 29, 2007, in Sonoma, Calif.

----- Venus Celeste Faustino, born May 17, 1957, Arcata, Calif. Married May 27, 1978, Arcata, Calif. to Irwin Dean Brown, born Mar. 15, 1959. (They had 1 child: .) He left right after the 3-lb. baby was born and they divorced. She married Nov. 22, 1983, to Marvin Eugene Thurston, born Oct. 29, 1960. (They had 2 children.)

------ Christina Celeste Brown, born Aug. 24, 1979. Married Aug. 29, 2001, to Dustin Ward. (They had 3 children, all born in Eureka, Calif.)

------- Douglas Ward, birthday unknown.

------- Monica Ward, birthdate unknown.

------- Daphane Michelle Ward, born May 23, 2005.

------ Kirk Eugene Thurston, born Mar. 24, 1982.

------ Joey B. Thurston, born Apr. 5, 1985.

---- Nicholas Joseph Kruger, born Apr. 21, 1926, White Oak Township, Minn. Died May 19, 2001. Married Oct. 19, 1951, Eureka, Calif., to Olive May Watson, born Oct. 22, 1933, Los Angeles, Calif.; died June 2007. (They had 4 children.) Olive May married Omar Bekkedakl, Mar. 25, 2006, Spokane, Wash., and died the following year.

----- Olive Ellen Kruger, born Aug. 9, 1953, Eureka, Calif. Married May 5, 1973, to Gary Alan Ashcraft. (They had 3 children.)

------ Daniella Ashcraft, birthdate unknown.

------ Jonathon Ashcraft, birthdate unknown.

------ Cory Ashcraft, born Mar. 30, 1975, Ferndale, Calif.

----- Nancy LeAnne Kruger, born Nov. 13, 1956, Eureka, Calif. Married June 17, 1975, Blain, Wash., to Daniel LeRoy Phillips. (They had 2 children born in Washington.)

------ Charity Lennie Phillips, born Nov. 22, 1979.

------ Channel Phillips, born Sept. 1989.

----- Todd Nicholas Kruger, born July 11, 1960, Arcata, Calif. Married Dec. 15, 1979, to Laurie Kay Little, born July 25, 1959, killed in car accident on June 14, 1986. (They had 1 child.) Later married in Reno to Sherry Maker. (They had 1 child.)

------ Shalise Darlelne Kruger. Married Nov. 12, 2005, Bellingham, Wash. to Justin Holdaas.

------ Katelyn Kruger.

----- Karen Louise Kruger, born June 8, 1965, Eureka, Calif. Married Mar. 26, 1988, Fresno, Calif., to Richard M. Hernandez. (He had 2 children, no names avail.) (They had 1 child together and later divorced.) Karen married Paul L. Perras on July 14, 2003.

------ Hernandez, unknown child

------ Hernandez, unknown child

------ Ira Hernandez, born summer of 1989, Fresno, Calif.

---- Joseph (Joe) Evenson, born Apr. 8, 1912, Bemidji, Minn. Died Jan. 21, 1953, Eureka, Calif. Married in Akeley, Minn. to Esther; she died sometime in the 1980s. (They had 6 children all born in Minn.) About 1950 Esther and the children came to Calif. to join Joe.

----- William Evenson, born in Akeley Minn.

----- Fredrick Evenson, born Apr. 1933, Akeley, Minn.

Married Terri in Eureka, Calif.

----- Joseph Jr. Evenson.

----- Raymond Evenson. Married Betty.

----- Richard Evenson.

----- Joyce Evenson.

(These children all married and had children but I don't have any information on them.)

---- Arthur (Art) Louise Evenson, born Mar. 7, 1914, Walker, Minn. Married Jane Hurley, Akeley, Minn.; divorced 1968. (He said they had 6 children, 22 grandchildren, and 14 great-grandchildren when I saw him in June of 1992 at the age of 77.) Married again sometime in the 1970s. They lived in Laurel, Montana. He died sometime between 2004-05. All the children married and had children but I have no information on them. Then in the fall of 2005, my brother Jim's son Raymond received a phone call from Arthur's oldest daughter Agnes in Gilroy, Calif., to find out if they were related. He said, "Let me call my aunt right away," so he phoned me that night and gave me the information that she had given him. I said, "Yes, you are related." I told him I have a picture of her mother, Jane, and me together in Minn. when I was about age 11 and she maybe 14.

----- Agnes Walczak.

----- Arthur.

----- Kay.

----- Julius.

----- Carol.

----- Myron.

* * * * *

These are all of **Nellie Fanny Andress-Kruger-Evenson's** offspring. Later she married Victor (Vic) Emanuel Hilton, June 28, 1947, at Eureka, California. He was born Oct. 13, 1902; died June 15, 1976, Crescent City, Calif. (He had a son from an earlier marriage.)

* * * *

--- Harry George Washington Andress, born Feb. 22, 1904, Hubbard Co., Minn. Died, Feb. 18, 1992, at Bronson MO. Married May 12, 1920, to Eva Nixon, born Nov. 2, 1900; died Feb. 20, 1961. (They had 1 adopted child, Harold.) Later, Harry married Genevieve and she outlived him.

---- Harold Andress; died 1975, Berkeley, Calif. Married about 1947 to Bessie. (They had 2 children.) Shirley and one other.

----- Shirley, born 1947.

----- Unknown.

--- Burtran (Burt) LeRoy Andress, born June 12, 1908, Akeley, Minn. Died May 18, 1983, Akeley, Minn. Married Dec. 15, 1932, to Edith Evelyn Holland, born about 1915; died Sept. 16, 2006. (They had 5 children, all born in Akeley, Minn.) She married Sept. 22, 1987, to Dick Breezee.

---- Leonard E. Andress, born Mar. 15, 1934. Married Mar. 1958 to June Gayque. (They had 2 children.)

----- boy and a girl, no names.

---- Leta Lorraine Andress, born June 20, 1935. Married Aug. 1960 to Gene Tabias.

---- Robert Leland Andress, born Feb. 3, 1937; died May 10, 1992, Park Rapids, Minn. Married Nov. 1958 to Sharon Eskelson. (They had 1 child.)

----- David Andress.

---- Lois Grace Andress, born Sept. 27, 1939. Married July 1960 to DeWayne Ostenoa.

----Irvin (Keith) Andress, born June 21, 1942. Married Karen Gusstad. (They had twins.)

-----Jan Andress.

-----Judy Andress.

--- Eva LaVena Andress, born Sept. 6, 1910, Akeley, Minn. Married Feb. 6, 1932, to Harold Vik, born Oct. 4, 1904; died Oct. 7, 1996, Park Rapids, Minn. (They had 6 children, all born in Akeley, Minn.)

---- Rodney L. Vik, born Aug. 20, 1932. Married Dec. 30, 1956, to Evon Fattig. (They had 5 children.)

----- Debby Vik.

----- Julie Vik.

----- Rod Jr Vik.

----- Andrew Vik; died.

----- Kathy Vik.

---- Lorna Jean Vik, born Apr. 23, 1935. Married Mar. 19, 1958, to Duane Cunningham. (They had 3 children.)

----- Laurie Cunningham.

----- Steve Cunningham.

----- Liza Jean Cunningham. Married June 21, 1997, Park Rapids, Minn., to James Rudolph Roden.

---- Audrey Lenore Vik, born Jan. 20, 1936. Married Nov. 9, 1965, to Jerry Doherty. (They had 2 children.)

----- Cindy Doherty.

----- Jerry Doherty.

---- Gary Allen Vik, born Apr. 1, 1939. Married Feb. 16, 1958, to Claudia Mae. (They had 1 child.)

----- Mark Vik Married Marjie. (They had 3 children.)

------ Jacob Vik.

------ Matthew Vik.

------ Nichole Vik, born Nov. 22, 1992.

---- Sandra Rae Vik, born Jan. 18, 1947. Married Jan. 21, 1969, to Charles Weaver. (They had 1 child.)

----- Jeff Weaver. Married Amber. (They had 1 child.)

------ Gage Weaver.

---- Linda Kae Vik, born Sept. 6, 1951. Married Mike McDowell. (They had 2 children.)

----- Mac McDowell, born 1987.

----- Michael McDowell, born Nov. 1990.

This is the end of the list I have of Martha Amelia and Charles Henry Andress's children, grandchildren, and through to the great-great-great-great-grandchildren, as of November 2010.

* * * * *

Back to the rest of the JOHN MILLER VOSHELL family of 11.

After Martha, who was 6th in line of 11, comes:

-- Allie B. Voshell, born Jan. 5, 1872; died Apr. 3. 1873, Arlington, Iowa.

-- Nancy Abigal Voshell, born Sept. 15, 1873; died Mar. 10, 1899, Arlington, Iowa. Married Jan. 1, 1895 to C. A. Bendict.

-- William Martin Voshell, born Dec. 17, 1875, Arlington, Iowa; died Apr. 12, 1959. Married Aug. 22, 1908, Park Rapids, Minn. to Ada Anne Miller, born May 5, 1889, Wadena, Iowa, died July 20, 1930, Spirit Lake, Iowa, buried Arlington Cemetery. (They had 3 children.) Second wife, married Oct. 24, 1947 to Lide Eliza Ann Lockard Voshell, born Sept. 29, 1973; died Feb. 25, 1953, Oelwein, Iowa. (She was the widow of his fifth brother Marion Markeley Voshell.) (They had 2 children.)

--- Claude William Voshell, born Mar. 15, 1910, Akeley, Minn. Married Mar. 22, 1930, to Mary Irene Longergan, born Mar. 2, 1915, Rose Creek, Minn. (They had 3 children.)

---- Beverly Jean Voshell, born Aug. 2, 1934, Mitchell, Iowa. Married Mar. 2, 1952 to Eugene Darold Whitney born July 7, 1922. (They had 3 children.)

----- Mark Eugene Whitney, born Dec. 15, 1955, Charles City, Iowa.

----- Sheila Jane Whitney, born Feb. 5, 1957, Seattle, Washington.

----- Jennefer Lee Whitney, born May 7, 1963, Charles City, Iowa.

--- Edith Ione Voshell (this is the person that did all the research on the Voshell roots and sent it to me, LaVonne Kruger, and I took over Nellie Andress's side of the family.) She was born Sept. 29, 1914, Akeley, Minn. Married Nov. 25, 1933, to Harley Moore, born June 20, 1902, Fayette, Iowa. (They had 2 children.)

---- Delores Elaine Moore, born Sept. 29, 1938, Wadena, Iowa. Married Oct. 24, 1956, to Duane O. Brandt, born Aug. 14, 1934, Wadena, Iowa. (They had 5 children, all born at West Union, Iowa.)

----- Gilbert LeRoy Brandt, born Aug. 9, 1957.

----- Dawn Lynn Brandt, born Oct. 12, 1958.

----- Daryl Duane Brandt, born Oct. 9, 1959.

----- Troy Alan Brandt. Born Jan. 30, 1962.

----- Aaron Brandt, born June 1971; died June 14, 1971, buried Oelwein, Iowa.

---- Judith Ann Moore, born Aug.1, 1940, Fayette, Iowa. Married Wayne A. Bentley, Fayette, Iowa. (They had 2 children, born West Union, Iowa.)

----- Greg Alan Bentley, born Aug.20, 1956.

-- (twin) Pamelia Robecca Crane, born June 18, 1871; died Sept. 5, 1934. Married, Abe Eller. (Pamelia and Peter were twins.)

-- (twin) Peter Arphaxed Crane, born June 18, 1871, died Dec. 2, 1943, Iowa. Married Margaret Isaac.

-- Ellen M. Nellie Crane, born May 13, 1876; died Feb. 18, 1933, Fayette, d Jan. 10, 1891, Stephen Corbin.

ure these people had families, but I do not have any record of it.

o ends the Mary Miller and Peter Voshell family tree from 1798-2010, including ions of grandchildren.

----- Julie Rae Bentley

--- Kenneth Harry (adopted Thomp:
Frazel, Minn. Married July 27, 1940, to Harriet Louise McC
Concord, Minn. (They had 2 children, both born in Albert

---- Judith Diane Voshell, boi
to Dan Ver Doarn, born Jan. 12, 1939, Hasper, Iowa. (They

----- Wendy Sue Ver I
Minn.

----- Tammy Jo Ver D
Minn.

---- Kenneth Jerome Voshell,
1961, to Phyllis Bakken, born at Albert Lea, Minn. (They h

----- Todd Rodney Vo
View, Minn.

----- Troy Jerome Vosl
Minn.

-- Heman Voshell, born Feb. 27, 1879, Arling
Oak, Akeley, Minn. Married Aug. 5, 1902, to Harriet Eliza
Hazelton, Iowa; died Apr. 1, 19??, at the Sunset Rest Home
children.)

--- Glen Voshell, born Mar. 18, 1904;
Minn.

--- Clyde Voshell, born Oct.15, 1906.
--- Grant C. Voshell, born 1916.

-- Hannah Voshell, born Apr. 6, 1881; died F

This is the end of John Miller family of 11. His sister Eliz
Miller and Peter Voshell family.

*****

- Elizabeth Voshell the 5th, born June 16, 1833, Kent
buried at Prairie Flower Cemetery, Miner, South Dakota. M
born Aug 14, 1836; died Dec. 29, 1901, Carthage, South Dak(
children.)

-- Iwin S. Crane, born Aug. 15, 1858, Audabo:
1926. Married Aug. 31, 1877, to Mary Seward.

-- Mary LaVina Crane, born Nov. 6, 1860; die
1877, to Jasper Moore.

-- Edgar Crane, born May 17, 1863; died June
Iowa.

-- Annaple (Ann) Crane, born Feb. 15, 1866; d
Married Wilbur Mansell. Second husband, Joel Sturtevant.

-- Jesse V. Crane, born Oct. 25, 1868; died Jun
Anna Beards. Second wife, Lois Trusty.

June 1888 to

Fayette Co.,

Iowa. Marri

I'm

And
seven genera

APPENDIX E

Family Tree on Frank's Side:

Manuel Viera Cardosa (Amaral) branch:

1845 to 2010

Rosa Bettencourt branch:

1795 to 2010

---- Christopher Scott, born Oct. 24, 1963, Silverton, Ore. Married Aug. 10, 1991, Anaconda, Montana, to Lisa Marie Verstraete. (They had two children.)
----- Kelli Anne, born Feb. 27, 1995.
----- Gina Marie, born June 13, 1997.

--- Milton Viera, born July 15, 1942, Stockton, Calif. Married July 7, 1974, to Dianne Sue Emmertson. Divorced 1978. Married Mary Margaret "Meme" Miller, born June 20, 1940. Milton and Meme were married on Dec. 19, 1982, Sacramento, Calif. (She had a son.)
---- Aaron Richard Miller, born Oct. 31, 1972. Married June 28, 2003, to Lauren Evelyn Wilbert. (They have two children).
----- Alexis Rachel Miller, born March 10, 2007.
----- April Marie Miller, born April 7, 2010.

-- George Viera Amaral, born Jan. 29, 1915, Milpitas, Calif. Died Apr. 17, 1960, at rest in Manteca, Calif. Married July 21, 1942, to Marie Gomes, Reno, Nev. She died Oct. 28, 1994, Manteca, Calif. (They had two children.)
--- George Viera, born Nov. 22, 1946, Stockton, Calif. Married Dec. 1966 to Terry Canfield at Fremont, Calif., born Nov. 3, 1948. (They had two children).
---- Ronald, born Dec. 15, 1968, Fremont, Calif.
---- Alicia Ann, born Apr. 15, 1970, Fremont Calif. Married Jan. 4, 1992, to Douglas Calcagno, at Hayward, Calif. (They had two children, but I have no names.)

--- Edward, born Aug. 3, 1949, Stockton Calif.

-- Frank Viera Amaral, born June 19, 1918, Orland, Butte County, Calif. Died Mar. 5, 2007, at home, Nevada City, Calif. Married Nov. 26, 1942, to (Gertrude) **LaVonne Kruger**, at Stockton, Calif. (They had two children.)
--- Julia Rose, born Apr. 10, 1944, Stockton, Calif. Married Markus Brent Strate, Oct. 9, 1993, at St. Helena, Calif. Born Mar. 26, 1953, Moline, Ill. (She kept the Amaral name, no children).
--- Laurence (Lance) Viera, born Apr. 27, 1946, Nevada City, Calif. Married Gloria Ann Morrison (Spencer, Angove) on Oct. 26, 1975, Miners Foundry, Nevada City, Calif. She was born May 3, 1936, Pasadena, Calif. (Gloria had three children. Laurence adopted Gloria's son, Bradley L. Angove, in 2000. Bradley changed his surname to Amaral.)
---- William Spence, born Aug. 1, 1956, Pasadena, Calif. Married Tracy sometime in the 1980s and divorced same year.
---- Stephanie Lynn, born Aug. 4, 1958, San Jose, Calif. Married May 19, 1984, Sacramento, Calif., to Jeff Clark. (They had two children.)
----- Collin Jeffson Clark, born July 31, 1986, Sacramento, Calif.
----- Evan Spence Clark, born Nov. 17, 1988, Sacramento, Calif.
---- Bradley Lawrence, born April 6, 1967, Roseville, Calif. Married Penny Kathleen Marsh, Feb. 7, 1998, at American Victorian Museum (also known as the Miners Foundry), Nevada City, Calif. Divorced, 2003. Married Lisa Marie Brown, at his parents' residence in Deer Creek Park, Nevada City, Calif., Sept. 25, 2004. Divorced in 2009.

III. Notes on the extended family tree
of Rosa Bettencourt

For readers of this book, particularly relatives, interested in some of the more distant branches of our ancestry, here is more detailed information on relations stemming from the great-grandparents in the Azores of Rosa Bettencourt, Frank's mother.

* **Maria Julia**, last name unknown. Born about 1795. Married about 1820 to **Manuel Mendes Pereira**, born about 1790. These are Frank's great-grandparents, on his mother's mother's side. (They had eight children: Manuel Mendes II, Francisco Mendes, José Mendes, John Mendes, Maria Julia, Maria José, Rosa, and Mariana.)

- Manuel Mendes II, no history avail.

- Francisco Mendes, did marry, wife's name is unknown, they had three children and all live in Brazil.

- Jose Mendes, no history avail.

- John Mendes, married, wife's name is unknown.

- **Maria Julia**, born about 1825, married about 1850 to Francisco Jose Bettencourt II, born about 1820. (They had 16 children.) *These are Frank Amaral's grandparents on his mother's side. Jose Francisco Bettencourt II's father was Francisco Jose Bettencourt I, born about 1790. Wife's name unknown. Married about 1820 and had two children. Francisco Jose II, whose name is above, and Antonio Jose, married, wife's name unknown.* (The 16 children were seven sets of twins, one of each died, and the two singles. Survivors were Rosa Julia (Frank Amaral's mother), Francisco Jose III, Manuel Jose, Jose Mendes, Maria Julia, Gertrude Julia and Candida de Jeseus.

-- **Rosa Julia Bettencourt**, born April 17, 1889, Riberinha, near Feteira and Angra, Terceiria, Azores Island. Died Nov. 12, 1943, Princeton Calif. Married Feb. 24, 1911, to Manuel Viera Cardosa, (changed his last name to *Amaral* about the time he came to the states.) Amaral born 1875, Siveira Lajes, Pico Island, died Nov. 6, 1924, Chico, Calif. (They had four children.)

--- Marie Julia Amaral, born May 11, 1912, Palo Alto, Calif., died Jan. 18, 2001. Married Nov. 26, 1933 to Manual Souza, born Aug. 10, 1903, Beira, Sao Jorge, Azores Islands. Died Feb. 14, 1999 at home in Princeton, Calif. (They had one adopted child.)

---- Anna Maria Silveira da Bettencourt, born Aug. 6, 1952, Island of Sao Jorge. (Came to this country in 1958 at age of 5, was adopted Dec. 12, 1958.) Married, Sept. 1, 1973 to Ronald Dillard, born Mar. 25, 1952 at Princeton, Calif. (They had two children.)

----- Amber Maria, born Oct. 16, 1975, married December 13, 1996, to Donald Brian Weathers. (They had three children.)

------ Colton Michael born Nov. 30, 1998.

------ (twin) Makenzie, born Mar. 7, 2002.

------ (twin) Makaela, born Mar. 7, 2002.

Born in Okinawa, Japan, where Ron was stationed.

IV. Additional notes on the extended family tree

* **Maria Julia Pereira**, born about 1825, married about 1850 to **Francisco José Bettencourt II**, born about 1820 (these are Frank Amaral's grandparents). They had 16 children: seven sets of twins, and of the seven sets, one of each died early. Both of the non-twins died early, as well. (By the way, José Bettencourt II's father was Francisco José Bettencourt I, born about 1790. Bettencourt II's mother's name is unknown. His parents were married about 1820. Bettencourt I and his wife are Frank Amaral's great-grandparents on his mother's father's side. They had two children, Francisco José II and Antonio José (married, wife's name is unknown.)

Rosa Julia Bettencourt, Frank's mother, was born April 17, 1889, in Ribeirinha, near Feteira and Angra, Terceira, Azores Island.

* * *

Since each of the seven surviving children of Maria Julia and Francisco José II left the Azores and settled in California, here is what information I have on each of them and their children, besides Rose Julia Bettencourt, Frank's mother.

-- **Francisco (Frank) José III, Bettencourt,** born Feb. 29, 1892, in Rebeirinha, Terceira, Azores Islands; died Sept. 3, 1965, Woodland, Calif. Married Oct. 8, 1921, in Modesto, Calif., to Rita Pereira Pires, born Feb. 28, 1903, Porto Jedew, Terceira, Azores; died Nov. 1, 1941, in Woodland, California. (They had six children.)

    --- Frank J., born Nov. 27, 1922, died March 9, 1946.

    --- Deolinda ("Dee") Bettencourt, born April 13, 1925. Married in 1946 to Stanley Duncan. They had two children:

        ---- Mike Duncan, who married Brenda.

        ---- Rita, who married Barry Turnbull.

    --- Alice Bettencourt, born March 26, 1926. Married Lewie Raddigan. He died Dec. 23, 1990. I do not have a record on any of their children or other members of the family.

    --- Manuel J., born Oct. 4, 1927.

    --- Lucille, born Dec. 1, 1931.

    --- Ida, born Jan. 28, 1935.

All six children married and had families of their own, and live around the Woodland, Calif. area.

-- **Manuel José (Joe)**, born 1896, Ribeirinha, Terceira, Azores; died Aug. 10, 1990, San José, Calif.

-- **José (Joe) Mendes**, born in Ribeirinha, Terceira, Azores; died 1944, in Woodland, Calif.

-- **Maria Julia**, born in Ribeirinha, Terceira, Azores. Married Joe Rocha, also from Terceira; she died in 1982 in Calif. (They had five children, all married and had children, except Doloris.)
   --- Mary
   --- Alvera
   --- Doloris
   --- Tony
   --- Joe

-- **Gertrude Julia,** born Jan. 1, 1891 in Ribeirinha, Terceira, Azores; died Dec. 29, 1974 in Concord, Calif. Married Tony Rocha, also from Port Judeau, Terceira Azores. He died Aug. 5, 1972 in Modesto, Calif. (They had four children, all married and had children.)
   --- Mary
   --- Tony
   --- Frank
   --- Elsie, born Sept. 4, 1929 in Orland, Calif. Married July 1949 in Carmel, Calif. to Robert J. Wright. Died Feb. 18, 2005.
    (Maria and Gertrude married Joe and Tony, two brothers.)

-- **Candida de Jeseus**, born in Ribeirinha, Terceira, Azores in 1902 and the last of the many children of Maria Julia and Francisco José II. Candida died March 18, 1981, in Modesto, Calif. Married Joe Fagundes from the Azores. He died in the Manteca-Modesto, California area. (They had five children, all married and had children of their own.)
   --- Mary Souza's first husband died. (They had three children.)
Later she married Arnold Scheer, I believe April 9, 1975. Years later she divorced him.
    ---- A girl, married.
    ---- A boy, married.
    ---- Michael, not married, died from some kind of a growth.
   --- Alice
   --- Velma
   --- Joe
   --- Evelyn

A bit more history:

Frank's mother, Rosa, had a cousin by the name of **Orvalina (Bettencourt) Laurenco.** She married **Antonio L. Homem, Laurenco Jr.** He died in 1993. (They had three children.)
  -- **Ermalinda** married Paulo Jorge Martina; (They had two children.)
   ---Thema.
   ---Paulo.
  -- **Joao da Silva Laurenco** married Lentina. (They had three children.)
   ---Joao.
   ---Diogo.
   ---Andrea.
  -- **Antonio Laurenco** married Zilda. (They had three children.)
   ---Antonio.
   ---Andre.
   ---Anna.

Made in United States
North Haven, CT
05 August 2023